Native American Women

A Biographical Dictionary

Native American Women
A Biographical Dictionary

Second Edition

Gretchen M. Bataille

Laurie Lisa

Editors

Routledge
New York London

Published in 2001 by
Routledge
29 West 35th Street
New York, NY 10001

Published in Great Britain by
Routledge
11 New Fetter Lane
London EC4P 4EE

Routledge is an Imprint of Taylor & Francis Books, Inc.

First edition published in 1993 by Garland Publishing.
Printed in the United States of America on acid-free paper.

10 9 8 7 6 5 4 3 2 1

Photo credits:
Elsie Allen: courtesy of Marion Steinbach; Paula Gunn Allen: courtesy of Rountry/Williams; Tsianina
Redfeather Blackstone: courtesy of Eugene Hutchinson; Gertrude Simmons Bonnin: courtesy of
Marquette University; Sr. Genevieve Cuny: courtesy of *Yankton Daily Press* and Dakotan; Joy Harjo:
courtesy of Diana Luppi; Vivien Hailstone: Beverly R. Ortiz; Charlotte Anne Wilson Heth: courtesy of
Amy Suber; Vi Hilbert: courtesy of Josef Scaylea; Joan Hill: courtesy of Joan Hill; Linda Hogan: courtesy
of Rich Powers; Josette Juneau: courtesy of Milwaukee Public Museum; Mable McKay: courtesy of
Beverly R. Ortiz; Julia F. Parker: courtesy of Beverly Ortiz; Essie Parrish: courtesy of Violet
Chappell/Greg Sarris; Agnes Picotte: courtesy of Ken Olson; Wendy Rose: courtesy of Arthur Murata;
Sacred White Buffalo, Mother Mary Catherine: courtesy of Marquette University; Leslie Marmon Silko:
©1981 courtesy of Linda Fry Poverman; Kathleen R. Smith: courtesy of Beverly R. Ortiz; Virginia
Driving Hawk Sneve: courtesy of Virginia Driving Hawk Sneve: Laura Somersal: courtesy of Marion
Steinbach.

Library of Congress Cataloging-in-Publication Data

Native American women : a biographical dictionary / Gretchen M. Bataille, Laurie Lisa,
editors.—2nd ed.
    p. cm. — (Biographical dictionaries of minority women)
  Includes bibliographical references and index.
  ISBN: 0-415-93020-0 (alk. paper)
   1. Indian women—North America. 2. Indians of North
America—Biography—Dictionaries. 3. Women—North
America—Biography—Dictionaries. I. Bataille, Gretchen M., 1944– II. Lisa, Laurie.
III. Series.

E98, W8 B38 2001
920.72'08997—dc21   2001019749

Contents

Preface to the First Edition

As series editor for Garland's Biographical Dictionaries of Minority Women, I have had the privilege to work with many outstanding colleagues in the field of women's history whose scholarship has expanded the scope of women's history to include and acknowledge the presence and contributions of all women in the pluralistic society of this nation. Each volume in this series focuses upon the biographic and bibliographic sources available to inform both lay and professional researchers from many academic disciplines about women within a particular ethnic group.

I first confronted the paucity and inadequacy of basic reference sources on minority women when I began to edit the *Handbook of American Women's History* in the late 1980s. My contributors and I had to use our best and most determined research techniques to track down biographical information and bibliographical sources for women who were significant historical participants, yet whose names appeared in general historical monographs in a few places, like UFO blips on a radar screen. When I lamented this appalling lack of collections of minimal facts and works on minority women, my editor at Garland, Kennie Lyman, offered me the opportunity to coordinate the collection of such basic historical and historiographical data on these neglected women.

Gretchen Bataille was one of the first to accept my invitation to edit one of our volumes. We are very fortunate that she agreed to undertake this ambitious but long overdue effort to restore to the historical record the names and contributions of Native American women whose lives influenced the development of the history of the United States. I am very proud to be associated with this much-needed reference work that is the result of the indefatigable efforts of its editor and her contributors. I applaud her execution of our mission to render accessible fundamental information and research sources for this significant group of American women.

I thank Professor Bataille for allowing her commitment to her field to overrule the wisdom of all previous editorial experience, which decrees that "no good deed goes unpunished," and welcome her into my informal support group of editors of reference works in Women's Studies who accept the challenge of the almost impossible task of restoring to public awareness all women whose lives have earned them the honor of being remembered by generations to come. Despite our knowledge that inevitably a few significant women still would not be found among the entries within each volume, we nonetheless strive to offer comprehensive coverage of minority women within this series.

Angela Howard Zophy, Series Editor

Preface to the Second Edition

The first edition of Gretchen M. Bataille's *Native American Women: A Biographical Dictionary* set a high standard for reclaiming portions of women's history that had been ignored or marginalized until the rise of women's history and Women's Studies made clear the demand for sources that offered basic biographical and bibliographical information about women. Reviewers and readers alike—librarians, historians, and Women's Studies scholars, teachers, and students—agreed that *Native American Women* collected and organized much-needed information on the Native American women who as individuals and members of an ethnic group have been woefully underrepresented in reference works on "notables" among Native Americans. In this edition of *Native American Women*, Professor Bataille and her coeditor, Laurie Lisa, have added new entries as well as reviewed and revised both the text and the bibliographical listings for the original entries. I predict that readers will approve their efforts to update this volume.

Angela Howard Zophy, Series Editor

Acknowledgments

What I described as a "monumental undertaking" the first time around was equally daunting the second time. Working closely with Angela Noelle Williams, a research assistant and Ph.D. candidate in English at the University of California, Santa Barbara, I began the process of communicating with the more than sixty contributors to the first edition. Given the itinerant life of many academics, we frequently found ourselves with multiple addresses—and sometimes one step behind our contributors! Ultimately, we were amazed by the positive responses, the quick replies to our letters, and the enthusiasm about the production of a revised and expanded edition.

I then turned to Laurie Lisa, the editorial assistant for the first edition. Laurie had completed her Ph.D. at Arizona State University with a dissertation on Gertrude Bonnin, and she agreed to take on the task of coeditor for the second edition. As always, Laurie's excellent writing and editing skills contributed to a final manuscript that was thorough and complete. After I took the position of Provost and Academic Vice President at Washington State University, Pullman, the book benefited from the help of research assistants Patti Verstrat and Bethany Blankenship. And throughout this project, the series editor, Angela Zophy, has been enthusiastic about the positive response to the volumes on minority women. This book is the result of the contributions of many scholars jointly supported by a circle of women who worked together to complete the project.

For the first edition, Arizona State University provided extensive institutional support, and for the second edition, research assistance was provided through support from the Office of the Executive Vice Chancellor at the University of California, Santa Barbara, and the Office of the Provost at Washington State University, Pullman. I am grateful to have had the support of universities that value the importance of documenting the lives of these women whose histories have been ignored for far too long.

To all those who contributed to the first and second editions, and to those whose lives this book documents, I am grateful.

Gretchen M. Bataille

Introduction

Although the lives of Native American women have been ignored by many historians, and Indian women have been stereotyped as "squaws" and "princesses" in children's books and many textbooks, ongoing research continues to establish the importance of their roles in both traditional and contemporary cultures. Many factors have combined to produce inaccurate images of American Indian women in today's society. Historically, cultural determinants and the diversity of Indian cultures established the traditional roles and positions of women within their tribes, but political mandates, educational reforms, and religious fervor often eroded tribal organization and women's roles, a contradiction that continues to define the lives of American Indian women. The histories of Native women from the past, such as Pocahontas, Sacagawea, Lozen, and Dahteste, resonate with fabulous tales of sacrifice or exploits, achieving for Native women explorer or warrior status, but much of what has been published perpetuates myths that have been repeated by scholars for so long that the complete truth probably will always remain hidden.

Since the earliest accounts, Native women's lives have been described by outsiders unfamiliar with the cultures or the women's roles within those cultures. In his earliest journals, Christopher Columbus praises the "gentle" people he encountered, but he quickly replaces his admiration with scorn when it becomes clear to him that he must subdue these people in order to achieve any recognition as a hero for his ambitious journeys to a "new world." Amerigo Vespucci, after whom two continents are named, observes in his letters that Indian men and women are "dirty and shameless," with "no modesty." Of the women, he writes, "They are very fertile women, and in their pregnancies avoid no toil." This view was resurrected by later writers and moviemakers, who consistently have shown Native women disappearing briefly into the trees to give birth and then returning to hoe the fields or tan hides without seeming to have suffered either pain or exhaustion. Vespucci also writes that Native women are "heartless and cruel," and go about "utterly naked," certainly a contrast to the heavily robed women of his contemporary Europe, and therefore unacceptable.[1] These descriptions by male outsiders with ethnocentric expectations began a pattern of describing Native American women that continues to influence biography, fiction, and visual images.

Later historians were influenced by such written accounts as well as by early woodcuts that portrayed Native women in ambiguous ways. While decrying the nakedness and cruelty of these women, early writers also referred to their generosity and attractiveness. John Smith, in his accounts of Pocahontas, portrays her as gentle and eager to please the white settlers. Many woodcuts showed Native women representing America itself, usually depicted as a seminaked woman in a bucolic setting. The image appeared frequently on seventeenth-century maps of the New World.

Since the 1960s scholars have attempted to develop and communicate realistic portrayals of Native American women, but much of their work has been fragmentary and undocumented. In spite of these efforts, many writers have been hampered by the inaccuracies and misconceptions of previous work. Carolyn Foreman, in *Indian Women Chiefs* (1954), relies on many earlier sources of dubious authenticity in an attempt to provide documentation of the lives of Indian women who had power within their tribes. Repeatedly she generalizes and perpetuates inaccurate data and terminology. For instance, Foreman calls Sarah Winnemucca (Hopkins) a "chief." Although Winnemucca was influential in her tribe, she never carried the title of "chief." Just as the terms "princess" and "queen" had been misused by Europeans who did not understand Indian tribal organization, so Foreman erroneously uses "chief" to designate women leaders who held positions of power and influence. Ten years later, Lela and Rufus Waltrip published *Indian Women*, a collection of thirteen embellished narratives about Indian women. The authors provided speeches for Pocahontas and Sacagawea, attempting to re-create the world of the 1600s and 1700s. Their bibliography is incomplete and often inaccurate. As a scholarly source, the book fails to provide accurate or even convincing information. These two books were followed in 1974 by Marion E. Gridley's *American Indian Women*. Gridley borrows heavily from the Waltrips' book in her generalizations about Indian women. She includes Pocahontas and Sacagawea along with seventeen other Indian women, from Wetamoo to contemporary figures such as Wilma Victor and Annie Dodge Wauneka, providing readable but often undocumented biographies.

It finally took the efforts of Indian women themselves to present an accurate account of Native women's histories and lives. Rayna Green's essay in *Signs* (1980), followed by her work with the Ohoyo Resource Center and her *Native American Women: A Contextual Bibliography* (1983), offers a substantial body of reliable historical, biographical, and ethnographic information on Indian women in traditional and contemporary tribal cultures. More recently, the feminist work of Paula Gunn Allen in *The Sacred Hoop* (1986) reinterprets Indian women's history within a contemporary framework that relies on sacred myth as well as Indian women's personal testimonies. Writers such as Louise Erdrich, Leslie Marmon Silko, Linda Hogan, Joy Harjo, Lee Maracle, Beverly Hungry Wolf, Wendy Rose, and others continue to contribute to a revisionist view of American Indian women's experiences. Many of these women use their bicultural training to communicate both the scholarly and the personal to define female experience within tribal communities threatened by external factors.

The lives of legendary and historical figures, as well as of contemporary American Indian women, presented in this dictionary reflect cultural continuities and changes. Information on the historical figures included herein was drawn from existing sources, some of which remain ambiguous and contradictory. Some women might have several names in their lifetime, and those names often have been spelled or translated differently in various sources, making the task of compiling accurate information more difficult. The biographies of contemporary women were often edited by the women themselves, providing verification and credibility to the entries.

These biographies present many American Indian women with diverse roles within their cultures. Every effort has been made, through networking and research, to present a broad cross section of Native women's experiences in both historical and contemporary contexts. Their roles reflect the historical times within which they lived, the degree of acculturation, or the level of education. The variety of gender roles and degrees of power experienced by Native American women is not easily represented in the precontact and early colonial periods in a collection such as this because so little is known about individual lives. Nevertheless, we have enough information to conclude that in agricultural societies such as the Iroquois or the Navajo, women were accorded more status than they received in the primarily hunting societies of the Great Plains. Women's status among the Iroquois has been a subject of much interest, yet little is known about specific Iroquois women in history except such exceptional figures as Kateri of the Mohawks and Molly Brant. The Iroquois organized their kinship groups into matrilineal clans whose members traced their descent from a common female ancestor. Iroquois women owned the longhouses in which they lived and passed them on to their descendants. They also had a great deal of power because they controlled the agricultural life of the tribes by managing the farming activities. They are but one example of Native women whose roles and responsibilities gave them significant power in traditional tribal societies, a power that is still evident in some contemporary accounts.

Prior to contact with whites, women had a great deal of power among the Cherokee in the South. They had the right to speak in village councils, and some accompanied the men when the tribe went to war. Cherokee tribal chairwoman Wilma Mankiller is a contemporary example of the strength of Cherokee women that continues to exist today. Women of the Southwest still live in matrilocal and matrilineal societies, where their roles in agriculture, female puberty ceremonies, and tribal government remain prominent. Myths of Spider Woman, Changing Woman, and Yellow Woman reinforce the position of women in these tribal societies.

Between 1790 and 1840 missionaries and government agents urged Native Americans to value individual ownership of land, European gender roles, and the patriarchal family. The traditional base of women's power among groups such as the Iroquois and the Cherokee was eroded by the imposition of Judeo–Christian values, the influence of which abated only with the passage of the American Indian Religious Freedom Act of 1978. The Act guaranteed legal recognition of sacred places such as Taos Blue Lake, sacred plants, and ceremonies such as the Sun Dance, and in doing so often reaffirmed the traditional roles of women in these societies.

Many of the negative images of Indian women developed as a result of contact with Euro–American society, and the assault on traditional practices took many forms. Fur trappers and traders changed the material culture of the tribes by introducing and developing a demand for iron, glass beads, cloth, and dyes. The missionaries judged Indian women by traditional Judeo–Christian views that denigrated the power women held in some tribes in favor of European-style patriarchy. Often Native women were judged on the basis of how helpful they could be to whites. Pocahontas, who saved Captain John Smith in 1607 and married John Rolfe, a leader of the English colony in Virginia, is one famous example of an Indian woman valued by whites. Sacagawea of the Shoshone, who traveled with the Lewis and Clark expedition between 1804 and 1806, gained a significant place in history for purportedly leading explorers across the country.

Efforts to assimilate Native women into Euro–American society through education changed the status of women. Schools run by missionaries and the Bureau of Indian Affairs established curricula along stereotypical lines, training women in homemaking skills while punishing them for speaking their native language or wearing traditional clothing. In the twentieth century Indian women have been victims of medical practices that resulted in mass sterilizations and dubious experimentation with Depo-Provera, a hormone given to mentally disabled Indian women, that have led to accusations of genocide. Such spokespersons as Connie Uri and groups such as Women of All Red Nations (WARN) brought media attention to these practices, and as a result regulations governing sterilization were issued by the Department of Health, Education, and Welfare (HEW) in 1979. The United States court system has interfered with tribal laws regarding child custody and hunting and fishing practices; and civil rights laws, although passed in support of minority rights, have conflicted with some tribal powers and traditions.

There has been some redress for grievances in recent times, and much of the pressure has been brought to bear by Indian women. Groups such as WARN and Ohoyo, and women within the National Indian Education Association, have urged that women's issues should receive attention from educators, the government, and tribes. The Indian Child Welfare Act of 1978, which mandated preference for placement of Indian children with Indian families and recognized tribal rights in adoption and placement of foster children, brought attention to one of contemporary Indian women's greatest concerns: the future of their children.

Today the rate of infant mortality of Indians exceeds that of the national rate of all races, the rate of fetal alcohol syndrome is three to six times higher than the national average, and Indian children suffer disproportionately from otitis media (inflammation of the middle ear), probably the leading cause of learning deficiencies among these children. Native American children with handicapping conditions are less likely to receive services than other American children. Until the passage of the Indian Child Welfare Act, preservation of the Indian family was not considered a priority by government agencies, and many Indian children were placed in non–Indian foster care and adoptive homes or boarding schools without consultation with the families or tribes involved.

All of the factors that have affected Indian peoples have impacted the women. These external influences are reflected in the choices they have made in their lives and in their ability to endure and to succeed. Many contemporary women have spoken out and have written their own stories, tribal histories, fiction, and poetry. Beth Brant has spoken for many of these women: "What good is this pen, this yellow paper, if I can't fashion them into tools or weapons to change our lives?"[2] These brief accounts cannot possibly provide all the details of these women's lives; however, the words are indeed "weapons" to change the popular impression that Indian women have no viable history and no recognizable present.

Accurate biographies, even if they are brief, are an effective means of gaining a true picture of the variety of experiences and of the powers and endurance of Indian women. This collection provides information that is missing from general biographical dictionaries of women, books that include sketches of only the most obvious and best-known figures. The European views that incorporated both fascination and repugnance obscured accurate depictions, and even the best-intentioned scholarship has often been flawed. This volume is part of a series of biographical dictionaries that will fill in the missing figures in history, the women of color who are as much a part of America's past and present as their lighter-skinned sisters and brothers.

From an original list of fewer than one hundred names, this project grew as each contributor became engaged in the process of adding new names. The list was made available to all contributors, and throughout the United States, Canada, and Europe, interested scholars corrected inaccurate data and provided alternate spellings for individual names, set the record straight on misinformation, and suggested additions or deletions. There are sure to be women who should have been included and were not, perhaps because of insufficient information or because contributors who volunteered to prepare certain entries were unable to complete the material. Every attempt was made to verify information; however, there are sure to be errors because of the difficulty of verifying the realities of women's lives. The involvement of many women in their own biographies is a beginning, however, and gives assurance that future accounts might be more accurate.

Notes

1. *Amerigo Vespucci: Letter to Piero Soderini Gonfaloniere*, translated and edited by George Tyler Northup (Princeton, NJ: Princeton University Press, 1916), 7–10.
2. *Beth Brant, Food & Spirits* (Ithaca, NY: Firebrand Books, 1991).

A

ABEITA, LOUISE [E-Yeh-Shure', Blue Corn] (b. 1926), is the author of *I Am a Pueblo Indian Girl,* a limited edition book prepared under the sponsorship of the National Gallery of the American Indian. She was born in Isleta Pueblo, New Mexico. When her father realized her natural talent as a poet, he brought together Indian artists—Navaho, Apache, and Pueblo—in a cooperative endeavor to make the first truly Indian book, which was printed when she was thirteen years old.

Abeita describes her way of life in both prose and poetry, and includes interesting insights into the Pueblo traditions. The illustrators present a stirringly beautiful picture of the surviving Pueblo culture.

Abeita is a member of one of the strong families of the Isleta Pueblo who wish to hold on to the good things of their culture and the ancient religion. Her publication was part of an effort to unite traditional words and implied ideas with illustrations to make Pueblo life understood in the simplest way possible. This was a first tentative step toward making their artistry understood by the English-speaking public.

Reference

Abeita, Louise. *I Am a Pueblo Indian Girl*. Introduction by Oliver La Farge. New York: William Morrow, 1939.

—Joyce Ann Kievit

ABEYTA, PABLITA (b. 1953), sculptor and activist. A native of New Mexico, she is the oldest daughter of Narciso (Ha-So-De) Abeyta, a world-renowned Navajo artist who studied under Dorothy Dunn at the Santa Fe Arts Institute. In a family of seven children and two artistic parents, each member established his or her own reputation in fields ranging from painting to sculpture to weaving. Each brother and sister was given an Indian middle name to help them identify with their Indian heritage. Pablita's Navajo name, "Ta-Nez-Bah," traces from her grandmother and translates as, "One Who Completes a Circle," a fitting name since many of the sculptures she has created are smooth, round, and sensuous.

In addition to her work as an artist, Abeyta has had a busy professional career in politics and Indian affairs. After earning her M.P.A. from the University of New Mexico in 1983, Abeyta became a lobbyist for the Navajo Nation Washington office, where she coordinated a nationwide effort to secure passage of comprehensive Indian amendments to the Safe Drinking Water, Clean Water, and Superfund acts. From 1986 to 1988, Abeyta worked as legislative assistant to Ben Nighthorse Campbell (later a U.S. senator from Colorado), and, in 1988, she joined the professional staff of the House Interior Committee's Indian Affairs Office. In 1991, Abeyta joined the Smithsonian Institution and became a congressional liaison for the National Museum of the American Indian, where she monitored funding for that institution, assisted in obtaining financial support for the NMAI Suitland Cultural Resources Center and the Mall Museum, and drafted, coordinated, and reviewed legislative proposals pertaining to American Indian cultural matters and repatriation. Since 1999, she has served as special assistant to the director of the National Museum of the American Indian.

Abeyta's art has been featured around the country, including galleries in San Francisco, Chicago, New York, Washington, D.C., and Durango, Colorado. Her work is also displayed in several congressional offices, including those of Senators Daniel Inouye and John McCain, as well as in permanent exhibits at the National Museum of the American Indian and the National Museum of American History.

References

Abeyta, Pablita. "Artist's Statement," March 2, 2001.
Abeyta, Pablita. "Curriculum Vitae," provided on March 2, 2001.
Telephone interview with the author, March 2, 2001.

—Michael Sherfy

ACKERMAN, MARIA JOSEPH [Ldaneit] (b. 1927), a Tlingit, was born in Juneau, Alaska, and is a member of the Raven tribe in the Cohoe clan. During her childhood, she lived with her maternal grandparents, who earned their living from traditional arts. Her grandmother did beadwork, and made moccasins and spruce root baskets; her grandfather carved totem poles. Ackerman attended school for four years at the Pius X Mission School in Skagway, Alaska, living with her aunt, Jessie Jacobs, during that time. From her, Ackerman learned sewing and heard the traditional Tlingit stories. These oral stories that had been handed down from one generation to the next are recorded in Ackerman's *Tlingit Stories*, a compilation of thirteen tales including "The Girl and Woodworm," "May the Best Animal Win," and "The Trapper and the Kooshd'aa K'aas."

Ackerman, the mother of five children, has worked as a resource Native artist for the Anchorage Borough School District Indian Education Program. She maintains a great interest in Tlingit arts and crafts, and has given courses on skin sewing and beadwork.

Reference

Ackerman, Maria. *Tlingit Stories*. Anchorage: Alaska Methodist University Press, 1975.

—Laurie Lisa

AHENAKEW, FREDA (b. 1932), a Plains Cree linguist and university professor, was born in Atâhkakohp (Sandy Lake), Saskatchewan. She resumed her interrupted high school education in 1968 and attended classes with nine of her twelve children. She became a Cree language teacher under the guidance of Ida MacLeod, received a BEd from the University of Saskatchewan in 1979, and took an MA in Cree linguistics at the University of Manitoba in 1984. After serving as director of the Saskatchewan Indian Languages Institute at Saskatoon from 1985 to 1989, she was associate professor and head of the Native Studies Department at the University of Manitoba until her retirement in 1996. She is widely recognized as a leader in the movement to preserve the indigenous linguistic and literary heritage of Canada.

In addition to articles on and teaching the Cree language, children's storybooks, and an introductory grammar book, *Cree Language Structures: A Cree Approach*, Ahenakew has published several volumes of Cree texts. In recent years, she has devoted much of her time and energy to the careful transcription, analysis, and translation of traditional stories and autobiographical accounts (especially women's life experiences), preparing them for publication in formal Cree (in both syllabic and Roman orthographies) and in vernacular Cree.

References

Ahenakew, Freda. *Cree Language Structures: A Cree Approach*. Winnipeg, MN: Pemmican Publications, 1987.

————, ed. *kiskinahamawâkan-âcimowinisa/Student Stories Written by Cree-Speaking Students*. Algonquian and Iroquoian Linguistics Memoir 2, 1986.

————. *wâskahikaniwiyiniw-âcimowina/Stories of the House People*. Told by Peter Vandall and Joe Doquette. Publications of the Algonquian Text Society. Winnipeg: University of Manitoba Press, 1987.

Ahenakew, Freda, and H. C. Wolfart. "The Reality of Cree Morpheme-Boundary Rules." *Algonquian and Iroquoian Linguistics* 16 (1991): 27, 32.

————, eds. *Kôhkominawak otâcimowiniwâwa/Our Grandmothers' Lives as Told in Their Own Words*. Saskatoon, SK: Fifth House Publishers, 1992.

Tootoosis, Kevin, ed. *Profiles: Professional Aboriginal Peoples of Saskatchewan*. Saskatoon: Saskatchewan Indian Cultural Centre, 1990.

Wolfart, H. C., and Freda Ahenakew, eds. *The Cree Language Is Our Identity: The LaRonge Lectures of Sarah Whitecalf*. Publications of the Algonquian Text Society. Winnipeg: University of Manitoba Press, 1992.

—John D. Nichols

AINSE, SALLY [Sally Montour, Sara Montour, Hands, Hains, Willson]. (c. 1728–1823), Oneida fur trader, landowner, and diplomat, was born probably in 1728 and raised in the Susquehanna River region of New York. At age seventeen she married Andrew Montour, an Indian interpreter for the British government, with whom she had several children. According to her own words, after several years of marriage she was left with her people, the Oneidas. This probably occurred between 1757 and 1758. From the Oneidas she acquired a deed to lands in the Fort Stanwix

(Rome, New York) area. Records indicate that by this time Ainse had begun her career as a trader. Sometime after the commencement of the American Revolution, she abandoned her New York lands and removed to the British-controlled Detroit District. Known until then as Sally or Sara Montour, in the Detroit region she became best known as Sally Ainse, although there are references to her as Hands, Hains, or Willson. By the spring of 1775, Ainse was doing business in the region, trading cider and other goods to the Indians for furs, and in 1778 she bought a house and lot in Detroit with the profits from that business. According to the 1779 Detroit records, she continued to prosper. Her holdings at that time were four slaves, three cows, four horses, and one hundred pounds of flour.

Ainse also became well known as a woodland diplomat and intermediary. After the 1794 defeat of the allied Indian tribes by United States forces commanded by General Anthony Wayne at the Battle of Fallen Timbers in Ohio, Ainse participated in the peace negotiations. She also acted on behalf of Chief Joseph Brant, transmitting messages and speeches between the various Indian tribes and the British government.

In 1783, through a Chippewa deed, Ainse acquired, land along the north shore of the Thames River at present-day Chatham, Ontario. By 1787 she had sold her land in Detroit and permanently settled on her Chatham lands. Her holdings there were extensive: three improved farms, an orchard, and a "mansion." The formal purchase from the Chippewas of the lands in this region by the British Crown in 1790 (the McKee Purchase) marked the beginning of what became a twenty-three-year legal struggle by Ainse to retain possession of her Chatham lands. The British Land Board, charged with the subsequent sale and distribution of these lands, refused to recognize her Chippewa deed. Ainse's claim rested not only on her Chippewa deed but also on a specific exemption of her property from the McKee Purchase. She was supported in her claim by seven Chippewa chiefs, who in 1791 signed a statement affirming that indeed their "sister's" lands had been exempted. Other prominent Indians and Europeans came to her defense: the influential Mohawk Chief Joseph Brant, Lieutenant Governor Simcoe, and the powerful head of Indian Affairs, Sir John Johnson. But, in the end, not even these personages could secure Ainse's claim against the rising tide of white settlers to the region. Ainse ultimately abandoned the fight for her lands. Sometime after 1806 she is said to have moved to Amherstburg, Ontario, where she resided until her death in 1823.

References

Hamil, F.C. *Sally Ainse, Fur Trader*. Detroit: The Algonquin Society, 1939.

———. *The Valley of the Lower Thames, 1640–1850*. Toronto: University of Toronto Press, 1951.

Kelsay, Isabel Thompson. *Joseph Brant 1743–1807: Man of Two Worlds*. Syracuse, NY: Syracuse University Press, 1984.

Surtees, Robert J. "Indian Land Cessions in Ontario, 1763–1862: The Evolution of a System." PhD diss., Carleton University, Ottawa, 1983.

Tanner, Helen Hornbeck, ed. *Atlas of Great Lakes Indian History*. Norman: University of Oklahoma Press, 1986.

—Faren R. Siminoff

AKERS, DONNA L. (b. 1954), completed her PhD in history at Arizona State University and is an Assistant Professor of American history at Purdue University. She is an enrolled member of the Choctaw Nation of Oklahoma and speaks, reads, and writes the Choctaw language. She received her bachelor's degree at the University of Houston and her master's degree in history at the University of Oklahoma. She has taught American history, Native American history, and western American history. Akers is currently completing two books: an edited anthology of research by Native American historians and a revisionist history of the Choctaw Nation in the nineteenth and twentieth centuries, *Living in the Land of the Dead: The Choctaw Nation in the 19th and 20th Centuries*. She is an expert on issues dealing with social history relating to Native Americans in Indian Territory and those involving race, class, and gender among American Indians. She has a special interest in environmental history among Native nations. Akers is a member of the Chancellor's Native American Advisory Committee for the University of California. She lives with her husband and two children in Mission Viejo, California.

Reference

Trafzer, Clifford E. Personal communication with Donna Akers, 1996.

—Clifford E. Trafzer

ALBERTY, ELIZA MISSOURI BUSHYHEAD (1839–1919), Cherokee educator and businesswoman, was the seventh child of Rev. Jesse Bushyhead (also called Unaduti), a Cherokee Baptist minister, and Eliza Wilkinson (spelled Wilkerson by some descendants), a woman of mixed white and Cherokee blood. Her father established a mission, originally known as Bread Town because of the rations given to people who passed through it, near present-day Westville, Arkansas. Alberty attended school at the Baptist mission until 1854, when she enrolled in the Cherokee Female Seminary at Park Hill, Cherokee Nation, from which she graduated in 1856. She then taught at the Post Oak Grove and Vann's Valley schools (two of the Cherokee Nation's public schools) until 1859. In 1858 she married David Rowe Vann, a mixed-blood Cherokee. Three years after his death in 1870, she married Bluford West Alberty, also a mixed-blood.

Soon after their marriage, the Albertys were appointed stewards of the Cherokee Insane Asylum. In 1885 they purchased a hotel in Tahlequah—the capital of the Cherokee Nation. After her husband's death in 1889, Alberty managed the hotel, making it one of the most successful in Indian Territory. She was active in the Baptist Church and, because of the members' affection for her, was known as Aunt Eliza. Her brother, Dennis Wolfe Bushyhead, served as principal chief of the Cherokee Nation from 1879 to 1888.

References

Foreman, Carolyn Thomas. "Aunt Eliza of Tahlequah." *Chronicles of Oklahoma* 9 (March 1931): 43–55.
Miner, H. Craig. "Dennis Bushyhead." In *American Indian Leaders: A Study in Diversity*. Edited by R. David Edmunds. Pp. 192–205. Lincoln: University of Nebraska Press, 1980.

West, Clarence William. *Tahlequah and the Cherokee Nation: 1841–1941.* Muskogee, OK: Muskogee Publishing, 1978.

—*Devon A. Mihesuah*

ALLEN, ELSIE (1899–1990), tribal scholar, cultural consultant, and renowned Pomo weaver, was born in a hop field outside Santa Rosa, California, to George (Ukiah Pomo) and Annie Comanche (Cloverdale Pomo). Elsie's father died when she was a young girl; her mother subsequently married Richard Burke (half Pomo), with whom she had a son and a daughter.

Allen, who spoke only Pomo as a youth, learned to read and write English between the ages of thirteen and sixteen. She spent her teens working as a field hand. At eighteen, she went to San Francisco, where she worked as a housekeeper, then secured a job at Saint Joseph's Hospital. In 1919 she married Arthur Allen (Pinoleville Pomo), with whom she had three children.

Allen was active in the Pomo Women's Club (established in 1940 and disbanded in 1957), through which Native American women provided social and financial support for their people. She helped with club fund-raisers and headed the Basket Committee. In the 1940s the club supported a successful lawsuit by Steven Knight against a Ukiah theater that denied Indians the right to sit on its lower floor. To avoid future lawsuits, other Ukiah business owners ended their "No Indians Allowed" policies. Later, Allen was active in the Hintil Women's Club, which did charitable work and awarded scholarships to local Indians.

Allen's mother broke with Pomo tradition on her deathbed when she begged Allen to keep the family's baskets rather than burying them with her. She told her daughter the baskets would take Allen traveling, bring people enjoyment, and

Elsie Allen

create an understanding that the Pomo weren't "dumb." These baskets and others from the Allen collection are now on loan to the Mendocino County Museum in Willets, California.

At age sixty-two, Allen took up the Pomo basketmaking she had learned in her youth, a tradition she has demonstrated to a wide audience. In 1972 her book, *Pomo Basketmaking: A Supreme Art for the Weaver*, brought widespread recognition of Pomo basketry. From 1979 to 1981 Allen was a primary consultant for the Warm Springs Cultural Resources Study, which detailed the history and culture of the Dry Creek and Cloverdale Pomo. For her cultural work, she received an honorary Doctorate of Divinity as "Pomo Sage."

Allen's most enduring contribution was to become the first Pomo weaver to teach Pomo basketry to people outside her family, including non–Indians, against all tradition. According to Kathleen Smith (Bodega Miwok/Dry Creek Pomo), "Elsie Allen felt this urge that if she didn't share what she knew, it would die. She didn't want it to die, so she broke with the real strong tradition of not teaching to those outside your family. She got a lot of flak, but the time was right for people to listen to her." According to her grandniece, Susan Billie (Hopland Pomo), who is carrying on Allen's basketmaking tradition, "Elsie just loved people. She didn't care about money and material things. She cared about people."

References

Allen, Elsie. *Pomo Basketmaking: A Supreme Art for the Weaver*. Edited by Vinson Brown. Healdsburg, CA: Naturegraph Publishers, 1972.

Eisenberg, Bonnie, and Marylynne Slayen. "An Interview with Kathleen Smith." *Women's Voices* 6 (March 1981): 16–17.

Frederickson, Vera Mae, ed. "School Days in Northern California: The Accounts of Six Pomo Women." *News from Native California* 4 (Fall 1989): 40–45.

McGill, Marsha Ann. "California Indian Women's Clubs: Past and Present." *News from Native California* 4 (Spring 1990): 22–23.

Ortiz, Bev. Personal communication with Elsie Allen, June 7, 1986.

———. Personal communication with Susan Billie, December 24, 1990.

———. Personal communication with Kathleen Smith, December 24, 1990.

—Bev Ortiz

ALLEN, MINERVA (b. 1935), is an Assiniboine from Lodgepole, on the Fort Belknap Reservation near the Canadian border in northern Montana. She has been a poet, historian, educator, and activist on behalf of her family and community. A mother of eight children, she returned to school in her thirties, receiving a BS from Central Michigan, an MA in career guidance at Northern Montana State, and an MAT in early childhood education from Weber State College. Allen spent five years with Montana Legal Services and ten years as a Head Start director. Successfully bringing traditional language and practices into the classroom, she has spent the last several years working with the students of the Hayes-Lodgepole School District.

In 1974 Allen published her first chapbook of poetry, *Like Spirits of the Past Trying to Break Out and Walk to the West*. She was encouraged by a VISTA worker, who told her that the poems she had been producing since childhood were good. She began writing in response to the loneliness and isolation of being raised as the only child of her grandparents; an Assiniboine tradition dictates that the first grandchild is raised by the grandparents in the traditional way. Also in 1974, Dick Lourie included her poetry in his collection of emerging Native voices, *Come to Power*. Since then, she has published a second chapbook, *Spirits Rest* (1981), and a collection of prayers and devotions for children, *The Effectual Fervent Prayer* (1997).

At the time of her retirement from the Lodgepole–Hayes School District, Allen was engaged in several projects, including her ongoing responsibilities as tribal historian. In connection with this position, she has been collecting the materials to write a tribal history from various sources and tribal elders for over fifteen years. She is also working with Buffalo Chasers, retrieving Assiniboine artifacts that have been held by the Smithsonian and other museums, and with Macro International in Maryland, on a study involving young Indian girls in the Harlem area of New York City and in Browning, Montana. The project hopes to compare the results of substance abuse prevention and intervention programs that are culturally specific. Her work on an herbal book describing the medicinal, nutritional, and spiritual aspects of local plants like sage, including the Indian, Latin, and English names for each plant, is nearly complete, and she is hoping to add photographs of each plant.

About her poetry, Allen says, "I write anytime and anywhere." Given the scope of her contributions in literature, history, and education, she also writes and works anytime and anywhere for her tribe and culture.

References

Allen, Minerva. *The Effectual Fervent Prayer*. Orlando, FL: Great House Publishing, 1997.
———. *Like Spirits of the Past Trying to Break Out and Walk to the West*. Albuquerque, NM: Wowapi, 1974.
———. *Spirits Rest*. Los Angeles: By the author, 1981.
Bredin, Renae Moore. Personal communication with Minerva Allen, February 17, 1997.
Hobson, Geary. *The Remembered Earth*. Albuquerque: University of New Mexico Press, 1980.
Kittredge, William, and Annick Smith, eds. *The Last Best Place: A Montana Anthology*. Seattle: University of Washington Press, 1988.
Lourie, Dick, ed. *Come to Power*. Trumansburg, NY: The Crossing Press, 1974.
Scholer, Bo. "Minerva Allen: A Few Good Words." *Wicazo Sa Review* 3 (Spring 1987): 1–7.

—*Renae Moore Bredin*

ALLEN, PAULA GUNN (b. 1939), was born at Cubero, New Mexico, to a Lebanese–American father and a Laguna–Sioux–Scottish mother, both of whom were native New Mexicans. She is divorced and the mother of three children. In 1966 she received her BA from the University of Oregon; in 1968; an MFA from the same university; and in 1975, a PhD in American Studies from the University of New Mexico.

Allen taught at San Francisco State University in 1975–1976; at the University of New Mexico in 1977–1978; at Fort Lewis College, Durango, Colorado, in 1978–1979; and at the University of California, Berkeley, in 1982–1986. Currently, she teaches English at UCLA. Her research and writing fellowships include an NEA fellowship in creative writing (1977–1978); a research fellowship, Institute of the Americas–American Indian Center for Research, UCLA (1981–1982); and a National Research Council senior postdoctoral fellowship for minority scholars (1984–1985). She has received the Kappa Kappa Gamma Prize for Poetry, University of New Mexico (1964); the Julia Burgess Prize for Poetry, University of Oregon (1967); a creative writing award from the National Endowment for the Arts (1977–1978); nominations for the Pushcart Poetry Prize (1979 and 1981); and, for *The Woman Who Owned the Shadows*, a citation from the San Francisco Board of Supervisors for contributions to the San Francisco Native American community (1983).

Allen is one of the most important American Indian intellectuals and artists. She is an avowed feminist and very active in women's movements as well as in antiwar and antinuclear organizations. A prolific writer, she has produced seven collections of poems, a novel, and a huge body of critical essays. As a poet, she uses a remarkable range of techniques and languages to convey to the reader the basic thematic elements of her poetry: her Pueblo reality versus white dominant culture, the role of women in the traditional Indian worldview, the sense and meaning of her own Indianness, and powerful mythic imagery as a means of resistance, regeneration, and survival. Her novel, *The Woman Who Owned the Shadows* (1983), is a stream-of-consciousness narrative of an Indian woman caught between cultures as she undertakes a quest to become whole, surrounded by the shadows of her tribal and personal past. Innovative in its structure, and influenced by writers such

Paula Gunn Allen

as Gertrude Stein and Virginia Woolf, the novel remains distinctly Native American; its thematic interaction between past and present, the Pueblo ceremonial
life/culture and the storytelling tradition plays a fundamental role in shaping the
main character's new identity.

Allen's outstanding work as a critic centers on American thought and on
American history from a minority perspective, a comprehensive introduction to Indian spiritual beliefs, a mythopoetic approach to American Indian literature, and
the theme of alienation in Indian prose and poetry. *Studies in American Indian
Literature*, which she edited in 1983 for the Modern Language Association, is a
standard work in the cross-disciplinary field. *The Sacred Hoop: Recovering the
Feminine in American Indian Traditions* is a collection of seventeen essays dealing
with cultural history, ethnic feminism, literary criticism, and the spirituality of traditional tribes and their use of the feminine.

Allen also has edited one of the most praised anthologies, *Spider Woman's
Granddaughters: Traditional Tales and Contemporary Writing by Native American Women*, a collection of short fiction, stories from the oral tradition, and excerpts from autobiographies. *Grandmothers of the Light: A Medicine Woman's
Sourcebook* includes twenty-one stories from the Cherokee, Navajo, Aztec, Maya,
and other Native civilizations. In a fine and extended introduction, "The Living
Reality of the Medicine World," Allen stresses the complexity of the word and the
concept of "medicine." Offering a real sourcebook for medicine women of the
twenty-first century and their spiritual beliefs, Allen discusses definitions and
analyses, then illustrates them with stories to make up a female shamanic tradition
and a powerful body of spiritual guides.

References

Aal, Katharyn Machan. "Writing as an Indian Woman: An Interview with Paula
    Gunn Allen." *North Dakota Quarterly* 57 (Spring 1989): 148–161.
Allen, Paula Gunn. "Beloved Woman: The Lesbians in American Indian Cultures."
    Conditions 3 (Spring 1981): 67–87.
———. *The Blind Lion*. Berkeley, CA: Thorp Springs Press, 1974.
———. *A Cannon Between My Knees*. New York: Strawberry Press, 1983.
———. *Coyote's Daylight Trip*. Albuquerque, NM: La Confluencia, 1978.
———. "The Grace That Remains: American Indian Women's Literature." *Book
    Forum* 5 (1981): 376–382.
———. *Grandmothers of the Light: A Medicine Woman's Sourcebook*. Boston:
    Beacon Press, 1991.
———. *Life is a Fatal Disease: Selected Poems 1964–1994*. Albuquerque, NM:
    West End Press, 1996.
———. *Off the Reservation: Reflections on Boundary-Busting, Border-Crossing
    Loose Canons*. Boston: Beacon Press, 1998.
———. "The Sacred Hoop: A Contemporary Indian Perception of American In-
    dian Literature." In *Literature of the American Indians: Views and Interpreta-
    tions*. Edited by Abraham Chapman. Pp. 111–135. New York: New American
    Library, 1975.
———. *The Sacred Hoop: Recovering the Feminine in American Indian Tradi-
    tions*. Boston: Beacon Press, 1986. Rev. ed., 1992.

———. *Shadow Country*. Los Angeles: American Indian Studies Center, 1982.

———. *Skins and Bones: Poems 1979–1987*. Albuquerque, NM: West End Press, 1988.

———, ed. *Song of the Turtle: American Indian Literature, 1974–1994*. New York: Ballantine Books, 1996.

———, ed. "Special Issue: Native Women of New Mexico." *A: A Journal of Contemporary Literature* 3 (Fall 1978).

———, ed. *Spider Woman's Granddaughters: Traditional Tales and Contemporary Writing by Native American Women*. Boston: Beacon Press, 1989.

———. *Star Child*. Marvin, SD: Blue Cloud Quarterly Press, 1981.

———. "A Stranger in My Own Life: Alienation in Native American Prose and Poetry." *ASAIL Newsletter* 3 (Spring 1979): 16–23.

———, ed. *Studies in American Indian Literature: Critical Essays and Course Designs*. New York: MLA, 1983.

———, ed. *Voice of the Turtle: American Indian Literature, 1900–1970*. New York: Ballantine Books, 1994.

———. "Where I Came from Is like This." In *Rereading America: Cultural Contexts for Critical Thinking and Writing*. Edited by Gary Colombo, Robert Cullen, and Bonnie Lisle. Pp. 273–281. New York: St. Martin's Press, 1990.

———. *The Woman Who Owned the Shadows*. San Francisco: Spinster's Ink, 1983.

———. *Wyrds*. San Francisco: Taurean Horn, 1987.

Allen, Paula Gunn, and Patricia Clark Smith. *As Long as the Rivers Flow: The Stories of Nine Native Americans*. New York: Scholastic, 1996.

Ballinger, Franchot, and Brian Swann. "A MELUS Interview: Paula Gunn Allen." *MELUS* 10 (Summer 1983): 3–25.

Bruchac, Joseph. "I Climb the Mesas in My Dreams: An Interview with Paula Gunn Allen." In *Survival This Way: Interviews with American Indian Poets*. Edited by Joseph Bruchac. Pp. 1–21. Tucson: University of Arizona Press, 1987.

Coltelli, Laura. "Paula Gunn Allen." In *Winged Words: American Indian Writers Speak*. Edited by Laura Coltelli. Pp. 10–39. Lincoln: University of Nebraska Press, 1990.

Eysturoy, Annie O. "Paula Gunn Allen." In *This Is about Vision: Interviews with Southwestern Writers*. Edited by William Balassi, John F. Crawford, and Annie O. Eysturoy. Pp. 94–107. Albuquerque: University of New Mexico Press, 1990.

Keating, Ana Louise. *Women Reading Women Writing: Self-Invention in Paula Gunn Allen, Gloria Anzaldúa, and Audre Lorde*. Philadelphia: Temple University Press, 1996.

Perry, Donna. "Paula Gunn Allen." In *Backtalk: Women Writers Speak Out*. Edited by Donna Perry. Pp. 1–18. New Brunswick, NJ: Rutgers University Press, 1993.

Van Dyke, Ann. "The Journey Back to Female Roots: A Laguna Pueblo Model." In *Lesbian Texts and Contexts: Radical Revisions*. Edited by Karla Jay and Joanne Glasgow. Pp. 339–354. New York: New York University Press, 1990.

—Laura Coltelli

ANAHEREO [Gertrude Benard] (1906–1986), married Archie Belaney (Grey Owl) in 1925. Her Mohawk ancestors lived at Lake of Two Mountains (Oka). Her Scottish great-great-grandmother had been taken captive during the French–Iroquois war and married Naharrenou (from which the name Anahereo is derived). Anahareo's grandparents left Oka to farm in Ontario, eventually settling at Mattawa on Lake Tamagami. She was raised by her grandmother, who taught her Indian crafts and medicine lore. Unhappy when an aunt with many children moved in to look after the aging grandmother, Anahereo skipped school and grew up to be a strong-willed, independent tomboy.

She met Belaney at Mattawa, joined him on the trapline, and married him in an Indian ceremony. Anahareo had no survival skills but eventually became a highly proficient prospector and dog team driver. Life changed dramatically when Belaney brought home two beaver kittens. He scoffed at Anahereo's idea of keeping them for pets, but her stubborness prevailed. She had long abhorred the cruelty of the trapline, and after considerable introspection, Belaney decided to devote his life to conservation instead of trapping.

He began to lecture and write, and eventually was appointed naturalist by the Canadian federal government. However, Anahereo found Belaney's sedentary life boring, even when their only child, Shirley Dawn, was born. Though dearly loved by both her parents, a baby did not fit into their lifestyle. A friend cared for Dawn when Anahereo returned to prospecting.

The marriage faltered, and after a final stormy meeting at which Belaney claimed Anahereo had tried to choke him for forty minutes, they separated permanently. After his death Anahereo learned that he was an Englishman. (He had told her he was part Mexican.) Hurt and bewildered, she felt that she had not known the man who had been her partner for so many years. She had supported his Indian image because she believed that he could more effectively convey his conservation message as an Indian.

Though there were other women in Belaney's life, he asked for Anahereo on his deathbed. History has focused almost exclusively on Grey Owl. Nevertheless, he made two movies of his beavers that featured Anahereo, and after a lecture, the questions were almost entirely about her.

Anahereo married Count Eric Moltke Huitfeldt in 1939 and drifted into relative obscurity. She was admitted to the Order of Nature of the International League of Animal Rights in 1979. With her daughter Dawn's encouragement, she wrote *Devil in Deerskins* (1972), which described her life with Grey Owl.

References

Anahereo. *Devil in Deerskins: My Life with Grey Owl*. Toronto: New Press, 1972.
"Mrs. Grey Owl's Amazing Life Story." *Vancouver Sun*, October 6, 1936.
Smith, Donald B. *From the Land of Shadows: The Making of Grey Owl*. Saskatoon, SK: Western Producer Prairie Books, 1990.

—Agnes Grant

ANAUTA [Anauta Ford Blackmore, A Stick For Beating Snow From Your Clothes], an Inuit, was born on Baffin Island, the third child and first daughter of Yorgke

(George Ford) and Alea. She does not know the exact date of her birth, but she does know that it occurred during a blizzard in which a respected hunter was lost. She was named Anauta after him, and was expected to follow in his footsteps and to excel. Consequently, her mother allowed the hunter Anauta's mother, Oomiálik, to raise Anauta.

Anauta dressed as a male for the first years of her life and learned the skills of hunting and trapping. Later, she wore women's clothing and learned the sewing and domestic skills of her people. She had a traditionally arranged wedding to Uille, a man who respected her abilities as a hunter and trapper. They had two daughters; a third was born after Uille drowned. Anauta then traveled to Labrador, then through Canada, finally settling in Indianapolis. She married Blackmore, a union that produced one daughter and later was amicably ended.

Anauta's autobiography details her difficulties in adjusting to a new culture, the problems she had with money, her struggle to learn English, and the illnesses of her family. She worked for five years in a factory before finding a career as a lecturer on the Baffin Island culture and way of life. She spoke at churches and schools throughout the Midwest.

At the request of Rev. E. J. Peck in Toronto, Anauta translated the Psalms and the Lord's Prayer into his Inuit language. The task was difficult because the English words often had no Inuit equivalent; she worked on this project for several years. Anauta is the coauthor, with Heluiz Washburne, of three books. *Land of Good Shadows* is her autobiography; *Wild like the Foxes* is based on the childhood of Anauta's mother, Alea; and *Children of the Blizzard* is a collection of stories depicting the life of Eskimo children.

References

Washburne, Heluiz, and Anauta. *Children of the Blizzard*. London: Dennis Dobson, 1960.
———. *Land of Good Shadows: The Life Story of Anauta, an Eskimo Woman*. New York: John Day, 1940. Reprint, New York: AMS Press, 1976.
———. *Wild like the Foxes: The True Story of an Eskimo Girl*. New York: John Day, 1956.

—Laurie Lisa

ANDERSON, MABEL WASHBOURNE (1863–1949), a writer and teacher, was descended from two well-known Cherokee families. Her maternal grandfather was John Rollin Ridge, a leader of the Treaty Party, and her paternal grandfather was Cephus Washburn (Anderson's father changed the spelling), an early missionary and founder of the Dwight Mission among the Cherokee. Although she was born in Arkansas, Anderson lived from early childhood in the Cherokee Nation, later Oklahoma. She was educated in the Cherokee public school system, graduating from the Cherokee Female Seminary in 1883 and later becoming a teacher at Vinita.

After her marriage to John Carlton Anderson in 1891, she continued to teach and began to write. She wrote for the local newspaper on education and school systems. She was also a member of the local Sequoyah Literary Society, for which she wrote and read presentations on Cherokee history and lore, and contributed articles and poems on such topics to local and out-of-territory newspapers. In 1904 the Andersons moved to Pryor Creek. There Mabel continued to write biographies, histories, and articles about folklore, art, and literature, for the most part concerning American Indians, and she taught English in the local high school. She was also active in civic affairs, the Christian church, and the United Daughters of the Confederacy (UDC).

In relation to the latter, one of her life's goals was to have a monument erected to the memory of the Cherokee general Stand Watie, her grandfather's cousin. In 1913 she organized a UDC chapter in his name, and in 1915 she published a short biography to promote interest in his memory. She revised and republished the work in 1931.

After the Andersons moved to Tulsa in 1930, she wrote little and dropped from public view. When she died, she was described by a local newspaper as a "colorful pioneer." No emphasis was placed on the distinguished Cherokee family from which she descended.

References

Anderson, Mabel Washbourne. *The Life of General Stand Watie, the Only Indian General of the Confederate Army and the Last General to Surrender*. Pryor, OK: Mayes County Republican, 1915. 2nd rev. ed., Pryor, OK: By the author, 1931.
Boren, Lyle H., and Dale Boren. *Who Is Who in Oklahoma*. Guthrie, OK: Cooperative Publishing, 1935.
Littlefield, Daniel F., Jr., and James W. Parins. *A Biobibliography of Native American Writers, 1772–1924*. Metuchen, NJ: Scarecrow Press, 1986.
Pryor Jeffersonian [Pryor OK], September 22, 1949; 8.
"Sketch of Mrs. Mabel W. Anderson." *Twin Territories* 3 (June 1901): 99.
Vinita Weekly Chieftain [Vinita, Cherokee Nation], March 5, 1903; 8.

—*Daniel F. Littlefield, Jr.*

ANDERSON, OWANAH (b. 1926), editor, author, and administrator, was born to Choctaw parents in Choctaw County, Oklahoma. A priority in Anderson's career has been helping to advance the status of American Indian/Alaska Native women. In pursuit of this goal, she founded and directed the Ohoyo (Choctaw for "woman") Resource Center in 1979 and served as its director. Anderson's other leadership posts include chairperson of the National Committee on Indian Work in 1979–1980 and cochairperson of the Texas delegation during the Houston Women's Conference in 1977. She was a member of President Carter's Advisory Committee on Women from 1978 to 1981, and was the only American Indian appointed to the Commission on Security and Cooperation that met in Madrid, Spain, in 1980. In 1981 Anderson received the Anne Roe Award from the Harvard University Graduate School of Education.

Anderson's *Ohoyo One Thousand: A Resource Guide of American Indian/ Alaska Native Women* assists interested individuals in locating female Indian leaders. The resource guide identifies 1004 women with skills in sixty-two Indian programs; it also lists individuals with expertise in twenty-eight women's issues, including domestic violence, adolescent pregnancy, educational equity, affirmative education, and child care. The work identifies women who have attained postgraduate degrees and are professionals in the fields of art, business, communications, education, health care, law, sciences, and social work. It also lists individuals who have made cultural contributions in traditional arts, *mediums*, ceremonials, and dance. Seeking to strengthen all Native women, the work includes individuals from 231 tribes and bands. Anderson also has edited *Words of Today's American Indian Women: Ohoyo Makachi*, a volume of speeches and discussions from a 1981 conference held in Tahlequah, Oklahoma.

References

Anderson, Owanah. *400 Years: Anglican/Espiscopal Mission Among American Indians*. Cincinnati, OH: Forward Movement Publications, 1997.
———, ed. *Ohoyo One Thousand: A Resource Guide of American Indian/Alaska Native Women, 1982*. Wichita Falls, TX: Ohoyo Resource Center, 1982.
———. *Words of Today's American Indian Women: Ohoyo Makachi*. Wichita Falls, TX: Ohoyo Resource Center, 1982.
Green, Rayna. *Native American Women: A Contextual Bibliography*. Bloomington: Indiana University Press, 1983.
"Keynote: Charting New Directions." In *American Public Discourse: A Multicultural Perspective*. Pp. 3–7. Edited by Ronald K. Burke. Lanham, MD: University Press of America, 1992.

—Steven R. Price

AQUASH, ANNA MAE PICTOU (1945–1976), Micmac Indian rights activist, was born on March 27 in Shubenacadie, Nova Scotia, the third daughter of Mary Ellen Pictou and Francis Thomas Levi. In 1949 her mother married Noel Sapier, the son and the brother of traditional Micmac chiefs, and the family moved to Pictou's Landing on Northumberland Strait, where Aquash was raised in poverty. In 1962 she married a fellow tribesman, Jake Maloney, and moved to Boston. In the early 1970s, she taught at the Teaching and Research in Bicultural Education (TRIBE) school in Maine, enrolled in the New Careers Program at Wheelock College in Boston, worked at the Ruggles Street Day Care Center in Roxbury, helped to establish a job placement program, and was offered a scholarship to Brandeis University. She turned down the scholarship in order to care for her two daughters.

In 1972, along with members of the Boston Indian Council, Aquash participated in the American Indian Movement's (AIM) occupation of the Bureau of Indian Affairs headquarters in Washington, D.C. The next year, she joined the occupation at Wounded Knee, South Dakota, and married a Chippewa artist, Nogeeshik Aquash. For the next four years, Aquash worked as an AIM organizer. At the same time that she was traveling throughout the country carrying information, establishing support groups, and participating in protests, she also was dodging the FBI, who believed she could identify the killers of two FBI agents who were shot near Oglala, South Dakota, on June 26, 1975. She also fought rumors that were circulating among AIM members that she was an FBI informant.

On February 24, 1976, Aquash's body was found on the Pine Ridge Reservation in South Dakota; she had been shot in the back of the head. The circumstances of her death remain a mystery. The FBI accused AIM of killing her because it believed she was working for the FBI, and AIM accused the FBI of murdering her in retaliation for the deaths of their agents. Another theory is that AIM members killed her at the behest of the FBI.

References

Brand, Johanna. *The Life and Death of Anna Mae Aquash*. Toronto: James Lorimer, 1978.

Matthiessen, Peter. *In the Spirit of Crazy Horse*. New York: Viking Press, 1983.

Weir, David, and Lowell Bergman. "The Killing of Anna Mae Aquash." *Rolling Stone*, April 7, 1977; 51–55.

Witt, Shirley Hill. "The Brave-Hearted Women: The Struggle at Wounded Knee." *Civil Rights Digest* 8 (1976): 38–45.

—Devon A. Mihesuah

AQUINO, ELLA PIERRE (1902–1988), of Lummi and Yakima descent, is one of twelve children. She is survived by one sibling, Margaret Pierre. Aquino, a product of the boarding school system, attended Tulalip Indian School and St. George Catholic Boarding School. Her first marriage, to Owen Ringer, ended with his death in 1937; she married George Aquino (Filipino) of Seattle, Washington, in 1944. She had six children and is survived by two daughters, Alma and Geraldine.

Known throughout the Seattle area as the matriarch of the Seattle Native American community, Aquino was an extremely compassionate, humble, and caring woman. These characteristics led her to become a very public Indian civil rights activist. Before the enactment of the Indian Childhood Welfare Act (ICWA) in 1978, her earliest stand was on the issue of Indian children being placed in Indian foster homes. Aquino became politically active, pressuring Washington State to respond to and stop cross-racial foster placements. She diligently raised funds for political action and dedicated her life to recruiting Indian foster parents. Aquino and her husband personally fostered many children of color. She was one of eight nominated by Region Ten of the federal government as a "Beautiful Activist."

Noting the loss of the traditional male roles in Indian communities and the damaging consequences of Bureau of Indian Affairs (BIA) "relocation" efforts, Aquino struggled to address these issues as one of the founders of the Seattle Indian Center and the American Indian Women's Service League. The far-reaching impact of Aquino's caring was evident in the struggle with the Asian community over the expansion of the Seattle Indian Center. The primary speaker for the Asian community acknowledged, in a large community debate, that he couldn't speak against the expansion because his foster mother (Aquino) was a key instigator of this expansion.

Aquino was a key member of the early organized efforts to regain federal recognition of tribal treaty and fishing rights, and an advocate for the Puyallup tribe's regaining title to tribal land. She spearheaded the movement to gain the Fort Lawton property and the Cushman Hospital. Earning the title "Give 'em Hell Ella," she was photographed scaling the hill and barbed wire fence when the movement faced off with the National Guard and local police in a nonviolent sit-in at Fort Lawton.

A supporter of Indian journalism, Aquino edited the column "Teepee Talk" in the *Northwest Indian* newspaper. A video honoring her many contributions, *Princess of the Pow Wow*, is available.

References

Running Wolf, Paulette. Telephone interview with Ramona Bennett, July 1998.
————. Telephone interview with Margaret Pierre, September 1998.

—Paulette Running Wolf and Susan Rae Banks

ARCHAMBAULT, JOALLYN (b. 1943), a Standing Rock Sioux, was born in Claremore, Oklahoma, to a family of Sioux–Creek–Irish–French ancestry. She received her PhD in anthropology from the University of California, Berkeley and then served on the faculties of the University of California, Berkeley; California College of Arts and Crafts; and University of Wisconsin, Milwaukee. While at Berkeley, she served as curator of the Lowie Museum of Anthropology.

Among Archambault's many acts of service to the Indian community, she has been a member of the board of directors of the California Indian Education Advisory Board, the Native American Scholarship Fund, the Native American Arts Studies Association, the Milwaukee Indian Economic Development Association, and the Northern Plains Tribal Arts Association.

Archambault has frequently been honored for her efforts to preserve and promote Indian arts and culture. While still a student, she won a Ford Foundation doctoral fellowship. Her artwork has appeared in such venues as the Heard Museum in Phoenix, Arizona.

Currently the director of American Indian Programs at the Smithsonian Institution's National Museum of Natural History, Archambault has worked on special events, such as curating the Plains Indian Arts Exhibit that toured the country in the late 1980s as part of SITES (Smithsonian Institution Traveling Exhibits Series). She also has been editor for a collection of tribal catalogs.

References

Anderson, Owanah, ed. *Ohoyo One Thousand: A Resource Guide of American Indian/Alaska Native Women, 1982*. Wichita Falls, TX: Ohoyo Resource Center, 1982.
Fixico, Michelene, comp. *Resource Directory of American Indian Professionals*. Milwaukee: University of Wisconsin Press, 1987.
Who's Who Among the Sioux. Vermillion: University of South Dakota, Institute of Indian Studies, 1988.

—Cynthia Kasee

ARMSTRONG, JEANNETTE (b. 1948), was born on the Okanagan Reserve near Penticton, British Columbia, where she received instruction from her parents and traditional elders, and also attended to local schools. She is a grandniece of Humishuma (Mourning Dove, 1888–1936), the author of an early Native American novel, *Co-Ge-We-A, The Half-Blood* (1927).

Armstrong earned a diploma of fine arts from Okanagan College, and later a BFA in creative writing from the University of Victoria. An active participant in the political and cultural life of the Okanagan Nation, she has worked in various capacities in the curriculum development and cultural programs of her people. Two books of juvenile fiction came out of this involvement: *Enwhisteetkwa: Walk on Water* and *Neekna and Chemai*.

Jeannette Armstrong was an elected council member of the Penticton band. Since 1978 she has been working with the Okanagan people's En'Owkin Cultural Center, serving as its director since 1985. The En'Owkin Center also houses Theytus Books, the first Native-owned and -operated publishing house in Canada. In 1985 Armstrong's first novel (for young and adult readers), *Slash*, was published by Theytus Books. The novel combines historiography (of the American Indian Movement and related Native struggles in Canada) with the fictional biography of a young Okanagan man, Thomas Kelasket, who moves from a very traditional upbringing on the reserve through skid row, addiction, crime, and prison, toward political awakening and active involvement in the Red Power Movement. Kelasket finally comes to realize that unless he observes, follows, and practices a traditional Indian way, even in a modern setting, there is no Indian identity and no survival worth struggling for.

Besides her internationally acclaimed novel, Armstrong has published a book of poetry, *Breath Tracks* (1991), and written a collaborative discourse, *The Native Creative Process* (1991), with Métis architect Cardinal Douglas. Her poetry and essays have appeared in numerous anthologies and magazines. She has won artistic achievement prizes such as the Mungo Martin Award (1974), the Helen Pitt Memorial Award (1978), and the Vancouver Foundation Graduate Award (1978). A brilliant orator, she has addressed Native and non–Native audiences across North America on issues of cultural self-determination, ethnic pride, Native voice, and Indian self-expression through the arts, especially literature. In 1993 she edited the first all-Native anthology of literary criticism, *Looking at the Words of Our People: First Nations Analysis of Literature*.

Armstrong was responsible for the establishment of the En'Owkin School of International Writing, the first creative writing program designed and operated by Native people, affiliated with the University of Victoria. Since September 4, 1989, when the En'Owkin School started to operate, she has been its director; the program, is attracting increasing numbers of students. Since 1990 the En'Owkin School has published an annual collection of First Nations fiction, poetry, and criticism, *Gatherings: The En'Owkin Journal of First North American Peoples*.

Jeanette Armstrong stands alone as Canada's most active, determined, and diligent promoter of First Nations literature and of cultural and political self-determination. She has traveled and read widely in North and South America, Russia, Switzerland, and Germany.

References

Armstrong, Jeannette. *Breath Tracks*. Vancouver, BC: Williams-Wallace/Theytus Books, 1991.

———. *Enwhisteetkwa: Walk on Water*. Penticton, BC: Okanagan Indian Curriculum Project, 1982.

———, ed. *Looking at the Words of Our People: First Nations Analysis of Literature*. Penticton, BC: Theytus Books, 1993.

———. *Neekna and Chemai*. Penticton, BC: Theytus Books, 1984.

———. "Rights on Paper: An Interview with Victoria Freeman." *Fuse* (March/April 1988): 36–38.

———. *Slash*. Penticton, BC: Theytus Books, 1985. Rev. ed., 1988.

———. *Whispering in Shadows: A Novel*. Penticton, BC: Theytus Books, 2000.

———. "Words." In *Telling It: Women and Language Across Cultures*. edited by the Telling It Book Collective. Pp. 23–30. Vancouver, BC: Press Gang Publishers, 1990.

Cardinal, Douglas, and Jeannette Armstrong. *The Native Creative Process: A Collaborative Discourse Between Douglas Cardinal and Jeannette Armstrong*. Penticton, BC: Theytus Books, 1991.

Currie, Noel Elizabeth. "Jeannette Armstrong and the Colonial Legacy." *Canadian Literature* 124–125 (Spring/Summer 1990): 138–152.

Dube, Pamela Z. "Breaking the Silence: Concepts of Anger and Identity Assertion in Contemporary English Poetry Writing of First Nations Women." In *Ahornblätter: Marburger Beiträge zur Kanada-Forschung*, no. 9. Pp. 145–156. Marburg, Germany: Universitätsbibliothek Marburg, 1996.

Fee, Margery. "Upsetting Fake Ideas: Jeannette Armstrong's 'Slash' and Beatrice Culleton's 'April Raintree.'" *Canadian Literature* 124–125 (Spring/Summer 1990): 168–180.

"Jeannette Armstrong." In *Contemporary Challenges: Conversations with Canadian Native Authors*. Edited by Hartmut Lutz. Pp. 13–32. Saskatoon, Sask.: Fifth House, 1991.

Lutz, Hartmut. "Contemporary Native Literature in Canada and 'The Voice of Mother.'" In *O Canada: Essays on Canadian Literature and Culture*. Pp. 79–96. Aarhus, Denmark: Aarhus University Press, 1995.

———. "First Nations Literature in Canada: Writing Back and Writing Home." In *Ahornblätter: Marburger Beiträge zur Kanada-Forschung*, no. 9. Pp. 129–141. Marburg: Universitätsbibliothek Marburg, 1996.

Petrone, Penny. *Native Literature in Canada: From the Oral Tradition to the Present*. Toronto: Oxford University Press, 1990.

Witalec, Janet, ed. *Native North American Literature*. New York: Gale Research, 1994.

—Hartmut Lutz

ARRINGTON, RUTH (b. 1924), was born in Tulsa, Oklahoma. She is a member of the Creek tribe. She received her bachelor's degree in speech at the Oklahoma College for Women (Chickasha), her MA in speech at the University of Michigan, and her PhD in speech at Louisiana State University (1971). She taught speech and co-ordinated the Indian Studies Program at Northeastern State University in Tahle-quah, Oklahoma, until her retirement in 1988. Besides producing and directing plays, musicals, and a film on Indian governments, she portrayed the Cherokee Beloved Woman Nancy Ward in *Horn of the West*, an outdoor drama staged in Boone, North Carolina.

Arrington has served on a number of boards and commissions, including the Oklahoma Indian Affairs Commission (1982–87), the Headlands Indian Health Program Board and staff, the Oklahoma Humanities Committee, and the Advisory Board of the American Indian Institute at the University of Oklahoma. She has published a number of articles, including "Alex Posey: Creek Statesman, Journal-ist, and Poet," in *Essays on Minority Folklore* (1977), and "Some American Indian Voices," in *The Speech Teacher* (1975). She was named Outstanding Indian Woman by the Oklahoma Federation of Indian Women in 1972 and Outstanding College Theatre Educator by the Oklahoma Speech/Theatre/Communication As-sociation in 1987. She remains active in professional organizations and cultural events in Oklahoma.

Reference

Anderson, Owanan. *Ohoyo One Thousand: A Resource Guide of American Indian/Alaska Native Women*. Wichita Falls, TX: Ohoyo Resource Center, 1982.

—Clara Sue Kidwell

ARTHUR, CLAUDEEN BATES (b. 1942), Navajo attorney, was born in Ganado, Ari-zona. After graduating with a JD degree from Arizona State University in 1974, Arthur worked for two years at Navajo Legal Services in the reservation town of Shiprock, New Mexico. In 1978, following the establishment of her private prac-tice, she became the only Indian woman lawyer to attain the rank of field solicitor for the United States Department of the Interior, a post she held for four years.

Because of her career accomplishments and her strong belief in the ability of the Navajo woman, Arthur is seen as a role model for Indian women considering a career in law. Concerned also with the entire Navajo Nation, she recognizes the need for Navajos, male and female, to make careful decisions about their future. To ensure the self-determination of her people, Arthur stresses the need for educa-tion to combat the poverty and unemployment that the Nation faces.

References

Anderson, Owanah, ed. *Ohoyo One Thousand: A Resource Guide of American Indian/Alaska Native Women, 1982*. Wichita Falls, TX: Ohoyo Resource Cen-ter, 1982.
Wood, Beth, and Tom Barry. "The Story of Three Navajo Women." *Integrateduca-tion* 16 (March/April 1978): 33–35.

—Steven R. Price

ASHEVAK, KENOJUAK [Kenoyuak, Kinoajuak] (b. 1927), was born at Ikarasak, near Cape Dorset on Baffin Island, in Arctic Canada. After her father died, Kenojuak and her younger brother were raised by their maternal grandmother, Quisa. In 1949 she married Johnniebo, an artist and hunter with whom she reared sixteen children (five of them adopted). Probably the best-known woman Inuit printmaker, Kenojuak resides at Cape Dorset.

In the late 1950s the Canadian artist and author James A. Houston, serving as a civil administrator for the Department of Northern Affairs and National Resources, introduced drawing and printmaking to the Inuit people of Cape Dorset. Although not residing in Cape Dorset at the time (but in a nearby fishing village), Kenojuak, encouraged by Houston, began drawing. By the time she and Johnniebo moved to Cape Dorset around 1967, printmaking was a well-established way to earn a living. Kenojuak's graphic designs have appeared in almost every collection of Inuit art since 1959. Her work has been exhibited, collected, and sold internationally.

As early as 1961 the National Film Board of Canada produced a film about Kenojuak's life and environment, of *Eskimo Artist—Kenojuak*. Like other Cape Dorset artists, Kenojuak depicts scenes of seasonal activities and figures from Inuit myths. Her images are memorable, filled with grace and spirit. In 1967 (one source says 1970) Kenojuak received the Order of Canada, the nation's highest civilian honor, for her artistic contributions. Frequently she creates bird and sun designs, for which she is well known. Her most renowned piece is a stonecut, *The Enchanted Owl*, which appeared in the 1960 collection of Inuit art. In 1970 this dazzling bird was used as the design for the six-cent Canadian postage stamp commemorating the centennial of the Northwest Territories. Often Kenojuak and Johnniebo collaborated on prints. Together they created a ninety six-foot-square plaster carved wall panel that was displayed at the Canadian Pavilion at Expo '70 in Osaka, Japan. In 1974 Kenojuak became a member of the Royal Canadian Academy.

In addition to museum curators and art collectors, Kenojuak's designs have been sought by religious and commercial organizations: the Roman Catholic Church used one of her designs in their Sunday missal (1976), and the retail store Northern Images used a Kenojuak design for its logo (1978). In 1980 her 1961 print *Return of the Sun* was the design for a seventeen-cent Canadian stamp. Two years later she was appointed a Companion of the Order of Canada. After Johnniebo's death, Kenojuak remarried. She continues her work as a graphic artist, occasionally producing stonecuts and engravings.

References

Barz, Sandra B., comp. *Inuit Artists Print Workbook*. New York: Arts and Cultures of the North, 1981.

Blodgett, Jean. *Graphic Masterworks of the Inuit: Kenojuak*. Toronto: Mintmark, 1981.

Dorset 79: The Twentieth Annual Cape Dorset Graphics Collection. Toronto: M. F. Feheley, 1979.

Furneaux, Patrick. "Evolution and Development of the Eskimo Print." In *Arts of the Eskimo: Prints*. Edited by Ernst Roch. Pp. 9–16. Barre, MA: Barre, 1975.

Leroux, Odette, Marion E. Jackson, and Minnie Aodla Freeman, eds. *Inuit Women Artists: Voices from Cape Dorset*. Vancouver, BC: Douglas & McIntyre, 1994.
Rosshandler, Leo. "The Eskimo Print, an Appreciation." In *Arts of the Eskimo: Prints*. Edited by Ernst Roch. Pp. 17–19. Barre, MA: Barre, 1975.
Schuldberg, Jane. *Kenojuak Ashevak*. Seattle: Snow Goose Associates, n.d.

—Hertha D. Wong

ASHOONA, PITSEOLAK (1904–1983), was born on Nottingham Island in Hudson Strait in Arctic Canada. As a child, she lived with her father, Ottochie, and her mother, Timangiak, near Frobisher Bay and Cape Dorset, and later on Akudluk Island. One of the best-known Inuit printmakers, she spent much of her adult life at Cape Dorset and is referred to as a Cape Dorset artist. Because in Inuit societies surnames are not traditional, and because there are various spellings of names, there is sometimes considerable confusion about individuals and their relationships to others with the same name. Although Pitseolak is a fairly common name, Pitseolak Ashoona is widely known simply as Pitseolak. Following in her footsteps, Pitseolak's children are also Cape Dorset artists. Her four sons, Ottochie, Kumwartok (variant Koomwartok), Kaka, and Kiawak, are sculptors, and her daughter Nawpachee (sometimes spelled Nawpashee, Napachee, Napatchie, or Napassie) is a printmaker.

In the late 1950s, when Canadian artist and author James A. Houston, serving as a civil administrator for the Department of Northern Affairs and National Resources, introduced drawing and printmaking to the Inuit people of Cape Dorset, Pitseolak Ashoona was among the first to learn. A widow trying to support her children, she began drawing to supplement the income she made from sewing. According to some sources, she produced over seven thousand original drawings, only some of which have been made into prints.

Pitseolak's graphic designs appeared in every annual Cape Dorset print collection from 1960 to 1984. Her prints have been exhibited internationally, and some of them are in the National Gallery of Canada. Like other Inuit artists, Pitseolak's drawings often include animals, birds, mythical figures, and seasonal activities, such as hunting, kayaking, or tanning hides. According to Leo Rosshandler, Pitseolak combines "imagination and recollection in well-organized patterns," and her prints convey movement and spirit.

In 1971 she traveled to Ottawa for the formal presentation of the book about her life, *Pitseolak: Pictures Out of My Life*, to the National Library by the Honorable Jean Chrétien. Later that year she traveled to Montreal to attend the opening of an exhibition of her work at the Canadian Guild of Crafts. Elected a member of the Royal Canadian Academy of Arts in 1974, Pitseolak received a Canada Council Senior Arts Grant in 1975. That same year the International Cinemedia Centre made two films about her work: *The Way We Live Today* and *Spirits and Monsters*. In recognition of her contribution to Canadian art, in 1977 she received the Order of Canada, Canada's highest civilian honor. "To make prints is not easy," Pitseolak once explained, "but I am happy doing prints. . . . If I can, I'll make them even after I am dead." Even when ill, Pitseolak continued to draw. She died on May 28, 1983.

References

Barz, Sandra B., comp. *Inuit Artists Print Workbook*. New York: Arts and Cultures of the North, 1981.

Dorset 79: The Twentieth Annual Cape Dorset Graphics Collection. Toronto: M. F. Feheley, 1979.

Eber, Dorothy, ed. *Pitseolak: Pictures Out of My Life*. Toronto: Oxford University Press, 1971.

Furneaux, Patrick. "Evolution and Development of the Eskimo Print." In *Arts of the Eskimo: Prints*. Edited by Ernst Roch. Pp. 9–16. Barre, MA: Barre, 1975.

Katz, Jane B. *This Song Remembers: Self-Portraits of Native Americans in the Arts*. Boston: Houghton Mifflin, 1980.

Leroux, Odette, Marion E. Jackson, and Minnie Aodla Freeman, eds. *Inuit Women Artists: Voices from Cape Dorset*. Vancouver, BC Douglas & McIntyre, 1994.

Rosshandler, Leo. "The Eskimo Print, an Appreciation." In *Arts of the Eskimo: Prints*. Edited by Ernst Roch. Pp. 17–19. Barre, MA: Barre, 1975.

Schuldberg, Jane. "The Matriarchs." *Snow Goose Flyer* 102 (January/February 1987).

———. *Pitseolak Ashoona*. Seattle: Snow Goose Associates, n.d.

—Hertha D. Wong

AWASHONKS [The Queen] was one of at least three women chieftains in New England during King Philip's War (1675–1676). Her husband, Tolony, is believed to have died before this time because she was already the squaw sachem of the Saconnet (or Sakonnet) band in the vicinity of present-day Little Compton, Rhode Island, having succeeded her brother after his death. Her band was originally part of the Wampanoag Confederacy. Unlike two other women chieftains of the period, Wetamoo and Magnus, Awashonks agreed in 1671 to a nonaggression pact with the colonial officials. She allied her tribe with the white settlers (c. 1676), committing some of her warriors to the English advances against King Philip and his confederates. In this way, Awashonks was able to preserve the integrity of her tribe, and during the fighting she led her band to the settlement of Sandwich, Massachusetts.

References

Biographical Dictionary of Indians of the Americas. Vol. 1. Newport Beach, CA: American Indian Publishers, 1983.

Mathes, Valerie Sherer. "Native American Women in Medicine and the Military." *Journal of the West* 21 (April 1982): 41–48.

Waldman, Carl. *Who Was Who in Native History: Indians and Non–Indians from Early Contacts Through 1900*. New York: Facts on File, 1990.

—Laurie Lisa

AWIAKTA, MARILOU (b. 1936), is an Eastern Cherokee poet whose unique mixing of themes from Cherokee mythology and antinuclear messages reflects the milieu in which she was raised. In the foothills of the Smoky Mountains, not far from the Cherokee Reservation of Qualla, lies Oak Ridge, Tennessee, the site of nuclear experimentation, key to the success of the Manhattan Project in World War II, the place where her father worked. Still a leading research area in nuclear energy, Oak Ridge is also federal land, what Awiakta describes as "a reservation for atoms, not Indians."

After graduating magna cum laude with a BA in English from the University of Tennessee in 1958, Awiakta went on to a distinguished career as a poet, lecturer, and folklorist. In 1986 her books *Abiding Appalachia: Where Mountain and Atom Meet* and *Rising Fawn and the Fire Mystery* were chosen for inclusion in the United States Information Agency's global tour, Women in the Contemporary World. She was the only American to have her work featured at the Ceremony for the Survival of the World in Le Havre, France (the poem was "Out of Ashes, Peace Will Rise").

Tennessee celebrated the Homecoming '86 Literary Festival in Nashville, and once again Awiakta was honored for her unique contributions to the preservation of traditional culture and its incorporation with atomic age issues. From the works read at this event, her "Motheroot" was chosen by Alice Walker to begin a section of her book *In Search of Our Mothers' Gardens*.

Awiakta has appeared on PBS programs such as *Natchez Trace Parkway: A Microcosm of America* (1988) and *American Indian Stories* (1989). She has lectured at Boston University, the Memphis Arts-in-the-Schools Program, and Tufts University's Conference to Develop a New Model for American Studies, Using Black, Ethnic and Feminist Perspectives. Numerous commissioned articles have appeared in such journals and periodicals as *Southern Exposure, Mandala, Fireweed*, and *Tennessee Conservationist*.

Awiakta's latest release is *Selu: Seeking the Corn-Mother's Wisdom*, a commingling of Cherokee stories and modern conservationist themes. She lives in Memphis, Tennessee, with her husband, Paul Thompson, and their three children.

References

Awiakta, Marilou. *Abiding Appalachia: Where Mountain and Atom Meet*. Memphis, TN: St. Luke's Press, 1978.
———. *Rising Fawn and the Fire Mystery*. Memphis, TN: St. Luke's Press, 1983.
———. *Selu: Seeking the Corn-Mother's Wisdom*. Golden, CO: Fulcrum, 1993.
———, and Phyllis Tickle. *Confessing Conscience: Churched Women on Abortion*. Nashville, TN: Arlington Press, 1990.
Cherokee Nation of Oklahoma, ed. *Proceedings of the National Women's Symposium, Tahlequah, OK, 1989*. Tahlequah: Cherokee Nation of Oklahoma, 1990.
Radford University, comp. *Appalachian Studies Conference Proceedings, 1985*. Radford, VA: Radford University, 1985.
Tennessee Arts Commission. *Homewords '86: An Anthology of State Writers*. Knoxville: University of Tennessee Press, 1986.
Walker, Alice. *In Search of Our Mothers' Gardens*. New York: Harcourt Brace Jovanovich, 1983.

—*Cynthia Kasee*

AYOUNGMAN, VIVIAN (b. 1947), was born into the Siksika (Blackfoot) Indian Nation, east of Calgary, Alberta, Canada. She attended the Old Sun Anglican Boarding School until the seventh grade, when she was transferred to the public school system as a result of a Department of Indian Affairs "integration initiative." Encouragement from her family and her own desire to learn helped her to graduate near the top of her class. After graduating from Western Canada High School in Calgary, in 1966, she attended the University of Calgary, where she majored in secondary education with an emphasis in second languages, graduating in 1970 with a BEd degree. Ayoungman then worked for three years as a teacher at the Ermineskin Morley Indian School before returning to the University of Calgary, where she served as a counselor in the Indian Student University Program, which she helped to establish. In 1974 she was elected to the board of directors of Old Sun Community College, and later served as academic vice president. Ayoungman received her MA and PhD degrees from Arizona State University. She now serves as the director of education for the Treaty Seven Tribal Council in Calgary. While engaged in her doctoral studies, she was the principal writer for the Sisiai'powashin Curriculum Project of the Siksika Curriculum Committee.

Ayoungman's interest in education goes beyond the classroom to include the community. At the University of Calgary, her interest in cultural diversity led her to join the International Students' Association, where she was exposed to different peoples and lifestyles. Her association with the campus civil liberties organization increased her awareness of problems within the community, particularly the negative image of American Indians found in textbooks and the media. She worked to dispel this image through speaking engagements at community and educational organizations as well as in the school classroom. Her selection as Indian Princess of Canada in 1968 gave her the opportunity to travel throughout Canada, speaking in a more official capacity. Personal knowledge of the social and financial hardships faced by the Native American community has served to strengthen her commitment to education.

Throughout her life, Ayoungman has maintained strong ties with her family and community. As part of a family that ranched on the Siksika Nation, she attended the rodeos, powwows, and ceremonies, including the Sun Dance, that were a part of community life. When away at school, she retained her ties by returning on weekends and spending vacations at home with her family. She attributes much of her success as an educator to her ability to blend formal education with traditional Indian values and cultural traits.

References

Axford, Roger W. "Vivian Ayoungman: Canadian Blackfoot Counselor." In *Native Americans: 23 Indian Biographies*. Pp. 77–81. Indiana, PA: A. G. Halldin, 1980.

Benson, Arlon. Personal communication with Vivian Ayoungman, March 20, 1992.

—Arlon Benson

B

BAHE, LIZ SOHAPPY [Om-na-ma, Cheshuts] (b. 1948), a Yakima poet, was born and spent her childhood near Toppenish, Washington. In 1969, at the age of twenty-one, she was assigned her Native American name, Om-na-ma. According to Bahe, this was a crucial moment in her experience: "My Indian name has made a great difference in my life. I really felt like a floating body until I received my name."

Before studying art for a time in Portland, Oregon, Bahe attended the Institute of American Indian Arts in Santa Fe, New Mexico, where, in addition to poetry, she was schooled in painting, sculpture, weaving, ceramics, music, and drama. She returned to the Institute in the summer of 1970 to study in a postgraduate poetry workshop.

Bahe's poetry is included in several anthologies and has appeared in *Suntracks* and *The South Dakota Review*. Her verse, which draws its form from modern Western poetry, also conveys a concern for her Native American heritage through subject matter ranging from a tribal parade to a Blackfoot ration card to a cornhusk bag. Kenneth Lincoln has suggested that the significance of her work, and that of other poets from the Institute of American Indian Arts, is that it "mark[s] the beginning of artists fusing old tribal names, new tongues, and adopted literary forms."

References

Allen, Terry, and Mae Durham, eds. *The Whispering Wind: Poetry by Young American Indians*. Garden City, NY: Doubleday, 1972.

Blicksilver, Edith. *The Ethnic American Woman: Problems, Protests, Lifestyle*. Dubuque, IA: Kendall/Hunt, 1978. Enl. ed. 1989.

Jacobson, Angeline, comp. *Contemporary Native American Literature: A Selected and Partially Annotated Bibliography*. Metuchen, NJ: Scarecrow Press, 1977.

Lincoln, Kenneth. *Native American Renaissance*. Berkeley: University of California Press, 1983.

Milton, John R., comp. *The American Indian Speaks*. Vermillion: University of South Dakota Press, 1969.

Niatum, Duane, ed. *Carriers of the Dream Wheel*. New York: Harper & Row, 1975.

—*Eric Severson*

BAKER, MARIE ANNHARTE [Anishinaabe] (b. 1942), an Ojibwa, was born and raised in Winnipeg, Manitoba. After attending university for a while, she went to Los Angeles and later to Minneapolis, which at the time, was the center of the American Indian Movement. She became involved in Native American activism and taught Native Studies at a number of colleges in Minneapolis. At Augsburg College she was one of the first people in North America to teach a course on Native American women. In 1980 she returned to Winnipeg and worked as a community family advocate.

In 1990 Baker published her first book of poetry, *Being on the Moon*. In the same year she won a National Film Board grant for *Too Tough*, a five-minute film in which she celebrates the spiritual power of Native women in order to counter their pervasive victim image. In 1991 she won the city of Regina's writing award for *Albeit Aboriginal*, a script presented in a workshop by the Nokomis Players, that was designed to reclaim the voices of Native women which had been appropriated by the New Age "shamans." A chapbook of poetry, *Coyote Columbus Cafe*, appeared in 1994. In 1995 her poem "Porkskin Panorama," which first appeared in *Callaloo*, was chosen by Adrienne Rich for her collection *Best American Poetry*. In the same year Baker received her BA from the University of Winnipeg and produced a video, *Moon Pause*, that draws on a recurring childhood dream in which she brings spotted horses back to her people.

In her essays "Medicine Lives" and "Borrowing Enemy Language" Baker contends that Native writing does not fit the criteria which govern the literary genres of the Western tradition, and advocates a redefining of the traditional concepts of orality and literacy. This concern for a First Nation's aesthetics has led her to volunteer for a Vancouver weekly radio program, *When Spirit Whispers*, where in "moc-talk" she interviews Native people, discussing what is and what is not Native literature and art. Baker is currently studying for her MA in art education at Simon Fraser University in Vancouver and working on her poetry collection *Blueberry Canoe*, which reclaims ancestral Ojibwa voices. She calls out for change with uncompromising honesty, irreverence, and a trenchant sense of humor.

References

Baker, Marie Annharte. *Being on the Moon*. Winlaw, BC: Polestar, 1990.
———. "Borrowing Enemy Language: A First Nation Woman Use of English." *West Coast Line* 27 (1993): 59–66.
———. *Coyote Columbus Cafe*. Winnipeg, MN: Moonprint, 1994.
———. "Medicine Lives: The Doctoring of Story and Self." *Canadian Woman Studies* 14 (Spring 1994): 114–118.
Petrone, S. Penny. Personal communication with Marie Baker, April 5 and 16, 1997.

—*S. Penny Petrone*

BELL, BETTY LOUISE (b. 1949), a scholar and fiction writer of Cherokee ancestry, is director of the Native American Studies Program and assistant professor of American culture, English, and Women's Studies at the University of Michigan, Ann Arbor. Her areas of scholarly interest include Native American literature,

Women's Studies, nineteenth-century American literature, and creative writing. She earned her PhD in 1985 from Ohio State University. Her first novel, *Faces in the Moon*, was published in 1994 and received favorable reviews. The work describes the homecoming of Lucie Evers and examines how she reestablishes connections with her past, her heritage, and her family. In addition, Bell has published critical articles on Native American literature that emphasize the political and personal aspects of Native American identity. Her projects in progress include writing *A Red Girl's Reasoning: Native American Women Writers and the Twentieth Century*; editing *Reading Red: Feminism in Native America*, (forthcoming from the Smithsonian Institution Press); and coediting the *Norton Anthology of Native American Literatures* (forthcoming).

References

Bell, Betty Louise. "Almost the Whole Truth: Gerald Vizenor's Shadow-working and Native American Autobiography." *A-B: Auto-Biography Studies* 7 (Fall 1992): 180–195.

————. *Faces in the Moon.* Norman: University of Oklahoma Press, 1994.

————, ed. *Linda Hogan: Calling Us Home.* Special issue of *Studies in American Indian Literatures* 6 (Fall 1994).

————. "Pocahontas: 'Little Mischief' and the 'Dirty Men.'" *Studies in American Indian Literatures* 6 (Spring 1994): 63–70.

—Dorie S. Goldman and Vanessa Holford Diana

BENNETT, KAY CURLEY [Kaibah] (1922–1997), a Navajo artist, author, and dollmaker, was born in a hogan at Sheepsprings Trading Post, New Mexico. Her father was Keedah, a silversmith, and her mother was Mary (Chahiilbahi) Chischillie. She attended Toadlena Boarding School in Toadlena, New Mexico, where she was later employed as a dormitory attendant (1945–1946). From 1946 to 1952 she was a teacher-interpreter at the Phoenix Indian School. Bennett lived in Afghanistan from 1958 to 1960 and traveled in the Far East, Middle East, and Europe.

Bennett's autobiography and first book, *Kaibah: Recollections of a Navajo Girlhood*, covers the period 1928 to 1935 and chronicles the everyday life of her New Mexico girlhood. In the introduction, she states that this is a true story, one that gives the history of her people by recording everyday family life as it was lived during that period. Bennett illustrated the heading of each vignette. Her second book, *A Navajo Saga*, written with her husband, Russell Bennett, is another family chronicle, spanning the years 1845 to 1868. The central figure is Shebah, based on Bennett's grandmother, and the story focuses on the Bosque Redondo experience and the Long Walk back. Bennett wrote, she said, to preserve part of Navajo history and culture.

Bennett was the New Mexico Human Rights Commissioner from 1969 to 1971, a member of the Inter-Tribal Indian Ceremonial Association, and a member of the advisory board of McKinley County Hospital. She has won numerous prizes for her dolls at state fairs in Arizona and New Mexico, as well as at the Navajo Tribal Fair. Bennett was appointed colonel-aide-de-camp, staff of the governor of New Mexico, and in 1968 she was chosen New Mexico's Mother of the Year.

References

Bennett, Kay. *Kaibah: Recollections of a Navajo Girlhood*. Los Angeles: Western-lore Press, 1964.

———. "Letter to the Editor." In *The American Indian Speaks*. Edited by John R. Milton. Pp. 171–172. Vermillion: University of South Dakota Press, 1969.

Bennett, Kay, and Russ Bennett. *A Navajo Saga*. San Antonio, TX: Naylor, 1969.

Kinsman, Clare, ed. *Contemporary Authors*. First revision series. Vols. 17–20, 68–69. Detroit: Gale Research, 1976.

Klein, Barry T. *Reference Encyclopedia of the American Indian*. 6th ed. West Nyack, NY: Todd Publications, 1993.

Stensland, Anna Lee. *Literature by and About the American Indian: An Annotated Bibliography*. 2nd ed. Urbana, IL: National Council of Teachers of English, 1979.

—Laurie Lisa

BENNETT, RAMONA (b. 1938), an enrolled Puyallup and descended from the Swinomish and Yakima nations, was born and raised in the Seattle and Bremerton areas of Washington State. She obtained her BA degree from Evergreen State College and her master's in education/counseling from the University of Puget Sound. Bennett was active in the first American Indian Women's, Service League in Seattle and a member of the Seattle All-American Indian Dance Troupe. She was highly involved in Indian rights in the Seattle area as well.

Bennett moved to the Tacoma and Puyallup Reservation in 1968 to support her tribe's rights and correct wrongs that had been perpetuated against her tribe. Elected to the Tribal Council in 1968, she realized that her tribe had been dying of federal neglect since the last certified tribal enrollment in 1929. The reservation at that time was almost entirely under the control of nonmembers who had been assigned as legal "guardians" of Puyallup family allotments—they stole them, sold them to each other, and sent the sheriff to evict or kill tribal members who refused to leave their land. Bennett's activism followed the example of her grandfather John McKinny, who died attempting to advocate for tribal members. She married Clyde Bill in 1971; they had six children and were foster parents and mentors to many more.

Bennett was the primary figure in what is known as the "cleanest"—in terms of legalities and public relations—one-week occupation of and eviction from the hospital on the Puyallup Reservation, in which over fifteen hundred local Indians participated. She was also a key figure in the armed camp set up to protect Indian fishing rights in the Columbia River, where Pauline Matheson made a one-woman stand with a gun while her nineteen-year-old son David utilized his treaty rights to fish the river. Multiple state and federal law enforcement agencies (the National Guard was placed on standby) responded. The protest resulted in intergovernmental and international agreements to protect fishing rights and the habitat of fish. As a result, the Puyallup tribe became strong, "rising from the ashes" with more than two thousand members.

While a member of the Tribal Council, Bennett developed and instituted the first tribally managed clinic, educational programs, and child placement group in the nation. In 1979 she was recalled from the council. She continued her work in the public sector, where she developed Rainbow Youth and Family Services in 1989. The focus of this agency is to recruit and license foster homes and provide adoption services for families and children of diverse ethnic backgrounds, one-third of them American Indian.

Reference

Running Wolf, Paulette. Personal communication with Ramona Bennett, June 1998.

—Paulette Running Wolf and Susan Rae Banks

BIG EYES [Tattooed Woman] (b.c.1520–), Wichita Indian, was captured around 1535 by the Tejas Indians near the Red River in what is today east Texas. The Wichita women had a custom of decorating their faces, and Big Eyes had two lines tattooed just under her eyes that accentuated her high cheekbones. The Tejas later sold her to the Tiguex Indians in Arizona as a slave. Big Eyes remained with the Tiguex until the summer of 1540, when the Spanish explorer Francisco Vásquez de Coronado made contact with the Natives. A battle ensued between the Spanish and the Tiguex, and Big Eyes was taken captive, becoming the possession of Juan de Zaldivar, a captain under Coronado.

Coronado's expedition headed north and then east, following the Pecos and then the Red River, in search of the Seven Cities of Cibola and gold. In the spring of 1541, it reached what is now the panhandle of Texas. Big Eyes recognized the country and slipped away from Zaldivar. When she arrived in her Wichita village, she told the people of the Spanish explorers and the strange foods, sights, and sounds she had experienced.

In the summer of 1542, members of Hernando de Soto's Florida expedition arrived in the Mississippi valley. The Natives told them of a Wichita woman who had traveled westward and back and had seen the great Coronado. Luis de Moscovo located Big Eyes and asked for news of the Coronado expedition. She told him that she had fled the other Spaniards about a year earlier, from a location nine days distant, and was able to name the captains in Coronado's camp. When the Spanish pressed her for more information, she sketched a crude map in the dirt that illustrated the route Coronado had followed from the Rio Grande and the route she had followed after she had left the Spaniards on the plains near Tule Canyon. One of Moscovo's men copied her crude map on a piece of parchment, and in time that map reached Europe and the mapmakers of the world.

The chronology of Big Eyes's story has raised some questions among historians concerning discrepancies in times, dates, and places. However, because of her flight across Texas, Big Eyes was a personal link between the exploration of Coronado in the west and the men of de Soto in the east. The two expeditions had nearly spanned the continent, and for the first time the width of North America could be estimated.

References

Bolton, Herbert E. *Coronado, Knight of the Pueblos and Plains*. Albuquerque: University of New Mexico Press, 1949.

Coronado, Francisco Vásquez de. *The Journey of Coronado 1540–1542 from the City of Mexico to the Grand Canyon of the Colorado and the Buffalo Plains of Texas, Kansas and Nebraska*. Edited and translated by George Parker Winship. New York: A. S. Barnes, 1904.

Waltrip, Lela, and Rufus Waltrip. *Indian Women: Thirteen Who Played a Part in the History of America from the Earliest Days to Now*. New York: David McKay, 1964.

—Joyce Ann Kievit

BIGHORSE, TIANA (b. 1917), Navajo weaver and writer belonging to the Deer Spring clan, was born into the Bitter Water clan north of Tuba City, Arizona. At the age of seven she learned weaving from her mother, who taught her not only the skills but also the pride of weaving. Although her married name is Butler, she uses the last name of Bighorse to honor her father. He was of the Rock Gap clan, and his father was Edgewater clan. She is the mother of seven children and has spent her life in the western part of the Navajo Reservation.

In 1971, with Noel Bennett, Bighorse published *Working with the Wool*, an introduction to the art and technique of Navajo weaving. In 1990 Noel Bennett edited Bighorse's letters and recollections about her father into *Bighorse the Warrior*. His life spanned the Long Walk period of the 1860s and the stock reduction period of the 1930s. From his memory of finding his parents murdered when he was just sixteen to his account of the white-clad figure of death, Tiana Bighorse tells her father's story in his own voice with the subtlety, precision, and artistry characteristic of a people for whom memory is a vital means of valuing life. "I don't want to throw away what he told us," says Tiana Bighorse in *Bighorse the Warrior*. "Right now the young generation knows nothing. . . . I want the world to know that the Navajo warriors were heroes. . . . I want everyone to remember how the Navajo got this big reservation. They will tell their grandchildren, and our warriors will not be forgotten."

References

Bennett, Noel, and Tiana Bighorse. *Navajo Weaving Way: The Path from Fleece to Rug*. Loveland, CO: Interweave Press, 1997.

———. *Working with the Wool: How to Weave a Navajo Rug*. Flagstaff, AZ: Northland Press, 1971.

Bighorse, Tiana. *Bighorse the Warrior*. Edited by Noel Bennett. Tucson: University of Arizona Press, 1990.

—Rhoda Carroll

BILLIE, SUSIE (c. 1900) is a renowned and highly respected medicine woman of the Seminole people in Florida. She was born in Collier County and now lives on the Big Cypress Reservation. She is a matriarch of the large Panther clan, which has traditionally provided most of the medicine men for the Seminole and Micco-sukee tribes in Florida. She learned the medicine from her father, uncles, and grandfather; her brother, Buffalo Jim, is one of the oldest living medicine men.

Susie Billie practices "healing medicine," which is a combination of an exten-sive knowledge of herbs and their medicinal properties, and the songs and rituals that give the preparations their power. This is distinct from the spiritual "big medi-cine" practiced during the Green Corn Dance, which is strictly secret and limited to males. Her life has spanned one of the most tumultuous periods in the history of her people; within a century the Seminoles moved from a hunting-trapping society to modern tribal government and highly prosperous business enterprises. To assure that the old ways are not lost, Billie actively transmits her knowledge of herbal medicine and rituals to her children and grandchildren. In 1984 the Florida Folk-life Program, the Florida Endowment for the Humanities, and the National En-dowment for the Humanities collaborated to produce a video documentary for public television, *Four Corners of Earth*, which featured Susie Billie and the women of her family. Its focus was the woman's role in ensuring cultural continu-ity in Indian life. In 1985 she was designated an official Florida Folk Artist by the Florida Department of State.

References

Florida Department of State. *Florida Folk Artists and Apprentices 1984–1985*. Tallahassee: Florida Folklife Program, 1985.

Four Corners of Earth. Florida Folklife Program/WFSU-TV. 30 min. 1984. Docu-mentary.

Kersey, Harry A., Jr. *The Florida Seminoles and the New Deal, 1933–1942*. Boca Raton: Florida Atlantic University Press, 1989.

———. Interview with Susie Billie (translation), May 6, 1984. Tape recording SEM 187A. Oral History Archives, University of Florida, Gainesville.

—Harry A. Kersey, Jr.

BIRD, GAIL (b. 1949), is a jeweler of Laguna/Santo Domingo descent. Born in Cal-ifornia, she attended the University of California at Berkeley and the University of Colorado in Boulder before settling in New Mexico. She currently lives in Ojo Caliente with her partner and collaborator, Yazzie Johnson (Navajo).

Bird designs and Johnson fabricates jewelry characterized by the use of over seventy different types of stones and gems, including Coyomito white agate, iolite, Ceylon blue moonstone, hematite, Chinese turquoise, snowflake obsidian, psilomelene, covellite, coral, dinosaur bone, banded onyx, Deschutes and Wild Horse jasper, crysocholla, charoite, and several varieties of pearls.

Bird sketches all of her designs in great detail, creating intricate patterns for both the front and the back of her primarily 14k gold pins, necklaces, earrings, and bracelets. The images chosen for the underlay or overlay designs on the backs of the metal casings of buckles, pendants, and clasps include Pueblo pottery designs, Southwest petroglyphs, animals and birds, textile patterns, shooting stars, and ele-gant abstract designs.

Bird's necklaces are characterized by their versatility. Because of the unusual clasp designs, a single necklace may be worn in three distinct ways. Often, the clasp can be removed and worn as a pin. Asymmetry is another stylistic device used to great advantage. Bracelets, for example, are designed with stones slightly off center so they can be stacked in multiples.

Each year, Bird and Johnson concentrate their major creative effort in designing and making one or two concha belts that reflect their ideas and experiences in a given period. The belts have a single theme carried out by the design and choice of stones.

In 1981 Bird and Johnson won the Best of Show, Best of Class, and Best of Division awards at the prestigious, juried Santa Fe Indian Market, sponsored by the Southwest Association on Indian Affairs. Their work has been widely collected by corporations, individuals, and museums, including the Museum of Man (San Diego), the Wheelwright (Santa Fe), the Millicent Rogers (Taos), the Museum of New Mexico, and the Indian Arts and Crafts Board in Washington, DC.

Bird is a prominent authority on American Indian art and culture. She lectures widely on historic and contemporary jewelry and is a consultant to New Mexico arts organizations, such as the Eight Northern Pueblos, the Museum of New Mexico, the Laboratory of Anthropology, and the Southwestern Association on Indian Affairs.

Bird is currently a member of the board of trustees of the Institute of American Indian and Alaska Native Culture and Arts Development, a position to which she was appointed by President of the United States, and of the board of the Wheelwright Museum of the American Indian, both in Santa Fe. For five years she was on the board of the Southwestern Association on Indian Affairs.

References

Cirillo, Dexter. *Southwestern Indian Jewelry*. New York: Abbeville Press, 1992.

Jacka, Jerry, and Lois Essary Jacka. *Beyond Tradition: Contemporary Indian Art and Its Evolution*. Flagstaff, AZ: Northland Press, 1988.

Mather, Christine. *Native America*. New York: Clarkson Potter, 1990.

McGrew, Kate. "Partners in Art and Life: Gail Bird and Yazzie Johnson, Master Jewelers." *New Mexico Magazine* 67 (August 1989): 60–65.

—Dexter Fisher Cirillo

BIRD, GLORIA (b. 1951), poet, essayist, and fiction writer, is an enrolled member of the Spokane tribe. Born in Sunnyside, Washington, which is in the Yakima valley, Bird divided her childhood between the Spokane and Colville reservations, where she attended both mission and BIA boarding schools. She received her BA from Lewis and Clark College in Portland, Oregon, in 1990 and her MA in English from the University of Arizona in 1992. Soon after, Bird taught creative writing and literature at the Institute of American Indian and Alaska Native Culture and Arts Development Santa Fe, New Mexico.

Bird's first collection of poetry, *Full Moon on the Reservation*, published in 1993, received the Returning the Gift/Diane Decorah First Book Award. In that year, Bird also was awarded the Witter-Bynner Foundation grant for individual writers. Since then, she has published a second collection of poetry, *The River of History* (1997), and has edited and been featured in numerous publications, including *Reinventing the Enemy's Language*; *Speaking for the Generations*; *Blue Dawn, Red Earth*; *Returning the Gift*; *Indian Artist Magazine*; and the *Wicazo Sa Review*. Bird is one of the founding members of the Northwest Native American Writers Association.

Bird's poetry and fiction place themes about the nature of gender relations and birth/death/rebirth cycles in naturalistic settings. In "Sunset" the narrator states: "Sunset is a reddened fish,/cutthroat trout. She swallows your bullfrog heart." Bird's use of metaphor constructs a world in which nature acts as a mirror for humans. She also experiments with poetic form, dividing her poetry between two types of blank verse—one that uses short, enjambed lines and one that uses a single and multiple paragraph format. The effect of these different forms is powerful; tone and voice are dramatically altered to offer a narrator with a realistic and personable demeanor.

Bird is also a prolific essayist who calls for authors to portray the Native culture responsibly and accurately. In her article "The Exaggeration of Despair in Sherman Alexie's *Reservation Blues*," Bird takes Alexie to task for his interpolation of popular culture that makes his novel, she claims, "cut and paste . . . [creating] a pan-Indian, nonspecific representation of an Indian community that is flawed because of its exaggerated 'Indian' qualities." Bird believes the responsibility of all Native authors is "to accurately represent our communities without exploiting them." In her article "Breaking the Silence: Writing as Witness," Bird offers advice to Native writers and celebrates the autobiography as a method for Native writers to "[undo] the process of colonization of our minds."

Gloria Bird lives in Nespelem, Washington, where she works for the Spokane tribe and teaches at the Wellpinit campus of Salish-Kootenai College.

References

Bird, Gloria. "Breaking the Silence: Writing as Witness." In *Speaking for the Generations: Native Writers on Writing*. Edited by Simon Ortiz. Pp. 27–48. Tucson: University of Arizona Press, 1998.

———. "The Exaggeration of Despair in Sherman Alexie's *Reservation Blues*." *Wicazo Sa Review* 11 (1995): 47–52.

———. *Full Moon on the Reservation*. Greenfield Center, NY: Greenfield Review Press, 1993.

———. *The River of History*. Portland, OR: Trask House Books, 1997.

Bird, Gloria, and Joy Harjo. *Reinventing the Enemy's Language: Contemporary Native Women's Writing of North America*. New York: W. W. Norton, 1998.

Bird, Gloria, and Carroll Warner Williams. *A Filmography for American Indian Education*. Santa Fe, NM: Zia Cine, 1973.

Bruchac, Joseph, ed. *Returning the Gift: Poetry and Prose from the First North American Native Writers' Festival*. Tucson: University of Arizona Press, 1994.

Trafzer, Clifford E., ed. *Blue Dawn, Red Earth: New Native American Story Tellers*. New York: Anchor Books, 1996.

—*Bethany Blankenship*

BIRD, JOANNE (b. 1945), was born JoAnne Maestas in Oakland, California. Before her first birthday, her mother took her to Sisseton, South Dakota, to live with her maternal grandparents, Mr. and Mrs. Charles White. She remembers her childhood with great pleasure.

Her education began with the first grade in Wahpeton, North Dakota. Her next six years were spent in the Sisseton public school. Her high school years were spent at the Flandreau Indian School, from which she graduated in 1964. In 1965 she attended the Institute of American Indian Art in Santa Fe, New Mexico. She returned to Sisseton before finishing school, however, and married Gordon Bird in 1965. From 1967 to 1970 she worked for the 3M Corporation in Minneapolis as a design artist.

Returning home to Sisseton, Bird worked there as an independent artist until 1972, when she enrolled at Macalester College in St. Paul, Minnesota, to study art. In 1974 she transferred to Dakota State College in Madison, South Dakota, where her husband was a counselor. She left South Dakota in 1976.

During these years Bird continued to paint and to sculpt, and her reputation as an artist grew. Her main theme is the old Sioux culture, with a focus on the horse and warrior as main subjects. In 1987, disgusted with her painting, she took a brush and threw paint at her canvas. She was astonished at what she saw. She has developed this action into a new technique and style that have caused her recent work to be in great demand. Bird has had exhibitions of her work in many of the major cities of the United States, as well as in Canada and Europe. Her paintings are in galleries in Arizona, the Midwest, and New York. She has had numerous commissions, including some for bronze busts of Chief Gall for Manitoba, of Wabasha for the Minnesota Historical Society, and of Winnetou for the city of Bad Segeberg in Germany. In the summer of 1996, the Franklin Mint commissioned her to create four sculptures and paintings.

Although she had won awards earlier, they have become more numerous since 1987. She won first place in traditional painting at Sioux Falls in 1988, and Best of Show in painting at Minneapolis and at Bartlesville, Oklahoma, in 1990. She received an Honorable Mention at the Northern Plains Tribal Art Show in Sioux Falls in 1990 and a Special Merit Award at the Tulsa Indian Art Show in 1990. In 1992 she was selected as South Dakota Hall of Fame Artist of the Year. Perhaps her greatest honor was her inclusion as one of twenty Native Masters chosen by the Southwest Indian Art Association, which sponsors and produces the largest and oldest Indian art market, in Santa Fe, in 1996.

Bird's works have been featured in numerous art shows and exhibitions in the United States, Europe, and Canada. She, her husband, and their children reside in the village of Bushnell, South Dakota. There they have established a studio that they call Featherstone.

References

———. "Plains Warrior Representing July." *Wounded Knee Commemorative Sioux Art Calendar 1990*. St. Joseph's Indian School, Chamberlain, SD: Tipi Press, 1990.

Grauvogl, Ann. "Art Show Changed Bird's Career." *Argus Leader* [Sioux Falls SD], September 22, 1989, 38.

———. "She Splashes Easel with Life." *Argus Leader* [Sioux Falls SD], September 19, 1996, sec. B, 1.

Marken, Jack. Personal communication with Gordon Bird, July 18, 1996.

———. Personal communication with JoAnne Bird, July 18, 1996.

—Jack Marken

BLACK BEAR, MATILDA [Tillie] (b. 1946), is a leader in education, politics, and social services on the Lakota Sioux Rosebud Reservation. She is especially interested in mental health, domestic violence, and women's issues.

Black Bear was director of student services (1974–1977), a board member (1975–1976), and an instructor in the Human Services Department (1981) at the Sioux Sinte Gleska College. She also served on the board of the St. Francis Indian School (1974–1977, 1980–?), and was director of the Rosebud Sioux tribe's Education Department (1981).

As an officer of the state and national Coalition Against Domestic Violence and member of the Indian Health Management Board, the Child Abuse Training Team of the South Dakota WPC, South Dakota National Organization for Women, and the White Buffalo Calf Women's Society, Black Bear has made significant contributions to the position of women on the Rosebud Reservation. The White Buffalo Calf Women's Society—named for the deity who brought the Sioux the sacred pipe and who serves as a guide for proper conduct—addresses women's and children's issues on the reservation. Under Black Bear's directorship, the society has provided services and a shelter for battered women. Black Bear has worked closely with Viola Burnette, attorney general for the Rosebud Sioux tribe, in implementing a Tribal Council policy requiring mandatory arrest of perpetrators of violence against women and children.

Black Bear's social concerns include redressing past mistreatment of Indians. She led a drive for the rescinding of thirty Congressional Medals of Honor awarded to Seventh Cavalry members who fought at Wounded Knee.

Black Bear was named an Outstanding Young Woman in America in 1973 and 1977. In 1989 her work with the White Buffalo Calf Women's Society was recognized with an award from the Victims of Crimes Office, a division of the United States Justice Department. It was presented in Washington, D.C., by Attorney General Richard Thornburgh.

References

Anderson, Owanah. "Black Bear, Matilda L." In *Ohoyo One Thousand: A Resource Guide of American Indian/Alaska Native Women, 1982*. Wichita Falls, TX: Ohoyo Resource Center, 1982.

"Dishonor." *Time*, December 31, 1990, 8.

Kachel, Douglas. "The Rosebud Sioux Confront Domestic Violence and Women's Issues." *Akwesasne Notes* (Summer 1989): 11.

—Pattiann Frinzi

BLACKGOAT, ROBERTA (b.c. 1920), of the Big Mountain Diné (Navajo) Bitter Water clan, lives on Big Mountain land where she was born and where her great-grandmother, grandmother, mother, and one of her children are buried. In 1941, she married Benny Blackgoat, who died in 1966. Six of their children are living.

Blackgoat is a traditional Navajo woman in that she raises sheep and goats and weaves rugs from her sheep's wool. She is somewhat nontraditional in that, along with other Big Mountain elders, she has taken a very vocal and sometimes militant stand in opposing the forced relocation of Diné from their homeland.

Natural resource companies, such as Peabody Coal, interested in the large deposits of oil, natural gas, uranium, and coal on the reservation, promoted the Navajo–Hopi land dispute, which prompted the passing of Public Law 93-531 in 1974. Under this law, the Joint Use Area of Navajo–Hopi reservation land was "divided" by a barbed wire fence that sometimes went between a family's house and corral. Grazing lands—and sacred shrines and grave sites—were bulldozed and dragged with customized ship anchor chains to remove trees and plants. Approximately one hundred Hopi and ten thousand Navajo caught on the "wrong side of the fence" were told they had to relocate.

The Big Mountain Diné resisted fencing and defended their homes. Traditional Diné have taken their protest to Washington, D.C. Pauline Whitesinger, an elder and a leader of the Big Mountain resistance, said: "There is no word for relocation in the Navajo language; to relocate is to disappear and never be seen again." Roberta Blackgoat says that "[t]he Creator is the only one who can relocate me."

Like many of the relocatees, Blackgoat's children, most of whom chose to move, are having a hard time adjusting to life off the reservation. One daughter has lost her home, and a son has returned to Big Mountain in order to heal the scars caused by his relocation experiences. Blackgoat wants her children and grandchildren to return to their ancestral land.

In the 1930s Blackgoat experienced the government stock reduction program, designed to reduce Navajo self-sufficiency and to open up more land to mining interests. The program destroyed about one-third of all Navajo livestock. In this latest relocation effort, the government again ordered sheep to be taken away, thereby attempting to force the traditional Navajo to make a "starve or move" choice. Blackgoat and other Big Mountain Diné have refused to move or to give up their way of life.

References

Florio, Maria, and Victoria Mudd. *Broken Rainbow*. Distributed by Earthworks Films. 1985.

LaDuke, Winona. "Interview with Roberta Blackgoat, a Diné Elder." *Woman of Power* 4 (Fall 1986): 29–31.

———. "Words from the Indigenous Women's Network Meeting." *Akwesasne Notes* 17 (Winter 1985): 8–10.

—*Elizabeth A. McNeil*

BLACKSTONE, TSIANINA REDFEATHER [Florence Tsianina Evans] (c. 1882–1985), was born into a large Creek/Cherokee family in Indian Territory (later Oklahoma).

Tsianina Redfeather Blackstone

Listed on the Creek tribal rolls as Florence Evans, she was known to family and friends by her Creek name, Tsianina, which she used in a long and distinguished career as a professional singer and entertainer. She attended public primary school near Muskogee, Oklahoma, and a federal Indian school in Eufaula, Oklahoma. Encouraged by her piano teacher, and with the assistance of Alice Robertson, Oklahoma's first congresswoman, Tsianina traveled as a young woman to Denver, Colorado, to study voice and piano.

In Denver, she met Charles Wakefield Cadman, an "Indianist" composer inspired by Native American melodies; his best-known work was *From the Land of the Sky Blue Water*. He toured the country presenting his "Indian Music Talk" lecture and recital; it reached its greatest popularity when Tsianina became the principal soloist in 1913. Cadman's third opera, *Shanewis: The Robin Woman*, was based quite loosely on Tsianina's life; as Cadman himself admitted, her life was colorful, but not dramatic enough for opera. *Shanewis* was the first American opera with a modern setting to be produced in two consecutive seasons (1918 and 1919) at the Metropolitan Opera in New York City. In 1926 Tsianina sang the title role when the opera was staged at the Hollywood Bowl in Los Angeles. Critical reviews did not comment so much on the fineness of her mezzo-soprano voice as on the forcefulness of her personality.

In addition to her tours with Cadman, Tsianina was invited to sing in the Santa Fe Fiesta Program by the program's organizer, Edgar Hewett, a noted anthropologist and founder of the School of American Research and Museum of New Mexico. Tsianina left the Cadman tour in 1918 to answer General John Pershing's call for volunteer entertainers; she sailed to England and Europe, arriving in Paris shortly before the armistice was signed. She rejoined Cadman late in 1919 for another national tour that was highlighted by her appearance at the Greek Theater in Berkeley, California.

Her marriage to Albert Blackstone (French–Indian?) ended in separation due to his alcoholism, and she went on tour yet again. Tsianina was plagued by illness after her European tour during World War I, and she turned to Christian Science.

She retired in the 1930s and devoted her energies to religious activities in southern California, as well as to political work. She was an active fund-raiser for the Republican Party for many years. She also took a vital interest in Indian issues, organizing a group of friends in Los Angeles to establish the Foundation for American Indian Education and serving on the board of managers of the School of American Research from 1933 to 1963. Tsianina died in San Diego on January 10, 1985.

References

Blackstone, Tsianina. *Where Trails Have Led Me*. Santa Fe, NM: Vergara Printing, 1968.

Index to and the Final Rolls of Citizens and Freedmen of the Five Civilized Tribes in Indian Territory. Census card #1117, November 11, 1899. Federal Records Center, Fort Worth, TX.

Lomawaima, K. Tsianina. Personal communication with Marjorie F. Lambert, January 4, 1991.

——. Personal communication with Martha Noss, January 4, 1991.

Maddox, Brent. Review of PhD diss. *Charles Wakefield Cadman: His Life and Works* by Harry Perison. *Inter-American Music Review* 4 (1982): 100–103.

Perison, Harry D. "The 'Indian' Operas of Charles Wakefield Cadman." *College Music Symposium* 22 (Fall 1982): 20–48.

Who's Who of American Women. 4th ed. Chicago: A. N. Marquis, 1966–1967.

—*K. Tsianina Lomawaima*

BLAESER, KIMBERLY M. (b. 1955), is a widely published poet and an associate professor of English at the University of Wisconsin-Milwaukee, where she has taught Native American literature, creative writing, and American nature writing since 1987. Of Anishinaabe and German heritage, she was born in Billings, Montana, and was raised on the White Earth Reservation in Minnesota. She is an enrolled member of the Minnesota Chippewa tribe.

In her 1994 collection of poems, *Trailing You*, Blaeser explains her intent to "explore the way writing can cross the boundaries of print" in both her scholarly and her creative writing. *Trailing You* received the North American Native Authors First Book Award and the Diane Decorah Award for Poetry. In addition to poems, Blaeser has published numerous works of short fiction, essays, and scholarly articles, in forums ranging from local newspapers to literary anthologies. She published *Gerald Vizenor: Writing in the Oral Tradition* in 1996, and currently is editing a collection of Vizenor's haiku, a collection of Anishinaabe prose, and *A Resource Guide to Native American Literature*. Consistently, she has noted in her works the importance of family and of nature as influences on her writing.

Blaeser has served as vice president of the Wordcraft Circle of Native Writers and Storytellers (1995–1997) and, since 1995, as a member of the Native American Series Board of Michigan State University Press. She also founded and is faculty adviser for the Word Warrior Society, a multicultural writers' group at the University of Wisconsin-Milwaukee that has helped members become published, be accepted into creative writing programs, and be hired as writers and writing instructors. Prior to her employment at the University of Wisconsin, Blaeser worked as a reporter and photographer. She received her MA in 1982 and her PhD in 1990 from the University of Notre Dame, where she served as a visiting professor of American Studies in 1990.

References

Blaeser, Kimberly M. *Gerald Vizenor: Writing in the Oral Tradition*. Norman: University of Oklahoma Press, 1996.

————. "On Mapping and Urban Shamans." In *As We Are Now: Mixblood Essays on Race and Identity*. Edited by William S. Penn. Pp. 115–125. Berkeley: University of California Press, 1997.

————. "Rituals of Memory." In *Everything Matters: Autobiographical Essays by Native American Writers*. Edited by Arnold Krupat and Brian Swann. New York: Random House, 1998.

————. *Trailing You*. Greenfield Center, NY: Greenfield Review Press, 1994.

—*Ryan Simmons*

BLUE LEGS [Alice New Holy] (b. 1925) was born on July 25 at Grass Creek on the Pine Ridge Reservation, the daughter of Julia and Joseph New Holy. She has lived all her life in the house of her birth, near Oglala, South Dakota. She was educated in the Oglala Community School through the twelfth grade.

Her mother died when Blue Legs was very young. She remembers that both her mother and her grandmother used porcupine quills in decorating skins and cloth and in making medallions and other objects. As a girl, she found that no one was doing this kind of artistry. She believed that the process should be resurrected, but there was no one to teach her except her father. He gave her as much instruction as he could remember, but he would not touch the quills because he believed that was women's work.

Through trial and error Blue Legs succeeded in resurrecting the lost art of quilling. With the help of her husband, Emil Blue Legs, and her daughters, she prepares the quills by collecting, boiling, dyeing, and drying them carefully. When using them in decorations, she softens them in her mouth, as her predecessors did. Softening them in water does not work, she says, because the additives and minerals in water dry them too much.

Blue Legs does most of her work at night because everyone is asleep, there is no noise, and it is calm. Her artistry and skill have earned her many awards, the chief one being a cash award from the National Endowment for the Arts in 1985. She was the only Indian artist from South Dakota to win such an award that year. In that year she and her daughters and husband were the subject of a film by Nauman Productions of Rapid City. *Lakota Quill Work* shows them preparing the quills at her house.

In recent years Blue Legs has traveled to teach Indian youth how to use quills because she thinks the art is in danger of being lost. She goes to museums and schools and workshops to give demonstrations. She has traveled as far west as the Hopi Reservation and as far east as New York and New England for this purpose. She has had exhibits of her work in these places, as well as at Anadarko, Oklahoma, Indianapolis, and St. Louis.

Two of her daughters, Bernadine and Catherine, have learned the art from their mother and have their own traveling exhibits. They live near their mother in Oglala, where they can be found quilling in the evenings when they are not traveling.

References

Lakota Quill Work. 16mm, 27 min. Nauman Productions, Rapid City, SD, 1985.
Marken, Jack. Personal communication with Blue Legs, September 29, 1990.

—Jack Marken

BONNIN, GERTRUDE SIMMONS [Zitkala Sa, Red Bird] (1876–1938), has been called the most important figure in reform Pan-Indianism during the 1920s. A highly visible Indian rights activist, she was also an important early Native American writer, publishing essays and short stories and a volume of Indian legends. In addition, she was an award-winning orator.

Born a Sioux at the Yankton Agency in South Dakota in 1876, Bonnin was taken at age seven to a Quaker school in Wabash, Indiana. Although her initial experiences there were traumatic, she remained for the full three-year course before returning to the reservation for four years. She then returned to Wabash and completed another three-year course. In 1895, at the age of nineteen, she entered Earlham College at Richmond, Indiana, where she distinguished herself as a skillful orator, winning a statewide speech contest.

After she left Earlham in 1897, Bonnin obtained a teaching job at the government's showpiece Indian school at Carlisle, Pennsylvania. While at Carlisle, she began cultivating literary contacts and published essays and short stories under the Sioux name Zitkala Sa, or Red Bird, in such prestigious publications as the *Atlantic Monthly* and *Harper's*.

Gertrude Simmons Bonnin

After two difficult years at Carlisle, Bonnin resigned in order to study the violin at the New England Conservatory of Music in Boston. She treasured her life in Boston, where she studied music, wrote, and moved in literary circles but felt a great sense of responsibility to her people. She resolved to spend at least a year at the Yankton Agency, during which time she gathered material for her stories and cared for her mother. This period at Yankton contributed to the end of her engagement to Dr. Carlos Montezuma, whom she had met at Carlisle; he was reluctant to give up his Chicago medical practice to accept a position as a reservation doctor, as Bonnin wished him to do.

Her plans to stay in South Dakota changed in 1902, when she met and married Raymond T. Bonnin, also a Yankton Sioux, who had accepted a Bureau of Indian Affairs clerk position on the Uintah and Ouray Reservation in Utah. There, she became involved with the Society of American Indians and did community center work under its auspices. In 1916 she was elected secretary of the organization, and shortly thereafter, the Bonnins moved to Washington, D.C., where Gertrude assumed the duties of secretary from 1916 until 1919. She was also editor of the society's *American Indian Magazine* and wrote numerous editorials for that publication. In Washington, she allied herself with other important Indian rights organizations, including John Collier's American Indian Defense Association and the Indian Rights Association of Philadelphia.

Bonnin was instrumental in the creation of the Indian Welfare Committee within the General Federation of Women's Clubs of America, and as its research agent she participated in a 1923 investigation that exposed the widespread corruption associated with white guardianships of Indian properties and oil leases in Oklahoma. In 1922 and 1923 she made a speaking tour of the Midwest and South, addressing women's clubs in order to crystallize public opinion in favor of Indian citizenship.

In addition to their association with these formal organizations, Gertrude and Raymond Bonnin devoted considerable time to lobbying governmental departments and congressional committees on behalf of Indian individuals and tribes. The Bonnins testified before congressional committees to promote peyote suppression, Indian citizenship, Indian educational reforms, and Native land claims. Although often at odds with him, Gertrude Bonnin also served as an informal adviser to John Collier after he became the head of the Bureau of Indian Affairs under President Franklin D. Roosevelt.

In 1926 Bonnin and her husband organized the National Congress of American Indians (NCAI). For the twelve years it existed, it was the only nationally organized reform group with exclusively Native American membership. The Bonnins tirelessly traveled the United States, combining speaking tours with visits to reservations to organize NCAI chapters and enroll members. Her work came to an end in 1938, when she died in Washington, D.C. She is buried in Arlington National Cemetery.

References

Bonnin, Gertrude [Zitkala Sa]. *American Indian Stories*. 1921. Reprint, Lincoln: University of Nebraska Press, 1985.

———. *Old Indian Legends*. 1901. Reprint, Lincoln: University of Nebraska Press, 1985.

Bonnin Gertrude, Charles H. Fabens, and Matthew K. Sniffen. *Oklahoma's Poor Rich Indians: An Orgy of Graft and Exploitation of the Five Civilized Tribes— Legalized Robbery*. Publications of the Indian Rights Association, 2nd Series, no. 127. Philadelphia: Indian Rights Association, 1924.

Bonnin, Gertrude Simmons. Papers (MS 1704). Brigham Young University, Provo, UT.

Cutter, Martha J. "Zitkala-Sa's Autobiographical Writings: The Problems of a Canonical Search for Language and Identity." *MELUS* 19 (Spring 1994): 31–44.

Fisher, Dexter. "The Transformation of Tradition: A Study of Zitkala-Sa and Mourning Dove, Two Transitional American Indian Writers." In *Critical Essays on American Indian Literature*. Edited by Andrew Wiget. Pp. 202–211. Boston: G. K. Hall, 1985.

———. "Zitkala-Sa: The Evolution of a Writer." *American Indian Quarterly* 5 (August 1979): 229–238.

Johnson, David L., and Raymond Wilson. "Gertrude Simmons Bonnin, 1876–1938: 'Americanize the First Americans.'" *American Indian Quarterly* 12 (Winter 1988): 27–40.

Lisa, Laurie. "The Life Story of Zitkala-Sa/Gertrude Simmons Bonnin: Writing and Creating a Public Image." PhD diss., Arizona State University, 1996.

Okker, Patricia. "Native American Literatures and the Canon: The Case of Zitkala Sa." In *American Realism and the Canon*. Edited by Tom Quirk and Gary Scharnhorst. Pp. 87–101. Newark: University of Delaware Press, 1994.

Smith, Jeanne. "A 'Second Tongue': The Trickster's Voice in the Works of Zitkala-Sa." In *Tricksterism in Turn-of-the-Century American Literature*. Edited by Elizabeth Ammons and Annette White-Parks. Pp. 46–60. Hanover, NH: Tufts University/University Press of New England, 1994.

Susag, Dorothea M. "Zitkala-Sa (Gertrude Simmons Bonnin): A Power (full) Literary Voice." *Studies in American Indian Literatures* 5 (Winter 1993): 3–24.

Welch, Deborah. "Zitkala Sa: An American Indian Leader, 1876–1938." PhD diss., University of Wyoming, 1985.

Willard, William. "Zitkala Sa: A Woman Who Would Be Heard." *Wicazo Sa Review* 1 (Spring 1985): 11–16.

Williams, Walter L. "Twentieth Century Indian Leaders: Brokers and Providers." *Journal of the West* 23 (July 1984): 3–6.

Zitkala-Sa [Gertrude Bonnin]. "America, Home of the Red Man." *American Indian* 6 (Winter 1919): 165–167.

———. "Why I Am a Pagan." *Atlantic Monthly* 90 (December 1902): 802–803.

———. "A Year's Experience in Community Service Work Among the Ute Tribes of Indians." *American Indian* 4 (October/December 1916): 307–310.

Zitkala-Sa and William Hanson. *The Sun Dance*. Vernal, UT: Orpheus Hall, February 20, 1913.

—*Catherine Udall*

BORDEAUX, SHIRLEY (b. 1950), a business analyst with the University of South Dakota (USD) Business Opportunity Center, works with a variety of organizations and businesses to promote economic development for Native Americans. She serves on the boards of South Dakotans for the Arts, the South Dakota Community Foundation, and the Lakota Development Council. She also has started her own small business and management consulting business.

Born at Valentine, Nebraska, Bordeaux grew up near Mission, South Dakota, on the Rosebud Reservation. Her parents, Catherine Robinson, a Choctaw from Oklahoma, and Ralph Carlson Bordeaux, a Sicangu (Brulé) Sioux, worked at the Old Rosebud Boarding School; the family lived there when Bordeaux was a child. She attended St. Mary's School for Indian Girls, an Episcopal boarding school, from the seventh through ninth grades. She then entered Todd County High School, from which she graduated in 1968.

After her daughter, Ann, was born in 1970, Bordeaux enrolled in Black Hills State College, graduating with a BS in social sciences in 1974. She then worked as an information officer for Sinte Gleska College until 1976.

She spent the following two years in Arcata, California, at Humboldt State University, where she worked in natural resource planning and interpretation for the California state parks. She would have begun work as a forest ranger in the fall of 1978, but the passing of Proposition 13 caused a statewide hiring freeze. Bordeaux returned to the Dakotas.

In 1979 Bordeaux served as director of public information for United Tribes Technical College in Bismarck, North Dakota, and continues to serve as a consultant for the college, writing grants, promotional materials, and conference newsletters, and planning programs.

Bordeaux left Bismarck in 1980 and returned to Rosebud, where she was an information officer for the Rosebud tribe for the following two years. Then, from 1982 through 1984, she was regional editor of the *Lakota Times*. Still at Rosebud, she worked for the next three years for First Computer Concepts (and continues to serve as a consultant for the firm).

From the fall of 1986 through the spring of 1987, Bordeaux was managing editor of the *Lakota Times*. She wrote editorials and news articles for the newspaper during this period.

In 1987 she moved to Sioux Falls, South Dakota, to work with American Indian Services as the first director of the Northern Plains Tribal Arts Project. With a diverse, cross-cultural group of art enthusiasts, Bordeaux helped to plan and implement a market for Native American visual artists from North and South Dakota, Montana, Nebraska, Wyoming, and Canada. The Project's show has grown from seventy-one artists exhibiting in 1988 to over one hundred. Working with USD's Small Business Development Center, Bordeaux continues to be involved in the long-range development of the Project.

Having served on the first South Dakota Reconciliation Council in 1990–1991, Bordeaux continues to work interculturally for better access to and implementation of economic resources necessary for the benefit of Native American people.

At USD, Bordeaux earned a second bachelor's degree in history with a minor in business, and then went on to receive a master's degree in business administration from USD in 1996.

Looking back on her own life, Bordeaux is glad that her daughter, Ann, never had to endure the boarding school experience. She works with the vision of a better life for her granddaughter, Vanessa McDaniel, and future generations.

Reference

Giago, Doris. "Many Find Road to City Paved with Hardship." *Argus Leader* [Sioux Falls, SD], August 21, 1988; A1.

—Norma C. Wilson

BRANT, BETH [Degonwadonti] (b. 1941), was born in Melvindale, Michigan. She is a Mohawk of the Bay of Quinte who began writing at the age of forty as the result of an encounter with a bald eagle. She first gained national recognition as the editor of *A Gathering of Spirit*, the first anthology of contemporary Indian women's art and literature. *A Gathering*, now in its fourth printing, continues to be an important collection of Indian women's writing. In order to assemble a representative sampling of Indian women's work, Brant not only contacted established writers but also ran ads in tribal newspapers and contacted women's prisons with large Indian inmate populations. Some of the correspondence from her experience as editor and compiler is included in the volume.

In her first book, *Mohawk Trail*, Brant draws on memories of her grandparents, her family, and her own experiences of being a mixed-blood, a lesbian, and a feminist to seed new ground in Native literature. Brant has no academic degrees—in fact, she did not complete high school—but she has had a tremendous education in living, writing, and reading. Her "education" has led her to form creative writing workshops for Indian women and Indian high school students. For Brant, writing can be the act that frees Indian people from institutionalized racism and the internalized self-hatred they have been taught to inflict on themselves. Indian writers are in a constant state of translation—from oral to written—and it is this act of translation that gives such power to the works of Indian artists. Her work reflects the many identifications that come from being Mohawk, and she feels that being a feminist is a natural reflection of her own matrilineal and matriarchal heritage.

Brant has been a speaker and lecturer on Indian literature and against the appropriation by non–Indians of Native belief systems and religions. She has written several essays on Native women who are considered "traitors" to their people—such as Pocahontas, Nancy Ward, and Malinche—and has brought new understanding of the motives of these women. "Grandmothers of a New World," one such essay, has been widely reprinted in scholarly journals, Native magazines, and feminist anthologies. In addition to writing full-time, Brant has served as mentor to many emerging Native writers and has conducted writing workshops for women in prison. She is also an activist for People with AIDS and has given AIDS education workshops in the Indian community. She has lectured and given readings at many universities and Indian cultural centers, and has received grants from the Michigan Council for the Arts, the Ontario Arts Council, Money for Women, and the National Endowment for the Arts.

References

Allison, Dorothy. "Beth Brant." In *Contemporary Lesbian Writers of the United States: A Bio-Bibliographical Critical Sourcebook*. Edited by Sandra Pollack and Denise Knight. Westport, CT: Greenwood Press, 1993.

Brant, Beth. *Food & Spirits*. Ithaca, NY: Firebrand Books, 1991.

———. *A Gathering of Spirit*. Special issue of *Sinister Wisdom* 22/23 (July 1983). Reprint, Ithaca, NY: Firebrand Books, 1988.

———. "Grandmothers of a New World." *Women of Power* 16 (Spring 1990): 40–47.

———. *I'll Sing 'til the Day I Die: Conversations with Tyendinaga Elders*. Toronto: McGilligan Books, 1996.

———. *Mohawk Trail*. Ithaca, NY: Firebrand Books, 1985.

———. *Sweet Grass All Around Her*. Toronto: Native American Women in the Arts, 1996.

———. *Writing as Witness: Essay and Talk*. Toronto: Women's Press, 1995.

Bruchac, Carol, Linda Hogan, and Judith McDaniel, eds. *The Stories We Hold Secret: Tales of Women's Spiritual Development*. Greenfield Center, NY: Greenfield Review Press, 1986.

Bruchac, Joseph, ed. *Songs from This Earth on Turtle's Back: Contemporary American Indian Poetry*. Greenfield Center, NY: Greenfield Review Press, 1983.

Cochran, Jo, et al., eds. *Bearing Witness/Sobreviviendo: An Anthology of Native American/Latina Art and Literature*. Special issue of *Calyx: A Journal of Art and Literature by Women* 8 (1984).

Cullum, Linda. "Beth Brant." In *Notable Native Americans*. Edited by Sharon Malinowski. Pp. 51–53. Detroit: ITP, 1995.

Roscoe, Will, comp. *Living the Spirit: A Gay American Indian Anthology*. New York: St. Martin's Press, 1988.

—Kathryn W. Shanley

BRANT, MOLLY [Mary Brant, Gonwatsijayenni] (c. 1736–1796), was the most influential Iroquois woman on the New York frontier from 1759 to 1776. In part her power flowed from the traditionally influential position of women in the matrilineal society of the Iroquois, but Molly Brant parlayed her opportunities to the highest advantage. At the age of twenty-three, she became the mistress of William Johnson, the powerful official in charge of the British Indian Department's Northern District. She relished this role and fulfilled it so effectively for fifteen years that she was not only the mother of several children with Johnson but also his political consort and the hostess at his estate.

Because the women of Iroquois villages brokered power by influencing the nomination of sachems, as well as decisions favoring war or peace, Molly Brant proved an invaluable asset to William Johnson's forest diplomacy. British visitors were so impressed by her hospitality that she was sent gifts and mentioned by name in notes of thanks. In her position of influence she could see to it that her younger brother Joseph Brant, or Thayendanegea, was one of the young Mohawks chosen to attend a missionary school in Connecticut. And, she had no qualms about ordering her brother home when she thought the threat of frontier warfare threatened his safety. Thus she repeatedly advanced the ends of her lover, her brother, and her Mohawk people. She was generous in using credit at local merchants to satisfy the needs of relatives and friends who came to her seeking help.

When she had to leave her Johnson's baronial home after his death in 1774, she took with her numerous expensive dresses and luxury items. Invaders who drove her from her village during the American Revolution reportedly dug up several barrels of dresses from the backyard of her abandoned home. Prior to her flight into exile, when American representatives sought means to neutralize the power of the Iroquois in 1775 and 1776, frontier diplomats understood that Molly Brant was the deus ex machina. One observer impressed by her political prowess concluded, "Women govern the Politics of Savages as well as the refined part of the world."

Even after she was driven from her homeland, Brant encouraged Iroquois support of the British. She was instrumental in inspiring continued loyalty to the English king by her people; as one official noted, one word from Molly Brant was far more persuasive than a thousand words from a British official. Indeed, Brant's effectiveness during her term as William Johnson's mistress had established sufficient connections with British officialdom that she was be supported financially for the rest of her life. Her claims for damages of £1206 and her yearly pension of £100 exceeded those of her brother Joseph Brant, the faithful Mohawk war captain. Forced by the fortunes of war to remain away from her homeland, she eventually settled in Kingston, Ontario, where she died in 1796.

References

Green, Gretchen. "Molly Brant, Catharine Brant, and Their Daughters: A Study in Colonial Acculturation." *Ontario History* 81 (1989): 235–250.
Gundy, H. Pearson. "Molly Brant—Loyalist." *Ontario History* 14 (1953): 97–108.
Hamilton, Milton W. *Sir William Johnson: Colonial American, 1715–1763*. Port Washington, NY: Kennikat Press, 1976.
Kelsay, Isabel T. *Joseph Brant, 1743–1807: Man of Two Worlds*. Syracuse, NY: Syracuse University Press, 1984.
Seymour, Flora Warren. *Women of Trail and Wigwam*. New York: Woman's Press, 1930.

—*James H. O'Donnell III*

BRASS, ELEANOR (1905–1992), the daughter of Frederick Charles Dieter (Cree, German) and Marybelle Cote (Saulteaux [Ojibwa] French), was born on May 1 on the Peepeekisis Reserve in the Balcarrer district, east of Regina, Saskatchewan. She was the direct descendent of two signatories of Treaty No. Four (Fort Qu'Apelle, 1874), Cree Chief Okanese (her father's grandfather) and Saulteaux Chief Gabriel Cote (her mother's grandfather). She attended the Presbyterian File Hills Indian Boarding School and later went to high school in Kenora, Saskatchewan, leaving after the tenth grade in 1921. On January 12, 1925, she married her childhood friend Hector Brass, with whom she farmed on the File Hills Colony on the Peepeekisis Reserve until 1949. At the same time she started writing articles on Native issues and Native/non–Native relations for the *Regina Leader Post* and other newspapers and magazines in Saskatchewan.

After leaving the reserve for the city, Eleanor and Hector Brass worked in Regina in various capacities, ranging from menial to secretarial work. In the city,

Eleanor became increasingly involved in human rights issues pertaining to Native people. Through the YWCA, her employer for many years, she organized social events for urban Natives, founded the Regina Native Society, and in 1960, with four other activists (including her husband), she established the Regina Indian Friendship Center. Her increasing involvement in Native affairs, and her dedication to reeducating uninformed and prejudiced non–Natives, led to further publishing and CBC broadcasting for public schools, including the retelling of Cree legends from the oral tradition.

In 1965 Brass was hired by the provincial government as an information writer for the Department of Agriculture. Her husband died on October 17, 1965, and Brass soon transferred to the provincial government's Indian and Métis Branch, where she did counseling and served as placement officer, checking the quota of Native employees in government institutions and finding employment opportunities for Native youth in the private sector. In 1970 she transferred to Saskatoon, and officially retired from government service a year later.

Brass then started a fourth career, working as executive director of the Sagitawa Indian Friendship Center until 1975, when the Alberta Native Communications Society hired her as a news correspondent for the Peace River region, where she helped establish an Indian Friendship Center. All the while, Brass was actively campaigning for a better understanding between Native and non–Native people by addressing schoolchildren, the inmates of correctional institutions, and the public at large via publications and broadcasts. These included her collection of Cree narratives, *Medicine Boy and Other Cree Tales* (1978). In 1982 she addressed the World Assembly of First Nations in Regina. Failing health forced her to retire again in 1985.

Brass continued to lived in Regina, a far from inactive elder, using her time to write her autobiography, *I Walk in Two Worlds* (1987), and to serve the Native community as a speaker and writer campaigning for demolition of the barriers of mistrust and ignorance that keep many non–Natives from respecting her and her people as humans and equals. She viewed publishing Cree tales from the oral tradition in English and writing down her own life's experiences as an extension of the traditionally didactic function of storytelling: teaching coming generations how to act properly and which mistakes to avoid, and strengthening identity and pride in one's heritage.

Besides her two published books, Brass produced countless articles and essays. She also wrote a play (unpublished), *Strangers in Their Own Land*, which was performed by the Fort Qu'Apelle Drama Group.

References

Brass, Eleanor. "Eleanor Brass." In *Speaking Together: Canada's Native Women.* Pp. 42–43. Ottawa: The Secretary of State, 1975.

————. *I Walk in Two Worlds*. Calgary: Glenbow Museum, 1987.

————. *Medicine Boy and Other Cree Tales*. 1982. Reprint, Calgary: Glenbow Museum, 1978. Livingston, Donna. "She Walks in Two Worlds." *Glenbow* 8 (Spring 1988): 8–9.

—*Hartmut Lutz*

BRAVE BIRD, MARY [Mary Crow Dog, Mary Olguin, Ohitika Win, Brave Woman] (b. 1953), a political activist, is a Sioux born on the Rosebud Reservation in South Dakota. She is a member of the "Burned Thigh" or Brulé Sioux. Brave Bird tells a compelling story of what it is like to be a Native American woman in her autobiography, *Lakota Woman*, which was written under the name Mary Crow Dog and tells of her life until 1977. *Lakota Woman* won the American Book Award in 1991. The narrative that she delivers in this work is not chronological; rather, it is a cyclical account told in colloquial language. This same pattern of development, along with the same passionate voice, can be found in *Ohitika Woman*, the continuation of her story under the name Mary Brave Bird.

In *Lakota Woman*, Brave Bird describes herself as an *iveska*, or half-blood, and relates a childhood and adolescence of dismal realities: alcoholism, rebelliousness, and poverty. She was raised primarily by her grandparents while her mother trained as a nurse. She also had close contact with members of her extended family, such as her granduncle Dick Fool Bull, who took her to her first peyote meeting when she was still a young girl, and her aunt Elsie Flood, a medicine woman. From them, she learned the oral tradition of her people. During the early 1960s, she attended the mission school at St. Francis, an unhappy experience of beatings and racism that caused her to drop out before she graduated.

The turning point in Brave Bird's life came with her first encounter with the American Indian Movement (AIM, founded in 1968) at a powwow held in 1971 at Leonard Crow Dog's home after a Sun Dance. According to her, the AIM boosted the morale of Native Americans at a time when it was critically needed, and the Indian rights movement was first of all a spiritual movement with ancient religion at its heart. Brave Bird joined the Trail of Broken Treaties, a caravan that followed the Cherokees' Trail of Tears, and was in the group that took over the Bureau of Indian Affairs building in Washington, D.C., in 1972. She was also present at the siege of Wounded Knee in 1973, and gave birth to her first child there. This siege, with its echoes of the past injustices forced upon Native Americans, forms the focal point of her narration. Brave Bird married Leonard Crow Dog, a medicine man, in 1973. As a medicine man's wife, she learned more of the traditions and rituals of the Sioux, looking to Native American religion as the cornerstone of her life. She and Leonard had three children.

Ohitika Woman continues Brave Bird's compelling story, beginning with a car accident that occurred after she had been drinking heavily. Her life with Leonard at Crow Dog Paradise had ended some years before. Although she appreciated his tutelage in Sioux tradition and ceremony, the uncertainty of their way of life finally became too much for her. The book recounts her battle with alcoholism and the grinding poverty and despair of reservation life. However, these facts are contrasted with the value of Sioux culture and traditional ceremonies, and her faith in the Native American Church. In 1991 she married Rudi Olguin, with whom she had her fifth child.

Brave Bird's story, as told in *Lakota Woman* and *Ohitika Woman*, is one of a Lakota woman, an activist, and an "Indian feminist." However, like other Native American women, she has been in a double bind of victimization, caught between eroding traditions and a neglectful and misinformed white dominant culture. She has been beaten, jailed, and oppressed. However, Mary Brave Bird's life story is ultimately one of triumph. Not only does she survive but she also emerges strong and whole because she can balance injustice with humanity and anger with faith in herself and her culture.

References

Brave Bird, Mary, with Richard Erdoes. *Ohitika Woman.* New York: Grove Press, 1993. Reprint, New York: HarperPerennial, 1994.

Crow Dog, Mary, with Richard Erdoes. *Lakota Woman.* New York: GroveWeidenfeld, 1990.

Wise, Christopher, and R. Todd Wise. "Mary Brave Bird Speaks: A Brief Interview." *SAIL* 10 (Winter 1998): 1–8.

—Laurie Lisa

BRIGHAM, BESMILR MOORE (b. 1913), the daughter of Monroe I. and Bessie May Emmons Moore, was born near Pace, Mississippi. She lived in this area and in Jonesboro, Arkansas, for ten years before moving to Donna, Texas, where she finished high school. Later she attended Mary Hardin-Baylor Women's College in Belton, Texas, from which she graduated in 1935 with a BA degree in journalism. There she met Roy Brigham, who was working for a local printer. They married in 1936 and spent the next few years moving from place to place in Texas, Oklahoma, and Mississippi. During these years Roy worked as a typesetter and Brigham wrote copy for local newspapers.

In the early 1940s they moved to New York City, where Brigham studied for two years at the New School for Social Research. "There is no school like it," she says. Her major teachers there were Horace Gregory and Sidney Alexander. She took courses in poetry and fiction and tried "to get as far away from journalism as possible," writing her works without punctuation or capitals. She also became interested in the theater, particularly mime, and left journalism forever.

Always restless, she and Roy traveled frequently, going to Mexico, Central America, and Europe. Brigham was fascinated by her father's trips to work with the Meskito Indians in Nicaragua and succeeded in tracing the same routes he had followed there. These trips and their experiences among the Indians in the Americas and Mexico provided material for the increasing amount of writing Brigham was doing. Her own ancestry (her mother's father was half Choctaw) strongly influenced her. During the 1940s and 1950s, she thought of herself as a writer, and she continued to fill notebooks with poems, essays, and stories that Roy helped her with by collaborating, editing, and typing.

Brigham's first work was published in 1965 when her poem "Yaqui Deer" was accepted for publication by *Corno emplumada* in Mexico City. Since then her work has been included in numerous anthologies, including *31 New American Poets* (Hill and Wang, 1969), *From the Belly of the Shark* (Vintage Books, 1973), and *New Generation: Poetry* (Ann Arbor Review, 1971). She is included in Dorothy Abbot's *Mississippi Writers* (University Press of Mississippi, 1985), and her work has appeared in many American literary magazines, from *The Atlantic* to the *Southern Review*, from *American and Canadian Poetry* to *West Coast Review*. Her stories have also selected for Martha Foley's *Best Short Stories of 1972, Best Short Stories of 1973*, and *Best Short Stories of 1983*.

Brigham is an interesting speaker whose observations and reminiscences have fascinated audiences for many years. Her readings and conversations have been recorded at Southwest Minnesota State University, the University of Wisconsin at LaCrosse and Green Bay, and at the Library of Congress.

In the early 1990s Roy and Besmilr moved to Las Cruces, New Mexico, to be near their daughter and her husband. Shortly afterward Besmilr was stricken with Alzheimer's disease. Roy died in the fall of 1996.

References

Brigham, Besmilr. *Agony Dance: Death of the Dancing Dolls*. Portland, OR: Prensa de Lagar/Wine Press, 1969.
————. *Heaved from the Earth*. New York: Alfred A. Knopf, 1971.
Kopp, Karl, and Jane Kopp, eds. *Southwest: A Contemporary Anthology*. Albuquerque, NM: Red Earth, 1977.
Marken, Jack. Personal communication with Besmilr Moore Brigham, November 19, 1990.
————. Personal communication with Roy Brigham, summer 1996.

—Jack Marken

BRINK, JEANNE (b. 1944), was born in Montpelier, Vermont, and is a member of the Obomsawin family of Thompson's Point, Vermont, and the Abenaki Nation of Missisquoi. Continuing in the family tradition of ash splint and sweetgrass basketry, she has original work in collections in the Memorial Hall Museum and the Worcester Art Museum in Massachusetts; the New Hampshire Historical Society; and in the Chimney Point State Historic Site and the St. Albans Historical Society in Vermont. She has been artist-in-residence at Dartmouth College, the Arts Center at Old Forge, New York, and the Worcester (Massachusetts) Art Museum. She also has consulted on Abenaki culture and education with public and private schools and colleges throughout New England. As the cultural awareness director of the Dawnland Center in Montpelier, she coordinates powwows and traditional arts and crafts workshops for intertribal programs and the W'Abenaki Dancers, an adult traditional dance group that gives presentations at regional schools, colleges, and powwows.

Brink was the project director and curator of the material culture and art exhibit "Spirit of the Abenaki," and codirector and curator (with Gerard Tsonakwa) of the Abenaki art exhibit "Shamanism, Magic, and the Busy Spider." A recipient of grants from the Vermont Council on the Arts and the Vermont Council on the Humanities, she creates and coordinates exhibits, presentations, lectures, and programs on western Abenaki history, language, culture, basket making, oral tradition, dance, games, and current issues for the Vermont Council on the Humanities, the Vermont Department of Libraries, and schools and colleges in New England.

Besides being author, with Gordon Day, of *Alnôbaôdwa: A Western Abenaki Language Guide*, Brink has digitized Day's *Western Abenaki Dictionary* (volume 1 is Abenaki–English; volume 2 is English–Abenaki) for publication by the Museum of Civilization in Ottawa, Canada. A recipient of the Vermont Council on the

Arts Award of Merit, she serves on the board of directors for the Robert Hull Fleming Museum at the University of Vermont and the Vermont Historical Society in Montpelier. She is listed in the New England Foundation for the Arts' *Directory of Native American Artists and Resources of New England*. Brink holds an MA in Native American Studies, a BA in liberal studies, and an AS in executive administrative assistance from Vermont College of Norwich University.

The mother of three and grandmother of six, Jeanne Brink lives with her husband in Barre, Vermont. She says, "I am committed to the preservation of Western Abenaki language, traditions, and culture."

Reference

Brink, Jeanne, and Gordon M. Day. *Alnôbaôdwa: A Western Abenaki Language Guide*. Swanton, VT: Franklin Northwest Supervisory Union, Title V Indian Education Office, 1990.

—Rhoda Carroll

BROKER, IGNATIA (1919–1987), was born and raised on the White Earth Reservation in Minnesota. She attended Wahpeton Indian Boarding School in North Dakota, Haskell Institute in Lawrence, Kansas, and public school in Park Rapids, Minnesota. She received business training at North Star College in Warren, Minnesota.

During World War II, Broker worked in a defense plant and took night classes in journalism. When the war ended, she married a veteran and moved to St. Paul's River Flats district, an area with a large Indian population. After her husband was killed in the Korean War, she moved to Minneapolis and worked in a health clinic.

In 1953 Broker attended the Minnesota School of Business in Minneapolis. She was an active volunteer in Indian organizations concerned with Indian rights issues, such as American Indians Incorporated, Service to American Indian Resident Students, Indian Upward Bound, halfway houses, and the Minority Task Force of the Minneapolis public schools. Broker was also a founder and active member of the Upper Midwest American Indian Center of Minneapolis, the Urban American Indian Federation of the State of Minnesota, the Department of Indian Work of the United Church Committee, and the Minnesota Indian Historical Society.

As a member of Concerned Indian Citizens, Broker headed a study of welfare abuses directed at Indians. The research uncovered the bus ticket policy—when Indians requested welfare support, the common policy was to give them bus tickets back to the reservations. The Concerned Indian Citizens, working with the United Church Committee, used this research to help change attitudes toward Indians and rescind the bus ticket policy.

In 1982 Broker retired and moved with her mother to Bemidji, Minnesota, near the White Earth Reservation. She continued to be active, participating in the Minnesota Indian Council on Aging and local senior citizens' organizations.

Broker was concerned with bridging generation gaps for the Ojibwa. She produced films and stories on Ojibwa culture for the Minneapolis public schools' Indian Elementary Curriculum Project and the Indian Education Program at Cass Lake in northern Minnesota. In 1983 she published a biography of her great-great-grandmother, Night Flying Woman. Her goals were to teach the younger generation about the lifestyle of earlier generations of Ojibwa, create a sense of identity for the present generation, ensure the continuity of the Ojibwa tribal customs, and dispel stereotypes of Indians. In *Night Flying Woman*, Broker explains that telling these stories to her grandchildren ensured the continuity not only of the customs but also of the Ojibwa people themselves. She believed her grandchildren's generation would close the circle of seven generations that began with Night Flying Woman. According to Ojibwa traditions, this closure would return the Ojibwa to their traditional ways.

In 1984 Broker was awarded the National Wonder Woman Award for her efforts in furthering equality and peace.

References

Broker, Ignatia. *Ahmik Nishgahdahzee, the Story of an Angry Beaver*. Minneapolis: Minneapolis Public Schools, Indian Elementary Curriculum Project. Filmstrip and poster story.

————. *Night Flying Woman, an Ojibway Narrative*. St. Paul: Minnesota Historical Society Press, 1983.

————. *Our People*. Cass Lake, MN: Indian Education Program. Film series, booklets and teachers' guides.

————. Personal papers. Minnesota Historical Society Manuscripts Collections (1908–1920, 1931, 1978, 1982–1987). St. Paul.

————. *Weegwahsimitig, the Story of a Birch Tree*. Minneapolis: Minneapolis Public Schools, Indian Elementary Curriculum Project.

—Pattiann Frinzi

BRONSON, RUTH MUSKRAT [Ruth Margaret Muskrat] (1897–1982), was born in the Delaware district of the Cherokee Nation, Indian Territory (now Oklahoma). As a child she experienced the hardships caused by the allotment of Cherokee lands and the dismantling of Cherokee institutions. In her search for answers to the problems of her generation, she sought an advanced education. At fourteen, Bronson left home for Tonkawa, Oklahoma, where she received a college preparatory education. After graduating in 1919, she taught in Oklahoma's rural schools and spent a year each at the universities of Oklahoma and Kansas. In 1923 she entered Mount Holyoke College in Massachusetts with advanced standing and a full scholarship. In 1925 she became the first Indian woman to attend and graduate from that institution.

Bronson received national attention when she became the first American Indian student delegate at the World Student Christian Federation's annual conference, which in 1922 was held in Beijing, China. A year later, she presented her views on Indian affairs when she spoke during the so-called Committee of 100 meeting in Washington, D.C. After graduating from college, Bronson spent a summer as dean of women at Northeastern State Teachers College in Tahlequah, Oklahoma. In September, she left for Lawrence, Kansas, where she taught at Haskell Indian Boarding School. Now, she felt, she could really begin encouraging the development of Indian leadership, for she believed that only Indians could find adequate solutions to Indian problems.

In 1930 Bronson benefited from a reform movement within the Bureau of Indian Affairs' Education Division when she accepted an offer to fill the newly created position of guidance and placement officer. From her office in Kansas City, and later from Washington, D.C., she disbursed educational loans and promoted Indian student success in postsecondary educational institutions. She retired in 1944. In the interim she married John F. Bronson, and they adopted a two-year-old Laguna girl named Delores. In 1944 Bronson wrote and published her only book-length work, *Indians Are People Too*.

Having lived and worked in Washington, D.C., since 1936, Bronson possessed the experience and contacts necessary to help the fledgling National Congress of American Indians (NCAI). Between 1945 and 1957, she established an effective Washington bureau for the NCAI, edited its *Washington Bulletin*, and served the organization as its executive director, treasurer, delegation coordinator, lobbyist, and general problem solver. In 1949 Bronson became one of the three original trustees of NCAI's nonprofit educational affiliate, ARROW, Inc. (Americans for the Restitution and Righting of Old Wrongs).

As a result of her involvement with ARROW's educational work, Bronson became interested in leadership development at the community level. Thus, in 1957, she and her husband left Washington and national politics for community education work on the San Carlos Apache Reservation in Arizona. Bronson had accepted another newly created government position, health education specialist for the United States Indian Health Service. In this position she encouraged a fundamental type of adult education that went beyond preventive medicine to the nurturing of leadership skills among Apache women. During her five years at San Carlos, Bronson helped empower some of these women, thereby enabling them to become more involved in determining the health of their community. For her efforts at San Carlos, Bronson received the Department of Health, Education and Welfare's Superior Service and Oveta Cult Hobby awards in 1962. When she and her husband retired to Tucson shortly thereafter, she remained supportive of community development programs in the region until ill health in the 1970s finally made activism impossible.

References

Bernstein, Alison. "A Mixed Record: The Political Enfranchisement of American Indian Women During the Indian New Deal." *Journal of the West* 23 (July 1984): 13–20.

Bronson, Ruth Muskrat. Clipping file. Mount Holyoke College Library/Archives, South Hadley, MA.

———. *Indians Are People Too*. New York: Friendship Press, 1944.

———. "San Carlos Apache Community Development." In *Indian Communities in Action*. Edited by Broderick H. Johnson. Pp. 132–154. Tempe: Bureau of Publications, Arizona State University, 1967.

Harvey, Gretchen. "Cherokee and American: Ruth Muskrat Bronson, 1897–1982." PhD diss., Arizona State University, 1996.

—Gretchen G. Harvey

BROWN, CATHARINE (1800–1823), was one of the first Cherokee converts to Christianity. She and her brother John, children of James Brown, one of the headmen of the Creek Path community, entered the school established at Brainard Mission in the Cherokee Nation by the American Board of Commissioners for Foreign Missions in 1818. Although she was described as "proud and haughty" when she first arrived, she was later described as "modest and amiable." She showed signs of Christian conversion and was received into the mission church established at Brainard in November 1818.

The following year, Brown's father called her home because he wanted to move his family to the Arkansas Territory west of the Mississippi River. Although Brown considered leaving "more bitter than death," she dutifully followed her father's wish. However, four months later her family still had not moved, and her parents gave her permission to return to the school and to remain even after they moved. Brown attributed her father's change of heart to "the special providence of God" and to her own "fervent believing prayer." Her father evidently did not emigrate to Arkansas; in January 1820 Brown and her brother David went to Creek Path to visit him because he was sick. David, who also had converted to Christianity, read the Bible to his father and exhorted him to repent of his sins. Following his recovery, James Brown wrote to the American Board in February, asking that a school be established in his community. Several missionaries from Brainard went to Creek Path, and the school opened in March 1820. By June it was full, and a second school was proposed.

Catharine Brown offered to teach a school for girls if the community would erect a building for it. Her offer was accepted, and in May 1820 she left Brainard to return to Creek Path and commence her teaching career. She became ill with tuberculosis and finally went to a physician in Limestone County, Alabama, for treatment. She died at his home on July 18, 1823. Her passing was mourned by the missionaries. Because she was one of the earliest Cherokee converts and served as a pious example to her students, her life was glorified by the American Board in a number of pamphlets and textbooks used in American Board mission schools. Choctaw children read about her in *Chahta Holisso a tukla, or the Second Chahta Book*, written by Alfred Wright and Cyrus Byington.

References

American Board of Commissioners for Foreign Missions. *First Ten Annual Reports of the American Board of Commissioners for Foreign Missions, with Other Documents of the Board*. Boston: Crocker and Brewster, 1834.

Missionary Herald 19 (October 1823): 336.

Tracy, Joseph. "History of the American Board of Commissioners for Foreign Missions. Compiled Chiefly from the Published and Unpublished Documents of the Board." In *History of American Missions to the Heathen from Their Commencement to the Present Time*. Worcester, MA: Spooner & Howland, 1840.

Wright, Alfred, and Cyrus Byington. *Chahta Holisso a tukla, or the Second Chahta Book: Containing Translations of Portions of the Scriptures, Biographical Notices of Henry Obokiah and Catharine Brown, a Catechism, and Dissertations on Religious Subjects*. Cincinnati, OH: Morgan, Lodge and Fisher, 1827.

—Clara Sue Kidwell

BROWN, EMILY IVANOFF [Ticasuk] (1904–1982), was born in Unalakleet, Alaska, and died in Fairbanks, Alaska. She was the granddaughter of Sergei Ivanoff, a Russian immigrant to Alaska, and his Yupik Eskimo wife, Chikuk, and the daughter of Stephan Ivanoff and his wife, Malquay. She began school in Shaktoolik, a village her father helped to establish in 1907. After graduating from high school, Brown obtained a provisional teaching certificate and became a grade school teacher and an advocate of bilingual education. She enrolled at the University of Alaska in 1959 to obtain a formal college degree because she felt that her provisional credentials had never been fully accepted by fellow teachers; she ultimately received two BA degrees from the university. Her master's thesis at the University of Alaska was published as a book, *Grandfather of Unalakleet*, in 1974. Brown later revised the book, and it was republished in 1981 as *The Roots of Ticasuk: An Eskimo Woman's Family Story*.

Brown was widely recognized by Alaska Native people as an educator and writer of articles about Eskimo cultures and education. Among her many honors were a Presidential Commendation from Richard M. Nixon for exceptional service and recognition by the Alaskan legislature and the National Federation of Press Women. Her death came two weeks before she was to receive an honorary doctorate from the University of Alaska.

References

Ticasuk [Emily Ivanoff Brown]. *The Roots of Ticasuk: An Eskimo Woman's Family Story*. Anchorage: Alaska Northwest Publishing, 1981.
———. *Tales of Ticasuk: Eskimo Legends and Stories*. Illustrated by Eugene C. Trotten and Mary Lou Trotten. Fairbanks: University of Alaska Press, 1987.

—Clara Sue Kidwell

BUFFALO BIRD WOMAN [Maxidiwiac, Waheenee] (c. 1839–1932), a Hidatsa who experienced the traditional life of her people in what is now North Dakota, is known through the work of Gilbert Wilson, who first interviewed her in 1906 and wrote two books about her life: *Waheenee* and *Buffalo Bird Woman's Garden*. Additional information can be found in Wilson's book about her son, *Goodbird the Indian*, and in Gilman and Schneider's *The Way to Independence*, a chronicle of her family's life from 1840 to 1920.

During a series of interviews over a period of twelve years, Buffalo Bird Woman told Wilson the history of the Hidatsa that had been transmitted to her through the oral tradition, and she described her own experience and the lives and work of women in Hidatsa culture. She spoke only the Hidatsa language, and her accounts were translated into English by her son.

In 1837 a smallpox epidemic killed over half the Hidatsa. Buffalo Bird Woman told Wilson that she was "born in an earth lodge by the mouth of the Knife River, in what is now North Dakota, three years after the smallpox winter." She was with the Hidatsa and Mandan tribes in 1845 when they relocated and built Like-a-Fishhook Village overlooking the Missouri River, upstream from their traditional homeland.

Her mother, Weahtee, was one of four sisters—all wives of Small Ankle—and the three aunts were like mothers to her. When she was six, Weahtee died; thereafter, her primary caretaker was her grandmother, Turtle, who taught her proper values and behavior. Her grandfather, Missouri River, a medicine man, taught her of the spirits.

The family's earth lodge was also the community meeting place and church. Kept within it were the holy objects of their clan, the Midipadi or Waterbusters. Missouri River had brought these holy objects, the Maa-duush, from the Knife River villages.

When she was ten, a naming ceremony was held for her and she was given the name Waheenee (Good Way). But later her father, Small Ankle, gave her the name Maxidiwiac, meaning Buffalo Bird Woman, in an effort to help her recover from sickness. She learned and practiced all the traditional skills of Hidatsa women— gardening, preparing food, building earth lodges, weaving mats and baskets, and many others. Her aunt Sage honored Buffalo Bird Woman with the gift of a woman's belt as a reward for tanning hundreds of hides.

When she was fourteen, Buffalo Bird Woman joined the Skunk Society. Among the activities of this group of girls was dancing and singing to celebrate the return of a successful war party. At sixteen, Buffalo Bird Woman was married in the traditional way, with an exchange of gifts. She and her half sister agreed to marry Magpie, the stepson of a Crow man named Hanging Stone, who also lived in Like-a-Fishhook Village. After the ceremonial gifts had been given, Magpie went to live with the two young women in their lodge, according to the matrilocal Hidatsa custom. Buffalo Bird Woman lived with Magpie for the next thirteen years, until he died of tuberculosis.

Her second marriage, to Son of a Star, was to last the rest of her life. In the autumn of 1869, when she was thirty, she gave birth to their son, her first and only child, Tskaka-sakis, Goodbird. Life at Like-a-Fishhook Village continued until 1885, when Hidatsa, Mandan, and Arikara families began to spread out on allotments along the Missouri River, usually settling according to tribal affiliation on land that became the Fort Berthold Reservation.

Buffalo Bird Woman held to the traditional ways of her culture and generously and tirelessly transmitted them. Her information is valuable for its detailed description of the lifestyle her people had developed to sustain themselves in balance with nature. As important as her explanation of how to garden in the traditional Hidatsa manner is her transmission of the philosophical views of her people in statements such as these: "We thought that the corn plants had souls as children have souls" and "We thought an earth lodge was alive and had a spirit like a human body, and its front was like a face, with the door for mouth."

References

Gilman, Carolyn, and Mary Jane Schneider. *The Way to Independence*. St. Paul: Minnesota Historical Society Press, 1987.

Goodbird, Arnie. Personal communication to Norma C. Wilson, February 27, 1991.

Goodbird, Edward. *Goodbird the Indian: His Story, Told by Himself to Gilbert L. Wilson*. New York: Fleming H. Revell, 1914.

Jensen, Joan M. *With These Hands: Women Working the Land.* Old Westbury, NY: Feminist Press, 1981.

Wilson, Gilbert L. *Agriculture of the Hidatsa Indians: An Indian Interpretation.* Studies in the Social Sciences, no. 9. Minneapolis: University of Minnesota, 1917.

————. *Buffalo Bird Woman's Garden: Agriculture of the Hidatsa Indians.* St. Paul: Minnesota Historical Society Press, 1987.

————. *Waheenee: An Indian Girl's Story Told by Herself to Gilbert L. Wilson.* Lincoln: University of Nebraska Press, 1987.

—Norma C. Wilson

BURNS, DIANE M. (b. 1957), poet and artist, was born in California to a Chemehuevi father and an Anishinaabe/Chippewa (Ojibwa) mother; she was educated at the Sherman Institute, the Institute of American Indian Arts (where she was awarded the Congressional Medal of Merit for artistic and academic excellence), an alternative school in Scarsdale, New York, and Barnard College of Columbia University (class of 1978), where she majored in political science. A painter and illustrator who has written book reviews for the Council on Interracial Books for Children and has taught a course in poetry at St. Marks Poetry Project in New York City, she is a member of the Poet's Overland Expeditionary Troupe, the Third World Writers Association, and the Feminist Writers Guild. She has read her poetry throughout the country and has been published in *Greenfield Review, Blue Cloud Quarterly, White Pine Journal, Hard Press, Sunbury, New York Waterways,* and *Contact/II.*

Burns's first volume of poetry, *Riding the One-Eyed Ford* (1981), nominated for the William Carlos Williams Award, marks Burns as one of the most important contemporary Indian poets. This collection of narrative verse, examining issues of conformity and nonconformity from a particularly urban and female Indian perspective, is strongly influenced by popular culture and performance theory. Her poetry is distinctly rhythmic, shaped by both contemporary and traditional music—for her a primal force, a reflection of Native ceremony and the storytelling tradition. Burns believes that women, particularly, have "tapped into a more creative and individual persona. They've got their own voice, only more so. They're more on the cutting edge, more avant-garde," especially Native women, who have a heritage of power and creativity. Recognizing the possibility of paradox in her dual emphasis on individuality and community, she asserts that "creativity is the force that propels everything. That's the energy of the universe."

Burns is a resident of New York City, the setting of much of her work. Her projects include completing another volume of poetry and a science fiction novel about a conquest from Jupiter. Of the latter she says, "I like the irony of the second invasion."

References

Bruchac Joseph. "That Beat, That Pulse: An Interview with Diane Burns." In *Survival This Way: Interviews with American Indian Poets.* Pp. 42–56. Sun Tracks, vol. 15. Tucson: University of Arizona Press, 1987.

————, ed. *Songs from This Earth on Turtle's Back: Contemporary American Indian Poetry*. Greenfield Center, NY: Greenfield Review Press, 1983.

Burns, Diane M. *Riding the One-Eyed Ford*. 1981. Reprint, Brooklyn, NY: Strawberry Press, 1982.

Green, Rayna, ed. *That's What She Said: Contemporary Poetry and Fiction by Native American Women*. Bloomington: Indiana University Press, 1984.

—Rodney Simard

BURTON, JIMALEE CHITWOOD [Ho-Chee-Nee] (b. 1920), was born in eastern Oklahoma. A Cherokee, she came to prominence with her volume of collected poetry, prose, and traditional stories, *Indian Heritage, Indian Pride: Stories That Touched My Life*. Her most prolific period was from 1967 to 1974, during which she wrote several well-received poems in addition to *Indian Heritage, Indian Pride*. Aside from her poetry and prose, Burton is known as a graphic artist who melds traditional motifs with contemporary themes and media. She was editor of the intertribal newspaper *The Native Voice* for fifteen years.

References

Brumble, David H. III. *An Annotated Bibliography of American Indian and Eskimo Autobiography*. Lincoln: University of Nebraska Press, 1981.

Burton, Jimalee. *Indian Heritage, Indian Pride: Stories That Touched My Life*. Norman: University of Oklahoma Press, 1974.

Green, Rayna, ed. *That's What She Said: An Anthology of Contemporary Native American Women*. Bloomington: Indiana University Press, 1984.

—Cynthia Kasee

C

CALLAHAN, SOPHIA ALICE (1868–1894), a teacher and writer in the Creek Nation, was a member of a family prominent in Creek national political affairs. Qualified to teach grammar, arithmetic, geography, history, and physics, in 1892–1893 she taught at Wealaka Mission School, and during the fall of 1893 at Harrell Institute, a Methodist school at Muskogee. At the time of her death in January 1894, she was serving in a minor official capacity in the Indian Mission Conference of the Methodist Episcopal Church, South.

Although Callahan wrote verse, her most ambitious literary effort was *Wynema: A Child of the Forest*, a loosely constructed novel that she published at age twenty-three. She dedicated the work to the oppressed Indian tribes of North America, hoping it would help to bring about an era of goodwill and justice for the American Indian. Thin, and sometimes highly improbable, plots are woven through with themes concerning the importance of Christianity and education in English, fraud in Indian administration, allotments, temperance, women's rights, the Ghost Dance movement, and atrocities committed upon the Sioux at Wounded Knee. Though her novel is extremely flawed, Callahan stands as the first Indian woman known to have written a novel. *Wynema* appeared in a new edition in 1997.

References

Callahan, S. Alice. *Wynema: A Child of the Forest*. Chicago: H. J. Smith, 1891. Reprint, edited by A. LaVonne Brown Ruoff, Lincoln: University of Nebraska Press, 1997.

Foreman, Carolyn Thomas. "S. Alice Callahan: Author of *Wynema: A Child of the Forest*." *Chronicles of Oklahoma* 33 (Autumn 1955): 306–315, 549.

Ruoff, A. LaVonne Brown. "Introduction." In *Wynema: A Child of the Forest*. Lincoln: University of Nebraska Press, 1997.

———. "Justice for Indians and Women: The Protest Fiction of Alice Callahan and Pauline Johnson." *World Literature Today* 66 (1992): 249–255.

Van Dyke, Annette. "An Introduction to *Wynema, A Child of the Forest*, by Sophia Alice Callahan." *SAIL* 4 (Summer/Fall 1992): 123–128.

—Daniel F. Littlefield, Jr.

CAMPBELL, MARIA (b. 1940), a Métis born in Saskatchewan, is best known for her autobiography *Halfbreed*, published in 1973. The autobiography is a loving, bitter, and comic portrait of a cultural and individual life during a transitional period in Métis culture. Campbell recalls the happy family times and close community ties. Among the most influential people in her early life was her great-grandmother Cheechum, who taught her traditional Métis ways and who served as a conscience for the community by encouraging Métis political activism against the racism of the Canadian government. Following the death of Campbell's mother, the family became Maria's responsibility, and at the same time they were forced into extreme poverty. Eventually, the younger children were removed from the home by a misguided social welfare system, and Campbell married a Euro–Canadian in an effort to reclaim the children. At the same time Campbell was descending into alcoholism, drug abuse, prostitution, and drug smuggling, the parallel disintegration of Métis cultural life was occurring through the loss of their traditional hunting and trapping lands and the demoralizing effect of a paternalistic welfare system. Eventually, Campbell realized that "if I was to know peace, I would have to search within myself." She embarked on a career of political activism based upon traditional Métis spiritual values.

Campbell's political concerns since the publication of *Halfbreed* have been for the welfare of Métis women and children. Sometimes referred to as "the mother of us all," she also has conducted numerous workshops for young Native writers. In an effort to teach young Métis about their history, she has written three children's books: *People of the Buffalo, Little Badger and the Fire Spirit*, and *Riel's People*. *Jessica: A Transformation*, a play based upon *Halfbreed*, was performed by the Great Canadian Theatre Company of Toronto in October 1986. The play was published as *The Book of Jessica* in 1989 by Campbell and her collaborator, Linda Griffiths. She also worked on a television film, *The Road Allowance People*.

References

Bataille, Gretchen M., and Kathleen M. Sands. *American Indian Women Telling Their Lives*. Pp. 113–126. Lincoln: University of Nebraska Press, 1984.

Campbell, Maria. *Achimoona*. Saskatoon, SK: Fifth House, 1985.

———. *Halfbreed*. Toronto: McClelland and Stewart, 1973. Reprint, Lincoln: University of Nebraska Press, 1982.

———. *Little Badger and the Fire Spirit*. Toronto: McClelland and Stewart, 1977.

———. *People of the Buffalo*. Toronto: Douglas & McIntyre, 1976.

———. *Riel's People*. Toronto: Douglas & McIntyre, 1978.

———. *Stories of the Road Allowance People*. Penticton, BC: Theytus Books, 1995.

———, and Linda Griffiths. *The Book of Jessica: A Theatrical Transformation*. Toronto: Coach House Press, 1989.

Godard, Barbara. "The Politics of Representation: Some Native Canadian Women Writers." *Canadian Literature* 124–125 (Spring/Summer 1990): 183–225.

Grant, Agnes. "Contemporary Native Women's Voices in Literature." *Canadian Literature* 124–125 (Spring/Summer 1990): 124–132.

Hillis, Doris. "You Have to Own Yourself: An Interview with Maria Campbell." *Prairie Fire* 9 (Autumn 1988): 44–58.

"Maria Campbell." In *Contemporary Challenges: Conversations with Native Canadian Writers*. Edited by Hartmut Lutz. Pp. 41–66. Saskatoon, SK: Fifth House, 1991.

Petrone, Penny. *Native Literature in Canada: From the Oral Tradition to the Present*. Toronto: Oxford University Press, 1990.

Tsosie, Rebecca. "Changing Woman: The Cross-Currents of American Indian Feminine Identity." *American Indian Culture and Research Journal* 12 (1988): 1–37.

Vangen, Kate. "Making Faces: Defiance and Humour in Campbell's *Halfbreed* and Welch's *Winter in the Blood*." In *The Native in Literature*. Edited by Thomas King, Cheryl Cates, and Helen Hog. Pp. 188–205. Winnipeg, MN: ECW Press, 1987.

—*Kathleen McNerney Donovan*

CARDIFF, GLADYS (b. 1942), a prolific poet, is an Eastern Cherokee who was born in the area of Browning, Montana. She studied English, literature, and creative writing at the University of Washington. A frequent participant in seminars, workshops, and conferences in the Pacific Northwest, she reads her poetry (much of it devoted to themes from her tribal legends) and teaches others about creative writing through venues such as the Poetry in the Schools Program, an official program of Washington State.

Her first book, *To Frighten a Storm*, received the Governor's Writers Award for a First Book. Cardiff won several other state-sponsored writing awards, as well as independent literary awards, such as the Louisa Kern Award and the Nelson Bentley Award for Poetry (both in 1988).

Working almost exclusively in the genre of poetry, Cardiff has published works in journals, periodicals, and anthologies, including *Songs from This Earth on Turtle's Back, That's What She Said: An Anthology of Contemporary Native American Women*, and *Dancing on the Rim of the World*. Cardiff is currently writing a play in dramatic verse based on the creation story and modern myths of the Eastern Cherokee. She makes her home in Seattle, Washington.

References

Bruchac, Joseph, ed. *Songs from This Earth on Turtle's Back*. Greenfield Center, NY: Greenfield Review Press, 1983.

Cardiff, Gladys. *To Frighten a Storm*. Port Townsend, WA: Copper Canyon Press, 1976.

Green, Rayna, ed. *That's What She Said: An Anthology of Contemporary Native American Women*. Bloomington: Indiana University Press, 1984.

Lerner, Andrea, ed. *Dancing on the Rim of the World: An Anthology of Contemporary Northwest Native American Writing*. Tucson: University of Arizona Press, 1990.

Niatum, Duane, ed. *Carriers of the Dream Wheel: Contemporary Native American Poets of the Twentieth Century*. New York: Harper & Row, 1975.

—*Cynthia Kasee*

CARIUS, HELEN SLWOOKO (1928–1998), a Sevukakmet Inuit, was born at Camp Noosak on Boxer Bay in Alaska. For the first few years of her life, she thought that her family members were the only people on earth. Life changed for her around 1930, when her father became ill and the family moved to Gambell to get aid from the missionaries.

When Carius was about ten years old, she contracted polio. She was given therapy at the Indian Hospital in Tacoma, Washington, and in Mt. Edgecumbe, Alaska. After high school she married an airman, and they left Alaska in 1954. They had two sons and a daughter.

For the next twenty-three years, Carius lived in California, Arizona, and Missouri. She made and sold leather art, such as Eskimo dolls, slippers, and hassocks decorated with whales, walruses, and polar bears. She gave a series of lectures in the Kansas City schools about the Sevukakmet way of life on St. Lawrence Island. In 1976, at the Chicago National Council of Teachers of English Convention, she presented a lecture on her life as one of the Sevukakmet and illustrated it with slides of the drawings she had made.

In 1977 Carius returned to Alaska and worked as a resource person in the Anchorage public schools. She also helped direct, and was technical adviser for, a television show on Eskimo heritage.

In 1979 Servius wrote and illustrated *Sevukakmet*, a book that describes the way of life of the Siberian Eskimo. The last fifteen years of her life were dedicated to preserving the knowledge and heritage of the St. Lawrence Island Eskimos.

Reference

Carius, Helen Slwooko. *Sevukakmet*. Anchorage, AK: Alaska Pacific University Press, 1979.

—*Joyce Ann Kievit*

CARLO, POLDINE DEMOSKI (b. 1920), Yukon Athabascan author, was born at Nulato, Alaska, the daughter of Priscilla Stickman and James Demoski. Her father drowned while crossing the Yukon River in a canoe. Priscilla remarried and had two more daughters, Anna and Florence. After Priscilla died in 1928, Poldine and her sisters were raised by their grandparents, Joseph and Anna Stickman (Otzosia and K'Oghotaaineek), two of the most powerful medicine people in the Yukon. Baptized at Nulato, Carlo was named after Sister Mary Leopoldine, the mother superior of the St. Ann Order of Nuns of Alaska. Although she attended the Catholic school at Nulato and spent a short time at the high school in Eklutna, much of her knowledge came from her grandparents. On March 19, 1940, she moved to Tanana, Alaska, where she met and married Bill Carlo. The couple had five sons and three daughters, and have lived in Ruby, Galena, Rampart, and Fairbanks, Alaska.

Carlo's accomplishments include serving as a charter member of the Fairbanks Native Association, a board member of the State of Alaska Bicentennial Commission, and a consultant for the Tanana Chiefs Conference. She dedicated her book, *Nulato: An Indian Life on the Yukon*, to her son Stewart Allen, who died in 1975, in an auto accident. Praised by Alaskan Senator John C. Sackett for recording "the vital elements of the Yukon Indian culture," the book shows a society steeped in tradition, yet still living with the modern influences of gold mining, fur trading, and missionaries. Divided into chapters titled "Growing Up," "Beliefs and Remedies," "Work," "Celebration," and "Old Ways and New," and including a helpful index, the biography provides an insightful examination of the Athabascan Indian way of life in Nulato, Alaska.

Reference

Carlo, Poldine. *Nulato: An Indian Life on the Yukon.* Caldwell, ID: Caxton Publishers, 1978.

—Steven R. Price

CHILD, BRENDA J. (b. 1959), historian and author. She is an enrolled member of the Red Lake Band of the Chippewa tribe in northern Minnesota. She received her Ph.D. in History from the University of Iowa in 1993 and taught at the University of Wisconsin at Milwaukee until 1996. At that time, Child became an associate professor of American Studies and American Indian Studies at the University of Minnesota. Specializing in Great Lakes history and American Indian education, Child has taught courses on multiculturalism and American Indian history. In 1995 and 1996, she co-taught a National Endowment for the Humanities seminar, "The Construction of Gender and the Experience of Women in American Indian Societies," with Professor Patricia Albers at the D'Arcy McNickle Center for the History of the American Indian at the Newberry Library. Her first book, *Boarding School Seasons: American Indian Families, 1900–1940*, was published by the University of Nebraska Press in 1998 and won the 1996 North American Indian Prose Award. In this work, inspired by conversations with relatives who attended government schools, Child uses letters written by Indian students, Indian parents and school administrators, student newspapers, and other previously underutilized documents to provide broader insights into the resistance strategies and survival tactics that operated within the government-run Indian schools at Flandreau, South Dakota, Pipestone, Minnesota, and the Haskell Institute in Kansas. Her study reveals the ambiguous and mixed meanings of boarding schools for the Ojibwes and other Native peoples.

References

University of Minnesota American Indian Studies Web page: <http://www.cla.umn.edu/amerind/child.html>

Coleman, Michael C. "Book Review: *Boarding School Seasons.*" *Journal of American History* 87:3 (December 2000).

Crum, Steven J. "Book Review: *Boarding School Seasons.*" *American Historical Review* 105:1 (February 2000).

—Michael Sherfy

CHONA, MARIA (c. 1845–1936), was born at Mesquite Root village in the Spanish province of Upper Pimeria several years before the U.S. government acquired the Arizona Territory through the Gadsen Purchase in 1853. A daughter of José María, who was appointed village governor when the Papagos came under American supervision, Chona spent her girlhood in a traditional Papago setting little changed since the coming of the expedition of Father Eusebio Kino in the late seventeenth century. Her father's status in the village made her privy to important events and led to her later characterization of herself as "a woman who knows things." Raised in a family of medicine men, she exhibited signs of medicine power in childhood but was not permitted to develop her gift. She participated in a traditional puberty ceremony and was married into another medicine family, but returned to her family when her husband accepted a second wife, a common practice for medicine men at the time but one that she found impossible to accept. She later married a man considerably older than she who encouraged her to develop her healing powers; she was able to fulfill her medicine gift in her later years and became well known as a curer of infant maladies.

In the early 1930s Chona became the guide and primary informant for anthropologist Ruth M. Underhill, who was compiling the first comprehensive study of Papago culture. In the course of their work and travels together, Chona narrated her life story, which was first published under the title *The Autobiography of a Papago Woman* in 1936, and reissued with a comprehensive introduction by Underhill as *Papago Woman* in 1979. Focusing on traditional Papago village life, the autobiography is a striking and lyrical narrative of a woman Underhill characterizes as "executive" for her capacity to satisfy her personal goals and desires within the limits of her culture. The published text was hailed as a breakthrough in ethnographic life history for its literary style and depiction of a complex narrative persona.

Chona's autobiography provides an intimate portrait of traditional Papago culture from a distinctly female viewpoint, with emphasis on family life, seasonal cycles, ceremonial events, and movement across the desert landscape. The collaboration of Chona, a woman exceptionally knowledgeable about her culture, and Underhill, an ethnographer with a literary bent, produced a text that has been consistently praised for its historical, anthropological, and literary quality.

Chona spent the last years of her life alternating between living in Tucson and with her daughter in Santa Rosa village on the Papago Reservation. She was well known for her basketry, and though she was acquainted with modern American ways, she chose to pursue a traditional way of life.

References

Bataille, Gretchen M., and Kathleen M. Sands. "Maria Chona." In *Native American Women Telling Their Lives*. Pp. 447–482. Lincoln: University of Nebraska Press, 1984.

Carr, Helen. "In Other Words: Native American Women's Autobiography." In *Life/Lines*. Edited by Bella Brodzki and Celeste Schenke. Pp. 131–153. Ithaca, NY: Cornell University Press, 1988.

Lurie, Nancy Oestreich. "A Papago Woman and a Woman Anthropologist." *Reviews on Anthropology* 7 (Winter 1980): 120.

Moore, David L. "Colonizing Criticism: Reading Dialects and Dialogics in Native American Literature." *SAIL* 6 (Winter 1994): 7–35.

Sands, Kathleen M. "Ethnography, Autobiography and Fiction: Narrative Strategies in Cultural Analysis." In *Native American Literature: Forum I*. Edited by Laura Coltelli. Pp. 39–52. Pisa: Serrizo Editoriale Universitario, 1989.

Staub, Michael E. *Voices of Persuasion: Politics of Representation in 1930s America*. New York: Cambridge University Press, 1994.

Underhill, Ruth M. "The Papago Family." In *Comparative Family Systems*. Edited by M. F. Nimkoff. Pp. 147–162. Boston: Houghton Mifflin, 1965.

———. *Papago Woman*. New York: Holt, Rinehart, and Winston, 1979.

———. *Social Organization of the Papago Indians*. Columbia University Contributions to Anthropology 30. New York: Columbia University Press, 1936.

—Kathleen Mullen Sands

CHOUTEAU, YVONNE (b. 1929), a Cherokee, is a celebrated Indian ballerina. Chouteau was born to parents of Cherokee/Shawnee ancestry in Fort Worth, Texas. She began her illustrious career by receiving her general education at the Professional Children's School in New York City. This allowed her to attend school while still focusing on her dancing, for she had already won a scholarship to the School of American Ballet. Beginning in 1941, at the age of twelve, she studied over a two-year period with such ballet luminaries as Anatole Vilzak and Ludmilla Sholler. Other noted tutors included Fronie Asher and Veronine Vestoff.

At the age of fourteen (1943), Chouteau joined the Ballet Russe de Monte Carlo as a member of the corps de ballet. In 1945 she first soloed as Prayer in *Coppelia*, followed by other noted roles, such as the title character in *Paquila*, Fanny Cerito in *Pas de Quatre*, and Jota in *Capriccio Espagnol*. Her 1950 elevation to the position of ballerina was made official when she danced Juliette in *Romeo et Juliette*.

In the mid-1950s, Chouteau married fellow dancer Miguel Terekhov. In 1957 they moved to Montevideo, Uruguay, where they worked with ballet troupes for two years. In 1959 they moved to Norman, Oklahoma, to become artists-in-residence at the University of Oklahoma. In 1962 the college instituted a full degree in dance, and Chouteau and Terekhov designed its first curriculum. They continued to teach in their school in Oklahoma City and organized their own ballet troupe. They have served as guest artists with other troupes, and have worked tirelessly to foster interest in Oklahoma's performing arts.

In 1976 Chouteau was again in the national spotlight, dancing in her work *Indian Trail of Tears* at the Kennedy Center in Washington, D.C. She continued to dance in performance until 1978. On September 16, 1983, she received Oklahoma's Governor's Arts Award for lifetime achievement in the arts. Oklahoma Governor Walters declared 1992 the Year of the Indian, and in honor of Chouteau and other Indian ballerinas, artist Mike Larsen painted a mural depicting their lives. It was unveiled in the capital rotunda on November 17, 1991.

Chouteau, and her husband, parents of two and grandparents of two, still teach ballet at their school. In 1974 Phillips University in Oklahoma awarded her an honorary Doctor of Humanities degree. She lives in a suburb of Oklahoma City.

References

Chujoy, Anatole, and P. W. Manchester, comps. *The Dance Encyclopedia*. New York: Simon and Schuster, 1967.
Gridley, Marion. *American Indian Women*. New York: Hawthorne Books, 1974.
Koegler, Horst. *Concise Dictionary of Ballet*. New York: Oxford University Press, 1977. "Moon-Maidens: Five Part Indian Ballerinas." *Newsweek* 70 (November 1967): 101–102.

—Cynthia Kasee

CHRYSTOS (b. 1946), poet, artist, and activist, was born and raised in San Francisco by her Menominee father and Lithuanian/French mother. Active with Women for Big Mountain in Seattle, she lives on Bainbridge Island, Washington.

Influenced and encouraged by Kate Millett and Audre Lorde, Chrystos has published her work in such publications and collections as *A Gathering of Spirit, Sinister Wisdom, Living the Spirit, Fireweed, Naming the Violence: Speaking Out on Lesbian Battering*, and *Making Face, Making Soul/Haciendo Caras*. Her book *Not Vanishing* collects seventy-two of her highly imagistic poems marked by her experiences as a drug addict, prostitute, and mental patient. *Dream On* delivers a more forceful and feminist voice, one more confidently engaged in Indian and lesbian matters from a more pointedly political perspective.

Always aware of the duality of being both Native American and urban, in her passionate verse Chrystos explores the issues of colonialism, genocide, class, and gender, and how they affect women and Indian peoples, specifically from a feminist and lesbian perspective. Her work ranges from the anger of "Today Was a Bad Day like TB," to the humor of "Poem for Lettuce," to the eroticism of "O Honeysuckle Woman," to the social and political outrage of "For Eli." Her subjects are inevitably the disenfranchised—Indians, women, lesbians, prostitutes, alcoholics, abused children, mixed-bloods, gays, the homeless, African Americans—whom she champions with an insider's awareness and sensitivity. Simultaneously, she rages vigorously against the victimizers in contemporary society, never flinching from the gritty realities that have shaped many current social and political conditions. Both harsh and lyrical, her free verse is frequently prosaic in form, and her contributions are primarily the force of her message and social vision, as well as her romantic and lyric eroticism.

References

Chrystos. *Dream On*. Vancouver, WA: Press Gang, 1991.
———. *Fire Power*. Vancouver, WA: Press Gang, 1995.
———. *Fugitive Colors*. Cleveland, OH: Cleveland State University Poetry Center, 1995.
———. *In Her I Am*. Vancouver, WA: Press Gang, 1993.
———. *Not Vanishing*. Vancouver, WA: Press Gang, 1988.
Lerner, Andrea, ed. *Dancing on the Rim of the World: An Anthology of Contemporary Northwest Native American Writing*. Tucson: University of Arizona Press, 1990.

May, Barbara Dale. "Chrystos." In *Contemporary Lesbian Writers of the United States: A Bio-Bibliographical Critical Sourcebook*. Edited by Sandra Pollack and Denise Knight. Pp. 118–121. Westport, CT: Greenwood Press, 1993.

Roscoe, Will, ed. *Living the Spirit: A Gay American Indian Anthology*. New York: St. Martin's Press, 1988.

—Rodney Simard

CLEGHORN, MILDRED IMOCH (1910–1997), a Fort Sill Apache, was born to Richard Imoch and Amy Wratten, prisoners of war confined by the U.S. military at Fort Sill, Oklahoma, on December 11, 1910. Cleghorn attended public school in Apache, Oklahoma, and the Haskell Institute in Lawrence, Kansas, then worked for the Kansas Bureau of Indian Affairs until 1937. In 1941 she received her college degree in home economics and was a school teacher for one and a half years at the Riverside School in Oklahoma. While working with Pawnees in Kansas, Cleghorn met her future husband, Bill. After an extended courtship, they were married in a double ceremony Cleghorn's cousin, Kathleen Smith Kanseah, on the Mescalero Apache Reservation in New Mexico. Cleghorn, one of only approximately ten Apaches living in the 1990s who was born in captivity, served as the chairperson for the Fort Sill Apaches. She was an admired, outspoken leader who strongly believed in preserving Native traditions. She actively participated in such tribal activities as dancing, beadwork, game playing (slapstick), cooking, singing, storytelling, praying, reading, and dollmaking. Cleghorn was elected Indian of the Year in 1989. She died in an auto accident on April 15, 1997, in Apache, Oklahoma.

Reference

Stockel, Henrietta H. *Women of the Apache Nation: Voices of Truth*. Reno: University of Nevada Press, 1991.

—Julie LaMay Abner

CLEMENTS, SUSAN DEER CLOUD (b. 1950), of Blackfeet, Mohawk, Seneca, and European descent, is one of the finest writers in the United States. In addition to producing two volumes of poetry, she has published poems, short stories, essays, and reviews in dozens of magazines, literary journals, and anthologies. Her work provides a provocative and insightful mosaic of contemporary life in which she interweaves the landscapes, histories, and memories of Andalusia, Florida, the Middle East, Great Britain, and Guatemala with her native upstate New York. In all of her writing, particularly her poems, she successfully explores the tenuous threads that connect public and private spheres. Born in Livingston Manor, New York, in the Catskill Mountains, Clements grew up profoundly aware of her otherness—both in terms of her ethnicity and in terms of her desire to write. It has been a fortuitous and somewhat unexpected bonus that her literary success has forged modes of connection not only with fellow Native Americans but also with non–Indians, including residents of Livingston Manor. According to Clements, the most rewarding aspect of her career has been how her written work has participated in the inter-change of the storytelling tradition; her stories have prompted others to share *their* stories with her.

In 1980 Clements earned a BA in creative writing and general literature (summa cum laude) from the State University of New York at Binghamton, and in 1982 she received her MA in creative writing and English literature from Bing-hamton's Graduate Program in Creative Writing. Since then, she has served on the faculty at Binghamton in a number of capacities, including as a distinguished writer in their Reader's Series. Her first book, a chapbook of Native American poems titled *The Broken Hoop* (1988), explores the relationship between the self and nature and the communities both engender. Her second collection, *In the Moon When the Deer Lose Their Horns*, not only extends her interest in Native American thematics but also expresses broader personal, social, and political concerns. Her poems and stories have been published in journals as diverse as *The Greensboro Review, Kentucky Poetry Review, Mid-American Review, North Dakota Quarterly, Negative Capability, Paterson Literary Review, Portland Review, Nimrod, Stand,* and *Ms*. She also has had work selected for two anthologies, *Unsettling America: An Anthology of Contemporary Multicultural Poetry* (Viking-Penguin, 1994) and *American Mixed Race: The Culture of Microdiversity* (Rowman & Littlefield, 1995). Clements has won several awards, including two Pushcart Prize nomina-tions for her poems "Snow Country" (1987) and "After Chernobyl" (1989). Hon-ors include a New York State Foundation for the Arts poetry fellowship (1993) and first prize in the Allen Ginsberg Poetry Awards for her poem "Tree" (1996).

Clements is at work on a collection of poems and short stories. She lives and writes with her husband, Arthur Clements, in a wildlife safety zone in Vestal, New York.

References

Clements, Susan. *The Broken Hoop*. Marvin, SD: Blue Cloud Press, 1988.
———. *In the Moon When the Deer Lose Their Horns*. Midland Park, NJ: Chantry Press, 1993.
Gillan, M. Review of *In the Moon When the Deer Lose Their Horns*. *Choice* 30 (1993): 790–791.

—Dean Rader

COBB, ISABELLE (1858–1947), physician and educator, was born in Morgantown, Tennessee, the eldest child of Joseph B. Cobb, a white man, and Evaline Clingan Cobb, of mixed Cherokee and white lineage. She was educated in the schools of Cleveland, Tennessee, until 1870, when her family moved to the Cherokee Nation in Indian Territory (today Oklahoma). Cobb then studied at the Cherokee Female Seminary, from which she graduated in 1879. She next enrolled in the Glendale Female College in Ohio for two years, then returned to Cherokee Female Semi-nary to teach from 1882 to 1887, along with her younger sister, Martha Cobb Clarke. Cobb graduated from the Women's Medical College of Pennsylvania with her medical degree in 1892, "specializing in women and children." She practiced medicine at the Nursery and Children's Hospital in West New Brighton, New York, and in Wagoner, Indian Territory, where she often performed surgery at her patients' homes because there were no hospitals in the vicinity. Cobb was an active Presbyterian and Republican, served as superintendent of the Oklahoma rural Sunday schools, and was a member of numerous literary societies in Wagoner County, Oklahoma.

References

"Cobb, Isabelle." In *Indian and Pioneer Histories*. Vol. 65. Edited by Grant Foreman. Pp. 184–218. Oklahoma City: Oklahoma Historical Society, n.d.

The Record-Democrat [Wagoner, OK], August 14, 1947, 1.

Starr, Emmett. *History of the Cherokee Indians and Their Legends and Folklore*. Oklahoma City: The Warden, 1979.

Who's Who Among Oklahoma Indians. Oklahoma City: Travis, 1928.

—*Devon A. Mihesuah*

COCHRAN, JO WHITEHORSE (b. 1958), author, editor, and educator who sees herself as an Indian/lesbian/feminist, was born in Seattle, Washington, to parents of Lakota and Norwegian descent. She is a Reiki practitioner and a Seichim master, and among her environmental interests is a wish to heal the planet. While working for her MA in creative writing at the University of Washington, she coinstructed an introductory course in Women's Studies.

Cochran has served as editor for a variety of publications, including *Changing Our Power*, an introductory text for women's studies; *Gathering Ground*, an anthology of writings by Northwest women of color; and *Calyx*, a journal of Native American literature. In her editorial statement in *Calyx*, Cochran outlines her desire to create a community voice bringing together the differing experiences and voices of Indian women. She adds that individuals must demonstrate the strength to write the truths found in their worldly experiences.

Cochran's poetry not only presents a commitment to nature and the earth but also vividly reflects human experience associated with being a Native American, a woman, and a contemplative individual. For example, "Halfbreed Girl in City School" speaks of the alienation one feels while living in diverse cultures that are still learning to coexist. "First of February, New Snow," and "Nearing Winter" express Cochran's understanding of the relationship that exists between nature and the experiences of life. Finally, "From My Grandmother" illustrates Cochran's ability to listen to the voices around her. Throughout her work, Cochran's commitment to an authentic representation of life presents itself clearly.

References

Cochran, Jo, ed. *Changing Our Power: An Introduction to Women's Studies*. Dubuque, IA: Kendall/Hunt, 1987.

Cochran, Jo, et al., eds. *Bearing Witness/Sobreviviendo: An Anthology of Native American/Latina Art and Literature. Special issue of Calyx: A Journal of Art and Literature by Women* 8 (1984).

Cochran, Jo, J. T. Stewart, and Mayumi Tsutakawa. *Gathering Ground: New Writing and Art by Northwest Women of Color*. Seattle: Seal Press, 1984.

Cochran, Jo Whitehorse. "Half-Breed Girl in City School." *Backbone: A Journal of Women's Literature* (Fall 1984).

Lerner, Andrea, ed. *Dancing on the Rim of the World: An Anthology of Contemporary Northwest Native American Writing*. Tucson: University of Arizona Press, 1990.

—Steven R. Price

COOCOOCHEE (c. early 1740s–post 1800), a Mohawk medicine woman and visionary, was born into the Bear clan at an Indian village southeast of Montreal but lived most of her life among Chief Blue Jacket's Shawnees in the Ohio country. Much of our knowledge of Coocoochee is from the writings of Oliver Spencer, who at age eleven was captured by Coocoochee's son, White Loon, near Cincinnati. Spencer lived with Coocoochee and her family from July 1792 until February 1793 and maintained contact with the family throughout his life.

Following her marriage to the Mohawk warrior Cokundiawsaw, and the birth of a daughter and three sons, Coocoochee and her family emigrated to the Ohio country in 1769. There they settled among the Shawnee on the west bank of the Scioto River. Coocoochee and her family hoped this move would distance them from the persistent encroachments of white colonists, but by 1774 there was nothing left of this dream. In that year the governor of Virginia, Lord Dunmore, destroyed the Shawnee villages in the Muskingum valley, halting a mere one hundred miles from the Shawnee enclave where Coocoochee resided. In 1777, Chief Blue Jacket and his people removed to the Mad River, along the Ohio–Kentucky frontier. Coocoochee and her family followed. Coocoochee's husband and eldest son, Wapanoo, who were pro–British, participated in anti–American expeditions during the American Revolution. Hostilities in the region continued unabated even after the Revolution, due to ever increasing pressure by Kentuckians for the Native population's land. As a result, more and more Indians of diverse tribal affiliations settled in the Mad River valley and joined in the battle against the encroachers.

Despite this alliance the Indians gave way before Benjamin Logan's expedition of 1786, which forced many of the inhabitants, including Coocoochee and her family, to flee. Again Coocoochee and her family followed Blue Jacket's Shawnees, and in 1787 settled near the Miami towns along the Maumee River, near Fort Wayne, Indiana. There they lived in relative peace until 1790, when the Miami towns were torched by a military expedition led by General Josiah Harmar. Coocoochee's spouse was killed during this raid. This resulted in Coocoochee's fourth removal, and with Blue Jacket and others of the allied Indian forces, she sought refuge at the Glaize, at the junction of the Maumee and Glaize rivers, at present-day Defiance, Ohio.

During her years among the Shawnee, Coocoochee developed special skills as a healer knowledgeable in the preparation and use of herbal medicines. She was also esteemed as a person of vision and wisdom, and was often consulted before the start of a military expedition. Specific examples of this were recorded by Spencer. In the fall of 1792, the Glaize's intertribal council consulted Coocoochee on the prospects for success of a contemplated raid on a supply shipment being sent to three American outposts north of Cincinnati. After communing with the spiritual world on behalf of the intertribal council, she declared that the raid would be successful. It was.

The final dispersion of the Glaize's mixed-tribal community came in the summer of 1794 when a raid (the battle of Fallen Timbers), led by General Anthony Wayne, forced the community to scatter. It is unclear what happened to Coocoochee after this event. Her daughter eventually took up residence near Malden, Ontario, where her husband, George Ironside, became a British Indian superintendent. Coocoochee's sons, White Loon and Black Loon, resided in various Shawnee towns in Ohio. Although the exact date is not known, she probably died early in the nineteenth century, before the commencement of the War of 1812.

Coocoochee's position as medicine woman and seer gave her a special status within her mixed tribal community. This, and her ability to maintain her family and traditional way of life despite periodic removals and the ever present threat of frontier warfare, give Coocoochee's life a special significance within the annals of colonial and frontier Euro–Indian relations.

References

Spencer, Oliver M. *The Indian Captivity of O. M. Spencer*. Edited by Milo Milton Quaife. Chicago: R. R. Donnelley, 1917. Reprint, New York: Citadel Press, 1968.

Tanner, Helen Hornbeck. "Coocoochee: Mohawk Medicine Woman." *American Indian Culture and Research Journal* 3 (1979): 23–41.

———, ed. *Atlas of Great Lakes Indian History*. Norman: University of Oklahoma Press, 1986.

—Faren R. Siminoff

COOK-LYNN, ELIZABETH (b. 1930), a Crow Creek Lakota Sioux, was born in Fort Thompson, South Dakota, and holds a BA degree in English and journalism and an MA in educational psychology and counseling. For almost twenty years she taught English and Indian Studies at Eastern Washington University, where she was a founding editor of the nationally recognized Indian studies journal *Wicazo Sa Review*. Students of contemporary Native American literature initially knew her for her poetry and mixed-genre experiments in prose and poetry, especially *Then Badger Said This*. By the beginning of the 1990s, her fiction began to attract attention. A collection of stories, *The Power of Horses*, appeared in 1990, and a novel, *From the River's Edge*, in 1991.

Cook-Lynn identifies three dominant influences on her creative writing: a rich family-tribal heritage, a powerful northern Plains landscape, and N. Scott Momaday's writings. Her father's and grandfather's experiences on the Crow Creek Tribal Council helped to shape her social and political attitudes. Just as important was the example of her grandmother and namesake, Eliza Renville, a bilingual writer for Christian newspapers. Besides these specific family influences, Cook-Lynn often notes the impact of family and reservation stories. She's thankful she listened and remembered. She also remembers the land. Strong visual images of skies and rivers, primarily the Missouri, and of powerful animals, particularly horses, as well as recollections of sounds as delicate as a meadowlark's call define her sense of place. So do histories as old as Wounded Knee and as recent as Wounded Rivers (a Missouri River dam project), and stories as ancient as Dakota creation narratives of Inyan, the rock, and as recent as destruction narratives of brutal reservation murders. Momaday's *The Way to Rainy Mountain* (1969) inspired Cook-Lynn to mix poetry, history, tribal narratives, and personal memories, and to perceive herself as a consecrator of past and current events that testify to the tragedies and successes of tribal and individual survival.

Family, tribe, place, and Momaday helped shape Cook-Lynn's literary imagination; so did gender. Repeatedly in her poems and fiction the narrative voice or focus is feminine. But this is no monotone performance. The viewpoint can be the insider's voice of a little girl riding on a reservation wagon (section XI of *Badger*); the insider/outsider voice of a young mother trying to get her children back from the mother of her ex-husband ("A Family Matter"); and a girl watching the sins of the father repeated in the drunken acts of her siblings ("Last Days of a Squaw Man"); the mature voice of the outsider Indian scholar desperately trying to locate a scholarship recipient and finding instead stares of cold hatred, handfuls of gravel thrown at her car, and the corpse of the young man she sought ("A Good Chance"); or the sympathetic voice of the poem "At Dawn, Sitting in My Father's House" that recalls Cook-Lynn's father with the vitality of a young daughter and with the wisdom of a woman who has accepted the natural processes of life and death. The range and the intensity of these women's voices make many of Cook-Lynn's Crow Creek portraits accessible and moving for readers who have little knowledge of Dakota tribal history, reservation life, or the banks of the Missouri.

In *From the River's Edge*, we again encounter powerful female perspectives, especially in Cook-Lynn's portrayal of the strong, beautiful, and independent Aurelia. The narrative focus of the novel, however, is the trial of John Tatekeya. Cook-Lynn uses the trial as a unifying device to satirize the legal system. John is the victim of cattle rustling, but during the trial, he (not the white rustler) is presented as the guilty one (a careless ranch manager, drinker, and adulterer) and "winning" the case brings him no recompense. Cook-Lynn also uses the trial to examine the decay of Dakota community and family relationships, the effects of damming the Missouri, and the impact of traditional Dakota values. For John, some ceremonials and some family values still work (sometimes), despite the severe tensions exposed by the trial. For Aurelia, John's longtime lover, Dakota values have lost their ability to sustain her against the separation from John, weak family support, the oppression of Dakota people and land, and the harsh South Dakota winds. *From the River's Edge* is a tough book. It implies that sometimes, and for some Indian people, tribal traditions can still sustain and enrich life. Nonetheless, in a pragmatic, honest, and tragic way, Aurelia realizes that tribal values and landscapes cannot heal her, despite her strengths and strong desire for healing.

References

Bruchac, Joseph. "As a Dakotah Woman." Interview with Elizabeth Cook-Lynn. In *Survival This Way: Interviews with American Indian Poets*. Edited by Joseph Bruchac. Pp. 57–71. Tucson: University of Arizona Press, 1987.

Cook-Lynn, Elizabeth. *From the River's Edge*. New York: Arcade Little, Brown, 1991.

———. *I Remember the Fallen Trees: New and Selected Poems*. Cheney, WA: Eastern Washington University Press, 1998.

———. *The Power of Horses and Other Stories*. New York: Arcade Little, Brown, 1990.

———. "The Radical Conscience in Native American Studies." *Wicazo Sa Review* 7 (Fall 1991): 9–13.

———. *Seek the House of Relatives*. Marvin, SD: Blue Cloud Quarterly, 1983.

———. *Then Badger Said This*. 1977. Reprint, Fairfield, WA: Ye Galleon Press, 1983.

———. *Why I Can't Read Wallace Stegner and Other Essays: A Tribal Voice*. Madison: University of Wisconsin Press, 1996.

———. "'You May Consider Speaking About Your Art. . . .'" In *I Tell You Now: Autobiographical Essays by Native American Writers*. Edited by Brian Swann and Arnold Krupat. Pp. 55–63. Lincoln: University of Nebraska Press, 1987.

Cook-Lynn, Elizabeth, and Mario Gonzalez. *The Politics of Hallowed Ground: Wounded Knee and the Struggle for Indian Sovereignty*. Urbana: University of Illinois Press, 1998.

Roemer, Kenneth M. Review of *Then Badger Said This*, by Elizabeth Cook-Lynn. *ASAIL Newsletter* n.s. 2 (Winter 1978): 55–58.

Ruppert, James. "Elizabeth Cook-Lynn." In *Dictionary of Native American Literature*. Edited by Andrew Wiget. Pp. 407–409. New York: Garland, 1994.

———. "The Uses of Oral Tradition in Six Contemporary Native American Poets." *American Indian Culture and Research Journal* 4 (1980): 87–110.

Sullivan, Jamie. "Acts of Survival: An Interview with Elizabeth Cook-Lynn." *Bloomsbury Review* 13 (January/February 1993): 1, 6.

Wilson, Norma C. "Elizabeth Cook-Lynn." In *Native American Writers of the United States*. Edited by Kenneth M. Roemer. Pp. 38–42. Detroit: Bruccoli Clark Layman/Gale, 1997.

—Kenneth M. Roemer

CORDERO, HELEN QUINTANA [Daiyrowitsa] (1915–1994), famous Native American potter and inventor of the Storyteller doll, was the second daughter of Pablo and Caroline Trujillo Quintana from the Keres Pueblo of Cochiti, New Mexico. Unlike most Pueblo women, she did not learn pottery making as a child, preferring farming and men's work to housework and schoolwork. She did, reluctantly, attend St. Catherine's Indian School in Santa Fe from the third to the eighth grade. The most important teacher in her youth was her grandfather Santiago Quintana, a respected storyteller and religious leader in the Pueblo. In addition to telling stories to his many children, grandchildren, and great-grandchildren, Santiago Quintana shared his wisdom with several generations of anthropologists, notably Adolph Bandelier, Edward S. Curtis, and Ruth Benedict, who published many of his stories in *Tales of the Cochiti Indians*. It was the image of him telling stories to the children that Cordero remembered in 1964 when the folk art collector Alexander Girard asked her to make a larger "singing mother" with more children, and she shaped the first Storyteller figure.

In 1932 she married Fernando (Fred) Cordero, who was a leading drummer and drum maker in the Pueblo and who held many tribal offices, including governor. In addition to four children of their own—Dolly, Jimmy, George, and Tony—they raised two foster sons, Gabriel and Leonard Trujillo. Cordero did not begin working with clay until the late 1950s, as an alternative to beadwork and leatherwork. She spent six months studying with Juanita Arquero, her husband's cousin, but could not master bowls and jars. Arquero suggested she try figures instead. Cordero's creativity blossomed, and her "little people" revived a long-standing but moribund Cochiti figurative tradition and began what has become a revolution in Pueblo ceramics. She shaped the first Storyteller in 1964 and took first, second, and third prizes that year at the New Mexico State Fair. In 1965 she won the first of many first prizes at the Santa Fe Indian Market, and in 1968, the first of many at the Annual Indian Arts and Crafts Exhibit at the Heard Museum in Phoenix, where she had her first one-person show in 1976. After that she demonstrated her pottery making from Bandelier National Monument in New Mexico to Kent State University in Ohio, and had countless shows at galleries and museums throughout the country, notably the "Tales for All Seasons" exhibit at the Wheelwright Museum in Santa Fe (1981–1982).

In addition to countless prizes for her figures, Cordero was much honored. In 1982 she received the New Mexico Governor's Award, and in 1986 a Heritage Fellowship from the National Endowment for the Arts. The popularity and success of Cordero's figures changed the shape of Pueblo pottery, resulted in a new valuation of figurative ceramics, and brought economic benefits to her own and other Pueblos. By 1973 at least six other Cochiti potters were making Storytellers and related figurines; ten years later there were ten times that number at Cochiti—including her own children and grandchildren—and hundreds of other potters from Taos to Hopi.

References

Babcock, Barbara A. "'At Home, No Women Are Storytellers': Potteries, Stories, and Politics in Cochiti Pueblo." *Journal of the Southwest* 30 (1988): 356–389.

———. "Clay Changes: Helen Cordero and the Pueblo Storyteller." *American Indian Art* 8 (1983): 30–39.

———. "Helen Cordero, the Storyteller Lady." *New Mexico Magazine* 56 (1978): 6–8.

———. "Modeled Selves: Helen Cordero's 'Little People.'" In *The Anthropology of Experience*. Edited by E. Bruner and V. Turner. Pp. 316–343. Urbana: University of Illinois Press, 1986.

———. "Taking Liberties, Writing from the Margins, and Doing It with a Difference." *Journal of American Folklore* 100 (October/December 1987): 390–411.

———, Guy Monthan, and Doris Monthan. *The Pueblo Storyteller: Development of a Figurative Ceramic Tradition*. Tucson: University of Arizona Press, 1986.

Benedict, Ruth Fulton. *Tales of the Cochiti Indians*. 1931. Reprint, Albuquerque: University of New Mexico Press, 1981.

Monthan, Guy, and Doris Monthan. "Helen Cordero." *American Indian Art* 2 (1977): 72–76.

—Barbara A. Babcock

COVINGTON, LUCY FREIDLANDER (1910–1983), born in Nespelem, Washington, a member of the Colville Confederated Tribes (Moses Columbian, Wenatchee, Palous, Entiat, Sanpoil), was a descendent of Chief Moses, Chief Kamiakin (Palous), and Chief Owhi (Yakima). She attended Nespelem schools and graduated from Haskell Indian Boarding School. She also attended Kinman Business School in Spokane, Washington. She married Johnny Covington, who served in World War II as a Seabee. They ran a cattle ranch most of their lives and assisted in raising numerous nieces and nephews.

Covington served on the Colville Tribal Business Council, beginning in the 1950s as a minority member who actively resisted termination of federal status to those tribes who were not yet ready for self-determination. At a tribal leaders' conference in 1966, she challenged Tribal Chairman Nicholson's reports on the health, education, and welfare of tribal members on the reservation with statistics that revealed the true conditions on the reservation (high unemployment, little education, substandard housing, and poverty). This led to political activism within the tribe to reject termination efforts and promote tribal sovereignty, which included publishing the Colville tribal newspaper *Our Heritage*. The focus of the paper was to communicate information about tribal council candidates who opposed termination and to report lobbying efforts. Covington's successful battle against termination resulted in a majority Tribal Council membership in support of tribal sovereignty and contributed to an era across the nation of tribal self-determination.

Covington's federal lobbying efforts for tribal sovereignty and Indian education continued throughout her lifetime. Her contributions were recognized in an award by the Association on American Indian Affairs, the Lucy Covington Award.

References

Hoxis, Frederick E., and Peter Iverson. *Indians in American History*. Wheeling, IL: Harlan Davidson, 1998.
Running Wolf, Paulette. Telephone interview with Barbara Freidlander Aripa, September 1998.
———. Telephone interview with Michael Jordan, September 1998.
———. Telephone interview with Sandra Lafontaine, September 1998.

—Paulette Running Wolf and Susan Banks

CRYING WIND [Linda Stafford, Gwendlelynn Lovequist] (b. 1943) was abandoned by her mother and raised by her Kickapoo grandmother, Shima Sani, on the Kickapoo Indian Reservation in Eagle Pass, Texas. She attended the University of Colorado (1961), the University of Texas (1966), the University of New Mexico (1967), and the University of Alaska (1969).

Under the name Crying Wind she has published a historical novel, *I Remember Divide*, and two autobiographical novels, *Crying Wind* and *My Searching Heart*. The autobiographies are based on her experiences with poverty and prejudice, her conversion to Christianity, and her search to find herself. These books have been translated into over a dozen foreign languages.

Using the pseudonym Gwendlelynn Lovequist, she has published numerous love stories and romances and has contributed over two hundred stories to magazines such as *Writer's Digest*. As Linda Stafford, she has written articles on child rearing, home life, and humor. She is the proprietor of art galleries in Santa Fe, New Mexico; Anchorage, Alaska; and Oklahoma City.

She married Don B. Stafford, a steelworker, in 1965, and they live in Anderson, Missouri, with their four children. All of her books have a message of hope and the optimistic theme of not giving up, because things will get better. She likes to leave the reader with a smile and a happy ending.

References

Crying Wind. *Crying Wind*. Chicago: Moody Press, 1977. Reprint, Irvine, CA: Harvest House, 1980.

———. *I Remember Divide*. Stafford Publishers, 1978.

———. *My Searching Heart*. Eugene, OR: Harvest House, 1980.

Fraser, Gordon. *Rain on the Desert*. Chicago: Moody Press, 1975.

—Joyce Ann Kievit

CUERO, DELFINA (c. 1900–1972) was one of the survivors of forced displacement of Kumeyaaye (Diegueño) people by non–Indian (Anglo–American and immigrant Asian) settlers in the San Diego area at the beginning of the twentieth century. In the 1960s Cuero narrated her life history to Florence Shipek. In doing so, she contributed not only an account of personal courage and endurance but also invaluable knowledge of the ecology of coastal southern California and traditional Kumeyaaye arts and sciences.

Cuero was born near Mission San Diego, but she and her family were considered squatters on the land they had occupied for centuries. Their band had to move frequently as more and more land was claimed for non–Indian agriculture, ranching, and settlement. She was married in her early teens to Sebastian Osun, a hardworking man chosen by her parents, and they had five surviving children: Aurelio, Lupe, Eugenia, Lola, and Santos. Shortly before her marriage, Cuero's parents had moved with her to Baja California (Mexico), where the displaced Kumeyaaye were relatively unharassed and could maintain crops and domestic animals on the land they occupied. Sebastian Osun died when their oldest child was eleven years old; Cuero remained in Mexico, where she raised her children under harsh circumstances. Wage labor brought little income, generally food or secondhand clothing rather than money, and previous sources of sustenance were no longer accessible. Some of Cuero's children were indentured in abusive homes, and she herself suffered from more than one abusive companion. One of her purposes in telling her life story, according to Florence Shipek, was to validate her claim to U.S. citizenship by birth, and thus to secure the right to return to live with relatives in southern California. In 1967 she was able to return permanently to the San Diego area, where she lived until her death in 1972.

References

Cuero, Delfina. *The Autobiography of Delfina Cuero*. Edited by Florence Shipek. Translated by Rosalie Pinto Robertson. Pasadena: Dawson's Book Shop, 1968. Reprint, Banning, CA: Malki Museum Press, 1970.

―――. *Delfina Cuero: Her Autobiography, An Account of Her Last Years and Her Ethnobotanic Contributions*. Edited by Florence Connolly Shipek. Ballena Press Anthropological Papers no. 38. Menlo Park, CA: Ballena Press, 1991.

Kelly, Isabel. Review of *The Autobiography of Delfina Cuero: A Diegueño Indian*. *American Anthropology* 71 (1969): 111–112.

Levi, Jerome M. Review of *Delfina Cuero: Her Autobiography, An Account of Her Last Years and Her Ethnobotanic Contributions*. *American Indian Culture and Research Journal* 16 (1992): 208–215.

—Helen Jaskoski

CULLETON, BEATRICE [Beatrice Mosionier] (b. 1949), a Métis author, was born in St. Boniface, near Winnipeg, Manitoba, the youngest child of Louis and Mary Clara Mosionier. When she was three, she and her two sisters and one brother became wards of the Children's Aid Society, who put them into different foster homes. Culleton grew up near Winnipeg with a non–Native foster family. She attended the first ten grades in the Catholic schools of St. Norbert, Manitoba, then transferred to St. Charles Academy, near Winnipeg. She began the twelfth grade at Gordon Bell High School but dropped out before graduation. Later, she attended George Brown College in Toronto.

Though Culleton's personal experiences in a foster home were positive, her sisters fared much worse. They experienced racism, cruelty, and abuse that forced them into the "Native girl syndrome." Both sisters committed suicide, traumas that affected profoundly. After the death of her second sister in October 1980, she decided to write fiction as a therapeutic inward quest for identity. The result of this inward journey was her first novel, *In Search of April Raintree*, which was published in 1983. A slightly edited school edition, *April Raintree*, followed a year later. The novel is the fictional account of the lives of two Métis sisters, who grow up in foster families, and who try to find a meaningful way of life in a society that is marked by prejudice, racism, and sexual violence. Whereas the narrator, April, "passes" as white for years and marries into a rich Torontonian family, Cheryl develops pride in her Métis roots but is unable to achieve her goal of improving the lot of her people. Instead, she ends up on skid row and commits suicide; April separates from her husband, returns to Winnipeg, and decides to raise Cheryl's son, conscious and proud of their Native heritage. The straightforwardly told, realistic novel gives a graphic depiction of the plight of Native children who become wards of the government due to their parents' addictions. Their immense struggle to retain their humanity, within an environment bent on making them fail, provides a plot that is both moving and full of suspense.

After the publication of the novel, Culleton served as an editor for Pemmican Publications, a publishing house affiliated with the Manitoba Métis Federation. Her historical novella, *Spirit of the White Bison*, came out in 1985. It depicts the wanton slaughter of the North American bison by the white intruders as a parable of the genocide against Native Americans, to which it was so closely and consciously linked. This book for young readers addresses issues of ecology and international solidarity vis-à-vis Western linear concepts of growth and progress threatening the survival of all people.

Since Culleton has lived in Toronto, working in the firm of her husband, George Moehring, and doing woodwork, exterior design, and carving. In 1991–1992 she was playwright-in-residence at Native Earth Performing Arts. Her drama about a group of women fighting against rape, *Night of the Trickster*, was performed by Native Earth Performing Arts at Toronto in 1993. She also wrote a screenplay, *Walker*, for an educational film against racism, in 1993.

Culleton has lectured widely in Canada and the United States. In 1994 she visited Germany on a reading tour to launch the German translation of *In Search of April Raintree*.

References

"Beatrice Culleton." In *Contemporary Challenges: Conversations with Canadian Native Authors*. Edited by Hartmut Lutz. Pp. 97–105. Saskatoon, SK: Fifth House, 1991.

Bohlinger, Janine. "Zeitgenössische Autobiographien Kanadischer Ureinwohnerinnen." Inaugural diss., University of Mainz, 1995.

Culleton, Beatrice. *Halbblut! Die Geschichte der April Raintree*. Translated by Annette Kohlbeyer. Wuppertal, Germany: Hammer Verlag, 1994.

———. *In Search of April Raintree*. Winnipeg, MN: Pemmican Publications, 1983.

———. *Spirit of the White Bison*. Winnipeg, MN: Pemmican Publications, 1985.

———. Screenplay for *Walker*. Directed by Alanis Obomsawin. Educational Films, National Film Board of Canada, 1993.

Damm, Kateri. "Dispelling and Telling: Speaking Native Realities in Maria Campbell's *Halfbreed* and Beatrice Culleton's *In Search of April Raintree*." In *Looking at the Words of Our People*. Edited by Jeannette Armstrong. Pp. 93–113. Penticton, BC: Theytus Books, 1993.

Fee, Margery. "Upsetting Fake Ideas: Jeannette Armstrong's 'Slash' and Beatrice Culleton's 'April Raintree.'" *Canadian Literature* 124–125 (Spring/Summer 1990): 168–180.

Garrod, Andrew. "Beatrice Culleton." In *Speaking for Myself: Canadian Writers in Interview*. Edited by Andrew Garrod. 79–96. St. John, NF: Breakwater Books, 1986.

Grant, Agnes. "Contemporary Native Women's Voices in Literature." *Canadian Literature* 124–125 (Spring/Summer 1990): 124–132.

Hoy, Helen. "'Nothing but the Truth': Discursive Transparency in Beatrice Culleton." *ARIEL* 25 (January 1994): 155–184.

Klooss, Wolfgang. "Fictional and Non-Fictional Autobiographies by Métis Women." In *Minority Literatures in North America: Contemporary Perspectives*. Edited by Wolfgang Karrer and Hartmut Lutz. Pp. 205–225. Frankfurt: Peter Lang, 1990.

Lundgren, Jodi. "'Being a Half-Breed': Discourses of Race and Cultural Syncreticity in the Works of Three Métis Women Writers." *Canadian Literature* 144 (Spring 1995): 62–77.

Lutz, Hartmut. "Nachwort." In *Beatrice Culleton, Halbblut! Die Geschichte der April Raintree*. Pp. 265–288. Wuppertal: Hammer Verlag, 1994.

Petrone, Penny. *Native Literature in Canada: From the Oral Tradition to the Present*. Toronto: Oxford University Press, 1990.

Witalec, Janet, ed. *Native North American Literature*. New York: Gale Research, 1994.

—Hartmut Lutz

CUNY, SISTER GENEVIEVE (b. 1930) is a Franciscan educator and administrator who herself was a product of a Franciscan education. She was one of fifteen children born into an Oglala Lakota family homesteading the Badlands of Pine Ridge Reservation, South Dakota. She attended Catholic boarding schools staffed by Franciscan Sisters, first in Pine Ridge for twelve years, then in Sioux City, Iowa, for college. In 1954 she professed her vows. For several years thereafter she taught, and later administered, at Franciscan-staffed schools in the Rosebud and Pine Ridge Reservation vicinities and furthered her studies with a BS degree in history from Regis College, Denver, Colorado, and an MS degree in business education from the University of Detroit.

Sr. Genevieve Cuny

During the 1970s, the Catholic Church created new opportunities for Indian church leadership and participation in response to demands for self-determination and the declining availability of non–Indian church personnel on reservations. Cuny reacted to these needs by redirecting her work toward religious education, where she became an advocate for including Native spirituality and values in the teaching of the Catholic faith. She first served as a local church educator and pastoral minister in the Rosebud Reservation area. Then, after completing an advanced religious education degree at Loyola University, Chicago, she became a Native religious education consultant for the diocese of Rapid City, South Dakota, a support position for local educators within five rural reservations and one urban Indian church.

Since 1976 Cuny has been a national advocate for more Indian self-determination within the Catholic Church. As a member of the Tekakwitha Conference Board of Directors, she has been a principal architect in transforming it from a regional missionary support group into a Native North American Catholic association for revitalizing local urban and rural Indian Catholic parishes. Moreover, she has served on several teams to further religious education among Native American Catholics, including a traveling national training team for catechists, the U.S. Catholic Conference Multi-Cultural Catechesis Task Force, and a writing team for Seasons of Faith, a preschool-to-adult textbook series for family-centered multicultural catechesis. From 1989 to 1991 she served as director of catechetics at the Tekakwitha Conference National Center, Great Falls, Montana. This was followed by five years as province secretary-treasurer for her religious order in Denver. In 1996 Cuny returned to the Pine Ridge Reservation to coordinate the training of catechists for the sixteen Catholic parishes across the reservation.

References

Cross and Feather News (Great Falls, MT: Tekakwitha Conference National Center) 1–10 (1982–1991).

Cuny, Genevieve. "Leadership and Professional Development in the Light of the Native American Experience." In *Faith and Culture: A Multicultural Catechetical Resource*. Edited by United States Catholic Conference, Department of Education. Pp. 53–61. Washington, DC: United States Catholic Conference, 1987.

"Cuny Authors Article About Native Catechesis." *West River Catholic* [Rapid City, SD] 15 (1987): 17.

"Cuny to Coordinate Catechist Formation on P.R. Reservation." *West River Catholic* [Rapid City, SD] 24 (1996): 22.

Freye, Mariella, ed. *The Story and Faith Journey of Seventeen Native Catechists*. Great Falls, MT: Tekakwitha Conference National Center, 1982.

—Mark G. Thiel

D

DAHTESTE [Tah-Des-Te] (b. 1865?–?), Apache, was a woman warrior who actively participated in battles and raiding parties with her husbands, Anandia and Coonie, and Geronimo. According to one source she was as "courageous, daring, and skillful as the men." Apaches are traditionally matrilocal societies, and women were taught warfare skills without ridicule and were praised for mastering them. Women were also responsible for providing moral and spiritual support, as well as for cooking, cleaning, and nursing (when necessary) during these raiding parties. Dahteste was also a skillful rider and hunter, and became a trusted scout, messenger, and mediator between the U.S. Cavalry and Geronimo and his band. She was instrumental, along with Lozen, in bringing about the final surrender of Geronimo in 1886; she was incarcerated in Florida along with Geronimo and his followers, and in 1884 was transferred to Fort Sill in Indian Territory (now Oklahoma). She lived on that military facility until 1913, when she and her family moved to the Mescalero Apache Reservation, living in a tent until their home was built.

Dahteste was able to win personal as well as military battles. She survived both pneumonia and tuberculosis. After her divorce from Anandia in the "Indian way"—he left her to return to his previous wife—Dahteste married Kuni (Coonie), a widower with three children who was a scout for Fort Apache: Besides Kuni's children, his nephew and two orphans (or three nephews) lived with them. A beautiful woman, Dahteste has been described as wearing her long, dark hair straight and as always dressing well in the traditional way, with beads, turquoise, belts, and bags. The elderly Dahteste lived at Whitetail, with her niece, Elizabeth Coonie, and at the Mescalero Indian Reservation until she died of old age.

References

Ball, Eve, and Lynad Sanchez. "Legendary Apache Women." *Frontier Times* (October/November 1980): 8–12.

Buchanan, Kimberly Moore. *Apache Women Warriors*. El Paso: Texas Western Press, 1986.

Stockel, Henrietta H. *Women of the Apache Nation: Voices of Truth*. Reno: University of Nevada Press, 1991.

—Julie LaMay Abner

DAT-SO-LA-LEE [Louisa Kizer or Keyser] (c. 1835–1925), a famous basket maker, was a full-blooded Washo born near Woodfords, California. Her parents named her Dabuda, but she eventually came to be known as Dat-So-La-Lee or "Big Hips" (some sources state that the name was given to her by S. L. Lee, a prominent Carson City, Nevada, physician). She is mentioned in the journals of John C. Frémont, which record his journey through the Carson valley in January 1844. She first married a Washoe man named Assu, but he and their two children died. She then married Charley Kizer, a Washoe-Miwok craftsman, in 1888, and became Louisa Kizer. Later she and her husband lived with Abram and Amy Cohn in Carson City, where she worked first as a laundress. Her basket weaving fascinated Amy Cohn, and the Cohns came to monopolize ownership of all Washo basketry for a time, especially the baskets of Louisa Kizer. They supported the Kizers in return for ownership of every basket Dat-So-La-Lee wove, so she never received any money for her work. It is generally agreed that Louisa Kizer single-handedly transformed Washo basket making, introducing curio functions and the incurving *degikup* shape (which begins with a small, circular base, extends up and out to a maximum circumference, then becomes smaller until the top opening is roughly the same diameter as the base), the hallmark of the coiled basket style.

Dat-So-La-Lee adopted some ideas and materials from the neighboring Maidu and Pomo, and then dramatically transformed her own already innovative style. She used a piece of glass, or her teeth and fingernails, to scrape the willow. Later, she used a tin can lid to evenly size narrower splints, ultimately achieving thirty stitches per inch. Dat-So-La-Lee made her most significant contribution in the finely stitched, two-color *degikup*, often with flame motifs in a scatter design or decorative bands in symmetrical or alternating formats. In her baskets she created "art for art's sake," but nevertheless maintained the reserved, ordered, and integrated look of "tradition."

Dat-So-La-Lee journeyed to the St. Louis Exposition in 1919 with Abram and Amy Cohn to exhibit her baskets and demonstrate her artistry, but such large public demonstrations were uncomfortable to her. She believed basket art should be passed to family members only. She died in Carson City, Nevada, in the house the Cohns had provided.

References

Cohodas, Marvin. "Dat-So-La-Lee and the 'Degikup.'" *Halcyon: A Journal of the Humanities* 4 (1982): 119–140.

Dat-So-La-Lee. In Inter-Tribal Council of Nevada, *Life Stories of Our Native People: Shoshone, Paiute, Washo*. Salt Lake City: University of Utah Printing Service, 1974.

"Dat-So-La-Lee's Basketry Designs." *American Indian Art Magazine* (Autumn 1976): 22–31.

Gigli, Jane Green. *Dat-so-la-lee, Queen of the Washo Basket Makers*. Nevada State Museum Anthropological Papers. Carson City: Nevada State Museum, 1974.

James, George Wharton. *Indian Basketry*. New York: Dover Publications, 1972.

Porter, Frank W., ed. *The Art of Native American Basketry: A Living Legacy*. Contributions to the Study of Anthropology no. 5. New York: Greenwood Press, 1990.

Price, John A. *The Washo Indians: History, Life Cycle, Religion, Technology, Economics, and Modern Life.* Nevada State Museum Occasional Papers, no. 4. Carson City: Nevada State Museum 1980.

Waltrip, Lela, and Rufus Waltrip. *Indian Women.* New York: David McKay, 1964.

—*Gretchen Ronnow*

DAUENHAUER, NORA MARKS (b. 1927), was born in Juneau, Alaska; she grew up in Juneau and Hoonah, as well as on the family fishing boat and in seasonal subsistence sites around Icy Strait, Glacier Bay, and Cape Spencer. She was raised speaking the Tlingit language, and it was not until she entered school at the age of eight that she began to learn English. Almost all of her work as a writer, an anthropologist, and a cultural conservationist has grown from and is flavored by her sense of living in two languages.

Dauenhauer received her BA in anthropology from Alaska Methodist University in 1976. She is married to Richard Dauenhauer, a writer and former poet laureate of Alaska. They have four children and thirteen grandchildren. Although her family maintains a central place in her life, she has earned an international reputation for her transcription, translation, and explication of Tlingit oral literature.

Dauenhauer's extensive research in Tlingit oral literatures culminated in 1987 with the publication (with Richard Dauenhauer) of *Haa Shuka, Our Ancestors: Tlingit Oral Narratives.* Carefully transcribed and produced in both English and Tlingit, the work not only is an invaluable text for anthropologists and those interested in Northwest languages and cultures, is also distinguished by its artistic appeal. Its imaginative freshness, its imagery, and its vision make the collection an outstanding work of literature. The Dauenhauers' sensitivity and expertise in the Tlingit language produce an authentic version of the narratives. Finally, their decision to produce the collection in a bilingual format reveals their sense of the two audiences for the text. Their work challenges the classic anthropological tradition of appropriating Native materials for presentation to mainly white audiences. This text is perhaps most strongly geared to a Tlingit audience, and thus it has served as a model for other indigenous communities seeking to take control of collecting and preserving their cultural legacies. Dauenhauer, in collaboration with her husband, continues to work on Tlingit language projects in her capacity as principal researcher for the Sealaska Heritage Foundation. Their years of commitment to and interest in Alaska's indigenous peoples and their languages have resulted in three additional publications. The first, *Because We Cherish You: Sealaska Elders Speak to the Future* (1981), offers elders' stories and perceptions of the delicate balance between traditional life and the contemporary world. The Dauenhauers have also produced two language texts: *Beginning Tlingit* (1976) and *Tlingit Spelling Book* (1974).

Dauenhauer has received much acclaim for her prose and poetry. In 1988 she published her first volume of poetry, *The Droning Shaman.* This volume is thoroughly infused with her interest in place, particularly the Alaskan landscape, as well as her interest in language and translation. Though many of the poems written in English use phrases and words from Tlingit, she also demonstrates her facility and interest in translation by presenting a number of her own translations into

Tlingit of poems by Basho, ee cummings, and Gary Snyder's reworkings of Han Shan. Her poetry and prose have appeared in a number of anthologies, including *New Worlds of Literature, Harper's Anthology of 20th Century Native American Poetry, Earth Power Coming: Short Fiction in Native American Literature,* and *Alaska Native Writers, Storytellers, and Orators*, the last edited by Dauenhauer with her husband and Gary Holthaus.

Dauenhauer's work has brougt her many prizes; in 1989 she received the Governor's Award for the Arts, and in 1980 the Alaska Humanities Forum voted her Humanist of the Year. Her poetry, her prose, and her texts in Tlingit oral history and language resonate with her commitment to her traditions, her ancestry, and her language.

References

Dauenhauer, Nora Marks. *The Droning Shaman*. Haines, AK: Black Currant Press, 1988.

Dauenhauer, Nora Marks, and Richard Dauenhauer. *Beginning Tlingit*. 4th ed. Juneau, AK: Sealaska Heritage Foundation, 2000.

———, eds. *Because We Cherish You: Sealaska Elders Speak to the Future*. Juneau, AK: Sealaska Heritage Foundation, 1981.

———, eds. *Haa Kusteeyi, Our Culture: Tlingit Life Stories*. Seattle: University of Washington Press, 1994.

———, eds. *Haa Shuka, Our Ancestors: Tlingit Oral Narratives*. Seattle: University of Washington Press, 1987.

———, eds. *Haa Tuwunaagu Yis, for Healing Our Spirit: Tlingit Oratory*. Seattle: University of Washington Press, 1990.

———, eds. *Tlingit Spelling Book*. Juneau, AK: Sealaska Heritage Foundation, 1974.

Dauenhauer, Nora Marks, Richard Dauenhauer, and Gary Holthaus, eds. *Alaska Native Writers, Storytellers, and Orators*. Special issue of *Alaska Quarterly Review* (1986).

Green, Rayna, ed. *That's What She Said: Contemporary Poetry and Fiction by Native American Women*. Bloomington: Indiana University Press, 1984.

Niatum, Duane, ed. *Harper's Anthology of 20th Century Native American Poetry*. San Francisco: Harper & Row, 1988.

Ortiz, Simon, ed. *Earth Power Coming: Short Fiction in Native American Literature*. Tsaile, AZ: Navajo Community College Press, 1983.

—Andrea Lerner

DAVIDSON, FLORENCE EDENSHAW [Story Maid] (1896–1993), a Haida, was born on September 15, 1896, in the village of Masset, on one of the Queen Charlotte Islands off the coast of British Columbia. She was born in her father's home with her grandmother, Amy Edenshaw, as midwife. Because her parents, Chief

Charles (the carver) and Isabella Edenshaw, believed in both traditional religion and Christianity, Davidson had her ears pierced at four days of age and was also baptized into the Anglican Church. Chief Charles always favored her because he believed her to be the reincarnation of his mother, Qawkuna, for the first words Florence spoke were "Dad, I'm your mother." Davidson sporadically attended the mission school at Masset until the fourth level because she was often needed at home or to assist her Aunt Martha. Because Haida culture has defined gender roles and is a matrilineal society, Davidson's childhood ended with her puberty seclusion and arranged marriage to Robert Davidson, a man twice her age, on February 23, 1911, when she was fourteen years old. She defiantly announced to her mother that she would not marry "that old man," and later said, "I wish I were dead." The years melted her bitterness, however, and Davidson began to speak fondly of her husband; they had nineteen children.

In her adult life, Davidson was an active member of the local Anglican church, its choir, and its women's auxiliary; she also worked in a cannery, yet found time to fish and to bake much of her family's food. In 1929 the entire family moved from their small cottage into the large two-story house that Robert built for them. Two elders named the new home "It's Summertime Inside" and "The Main Road Runs by the House." In 1952 their home was destroyed by fire, and the family began a two-year project of rebuilding it. Throughout her life, Davidson strove to preserve her heritage, which was so important to her. Most of her life was devoted to caring for her children; her home was often filled with visitors, and her warmth and kindness were well known among her people.

Reference

Blackman, Margaret B. *During My Time: Florence Edenshaw Davidson, a Haida Woman*. Seattle: University of Washington Press, 1982.

—*Julie LaMay Abner*

DE CLUE, CHARLOTTE (b. 1948), is an Osage poet originally from Enid, Oklahoma. She attended Oklahoma State University at Stillwater and the University of Missouri at Kansas City. Her poetry reflects her strong interest in Osage history and culture. Her works have appeared in many collections, such as *Songs from This Earth on Turtle's Back, A Gathering of Spirit*, and *That's What She Said*. De Clue and her husband have a grown son and make their home in Lawrence, Kansas.

References

Brant, Beth, ed. *A Gathering of Spirit*. Rockland, ME: Sinister Wisdom, 1984.
Bruchac, Joseph, ed. *Songs from This Earth on Turtle's Back*. Greenfield Center, NY: Greenfield Review Press, 1983.
———. Special issue on Native American writers. Greenfield Review 9 (Fall 1981).

Cochran, Jo, et al., eds. *Bearing Witness/Sobreviviendo: An Anthology of Native American/Latina Art and Literature.* Special issue of *Calyx: A Journal of Art and Literature by Women* 8 (1984).

De Clue, Charlotte. *Stiletto 2: The Disinherited.* Kansas City, KS: Howling Dog, 1991.

———. *Without Warning.* New York: Strawberry Press, 1985.

Fife, Connie, ed. *The Colour of Resistance: A Contemporary Collection of Writing by Aboriginal Women.* Toronto: Sister Vision, 1993.

Green, Rayna, ed. *That's What She Said.* Bloomington: Indiana University Press, 1984.

—Cynthia Kasee

DEER, ADA (b. 1935), was born and raised on the Menominee Reservation in northern Wisconsin. She is the eldest of five children of a Menominee father and Euro–American mother. For the first eighteen years of her life, Deer lived with her family near the Wolf River in a small log cabin without electricity or running water. In 1957 she earned a BA degree in social work, the first Menominee to graduate from the University of Wisconsin at Madison. In addition, she was the first Native American to earn an MSW from the Columbia University School of Social Work (1961). Deer also studied law briefly at the University of Wisconsin at Madison and the University of New Mexico at Albuquerque, and was a fellow at the Harvard Institute of Politics, John F. Kennedy School of Government, in 1977. Since 1977 she has been a senior lecturer in the School of Social Work and the Native American Studies Program at the University of Wisconsin at Madison. In 1991 she added a third academic affiliation, this one with the Women's Studies program. She was a member of the board of directors of the Native American Rights Fund from 1984 to 1990 and served as its chair in 1989–1990.

A social worker, educator, and activist, Deer is best known for her political activism in the 1960s and early 1970s, when she led the struggle to regain federal recognition for her tribe. As part of the federal government's policy of forced Indian assimilation, the U.S. Congress passed an act terminating the Menominee Reservation (1954). Known as the Menominee Termination Act, this legislation (which was fully implemented by 1961) meant the end of federal control over tribal affairs. In short, the Menominee were no longer recognized by the federal government as Indians. The consequences for the Menominee were drastic: the loss of the health and education services and the potential loss of their tribal land. In an effort to reorganize during the implementation period following passage of the Termination Act, the Menominees voted to become a separate county and were soon in serious financial difficulty. In 1970 Deer, Jim White, and others created a new Menominee political organization known as Determination of the Rights and Unity for Menominee Shareholders (DRUMS). Its long-term goal was repeal of the Termination Act, but first DRUMS leaders replaced the generally discredited Menominee government officials. With legal assistance from the Native American Rights Fund, Deer and other DRUMS leaders headed the long fight to regain federal recognition for the Menominee. In 1972–1973 Deer was vice president and chief lobbyist for the DRUMS-originated National Committee to Save the Menominee People and Forest, Inc. Their efforts were rewarded in 1973, when President Richard Nixon signed into law the Menominee Restoration Act, which restored federal recognition, and thus health and education benefits, to the tribe.

After the Restoration Act, Deer was elected chair of the Menominee Restoration Committee, a position she held from 1973 to 1976. Her job was to complete the transition back to reservation life. Throughout the process she had to deal with the criticism of some Menominee detractors, the bias of some of the media, and the alternative strategies of more radical activists who became known as the Menominee Warriors. By 1976 the new structure for the Menominee tribal government was set up and adopted. Her work completed, Deer resigned.

In addition to her well-known efforts to regain federal recognition for her people (a historic reversal of Indian policy in the United States), Deer has labored diligently on behalf of numerous causes. Since 1958 she has worked to provide community services, particularly education, health, and legal services, for youth, women, and Native Americans. Deer has a contagious belief in the possibility of pursuing social and political change from the bottom up. She does not wait for political powers at the top to initiate action. Over the years, Deer has received numerous awards for her activism. In 1982 she was one of eighteen women presented the Wonder Woman Award by the Wonder Woman Foundation in New York City. That same year, the Girl Scouts USA honored Deer with their Woman of the Year Award. The prestigious Indian Achievement Award was presented to her in 1984, and in 1985 she was named Poster Woman by the National Women's History Project, one of twelve women to be depicted on the Heroine Calendar, and (along with other valiant women like Ida B. Wells and Amelia Earhart) was selected for the Gallery of Women by the Adolph Coors Company. In addition, she has received the Politzer Award of the Ethical Culture Society (1975), the White Buffalo Council Achievement Award (1974), and the Distinguished Service Award of the American Indian Resources Institute (1991).

Deer has served as a board member of such national organizations as Girl Scouts USA, the American Indian Policy Review Commission, the National Association of Social Workers, Americans for Indian Opportunity, and the Housing Assistance Council. She also has contributed her energies to the National Women's Education Fund, the National Indian Advisory Committee of Honor, and the Quincentenary Committee for the Smithsonian Institution. Deer has remained active in such local and state political organizations as the Wisconsin Women's Council and the Democratic Party of Wisconsin. In 1978 and 1982, she was a candidate for Wisconsin secretary of state. She is past president of the Wisconsin chapter of the National Association of Social Workers. From 1981 to the present, Deer has served as a national board member on the Hunt Commission for the Democratic National Committee, studying the presidential nominating process. Deer was chosen by President Clinton to be assistant secretary of the Interior for Indian affairs and was confirmed by the U.S. Senate on July 16, 1993. She is the first woman to hold this position. She also is active in many of the initiatives undertaken by the Clinton administration.

Deer has devoted her life to working for social justice, particularly with and for Native people and women. With her indomitable spirit and contagious optimism, she continues to serve as a role model, exhorting and inspiring individuals to become politically active.

References

Anderson, Owanah, ed. *Ohoyo One Thousand: A Resource Guide of American Indian/Alaska Native Women, 1982*. Wichita Falls, TX: Ohoyo Resource Center, 1982.

Bletzinger, Andrea, and Anne Short, eds. *Wisconsin Women: A Gifted Heritage*. Milwaukee: American Association of University Women, Wisconsin State Division, 1982.

Deer, Ada, with R. E. Simon, Jr. *Speaking Out*. Chicago: Children's Press/Open Door Books, 1970.

Directory of Significant 20th Century American Minority Women. Nashville, TN: Fisk University Press, 1978.

Fanlund, Lari. "Indians in Wisconsin: A Conversation with Ada Deer." *Wisconsin Trails: The Magazine of Life in Wisconsin* 24 (March/April 1983): 8–21.

Graf, Karen. "Ada Deer: Creating Opportunities for Minority Students." *On Wisconsin* 9 (April 1987): 8.

McClanahan, A. J. "Indian Leader Says Keep Tribal Ties." *Anchorage Times* March 9, 1984, B6.

Peroff, Nicholas C. *Menominee Drums: Tribal Termination and Restoration, 1954–1974*. Norman: University of Oklahoma Press, 1982.

Who's Who in American Politics. New York: R. R. Bowker, 1979.

Wong, Hertha. Written Personal communication with Ada Deer, February 25, 1991.

Zweifel, Dave. "Ada Deer Is Finally Given 'Heroine' Status." *Capital Times* [Madison, WI], March 18, 1985, 2.

—Hertha D. Wong

DELORIA, ELLA CARA (1889–1971), a linguistic anthropologist, was a Yankton Sioux born at White Swan, South Dakota, on the Yankton Sioux Reservation. In 1890 her father was assigned to St. Elizabeth's Mission as a deacon of the Episcopal Church, and the family moved to the Standing Rock Reservation; he was ordained to the priesthood in 1892. Deloria and her siblings were taught according to the doctrines of Episcopalian Christianity and also were greatly influenced by the Sioux culture and language with which they lived.

Deloria attended St. Elizabeth's Mission in Wakpala, South Dakota, and All Saints' School in Sioux Falls, South Dakota, taking the college preparatory course (1906–1910). She attended the University of Chicago (1910–1911) and completed her course work at Oberlin College in Ohio. She then enrolled at Columbia University and began her lengthy association with Dr. Franz Boas. She graduated from Columbia with a BS degree in June 1915.

Deloria returned to South Dakota and taught at All Saints' from 1915 to 1919. She then accepted a job with the Young Women's Christian Association (YWCA) in an experimental program that would demonstrate to the Bureau of Indian Affairs the value of physical education for Native American girls. The Haskell Indian School in Lawrence, Kansas, employed her to teach physical education in 1923.

In 1927 Deloria reestablished her connection with Franz Boas, the preeminent American anthropologist of the time, and assisted him as a research specialist in American Indian ethnology and linguistics until his death in 1942. The first project began when Boas asked her to translate and edit some written Sioux texts. She gathered and translated additional stories, legends, and works as well. As a result of these efforts, "Sun Dance of the Oglala Sioux" was published in *Journal of American Folklore* in 1929. This was followed by *Dakota Texts* (1932), a bilingual collection of Sioux tales, and *Dakota Grammar* (1941), a collaboration with Boas. *Speaking of Indians*, a description of Indian, particularly Sioux, culture was published in 1944. *Waterlily*, a novel of a Teton Sioux woman's life, was written during the early 1940s and published posthumously in 1988.

Deloria received the 1943 Indian Achievement Medal, and during the 1940s she was recognized as the leading authority on the Sioux. She continued her scholarly research, writing, and lecturing throughout her life, collecting large amounts of folkloristic and linguistic materials and translations. She also was director of St. Elizabeth's Mission from 1955 to 1958. At the time of her death, on February 12, 1971, she was working on a Lakota dictionary.

Deloria is buried beside her sister, Susan Marble, and her mother, Mary Sully Deloria, in St. Phillip's Cemetery at Lake Andes, South Dakota. Deloria's upbringing among the Sioux, her devotion to Christianity, and her training as an ethnologist give her work a unique and invaluable place in the study of her culture.

References

Deloria, Ella Cara. *Dakota Texts*. New York: G. E. Stechert, 1932. Reprint, edited by Agnes Picotte and Paul N. Pavich, Vermillion, SD: Dakota Press, 1978.

———. *Speaking of Indians*. New York: Friendship Press, 1944. Reprint with introductory notes by Agnes Picotte and Paul N. Pavich, Vermillion, SD: Dakota Press, 1979.

———. Waterlily. Lincoln: University of Nebraska Press, 1988.

Deloria, Ella Cara, and Franz Boas. *Dakota Grammar*. Washington, DC: U.S. Government Printing Office, 1941. Reprint, Vermillion, SD: Dakota Press, 1982.

Medicine, Bea. "Ella C. Deloria: The Emic Voice." *MELUS* 7 (Winter 1980): 23–30.

Miller, Carol. "Mediation and Authority: The Native American Voices of Mourning Dove and Ella Deloria." In *Multicultural Education, Transformative Knowledge, and Action*. Edited by James A. Banks, Pp. 141–155. New York: Teachers College Press, 1996.

Murray, Janette K. "Ella Deloria: A Biographical Sketch and Literary Analysis." PhD diss., University of North Dakota, 1974.

Prater, John. "Ella Deloria: Varied Intercourse." *Wicazo Sa Review* 11 (Fall 1995): 40–46.

Rice, Julian: *Deer Women and Elk Men: The Lakota Narratives of Ella Deloria*. Albuquerque: University of New Mexico Press, 1992.

———. "Why the Lakota Still Have Their Own: Ella Deloria's *Dakota Texts*." *Western American Literature* 19 (November 1984): 205–217.

Rice, Julian, ed. *Ella Deloria's Iron Hawk*. Albuquerque: University of New Mexico Press, 1993.
———. *Ella Deloria's The Buffalo People*. Albuquerque: University of New Mexico Press, 1994.

—Laurie Lisa

DICK, LENA FRANK (c. 1889–1965), was born in Coleville, in the Antelope valley of California, the daughter of Charley and Lucy Frank, and belonged to the Washoe tribe. She was a teenager when she married George Emm and had her only child, Juanita. She married Levi Dick around 1906, after George Emm left her following the birth of Juanita.

Dick learned basket weaving from her mother, a skilled basket maker. Her sisters, Lillie Frank James and Jessie Frank Wade, also became known as accomplished basket weavers. Although Dick was a very traditional Washoe woman, she became an innovator in the techniques, designs, and use of color in basket weaving. While she was actively weaving, from around 1920 to 1935, she acquired the patronage of Roscoe A. Day, a San Francisco-area orthodontist, through an agent, Fred Settelmeyer, a Carson valley rancher. Neither Day nor Settelmeyer promoted Dick's work to other collectors or took the time to meet her. Due to their interest in the art and not in the artist, much of Dick's work was mistakenly identified as that of other weavers after baskets had passed out of her possession. She was not given credit for all of her work until the late 1970s.

Dick's excellence as a weaver was centered in an extreme fineness of technique, usually finer than twenty-five stitches per inch; conservation and expansion of serrated diamond and V-designs, triangles or nested Vs, and characteristic non-standardized arrangements of lines and triangles, and juxtaposition of red and black in the same motif in the creation of a traditional *degikup* basket.

After about 1935, due to failing eyesight from years of fine and detailed basket weaving, Dick gave up making the extremely fine baskets in favor of utilitarian ones.

References

Cohodas, Marvin. "Lena Frank Dick: An Outstanding Washoe Basket Weaver." *American Indian Art* 4 (Autumn 1979): 32–41, 90.
———. "Washoe Innovators and Their Patrons." In *The Arts of the North American Indian: Native Traditions in Evolution*. Edited by Edwin L. Wade. Pp. 203–220. New York: Hudson Hills, 1986.

—Julie A. Russ

DIETZ, ANGEL DeCORA [Hinookmahiwi-Kilinaka, Henook-Makhewe-Kelenaka] (1871–1919), was a prominent personality of the Allotment Era (when the federal government parceled land to families, which was designed to break the economic base that supported tribalism) at the turn of the twentieth century. She was an institutionally trained professional artist, a teacher, a popular lecturer on Indian affairs, an occasional writer, and an active member of the Society of American Indians

Dietz was born on May 3, 1871, on the Winnebago Reservation in Nebraska. Her father, David DeCora, a descendant of the Dakaury family, was of French–Winnebago ancestry; her mother was a member of the La Mere family. According to Frederick Dockstader, her parents died when she was still a young girl, and she was brought up by her maternal relatives.

Dietz first attended the local reservation school, then, at the age of twelve, was sent to Hampton Institute, where she graduated in 1891. According to her autobiographical sketch written in 1911, her transfer to Hampton was arranged by some "strange white man" without the consent of her relatives. Dietz continued her education at the Burnham Classical School for Girls in Massachusetts and then enrolled in a four-year course at Smith College, studying art under Dwight T. Tryon. Later she entered Drexel Institute in Philadelphia to study illustration with Howard Pyle for approximately two years. Following a brief sojourn at the Cowles Art School, she perfected her artistic skills for another two years at the Boston Museum of Fine Arts School.

Following completion of her academic training, Dietz set up a private studio in Boston and did illustrations for a number of major publishing firms there before moving to New York City. There she established herself as a book illustrator, working on Francis La Flesche's *The Middle Five*, Gertrude Bonnin's *Old Indian Legends*, Natalie Curtis's *The Indian's Book*, and Elaine Goodale Eastman's *Yellow Star*. While preparing the illustrations for *Old Indian Legends*, she struck up what would become a long-lasting friendship with Gertrude Bonnin, with whom she would later cooperate in matters of Indian politics.

Dietz's most important role during the Allotment Era was as director of the Leupp Art Department at Carlisle Indian School from 1906 to 1915. Here she developed an intensive art program for Indian students, encouraging them to apply Indian designs to modern art media. This was at a time when practically all things Indian were viewed as mere hindrance to the progress of Indian "civilization." She firmly believed that young Indians had a special "talent for pictorial art," and that her students at Carlisle could possibly develop it to the point of someday making a marked contribution to American art. Her work at Carlisle must not always have been easy because it was vehemently opposed by its former superintendent, Richard Pratt, who referred to it as plain "humbug." Nevertheless, Dietz's views were already becoming manifest with the emergence of the San Ildefonso School of Indian artists in the Southwest at about that time (1910), a period which is viewed by art historians as the "renaissance" of Indian art. The artists became a part of official Indian policy during the New Deal era with the creation of an Indian Arts and Crafts Department in 1935.

At Carlisle, she met Sioux artist William Dietz, whom she married in 1908. They moved to New York State at the outbreak of World War I, and Angel worked at the New York State Museum in Albany as draftswoman. She divorced Dietz in 1918 and then moved to New York City, to continue her illustrating work. She lectured widely on Indian affairs in general, as well as on Indian art in particular, and was an active supporter of the Society of American Indians (SAI). On October 13, 1911, Dietz delivered a talk titled "The Preservation of Native Indian Art" at the first annual conference of the SAI held at the University of Ohio; it was published in the

Report of the Executive Council the following year. Dietz wrote a number of articles, including several on Indian art, as well as a short story, "The Sick Child," published in *Harper's Monthly* in 1899, and an autobiographical sketch for Carlisle's *The Red Man, by Red Men* in 1911. She died in New York City on February 6, 1919.

References

Bonnin, Gertrude. *Old Indian Legends*. Boston: Ginn, 1901. Reprint, Lincoln: University of Nebraska Press, 1985.

Curtis, Natalie. "An American Indian Artist." *Outlook* 124 (January 1920): 64–66.

———. *The Indian's Book*. New York: Harper & Brothers, 1907.

Dietz, Angel DeCora. "Angel DeCora—An Autobiography." *The Red Man, by Red Men* 3 (March 1911): 279–285.

———. "Native American Arts." *The Indian Historian* 3 (Winter 1970): 27–29.

———. "The Sick Child." *Harper's Monthly* (February 1899): 446–448. Reprinted in *The Singing Spirit*. Edited by Bernd Peyer. Pp. 45–47. Tucson: University of Arizona Press, 1989.

Dockstader, Frederick J. "Angel DeCora Dietz." In *Great North American Indians*. Edited by Frederick J. Dockstader. P. 71. New York: Van Nostrand Reinhold, 1977.

Eastman, Elaine G. "In Memoriam: Angel DeCora Dietz." *American Indian* 7 (Spring 1919): 51–52.

———. *Yellow Star*. Boston: Little, Brown, 1911.

La Flesche, Francis. *The Middle Five*. Boston: Ginn, 1900.

Littlefield, Daniel F., and James W. Parins. *A Biobibliography of Native American Writers, 1772–1924*. Metuchen, NJ: Scarecrow Press, 1981. Enl. ed., 1985.

McAnulty, Sarah. "Angel DeCora: American Indian Artist and Educator." *Nebraska History* 57 (1976): 143–199.

Society of American Indians. *Report of the Executive Council on the Proceedings of the Annual Conference of the Society of American Indians*. Washington, D.C.: The Society, 1912.

—*Bernd Peyer*

DIXON, LORENA LUCILLE MAJEL (b. 1922), was born on the Rincon Indian Reservation in southern California, the second of five children. She is a Luiseño Indian who lives on the Pauma Indian Reservation. Both of her parents were educated at Sherman Indian Boarding School in Riverside, California. Although their treatment at Sherman was harsh, they came from a tribal tradition that valued learning. At an early age, they taught Dixon the importance of formal education and of reading. In 1947 she married Gene E. Dixon, and they both passed along a love of learning to their children. They sacrificed to send their children to private schools so that they could "avoid the prejudices of public schools against Indian children and to ensure quality education for their children." Two of their children have earned master's degrees, one is completing her PhD, and another received a bachelor's degree and attended law school for one year. After her children were grown, Dixon continued her own education, earning an associate of arts degree at Palomar College, an institution that recognized her contributions to education by awarding her an honorary degree. Since then Dixon has continued to take classes toward her bachelor's degree.

Dixon was the first director of the American Indian Education Center, a satellite campus of Palomar College, located first on the Pala Indian Reservation and then on the Pauma Indian Reservation. She directed the American Indian Education Center, which offered college courses, tutoring, academic counseling, and financial assistance to Native Americans. Dixon also was instrumental in opening the first tribal library (with public access) on the Pauma Indian Reservation, encouraging readers of all ages to take advantage of the convenient facilities. For many years she has served as a tribal leader, working on every committee. She has focused her work primarily on committees to foster better education for all Native Americans. Dixon served four terms as tribal chair, navigating her tribe through difficult times and distinguishing herself as one of the most important tribal leaders in the state of California. She has been a member of her tribe's education committee, the Sherman Indian High School board, the American Indian Advisory Board of the University of California, San Diego, and the Learning Circle, a consortium of educators and community leaders interested in Native Americans and higher education. Although she has suffered a stroke, Dixon continues to serve her tribe and community by volunteering at the tribal library and education center.

References

American Indian Education Center. *Biography of Lorena Lucille Majel Dixon.* Pauma Valley, CA: The Center.
Trafzer, Clifford E. Personal communication with Lorena Dixon, March 1, 1996.

—Clifford E. Trafzer

DIXON, PATRICIA A. (b. 1948), is an associate professor of American Indian Studies and history at Palomar College, where she periodically serves as chair of Native American Studies. She is also a lecturer in American Indian Studies at San Diego State University. She is a Luiseño Indian and member of the Pauma Band of Mission Indians. She has served two terms as tribal chair and is active in tribal affairs. Dixon received her bachelor's and master's degrees in history at the University of San Diego, and she is currently pursuing graduate work in history at the University of California, Riverside, where she also serves on the Chancellor's Native American Advisory Committee. She is an active member of the Native American community in southern California, serving on the University Council of California State University, San Marcos, and as chair of the Sherman Indian High School board and of the Education Committee for the Pauma Band of Mission Indians. Dixon has lectured on many topics, including Native American history, the American West, and Native Americans in southern California. She has spoken before the Senate Select Committee on Indian Affairs and the World Conference for Indigenous People. She has offered workshops on Native American history and culture to numerous groups, including teachers and prisoners, giving of her time to improve knowledge about the Native peoples of America. Dixon lives on her reservation in the Pauma valley of southern California.

Reference

Trafzer, Clifford E. Personal communication with Patricia Dixon, March 1, 1996.

—*Clifford E. Trafzer*

DORION WOMAN [Marie Iowa, Marie LaGuivoise, Madam Marie Iowa, Dorion Venier Toupin] (1786–1853), an Iowa Indian, was born near the Arkansas River or the Red River. Referred to as the Dorion Woman, she appears in the narratives of various members of the Wilson Price Hunt expedition from St. Louis, Missouri, to the Pacific Northwest, which began in 1811. Her husband, Pierre Dorion, a mixed-blood Métis and Yankton Sioux, was employed by Hunt because of his command of several American Indian languages.

When the group set out for the West, the Dorion Woman accompanied them with her two children, Baptiste and Paul—a circumstance that would not have been allowed had Hunt not needed Pierre Dorion's services so badly. Along the way Dorion Woman gave birth to a third child, which died a week after it was born due to the harsh winter weather and starvation the group experienced passing over the mountains. Once the group successfully traversed the Rockies, they split into two groups to set up posts for trading and trapping; Pierre Dorion and his family went with John Reed. The Reed group then split into three parties. While Pierre was out hunting, Dog Rib Indians attacked and killed all in his party and at the two other posts. When the Dorion Woman was warned of the attacks, she fled with her children. She found one badly wounded man from her husband's party still alive and heard of her husband's death. She attempted to save both the man from Pierre's party and her children by hiding, but he died in the night. She headed out with her children, eventually set up camp for the winter, and kept them all alive by killing her two horses and smoking and drying the meat. After a long, arduous journey east in the spring, she found a new home among the Walla Wallas.

On April 17, 1814, when the rest of the original party stopped at the Walla Walla camp, Dorion Woman told her story to Gabriel Franchere, who carried the news with him to Montreal and published his narrative version five years later. Alexander Ross heard the Dorion Woman's story and published it in London in 1849; others took the story back with them to St. Louis. None of the men knew her Indian name, but later, after her third marriage, she took the name Marie LaGuivoise when she was baptized for her marriage to John Toupin, a mixed-blood Canadian. (Venier was her second husband's name.) She died in the Willamette Valley near Salem, Oregon, in 1853.

The Dorion Woman, as her name suggests, became legendary more for the role she played in relation to Anglo–American efforts to "win the West" than she did as a person in her own right. Nevertheless, she was by all accounts a woman of courage, dignity, and fortitude.

References

Allen, A. J. *Ten Years in Oregon: Travels and Adventures of Dr. E. White and Lady.* Ithaca, NY: Mack-Andrus, 1848.

Barry, J. Neilson. *Redskin & Pioneer: Brave Tales of the Great Northwest.* New York: Rand McNally, 1932.

Defenbach, Byron. *Red Heroines of the Northwest.* Caldwell, ID: Caxton, 1929.

Franchere, Gabriel. *Narrative of a Voyage to the Northwest Coast of America in the Years 1811, 1812, 1813, and 1814.* Translated and edited by J. V. Huntington. New York: Redfield, 1854.

Irving, Washington. *Astoria or Anecdotes of an Enterprise Beyond the Rocky Mountains.* Chicago: Belford-Clark, 1836.

Ross, Alexander. *Adventures of the First Settlers on the Oregon or Columbia River, Being the Narrative of the Expedition Fitted by John Jacob Astor to Establish the "Pacific Fur Company. . . ."* London: Smith-Elder, 1849.

—Kathryn W. Shanley

E

EATON, RACHEL CAROLINE (1869–1938), historian, was the eldest child of George W. Eaton, a white man, and Nancy Elizabeth Williams Eaton, of mixed Cherokee and white lineage. She was born in Indian Territory and was educated in the Cherokee public schools, including the Cherokee Female Seminary, from which she graduated in 1887. She received her BA degree in 1895 from Drury College in Springfield, Missouri, graduating cum laude. Eaton then returned to the Cherokee Nation to teach in the public schools and at the Female Seminary, along with her sister, Pauline. She later earned her MA (1911) and PhD (1919) degrees in history from the University of Chicago.

During her long and productive career, Eaton served as the head of the History Department at the State College for Women in Columbus, Missouri, professor of history at Lake Erie College in Painesville, Ohio, dean of women and of the History Department head at Trinity University in San Antonio, Texas, and as superintendent of schools in Rogers County, Oklahoma. She wrote *Domestic Science Among the Primitive Cherokees, Historic Fort Gibson, John Ross and the Cherokee Indians, Oklahoma Pioneer Life, The Battle of Claremore Mound*, and *History of Pioneer Churches in Oklahoma*. She was an active member of the Presbyterian Church and also a member of the Order of the Eastern Star, the Rebekah Lodge, the Oklahoma Authors' League, the Tulsa Women's Indian Club, and the La-kee-kon Club. In 1932 the Tulsa Historical Society formed the Rachel Caroline Eaton chapter, and in 1936 Eaton was inducted into the Oklahoma Hall of Fame.

References

Eaton, Rachel Caroline. *John Ross and the Cherokee Indians*. New York: Ams. Press, 1978.

Editorial. *Chronicles of Oklahoma* 10 (March 1932): 8.

Starr, Emmett. *History of the Cherokee Indians and Their Legends and Folklore*. Oklahoma City: Warden, 1979.

Who's Who Among Oklahoma Indians. Oklahoma City: Travis, 1928.

Wright, Muriel. "Rachel Caroline Eaton." *Chronicles of Oklahoma* 16 (March/December 1938): 509–510.

—*Devon A. Mihesuah*

ENDREZZE, ANITA [Endrezze-Danielson, Endrezze-Probst] (b. 1952), of European and Yaqui heritage, is a widely acclaimed visual artist, poet, and short story writer. She was born in Long Beach, California, and was raised in California, Hawaii, Oregon, and Washington; she now makes her home in Spokane, Washington.

Collections of poetry including *Burning the Fields, The North People*, and *The Humming of Stars and Bees and Waves* have brought Endrezze wide recognition for their imagistic and deeply spiritual artistry. Her poetry draws heavily upon her Native American heritage, and infused throughout it is a distinctly feminist vision. At times rooted in the daily domestic realm, the poems make startling jumps to a universal realm. At the center of much of her work is the artist's deeply felt relationship to the earth and the natural world. The poems successfully meld Endrezze's ecofeminist view to her own brand of American Indian spirituality and offer, in poignant and artistic frames, a new lens through which to posit the relationship between humans and the landscape, as well as the relations between men and women, the body and the spirit. Her words offer soaring insights and leaps of imaginative fancy that are truly transformative, yet the writer remains a craftswoman, never forsaking her scrutiny of form, of language, and of sound. Endrezze's writing has appeared in virtually all of the leading anthologies of Native American writing, including *Voices of the Rainbow, A Gathering of Spirit, Songs from This Earth on Turtle's Back, Dancing on the Rim of the World*, and *Harper's Anthology of 20th Century Native American Poetry*. Her work has been translated into a number of languages, including French, German, Danish, and Italian. She is fluent in Danish and published a children's novel, *The Mountain and the Guardian Spirit*, in that language.

Endrezze's writing has garnered awards and international praise. In 1990 she was invited to participate in a forum at the University of Milan; the year before, she was a featured speaker at Grenoble, France. More locally, she has received awards from the Northwest Writers' Conference and Seattle's Bumbershoot Writers-in-Performance Award.

Endrezze is equally well known as a painter and visual artist. As in her writing, much of the imagery in her art stems from dreams and visions, and works to capture something of the eternal feminine energy that, for Endrezze, is the basis of all healing. Her artwork has been used to illustrate a number of collections of American Indian writing, including the cover of *Harper's Anthology of 20th Century Native American Poetry*, as well as the cover of a special American Indian issue of *The Wooster Review*.

Endrezze has served as poet-in-residence with the Washington State Arts Commission and has edited newsletters for the Audubon Society and the Indian Artists Guild. She is a member of ATLATL, a Phoenix-based Native American arts organization. She has offered numerous workshops on poetry, painting, storytelling, and poetry and art as therapy.

References

Brant, Beth. *A Gathering of Spirit*. Rockland, ME: Sinister Wisdom, 1984.

Bruchac, Joseph, ed. *Songs from This Earth on Turtle's Back: Contemporary American Indian Poetry*. Greenfield Center, NY: Greenfield Review Press, 1983.

Endrezze, Anita. *At the Helm of Twilight*. Seattle, WA: Broken Moon Press, 1992.

————. *Burning the Fields*. Lewiston, ID: Confluence Press, 1983.

————. *The Humming of Stars and Bees and Waves*. Guildford: Making Waves, 1998.

————. *The Mountain and the Guardian Spirit*. Denmark: CDR Forlag, 1986. (In Danish).

————. *The North People*. Marvin, SD: Blue Cloud Quarterly Press, 1983.

————. *Throwing Fire at the Sun, Water at the Moon*. Tucson: University of Arizona Press, 2000.

Lerner, Andrea, ed. *Dancing on the Rim of the World*. Tucson: University of Arizona Press, 1990.

Niatum, Duane, ed. *Carriers of the Dream Wheel*. New York: Harper & Row, 1975.

————. *Harper's Anthology of 20th Century Native American Poetry*. San Francisco: Harper & Row, 1988.

Rosen, Kenneth, ed. *Voices of the Rainbow*. New York: Viking Press, 1975.

—Andrea Lerner

ERDRICH, ANGIE (b. 1965), physician and artist, a Turtle Mountain Ojibway born in Breckenridge, Minnesota, to an Ojibway mother and a German father. She was raised in a family of seven children in Wahpeton, North Dakota. In 1987, Erdrich earned a B.A. from Dartmouth College (in Hanover, New Hampshire) in visual studies and went on to medical school at the same institution. In 1994, she began her residency in pediatrics at the University of Washington Children's Hospital Medical Center in Seattle. She completed her residency in 1997.

Erdrich currently works for the Indian Health Service on the Navajo reservation in Chinle, Arizona. A staunch advocate for Native American children's healthcare, she has worked to promote breastfeeding and childhood safety and to prevent substance abuse among adolescent Native Americans. She is a member of the Association of American Indian Physicians. Erdrich's talents are not limited to medicine. Her watercolor painting graced the cover of Heid E. Erdrich's 1997 poetry collection, *Fishing for Myth*.

Reference

Telephone conversation with Angie Erdrich, March 3, 2001.

—Matthew Holt Jennings

ERDRICH, HEID E. (b. 1963), poet and creative writing teacher, a Turtle Mountain Ojibway born in Minnesota. She was raised in Wahpeton, North Dakota, where her parents taught at a Bureau of Indian Affairs boarding school. Erdrich earned a B.A. from Dartmouth College in 1986, and received two Master of Arts degrees from Johns Hopkins University in 1989 and 1990 in poetry and fiction.

Erdrich's poetry has appeared in numerous journals including *Tamaqua, The Maryland Poetry Review, Great River Review,* and *Cimarron Review*. Her poems also appear in several anthologies, including *Party Train* and *Prairie Volcano*. Erdrich's 1997 poetry collection, *Fishing for Myth*, met with critical praise and earned her a nomination for a Minnesota Book Award in 1998. One reviewer described *Fishing for Myth* as a "remarkable first book" and went on to credit Erdrich with demonstrating "the bonds between land, history and people." Erdrich has received numerous honors, including a career grant from the Loft and a New Voices Award from New Rivers Press. She has read her poetry in bookstores throughout the Midwest and Washington. Erdrich cites Joy Harjo, Toni Morrison, Linda Hogan, and Lorraine Hansberry as literary influences. Erdrich teaches at the University of St. Thomas and is active in the St. Paul community, where she coordinates reading series and mentors Native American youth. She also edits the Native American Alumni of Dartmouth College Newsletter. Erdrich lives in St. Paul with her husband John Burke and son Jules Ezra.

References

University of St. Thomas, faculty Web page.
<http://www.stthomas.edu/engl/Facultybios/HeidErdrich.htm>
Review of *Fishing for Myth* (quoted above) appeared in the January–February 1998 issue *Fodder*.
Personal correspondence with Heid E. Erdrich, February 27–28, 2001.

—*Matthew Holt Jennings*

ERDRICH, LOUISE (b. 1954), known for her poetry, novels, and short stories, was born in Little Falls, Minnesota, and raised in Wahpeton, North Dakota. Her mother, a Chippewa, and her father, of German descent, both taught at the Wahpeton Indian School, and her grandfather was tribal chair of the Turtle Mountain Chippewa Reservation in North Dakota for a number of years. Erdrich is a member of the Turtle Mountain band of Chippewa.

In 1976 Erdrich received her BA from Dartmouth, where she was awarded prizes for fiction and poetry. After graduating she returned to North Dakota and taught in the Poetry in the Schools Program, and was visiting poet and teacher for the North Dakota Council on the Arts in 1977 to 1978. In 1978 she received a fellowship to teach composition and creative writing at Johns Hopkins University. After completing her MA at Johns Hopkins in 1979, Erdrich moved to Boston, to become editor of the Boston Indian Council newspaper, *The Circle*. She was a MacDowell Colony fellow in 1980 and a Yaddo Colony fellow in 1981, and was awarded a National Endowment for the Arts fellowship in 1982.

Love Medicine (1984), often referred to as a "short story cycle," was the first in a series of novels chronicling the struggles of several generations of Chippewa, mixed-blood, and European–American families in various fictional settings in North Dakota. Following it were *The Beet Queen* (1986), *Tracks* (1988), *The Bingo Palace* (1994), and *Tales of Burning Love* (1996), and *The Last Report on the Miracles at Little No Horse* (2001, forth coming). In 1993 Erdrich published a new and expanded edition of *Love Medicine*, which contains four new chapters and other minor revisions.

In addition to this group of novels, Erdrich has produced a textbook called *Imagination* (1980); two collections of poetry, *Jacklight* (1984) and *Baptism of Desire* (1989); a limited-edition travel book, *Route Two* (1990); and a collection of essays—many of them previously published in magazines—titled *The Blue Jay's Dance: A Birth Year* (1995). She has contributed numerous stories, poems, essays, and book reviews to periodicals.

Erdrich won several awards for *Love Medicine*, including the National Book Critics Circle Award in 1984, the Sue Kaufman Prize, the *Los Angles Times* Award for best novel, the Virginia McCormack Scully Prize for best book of 1984, and the Best First Fiction Award from the American Academy and Institute of Arts and Letters. The book was also named one of the best eleven books of 1985 by the *New York Times Book Review*. In 1986 *The Beet Queen* was named one of *Publisher's Weekly*'s best books, won First Prize in the O. Henry Awards in 1986, and was nominated for the National Book Critics Circle Award. She also won the Pushcart Prize in 1983 and the National Magazine Fiction Award in 1983 and 1987. Erdrich was a Guggenheim fellow in 1985 to 1986, and in 1982 she won the Nelson Algren Short Fiction Award for "The World's Greatest Fisherman."

Erdrich was married to Michael Dorris (Modoc) and collaborated with him to write *Crown of Columbus* (1991) and *Route Two* (1990).

References

Bak, Hans. "Toward a Native American 'Realism': The Amphibious Fiction of Louise Erdrich." In *Neo-Realism in Contemporary American Fiction*. Edited by Kristiaan Versulys. Pp. 145–170. Atlanta: Rodopi, 1992.

Bonetti, Kay. "An Interview with Louise Erdrich and Michael Dorris." *Missouri Review* 11 (1988): 79–99.

Brewington, Lillian, Normie Bullard, and R. W. Reising. "Writing in Love: An Annotated Bibliography of Critical Responses to the Poetry and Novels of Louise Erdrich and Michael Dorris." *American Indian Culture and Research Journal* 10 (1986): 81–86.

Bruchac, Joseph. "Whatever Is Really Yours: An Interview with Louise Erdrich." In *Survival This Way: Interviews with Native American Poets*. Pp. 73–86. Tucson: University of Arizona Press, 1987.

Chavkin, Allan, and Nancy Feyl Chavkin, eds. *Conversations with Louise Erdrich and Michael Dorris*. Jackson: University Press of Mississippi, 1994.

Coltelli, Laura. *Winged Words: Native American Writers Speak*. Lincoln: University of Nebraska Press, 1990.

Dorris, Michael, and Louise Erdrich. *The Crown of Columbus*. New York: Harper-Collins, 1991.

Erdrich, Louise. *The Antelope Wife*. New York: HarperCollins, 1998.

———. *Baptism of Desire*. New York: Harper & Row, 1989.

———. *The Beet Queen*. New York: Henry Holt, 1986.

———. *The Bingo Palace*. New York: HarperCollins, 1994.

———. *The Blue Jay's Dance: A Birth Year*. New York: HarperCollins, 1995.

———. *Grandmother's Pigeon*. New York: Hyperion, 1996.

———. *Imagination*. Westerville, OH: Merrill, 1981.

———. *Jacklight*. New York: Holt, Rinehart and Winston, 1984.

————. *Love Medicine*. New York: Holt, Rinehart and Winston, 1984. New and enl. ed., New York: HarperPerennial, 1993.

————. *Tales of Burning Love*. New York: HarperCollins, 1996.

————. *Tracks*. New York: Henry Holt, 1988.

————, and Michael Dorris. *Route Two*. Northridge, CA: Lord John Press, 1990.

George, Jan. "Interview with Louise Erdrich." *North Dakota Quarterly* 53 (Spring 1985): 240–246.

Kroeber, Karl, ed. "Louise Erdrich: *Love Medicine*." *Studies in American Indian Literatures* 9 (Winter 1985): 1–41.

Nowik, Nan. "Interview with Louise Erdrich." *Belles Lettres* (November/December 1986): 9.

Towery, Margie. "Continuity and Connection: Characters in Louise Erdrich's Fiction." *American Indian Culture and Research Journal* 16 (1992): 99–115.

Wong, Hertha D. "Louise Erdrich's *Love Medicine*: Narrative Communities and the Short Story Sequence." In *Modern American Short Story Sequences: Composite Fictions and Fictive Communities*. Edited by J. Gerald Kennedy. Pp. 170–193. Cambridge: Cambridge University Press, 1995.

—Janet Peterson Gerstner

EVANS, MARY AUGUSTA TAPPAGE (b. 1888), elder and poet of the Soda Creek Indians of Cariboo country, British Columbia, was the granddaughter of William Longshem, hereditary Shuswap chief, and the daughter of Mary Ann Longsheim and Christopher (Alex) Tappage. She was educated at St. Joseph's Mission in Onward Valley, near Williams Lake, and married George Evans, half Indian and half Welsh (died 1931) in 1903, after which she lost her Indian status because she married a non–Indian. They established a ranch on the banks of Deep Creek, near her birthplace. They had two daughters (both stillborn) and two sons.

Evans's status as a "poet" is marginal in the conventional sense, for though her work has been anthologized and is collected in a volume along with photographs, tales, and children's stories, hers are "spoken poems," traditional narratives shaped into poetic form by her editor, Jean E. Speare. Nevertheless, her experiential stories, and the traditional tales she relates, often have mythic dimensions. Works such as "Smallpox," an account of the impact of various diseases on her family, and "Changes," a meditation about marriage and changing customs, are genuinely affecting as modern poetry.

References

Day, David, and Marilyn Bowering, eds. *Many Voices: An Anthology of Contemporary Canadian Indian Poetry*. Vancouver, BC: J. J. Douglas, 1977.

Speare, Jean E., ed. *The Days of Augusta*. Vancouver, BC: J. J. Douglas, 1973.

—Rodney Simard

F

FIFE, CONNIE (b. 1961), is a poet who has edited and contributed to numerous collections of writings by and about aboriginal women. In the introduction to her anthology *The Colour of Resistance* (1993), she asserts: "No matter the authors or their skills in the written word, European writers have failed miserably at conveying the essence behind our words; they have failed to transport the life we find in language onto the page." Her work represents an effort to remedy this situation by offering "in [their] own Indigenous voice[s]" the writings of aboriginal women from a variety of perspectives, including her own as a Cree and a lesbian.

From 1990 to 1992 Fife was writer-in-residence at the En'owkin International School of Writing in Penticton, British Columbia. She published a collection of poetry, *Beneath the Naked Sun*, in 1992, and in 1986 she edited the Native Women's issue of *Fireweed*. As of 2000 she is an outreach worker for the Urban Native Youth Association, working with street-entrenched and at-risk aboriginal youths in Vancouver, British Columbia. Originally from Saskatchewan, she now lives in Vancouver with her son.

References

Fife, Connie. *Beneath the Naked Sun*. Toronto: Sister Vision Press, 1992.
———. *Speaking Through Jagged Rock*. Fredericton, NB: Broken Jaw Press, 1999.
———, ed. *The Colour of Resistance: A Contemporary Collection of Writing by Aboriginal Women*. Toronto: Sister Vision Press, 1993.
Moses, Daniel David, and Perry Goldie, eds. *Anthology of Canadian Native Literature in English*. New York: Oxford University Press, 1998.

—*Ryan Simmons*

FOLWELL, JODY (b. 1942), is a member of the distinguished Naranjo family of artists and potters from Santa Clara Pueblo, New Mexico. Fluent in Tewa and English, Folwell was educated at Santa Clara Day School and in Taos, New Mexico. She also studied at the College of Santa Fe and the University of New Mexico, receiving her BA in history and political science from the latter.

After twelve years as a teacher and educator, Folwell turned to pottery making full-time in 1974. In a family noted for its artistic accomplishments (her sister is

Nora Naranjo-Morse), Folwell has emerged as an unparalleled innovator in design. Though her methods of pottery making are time honored—she gathers her own clay and tempers it with volcanic ash; she builds her pots by the coil method and hand polishes them to a high sheen; and she fires outside—her designs are distinctly individual, characterized by asymmetry, unusual color combinations of sienna, charcoal, amber, and ocher, and bold political and personal statements incised onto the surface through the *sgraffito* method.

Controversial for several years because of her departure from the classic polished red and black ware of Santa Clara Pueblo, Folwell began attracting major collectors and galleries in the late 1970s. She has received numerous awards, including the prestigious Best of Show at the 1985 Indian Market in Santa Fe, sponsored by the Southwestern Association on Indian Affairs, for a jar on which she and the sculptor Robert Haozous collaborated.

Upon the slightly irregular surface of her dome-shaped vessels, Folwell carves stories that reflect her concerns of the moment, such as airplanes that symbolize the overly rapid technological explosion of this country, or dogs, the abandoned strays of many Indian reservations, which she supports through the sale of her dog pots until she finds proper homes for them.

The subject of articles and a PBS-TV special on prominent American Indian artists, Folwell has opened the door for American Indian potters to explore the limits of their creativity and to build today the traditions of tomorrow. Her work is in numerous private and corporate collections, as well as museums, including the Heard Museum in Phoenix. In "Literary Pottery," by Ron McCoy, Folwell says: "Traditional and contemporary are the same. What's contemporary today is traditional tomorrow. What's traditional today becomes contemporary down the road. That's a perpetual cycle artists must go and grow through in order to succeed creatively. . . . Ancient Southwestern pottery represents abstract design. The thought behind a design is traditional. Yet as abstraction, it falls on the borderline of 'then' and 'now.'"

References

American Indian Artists 11. Distributed by the Native American Public Broadcasting Consortium, Lincoln, NE. 30 min. 1983. A video documentary.

Arnold, David. "Pueblo Pottery—2000 Years of Artistry." *National Geographic* (November 1982): 593–605.

Cortright, Barbara. "Jody Folwell, Potter." *Artspace* (Summer 1982): 33–35.

Jacka, Jerry, and Lois Essary Jacka. *Beyond Tradition: Contemporary Indian Art and Its Evolution*. Flagstaff, AZ: Northland Publishing, 1988.

Lichtenstein, Grace. "The Evolution of a Craft Tradition." *Ms.* 11 (April 1983): 58–60, 92.

McCoy, Ron. "Literary Pottery." *Southwest Profile* (January 1987): 14–17.

———. "Made in America." *America West* 1 (February 1987): 51–67.

Perlman, Barbara. "Courage: Her Greatest Asset." *Arizona Arts and Lifestyle* (Summer 1980): 20–21.

Trimble, Stephen. *Talking with the Clay—The Art of Pueblo Pottery*. Santa Fe, NM: School of American Research Press, 1987.

Women of Sweetgrass, Cedar, and Sage. Catalog for show curated by Harmony Hammond and Jaune Quick-to-See Smith. New York: Gallery of the American Indian Community House, 1985.

—Dexter Fisher Cirillo

FRANCISCO, NIA (b. 1952), is a Navajo poet whose book *Carried Away by the Black River* is intended to be a solace and an ally for children who have suffered sexual abuse, especially incest. The personae of these harrowing, direct poems speak for children like "janelle, nellie, and janet," who have lost their voices in sorrow and fear: "shocked she stood wordless choked/facing a black figure with large rough hands/groping her childlike thighs." In her Afterword, Francisco writes, "A child sexually abused is like being carried away by a black river." This short volume acknowledges the power of that deadly current and the hope of rescue. "I must love again. . . I must survive" is an echo for each poem.

Nia Francisco was born in 1952 in Fort Defiance, Arizona, of the Red Bottom People and for the Salt People. Her first book, *Blue Horses for Navajo Women*, chronicles birth, death, motherhood, love, dreams, families, and the hard border between Navajo and Anglo culture. It is divided into four sections, each representing one of the four sacred directions (the sacred mountains) of the Navajo. Holy beings (blue horses, white shell, turquoise, black thunderclouds) reflect her deep spirituality and suggest the complexities of life lived on or near the Navajo homeland. Her beliefs include the assumption that there are holy beings in every religion. She credits her grandparents, who raised her, with instilling in her a reverence for traditional Navajo ways.

Francisco holds an associate in arts degree in Indian education and Navajo Studies from Navajo Community College and a certificate in graphic and performing arts from the Institute of American Indian Arts (IAIA) in Santa Fe. At the IAIA, exposure to other Native cultures helped her to appreciate the unique beauty of her own. She has worked in the Parent Aide Program of the Navajo Division of Social Services (Fort Defiance Agency) and as an educator in the Navajo Tribe Division of Education, the Fort Defiance Division of Child Development, the Chinle School District, the Navajo Academy, and Navajo Community College. She lives in New Mexico. "To me," Francisco wrote, "writing is my art form. I've refined it. I enjoy doing it. I also write Navajo language, speak it fluently. In the Navajo, when a person is bilingual—knows another tongue—it is said that person can 'hear.'"

References

Francisco, Nia. *Blue Horses for Navajo Women*. Greenfield Center, NY: Greenfield Review Press, 1988.

———. *Carried Away by the Black River*. Farmington, NM: Yoo-Hoo Press, 1994.

———. "Navajo Traditional Knowledge." In *The Sacred: Ways of Knowledge, Sources of Life*. Edited by Peggy Beck, Anna Lee Walters, and Nia Francisco. Pp. 277–300. Tsaile, AZ: Navajo Community College Press, 1977.

—Rhoda Carroll

FREEMAN, MINNIE AODLA (b. 1936), has been an editor, playwright, filmmaker, and translator for the Canadian government. Born on the Cape Hope Islands in James Bay, she was the granddaughter of an influential Inuit leader, Weetaltuk. She grew up in the towns of Moose Factory, Ontario, and Fort George, Quebec, and attended Anglican and Roman Catholic schools. She started translating for Inuit patients while hospitalized for tuberculosis in 1951 to 1952, and moved to Ottawa in 1957 to begin work as a translator of the Inuktitut and Cree languages for what was then known as the Department of Northern Affairs and National Resources. Her childhood in the North and early adulthood in the urban South are presented in her first book, *Life Among the Quallunaat* (1978), which serves doubly as an autobiography and an ethnography of southern Canadian culture in the 1950s. It has been translated into German and French.

Freeman's play *Survival in the South* was staged at the National Arts Centre in Ottawa in 1973, and several of her poems and short stories have appeared in the *Canadian Children's Annual*. Freeman has produced numerous documentary films about dimensions of Inuit life, including *Little Cornwallis Mining* (1978), *The Islands* (1980), and *America Mute* (1994), the last of which continues to be used for Inuit studies by the Anthropology Department of the University of California at Berkeley. Between 1973 and 1979 Freeman was Native cultural adviser and narrator for the Canadian Broadcasting Corporation in Toronto. Since then she has served as assistant editor of *Inuit Today* Magazine, executive secretary of the Land Claims Secretariat of the Inuit Tapirisat of Canada, and a founder and producer for the Inuit Broadcasting Corporation in Ottawa. She has held lectureships at the University of Alberta, the University of Western Ontario, Memorial University, and Arctic College, and was a facilitator and Inuktitut editor for the PEN eastern Arctic tour.

Since 1981 Freeman has lived in Edmonton, Alberta, where in addition to her filmmaking work, she has performed Inuit healing for prisoners at Bowden Institute and for a halfway house in Edmonton. In 1994 was coeditor of *Inuit Women Artists*. An elder for the Department of Indian Affairs and Northern Resources, she is married and has three children and five grandchildren.

References

Freeman, Minnie Aodla. "Dear Leaders of the World." In *Sharing Our Experience*. P. 186. N.p.: Canadian Advisory Council on the Status of Women, 1993.
———. *Life Among the Quallunaat*. Edmonton, AL: Hurtig, 1978.
———. "Living in Two Hells." In *Northern Voices: Inuit Writing in English*. Edited by Penny Petrone. P. 235. Toronto: University of Toronto Press, 1988.
Leroux, Odette, Marion E. Jackson, and Minnie Aodla Freeman, eds. *Inuit Women Artists: Voices from Cape Dorset*. Vancouver, BC: Douglas & McIntyre, 1994.

—*Ryan Simmons*

FRENCH, ALICE [Masak] (b. 1930), a Nunatakmuit Inuk, went to residential school in Aklavik in 1937 after her mother contracted tuberculosis. Her father, Anisalouk, was a trapper in the Mackenzie River delta. At school she was named Alice French.

She remained there for seven years and has described her school experience in the book *My Name Is Masak*.

French faced daunting challenges when she went home. She had a stepmother and younger siblings, and had to relearn a way of life. She had almost forgotten her native language. She was forced to acquire survival skills quickly in order not to be a burden to her family, and she overcame her fears of the bush, animals, the dark, and dogs. Traditional practices appeared strange. A great fear was that she would not find a suitable marriage partner.

French learned to trap, skin animals, sew, and perform the many tasks required to maintain family life. Much of her learning came from her very strict grandmother, who almost succeeded in arranging a marriage for the terrified girl when she was fourteen. Two years later her stepmother contracted tuberculosis, so sixteen-year-old Alice had to assume the role of mother for the family. After a year her father, missing his wife, accepted employment as a reindeer herder. The job gave him a regular salary and a real house. Though French missed the cooperation of the traditional families, she enjoyed the social life of the reindeer herders. A marriage to Jim Nahogaloak was arranged in the traditional way with French's consent. She believed this herder, whom she knew only by sight, would be better than a man chosen by her grandmother.

The marriage was doomed to failure. Jim had never been to school and spoke no English, and French's Inupeak was poor. He was twelve years older than she and came from a different culture. She was fascinated with the reindeer and loved the beauty of the natural world. She and Jim were the only humans living in a tent just big enough to accommodate the two of them. The loneliness, however, took its toll.

French has two sons, Charles and Gerry, and a daughter, Bunny; one child died of pneumonia. She and Jim moved to Aklavik to participate in the economic boom. Jim's parents largely looked after the two boys, so when Alice was asked to participate in the Pacific National Exhibition in Vancouver, she accepted. Once away from the North, she realized that an era of her life had ended. In 1960 she divorced Jim, taking Bunny with her.

In 1961 she married Dominick, a Royal Canadian Mounted Police officer. They lived in various locations in Manitoba, and briefly in Ireland after Dominick's father died. They had three children, Barry, Katherine, and Kevin, who died in infancy. French wrote two books about her experiences, and though today she lives with Dominick in Pinawa, Manitoba, she says, "My Northland in the Arctic has a fascination as no other for me."

References

French, Alice. *My Name Is Masak*. Winnipeg, MN: Peguis Publishers, 1976.
————. *The Restless Nomad*. Winnipeg, MN: Pemmican Publications, 1992.
Grant, Agnes. *No End of Grief: Indian Residential Schools in Canada*. Winnipeg, MN: Pemmican Publications, 1996.

—Agnes Grant

FRY, MAGGIE ANN CULVER (1900–1998), a widely known writer, was born at Vian, Cherokee Nation, and was educated in the elementary schools of the Indian

Territory and later Oklahoma. After four years as a salesclerk and telephone operator, she returned to high school but was forced to drop out. She married Merrit Fry, who like her was an enrolled Cherokee. They made their home near Claremore, Oklahoma, where she was a farm wife, mother, and active worker in agricultural economics clubs and 4–H clubs. From 1933 to 1935 she worked for the Oklahoma Emergency Relief Administration in Rogers County.

Though interested in writing since childhood, Fry did not pursue a writing career until after World War II. In 1954 she published her first volume of poetry, *The Witch Deer*, which was followed by five more books: *The Umbilical Cord*, which was nominated for the Pulitzer Prize, and *Buckskin Hollow Reflections*, collections of poetry; *A Boy Named Will*, a life of Will Rogers for juvenile readers; *Sunrise over Red Man's Land* (1981), an autobiography; and *Cherokee Female Seminary Years*, a collection of historical pieces and reminiscences. In addition, she published more than 750 articles, stories, and poems in publications as wide-ranging as religious and devotional magazines, the *Chicago Tribune* and other newspapers, literary magazines, agricultural publications, *American Mercury*, and *Organic Gardening*. Her writing won a number of awards, including the office of poet laureate of Oklahoma since 1977 and writer-in-residence at Claremore Junior College.

In addition to writing, Maggie Fry served as a Sunday school teacher for six decades after 1917, a church musician, a radio Sunday school teacher for station KWPR in Claremore (1962–1973), legislative assistant to the president pro tem of the Oklahoma Senate (1964–1965), editor of the *Rogers County Observer* (1968–1969), columnist for the same newspaper (1968–1971), and a teacher and civic leader.

Maggie Fry's writings and public careers reflect two strong influences: pride in her Cherokee heritage and an unfaltering Christian faith.

References

Authors in the News. Vol. 1. Detroit: Gale Research, 1976.

Claremore Progress [Claremore, OK], August 8, 1975, 1; July 21, 1977, 1; December 23, 1990, Spotlight sec., 1.

Fry files. Legislative Reference Division, Oklahoma Department of Libraries, Oklahoma City; Muskogee Public Library, Muskogee, OK; Will Rogers Public Library, Claremore, OK.

Fry, Maggie Culver. *A Boy Named Will: The Story of Young Will Rogers*. N.p.: Oklahoma Publishing, 1971.

———. *Buckskin Hollow Reflections*. Muskogee, OK: Five Civilized Tribes Museum, 1978.

———. *Cherokee Female Seminary Years: A Cherokee National Anthology*. Claremore, OK: Rogers State Press, 1988.

———. *The Umbilical Cord*. Chicago: Windfall Press, 1971.

———. *The Witch Deer: Poems of the Oklahoma Indians*. New York: Exposition Press, 1955.

Kay, Ernest, ed. *International Who's Who in Poetry*. 2nd ed. London: International Who's Who in Poetry, 1970.

—*Daniel F. Littlefield, Jr.*

G

GLANCY, DIANE (b. 1941), of German/English/Cherokee descent, was born in Kansas City, Missouri, and attended the University of Missouri. She holds an MA from Central State University in Oklahoma and an MFA from the University of Iowa (1988). As of 2000 she teaches at Macalester College in St. Paul, Minnesota, and has been artist-in-residence in Tulsa for the State Arts Council. She has published widely in leading literary journals. Her work has received the Pegasus Award from the Oklahoma Federation of Writers (for *Brown Wolf Leaves the Res*) and the Lakes and Prairies Prize from *Milkweed Chronicle* (for *One Age in a Dream*). She was poet laureate for the Five Civilized Tribes from 1984 to 1986. In addition to her literary and professional accomplishments, she is the mother of two children, David and Jennifer.

In her autobiographical essay "Two Dresses," in the anthology *I Tell You Now*, Glancy writes movingly of her mixed-blood heritage, her sense of history, and her relationship to the landscape of the Plains, all elements that infuse and inform her writing. Poetry reveals "underlying meanings and relationships" that permit her to "face the wilderness within." Part of that wilderness is the result of being a part of two cultures yet belonging wholly in neither. Another aspect of wilderness is the sense of being split between two dimensions, "between the visible and the invisible worlds, between earth and heaven," a split that characterizes both the Indian and poetry. "Poetry is a ghost dance in which one world seeks the other. Though the two worlds are opposed, they long to be united." This longing for fusion can be seen in the tension Glancy evokes between the smallness of the individual and the vastness of the landscape, and between the intersections of a people's sense of historical place and the mobility of the present, and in her use of contemporary English words and poetic forms interspersed with ancient Indian chants.

References

Bruchac, Joseph, ed. *Songs from This Earth on Turtle's Back: Contemporary American Indian Poetry*. Greenfield Center, NY: Greenfield Review Press, 1983.

Foss, Phillip. *The Clouds Threw This Light*. Santa Fe, NM: Institute of American Indian Arts Press, 1983.

Glancy, Diane. *Asylum in the Grasslands*. Wakefield, RI: Moyer Bell, 1998.

———. *Brown Wolf Leaves the Res and Other Poems*. Marvin, SD: Blue Cloud Quarterly Press, 1984.

————. *Boom Town*. Goodhue, MN: Black Hat, 1995.

————. *Claiming Breath*. Lincoln: University of Nebraska Press, 1992.

————. *The Cold-and-Hunger Dance*. Lincoln: University of Nebraska Press, 1998.

————. *Drystalks of the Moon*. Tulsa, OK: Hadassah Press, 1981.

————. *Firesticks: A Collection of Stories*. Norman: University of Oklahoma Press, 1993.

————. *Flutie*. Wakefield, RI: Moyer Bell, 1998.

————. *Fuller Man*. Wakefield, RI: Moyer Bell, 1999.

————. *Iron Woman: Poems*. Minneapolis, MN: New Rivers Press, 1990.

————. *Lone Dog's Winter Count*. Albuquerque, NM: West End Press, 1991.

————. *Monkey Secret*. Evanston, IL: Triquarterly/Northwestern University Press, 1995.

————. *Offering: Aliscolidodi*. Duluth, MN: Holy Cow! Press, 1988.

————. *One Age in a Dream*. Minneapolis, MN: Milkweed Editions, 1986.

————. *The Only Piece of Furniture in the House*. Wakefield, RI: Moyer Bell, 1996.

————. *Pushing the Bear*. New York: Harcourt Brace Jovanovich, 1996.

————. *Trigger Dance*. Boulder, CO: Fiction Collective Two, 1990.

————. *Traveling On*. Tulsa, OK: Myrtlewood Press, 1982.

————. "Two Dresses." In *I Tell You Now: Autobiographical Essays by Native American Writers*. Edited by Brian Swann and Arnold Krupat, Pp. 167–183. Lincoln: University of Nebraska Press, 1987.

————. *Visit Teepee Town: Native Writings After Detours*. Minneapolis, MN: Coffee House Press, 1999.

————. *The Voice That Was in Travel*. Norman: University of Oklahoma Press, 1999.

————. *War Cries: A Collection of Plays*. Duluth, MN: Holy Cow! Press, 1996.

————. *The West Pole*. Minneapolis: University of Minnesota Press, 1997.

Salisbury, Ralph, ed. *A Nation Within*. Hamilton, New Zealand: Outrigger, 1983.

Truesdale, C. W., and Diane Glancy, eds. *Two Worlds Walking: Short Stories, Essays, and Poetry by Writers with Mixed Heritages*. New York: New Rivers Press, 1994.

—*Kathleen McNerney Donovan*

GONZALES, ROSE [Rose Cata], (b. ?) was born and raised in the Tewa-speaking San Juan Pueblo of New Mexico's northern Rio Grande. The year of her birth is unknown. In 1920 she married Robert Gonzales and moved to his home, San Ildefonso Pueblo, where she learned the art of pottery making from her mother-in-law, Ramona Sanchez Gonzales. This personal training was expanded with study at the Institute of American Indian Arts in Santa Fe, New Mexico, the school of many San Ildefonso artists.

Gonzales continues to play a part in the San Ildefonso artistic renaissance that began in the 1930s with the movement from pottery with polychrome decorations to pottery with matte black designs on a polished black surface. This development had tremendous commercial success and revitalized the ceramic industry at San

Ildefonso Pueblo. Since that time, Gonzales has further enhanced the development of pottery making by being the first potter to use a carving technique as decoration, a style that has become quite popular among Pueblo potters.

Her work is characterized by the rounded edges of its carved areas and by the fine polishing throughout. Gonzales works in varied shapes ranging from closed bowls to canteens, consistently incorporating designs like "Awanyu" the serpent, "Kiva Steps," clouds, lightning, and "Thunderbird" into her black-on-black works.

Gonzales has shown widely throughout the United States as a contributor to specialized exhibits of Native American art. Her works can be found in the collections of the Museum of New Mexico, the Maxwell Museum of Anthropology in Albuquerque, Texas Tech University Museum at Lubbock, and the School of American Research in Santa Fe. Gonzales exhibits throughout the Southwest at the Heard Museum Arts and Crafts Show, the Southwestern Association of Indian Affairs Indian Market, the Gallup Ceremonial, and the Eight Northern Indian Pueblo Artists and Craftsmen Show.

Like her mother-in-law, Gonzales taught, and continues to inspire, potters who carry on the specialized art of pottery making at San Ildefonso Pueblo. As an artist and as an active member of the Pueblo, Gonzales has contributed to the artistic and cultural growth of the San Ildefonso Pueblo, as well as to the society at large.

References

Fox, Nancy. "Rose Gonzales." *American Indian Art Magazine* 2 (Autumn 1977): 52–57.

Maxwell Museum of Anthropology. *Seven Families in Pueblo Pottery*. Albuquerque: University of New Mexico Press, 1975.

—*Michelle Savoy*

GOOSE, MARY (b. 1955), was born in Des Moines, Iowa, and grew up around the Meskwaki Settlement near Tama. Her mother is a member of the Meskwaki tribe, and Mary Goose is Meskwaki and Chippewa, with most of her tribal influence coming from the Meskwaki. After attending public schools in Des Moines and Tama, she graduated from Tama High School in 1974. Goose then enrolled at Iowa State University, where she planned to study veterinary medicine. She found that her interests lay elsewhere, however, and graduated in 1980 with a BA in anthropology and minors in art and American Indian Studies. In 1985 she added a BS in speech communication with an emphasis in the telecommunication arts. She now lives in Des Moines, Iowa, with her son, Lucas.

Goose's love for creative fiction started with her mother translating comic books into Meskwaki for her before she was old enough to read. Although interested in a broad range of literature, she found that science fiction most stimulated her imagination. She received little encouragement from the public school system but was persuaded to try her hand at writing through college classes in creative writing and Native American literature. She found that poetry came very easily to her and provided an outlet for her creative talent. She lists the works of Ray Bradbury and the TV series *Star Trek* as two of her main sources of inspiration.

Goose's poetry has appeared in such anthologies as *The Remembered Earth, Songs from This Earth on Turtle's Back*, and *The Clouds Threw This Light*, as well as the spring 1985 issue of *North Dakota Quarterly*. Goose participated in the Oklahoma Writers Conference in July 1992.

References

Benson, Arlon. Personal communication with Mary Goose, March 17, 1992.
Hobson, Geary, ed. *The Remembered Earth: An Anthology of Contemporary Native American Literature*. Albuquerque, NM: Red Earth Press, 1979.

—Arlon Benson

GOULD, JANICE MAY (b. 1949), was born in San Diego, California, on April 1, 1949, the second of three daughters of a British immigrant father (Gould) and an Irish, French, and Maidu mother (Beatty). When Gould was nine years old, she moved from San Diego to Berkeley, California, where she lived until her graduation from Berkeley High School in 1967. During that tumultuous time of war protests and race riots, she was deeply affected by the civil rights movement and by the free speech movement that originated in Berkeley. Although her mother had told her that the family was Konkow, they were tribally enrolled as Maidu in the 1960s.

After high school, Gould moved back and forth between Portland, Oregon, and Boulder, Colorado. In 1979 she returned to Berkeley to attend the University of California, where she earned her BA degree in linguistics, with high honors and distinction, in 1983 and her MA degree in English in 1987. She completed her PhD in English at the University of New Mexico in Albuquerque in 1995. Her focus is Native American literature with an emphasis on poetry.

Gould has published numerous poems in journals such as *Sinister Wisdom; Calyx: A Journal of Art and Literature by Women; Berkeley Poetry Review; Conceptions Southwest*; and *Fireweed: A Feminist Quarterly*, as well as in anthologies including *A Gathering of Spirit; Naming the Waves; Living the Spirit: A Gay American Indian Anthology*; and *Spider Woman's Granddaughters*. In 1989 she received a National Endowment for the Arts Award for her poetry. Her first book of poems, *Beneath My Heart*, was published in 1990.

Although she is primarily a poet, Gould has published one somewhat autobiographical short story, "Stories Don't Have Endings," under the pseudonym Misha Gallagher (her grandmother's first husband's last name). The story appears in *Spider Woman's Granddaughters: Traditional Tales and Contemporary Writings by Native American Women*, an anthology edited by Paula Gunn Allen. Scholarly and creative essays by Gould are in *Reinventing the Enemy's Language*, edited by Joy Harjo; *Decolonizing the Subject: Politics and Gender in Women's Autobiography*, edited by Sidonie Smith and Julia Watson; *Growing Up Different*, edited by Christian McEwen; and *An Intimate Wilderness*, edited by Ruth Gundle.

In addition to writing, Gould is a gifted musician. Like her mother, who studied voice, piano, and flute at the Juilliard School of Music and who gave private music lessons, Gould has studied and worked as a musician. In contrast to her mother's classical training, Gould prepared to be a folk musician. She studied oboe, guitar, mandolin, and accordion, and has performed an eclectic selection of music, from folk to country to Irish to Tex-Mex. Her best-known contribution, though, is her graceful and sensitive writing about the search for a personal and Native identity, a central theme for many Native American women writers.

References

Cochran, Jo, et al., eds. *Bearing Witness/Sobreviviendo: An Anthology of Native American/Latina Art and Literature. Special issue of Calyx: A Journal of Art and Literature by Women* 8 (1984).
Gould, Janice. *Alphabet*. Vasion Island, WA: May Day Press, 1996.
———. "American Indian Women's Poetry: Strategies of Rage and Hope." *Signs: Journal of Women Culture and Society* 204 (Summer 1995): 797–817.
———. *Beneath My Heart*. Ithaca, NY: Firebrand Books, 1990.
———. "Between Two Realms: Problems of Return in American Indian Women's Literature." PhD diss., University of New Mexico, 1987.
———. "Disobedience (in Language) in Texts by Lesbian Native Americans." *ARIEL* 25 (January 1994): 32, 44.
———. *Earthquake Weather*. Tucson: University of Arizona Press, 1996.
Wong, Hertha. Personal communication with Janice Gould, November 1990.
———. Written personal communication with Janice Gould, January 1991.

—*Hertha D. Wong*

GREEN, RAYNA DIANE (b. 1942), a Cherokee, was born in Dallas, Texas, and raised in Oklahoma. She received her BA (1963) and MA (1966) from Southern Methodist University, and her PhD (1973) in folklore and American Studies from Indiana University. She has taught at the University of Arkansas, the University of Massachusetts, the University of Maryland, Yale University, George Washington University, and Dartmouth College. From 1980 to 1983 Green directed the Native American Science Resource Center at Dartmouth. She also has served as director of the Project on Native Americans in Science at the American Association for the Advancement of Science, and has been president of the American Folklore Society. Her board memberships include those of the Indian Law Resource Center, the Ms. Foundation on Women, and the Phelps-Stoke Fund.

As a folklorist and cultural historian, Green has published material on Native American women, folk and material culture, Native American stereotypes, and contemporary Native American literature and art. Her interests range from scholarly publications to poetry and scriptwriting. She wrote the script for the film *More Than Bows and Arrows* and has contributed to several television productions.

Green has contributed numerous articles and reviews to such publications as *Ms., Southern Exposure, Folklore Forum, Signs*, and *Southern Folklore Quarterly*. She edited and contributed to *That's What She Said: A Collection of Poetry and Fiction by Contemporary Native American Women*, and wrote *Native American Women: A Contextual Bibliography*. Green has been the planner (1983–1985), and is now the director, of American Indian programs for the National Museum of American History at the Smithsonion Institution. She continues to write, research, and lecture in many fields, including program and policy development for Indian tribes and institutions, folklife, Native American studies, women's studies, museum studies, and ethnoscience.

References

Green, Rayna. "The Beaded Adidas." In *Time and Temperature: A Centennial Retrospective*. Edited by Charles Camp. Pp. 66–67. Washington, DC: American Folklore Society, 1989. Reprinted in *The Messenger* (Wheelwright Museum newsletter), 1989; *The Runner* (Smithsonion American Indian newsletter), 1990; Joseph Bruchac, ed., *Contemporary Cherokee Prose Writing*. Greenfield, NY: Greenfield Review Press, 1991.

———. "Contemporary Indian Humor." In *American Public Discourse: A Multicultural Perspective*. Edited by Ronald K. Burke. Pp. 22–28. Lanham, MD: University Press of America, 1992.

———. "Diary of a Native American Feminist." *Ms.* (July/August 1982): 170–172, 211–213.

———. *The Encyclopedia of the First Peoples of North America*. Toronto: Douglas and MacIntyre, 1999.

———. "The Image of the Indian in American Popular Culture." In *The Handbook of North American Indians*. Vol. 4. Edited by Wilcomb Washburn. Pp. 587–606. Washington, DC: Smithsonian Institution Press, 1988.

———. *Mythologizing Pocahontas*. Washington, DC: Smithsonian Institution Press, 1993.

———. "Native American Women." *Signs* 6 (1980): 248–267.

———. *Native American Women: A Contextual Bibliography*. Bloomington: Indiana University Press, 1983.

———. "Native American Women: The Leadership Paradox." *Women's Educational Equity Communications Network News and Notes* 1 (1980): 1, 4.

———. "On Looking in the Mirror of an Institution." *Northeast Indian Quarterly* 7 (1990): 30–32.

———. "The Pocahontas Perplex: The Image of Indian Women in Popular Culture." *Massachusetts Review* 16 (1975): 698–714.

———. Resource guides *Museums as Educational Tools for Indian Education; Resources in American Indian Performing Arts*; and *Resources in American Indian Literature*. Washington, DC: ORBIS Associates, 1986.

———. *Women in American Indian Society*. New York: Chelsea House, 1992.

———, ed. *That's What She Said: Contemporary Poetry and Fiction by Native American Women*. Bloomington: Indiana University Press, 1984.

Green, Rayna, and Lisa Thompson, comps. *American Indian Sacred Objects, Skeletal Remains, Repatriation and Reburial: A Resource Guide*. Washington, DC: American Indian Program, National Museum of American History, Smithsonian Institution, 1992.

—Laurie Lisa

GREENE, ALMA [Gah-Wonh-Nos-Doh] (1896–1983), was the author of two books of Mohawk culture and legend, and a clan mother and active member of the Six Nations Reserve. The daughter of a Turtle clan mother and a Confederacy Council representative, she lived on the reserve near Brantford, Ontario, her entire life. As a child she attended political meetings with her father, gaining there a sense of the erosion of Mohawk culture in the twentieth century that would fuel her later activities. She also was identified as having been born with a gift that would allow her to become a medicine woman. Her education in traditional medicine is outlined in her *Forbidden Voice: Reflections of a Mohawk Indian* (1972), which also contains many of the traditional stories she was told as a child. The book's title is a translation of her name, Gahwonh-nos-doh.

A second book, *Tales of the Mohawks* (1975), and includes more Mohawk stories and legends. According to family members and others who knew Greene, her intent with both books was to keep alive Mohawk traditions and culture, and to foster understanding between Native people and non–Natives. In addition to her published writing, Greene was a storyteller, medicine woman, and political activist. She achieved local notoriety for annually renewing a curse on a Brantford shopping mall that, she maintained, was built on land the Mohawks still owned.

Forbidden Voice did not find a publisher for six years after it was completed, but finally was printed by a British publisher, Hamlyn. It quickly became a best-seller in Canada, but when the initial press run sold out, Hamlyn declined to issue a second printing. Greene's family—especially her granddaughter Lori, a current clan mother—lobbied for years to get *Forbidden Voice* reissued. Finally, in 1997, it was reprinted by Green Dragon Press.

References

Greene, Alma. *Forbidden Voice: Reflections of a Mohawk Indian*. London: Hamlyn, 1972. Reprint, Toronto: Green Dragon Press, 1997.
———. *Tales of the Mohawks*. N.p.: J. M. Dent & Sons, 1975.

—*Ryan Simmons*

H

HAIL, RAVEN [Awo, Go-la-nv, Lynn Davis] (b. 1921), was born north of Dewey, in Washington County, Oklahoma, on land leased for oil drilling, and is an active member of the Cherokee Nation. She attended West Anthracite and Prairie Center elementary schools while living with her mother on their Cherokee land allotment near Welch (Craig County), Oklahoma, and later spent two years at Oklahoma State University and one at Southern Methodist University. A member of the Cherokee River Culture Church, she married and was divorced from Henry Frank Davis. Their only child, Henry, Jr., married Paulette Blessing; they have two children, Megan and Adam. After her divorce, Hail legally changed her surname to her mother's maiden name.

Her poetry and essays on Cherokee culture have appeared in various publications, including *The Cherokee Advocate, Arizona Women's Voice, The Clouds Threw This Light, The Remembered Earth, Poetry Dallas, Fiction International, Cimarron Review, The Herb Quarterly, Bestways Magazine*, and *Circle of Motion*.

Among Raven Hail's diverse accomplishments are a recording, *The Raven Sings*, consisting of Native American songs; *The Raven and the Redbird*, a three-act play about the life of Sam Houston and his Cherokee wife, Talihina (Diana) Rogers; and *The Raven Speaks*, originally published as a monthly newsletter between April 1968 and March 1972. She also has written three novels and a cookbook: *Windsong*, the story of Rebecca Bowles (the daughter of a Texas Cherokee named Warlord and wife of Sequoyah's son) and her experiences on the Texas frontier; *The Raven's Tales*, bilingual Cherokee legends; *The Pleiades Stones*, about a mysterious circle of stones and a journey into the unknown through the use of a magic crystal; and *Native American Foods (Foods the Indians Gave Us) Coloring Book*, a book of traditional recipes combined with a coloring book. Hail also lectures on many aspects of Cherokee culture and is an instructor in such traditional fields as beadwork, basketry, singing, dancing, and folklore.

Hail's unique style of prose is living "literature," at once domestic and aesthetic, which embraces a multifaceted, participatory interaction between teller and audience as she mixes prose, poetry, and visual elements while using both the English and the Cherokee languages. Her primary literary accomplishment is seguing from the Native oral tradition to the Euro-American literary-based novelistic form, thus preserving her Native American heritage.

References

Hail, Raven. *Cherokee Sacred Calendar of Natal Days*. Mesa, AZ: Raven Hail Books, 1998.

———. *The Magic Word*. Marvin, SD: Blue Cloud Abbey, 1971.

———. *Native American Foods (Foods the Indians Gave Us) Coloring Book*. Mesa, AZ: Raven Hail Books, 1979.

———. *The Pleiades Stones*. Mesa, AZ: Raven Hail Books, 1988.

———. *The Raven and the Redbird: Sam Houston and His Cherokee Wife*. Mesa, AZ: Raven Hail Books, 1965.

———. *The Raven Sings*. Wayfarer 1001-1. (33-1/3 rpm).

———. *Ravensong: Cherokee Indian Poetry*. Mesa, AZ: Raven Hail Books, 1995.

———. *The Raven Speaks: Cherokee Indian Lore in Cherokee and English*. Mesa, AZ: Raven Hail Books, 1987.

———. *Windsong, Texas Cherokee Princess: The Adventures of Rebecca Bowles on the Texas Frontier*. Mesa, AZ: Raven Hail Books, 1986.

—*Julie LaMay Abner*

HAILSTONE, VIVIEN (b. 1915), businesswoman, cultural consultant, educator, artisan, and political activist, was born to Geneva Orcutt (Yurok/Karok) and David Risling (Karok and a member of the Hupa tribe) in Morek, California. During her youth, there were no roads or stores in this area, and it wasn't until Hailstone started school that she first saw a non–Indian, the schoolmaster.

Hailstone's, great-grandmother Jane Young (Yurok) and her parents educated her in her people's traditions. For a time she worked in a sawmill her father owned

Vivien Hailstone

at Hoopa, doing whatever was needed, from manual labor to keeping books. During World War II, she moved to Eureka with her husband, Albert Hailstone, and their son, Albert, Jr.; there she learned welding and worked in shipyards. Later, she and her brother Anthony established a logging operation and built a new sawmill at Hoopa. Still later, she owned and operated an Indian gift shop.

Seeking to raise Indians' cultural pride in an era when they were made to feel ashamed of who they were, and realizing that traditional basketry materials were difficult to obtain, Hailstone became a founding member of a 1940s pottery guild that incorporated Indian basketry designs into its pottery. She served on a human rights commission that met in Eureka and, as a member (and later chair) of the College of the Redwoods Extension board of directors (1950s), was key in opening the way for an elder to teach northwest California Indian basketry and jewelry classes to interested Indians at the college. Those classes have now expanded in scope and location. Hailstone teaches basketry classes that incorporate Indian stories, history, songs, and language at D-Q University in Winters. Her jewelry pieces have won many awards.

In the 1960s, while raising an adopted son, Damon, Hailstone became concerned about teaching methods that promoted Indian stereotypes and assailed Indian children's pride. She became a founding member of Northern Indian California Education (NICE), and with the encouragement of her brother, David, helped initiate a grassroots organizing and lobbying effort in support of establishing the California Indian Education Association (CIEA). Once established, CIEA was the foundation for California Indian Legal Services, the National Indian Legal Service, and the Indian Teachers Educators program at Humboldt State University.

Hailstone assisted in the 1971 establishment of CIEA's Shasta County chapter, Local Indians for Education (LIFE), which became an independent, nonprofit corporation in 1978. In an effort to expand educational and economic opportunities for Indians, Hailstone helped organize classes in leather working, knitting, jewelry, airbrush painting, basketry, and sewing through the LIFE Center. This was the basis for the establishment of the Indian Art & Design gift shop concession (1980s) at Old Shasta State Park as an outlet for locally produced Indian arts.

As the first Indian to serve on the State of California Department of Parks and Recreation Commission (1970s), Hailstone helped promote Indian names for two parks and several park locales, a reburial policy for Indian remains and associated grave goods, a traditional materials-gathering policy for Indians, and the elimination of Indian stereotypes from park displays. As a Friends of the Museum member, Hailstone promoted a California State Indian Museum and collaborations between Indians and the state parks.

Hailstone's efforts furthered Indian pride, education, and political opportunities. She helped revitalize Indian skills in northwest California by blending these skills with nontraditional media and forms to create opportunities for their continuation while acknowledging Indians as people of today.

References

Ortiz, Bev. "Baskets of Dreams." *News from Native California* 2 (September/October 1988): 28–29.

———. "Beyond the Stereotypes." *News from Native California* 5 (November 1990/January 1991): 32–33.

———. Oral and taped interviews with Vivien Hailstone, 1988–1990.
———. Personal communication with Darlene Marshall, February 1991.

—Bev Ortiz

HALE, JANET CAMPBELL (b. 1946), poet, novelist, and teacher, was born in Riverside, California, and is a member of the Coeur d'Alene tribe of northern Idaho. As a child, she lived on the Coeur d'Alene, Colville, and Yakima reservations, and continues to have a strong connection with reservation life and tribal cultures.

Hale attended Wapato High School in Washington and transferred as a junior to the Institute of American Indian Arts in Santa Fe, New Mexico, where she pursued her interest in writing and the arts. In 1974 she received her BA from the University of California at Berkeley, then studied law at the University of California at Berkeley and Gonzaga Law School in Spokane, Washington. Since that time, Hale has earned her MA in English from the University of California at Davis (1984) and has taught literature courses at the University of California at Berkeley and Davis, D-Q University in Davis, Western Washington State University in Bellingham, the University of Oregon, and Lummi Community College in Bellingham, Washington.

Throughout her career, Hale has contributed to anthologies of both Native American and minority literature; her poems, as well as her novels, address the complexities of the modern Native American living in a multicultural world. Hale received positive reviews for *The Owl's Song*, which was praised it for its potential influence on young Americans' perceptions of tribal cultures. *The Jailing of Cecilia Capture* was nominated for the Pulitzer Prize as well as five other literary awards.

References

Allen, Terry D., ed. *The Whispering Wind*. Garden City, NY: Doubleday, 1972.
Bruchac, Joseph, ed. *The Next World: Poems by 32 Third World Americans*. Trumansburg, NY: Crossing Press, 1987.
———. *Songs from This Earth on Turtle's Back: Contemporary American Indian Poetry*. Greenfield Center, NY: Greenfield Review Press, 1983.
Colonese, Tom, and Louis Owens. *American Indian Novelists: An Annotated Critical Bibliography*. New York: Garland, 1985.
Dodge, Robert K., and Jospeh B. McCullough, eds. *Voices from Wah'Kon-tah*. New York: International Publishers, 1974.
Fisher, Dexter, ed. *The Third Woman: Minority Women Writers of the United States*. Boston: Houghton Mifflin, 1980.
Hale, Janet Campbell. *Bloodlines: Odyssey of a Native Daughter*. New York: Random House, 1993.
———. *Custer Lives in Humboldt County and Other Poems*. Greenfield Center, NY: Greenfield Review Press, 1978.
———. *The Jailing of Cecilia Capture*. New York: Random House, 1985.
———. *The Owl's Song*. New York: Doubleday, 1974.
———. *Women on the Run*. Moscow: University of Idaho Press, 1999.
Hobson, Geary, ed. *The Remembered Earth: An Anthology of Native American Literature*. Albuquerque, NM: Red Earth Press, 1979.

Lerner, Andrea, ed. *Dancing on the Rim of the World: An Anthology of Contemporary Northwest Native American Writing*. Tucson: University of Arizona Press, 1990.

Rosen, Kenneth. "American Indian Literature: Current Condition and Suggested Research." *American Indian Culture and Research Journal* 3 (1979): 57–66.

———, ed. *Voices of the Rainbow: Contemporary Poetry by American Indians*. New York: Viking, 1978.

—Michelle Savoy

HAMPTON, CAROL CUSSEN McDONALD (b. 1935), was born in Oklahoma City. A Caddo Indian, she received a BA degree in philosophy, and MA and PhD (1984) degrees in history, at the University of Oklahoma. Her scholarly work has been on the Native American Church. She has taught courses on Native American religions and philosophy at the University of Oklahoma, and she served as director of the American Indian Studies program at the University of Science and Arts of Oklahoma in Chickasha from 1981 to 1984. Hampton also served the Caddo tribe as a member of the tribal council from 1976 through 1983, and as tribal historian from 1979 to 1984. She was appointed a member of the Advisory Committee on Social Justice of the Oklahoma State Regents for Higher Education in 1983. From 1985 to 1987 she was associate director of the Consortium for Graduate Opportunities for American Indians in Berkeley, California, and was codirector of a National Endowment for the Humanities summer institute for college teachers, "Great Traditions in American Indian Thought," held at Berkeley in the summer of 1987. She was appointed national field officer for the American Indian/Alaska Native Ministry of the Episcopal Church in 1987, and she is a member of the Joint Strategy Action Committee, of the Indian Ministries Task Force and a commissioner of the Programme to Combat Racism, a program of the World Council of Churches.

In addition to her work with Indian programs, Hampton has been active in a number of civic organizations in Oklahoma City, including the Junior League, the Oklahoma Symphony Board, the Oklahoma Art Center, the Oklahoma Heritage Association, and the Oklahoma Foundation for the Humanities. She is also a member of a number of professional societies in the field of history, including the Western History Association, the Organization of American Historians, and the American Historical Association. She is a founding member of the Association of American Indian Historians.

Hampton and her husband live in Oklahoma City. They have four children and four grandchildren. During the 1996 to 1997 academic year, Hampton studied at Phillips Theological Seminary in Oklahoma in preparation for ordination to the Episcopal priesthood.

Reference

Anderson, Owanah, ed. *Ohoyo One Thousand: A Resource Guide of American Indian/Alaska Native Women, 1982*. Wichita Falls, TX: Ohoyo Resource Center, 1982.

—Clara Sue Kidwell

HARDIN, HELEN BAGSHAW [Little Corn Tassels, Tsa-sah-wee-ah, Little Standing Spruce] (1943–1984), was born in Albuquerque, New Mexico, to a Santa Clara Pueblo mother, Pablita Velarde, and an Anglo father, Herbert Hardin. By the age of thirty-five, Hardin had become one of the leading contemporary Indian women artists. Much of her childhood was spent at Santa Clara Pueblo among her mother's people. This daughter of an internationally renowned painter (her mother) won her first prize for a drawing when she was six and, as a child, sold pictures at the Gallup Ceremonial with her mother. For most of her life, Hardin lived and was educated in the Anglo world, and frequently described herself as "Anglo socially and Indian in [her] art." She graduated in 1961 from St. Pius X High School in Albuquerque, where she concentrated on art. Subsequently, she studied art history and anthropology at the University of New Mexico and attended a special school for Indian Arts at the University of Arizona, funded by the Rockefeller Foundation. In 1962, at the age of nineteen, Hardin had her first one-woman show at Coronado Monument. Two years later she gave birth to a daughter, Margarete, and had her first "formal" gallery show at the Enchanted Mesa in Albuquerque.

In 1968 Hardin separated herself from difficult relationships with her mother and with Pat Terrazas, the father of her child, by visiting her father in Bogotá, Colombia. While there, she had a very successful show at the American embassy, which led to another, three years later, in Guatemala City. This was followed by numerous exhibitions at home and abroad and many Grand Awards, Best of Show, and First Prizes at the National Indian Arts Exhibition in Scottsdale, Arizona; the Santa Fe Indian Market, the Philbrook Art Center in Tulsa, Oklahoma; and the Inter-Tribal Ceremonial at Gallup, New Mexico, among others. Hardin has been featured in national magazines, including *Seventeen*, when she was in high school, and a cover story in *New Mexico Magazine*, in 1970. She was also featured in the 1976 PBS series on American Indian artists. Her art has been reproduced in many contexts, and during her lifetime she received several commissions, notably from the Franklin Mint, to design coins for the series History of the American Indian, and from Clarke Industries, to illustrate two of their children's books.

Eschewing the "tourist-pleasing clichés" of many Indian painters, Hardin developed a contemporary and highly individual art influenced by Joe H. Herrera—an art that seems both old and new, combining modern techniques with tribal images and mythic figures: "I use tradition as a springboard and go diving into my paints." Her point of departure is the "ancient art history of my own people, as evidenced on the walls of caves and pottery of the Pueblo." Using acrylics, acrylic varnish, inks, washes, and architects' templates with precision, discipline, and control, this "high priestess of the protractor" created spiritual surfaces that have frequently been likened to those of Klee and Kandinsky. In more Native terms, her paintings revitalized an "art," like kiva murals and sandpainting, that was/is a ritual to restore the harmony of natural forces through the intuitive placement of life and color. Her artistic recognition in the last decade of her life was combined with a happy marriage to an Anglo photographer, Cradoc Bagshaw; a highly successful venture into etching beginning in 1980; and civic work related to the arts. She served as a member of the Board of Directors of the Southwest Association of Indian Affairs and of the Wheelwright Museum in Santa Fe. They lived in Tesuque and then in Albuquerque, where she died of cancer in 1984.

References

Culley, LouAnn Faris. "Helen Hardin: A Retrospective." *American Indian Art* 4 (1979): 68–75.

DeLaurer, Marjel. "Helen Hardin." *Arizona Highways* 52 (August 1976): 28–29, 44–45.

Hardin, Helen. "Helen Hardin, Tewa Painter." In *This Song Remembers: Self-Portraits of Native Americans in the Arts*. Edited by Jane B. Katz. Pp. 116–123. Boston: Houghton Mifflin, 1980.

Scott, Jay. *Changing Woman: The Life and Art of Helen Hardin*. Flagstaff, AZ: Northland Publishers, 1989.

Wilks, Flo. "A Spiritual Escape from the World of Reality." *Southwest Art* (August 1978): 66–69.

—*Barbara A. Babcock*

HARJO, JOY (b. 1951), was born in Tulsa, Oklahoma, to Allen W. (Creek) and Wynema Baker Foster. She is the mother of two children, Phil Dayn and Rainy Dawn.

Harjo attended high school at the Institute of American Indian Arts in Santa Fe, New Mexico. In 1976 she received her BA at the University of New Mexico, Albuquerque, and in 1978 her MFA at the University of Iowa. In 1978 to 1979 she was an instructor at the Institute of American Indian Arts, and in 1980 to 1981 a part-time instructor in creative writing and poetry at Arizona State University. She has also taught at the University of Colorado, Boulder, and at the University of Arizona. Since 1991 she has taught creative writing at the University of New Mexico, Albuquerque.

Harjo is on the Board of Directors of the National Association for Third World Writers, on the policy panel of the National Endowment for the Arts, and a member of the Board of Directors of the Native American Public Broadcasting Consortium. She is also contributing editor of *Contact II* and *Tyuony*, and the poetry editor of *High Plains Literary Review*.

Joy Harjo

Her third book of poetry, *She Had Some Horses*, was highly praised, and her *In Mad Love and War* won the Poetry Society of America's William Carlos Williams Award; the Delmore Schwartz Memorial Poetry Prize, sponsored by New York University; and the PEN Oakland Josephine Miles Award.

Her Creek heritage, history, and mythology are very important elements in Harjo's creative process and her poetry. Her ethnic background deeply affects her relationship with the land, a geography of the remembered earth that in her work has three physical directions that are spectacular and complementary: the Oklahoma red earth, the land of her people and her childhood; the Southwest and the desert landscape, which in many instances convey the sense of a mythic womanhood; and a direction that has its center in Alabama—the tribal land of the Creeks before the Removal Act—a land that is the original place, lost forever and forever re-created in the original memory.

Harjo's powerful poetic language creates images of beauty and images of grief, looking for perfection of love in all its manifestations. The rhythm is very often the incantatory, ceremonial sound of the old Indian chants, that Indian oral tradition in which, in Harjo's words "the knowledge was kept by remembering." And for that very reason, memory "swims deep in blood/a delta in the skin. . . ."

Her creative abilities encompass not only poetry but also scriptwriting, filmmaking, and playing "tribal-jazz-reggae" with her band Poetic Justice.

Harjo's most recent poetry collection is *The Woman Who Fell from the Sky*, of which Adrienne Rich said: "I turn and return to Harjo's poetry for her heartbreaking, complex witness and for her world-remaking language: precise, unsentimental, miraculous."

The Spiral of Memory, a collection of her interviews, builds up a mosaic that brings Harjo as a poet and Harjo as an artist into ever sharper focus.

References

Allen, Paula Gunn. "Answering the Deer: Genocide and Continuance in the Poetry of American Indian Women." In *The Sacred Hoop*. Edited by Allen. Pp. 155–164. Boston: Beacon Press, 1986.

"Bibliography of Fourteen Native American Poets: Joy Harjo." *SAIL* 9 (supp.) (1985): 18–23.

Bruchac, Joseph. "The Arms of Another Sky: Joy Harjo." In *The Sacred Hoop*. Edited by Paula Gunn Allen. Pp. 165–183. Boston: Beacon Press, 1986.

———. "Interview with Joy Harjo." *North Dakota Quarterly* 53 (Spring 1985): 220–234.

———, ed. *Survival This Way: Interviews with American Indian Poets*. Pp. 87–103. Tucson: University of Arizona Press, 1987.

Coltelli, Laura. "Joy Harjo." In *Winged Words: American Indian Writers Speak*. Pp. 55–68. Lincoln: University of Nebraska Press, 1990.

———, ed. *The Spiral of Memory: Interviews. Joy Harjo*. Ann Arbor: University of Michigan Press, 1996.

Harjo, Joy. *Fishing*. Browerville, MN: Ox Head, 1992.

———. *In Mad Love and War*. Middletown, CT: Wesleyan University Press, 1990.

———. *The Last Song*. Las Cruces, NM: Puerto del Sol Press, 1975.

————. "Ordinary Spirit." In *I Tell You Now: Autobiographical Essays by Native American Writers*. Edited by Brian Swann and Arnold Krupat. Pp. 263–270. Lincoln: University of Nebraska Press, 1987.

————. *Secrets from the Center of the World*. Sun Tracks series, vol. 17. Tucson: University of Arizona Press, 1989.

————. *She Had Some Horses*. New York: Thunder's Mouth Press, 1983.

————. *What Moon Drove Me to This*. New York: I. Reed, 1979.

————. *The Woman Who Fell from the Sky*. New York: Norton, 1994.

Harjo, Joy, Gloria Bird, Patricia Blanco, et al., eds. *Reinventing the Enemy's Language: Contemporary Native Women's Writing of North America*. New York: W. W. Norton, 1997.

Jaskoski, Helen. "A *MELUS* Interview: Joy Harjo." *MELUS* 16 (1989–1990): 5–13.

Kallet, Marilyn. "In Love and War." *Kenyon Review* 15 (Summer 1993): 57–66.

Leen, Mary. "An Art of Saying: Joy Harjo's Poetry of Storytelling." *American Indian Quarterly* 19 (1995): 1–16.

Ruppert, James. "Paula Gunn Allen and Joy Harjo: Closing the Distance Between Personal and Mythic Space." *American Indian Quarterly* 7 (Winter 1983): 27–40.

Scarry, John. "Representing Real Worlds: The Evolving Poetry of Joy Harjo." In *From This World: Contemporary American Indian Literature*. Special issue of *World Literature Today* 66 (1991): 286–291.

Smith, Stephanie Izarek. "Joy Harjo." *Poets and Writers Magazine* 21 (July/August 1993): 22–27.

Wiget, Andrew. "Nightriding with Noni Daylight: The Many Horse Songs of Joy Harjo." In *Native American Literatures*. Edited by Laura Coltelli. Pp. 185–196. Pisa: Seu, 1989.

—Laura Coltelli

HARJO, SUZAN SHOWN (b. 1945), a Cherokee/Muskogee, is the president and executive director of the Morning Star Institute, which was founded in 1984 to secure statutory protection for Native peoples' sacred sites and religious freedom. An active leader on repatriation, she served as the executive director of the National Congress of American Indians from 1984 to 1989, acted as the national coordinator for The 1992 Alliance, served as trustee and chair of the Program Planning Committee for the National Museum of the American Indian, and was the cofounder of Native Children's Survival.

Harjo is married to Frank Ray Harjo and is the mother of Adriane and Duke. As a result of her personal interest in the arts (she is an actress, a singer, and a writer of poetry), Harjo has expanded the role of the Morning Star Institute to include the advancement of cultures, traditions, and arts of Native people. With her husband, she coproduced *Seeing Red* for WBAI-FM. She also was one of the founders of a New York City improvisational group, Spiderwoman Theatre Company.

Born and raised in rural Oklahoma, Harjo spent her early teen years in Naples, Italy, where her father was serving in the U.S. Army. She lived for many years in

New York City before relocating to Washington, D.C., in order to commit herself to more hands-on advocacy for Native peoples' rights. Before joining the National Congress of American Indians, she served as a legislative liaison for a law firm and a congressional liaison for Indian affairs during the Carter administration.

References

Gamarekian, Barbara. "Working Profiles: Suzan Harjo, Lobbying for a Native Cause." *New York Times*, April 2, 1986.

Harjo, Suzan Shown. "Guest Essay." *Native Peoples* 7 (Winter 1994): 5.

———. "Visions from Native America: Contemporary Art for the Year of Indigenous Peoples." *Encounters* 10 (Fall 1992): 40–41.

Howard, Jane. "An American Crusader: Suzan Shown Harjo of Washington, D.C." *Lear's* 2 (July/August 1989): 135–136.

—Susan L. Rockwell

HARNAR, NELLIE SHAW (1905–1985), a Neh-muh or Northern Paiute, was born in Wadsworth, Nevada, on the Pyramid Lake Reservation. Her parents, James and Margie Shaw, had nine children. Harnar attended day school in Wadsworth but also learned the songs and legends of the tribe from the elders. She attended Carson Indian School at Stewart, Nevada, and graduated from Carson City High School and the Normal Training Course at Haskell Institute in Lawrence, Kansas. She received a BA in elementary education degree from Northern Arizona University in 1936 and an MA degree from the University of Nevada at Reno in 1965. Her master's thesis, which she dedicated to her people, the Neh-muh, was *The History of the Pyramid Lake Indians—1843 to 1959*. Along with her formal education, she maintained her fluency in Paiute and her interest in the stories, history, and traditions of her tribe. She dedicated her life to teaching and counseling in Bureau of Indian Affairs schools in Arizona, Kansas, New Mexico, Wyoming, and Nevada.

Throughout her life Harnar was active in many state and national service, social, and honorary societies, supporting the movement in Nevada to get monuments erected to the memory of Sarah Winnemucca (Hopkins) and Louisa Kizer (Dat-So-La-Lee); in 1975 she was named Nevada's Outstanding Woman of the Year.

Baptized and confirmed in the Episcopal Church, she married Curtis Sequoyah Harnar; they had one son, Curtis, Jr. She and her husband spent their retirement years on the Pyramid Lake Reservation, and she died in Reno. She is respectfully remembered by educators and historians, Anglo and Indian alike, and she made a significant impression upon all who met her.

References

"Harnar, Nellie Shaw." Computer biography on file. Alumni Association, University of Nevada, Reno.

Harnar, Nellie Shaw. *The History of the Pyramid Lake Indians, 1843–1959, and Early Tribal History, 1825–1834*. Sparks, NV: Dave's Printing and Publishing, 1974.

————. *The Indians of Coo-Yu-Ee Pah (Pyramid Lake): The History of the Pyramid Lake Indians in Nevada.* Sparks, NV: Western Printing and Publishing, 1974.

"Nellie Shaw Harner." *Indian Historian* 2 (October 1965): 17.

—*Gretchen Ronnow*

HARRIS, LADONNA (b. 1931), president and executive director of Americans for Indian Opportunity, was born in Temple, Oklahoma, to a Comanche mother and an Irish–American father. She spent her early years with her maternal grandparents, speaking only Comanche until she started school. As a result of her involvement in civil rights issues and her political contacts, gained firsthand during her husband's (Fred R. Harris) tenure as state senator and as a U.S. Congressman, Harris organized the first intertribal organization in Oklahoma in the early 1960s. Oklahomans for Indian Opportunity (OIO) brought together sixty tribes for purposes of economic development. During this era, Harris's current hometown, Lawton, was not yet integrated, so OIO was a vanguard organization.

With her husband's move to Washington, D.C., Harris became involved with feminist issues and was one of the first members of the National Women's Political Caucus. In recognition of this and many other groundbreaking projects, Harris was named to President Gerald Ford's U.S. Commission on the Observance of International Women's Year. By this time she had nurtured her national version of OIO, Americans for Indian Opportunity (AIO), for several years. With the recognition of President Ford, and later of President Jimmy Carter, Harris's organization grew and became a very influential force in the economic development of Indian Country. Always busy with numerous intersecting plans, Harris simultaneously served as special adviser to Sargent Shriver in the Office of Economic Opportunity and on the National Committee for Full Employment and the National Commission on the Mental Health of Children. An outgrowth of her investigations into the various methods of reaching full employment and seeking economic development of depressed areas was the founding of the Council of Energy Resources Tribes, a controversial but still very influential group.

An untiring advocate of Indian self-determination, Harris has continuously revamped AIO to meet the changing needs of Native communities. The organization has been involved in Indian youth programs, conflict resolution, and the formation of venues in which Natives can identify, discuss, and determine problem-solving plans for local concerns. AIO is also involved in international indigenous concerns, with plans to study indigenous populations in Africa, the Pacific, Central America, and the former Soviet Union.

A frequent lecturer, Harris has also taught at the School of the Institute for Policy Studies in Washington, D.C. She has several honorary degrees, including a doctor of laws from Dartmouth. She is the mother of three, including Katherine Harris Tijerina, president of the newly reorganized Institute of American Indian Arts in Santa Fe, New Mexico. Harris is a board member of many organizations, among them the National Organization for Women, Save the Children, and the National Urban League. In 1979 *Ladies Home Journal* named her Woman of the Year and of the Decade.

References

Harris, LaDonna. "American Indian Education and Pluralism." In *Contemporary Native American Addresses*. Edited by John R. Maestas. Pp. 96–104. Provo, UT: Brigham Young University, 1976.

Josephy, Alvin M. *Now that the Buffalo's Gone*. New York: Alfred A. Knopf, 1982.

"LaDonna Harris." Americans for Indian Opportunity information packet. Pp. 23–25. AOI, 1987.

Morris, Terry. "LaDonna Harris: A Woman Who Gives a Damn." *Redbook* (February 1970): 74, 115, 117–118.

Philip, Kenneth, ed. *Indian Self Rule*. Chicago: Howe Brothers, 1986.

Who's Who of the American Indian. New York: Todd, 1986.

—*Cynthia Kasee*

HATCH, VIOLA (b. 1930), an Arapaho born on her grandmother's allotment near Gary, Oklahoma, was the daughter of traditional chiefs and was taught to conduct herself accordingly. Her activism began at Concho Indian Boarding School in the fifth grade. Left in unfamiliar surroundings, she comforted a tearful younger girl, overcoming her own worries by helping another. Thwarted in her educational pursuits by a Bureau of Indian Affairs (BIA) agent who insisted she study to be a matron, Hatch moved to Chicago under the BIA relocation program, which largely abandoned country-bred relocatees in fast-paced cities. Having two sisters there, Hatch immediately found work at the Spiegel Company.

After returning to Oklahoma, she married Don Hatch. While helping her husband with union organizing, Hatch began her work as an activist. She opened senior citizen and Indian youth centers, fed the homeless, and started a Native American women's beadwork cooperative. She also hosted VISTA volunteers and persuaded people to run for offices at all levels. This work often got her fired, but it also got her recognized. In 1968 she became one of six women on the American Indian Task Force.

In the early 1970s, with the National Indian Youth Council (NIYC) and American Indian Movement, (AIM), Hatch helped take over the Oklahoma State Department of Indian Education when they discovered and exposed the school system's misuse of millions of federal dollars intended for Native American students since 1935. When her fifth-grade son was expelled for wearing his hair in a traditional manner, Hatch won a ruling in the 10th Circuit Court that set a fairness precedent for all students.

Since 1981 Hatch has been elected to tribal offices: the Business Committee several times; vice chair (1987 – 1988); treasurer (1989 – 1990); and chair (1994). She obtained grants for wastewater treatment and stopped hazardous dumping sites. For questioning the previous chair's financial and managerial abuses, she was indicted and removed from office, but the 10th Circuit Court of Appeals dismissed the case. Nevertheless, the federal prosecutor told Hatch the government intended to make an example of her, then go after all the other tribes because "white taxpayers are tired of you Indians wasting their money."

In the midst of this court battle, Hatch organized the Women's Healing Walk for Family and Mother Earth, from Los Angeles to St. Augustine, Florida (February 11 to July 11, 1996). Challenging nuclear dumping, desecration of burial mounds, and other injustices, they held ceremonies along the way, a cleansing rite in St. Augustine, and a closing ceremony at the Arapaho Sundance at Wind River, Wyoming. She also formed Women Warriors, a group that continues her struggle to benefit children, her community, her nation, and all people. Hatch is supported in her work by her husband; their three children, Danita Sue, Holly, and Buddy; and their six grandchildren. Through it all she asks, "When will people realize that dark-skinned people are human beings? The Creator put us all here together for a reason. To mistreat anyone is to criticize the Creator."

Reference

Zweig, Bella. Personal communication with Viola Hatch, November 1996.

—Bella Zweig

HENRY, JEANNETTE (b. 1908), was born to the Turtle clan of the Carolina Cherokee. She married Rupert Costo in 1950. Together they founded the American Indian Historical Society in 1962 and the Indian Historian Press in 1969. They have been responsible for publishing *Wassaja*, a national newspaper; *The Indian Historian*, a quarterly journal; and *The Weewish Tree*, a children's magazine. The organizations and publications seek to educate and inform Indians on national Indian issues, controversies, and opportunities for cooperation between Indian media and people.

References

Bahr, Donald, and Susan Fenger. "Indians and Missions: Homage to and Debate with Rupert Costo and Jeannette Henry." *Journal of the Southwest* 31 (Fall 1989): 300–321.

Costo, Rupert, and Jeannette Henry. *Indian Treaties: Two Centuries of Dishonor*. San Francisco: Indian Historian Press, 1977.

——, *The Missions of California: A Legacy of Genocide*. San Francisco: Indian Historian Press, 1987.

——, eds. *American Indian Reader*. vol. 4 San Francisco: Indian Historical Press, 1974.

——, eds. *A Thousand Years of American Indian Storytelling*. San Francisco: Indian Historian Press, 1981.

——, eds. *Natives of the Golden State: The California Indians*. San Francisco: Indian Historian Press, 1995.

——, eds. *Textbooks and the American Indian*. San Francisco: Indian Historian Press, 1970.

Henry, Jeannette, ed. *American Indian Reader*. vols. 1–3 San Francisco: Indian Historian Press, 1972–1973.

—Julie A. Russ

HETH, CHARLOTTE ANNE WILSON (b. 1937), was born in Muskogee, Oklahoma, and is the former chair of the Department of Ethnomusicology and Systematic Musicology at the University of California at Los Angeles (UCLA). She is a member of the Cherokee Nation of Oklahoma. She received her BA and MA degrees in music at the University of Tulsa, and a Ford Foundation fellowship to complete her PhD in ethnomusicology at UCLA in 1975. Her doctoral dissertation was an analysis of Cherokee Stomp Dance music in Oklahoma. She has taught music at the high school and college level, and served for two-years in the Peace Corps in Ethiopia, where she taught English to high school students. She joined the faculty of the Music Department at UCLA in 1974, and she served as director of the American Indian Studies Center there from 1976 to 1987. During that period, she coordinated the development and implementation of the first American Indian Studies master's degree program. From 1987 to 1989 she was director of the American Indian Studies Program at Cornell University, then returned to UCLA in 1989. She retired in 1994 and became assistant director of public programs at the National Museum of the American Indian at the Smithsonian Institution.

In addition to teaching and administration, Heth has remained active in research. She has produced six record albums and eight videotapes of Indian music, and coauthored a needs assessment on American Indian higher education. She has received grants from federal and state agencies to do research on Cherokee hymns and the Iroquois condolence ceremony, as well as postdoctoral fellowships from the D'Arcy McNickle Center for the History of the American Indian at the Newberry Library in Chicago and from the Ford Foundation.

Heth has been a consultant to numerous arts organizations and media projects, and was the primary music consultant for the highly acclaimed television series *Roanoak*, which appeared on PBS in 1987. She has been a member of the Advisory Committee of the American Folklife Program at the Smithsonian Institution, the California Council for the Humanities, the Advisory Council of the D'Arcy McNickle Center for the History of the American Indian at the Newberry Library,

Charlotte Anne Wilson Heth

and numerous other advisory boards and committees. She is also active in the Society for Ethnomusicology. As a musician and educator, Heth has played a significant role in disseminating information about American Indian music to Indian and non–Indian audiences nationally. Through her work with the American Indian Studies Center at UCLA, she has been instrumental in offering opportunities for graduate study to many American Indian students. Her primary research interests are in American Indian music and dance and American Indian education. She is the general editor of *Native American Dance: Ceremonies and Social Traditions*, published by the National Museum of the American Indian.

References

Heth, Charlotte, ed. *Native American Dance: Ceremonies and Social Traditions*. Washington, DC: National Museum of the American Indian, Smithsonian Institution, with Starwood Pub., 1992.

————, ed. *Selected Reports in Ethnomusicology* vol. 3 of *Music of the American Indians*. Los Angeles: UCLA Dept. Ethnom.

Who's Who in American Music. New York: R. R. Bowker, 1983.

Who's Who in the West. Chicago: Marquis Who's Who, 1949–.

Who's Who of American Women. Chicago: Marquis Who's Who, 1958–.

—*Clara Sue Kidwell*

HIGHWALKING, BELLE (1892–1971), was born on the Northern Cheyenne Reservation in Montana. Because her mother died in childbirth, Highwalking was raised by her paternal grandmother while her father, Teeth, served in a special corps of Cheyenne scouts for the U.S. Army at Fort Keogh until they were disbanded in 1895. At that time he became a policeman on the reservation, and Highwalking and her grandmother lived with him and her stepmother in Lame Deer. Her father married six times; of all his children, only Highwalking and her brother, John Teeth, survived. One other brother, John Stands In Timber, from her mother's first marriage, was the author of *Cheyenne Memories*. Highwalking's maternal grandmother, Blackbird Woman, was a Crow, and Highwalking often visited the nearby Crow Reservation.

Highwalking attended Busby School, at which her uncle Red Hat taught. She and Floyd Highwalking were married by a Mennonite minister on January 23, 1912. They attended the Catholic Church briefly, but the death of her daughter and the priest's objections to her Cheyenne peyote meetings led Highwalking to leave. She was pleased that the Mennonite Church taught her to read the Bible in Cheyenne and included her on their committees even when she was old.

Highwalking had many children, all delivered at home; the last daughter, Theresa, was born when her youngest brother was fifteen. She and her husband often traveled to other reservations in North Dakota, Wyoming, Oklahoma, and New Mexico. Floyd died in July 1964, and in later life Highwalking lived with her oldest son, George Hiwalker, until her death on October 30, 1971.

Highwalking told her life history to Katherine M. Weist, partly in English and partly in Cheyenne, beginning the interviews at Weist's home in Missoula, Montana, in 1970 and finishing the recordings a month before she died. Her daughter-in-law, Helen Hiwalker, translated the Cheyenne tapes in preparation for Weist's editing of Highwalking's narrative, which was published in 1979.

References

Stands in Timber, John, and Margot Liberty. *Cheyenne Memories*. New Haven, CT: Yale University Press, 1967.

Weist, Katherine M. "Giving Away: The Ceremonial Distribution of Goods Among the Northern Cheyenne of Southeastern Montana." *Plains Anthropologist* 18 (1973): 97–103.

———. "The Northern Cheyennes: Diversity in a Loosely Structured Society." PhD diss. Ann Arbor, MI: University Microfilms, 1970.

———, ed. *Belle Highwalking: The Narrative of a Northern Cheyenne Woman*. Billings: Montana Council for Indian Education, 1979.

—*Thelma Shinn Richard*

HILBERT, VI [Taq^{WV}Seblu] (b. 1918), is an Upper Skagit elder born in Lyman, Washington. A linguist, educator, and storyteller, she has devoted much of her life to the study, promotion, and preservation of her childhood language, Lushootseed Salish, and the oral literature and culture of her people. A quarter-century of unflagging research has resulted in a remarkable collection of audiotapes and videotapes of Lushootseed language, oral history, and cultural information shared by elders from the Skagit and neighboring communities. Hilbert has carefully transcribed and translated the materials into English, making available information that otherwise would have been lost to future generations of Lushootseed people. Working with low-quality, early recordings, she also has transcribed and translated a large body of material in Lushootseed taped by anthropologists twenty years before she began her research, at a time when many elders still spoke only Lushootseed. Many of these elders were the best storytellers of their time, and Hilbert sought to preserve this art form by memorizing their works, and analyzing and emulating their traditional type in classes on Lushootseed language and literature at the University of Washington. She translated several such stories into English and edited them in *Haboo: Native American Stories from Puget Sound*.

Vi Hilbert

When Hilbert retired from teaching in 1988, her former students begged her to tell the stories publicly, and she became a storyteller. Her unique blend of the traditional language with line-by-line English translation, uncommon in oral performance, has delighted audiences all over the world; she is frequently invited to speak and tell stories by Native groups, the National Association of Professional Storytellers, various local storytelling groups, and educators at all levels. Throughout her public storytelling career, she has continued her research. Her collaboration with linguists and anthropologists has produced two grammars and several research papers, a volume of texts in Lushootseed with English translations, and a revised and expanded version of the only dictionary of the language. She is also involved in a project to archive her collection.

References

Bates, Dawn, Thom Hess, and Vi Hilbert. *Lushootseed Dictionary*. Seattle: University of Washington Press, 1994.

Bierwert, Crisca, ed. *Lushootseed Texts: An Introduction to Puget Salish Narrative Aesthetics*. Narrated by Emma Conrad, Martha Lamont, and Edward (Hagen) Sam. Translated by Crisca Bierwert, Vi Hilbert, and Thomas M. Hess. Lincoln: University of Nebraska Press American Studies Research Institute, 1996.

Hess, Thom, and Vi Hilbert. *Lushootseed I and II*. Seattle: Daybreak Star Press United Indians of All Tribes Foundation, 1976.

Hilbert, Vi. *Haboo: Native American Stories from Puget Sound*. Seattle: University of Washington Press, 1985.

———. "To a Different Canoe: The Lasting Legacy of Lushootseed Heritage." In *A Time of Gathering: Native American Heritage in Washington State*. Edited by Robin K. Wright. Thomas Burke Memorial Washington State Museum Monograph 7. Seattle: University of Washington Press, 1991.

—Dawn Bates

HILDEN, PATRICIA PENN (b. 1944), a Wallowa Nez Perce, was born in Los Angeles. She received her BA in English and history at the University of California, Berkeley, in 1965. After finishing her BA, she worked for EOP and other War on Poverty programs before returning to graduate school to earn her MA in American history in 1977. In 1981 Hilden was awarded an MA and PhD in history by Cambridge University. After a year as a fellow of Trinity Hall, Cambridge, she returned to the United States and taught at Emory University in Atlanta from 1982 to 1995. During 1993 to 1995 she was a visiting professor at New York University. Hilden has been at the University of California, Berkeley, since 1995 as a professor of comparative ethnic studies.

Hilden has written a book on socialist politics in France and another on women industrial workers in Belgium, titled *Women, Work, and Politics: Belgium, 1830 to 1914* (1993). *When Nickels Were Indians: An Urban, Mixed-Blood Story* was published by the Smithsonian Institution Press in 1993 and 1995. She has written a book with Shari Huhndorf titled *Fry Bread and Wild West Shows: American's "Indians," America's Museums*, which is currently being reviewed for publication.

Hilden has also published book reviews and several essays. Her most recent essays are "Ritchie Valens Is Dead: E Pluribus Unum," in *As We Are Now: Mixblood Essays on Race and Identity* and "Displacements: Performing Mestizaje" in *Everything Matters*. Hilden's current research work is on the North American Indian slave trade in the Caribbean from 1630 to 1750. She is the director of Ethic Studies at the University of Oregon.

References

Hilden, Patricia Penn. "Displacements: Performing Mestizaje." In *Everything Matters: Autobiographical Essays by Native American Writers*. Edited by Arnold Krupat and Brian Swann. New York: Random House, 1998.

———. "Ritchie Valens Is Dead: E Pluribus Unum." In *As We Are Now: Mixblood Essays on Race and Identity*. Edited by William S. Penn. Berkeley: University of California Press, 1997.

Tronsen, Kay. Electronic communication with Patricia Penn Hilden, April 16, 1998.

—*Kay Tronsen*

HILL, JOAN (b.?) originally from Muskogee, Oklahoma, is a painter and advocate for the arts. Her family lineage includes chiefs of the Cherokee and Creek nations. Her Indian name is Chea-se-quah, which means Redbird. She studied art with Dick West, a famous Cheyenne artist, at Bacone College in Muskogee, and taught for four years in the Tulsa public schools before resigning to devote herself full-time to her art. Her paintings are in the permanent collections of the United States Department of the Interior, the Philbrook Art Center in Tulsa, the Heard Museum in Phoenix, the Museum of the American Indian in New York City, and the Smithsonian Institution in Washington, D.C. She has won 255 awards, including the Grand Master Award from the Five Civilized Tribes Museum in Muskogee, the Waite

Joan Hill

Phillips Special Artists Trophy from the Philbrook Museum, a special commission award from the Daybreak Star Indian Center in Seattle, and a commemorative medal from Great Britain. She has traveled and studied in thirty-six foreign countries with the T. H. Hewitt painting workshops. Her most memorable participation was in the first Painters Cultural Interchange with the People's Republic of China. Photographs of a one-woman show of her work are still being circulated in China.

Hill's best-known work is characterized by a traditional style and content, which is sometimes inspired by dreams of incidents told to her by her parents and grandparents. It is also characterized by extensive research in historical documents to assure complete authenticity of detail. She works primarily in acrylics, but is also skilled with watercolors, which are generally abstract.

Hill has served the state of Oklahoma as a member of the Oklahoma Curriculum Improvement Commission and as a member of the Governor's Commission on the Status of Women.

The power of Hill's paintings comes from her natural talent, the support and encouragement of her parents during her youth, and her pride in her Indian heritage. She has honed her skill in painting and her scrupulous attention to historical detail to become one of the outstanding Indian painters of the twentieth century.

References

Strickland, Rennard. *Native American Art at Philbrook*. Tulsa, OK: Philbrook Art Center, 1980.

Who's Who in American Art. New York: American Federation of the Arts R. R. Bowker, 1978.

Who's Who of American Women. Chicago: Marquis Who's Who, 1958—.

—Clara Sue Kidwell

HOGAN, LINDA (b. 1947), was born in Denver to Charles Henderson (Chickasaw) and Cleona Bower. She is divorced and the mother of two adopted daughters, Sandra Dawn Protector and Tanya Thunder Horse.

She received her MA in English and creative writing in 1978 from the University of Colorado at Boulder. In 1979 Hogan was one of the organizers of the Colorado Cultural Program and was poet-in-the-schools for the states of Colorado and Oklahoma. In 1981 to 1984 she was assistant professor in the Tribes Program at Colorado College, Colorado Springs; and in 1982 to 1984, associate professor of American and American Indian Studies at the University of Minnesota. A member of the board of directors of the Denver Indian Center since 1984, she is currently an associate professor of Native American and American Studies at the University of Colorado at Boulder. She is also a volunteer worker at Colorado Wildlife Rehabilitation Clinic.

Hogan has received a Newberry Library fellowship, and in 1982, a Yaddo Colony fellowship. Other awards include the Five Civilized Tribes Playwriting Award (1980), the short fiction award from *Stand* magazine (1983); Western States Book Award honorable mention (1984); and a fellowship from Colorado Independent Writers (1984, 1985).

Linda Hogan

One of the most accomplished American Indian writers, Hogan began her literary career in 1979 as a poet with a chapbook, *Calling Myself Home*. Like much of her later poetry, most of the poems in this collection are derived from her experience in Oklahoma, evoking her ancestors and her Indian heritage.

A strong spirit of place pervades *Eclipse* (1983), poems of the earth and for the earth. In *Seeing Through the Sun* (1985) the theme of rebirth is always present with intensity and yet with conversational ease. *Savings* (1988) is grounded in a sense of kinship with nature; superb images and visions are incorporated into her poetry, through an elegant language, to create moments of true discovery. In her poetry collection *The Book of Medicines* (1993), Hogan draws on Native American legends, connecting the present to mythic time, offering words of "medicine" to restore balance between humanity and nature.

Hogan also has written two novels. *Mean Spirit* (1990), her first novel, which gained a Pulitzer Prize nomination in 1991, is an epic drama "about oil, land loss and grief." Set in 1922 and 1923, it tells how the discovery of oil in Oklahoma caused splitting and dislocation among Indian communities. But their respect for the earth rewards them with continuance, strength, and survival. In *Solar Storms* (1995) Hogan recounts the spiritual journey of the main character, Angela, to the land of her ancestors, a place that bears wounds and scars left by many generations of Europeans.

In her first nonfiction collection, *Dwellings: A Spiritual History of the Living World* (1995), Hogan discusses in a very lyrical prose how people "dwell" on earth, sharing a home with all other creatures.

Hogan is very active in antinuclear and pacifist movements. Her work reflects her deep involvement in her tribal history, the relationship between humans and other species, intense spirituality, and a profound understanding and concern for the human community.

Her views on the status of minority women are thus expressed: "To be a woman and a minority woman in this country is like a double-whammy, or maybe even a triple-whammy. It's hard enough to be one or the other. I think also here minority women and the white women's movement have completely different sets of priorities . . . it's like trying to break in and survive, versus trying to have a position equal to a white man in a corporation."

References

Allen, Paula Gunn. "Answering the Deer: Genocide and Continuance in the Poetry of American Indian Women." In *The Sacred Hoop*. Pp. 155–164. Boston: Beacon Press, 1986.

———. "Let Us Hold Fierce: Linda Hogan." In *The Sacred Hoop*. Pp. 165–183. Boston: Beacon Press, 1986.

Balassi, William, John F. Crawford, and Annie O. Eysturoy, eds. *This Is About Vision: Interviews with Southwestern Writers*. Albuquerque: University of New Mexico Press, 1990.

Bruchac, Joseph. "To Take Care of Life: An Interview with Linda Hogan." In *Survival This Way: Interviews with Native American Poets*. Pp. 119–134. Tucson: University of Arizona Press, 1987.

Coltelli, Laura. "Linda Hogan." In *Winged Words: American Indian Writers Speak*. Pp. 71–86. Lincoln: University of Nebraska Press, 1990.

Hogan, Linda. *The Book of Medicines*. Minneapolis, MN: Coffee House Press, 1993.

———. *Calling Myself Home*. Greenfield Center, NY: Greenfield Review Press, 1979.

———. *Daughters, I Love You*. Denver, CO: Loretto Heights College, 1981.

———. *Dwellings: A Spiritual History of the Living World*. New York: W. W. Norton, 1995.

———. *Eclipse*. Los Angeles: UCLA American Indian Studies Center Press, 1983.

———. *From Women's Experience to Feminist Theory*. Sheffield, UK: Sheffield Academic Press, 1997.

———. *Mean Spirit*. New York: Atheneum, 1990.

———. *Power*. New York: W. W. Norton, 1998.

———. *Red Clay: Poems and Stories*. Greenfield Center, NY: Greenfield Review Press, 1991.

———. *Savings: Poems*. Minneapolis, MN: Coffee House Press, 1988.

———. *Seeing Through the Sun*. Amherst: University of Massachusetts Press, 1985.

———. *Solar Storms*. New York: Scribners, 1995.

———. "The Two Lives." In *I Tell You Now: Autobiographical Essays by Native American Writers*. Edited by Brian Swann and Arnold Krupat. Pp. 233–249. Lincoln: University of Nebraska Press, 1987.

———. *The Woman Who Watches Over the World: A Native Memoir*. New York: Norton, 2001.

Hogan, Linda, and Charles Colbert Henderson. *That Horse*. Acoma, NM: Acoma Press, 1985.

Hogan, Linda, Judith McDaniel, and Carol Bruchac, eds. *The Stories We Hold Secret*. Greenfield Center, NY: Greenfield Review Press, 1986.

Hogan, Linda, Brenda Peterson, and Deena Metzger, eds. *Intimate Nature: The Bond Between Women and Animals*. New York: Ballantine, 1999.

"SAIL Bibliography, no. 6: Linda Hogan." *SAIL* 8 (Spring 1984): 1–2.

Scholer, Bo. "A Heart Made Out of Crickets: An Interview with Linda Hogan." *Journal of Ethnic Studies* 16 (Spring 1988): 107–117.

Smith, Patricia Clark. "Linda Hogan." In *This Is About Vision: Interviews with Southwestern Writers*. Edited by William Balassi, John F. Crawford, and Annie O. Eysturoy. Pp. 141–155. Albuquerque: University of New Mexico Press, 1990.

—*Laura Coltelli*

HOPKINS, SARAH WINNEMUCCA [Thocmetony, Tos-me-to-ne, Shell Flower, Sono-meta, Somitone, Sa-mit-tau-nee, White Shell] (c. 1844–1891), was a major figure in the history of the Paiute tribe and a spokeswoman for the plight of her tribe and of Indian peoples in the later part of the nineteenth century. Granddaughter of Chief Truckee, who had guided whites across the Great Basin, and daughter of Chief Winnemucca, an antelope shaman and leader, she became a legendary and controversial figure during her lifetime.

Because Sarah's first encounter with whites had terrified her, she did not want to travel from Humboldt Sink, in Nevada, to California with her family in 1847, but encounters with generous settlers along the way dissolved her fear. In California she attended a convent school, where she learned to write and speak English. She also learned Spanish and knew three Indian dialects. By adolescence her skill as a translator and her position in a prominent family brought Sarah the role of interpreter at Camp McDermitt in northern Nevada, and later at the Malheur Reservation in Oregon. She also became the personal interpreter and guide for General Oliver O. Howard during the Bannock War in 1878. She distinguished herself as a warrior in that conflict, taking her fallen uncle's place in battle.

Sarah's skills rapidly gained her recognition as spokeswoman for her people and led to lectures in major western cities on behalf of justice for Indians. In 1883 she went east to lecture and plead the cause of Indian rights. In Boston she became the protégée of Elizabeth Palmer Peabody and her sister Mary (Mrs. Horace) Mann, who volunteered to edit the manuscript of Winnemucca's autobiography, not only a record of her own life but also a history of her tribe and a strong plea for redress, as the title indicates: *Life Among the Paiutes: Their Wrongs and Claims*. The intent of her autobiography was to bring her crusade for justice to a wider audience and to convince white society that the Paiutes were decent people willing to coexist with whites. Her narrative ends with a plea to Congress to restore land and rights to her people.

Winnemucca's crusade for justice and an end to corruption in administration of reservations met with limited success—she was unable to regain land to the lost tribe when it was moved to the Yakima Reservation in Washington state. She was controversial because some of her white patrons were actually not advocates of Indian sovereignty and rights, and she was an unconventional representative of Indian women in white society and an unconventional woman within her tribe. Yet Winnemucca was an important lobbyist for reform in Indian policy, a woman who dared to make great personal sacrifices and take great risks for her causes. Before her death, she returned to her people to open a school for Paiute children.

References

Brimlow, George. "The Life of Sarah Winnemucca: The Formative Years." *Oregon Historical Quarterly* 53 (June 1952): 103–134.

Canfield, Gae Whitney. *Sarah Winnemucca of the Northern Paiutes*. Norman: University of Oklahoma Press, 1983.

Fowler, Catherine S. "Sarah Winnemucca Northern Paiute, ca. 1844–1891." In *American Indian Intellectuals*. Edited by Margot Liberty. Pp. 33–42. St. Paul, MN: West Publishing, 1978.

Gehm, Katherine. *Sarah Winnemucca*. Phoenix: O'Sullivan, Woodside, 1975.

Georgi-Findlay, Brigitte. "The Frontiers of Native American Women's Writing: Sarah Winnemucca's *Life Among the Piutes*." In *New Voices in Native American Literary Criticism*. Edited by Arnold Krupat. Pp. 222–252. Washington, DC: Smithsonian Institution Press, 1993.

Hopkins, Sara Winnemucca. *Life Among the Paiutes: Their Wrongs and Claims*. Edited by Mrs. Horace Mann. Boston: G. P. Putnam, 1883. Reprint, with foreword by Catherine S. Fowler. Reno: University of Nevada Press, 1994.

———. "The Pah-Utes." *California, a Western Monthly Magazine* 6 (1882): 252.

Morrison, Dorothy Nafus. *Chief Sarah: Sarah Winnemucca's Fight for Indian Rights*. New York: Antheneum, 1980.

Peabody, Elizabeth Palmer. *Sarah Winnemucca's Practical Solution of the Indian Problem*. Cambridge, MA: Wilcox, 1886.

Richey, Elinor. "Sagebrush Princess with a Cause: Sarah Winnemucca." *American West* 12 (November 1975): 30–33, 57–63.

Ruoff, A. LaVonne. "Nineteenth-Century American Indian Autobiographers: William Apes, George Copway, and Sarah Winnemucca." In *The New Literary History*. Edited by A. LaVonne Ruoff and Jerry Ward. Pp. 251–269. New York: MLA, 1991.

Sands, Kathleen Mullen. "Indian Women's Personal Narrative: Voices Past and Present." In *American Women's Autobiography: Fea(s)ts of Memory*. Edited by Margo Culley. Pp. 268–294. Madison: University of Wisconsin Press, 1992.

Scordato, Ellen. *Sarah Winnemucca: Northern Paiute Writer and Diplomat*. New York: Chelsea House, 1992.

Stewart, Patricia. "Sarah Winnemucca." *Nevada Historical Society Quarterly* 14 (Winter 1971): 23–38.

—*Kathleen Mullen Sands*

HORN, KAHN-TINETA (b. 1940), Mohawk activist, daughter of a Mohawk high-steel worker named Assennaienton Horn, of the Kahnawake Mohawk Nation Territory (Caughnawaga Reservation in Quebec, Canada), was born in Brooklyn, New York. She was primarily raised at Kahnawake and attended school both at Kahnawake and at Akwesasne (St. Regis Indian Reservation near Cornwall,

Ontario). As the daughter of a longhouse chief and member of the Bear clan, she was raised in the traditional Mohawk way of life. She has attributed her activism to childhood memories of both her father's activism and her grandfathers' struggle against the St. Lawrence Seaway, which ultimately expropriated 1,260 acres of Kahnawake land.

During the 1960s Horn was best known as a fashion model, actress, and seller of cosmetics who advocated Indian control of their lands, resources, and government, and a return to the traditional ways of the Hodinasaunnee (People of the Longhouse). On December 18, 1968, Horn was among a group of Mohawk Indians protesting Canada's failure to live up to the terms of Jay's Treaty (1794), which granted the Mohawks duty-free passage across the United States–Canadian border. During that protest Horn, along with sixty others, was arrested on Cornwall Island, Ontario, for blocking the entranceway to the International Bridge.

From 1973 to 1990 Horn worked for the Canadian Department of Indian Affairs as a program officer. In the spring of 1990, the town of Oka, Quebec, decided to extend a golf course onto fifty-five acres claimed by the Mohawks. This land included an Indian burial site and an area, known as "The Pines," considered sacred by the Mohawks. This decision resulted in the blockade of a dirt road traversing The Pines. Horn, who was on an educational leave from her job, became involved in this incident as part of a negotiating team that was seeking a peaceful resolution to the crisis. Its resolution on September 26, 1990, resulted in Horn's arrest. Among the casualties was Horn's fourteen-year-old daughter, Waneek, who, Horn says, was stabbed in the chest by soldiers while protecting her four-year-old sister, Ganyetahawi. Subsequently she was fired from her position with Indian Affairs and lost custody of Ganyetahawi. The Ministry of Indian Affairs cited her unauthorized absence from work during the time of the uprising as justification for her termination. Horn countered that the firing was politically and racially motivated, and was done in reprisal for her association with the Oka uprising. challenged her dismissal and has since regained custody of her daughter.

Horn founded and now runs the Canadian Alliance in Solidarity with the Native Peoples, a Toronto-based advocacy group. She is representative of the social and political leadership role that Mohawk women have filled within traditional Mohawk society.

References

Allan, Chris. "Baby By-the-Falling-Waters Joins the Fight." *Akwesasne Notes* 3 (March 1971): 27.

Broussand, C. "Mohawk Beauty with a Mission." *Look* (January 28, 1964): 91–94.

Platiel, Rudy. "Kahn-Tineta Wants Her Sister Evicted." *Akwesasne Notes* 3 (1971): 38.

—*Faren R. Siminoff*

HOWE, LEANNE (b. 1951), of the Choctaw Nation, is a writer and teacher. Born in Edmond, Oklahoma, she earned a bachelor's degree from Oklahoma State University. Her family name is Anolitubbee, which means "One Who Tells and Kills."

Her keen-edged voice is committed to a vision of cross-cultural understanding. Rooted in a tribal ethos, her writing dissects experiences of modern America, forging relations in moments of cultural division.

Howe has published two books, *Coyote Papers* and *A Stand Up Reader*. Her darkly funny "An American in New York" has been widely reprinted. About a displaced Native woman's sojoun in urban New York and her face-to-face encounters with present-day immigrants, the story explodes stereotypes of victimage embedded in the cultural narratives that have told who belongs in America— and to whom America belongs. "The Chaos of Angels" draws on Choctaw history and metaphysics, probing beneath an apparent separation in time and space to unearth the relatedness of all existence. For ten years Howe has researched Choctaw cultural history in primary documents held in the Newberry Library and the Smithsonian Institution. This work is the basis for *Porcupine Sash*, a forthcoming novel about the Choctaw's earliest contacts with Europeans and the persistence of these experiences in the present. A published excerpt, "Danse d'Amour, Danse de Mort," describes the traditional bone-picking ceremony, which for Howe is integral to the Choctaws' love of things that change into other things.

Howe is adept at narrative transformations, adapting old stories to new forms. She wrote and directed the film *Racism: A Look at Minorities in Education in Iowa* in 1993, and produced the video series *Handfuls of Earth* for Iowa Public Television in 1994. Also active in theater, she is the founder and director of the Wagon Burner Theatre Troupe for young Native American writers and actors. The group has toured in a production of her play *Indian Radio Days*, which it has performed at the Mark Taper Forum in Los Angeles. *Big Powwow*, a play she wrote with Roxy Gordon, was staged at Fort Worth, Texas, in 1987.

Howe has been employed in a variety of fields. From 1984 to 1989 she worked for investment firms in New York City and in New Orleans. Until 1994 she was as media producer in the Office of International Student Affairs at the University of Iowa. She helped to organize an American Indian Studies program there and served as an educational adviser on the governor of Iowa's American Indian Advancement Committee. In 1994 she moved to Texas, where she wrote for the *Dallas Morning News* and *USA Today*. She is a member of Choctaws for Democracy.

Howe continues to teach courses in American Indian literature, most recently at Grinnell College in Iowa in 1997. She has two sons and one granddaughter living in Oklahoma City.

References

Howe, LeAnne. "An American in New York." In *Spider Woman's Granddaughters*. Edited by Paula Gunn Allen. Pp. 212–220. Boston: Beacon Press, 1989.

———. "The Chaos of Angels." *Callaloo* 17 (Winter 1994): 108–114.

———. *Coyote Papers*. Dallas: Wowapi Press, 1985.

———. "Danse d'Amour, Danse de Mort." In *Earth Song, Sky Spirit*. Edited by Clifford E. Trafzer. Pp. 447–472. New York: Doubleday, 1993.

———. *A Stand Up Reader*. Dallas: Into View Press, 1987.

—Laura Adams

HUNGRY WOLF, BEVERLY [Sikski-Aki, Black-Faced Woman] (b. 1950), was born in the Blood Indian Hospital on the Blood Indian Reserve in Canada, a member of the Little Bear family of the Blood tribe of the Blackfoot Nation. She was educated at the boarding school on the reserve, and after finishing her college education, returned there as a teacher. Although her Catholic education discouraged adherence to her cultural traditions, her marriage to a German, born Adolph Gutöhrlein, led her to a new appreciation of and desire to preserve these traditions. Gutöhrlein had come to America in 1954, and as he matured, he pursued his interest in American Indians, finally adopting the name Adolph Hungry Wolf, which was given to him by an elderly Blackfoot Indian named Makes Summer. His appreciation of traditional Indian culture finally led him to Canada, where he met Beverly. He and his wife, Carol, first considered Beverly an "adopted sister," but after their marriage ended, Beverly and Adolph were wed.

Beverly and Adolph encountered some enmity among Indians who could not understand why a white man should choose to live as an Indian; their book *Shadows of the Buffalo* tells of their experiences. Earlier, Hungry Wolf had assisted her husband in gathering information for his book *The Blood People*, and he in turn encouraged her to collect the wisdom of the women of the Blackfoot Nation in her own book, *The Ways of My Grandmothers*. Adolph has also published independent works.

The women who served as sources for *The Ways of My Grandmothers* included Beverly Hungry Wolf's own grandmother, AnadaAki, whose name means Pretty Woman and who through later marriages was also known as Hilda Heavy Head, Hilda Beebe, and Hilda Strangling Wolf. Although she was the daughter of a German father named Joe Trollinger and was educated in a girls' school run by a British matron, AnadaAki grew up amid the songs and ceremonies of the Blackfoot Nation and shared their stories. She was in her nineties and living with Ruth Little Bear, Hungry Wolf's mother, when her stories were collected.

It is tribal custom, however, to consider all of the older women as grandmothers, and Beverly Hungry Wolf collected information and stories from these other "grandmothers" as well. A particularly important source was Paula Weasel Head, who was noted for her wisdom and her knowledge of the medicine pipe bundles important to the tribe, and who honored Hungry Wolf by taking her as an "adopted child." Additional stories came from Hungry Wolf's aunt, Mary One Spot, and other elders within the Blood clan. Other information is preserved in the book, such as recipes, crafts, dances, and childhood memories of the traditions and lifestyle of the Blackfoot Nation.

Beverly Hungry Wolf now lives with her husband and their five children in a cabin in the wilderness of the British Columbia Rockies. In 1987 she and her husband edited *Children of the Sun*, a collection of historical narratives that capture the stories and lives of Native Americans growing up in the early 1900s.

References

Hungry Wolf, Adolph. *The Blood People: A Division of the Blackfoot Confederacy.* New York: Harper & Row, 1977.
———. *Shadows of the Buffalo: A Family Odyssey Among the Indians.* New York: William Morrow, 1983.

Hungry Wolf, Adolph, and Beverly Hungry Wolf, eds. *Children of the Sun: Stories by and About Indian Kids.* New York: William Morrow, 1987.
———. *Daughters of the Buffalo Women: Maintaining the Tribal Faith.* Skookunchuck, BC: Canadian Caboose Press, 1996.
Hungry Wolf, Beverly. *The Ways of My Grandmothers.* New York: William Morrow, 1980.

—*Thelma Shinn Richard*

HUNTER, MARY JO BROOKS is a member of the Ho-Chunk Nation and a clinical instructor at the Hamline University School of Law. She received her B.A. from the University of Wisconsin and her J.D. from the UCLA School of Law. Brooks Hunter is an active member of the legal community and an advocate for children's rights within the legal system. At Hamline, she teaches Native American law and supervises the child advocacy clinic. Brooks Hunter has also been elected the first chief justice of the supreme court of the Ho-Chunk nation, and she is an associate justice of the Winnebago tribe of Nebraska.

Reference

http://web.hamline.edu/law/faculty/brooks.htm

—*Kerry Kennedy Wynn*

I

IGNACIO, CARMELLA (b. 1942), was the first registered nurse at Grossmont Hospital in San Diego, California, to reach Level IV for clinical nurses. She has worked there since 1968, and she has been in charge of the ophthalmology and orthopedic services in the operating room. She belongs to the National Association of Operating Room Nurses and the United Nurse Association of California. Ignacio is known nationally for her work in American Indian health. In 1984 she was elected to the board of directors of the San Diego American Indian Health Center, a very successful health care facility. She also has served as president of the Heartland Youth Symphony Orchestra.

Ignacio is Tohono O'odham (Papago) and was born at Sells, Arizona. Her mother was of the Chico family, and her father was a member of the Pablo family. As a child she attended Topawa Elementary School and St. John's Indian School. Upon graduation she attended the University of Arizona and St. Mary's School of Nursing, where she became a registered nurse. She has contributed significantly to the health of Native Americans by assuring quality medical service to thousands of Indians at the American Indian Health Center. She is well known to the Indian Health Service and has worked with state and federal agencies to improve health care to urban Indians throughout California.

Reference

Trafzer, Clifford. Personal communication with Carmella Ignacio, 1990.

—Clifford E. Trafzer

INDIAN EMILY (c.1856–1873) was a badly wounded Apache girl who was found by Lieutenant Tom Easton after an Apache raid on Fort David (in what is now Texas) in 1868. After being nursed back to health by his mother, Emily (the Eastons' name for her) spent the next several years with the lieutenant and his mother. The story goes that she learned to speak, read, and write in English and otherwise adapted to white ways, to the point of falling in love with Lieutenant Easton. About two years later, when his affections turned toward Mary Nelson, the daughter of a post family, Emily ran away. In 1873 the soldiers went on alert because Apaches had been attacking stagecoaches and wagon trains. One night a sentry, hearing approaching footsteps and getting no response to his challenge, fired on an apparent intruder; he shot and mortally wounded Emily, who had returned to warn Tom and his mother that her Apache band was going to attack the fort. Emily is remembered for giving her life for her friends, and saving the garrison from massacre.

References

Raht, Carlysle Graham. *The Romance of the Davis Mountains and the Big Bend Country*. El Paso, TX: Rahtbooks, 1919.

Twitchell, Ralph Emerson. *The Leading Facts of New Mexico History*. Cedar Rapids, IA: Torch Press, 1911.

Waltrip, Lela, and Rufus Waltrip. *Indian Women: Thirteen Who Played a Part in the History of America from the Earliest Days to Now*. New York: David McKay, 1964.

—*Kathryn W. Shanley*

ISOM, JOAN SHADDOX (b. 1940), was raised in the hills of eastern Oklahoma, learning all she could about her Cherokee people's myths, legends, and culture. As she matured, she developed equal interests in poetry and drawing. Isom saw both as ways to preserve Cherokee traditions and express her interpretations of them. She received a BA in education from Central State University (now Central Oklahoma State University) at Edmond in 1965 and an MFA from the University of Arkansas in 1970.

Isom's one-act plays, *The Living Forest, A Pound of Miracles, Paint Me a Memory, The Halloween Visitor*, and *Boy Medicine*, were all published in 1975 by Melody House in Oklahoma City. *Free Spirits*, published at Boston by Plays, Inc., also in 1975, won special recognition in the Best Plays of the Year contest. Isom was commissioned to write the bicentennial play for Fort Gibson, Oklahoma; it was first performed in 1976 and continues as an annual summer drama.

Isom is also an artist. Her work was exhibited in the 1968 Prix de Paris competition, where it won an award for representing current trends in American art. Also in 1968 her work placed fourth in the Olympic art competition held in Rimini, Italy.

A versatile artist and educator, Isom has taught all levels of school from elementary to college, was a producer for a children's theater group, and directed the fine arts program for her region in 1971. Bringing art to schoolchildren has always been a priority, and she has designed fine arts curricula, as well as serving as director of Oklahoma's Arts and Humanities Council.

Isom is most widely known for her collections of poems *Foxgrapes* and *The Moon in Five Disguises*, both of which she illustrated. She is a founding member of the Foxmoor Publishing Co-op, which published *The Moon in Five Disguises*. Individual works have appeared in many periodicals, such as *The Indian Historian*. Her poem "The Visit" creates a haunting picture of an adult Isom going through the ruins of her childhood home, lost during the Dustbowl. It won first place in the 1971 Beta Sigma Phi International Poetry Contest.

Isom makes her home in Tahlequah, Oklahoma.

References

Brant, Beth, ed. *A Gathering of Spirit*. Rockland, ME: Sinister Wisdom, 1984.

Campbell, Gilbert, ed. *Authors Files*. Palmer Lake, CO: Filter Press, 1991.

Isom, Joan Shaddox. *The First Starry Night*. Dallas, TX: Whispering Coyote Press, 1997.

———. *Foxgrapes*. Palmer Lake, CO: Filter Press, 1975.

———. *Home to Oklahoma*. Tahlequah, OK: Northeastern State University Press, 1990.

———. *The Moon in Five Disguises*. Tahlequah, OK: Foxmoor Publishing Co-op, 1981.

Isom, Joan Shaddox, and Mary Anne Maier. *The Leap Years: Women Reflect on Change, Loss, and Love*. Boston: Beacon Press, 1999.

—Cynthia Kasee

J

JARVIS, ROSIE (c. 1851–1955), was born on the Haupt Ranch in Sonoma County, California, where many of the Kashaya Pomo settled after the Russians abandoned Fort Ross in 1842. Her mother, Mollie, subsequently married Charlie Haupt, a squatter with a large tract of land, leaving her marriage to Chico Jarvis, Rosie's Indian father, to secure a home for her Kashaya people. Jarvis became a type of hand curer, massaging muscles and rubbing out pain. But her greatest contribution to the Kashaya Pomo and to other Indians was the vast knowledge she passed on as tribal historian. She raised her granddaughter, Essie Parrish, who would become the last great Kashaya religious and political leader, and schooled her in the history of the land and people. Because of Jarvis this oral history is alive and well today; every Kashaya person, if interested, can trace his or her heritage to ancestors living in specific locales at the time of European contact nearly two hundred years ago.

Jarvis married more than once. Her husband Tom Smith, a Kashaya Pomo/ Coast Miwok, was a well-known, powerful Indian doctor and dreamer. Their son, Robert, became chief of the Kashaya tribe. In 1919 Jarvis was among the first to settle on a plot of land, purchased by the U.S. government, to establish the Kashaya Reservation. She knew only a few words of English when she died in 1955. According to her great-granddaughter, Violet Chappell, daughter of Essie Parrish and current tribal historian, Jarvis "never stopped talking about the old days because it was important for us."

Reference

Sarris, Greg. Personal communication with Violet Chappell, May 1990.

—Greg Sarris

JEMISON, ALICE LEE (1901–1964), was born in the town of Silver Creek, just off the Cattaraugus Indian Reservation in New York state. The daughter of a Seneca mother and a Cherokee father, she identified more strongly with her Seneca heritage and with a long-standing tradition of politically significant Iroquois women. Jemison graduated from Silver Creek High School in 1919, but her ambition to continue her education and become a lawyer went unfulfilled for lack of money. After her marriage to LeVerne L. Jemison, a Seneca steelworker, ended in separation in 1928, she was forced to accept a wide variety of jobs, her choices determined almost solely by her responsibility to support her mother and two children. Thus began a struggle against poverty that would remain a constant throughout her life.

Jemison is best remembered as an outspoken critic of the Bureau of Indian Affairs and its New Deal program of the 1930s, and as a leader in the ultra-conservative American Indian Federation. Her use of inflammatory rhetoric and demagoguery, especially in opposition to New Deal legislation, led some of the government officials she criticized to cast her as an extremist. But a closer examination of Jemison's brand of conservatism reveals that it was complex and often misunderstood, especially when taken out of its cultural context. Her antigovernment positions were not rooted in an extreme ideology. Rather, her stances had two main sources: the general and widespread mistrust of non–Indian institutions that was typical of conservative Senecas, and the politically conservative climate prevalent in western New York.

To understand Jemison's point of view, more fully, it is important to recognize her commitment to preserving Iroquois treaty rights, which she and others believed safeguarded an independent Iroquois sovereignty, not a sovereign status protected at the pleasure of the Congress of the United States. Much affected by the problems all Iroquois faced during her lifetime, Jemison got involved in tribal politics in the 1920s and remained active well into the 1940s. She served the Seneca people as a legal researcher and lobbyist, and she also worked with members of the Iroquois Confederacy to organize Indian leaders into the Intertribal Committee for the Advancement of the American Indian.

References

Hauptman, Laurence M. "Alice Lee Jemison: Seneca Political Activist." *The Indian Historian* 12 (1974): 15–40.

———. "The Only Good Indian Bureau Is a Dead Indian Bureau: Alice Lee Jemison, Seneca Political Activist." In *The Iroquois and the New Deal*. Pp. 34–55. Syracuse, NY: Syracuse University Press, 1981.

Jemison, Alice Lee. *Buffalo Evening News*, April 1933, 18–21.

"Jemison, Alice Lee." File in office files of Commissioner John Collier. Bureau of Indian Affairs, Record Group 75, National Archives, Washington, DC.

—*Gretchen G. Harvey*

JENNINGS, VANESSA (b. 1952), artist and craftsman, born in the Kiowa community of Redstone near Ft. Cobb, Oklahoma, on land allotted to her family in the nineteenth century and on which she lives to this day. Her grandmother, Jeanette Berry Mopope (whose Kiowa name was "Tsotkeigope"), raised Jennings and her sisters and taught her a wide range of traditional Kiowa art and craftsmanship. As a result, Jennings now considers herself a generalist, since she produces everything from cloth dresses and leggings to beadwork, lances, and moccasins. Jennings is also the last active producer of Kiowa cradle boards, a skill she is currently passing on to her daughter-in-law and others through a series of classes offered freely to anyone interested. In 1989, Jennings was recognized as a National Heritage Fellow by the National Endowment for the Humanities and has received letters from both Presidents Bush and Clinton recognizing her as a living national treasure.

Despite such national recognition, Jennings continues to offer classes and to speak to young people throughout Oklahoma and Texas (often through workshops for teachers and students supported by the Texas Folklife Office), using her art and her storehouse of knowledge about Kiowa culture to interest young people in their own heritage and to give them a sense of belonging in order to give them the strength they will need to live their lives. Jennings believes that it is only by finding the courage and strength to face adversity and by tenaciously sharing one's skills and knowledge with others that any culture can survive.

Reference

Telephone interview with Vanessa Jennings, February 28, 2001.

—*Michael Sherfy*

JIMULLA, VIOLA PELHAME [Sicatuva, Born Quickly] (1878–1966), chieftess of the Yavapai tribe (mistakenly called the Mojave-Apache), was the third of three daughters of Who-wah and Ka-hava-soo-ah, who lived near Prescott, Arizona. Her father died when she was young, and Who-wah married Pelhame, under whose name Jimulla attended the Rice Arizona Indian School and the Phoenix Indian School. In 1901 she married Sam Jimulla ("Red Ants"), who died in 1940 after being thrown from his horse; they had five daughters, three of whom died young.

In 1935, approximately seventy-five acres were established as the Prescott Yavapai Indian Reservation (expanded to 1,327 acres in the early 1950s), the smallest Indian reservation in the United States. Sam Jimulla was appointed chief by the commissioner of Indian Affairs and simultaneously elected to the position by his people. After his death, his wife succeeded him as chieftess and primarily managed tribal affairs single-handedly for several years, despite the formation of a five-person tribal council in 1940. Following her death in 1966, her second daughter, Grace (Mrs. Don Mitchell), succeeded her; the appointment was confirmed by the tribal council in 1967.

A progressive and compassionate leader, Jimulla was also involved in her tribe's spiritual life. She was named an elder of the Yavapai Indian Mission (Presbyterian) in 1922 and was instrumental in the foundation of Trinity Presbyterian Church in Prescott in 1957. She was also an accomplished basket weaver and teacher of basketry under WPA programs.

Reference

Barnett, Franklin. *Viola Jimulla: The Indian Chieftess*. Prescott, AZ: Prescott Yavapai Indians, 1968.

—*Rodney Simard*

JOE, RITA (b. 1932), a Micmac poet, was born at Wycocomagh, Cape Breton Island, Nova Scotia, the daughter of Joseph Bernard and Annie Googoo. Her mother died in childbirth when Joe was five; the loss of her mother, and the feeling of desertion matched by a longing for her mother's love, run through Joe's poetry to this day. After her mother's death, Joe's aging father saw to it that she and her siblings had foster families, but without the attention of parents, Joe had a hard time learning the Micmac language and absorbing all the knowledge it transmits through the oral tradition. She had to make a conscious effort to reclaim that part of her heritage. When she was twelve, Joe entered Shubbenacadie Residential School, which she attended until eighth grade. In the early 1950s she moved to Boston, a city where many Micmac people found work then. There she met her husband, Frank Joe, also a Micmac (now deceased). They raised a large family, including adopted, biological, and foster children. Eventually they returned to Micmac territory, via Halifax, to Eskasoni Reserve on Cape Breton Island, where Joe now lives.

In the late 1960s, partly influenced by her children's experiences in public schools, and partly out of her own intellectual curiosity and creative exuberance, Joe began to write poetry. For years she also wrote a column, "Here and There in Eskasoni," for the *Micmac News*, a tribal newspaper that had readers all over the world. In 1971, when her eldest daughter, Evelyn, was subjected to racist slurs and ridicule by her teacher in an almost totally white public school, Joe decided to use her pen to counteract the devastating effects of mental colonization, such as the distortion and displacement of Native history and the stereotyping of Native persons. Her first volume of poetry, *Poems of Rita Joe*, came out in 1978. Without being aggressive or attacking on the political level, the poems gently present the Native experience within the dominant society, advocating love and understanding between peoples to overcome the barriers that impede communication and peace.

After the publication of her first book, Joe received many invitations to speak to Native and non–Native audiences in community centers, libraries, schools, and universities, including the University of British Columbia; the University of Maine; Acadia, Dalhousie, and McGill universities; and California State University at Chico. Her poem about making axe handles with her father, "untitled" in *Poems*, is now on display on tanned hide in the Canadian Museum of Civilization in Ottawa. Her second book of poetry, *Song of Eskasoni*, came out in 1988. Her poems have appeared in anthologies and periodicals, including *Canadian Women Studies/Les Cahiers de la femme* (1989).

Joe has received wide recognition for her literary and humanitarian efforts. In 1974 she won the poetry competition prize of the Nova Scotia Writers' Federation, which she accepted in Native dress, and in 1989 she was nominated for the Order of Canada, the highest honor Canada can bestow on her citizens. In April 1990, still suffering from the loss of her husband, Joe accepted the award from the governor general at Rideau Hall in Ottawa "on behalf of all the Native people," as she said in her acceptance speech.

Also in 1990, using her winnings from a bingo game, Joe established a small Micmac arts and crafts shop close to her house on the Eskasoni Reserve, where she sells products crafted by her community. The shop attracts customers from all over the world.

In 1991 Joe published her third volume of poetry, *Lnu and Indians We're Called*. Again she presents the richness of her Micmac heritage, blending Catholic and traditional beliefs and experiences into an idiosyncratic voice that carries love and respect for all peoples. The following year, in Ottawa, Joe was presented to

Queen Elizabeth II, who appointed her a member of the Queen's Privy Council. In 1996, despite having Parkinson's disease, Joe published her autobiography, *Song of Rita Joe: Autobiography of a Mi'kmaq Poet.*

Joe is a gentle but strong voice, a shining example of courage and dedication, an untiring community worker and supporter of her own people, and a lovable partner in conversation. As such she is an encouraging role model for young Native people.

References

Joe, Rita. "The Gentle War." *Canadian Women Studies/Les Cahiers de la femme* 10 (Summer/Fall 1989): 27–29.

———. *Lnu and Indians We're Called*. Charlottetown, PEI: Ragweed Press, 1991.

———. *Poems of Rita Joe*. Halifax, NS: Abanaki Press, 1978. Reprint, By the author, 1990.

———. *Song of Eskasoni: More Poems of Rita Joe*. Charlottetown, PEI: Ragweed Press, 1988.

———. *Song of Rita Joe: Autobiography of a Mi'kmaq Poet*. Lincoln: University of Nebraska Press, 1996.

———. *We Are the Dreamers: Recent and Early Poetry*. Wreck Cove: Breton Books, 1999.

Joe, Rita, and Lesley Choyce, eds. *The Mi'kmaq Anthology*. Lawrencetown Beach, NS: Pottersfield Press, 1997.

Lutz, Hartmut. "'Talking at the Kitchen Table': A Personal Homage to Rita Joe of Eskasoni Reserve, Cape Breton Island, Nova Scotia." In *Down East: Critical Essays on Contemporary Maritime Canadian Writing*. Edited by Wolfgang Hochbruck and James O. Taylor. Pp. 276–289. Trier, Germany: Wissenschaftlicher Verlag Trier, 1997.

"Rita Joe." In *Contemporary Challenges: Conversations with Canadian Native Authors*. Edited by Hartmut Lutz. Pp. 241–264. Saskatoon, Sk: Fifth House, 1991.

Ryga, George. *The Ecstasy of Rita Joe*. Vancouver, BC: Talonbooks, 1970.

Steele, Charlott Musical. "Rita Joe Wages Gentle War of Words." *Atlantic Advocate* 81 (January 1991): 11–13.

—*Hartmut Lutz*

JOHN, MARY (b. 1913), is a member of the Carrier Indian band on the Stoney Creek Reserve in northern British Columbia. She was born at Six-Mile-Lake, the home of her grandmother, to Anzell and Charlie Pinker, a white man. In 1920 she entered the mission school at Fort St. James, then transferred to the mission school at Lejac in 1922. Her memories of the seven years she attended school focus on the hunger and desolation she experienced. She married Lazare John in 1929; between 1930 and 1949 they had twelve children.

John's life is recounted in Bridget Moran's *Stoney Creek Woman*, an biography that chronicles the hardships endured by her people because of the Indian Act and a lack of government attention and funds, as well as John's personal struggles and victories over poverty, racism, and illness. In 1957 John went to work at the hospital in Vanderhoof, sometimes walking the nine miles when she lacked transportation. She worked at the hospital for thirteen years. In 1972 she was asked to teach the Carrier language and culture at St. Joseph's. The Stoney Creek Reserve began an Elders Society in 1978, and John was an active participant. The Rotary Club in Vanderhoof named her Citizen of the Year in 1979, acknowledging her contributions to Stoney Creek, other Native communities, and the entire community of Vanderhoof.

John says that if she had three wishes for her people, she would wish for improved living conditions on the reservations, more education for the children, and the opportunity to find employment on the reservations. Her life has been one of dedication to her family, loyalty to Stoney Creek, and service to the community at large.

Reference

Moran, Bridget. *Stoney Creek Woman: The Story of Mary John*. Vancouver, BC: Tillacum Library, 1988.

—*Laurie Lisa*

JOHNSON, EMILY PAULINE [Tekahionwake] (1861–1913), was born near Brantford, Ontario, on the Six Nations Reserve. The daughter of the Mohawk chief George Henry Martin Johnson and the English-born Emily Susanna Howells, who was a cousin of the American novelist William Dean Howells, Johnson absorbed Mohawk traditions from family members and Anglo–American traditions through reading such authors as Shakespeare, Byron, Emerson, and Longfellow. Her interest in theatrical performance and dramatic literary readings, stemming from family entertainments, increased during the years she attended the Central Collegiate School in Brantford.

Johnson began writing poetry around 1879 and to achieve recognition through publication and public readings of her work in the early 1890s. Building on family connections in England, she traveled to London in 1894 to find a publisher for her poems. The trip was a success, and the prestigious Bodley Head Press published her important collection *The White Wampum* in 1895. Following the publication of her first book, Johnson toured extensively. Though especially popular in western Canada, the "Mohawk Princess," as she was billed, found audiences for theatrical performances of her writings throughout Canada, as well as Great Britain and the United States. A second collection of poems, *Canadian Born*, was published at Toronto in 1903.

In 1904 Johnson turned more to prose writing and was able to place her stories and essays in *The Mother's Magazine* and other respected periodicals. Important collections of her prose works include *The Legends of Vancouver, The Shagganappi*, and *The Moccasin Maker*. A final verse collection, *Flint and Feather*, contains poems from *The White Wampum* and *Canadian Born* as well as later material.

Johnson is particularly noted for her memorable portrayal of American Indians and of women. Her stories often feature Indian heroines, and she frequently describes the victimization of Indian women in love relationships with white men. Her writings frequently serve to counteract negative stereotypes of Native Americans. In addition to her significance as a writer within the traditions of Native American and women's poetry and fiction, Johnson is regarded as an important figure in the development of the national literature of Canada. She never married. Johnson died in Vancouver, British Columbia, in 1913.

References

Foster, Mrs. W. Garland (Anne). *The Mohawk Princess, Being Some Account of the Life of Teka-hion-wake (E. Pauline Johnson)*. Vancouver, BC: Lion's Gate, 1931.

Gerson, Carole. "Some Notes Concerning Pauline Johnson." *Canadian Notes & Queries* 34 (1985): 16–19.

Johnson, Emily Pauline. *Canadian Born*. Toronto: Morang, 1903.

———. *Flint and Feather*. Toronto: Musson, 1912. Reprint, Markham, Ont., PaperJacks, 1973.

———. *Legends of Vancouver*. Vancouver, BC: Saturday Sunset Presses, 1911. Reprint, Vancouver, McClelland, 1912, 1961.

———. *The Moccasin Maker*. Toronto: William Briggs, 1913. Reprint, edited with introduction and notes by A. LaVonne Brown Ruoff, Tucson: University of Arizona Press, 1987.

———. *The Shagganappi*. Introduction by Ernest Thompson Seton. Vancouver, BC: Briggs, 1913.

———. *The White Wampum*. London: Bodley Head, 1895.

Keller, Betty. *Pauline: A Biography of Pauline Johnson*. Vancouver, BC: Douglas, 1981.

Loosely, Elizabeth. "Pauline Johnson." In *The Clear Spirit: Twenty Canadian Women and Their Times*. Edited by Mary Quayle Innes. Pp. 74–90. Toronto: University of Toronto Press, 1966.

Lyon, George W. "Pauline Johnson: A Reconsideration." *Studies in Canadian Literature* 15 (1990): 136–159.

McRaye, Walter. *Pauline Johnson and Her Friends*. Toronto: Ryerson, 1947.

———. *Town Hall To-night*. Toronto: Ryerson, 1929.

Mair, Charles. "Johnson: An Appreciation." *Canadian Magazine* 41 (July 1913): 281–283.

Ruoff, A. LaVonne Brown. "Justice for Indians and Women: The Protest Fiction of Alice Callahan and Pauline Johnson." *World Literature Today* 66 (1992): 249–255.

Shrive, Norman. "What Happened to Pauline?" *Canadian Literature* 13 (Summer 1962): 25–38.

Van Steen, Marcus, ed. *Pauline Johnson: Her Life and Work*. Toronto: Musson Book, 1965.

—James Robert Payne

JOHNSTON, VERNA PATRONELLA [Patronella Johnston, Patronella Verna Nadjiwon Johnston] (b. 1909), a Ojibwa, is called Verna by her family though she was christened Patronella Verna Nadjiwon when she was born at the Cape Croker Reserve in

Ontario, Canada. In 1926 she married Henry Johnston, and spent the next nineteen years raising her five children. From 1945 until 1959, she worked at odd jobs in Toronto and then returned to Cape Croker, where she was as a foster mother to Indian children. In 1965 Johnston returned to Toronto to "make a place in the city" for her two granddaughters, who were attending business courses, and in 1966 this initial endeavor led her to open the first boardinghouse for Indian students in Toronto. Over the next ten years, she developed her continuing interest in Indian adaptation to urban life as she taught her boarders how to value their Indianness, how to handle themselves off the reserve, and how to deal with the various governmental organizations concerned with Indian people.

In addition to her boardinghouse, Johnston ran a craft training program for Indian Affairs, which took her to 124 Canadian reserves and brought her into contact with Native peoples from all over Canada. As she puts it, she was "caught up in the upswing of Indian consciousness," and soon was in demand as a speaker who was knowledgeable about the reserve system and its flaws, as well as about Native urban life. This led to Johnston's being asked to teach Indian culture classes at Sheridan College, York University, and Seneca College. She also taught orientation classes for the Northern Corps teachers, and as a member of the board of the Indian Friendship Centre, she helped Indians from the reserves find places to live in the city.

In 1970 Johnston published *Tales of Nokomis*, the Ojibwa stories she had been told as a child by her grandmother. In 1973 ill health forced her to close her boardinghouse and return for a year to Cape Croker; she was back in Toronto in 1974, working as a voluntary consultant and housekeeper for Anduhyaun House, a hostel for young Indian girls. In 1976 she was named Indian Woman of the Year by the Native Women's Association of Canada. Since then, she has continued to be a resource person for the Native community. According to her niece by marriage, Carol Nadjiwon, in the fall of 1990 Johnston, at the age of eighty-one, was still very active at Cape Croker and "helping out wherever she could." She had just finished organizing a public assembly for peace and natural law.

References

Clark, Joni Adamson. Interview with Carol Nadjiwon, January 25, 1991.

Johnston, Patronella. *Tales of Nokomis*. Toronto: Musson Books, 1970.

Vanderburgh, Rosamund M. *I Am Nokomis Too: The Biography of Verna Patronella Johnston*. Don Mills, ON: General Publishing, 1977.

—Joni Adamson Clarke

JONES, ROSALIE MAE (b. 1941), was born in Browning, Montana. She was reared and educated in public schools in Cut Bank, Montana, then attended Fort Wright College of the Holy Names in Spokane, Washington, from 1959 to 1964. After earning the BFA in music from Fort Wright, Jones transferred to the University of Utah to study modern dance and received her master's degree in 1968. Jones's thesis, "The Blackfeet Medicine Lodge Ceremony: Ritual and Dance-Drama," explored the origins, history, and method of what whites renamed the Sun Dance. In conjuction with her thesis, Jones prepared a modern dance-drama based on the Blackfeet Medicine Lodge Ceremony, which was presented on April 23, 1968, in the University of Utah Dance Studio. In preparation for her thesis, Jones studied dance and attended the Hanya Holm School of Dance in Colorado Springs, during the summer of 1962, and took master classes and acted as concert dancer in Salt Lake City while completing her thesis.

Jones has participated in a number of dance performances, including those of Native dances at the Institute of American Indian Arts in Santa Fe, New Mexico. She also has been an instructor and choreographer of dance; in June 1966, she was the choreographer and assistant director of *Sipapu: A Drama of Authentic Dances and Chants of Indian America*, presented in Washington, D.C., and was a training instructor in dance arts for the Bureau of Indian Affairs.

References

Anderson, Owanah. *Ohoyo One Thousand: A Resource Guide of American Indian/Alaska Native Women 1982*. Wichita Falls, TX: Ohoya Resource Center, 1982.

Jones, Rosalie May. "The Blackfeet Medicine Lodge Ceremony: Ritual and Dance-Drama." MA thesis, University of Utah, 1968.

Magill, Gordon. "Rosalie Jones: Guiding Light of Daystar." *Dance* 72 (1998): 64ff.

—*Greg Grewell*

JUANA MARIA [Lost Woman of San Nicholas Island, Lone Woman of San Nicholas Island] (c.1815–1853) was found in 1853, living alone on San Nicholas Island in the Santa Barbara Island group. Under the auspices formulated by Junipero Serra, the inhabitants of these tiny islands were transported to the mainland, presumably to protect them from raids by Russian hunters from Alaska, and to eliminate priests' having to cross rough seas to minister to them; after transportation, these people were employed as agricultural and domestic workers.

According to several accounts, in 1835 or 1836, upon boarding the transport ship, a young Nicole;atno woman discovered that her nursing infant had been left on the island, so she jumped overboard into a stormy sea to retrieve it. (Some accounts say she discovered her child missing before boarding, and walked back to the village; others do not mention that she was nursing.) The rising storm required the ship's immediate departure, so it could not wait or return for the pair. After arrival on the mainland, all trace of the Nicoleños quickly disappeared. The priests offered a two hundred dollar reward for her safe removal from the island, but attempts at rescue, though considered, were never carried through, due to the treachery of tides and winds. Otter and seal hunters who worked on the island sometimes looked, but were never able to find her.

Finally, in 1853, Captain George Nidever and his men, hunting otter and seal, found Juana Maria's whale rib house on the island; the next day they encountered the woman, sewing with a bone needle and sealskin thread in front of her house. After they had hunted for a month, they persuaded her to board their ship, supposedly to follow her people. Her inability to communicate because no one could understand her language (though a few words were recorded) prevented anyone from finding out exactly how she had survived, or what had happened to her child. Baptized Juana Maria, or Juana Marie, at Mission Santa Barbara, she soon contracted a fatal case of dysentery. The Lone Woman of San Nicholas Island died seven weeks after her "rescue." One of her water baskets, her beads, and a stone mortar were presented to the California Academy of Sciences after her death; they were destroyed in the San Francisco earthquake and fire of 1906. A luxurious cape of sealskin and cormorant feathers, was reported to have been sent to the Vatican, was lost.

These artifacts and the mere fact of her survival continued to fascinate the mainlanders, who thought of Juana Maria as a real-life Robinson Crusoe. Several romantic and historical accounts about her were published. *Island of the Blue Dolphins* (1960), a children's novel based on her story, won the Newbery Medal for children's literature and was made into a film for children. Like Ishi, Juana Maria was frequently called the last member of her tribe. She was buried in the Mission Santa Barbara cemetery on October 19, 1853.

References

Hardacre, Emma Chamberlain. "Eighteen Years Alone." *Scribner's Monthly* (September 1880): 657–664. Reprint, Santa Barbara, CA: Schauer Printing, 1950.

Heitzer, Robert F., and Albert B. Elsasser, eds. *Original Accounts of the Lone Woman of San Nicholas Island*. Reports of the University of California Archaeological Survey, no. 55 (1961). Reprint, Ramona, CA: Ballena Press, 1973.

O'Dell, Scott. *Island of the Blue Dolphins*. Boston: Houghton Mifflin, 1960.

—*Jay Ann Cox*

JUMPER, BETTY MAE (b. 1923), was born at Indiantown, near Lake Okeechobee in southern Florida. Her mother was Ada Tiger, a full-blood Seminole. When she was five years old, the family moved to the Dania Indian Reservation near Fort Lauderdale. The Tiger family became devout members of the Baptist Church. Over the protest of her grandmother, she learned English and attended the reservation day school. The school was closed in 1936, but Jumper and a few other Seminole youngsters were sent to a federal residential school for Indians at Cherokee, North Carolina. There she made the adjustment to white man's clothing and schooling, as well as to living in the mountains and experiencing seasonal changes. In 1945 Jumper and her cousin became the first Seminoles to receive high school diplomas.

After graduation Jumper entered the Kiowa Indian Hospital in Oklahoma and completed a year of nurse's training in public health. She then returned to Florida and worked with the public health nurse serving the Seminole reservations. During this time she married Moses Jumper, a young Seminole who had also attended school at Cherokee. He was one of only three Seminoles who volunteered and served in the military during World War II. They raised a family of two sons and a daughter.

When the Seminole tribe was formally organized in 1957, Jumper was elected to the tribal council for a two-year term. This was followed by four years of service on the board of directors, which supervised tribal business enterprises. In

1967 the Seminole people elected Jumper the first—woman chairperson of the tribal council. During her four-year term she worked to improve health, employ-ment, education, welfare, law and order, and housing conditions for her people. The tribe also entered into a number of land leases and other financial arrange-ments to move toward economic self-sufficiency. At the national level Jumper was active in the National Tribal Chairman's Association, was a founder of United Southeastern Tribes, and served on the National Council on Indian Opportunities. In 1970 she was named one of the Top Indian Women of the year and attended the National Seminar for American Indian Women held in Colorado. Since leaving office Jumper has held a variety of positions with the Seminole tribe and is cur-rently associated with its Communications Department, which published her brief memoir, . . . and with the Wagon Came God's Word.

In 1994 Jumper was awarded an honorary doctorate by Florida State Univer-sity in recognition of her lifetime of leadership of the Seminole people.

References

Jumper, Betty Mae. . . . and with the Wagon Came God's Word. Hollywood, FL: Seminole Tribe, 1980.

———. Legends of the Seminoles. Sarasota, FL: Pineapple Press, 1994.

Kersey, Harry A., Jr. An Assumption of Sovereignty: Social and Political Trans-formation Among the Florida Seminoles, 1953–1979. Lincoln: University of Nebraska Press, 1996.

———. "Federal Schools and Acculturation Among the Florida Seminoles, 1927–1954." Florida Historical Quarterly 59 (1980): 165–181.

—. The Florida Seminoles and the New Deal, 1933–1942. Gainesville: University Press of Florida, 1989.

———. Interviews with Betty Mae Jumper, June 17, 1969, and January 2, 1985.

Kersey, Harry A., Jr., and Helen M. Bannan. "Patchwork and Politics: The Evolv-ing Roles of Florida Seminole Women in the Twentieth Century." In Negotia-tors of Change: Historical Perspectives on Native American Women. Edited by Nancy Shoemaker. Pp. 193–212. New York: Routledge, 1995.

Seminole Tribe of Florida and Seminole Tribe of Florida, Inc. "20th Anniversary of Tribal Organization, 1957–1977, Saturday, 20 August 1977." Hollywood, FL: Seminole Tribe, 1977. (Mimeo).

—Harry A. Kersey, Jr.

JUNEAU, JOSETTE (1803–1855), was a humanitarian known for promoting peace and hospitality in frontier Milwaukee, Wisconsin. Her public life spanned thirty-two years while the region was in transition from Indian to non–Indian control. Her charity and good works were acknowledged by a gift from Pope Leo XII, and she was eulogized by the local press upon her death.

Juneau was born into a family of twelve children at what is now Sheboygan, Wisconsin. She was the daughter of Jacques Vieau, an itinerant French Canadian fur trader, and a Menominee mother. Her maternal relatives included the influen-tial Menominee leaders Ahkanepoway and Onaugesa. She was reared a Catholic, and during her youth she served at the St. Francis Xavier Mission near Green

Josette Juneau

Bay, Wisconsin. She was fluent and literate in French, and she was also fluent in Menominee, Chippewa, Potawatomi, and Winnebago.

At age seventeen, she married Solomon Laurent Juneau, a French Canadian who worked under her father's supervision at Milwaukee. At that trade outpost, she proved to be an energetic woman who managed the home life and also the trading post when her husband was absent. Juneau bore at least seventeen children, of whom fourteen survived to adulthood. (Her son Joseph later became a cofounder of Juneau, Alaska, which was named for him.) In addition, she regularly accommodated guests within her home and extended nursing care, charity, and education in domestics and Christian doctrine.

In 1835 Juneau's influence within the Native community was tested severely. A few Americans squatting on local Potawatomi lands caused the Potawatomi to plan a revenge attack on the settlement during her husband's absence. Because none of the warriors wished to confront Juneau, she succeeded in foiling the plan by keeping an all-night vigil within the settlement.

Juneau mingled little with the incoming Americans and rarely spoke English, despite her husband's civic prominence throughout the region (he had a variety of business interests and served as Milwaukee's first mayor). She longed for the rural life and more contact with her Menominee kin. Later she persuaded her husband to build a second home at Theresa, Wisconsin, a village north of Milwaukee close to the Menominee Reservation. This home served as their summer residence and, after 1852, as their retirement home. In 1855 she returned to Milwaukee for treatment of a lingering illness. The treatment failed, and she died soon after.

References

Bruce, William G., ed. *History of Milwaukee: City and County.* Chicago: S. J. Clarke, 1922.

Fox, Isabella. *Solomon Juneau: A Biography, with Sketches of the Juneau Family*. Milwaukee: Evening Wisconsin Printing, 1916.

Gregory, John G. *History of Milwaukee, Wisconsin*. Chicago: S. J. Clarke, 1931.

Thwaites, Reuben G., ed. *Collections of the State Historical Society of Wisconsin*. Vol. 11. Madison, WI: Democrat Printing, 1888.

Waldman, Carl. *Who Was Who in Native American History: Indians and Non–Indians from Early Contacts Through 1900*. New York: Facts on File, 1990.

—Mark G. Thiel

K

KAVENA, JUANITA TIGER (b. 1925), was born to a Muskogee Creek father and an Anglo mother in Sasakwa, Oklahoma. Growing up in Oklahoma, she attended BIA schools, public schools, and Bacone Junior College, and graduated from East Central State College with a degree in home economics. In the summer of 1948, she accepted a teaching position at the Hopi Agency in Keams Canyon, Arizona, where she taught home economics and served as a girls' adviser. In 1949 she married a Hopi man named Wilmer Kavena and was adopted into the Hopi tribe. After over thirty years of experience and research with Hopi foods, Kavena published her only book, *Hopi Cookery*. She was included in the 1974 to 1975 *Who's Who of American Women*, and received the Lifetime Award and Distinguished Citizen Award from the University of Arizona in 1982.

In the early 1950s Kavena began gathering information for her book while she served as an Agricultural Extension Service home economist on the Hopi Reservation. In that capacity she worked with Hopi women on meal planning, food preparation and preservation, and food storage. Over the ensuing decades, Kavena continued to visit villages on the Hopi and Navajo reservations, learning all she could about traditional foods.

In *Hopi Cookery*, Kavena presents a number of recipes based on the traditional foods and preparation techniques that she encountered over the years. Significantly, she foregrounds how the recipes have changed both in her lifetime and in the lifetimes and memories of those who taught her the recipes. In this way Kavena traces the effects that supermarkets, food preparation machines, and other products of Anglo culture have had on the home economics of the Hopi. She also emphasizes the ceremonial significance of various recipes, and highlights the ways in which "modern" Anglo foods and food preparation methods are inadequate for numerous traditional meals. Overall, *Hopi Cookery* provides a fascinating picture of Kavena's life's work and serves as an important document of cultural change in the often ignored realm of food production.

References

Kavena, Juanita Tiger. *Hopi Cookery*. Tucson: University of Arizona, 1980. Reprint, 1987.

Laetz, Hans. "Hopi Culture Preserved Through Authentic Cooking." *Arizona Daily Wildcat*, October 23, 1980, 13.

Sharp, Patrick B. Personal communication with Juanita Tiger Kavena, February 18, 1997.

—Patrick B. Sharp

KEAMS, GERALDINE (b. 1951), was born on the Navajo Reservation in Castle Butte, Arizona, and attended twelve different boarding and public schools before graduating from high school. The oldest of nine children in a family of sheep-herders, she was most influenced by the storytelling of her grandmother and by her own love for reading, which laid the foundation for her interest in preserving traditional Navajo tales and rituals in her poetry.

Keams studied English and American Indian literature at the University of Arizona. While there, she was recruited in 1971 by La Mama Theater in New York City. Working there with Lee Breuer, later cochair of the Yale Drama School, and Robert Shorty, a Navajo visual artist, she translated her grandmother's version of the Navajo creation story into English as the basis of a theater piece that was first presented in New York and then toured the country in 1971 to 1972. She credits Breuer with her growing interest in "weaving words and visuals together," which led to her work in film, theater, and performance poetry with the Lee Strasberg School and Café La Mama in New York in the 1970s and in Los Angeles in the 1980s.

A member of the Writers Guild of America West and cofounder of the Big Mountain Support Group of Los Angeles, Keams has served as consultant on such films as *Broken Rainbow*; has produced her own full-length film, *Trail of Pollen*; and is probably best known for her performance in the Clint Eastwood film, *The Outlaw Josey Wales*, although she has also acted in such other films as *Born to the Wind* and *The Legend of Walks Far Woman*. Her ambition in film is to "do the classic cowboy and Indian movie in reverse and do it all from the Indians' side." Meanwhile, she writes and performs her poetry in Los Angeles and involves herself in theater projects, such as *Asian Eyes*, which was performed at Olio on three levels: both a video projection of Keams and her simultaneous appearance on stage performing poetry, and a Navajo ritual. Through such multimedia approaches, she succeeds in combining the oral traditions of her heritage with her desire to preserve those traditions in ongoing artistic formats such as film and poetry.

References

Bataille, Gretchen M. "An Interview with Geraldine Keams." *Explorations in Ethnic Studies* 10 (January 1987): 1–7.
Stein, Julia. "The New Ellis Island: L.A.'s Poet Innovators." *High Performance* 38 (1987): 40–45.

—Thelma Shinn Richard

KEESHIG-TOBIAS, LENORE (b. 1950), is an Ojibwa/Potawatomi writer, storyteller, and cultural activist who resides in Toronto. The daughter of Keitha and Donald Keeshig grew up on the Nawash Reserve on the Bruce Peninsula, where she received her schooling at St. Mary's Indian Day School. She attended York University, Toronto, between 1977 and 1984, and graduated with a BFA, general honors, with an emphasis on creative writing and presentation.

Throughout her adult life, Keeshig-Tobias has promoted the production and dissemination of Native literature in Canada, working in close connection with other Native authors (Daniel David Moses, Tomson Highway, Beatrice Culleton) and initiating and cofounding the Toronto-based Committee to Re-establish the Trickster.

Keeshig-Tobias has published articles, poetry, children's literature, and drama, and has helped develop curricular material for use in Native schools. She also has lectured and conducted workshops on Native literature and history and Native contributions to world cultures at universities and cultural centers in Canada and the United States. She has given public readings throughout Canada and has produced educational and literary audio and video recordings. Keeshig-Tobias was an editor of *Ontario Indian* (1981–1982), and was a cofounder and editor of *Sweetgrass— The Magazine of Canada's Native Peoples* (1982–1985). Since 1988 she has edited *The Magazine to Re-establish the Trickster*.

Her incessant and selfless literary campaigning has brought Keeshig-Tobias grants and awards from the Department of Indian Affairs and Northern Development (1979, 1980), the Ontario Arts Council (1986–1989), and an Author's Award for a Feature Article written with David McLaren and published by *This Magazine*.

Keeshig-Tobias has come out strongly on several occasions against the appropriation of Native culture and philosophy by non–Native writers like Anne Cameron and Lynn Andrews. The wide attention this issue receives from Native and non–Native writers alike is mainly due to Keeshig-Tobias's panel discussion at the Writer's Union of Canada annual general meeting in the spring of 1989.

After having lived in Toronto for many years, Keeshig-Tobias returned to her home reserve on the Bruce Peninsula in the early 1990s. In 1992 she published a bilingual children's book, *Bineshiinh Dibaajmowin: Bird Talk*, illustrated by her oldest daughter, Polly. In November of the same year, she was invited to make a speaking and reading tour of Denmark, Sweden, and Finland. Keeshig-Tobias has five children and shares her life with her partner, David McLaren.

References

Keeshig-Tobias, Lenore. *Bineshiinh Dibaajmowin: Bird Talk*. Illustrated by Polly Keeshig-Tobias. Toronto: Sister Vision, 1992.

———. "He Was a Boxer When I Was Small" (and other poems). In *Seventh Generation*. Edited by Heather Hodgson. Pp. 64–71. Penticton, BC: Theytus Books, 1989.

———."Stop Stealing Native Stories." *Globe and Mail* [Toronto], January 26, 1990, A7.

———. "White Lies?" *Saturday Night* 105 (October 1990): 67–68.

———. ed. *Into the Moon: Heart, Mind, Body, Soul. The Native Women's Writing Circle*. Toronto: Sister Vision, 1996.

"Lenore Keeshig-Tobias." In *Contemporary Challenges: Conversations with Canadian Native Authors*. Edited by Hartmut Lutz. Pp. 79–88. Saskatoon, SK: Fifth House, 1991.

Petrone, Penny. *Native Literature in Canada: From the Oral Tradition to the Present*. Toronto: Oxford University Press, 1990.

—Hartmut Lutz

KEGG, MAUDE MITCHELL [Naawakamigookwe, Middle of the Earth Lady] (1904–1996), Chippewa (Ojibwa) tradition-bearer, was born in a birch bark wigwam at a wild rice harvesting camp in Crow Wing County, Minnesota, near the Chippewa villages of Lake Mille Lacs. She learned tribal lore and skills from Aakogwan, her maternal grandmother, who raised her in ricing, maple sugar, and berry picking camps and in the family's winter house. She attended the local country school with white settlers and completed the eighth grade. She married Martin Kegg in 1922; they eventually made their home on the Mille Lacs Reservation and raised ten children.

For many years a guide at the Mille Lacs Indian Museum of the Minnesota Historical Society, Kegg was an interpreter of her people's traditional way of life to both Indians and non–Indians. In 1969 she began teaching the Ojibway language to scholars and dictating her memoirs and historical legends in Ojibway. This work has led to two bilingual books (both in several editions), as well as a technical grammar and a student dictionary, widely used in Ojibway language and culture classes in the United States and Canada.

Skilled in traditional crafts with birch bark, basswood bark fiber, deer hide, and beads, Kegg was featured in the 1986 exhibition "Lost and Found Traditions: Native American Art 1965 to 1985." In 1990 she received a National Heritage fellowship from the National Endowment for the Arts in recognition of her achievements as a folk artist and a cultural interpreter.

References

Coe, Ralph. *Lost and Found Traditions: Native American Art 1965–1985*. Seattle: University of Washington Press, 1986. (Exhibition catalog).

Kegg, Maude. *Gabekanaansing/At the End of the Trail: Memories of Chippewa Childhood in Minnesota*. Edited by John Nichols. Occasional Publications in Anthropology, Linguistic Series, no. 4. Greeley: University of Northern Colorado Museum of Anthropology, 1978.

———. *Gii-Ikwezensiwiyaan/When I Was a Little Girl*. Edited by John Nichols. Onamia, MN: Privately printed, 1976.

———. *Nookomis Gaa-inaajimotawid/What My Grandmother Told Me*. Edited by John D. Nichols. 2nd ed. Bemidji, MN: American Indian Studies, Bemidji State University, 1990.

———. *Portage Lake*. Edited by John D. Nichols. Edmonton: University of Alberta Press, 1991. Reprint, Minneapolis: University of Minnesota Press, 1993.

Nichols, John D. "Ojibwe Morphology." PhD diss., Harvard University, 1980.

Nichols, John D., and Earl Nyholm. *A Concise Dictionary of Minnesota Ojibwe*. Minneapolis: University of Minnesota Press, 1995.

—John D. Nichols

KELLOGG, LAURA CORNELIUS [Laura Miriam Cornelius, Minnie Kellogg] (1880–1947), was born into the Oneida Indian community of Wisconsin and became a baptized member of the Episcopal Church. She was descended from two influential Oneida leaders, Chief Daniel Bread and Chief Skenandore. Like her forebears, Kellogg built her reputation as an Oneida leader by using her gift for oratory. Unlike many of her contemporaries, who went to Indian boarding schools, she attended Grafton Hall, a private finishing school for girls in Fond du Lac, Wisconsin. After graduating in 1898, she spent two years traveling in Europe, and she later studied at institutions of higher learning including Stanford, Barnard College, Columbia, Cornell, and the University of Wisconsin.

As one of the founders of the Society of American Indians, Kellogg contributed to the emergence of a national Indian voice at the society's first meeting in 1911. In her address she asked the leadership for a commitment to Indian self-sufficiency and independence, goals she believed were attainable by instituting plans for self-sustaining economic development on Indian reservations. Though her message did not prove overwhelmingly popular among national Indian leaders, Kellogg did find a supportive constituency among the Iroquois. Thereafter she began more and more to devote her considerable talents, which included fluency in Oneida, to the recovery of New York and Wisconsin lands taken from the Oneida people.

Kellogg's special genius as a leader of the Oneida land claims struggle included her use of traditional Iroquois images and institutions to solve modern problems. The strategies she developed have influenced all subsequent twentieth-century campaigns to reclaim Iroquois lands. Unfortunately, her legacy as an Iroquois leader is marred by accusations of fraud and mismanagement of donations. Never able to recover her reputation, she died in obscurity in New York City in 1947.

References

Campisi, Jack. "Ethnic Identity and Boundary Maintenance in Three Oneida Communities." PhD diss., State University of New York, Albany, 1974.

Cornelius, Laura M. "Industrial Organization for the Indian." In *Report of the Executive Council on the Proceedings of the First Annual Conference, 12–17 October 1911, Society of American Indians*. Pp. 46–49. Washington, DC: Society of American Indians, 1912.

———. "Overalls and the Tenderfoot: A Story." *The Barnard Bear* 2 (March 1907): 5–18.

Hauptman, Laurence M. "Designing Woman: Minnie Kellogg, Iroquois Leader." In *Indian Lives: Essays on Nineteenth- and Twentieth-Century Native American Leaders*. Edited by L. G. Moses and Raymond Wilson. Pp. 158–186. Albuquerque: University of New Mexico Press, 1985.

Kellogg, Laura Cornelius. *Our Democracy and the American Indian*. Kansas City, MO: Burton, 1920.

———. "Some Facts and Figures on Indian Education." *The Quarterly Journal* 1 (April 15, 1913): 37.

McLester, Thelma Cornelius. "Oneida Women Leaders." In *The Oneida Indian Experience: Two Perspectives*. Edited by Jack Campisi and Laurence Hauptman. Pp. 108–125. Syracuse, NY: Syracuse University Press, 1988.

—*Gretchen G. Harvey*

KIDWELL, CLARA S. (b. 1941), has been a professor and director of the American Studies Department, University of Oklahoma, since 1995, as well as a researcher in Choctaw land claims against the United States. This work followed service as an associate professor of Native American Studies, University of California, Berkeley, from 1974 to 1992, and as assistant director for cultural resources of the National Museum of the American Indian at the Smithsonian Institution from 1992 to 1995. In that capacity, she supervised the development and conservation of collections and, when appropriate, the repatriation of specific objects to tribes.

Kidwell's professional career began in 1966. She served first as a college instructor in history and then as a publications coordinator for a university research unit. In 1970 Kidwell became an instructor and chair of the Social Science Division at Haskell Indian Junior College, Lawrence, Kansas. She was appointed assistant professor of American Indian Studies at the University of Minnesota, Minneapolis from 1972 to 1974.

At Berkeley, Kidwell's research and publication flourished. Her writings and lectures reflected her interest in the interaction between Europeans and Native Americans in North America, including civil rights, education, ecology, medicine, women, worldview, and the Choctaw tribe. She received fellowships from the Newberry Library, Chicago, and the Smithsonian Institution, among others. In 1980 Kidwell served as a visiting scholar and associate professor at Dartmouth College, and in 1989 became a trustee of the National Museum of the American Indian. At Berkeley she also served as chair of the Department of Ethnic Studies, associate dean in the Graduate Division, and director of the Consortium for Graduate Opportunities for American Indians.

Of Choctaw and Chippewa parentage, Kidwell was born in Tahlequah, Oklahoma, and was raised in Muskogee, Oklahoma. She attended a Catholic grade school and a public high school in Muskogee. She earned her BA in letters, and her MA and PhD in history of science, at the University of Oklahoma, Norman, the latter in 1970.

References

Kidwell, Clara S. "American Indian Attitudes Toward Nature: A Bicentennial Perspective." In *Contemporary Native American Address*. Edited by John R. Maestas. Pp. 277–293. Provo, UT: Brigham Young University Publications, 1975.

————. "Aztec and European Medicine in the New World, 1521–1600." In *Anthropology of Medicine*. Edited by Lola Romanucci-Ross, Daniel Moerman, and Lawrence Tancredi. Pp. 19–30. South Hadley, MA: J. F. Bergin, 1982.

————. "The Choctaw Struggle for Land and Identity in Mississippi, 1830–1918." In *After Removal: The Choctaw in Mississippi*. Edited by Samuel J. Wells and Roseanna Tubby. Pp.64–93. Jackson: University Press of Mississippi, 1986.

————. *Choctaws and Missionaries in Mississippi, 1818–1918*. Norman: University of Oklahoma Press, 1995.

————. "The Power of Women in Three American Indian Societies." *Journal of Ethnic Studies* 6 (Winter 1979): 113–121.

————. "Science and Ethnoscience." *The Indian Historian* 6 (Fall 1973): 43–54.

———. "Science and Ethnoscience: Native American World Views as a Factor in the Development of Native Technologies." In *Environmental History: Critical Issues in Comparative Perspectives*. Edited by Kendall E. Bailes. Pp. 277–287. Lanham, MD: University Press of America, 1985.

———. "What Would Pocahontas Think Now? Women and Cultural Persistence." *Callaloo* 17 (1994): 149–159.

Kidwell, Clara Sue, Homer Noley, and George E. "Tink" Tinker. *A Native American Theology*. Maryknoll, NY: Orbis Books, 2001.

———. Electronic correspondence from Clara Sue Kidwell, October 7, 1996.

Thiel, Mark G. Personal communication with Clara Sue Kidwell, December 12, 1990.

—Mark G. Thiel

KILPATRICK, ANNA GRITTS (b. 1917), was born in Echota, Oklahoma, and earned a BS from Southern Methodist University in 1958. She spent her professional life as a teacher in the Dallas, Texas, public school system, and pursued an active second career as a writer and collaborator with her husband, Jack Frederick Kilpatrick, a professor of music at Southern Methodist University.

As a result of their shared interest in ethnomusicology, the Kilpatricks investigated the relation of traditional Cherokee music patterns and tropes to symphonic music. This interest in blending the tribal and the European musical traditions led Jack Kilpatrick to compose a symphony for the Oklahoma semicentennial in 1957; at the time of his death, he was composing a symphony based on the rhythms and euphony of Native music. The Kilpatricks also brought to print many translations of Cherokee history, charms and love songs, folktales, and oral traditions. Theirs was apparently very much an intellectual and emotional partnership, one committed to both preserving and adapting the cultural heritage of the Oklahoma Cherokee. Their edited translation of *New Chota Letters* made available material from the first Native-language periodical in America, a Cherokee publication. After her husband's death in 1967, Kilpatrick continued to prepare their collaborative works on the Oklahoma Cherokee culture for publication.

References

Kilpatrick, Anna Gritts, and Jack F. Kilpatrick. *Friends of Thunder: Folktales of the Oklahoma Cherokees*. Dallas, TX: Southern Methodist University Press, 1964.

———. *Muskogean Charm Songs Among the Oklahoma Cherokees*. Smithsonian Contributions to Anthropology, vol. 2, no. 3. Washington, DC: Smithsonian Press, 1967.

———. *Notebook of a Cherokee Shaman*. Smithsonian Contributions to Anthropology, vol. 2, no. 6. Washington, DC: Smithsonian Institution Press, 1970.

———. *Run Toward the Nightland: Magic of the Oklahoma Cherokees*. Dallas, TX: Southern Methodist University Press, 1967.

———. *Walk in Your Soul: Love Incantations of the Oklahoma Cherokees*. Dallas, TX: Southern Methodist University Press, 1965.

172   KIMBALL, YEFFE

————, eds. *New Chota Letters*. Dallas, TX: Southern Methodist University Press, 1968.

————. *The Shadow of Sequoyah: Social Documents of the Cherokees, 1862–1964*. Translated by Anna Gritts Kilpatrick and Jack F. Kilpatrick. Civilization of the American Indian Series, vol. 81. Norman: University of Oklahoma Press, 1965.

—*Jennifer L. Jenkins*

KIMBALL, YEFFE [Mikaka Upawixe, Wandering Star] (1914–1978), was an accomplished and versatile artist whose work includes award-winning paintings, storybook illustrations, a cookbook, and designs in a variety of media. In her work for the National Congress of American Indians and as a consultant to museums and the United States State Department, she was an outspoken defender of American Indian art and culture. Commissioned by NASA, she was also recognized as one of the foremost painters of outer space. During the course of her long career, her work was included in more than one hundred exhibits and featured in over fifty solo shows.

Kimball was born March 30, 1914, in Mountain Park, Oklahoma, of mixed Osage ancestry. During the late 1930s and early 1940s she trained at the Art Students League in New York, studied in Europe during the summers, and worked intermittently with Fernand Léger and Jon Corbino. Her early work was concerned essentially with re-presenting Indian art in a modern form. In review articles for *Art Digest*, Kimball spoke for a group of painters trying to bridge the gap between traditional American Indian art and modern European painting. The struggle, as she saw it, was not only for recognition of "this most native of our many art expressions" by the dominant culture, but also "against traditionalism, tight-bound ceremonial functions, Chieftain rule and Kiva law." Thus, she writes, "the modern Indian artist has painted his own particular 'Declaration of Independence,' [and] now insists on participating in the 20th Century."

Kimball seemed to declare her own independence from Indian art during the late 1950s and 1960s. After marrying Dr. Harvey L. Slatin, an atomic scientist, she turned her artistic attention to outer space and greater experimentation with her medium and its use. For this she was sometimes faulted by her critics. One reviewer remarked, "The pyrotechnical use of the medium, which includes the intelligence of its use, somewhat exceeds anything else. . . . The imagery is anthropomorphic and descriptive; the paintings seem to be imagined close-ups of the cosmos—which is just too easy." But in turning to the cosmos for inspiration, Kimball may have been more indebted to her Indian heritage than her critics recognized. As she herself wrote, "The Indian artist, while documenting his people, finds it natural to invest his work with the cosmos, since every aspect of Indian life shows [the] concept of man's place in the universe and his relationship to everything in it."

Kimball's paintings and other work in a variety of media produced near the end of her life exhibit recognizably Indian themes and symbols, which during the 1970s seemed to appeal more than outer space to those in search of something beyond the visible world—what numerous reviewers referred to as Indian "magic." Kimball had earlier predicted such a turn of events. As early as 1948 she had written of "an aesthetic world in the midst of [a] struggle to re-establish contact with the rejuvenating world beyond actual vision." Kimball died at her vacation home in Santa Fe, New Mexico, on April 10, 1978.

References

Kimball, Yeffe. *Kimball*. Washington, DC: Center for Arts of Indian America, 1967.
———. "Tulsa Accords Recognition to Our Indian Art." *Art Digest* 21 (1947): 12, 30.
———. "Tulsa Surveys U.S. Indian Art." *Art Digest* 22 (1948): 11.
Lester, Patrick D. "Yeffe Kimball." In *The Biographical Directory of Native American Painters*. P. 293. Tulsa, OK: SIR Publications, 1995.

—Christopher Schedler

KIRKNESS, VERNA J. (b. 1935), holds BA, MEd, and DEd, degrees, and is the founder and director of the First Nations House of Learning at the University of British Columbia. She is widely known for her contributions to the development of Indian-controlled education. Her career has spanned thirty-seven years, during which she has been an elementary school teacher and principal, education supervisor, curriculum development researcher and consultant, and education director for the Manitoba Indian Brotherhood. Kirkness joined the Education Department faculty at the University of British Columbia in 1981, as the director of the Native Indian Teacher Education Program (NITEP). In 1983 she became the director of Native Indian Education and developed the Ts'kel Education Administration Graduate Program, which began in 1984. In 1987 she assumed the position as director of NITEP.

Kirkness's publication record spans eighteen years and includes three books and more than twenty articles and papers on various aspects of Indian education in Canada. Since 1986 she has edited one issue each year of the *Canadian Journal of Native Education*. She is also widely known for her research, writing, and campaigning for the development of the national Indian Post-Secondary Education Assistance Program (1977). The program has sponsored thousands of Indian students pursuing technical and professional training at the postsecondary level.

Much of Kirkness's spare time is devoted to private consultation work that involves evaluating and advising locally controlled Indian band schools, doing workshops, and lecturing. Kirkness has lectured and presented papers at a wide range of forums. A world traveler, she attended the World Conference: Indigenous People's Education in New Zealand (1990).

Kirkness has been widely recognized and applauded for her contributions to, and promotion of, Indian education issues. She has received the Golden Eagle Feather Award (1988) from the Professional Native Women's Association, the title of fellow (1988) from the Ontario Institute for Studies in Education, the title of president emeritus (1988) of the Mokakit Indian Education Research Association (which she founded in 1983), Canadian Educator of the Year Award (1990), an honorary doctorate of humane letters from Mount St. Vincent University (1990), the University of British Columbia Alumni Award (1990), the University of British

Columbia's Seventy-fifth Anniversary Medal (1990), and the British Columbia Educator of the Year Award (1990). One of the most outstanding honors she received from her own community was the opening of the Kirkness Adult Learning Centre (1984) in Winnipeg, Manitoba. It was named to honor Kirkness as "a distinguished teacher and author on education of Native Indians."

Kirkness, of Swampy Cree origins, is from the Fisher River First Nation at Koostatak, Manitoba. She speaks her language fluently. Her example as a role model and activist has been important in opening the doors for indigenous women in the professions and in making Indian education a national priority.

References

Kirkness, Verna J. "Indian Control of Indian Education: Over a Decade Later." In *Mokakit Indian Education Research Association—Selected Papers*. Pp. 74–79. Vancouver: University of British Columbia, 1986.

———, ed. and comp. *Khot-La-Cha: The Autobiography of Chief Simon Bake* Vancouver, BC: Douglas & McIntyre, 1994.

McGlaughlin, Peter. "MSVU Convocation Without Incident, Threats." *The Daily News* [Halifax, NS], May 12, 1990, 4.

"A Tribute to Verna Kirkness, President Emeritus, Mokakit." *Mokakit Newsletter* 1 (1989): 1. West, Doug. "Educator Wins National Award." *Kahtou* (May 1, 1990): 3.

—Winona Stevenson

KREPPS, ETHEL C. (b?), was born in Mountain View, Oklahoma, and is secretary of the Kiowa tribe. An active voice for the importance of education for Indian peoples, she holds both nursing and law degrees. She received her JD from the University of Tulsa College of Law in 1979. In addition to her duties within her tribe, Krepps has served as a national officer of American Indian/Alaskan Native Nurses Association, staff attorney for the Native American Coalition of Tulsa for the Indian Child Welfare Act, state chairperson for the Indian Child Welfare Association, and secretary of the Native American Chamber of Commerce.

Krepps provides legal services to Indian tribes and individuals, contributes free legal counsel to obtain custody of Indian children for Indian parents, and has served as a family crisis counselor. She has presented testimony before the Committee on Equality of Education for Women, has been an adviser to the Ohoyo Resource Center, served on the Region VI Adoption Task Force, was the national essay winner for the Trial Lawyers' Association of the American Bar Association in 1979, and participated in an Oklahoma Conference in 1981.

References

Krepps, Ethel C. "Equality in Education for Indian Women." *Wassaja/The Indian Historian* 13 (June 1980): 9–10.

———. "Indian Women as Change Agents in Indian Policy." *In American Public Discourse: A Multicultural Perspective*. Edited by Ronald K. Burke. Pp. 29–33. Lanham, MD: University Press of America, 1992.

————. "A Strong Medicine Wind." *True West* 26 (March/April 1979): 7–10, 40–42.

————. *A Strong Medicine Wind*. Austin, TX: Western, 1979.

————. "A Strong Medicine Wind." In *Oklahoma Memories*. Edited by Anne Morgan and Rennard Strickland. Pp. 145–161. Norman: University of Oklahoma Press, 1981.

—Julie A. Russ

L

LADUKE, WINONA (b. 1959), an Anishinaabe (Ojibwa/Chippewa), is an enrolled member of the Mississippi of the White Earth Reservation in northern Minnesota where she lives with her daughter, Waseyabin, and their son, Ajawak. LaDuke spends a few weeks, several times a year, on the Minnesota White Earth Reservation, her father's tribal homeland.

After her parents' divorce, when LaDuke was five years old, she was raised by her mother. Today her Anishinaabe father, Vincent LaDuke (Sun Bear), is a well-known New Age author. Her mother, Betty LaDuke, who is Jewish, is an artist and activist who has supported her daughter's exploration of and identification with her Native heritage.

In 1982 LaDuke received a BA from Harvard in Native economic development. She studied at the Massachusetts Institute of Technology in 1983, in the Department of Urban Studies' Community Fellows Program. LaDuke received her MA in rural development from Antioch University in 1989.

LaDuke is a tireless author, economist, legal researcher, lecturer, and activist. She has published extensively on Native economic development and on environmental and legal issues related to Native affairs. She speaks out for the social, political, economic, and environmental rights of other tribes as well as her own. She has been involved, for instance, in the resistance movement by the Big Mountain Diné (Navajo), who are fighting forced relocation from their ancestral homeland. LaDuke has also expanded her scope of concern to address concerns of indigenous peoples worldwide, and participated in the 1995 U.N. Conference on Women held in China.

In 1989 LaDuke received one of the first international Reebok Human Rights Awards, recognizing human rights activists under the age of thirty. With her award, she initiated the White Earth Land Recovery Project, an effort that will return to tribal members some of the 830,000 acres of the White Earth Reservation that were promised to the Anishinaabe who originally relocated to this first Minnesota reservation.

LaDuke has held leadership positions in many local, national, and international organizations. She helped found Ikwe (Woman), a cooperative that sells crafts and wild rice; is a member of Women of All Red Nations; has served as president of the continental Indigenous Women's Network; and has been a Steering Committee representative on the International Council of Indigenous Women, a global organization seeking nongovernmental organization status at the United

Nations. In addition, Ralph Nader chose her as his 1996 and 2000 vice presidential candidate for the Green Party, and *Ms.* magazine selected her as one of its 1997 Women of the Year.

References

Anishinabeg. "Winona LaDuke." *Nature Study* 46 (March 1994): 46.

Fireweed: A Feminist Quarterly 22 (Winter 1986). Special issue.

Florio, Maria, and Victoria Mudd. *Broken Rainbow*. Distributed by Earthworks Films. 1985.

LaDuke, Betty. "Winona: In Celebration of a Rite of Passage." *Woman of Power* 13 (Spring 1989): 32–33.

LaDuke, Winona. *All Our Relations: Native Struggles for Land and Life.* Cambridge, MA: South End Press, 1999.

———. "Environmental Work: An Indigenous Perspective." *Northeast Indian Quarterly* 8 (1991): 16–19.

———. "I Fight like a Woman: The UN Conference on Women in China, 1995." *Canadian Dimension* 30 (April 1996): 39–41.

———. "In Honor of the Women Warriors." *off our backs* 11 (February 1981): 3–4.

———. "Indian Treaty Rights Are a Critical Environmental Issue." *Utne Reader* 37 (January/February 1990): 57.

———. "Interview with Roberta Blackgoat, a Diné Elder." *Woman of Power* 4 (Fall 1986): 29–31.

———. *Last Standing Woman*. Stillwater, MN: Voyageur Press, 1997.

———. "Like Tributaries to a River: The Growing Strength of Native Environmentalism." *Sierra* 81 (November/December 1996): 38–45.

———. "They Always Come Back." In *A Gathering of Spirit: A Collection by North American Indian Women*. 2nd ed. Edited by Beth Brant. Pp. 62–67. Ithaca, NY: Firebrand Books, 1988.

———. "The White Earth Land Struggle." International Working Group on Indigenous Affairs, Document no. 62 (January 1989).

———. "Words from the Indigenous Women's Network Meeting." *Akwesasne Notes* 17 (Winter 1985): 8–10.

LaDuke, Winona, and Ward Churchill. "Native America: The Political Economy of Radioactive Colonialism." *Insurgent Sociologist* 13 (Spring 1986): 51–78.

Levy, Paul. "The Land and the Blood." *Star Tribune Sunday Magazine*, May 14, 1989, 8–15.

Paul, Sonya, and Robert Perkinson. "Winona LaDuke." *The Progressive* 59 (October 1995): 36.

—*Elizabeth A. McNeil*

LAFLESCHE FARLEY, ROSALIE (1861–1900), was born on the Omaha Reservation in Nebraska in 1861, the second daughter of Joseph LaFlesche (Insta Maza, Iron Eye), and Mary Gale (Hinnuagsnun, One Woman). Joseph was half white and half Ponca; Mary was white and Omaha. Iron Eye had become a chief of the Omahas in 1853 and remained in that position until 1866. He was an influential member of the tribe at a time of great transition and upheaval in its history. Joseph LaFlesche preached the doctrine of assimilation to his people and to his children, insisting that they must provide a white education for young members of the tribe, and adopt white ways of living.

LaFlesche was one of four sisters who had an impact on the history of their people, the others being Susette, Marguerite, and Susan. Their half brother Francis became a noted ethnologist. Like Iron Eye's other children, LaFlesche attended school on the reservation. While her three sisters went on to attend school in the East, LaFlesche remained behind; nonetheless, she played an important role in the drama that was unfolding on the reservation at the time. Two issues were hotly debated on the Omaha Reservation after the allotment of land in severalty was completed in 1884: leasing of unallotted tribal land and self-government for the tribe.

On one side of the issue stood LaFlesche and her husband, Ed Farley, along with her father and most of the rest of the LaFlesche family. Opposing them were Susette LaFlesche, or Bright Eyes, and her husband, Thomas H. Tibbles, a newspaperman and reformer. The Tibbleses were outspoken in their belief that the Indians' best interests lay in citizenship and immediate assimilation into white society. LaFlesche and other family members believed in self-government for the Omaha, a system that would make them independent of both the federal government and the state of Nebraska. They contended, further, that leasing pastureland not used by the Indians would yield badly needed income for the tribe. Ed and Rosalie became the managers of a large tract of unallotted lands that they leased to white cattlemen. They also managed the allotted lands of some Indians who wished to rent their property rather than work it. LaFlesche handled most of the business, including negotiating with the government and the tribe, handling accounts for individuals, and making contracts. The leasing of pasture led to several disagreements with white squatters and land speculators, in which LaFlesche defended the tribe's interests vigorously. The self-government question was settled in 1887 when the Omahas were made citizens and came under the jurisdiction of the state of Nebraska.

Although she did not attain national prominence, Rosalie LaFlesche Farley was recognized as a leader of her people who spoke eloquently on their behalf.

References

Green, Norma Kidd. *Iron Eye's Family: The Children of Joseph LaFlesche.* Lincoln, NE: Johnsen Publishing, 1969.
LaFlesche Family Papers. Nebraska State Historical Society, Lincoln.

—*James W. Parins*

LAFLESCHE PICOTTE, SUSAN (1865–1915), was born on the Omaha Reservation in Nebraska on June 17, 1865, the daughter of Joseph LaFlesche (Insta Maza, Iron Eye) and Mary Gale (Hinnuagsnun, One Woman). Iron Eye, a chief of the Omaha, was half white and half Ponca; his wife was white and Omaha. The influential LaFlesche family supported bringing white education to the reservation and made certain that each of their children received a good education.

Susan LaFlesche attended school on the reservation, then accompanied her elder sister Marguerite to the Elizabeth Institute for Young Ladies in New Jersey. Three years later, in 1882, she returned home to teach at the mission school. In 1884 LaFlesche began her studies at the Hampton Normal and Agricultural Institute in Virginia, a school for blacks and Indians, graduating with honors in the spring of 1886. In October of that year, she entered the Woman's Medical College of Pennsylvania in Philadelphia. LaFlesche graduated at the head of her class in 1889, becoming the first American Indian female doctor of medicine.

LaFlesche returned to the Omaha Reservation upon completing a four-month internship in Philadelphia and worked as a physician at the local school. A few months later, she was appointed physician for the Omaha Agency, a post she held until 1893. The work was difficult, and her duties extended beyond the purely medical; she also served as adviser, teacher, interpreter, and nurse. In 1893 the young physician temporarily left her position to care for her mother, who was infirm. LaFlesche was in ill health herself by then, her condition no doubt worsened by her regimen of hard work; travel over long distances, often in inclement weather; and exposure to diseases of every kind.

Despite her ill health and against the advice of family and friends, LaFlesche announced her intention to marry Henry Picotte in 1894. Picotte, a Yankton Sioux, was the brother of Charles Picotte, who had married her sister Marguerite six years earlier. Susan and Henry settled in Bancroft, Nebraska, where she practiced medicine and he farmed. The couple had two sons, Caryl and Pierre. Even though her practice placed demands on her, Picotte continued to serve her people during this period. She acted as interpreter and helped many families and individuals during the transition Omaha society was experiencing.

After Henry's death in 1905, Picotte was appointed missionary to the Omahas by the Presbyterian Board of Home Missions. She had been active in the church in Bancroft, and after her appointment she continued to minister to the needs of the area's people. She was politically active as well, and in 1910 headed a tribal delegation to the nation's capital, where she addressed the secretary of the Interior on the issues of Omaha citizenship and competency. But it was in the area of health care that Picotte made her biggest contribution. She insisted that the Omaha adopt modern hygienic practices and other preventive measures to halt the spread of disease. Further, soon after she moved to the new town of Walthill, she began a campaign to build a hospital for the people there. The facility was opened in 1913.

Picotte administered to her people's physical, spiritual, and personal needs. She also represented the Omahas in white society, serving, from time to time, as their representative to the government. But more often, Picotte was the one who spoke for the Omahas in an unofficial but nonetheless clearly recognized capacity. She represented them to groups from the East and from Nebraska, ranging from women's clubs to missionary, educational, and medical organizations. Until her death in 1915, she was an effective role model for hundreds of young Omahas.

References

Clark, Jerry E., and Martha Ellen Webb. "Susette and Susan LaFlesche: Reformer and Missionary." In *Being and Becoming Indian: Biographical Studies of North American Frontiers*. Edited by James A. Clifton. Pp. 137–159. Chicago: Dorsey Press, 1989.

Green, Norma Kidd. *Iron Eye's Family: The Children of Joseph LaFlesche.* Lincoln, NE: Johnsen Publishing, 1969.

LaFlesche Family Papers. Nebraska State Historical Society, Lincoln.

Mathes, Valerie Sherer. "Dr. Susan LaFlesche Picotte: The Reformed and the Reformer." In *Indian Lives: Essays on Nineteenth- and Twentieth-Century Native Americans.* Edited by L. G. Moses and Raymond Wilson. Pp. 61–90. Albuquerque: University of New Mexico Press, 1985.

———. "Susan LaFlesche Picotte: Nebraska's Indian Physician, 1865–1915." *Nebraska History* 63 (1982): 502–530.

—*James W. Parins*

LAFLESCHE PICOTTE DIDDOCK, MARGUERITE

LAFLESCHE PICOTTE DIDDOCK, MARGUERITE (1862–1945), was born on the Omaha Reservation in Nebraska, the daughter of Joseph LaFlesche (Insta Maza, Iron Eye) and Mary Gale (Hinnuagsnun, One Woman). Her father was Ponca and white, and her mother was Omaha and white. LaFlesche was schooled on the reservation and later attended the Elizabeth Institute for Young Ladies in New Jersey, following in the footsteps of her older sister Susette. She was accompanied east by her sister Susan, and the pair remained at the Institute for three years. In 1882, after completing their course of study, they returned to the reservation. LaFlesche took a job teaching at the Presbyterian mission school there.

In 1884 Marguerite and Susan again went east, this time to Hampton, Virginia. There they enrolled in the Hampton Normal and Agricultural Institute, a school for blacks and Indians. LaFlesche studied in the teaching course for a year before returning home. In 1886 she returned to Hampton, and graduated in 1887. As part of the commencement ceremonies, LaFlesche read her senior composition, "Customs of the Omahas," a piece for which she had received special honors.

After graduation LaFlesche began her career as a teacher on the Omaha Reservation. While at Hampton, she had met Charles Felix Picotte, Jr., a Sioux, who had also become a teacher and was now back at the Yankton Agency. In late 1888 they decided to marry. Picotte left Yankton to join his new wife in Nebraska, where she continued to teach, and he took up management of much of the family farm after the death of Joseph LaFlesche. During the winter of 1889 to 1890, Picotte accompanied Susette LaFlesche and her husband, Thomas H. Tibbles, to Pine Ridge, where they reported on the Ghost Dance movement and the later violence at Wounded Knee. Picotte acted as interpreter for the two journalists until January 1891, when he returned to the Omaha Reservation. By this time his health was failing rapidly; he died the next year.

LaFlesche continued to teach at the Omaha Agency government school. The agency's "industrial farmer" was Walter Diddock, who was in charge of the farm and of teaching agriculture to boys from the school. In time, the two became engaged and were married in June 1895. Eventually they built a house on the reservation at Walthill, near the home of Susan LaFlesche Picotte, and reared five children there. During the first decades of the twentieth century, LaFlesche was active in the social, political, and educational affairs of the Omahas. She participated in negotiations with the federal government at the end of the trust period in 1910 and worked hard to bring library facilities to the reservation. She also served on the election board after the Nineteenth Amendment came into effect, although she could not vote herself.

LaFlesche died in the Susan Picotte Memorial Hospital in 1945.

References

Green, Norma Kidd. *Iron Eye's Family: The Children of Joseph LaFlesche*. Lincoln, NE: Johnsen Publishing, 1969.
LaFlesche family papers. Nebraska State Historical Society, Lincoln.

—James W. Parins

LAFLESCHE TIBBLES, SUSETTE [Inshta Theamba, Bright Eyes] (1854–1903), was born on the Omaha Reservation in Nebraska. Her father, Joseph LaFlesche (Insta Maza, Iron Eye) was Ponca and French; through he spent some of his early life working with his father as a trader, he eventually made his home with his Ponca mother, who lived with the Omahas. LaFlesche's mother was Mary Gale (Hinnu-agsnun, One Woman), who was white and Omaha. The LaFlesche family was influential on the reservation because Joseph had become chief in 1853, and remained chief until 1866. He was an early advocate of white education for Omaha children, and supported efforts by missionaries and others to establish schools among his people. He also saw to it that his children—Louis, Susette, Rosalie, Marguerite, and Susan—received a white education; the children of his second wife, an Omaha woman named Ta-in-ne (Elizabeth Esau), were educated by white teachers as well.

LaFlesche attended the mission school on the reservation until 1869, when it closed. In 1872 she entered the Elizabeth Institute for Young Ladies in New Jersey, which was conducted by one of her former teachers. She was a good student, excelling in literature and writing; some of her school essays were published in a New York newspaper before her graduation in 1875. She returned to the reservation to teach, but two years passed before she was able to secure a position at the government school, in spite of an Indian Service policy to give preference to properly qualified Indian applicants. She taught at the reservation school from 1877 to 1879.

During this time, events were unfolding among the Poncas, a neighboring tribe. In 1878, the Poncas were forcibly removed to Indian Territory by the U.S. Army. This action was of particular concern for the Omahas, who feared that if a peaceful group like the Poncas could be forced off their land despite their treaties, so could they. In addition, many of the Omahas had relatives among the Poncas; Bright Eyes's uncle, Joseph's brother White Swan, was a Ponca leader. During the winter of 1878 to 1879, the Ponca chief, Standing Bear, led a party of his people back to the banks of the Niobrara River, their traditional home in Nebraska. When he was arrested and brought to trial in April 1879, the event caused a great stir among the Omahas. LaFlesche took up the Ponca cause and offered expert testimony at the trial. Her appearance there and her subsequent report on conditions among the Ponca people launched her career as a writer, orator, and defender of Indian rights.

During 1878 and 1879, LaFlesche and her half brother Francis, who later became a noted ethnologist, visited the East with Standing Bear to bring the Poncas' plight to the attention of the public. The tour, organized by Thomas Henry Tibbles, assistant editor of the *Omaha Herald*, featured appearances by Standing Bear in traditional garb and the eloquent oratory of Bright Eyes, as she was billed. Tibbles, a former army scout and preacher, organized the six-month tour, during which LaFlesche spoke to civic groups, Indian reform organizations, and literary clubs in Chicago, Pittsburgh, Boston, New York, and Washington, D.C. Her fame spread as the group proceeded on their mission. At one point, Henry Wadsworth Longfellow attended her lecture, declaring that he had found Minnehaha. On the journey, she became friends with Helen Hunt Jackson, who later published *A Century of Dishonor* (1881), and Alice C. Fletcher, who subsequently worked with Francis LaFlesche on several important ethnological projects. In March and December 1880, LaFlesche testified before the Senate concerning Ponca removal. Her clear and forceful remarks reflected her firsthand knowledge of the situation, acquired through her friendship with Standing Bear, her work as an interpreter among the Poncas, and her correspondence with Ponca leaders such as White Swan.

After the death of Tibbles's wife, he and LaFlesche married. She continued her efforts on behalf of American Indians, working for citizenship and the allotment of land in severalty. In 1887 LaFlesche and her husband visited England and Scotland, where she lectured extensively. In 1890 and 1891, the pair were at Pine Ridge, where they reported on the events surrounding the Ghost Dance movement there and on the subsequent tragedy at Wounded Knee. LaFlesche published works in *St. Nicholas* and *Wide Awake*, and contributed the introduction to William Justin Harsha's Indian reform novel *Ploughed Under* (1881). LaFlesche was a correspondent for the *Omaha World Herald* and later contributed to Tibbles's Populist newspaper, *The Independent*. Except for her year in Britain and a brief sojourn in Washington, D.C., LaFlesche lived on or near the Omaha Reservation. Until her death in 1903, she used her considerable writing and speaking skills to fight for what she considered right for her people, in spite of differences of opinion with other family members.

References

Clark, Jerry E., and Martha Ellen Webb. "Susette and Susan LaFlesche: Reformer and Missionary." In *Being and Becoming Indian: Biographical Studies of North American Frontiers*. Edited by James A. Clifton. Pp. 137–159. Chicago: Dorsey Press, 1989.

Green, Norma Kidd. *Iron Eye's Family: The Children of Joseph LaFlesche*. Lincoln, NE: Johnsen Publishing, 1969.

LaFlesche Family Papers. Nebraska State Historical Society, Lincoln.

Wilson, Dorothy Clarke. *Bright Eyes: The Story of Susette LaFlesche, an Omaha Indian*. New York: McGraw-Hill, 1974.

—*James W. Parins*

LAROQUE, EMMA (b. 1949), of Cree/Métis descent, was born in Big Bay, Alberta. She received her BA from Goshen College in Indiana (1973), and her MA in religion and peace studies (1976) and her MA in Canadian history (1980) from the University of Manitoba, where she is a professor of Native Studies.

LaRoque's 1975 handbook for educators of Native students, *Defeathering the Indian*, argues that since European contact Native peoples have been defined by outsiders of the dominant culture, a situation which has resulted in "psychological violence" against Native peoples in general and against Native schoolchildren in particular. Among the issues she explores with candor are the nature and result of stereotyping, the exclusion of Native and Métis people from Canadian history texts and the misinformation disseminated when they are included, the confusion between culture and heritage, and the possible negative results of intercultural education. She advocates the inclusion of peace studies in school curricula to end the cultural and individual stereotyping that is so damaging to the self-image of Indian children.

LaRoque is also a poet. Her work appeared in *Canadian Literature* (Spring/ Summer 1990). Her brief, imagist poems are inspired by her Cree heritage and the landscape of the Canadian plains. In "The Red in Winter," she evokes the beauty of the river in winter: "The blushing river the Cree called her/She wears no rouge today/She speaks no Cree/I ask about her other lifetimes/beneath her white mask." In "Nostalgia," she asks: "Where does it go/the log-cabins,/woodstoves and rabbit soups/we know/in our eight year old hearts?" And, in the ironically titled "Progress," she describes "Earth poet/So busy/weaving/magic/into words," whose artistry is obscured by "mad modern man" and his creations, the "cold steel spires/ stealing earth and sun/dance."

References

LaRoque, Emma. *Defeathering the Indian*. Agincourt, AB: Book Society of Canada, 1975.
———. "Long Way from Home." *Ariel* 25 (1994): 122–126.
———. "Racism/Sexism and Its Effects on Native Women." In *The Canadian Human Rights Commission Report on Women and Racial Discrimination* (1990).
———. "Tides, Towns, and Trains." In *Living the Changes*. Edited by Joan Turner. Winnipeg: University of Manitoba Press, 1990.

—*Kathleen McNerney Donovan*

LAVELL, JEANNETTE [Corbiere-Lavell, Jeanette Vivian] (b. 1942) an Ojibwa, was raised on the Wikwemikong Reserve, Manitoulin Island, Ontario, and has worked in Toronto as an executive secretary and a social worker at the Canadian Indian Centre. In 1965 she was selected as Indian Princess Canada, and later, with the Young Canadians, traveled extensively across Canada, working with Native communities. She was one of the founding members and president of the Ontario Native Women's Association, and was elected a vice president of the Native Women's Association of Canada. She also served as president of Nishnawbe Institute, an organization that promotes Native culture and its relevance to contemporary life, and Anduhyaun, Inc., a residence for Native women in Toronto. She studied for and received her teaching certificate, and is still teaching in 2000.

In 1970 Lavell lost her legal status as an Indian through marriage. Subsequently, she decided to contest section 12(1)(b) of the 1951 Indian Act, which set forth that an Indian woman who marries a non–Indian is automatically deprived of her Indian status and her band rights from the date of her marriage. Under this act, male Indians who marry non–Indians are still considered Indians, and their wives are also considered Indians; thus, the basis of Lavell's case was that the gender-discriminatory provisions of section 12(1)(b) were contrary to the Canadian Bill of Rights, which guarantees protection of the law to all citizens regardless of race, sex, or creed. The case, which lost in the County Court and won in the Federal Court of Appeals, became a political vehicle for both the government and Native peoples. In 1973 it came before the Supreme Court of Canada, where it lost by one vote.

Though Lavell lost her case, she felt it a "victory and worth all the worry and anxiety it produced, because now Native people as well as our political Native organizations are looking at the whole question of Indian status and [band] membership." Indeed, for many people, the issue of Indian women's status acquired the dimensions of a moral dilemma—the rights of all Indians against the rights of a minority of Indians, namely, Indian women. The case led, in 1975, to a joint Canadian National Indian Brotherhood–cabinet consultative committee to revise the Indian Act, and in 1985, to a revision of the Indian Act.

References

Cheda, Sherill. "Indian Women." In *Women in Canada*. Edited by Marylee Stephensen. Pp. 203–204. Toronto: General Publishing, 1977.

Jamieson, Kathleen. *Indian Women and the Law in Canada: Citizen Minus*. Ottawa: Canadian Government Publishing Centre, 1978.

Secretary of State. "Jeanette Corbiere-Lavell." In *Speaking Together: Canada's Native Women*. Toronto: Hunter Rose, 1975.

Whyte, John D. "The Lavell Case and Equality in Canada." *Queen's Quarterly* 81 (1974): 28–41.

—Joni Adamson Clarke

LAWSON, ROBERTA CAMPBELL (1878–1940), a noted leader in women's clubs, was born at Alluwe, Cherokee Nation, a member of the well-known Journeycake family of Delawares. She was educated at home, in Independence, Missouri, and finally, at Hardin College in Mexico, Missouri, where she studied music.

From the time of her marriage to Edward B. Lawson in 1901, she was active in numerous women's clubs and civic projects, first at Nowata and then at Tulsa, where her husband's law practice and oil and banking interests took them. In 1917 she was elected president of the Oklahoma Federation of Women's Clubs, and thereafter rose steadily through the ranks of the General Federation of Women's Clubs of America, holding a number of offices before she became president in 1935.

Lawson chose "Education for Living" as the theme of her administration, during which the General Federation favored the balancing of capital and labor, birth control, the merit system for civil service, and the control of venereal diseases. It also became the parent organization of the Women's Field Army for the American Society for the Control of Cancer, favored federal assistance to women who needed vocational training, and debated such issues as uniform marriage, divorce, and narcotics laws and revision of tax codes. Upon retirement from the presidency in 1938,

Lawson returned to Tulsa, where she remained active in club and civic affairs until her death.

Lawson's career included other significant achievements. She published *Indian Music Programs for Clubs and Special Music Days,* and served as executive chair of the Administrative Committee for the Will Rogers Charity Fund for Drought Relief (1931) and on Eleanor Roosevelt's Committee on Mobilization for Human Needs (1933–1934). In 1933 she was a member of the first World Federation tour to Europe, where she gave performances of Indian music. In 1934 she was one of the General Federation's first delegates to the Pan-Pacific Conference. She was active throughout her career in the Presbyterian Church and the Democratic Party, and she was for many years a member of the board of regents of Oklahoma College for Women and of the board of trustees of the University of Tulsa.

References

Debo, Angie. "Roberta Campbell Lawson." In *Notable American Women 1607–1950: A Biographical Dictionary.* Edited by Edward T. James. Pp. 376–377. Cambridge, MA: Belknap Press of Harvard University Press, 1971.

Lawson, Roberta Campbell. *Indian Music Programs for Clubs and Special Music Days.* Nowata, OK: N.p., 1926.

Rainey, Luretta. *History of Oklahoma State Federation of Women's Clubs.* Guthrie, OK: Cooperative Publishing, 1939.

Tulsa Tribune, December 31, 1940, 1, 12.

—*Daniel F. Littlefield, Jr.*

LEWIS, LUCY (c. 1895–1992), an Acoma, was born around 1895 to Lola Santiago and Martin Ortiz, and lived most of her life on High Mesa at Sky City, Acoma Pueblo, in New Mexico. She did not know her exact age or birthdate, but she celebrated her entrance into the world on November 2. In the 1960s Lewis was struck by lightning and survived. She attended McCarty Day School through the third grade and spoke Keresan. She married Toribio Lewis (Hashkaya), and together they reared nine children. She was a nationally renowned potter who at a very early age learned her craft in the traditional manner, by watching her great-aunt Helice Vallo. Lewis received the Award of Merit at the first exhibition she entered, the 1950 Intertribal Indian Ceremonial in Gallup, New Mexico, and First Place at the Santa Fe Indian Market Competition in the same year. She later received national acclaim and had permanent displays in museum collections and exhibitions. Her work toured the American embassies in Europe and the Near East, and she was invited to the White House.

References

Collins, John. *A Tribute to Lucy M. Lewis, Acoma Potter.* Fullerton, CA: Museum of North Orange County, 1975.

Oleman, Minnie. "Lucy Lewis: Acoma's Versatile Potter." *El Palacio* 75 (1968): 10–12.

Peterson, Susan. *Lucy M. Lewis: American Indian Potter.* Tokyo: Kodansha International, 1984.

———. *Master Pueblo Potters*. New York: ACA Gallery, 1980. (Exhibition catalog).

—*Julie LaMay Abner*

LITTLE COYOTE, BERTHA (b. 1912), Cheyenne, was born in Oklahoma. She attended the Cantonment Boarding School in Canton, Oklahoma, from 1919 until 1925. Her vocal and lyrical interpretations of Cheyenne and Christian songs have been recorded and studied by ethnomusicologists, and she has been recognized by the Smithsonian Institution for her beadwork.

Her memoirs, as told to Virginia Giglio and titled *Leaving Everything Behind: The Songs and Memories of a Cheyenne Woman*, describe in vivid detail life in a government-run boarding school, various Cheyenne musical and game traditions, conflicts with and abuses by white culture, her melding of traditional Cheyenne and Mennonite spirituality, and her musical artistry. A compact disc that accompanies her written memoirs contains Little Coyote's songs and recorded conversations.

Reference

Little Coyote, Bertha, and Virginia Giglio. *Leaving Everything Behind: The Songs and Memories of a Cheyenne Woman*. Norman: University of Oklahoma Press, 1997.

—*Patricia Verstrat*

LITTLEMAN, ALICE (1910–2000), bead worker and craftsman, born in Old Town, north of Anadarko, Oklahoma, to Tommy Jones and Anna Konad Jones. She lived in the Washita community and attended school there until the ninth grade. Littleman (whose Kiowa name was "Domebeahty" or "Standing Under") learned the art of bead work from her mother, a renowned craftsman and bead artist in her own right. Littleman won her first award in this area at the age of seventeen at the Intertribal Ceremonial in Gallup, New Mexico. She later exhibited and sold her bead and leather work throughout the United States and was extremely active in the Oklahoma Arts and Crafts Cooperative. In her later years, Littleman created and experimented with "narrative fringes": buckskin handbags that were ornamented with fringe and that featured scenes from traditional Kiowa stories intricately portrayed in beads. Littleman was especially proud of the fact that she was able to teach the art of Kiowa beadwork to her five grandchildren—Mary, Glenda, Kathy, Edith Ann, and Linda Littlechief. She was also the mother of the late Bobby Hill, a nationally known Kiowa artist who painted under the pseudonym "White Buffalo." In recognition of her bead work and knowledge of Kiowa culture, Littleman was designated a "state treasure" of the state of Oklahoma in 1997. She died in May 2000 and is buried in Oklahoma.

Reference

Anadarko Daily News August 9, 1979 and May 26, 2000.

—*Michael Sherfy*

LOLOMA, OTELLIE (b. 1922), like many Hopi children, made little unfired clay toys, but she received no instruction until 1945, when she was awarded a three-year scholarship to Alfred University in New York state to study ceramics. Ironically, she almost refused the scholarship in order to stay at Shipaulovi, her home on Second Mesa, Arizona, where she was a substitute teacher at Shungopovi, Keams Canyon, Polacca, and Oraibi day schools. After returning from Alfred, Loloma also attended Northern Arizona University, in Flagstaff, and the College of Santa Fe.

In the late 1950s, Loloma and her husband, Charles, moved to Scottsdale, Arizona, where they perfected their crafts and opened the Kiva Craft Center. During the summers she taught at Arizona State University, and in 1961 she was an instructor for the Southwest Indian Art Project at the University of Arizona. In 1962 Loloma joined the faculty of the newly created Institute of American Indian Arts (IAIA) in Santa Fe.

During the 1960s Loloma's ceramics brought her wide critical acclaim, and she won prizes for her work at the Arizona State Fair, the Scottsdale Indian Art Exhibition, and the Philbrook Art Center, Tulsa, Oklahoma. Her work was included in several exhibitions that traveled throughout the United States, Latin America, and Europe, and is held in both permanent collections (the Museum of the American Indian and the Heye Foundation, New York; the Heard Museum, Phoenix; the Philbrook Indian Art Center; and IAIA) and private collections.

Loloma has executed work on canvas and in bronze and has designed jewelry, but it is in ceramics that she excels. The subject matter is subtly Hopi. There are human female forms with characteristic maiden whorls or buns above the ears, and bowls with masks or faces, but Loloma's manipulation of the clay is anything but Hopi. Some pieces are wheel-thrown, whereas others, especially the sculptures, are constructed; surfaces are textured, and turquoise beads and leather dress the sculpture. However modern the treatment of the clay, Loloma's heritage infuses it, as recorded by Guy and Doris Monthan: "When I start making a piece of pottery or a ceramic sculpture, I begin with an idea drawn from Hopi life and legends. As the piece progresses, the idea becomes part of the clay, subordinated to the overall design. In the finished piece the symbols may not be obvious, but they are there. They are like the seed: they have given their strength to make the plant grow."

Loloma's creative energies and time, however, are subordinate to the demands of her students at IAIA: "I stick with my students pretty close because of the fact that they are just now starting out. . . . If I'm going to make a creative artist out of them, I've got to be working close with them. . . . I'd rather have them come out of my class knowing something than me going out and doing my own exhibits, because I'm hired as an instructor, as a teacher."

References

Hammond, Harmony, and Juane Quick-to-See Smith. *Women of Sweetgrass, Cedar and Sage.* New York: Gallery of the American Indian Community House, 1985. (Exhibition catalog).

Loloma, Otellie. Interview, January 8, 1988. Manuscript Collection, Wheelwright Museum of Indian Art, Santa Fe.

Monthan, Guy, and Doris Monthan. *Art and Indian Individualism: The Art of Seventeen Contemporary Southwestern Artists and Craftsmen.* Flagstaff, AZ: Northland Press, 1975.
Nordness, Lee. *Objects: USA.* New York: Viking Press, 1970.

—Laura Graves

LONE DOG, LOUISE (b. 1928), a resident of New York City and a spiritualist, is the author of *Strange Journey: The Vision Life of a Psychic Indian Woman*, a peculiar mixture of 1960s metaphysics, traditional Indian spirituality, and Christianity. Self-professed to be of Mohawk and Delaware heritage, Lone Dog evinces much stereotypical but little legitimate tribal thinking in her work, a chronicle of her experiences with her spiritual guide, Chief White Feather (others who speak to her include Joan of Arc and John Kennedy), along with various childhood reminiscences and psychic predictions. Though the book exhibits vestigial and possibly confused, if not fraudulent, Native American traces (such as herbalism), homogenized Christian beliefs predominate; also present are communion with "haunts" and astral projection. All are juxtaposed against ridicule of witchcraft and voodoo, and skepticism of reincarnation and metaphysical organizations. Her volume, which concludes with testimonial letters from several New York women about primarily domestic predictions of Lone Dog, is perhaps best viewed as an artifact of the subjective and individual spiritual movements of the 1960s, in part influenced by the renewed popularity of such works as *Black Elk Speaks*.

Reference

Lone Dog, Louise. *Strange Journey: The Vision Life of a Psychic Indian Woman.* Edited by Vinson Brown. Healdsburg, CA: Naturegraph, 1964.

—Rodney Simard

LOWRY, ANNIE (1866–1943), a Northern Paiute, was born to Sau-tau-nee, who was called Susie, and Jerome Lowry, a white man, in Lovelock, Nevada. She said that the whites considered her just "plain old Paiute," and her Indian neighbors thought she acted as though she were better than they because she had adopted certain white customs. Nevertheless, she associated herself with her Paiute bloodline, feeling a great affinity for her tribe. To the white teachings, she said, her mind was closed.

Under the auspices of the Writers' Project of the Works Progress Administration, Lalla Scott, a white woman, met Lowry to record her version of local history and culture. Scott ultimately published this work as *Karnee: A Paiute Narrative*. It records Lowry's memories of Sau-tau-nee's stories of Cap John's encounter with the first white men to enter the area of Pyramid Lake and the Humboldt River—men such as Peter Skene Ogden, Joseph Reddeford Walker, and John C. Frémont. Lowry speaks of the last great Paiute Council in Nevada, traditional Paiute life and legends, and the battles at Pyramid Lake. She delivers her personal observations of her people's encounters with ranchers, miners, gamblers, and Chinese immigrants in Nevada. She recalls boarding with whites in order to attend school in Lovelock, and the harshness of existence after she and her mother were abandoned by Jerome Lowry.

Lowry married a Paiute man named Sanny; they had nine children, four of whom died young. Even though the words of her story are Lalla Scott's, there is an eloquence in the procession of experiences in Lowry's life, including the deaths of these children and of Sanny. She later married John Pascal, an English-speaking Paiute and mediator among the bands, and they lived out their lives near Lovelock, Nevada.

In spite of, or perhaps because of, the "embeddedness" of the text—Lowry's story retold in Lalla Scott's words, "authenticated" by Eva Wasson Pancho and Mabel Summerfield (Lowry's daughters), introduced by Robert Heizer, obtrusively annotated and commented upon, even patronizingly contradicted, by Charles Craig—Lowry was a Paiute woman well worth knowing. Her story makes a fascinating analogue to that of Sarah Winnemucca (Hopkins).

References

Numa: A Northern Paiute History. Reno, NV: Inter-Tribal Council of Nevada, 1976.

Scott, Lalla. *Karnee: A Paiute Narrative*. Reno: University of Nevada Press, 1966.

—*Gretchen Ronnow*

LOZEN (c. 1840–1889), Chiricahua Apache warrior woman, was born in Apacheria (New Mexico, Arizona, northern Mexico) in the 1840s. The sister of Victorio, famous Warm Springs Apache war leader, she was remarkable in that she remained single, and achieved honor and respect as a warrior and person of power.

According to Apache informants recorded by Eve Ball, Lozen's uniqueness was visible early in her life, and she was revered by her people, who protected her from criticism for breaking gender behavior rules. As a child, she could outrun boys in footraces, but her ability was respected, not resented. At the time of her puberty ceremony, she was given power to find the enemy, sensing their direction and distance by the intensity of a tingling sensation in her palms as she prayed with hands outstretched. She decided not to marry but to devote her life to aiding her people, who needed her greatly in the difficult years of the late nineteenth century, when they were constantly fighting Mexico and/or the United States. In addition to her talent for reconnaissance, Lozen was reportedly an excellent shot, cunning strategist, dextrous horse thief, knowledgeable healer, and effective messenger. Often acting as a shaman, she sang war songs and directed dances of war parties prior to their going into battle.

At the time of the Tres Castillos massacre in Mexico in 1880, which decimated her brother Victorio's band and led to his death, Lozen was assisting a Mescalero Apache woman in childbirth and escorting her back to her people in New Mexico. Many Chiricahuas believed that the tragic ambush would not have happened if Lozen had been with them. She was with Geronimo at the time of his final surrender; in fact, she was one of two women he sent as messengers to arrange a meeting with the American troops when he had decided to surrender. Lozen was among the Apaches sent as prisoners of war to Fort Marion, Florida, in 1886, and to Mount Vernon Barracks, Alabama, in 1887. She died there in 1889, probably of tuberculosis.

References

Ball, Eve, with Nora Henn and Lynda Sanchez. *Indeh: An Apache Odyssey*. Provo, UT: Brigham Young University Press, 1980.

Ball, Eve, with James Kaywaykla. *In the Days of Victorio: Recollections of a Warm Springs Apache*. Tucson: University of Arizona Press, 1970.

Ball, Eve, and Lynda Sanchez. "Legendary Apache Women." *Frontier Times* 54 (October/November 1980): 8–12.

Boyer, Ruth McDonald, and Narcissus Duffy Gayton. *Apache Mothers and Daughters: Four Generations of a Family*. Norman: University of Oklahoma Press, 1992.

Buchanan, Kimberly Moore. *Apache Women Warriors*. Southwestern Studies Series, no. 79. El Paso: Texas Western Press, 1986.

Cole, D. C. *The Chiricahua Apache 1846–1876: From War to Reservation*. Albuquerque: University of New Mexico Press, 1988.

Stockel, H. Henrietta. "Lozen: Apache Warrior Queen." *Real West* 25 (December 1982): 20–22.

———. *Survival of the Spirit: Chiricahua Apaches in Captivity*. Reno: University of Nevada Press, 1993.

———. *Women of the Apache Nation*. Reno: University of Nevada Press, 1991.

—Helen M. Bannan

M

MALINCHE [Doña Marina, Malintzin, Malinali] (c. 1499/1505–1529) was born into a ruling family in a Nahuatl-speaking region near Coatzacoalcos. After her father died, her mother purportedly gave or sold Malinche in order to ensure that the son she bore her second husband would inherit all of the family's wealth and titles. La Malinche later became a possession of Tabascans, who in turn gave her, among a group of twenty Native women, to the party of Spanish conquistadors led by Hernán Cortés in 1519. She eventually became the mistress or slave of Cortés and gave birth to their son, Martín Cortés. The Spaniards had one interpreter, Gerónimo de Aguilar, who had previously been shipwrecked in the Yucatan and could translate from Spanish to Mayan. Because La Malinche could speak both Nahuatl, the language of the lands governed by the Aztecs, and the Mayan language of the Tabascans and the Yucatan, she played a pivotal role in Cortés's interactions with the indigenous population. The natives even began to refer to Cortés himself as Malinche. With her help, Cortés was able to take advantage of the dissension and unrest within Moctezuma's empire, finding indigenous allies such as the Tlaxcalans. She is also credited with alerting Cortés to the attack planned against the Spaniards by the people of Cholula. La Malinche's abilities as a translator were also relied on in the Spaniards' attempts at conversion. While a member of Cortés's 1524 to 1526 expedition to what is now Honduras, she married the Spaniard Juan Jaramillo, with whom she had a son. She is reported to have died in January 1529.

La Malinche is a problematic cultural icon. Was she an obedient slave translating what she was told to say, or was she an active participant and political figure in her own right—using her political acumen and personal attributes to nuance or even replace Cortés's words? In Cortés's and Gómara's accounts, her role is somewhat downplayed. Yet Bernal Díaz praises her abilities, particularly her intellect, beauty, and fortitude, as essential to the Spaniards' survival and their eventual conquest of Mexico. By contrast, some Mexicans and Chicanos have used Malinche's name to signify a person who sells out his or her own country or race: *malinchista*. Even in her role as the symbolic mother of the mestizo race, La Malinche has been mythologized as everything from the beautiful Indian princess who fell in love with the conqueror and produced a noble offspring to the Eve figure whose seduction stained the race she engendered. For some, La Malinche embodies the rape of Native peoples and lands by imperialist forces. The narratives surrounding her life have had a powerful effect on the representation of Native and mestiza women, and, indeed, on the structure of gender relations in the Americas to the present day.

Since the 1980s, La Malinche has been reappropriated and reevaluated as a symbolic ancestor of Native and mestiza feminists.

References

Alarcón, Norma. "Traddutora, Traditora: A Paradigmatic Figure of Chicana Feminism." *Cultural Critique* 13 (Fall 1989): 57–87.

Cypess, Sandra Messinger. *La Malinche in Mexican Literature: From History to Myth*. Austin: University of Texas Press, 1991.

Díaz del Castillo, Bernal. *The True History of the Conquest of Mexico*. Translated by Maurice Keatinge. London: J. Wright, 1800.

López de Gómara, Francisco. *The Life of the Conqueror by His Secretary*. Translated by Lesley Byrd Simpson. Berkeley: University of California Press, 1964.

Paz, Octavio. *Labyrinth of Solitude: Life and Thought in Mexico*. Translated by Lysander Kemp. New York: Grove Press, 1961.

Pratt, Mary Louise. "'Yo Soy La Malinche:' Chicana Writers and the Poetics of Ethnonationalism." *Callaloo* 16 (1993): 859–873.

Prescott, William H. *History of the Conquest of Mexico and History of the Conquest of Peru*, 1843–1847. New York: Modern Library, 1936.

—*Angela Noelle Williams*

MANKILLER, WILMA (b. 1945), was the first woman to become principal chief of the Cherokee Nation of Oklahoma. One of eleven children, she was born at Hastings Indian Hospital in Tahlequah, Oklahoma, to a full-blood Cherokee father and a Dutch–Irish mother. Her father was directly related to tribal members who were removed from the southeastern Appalachian states in the 1838 to 1839 Trail of Tears forced migration. In 1957, when Mankiller was twelve, her family was relocated to a low-income housing project in San Francisco because of a federal program that attempted to "urbanize" rural Indians. During the 1960s she married, had two children, and studied sociology at San Francisco State University. She credits the 1969 takeover of the former prison on Alcatraz island by the American Indian Movement, to protest the U.S. government's treatment of Native Americans, with changing the direction of her life.

While doing volunteer work among Native Americans in the Bay area during the 1970s, Mankiller became angry at the historical and contemporary treatment of the Cherokees. The U.S. government granted the Cherokees self-determination in 1975; two years later, she divorced her husband and returned to Oklahoma with her children. She worked in community development, helping to obtain grants and introduce services in housing, employment, education, and health care. In 1979 another event changed the course of her life. Returning home from graduate classes at the University of Arkansas, Mankiller was involved in a car accident that left her face crushed, her ribs broken, and her legs shattered. After a series of operations and plastic surgery, she developed myasthenia gravis in November 1980.

Mankiller returned to work in December 1980, a more introspective and dedicated advocate of the Cherokee Nation. Drawing upon humanistic and progressive precepts handed down by the Cherokee elders, she helped obtain a grant to revitalize a poor community in eastern Oklahoma. The Bell Community Revitalization Project became a model for other Native American tribes who wanted to become self-sufficient. In 1983 Mankiller was asked to run for deputy chief; she became principal chief in 1985 when Ross Swimmer resigned to head the Bureau of Indian Affairs. In 1987 Mankiller was elected the first women Cherokee chief, and was reelected in 1991 with 83 percent of the vote.

Mankiller's autobiography, *Mankiller: A Chief and Her People*, written with Michael Wallis and published in 1993, is more than the story of her own life. It is also a history of the Cherokee Nation, a history that is inseparable from Mankiller's personal experience. Each of the thirteen chapters begins with a traditional Cherokee story in order to pay tribute to the "eternal voices" of all Cherokee storytellers, past and present.

Mankiller's accomplishments in economic and community development, health care, and tribal self-governance are well known in the Native American community. Despite another health setback in 1990, when she received a kidney transplant, Mankiller continues her tireless advocacy of self-reliance and self-sufficiency to help her people achieve the goals so long denied them.

References

Griffin, Connie. "Relearning to Trust Ourselves: An Interview with Chief Wilma Mankiller, Tahlequah, Oklahoma." *Women of Power* 7 (Summer 1987): 38–40, 72–74.

Mankiller, Wilma, and Michael Wallis. *Mankiller: A Chief and Her People*. New York: St. Martin's Press, 1993.

Wallis, Michael. "Hail to the Chief: Wilma Mankiller Is the First Woman to Be Elected Cherokee Nation Chief." *Phillip Morris Magazine* (October 1989): 37–39.

Whittemore, Hank. "She Leads a Nation." *Parade*, August 18, 1991, 4–5.

—*Laurie Lisa*

MANN, HENRI [Henrietta Whiteman, The Woman Who Comes To Offer Prayer] (b. 1934), educator, was born in Clinton, Oklahoma, the elder child of Lenora and Henry Mann, Cheyenne farmers enrolled in the Cheyenne and Arapaho tribes of Oklahoma. She received a BA in English education from Southwestern Oklahoma State University and an MA in English from Oklahoma State University. The recipient of a Danforth Foundation fellowship, she earned her PhD in American Studies from the University of New Mexico in 1982.

Mann, who has played a leading role in the development of Native American Studies at the university level, has emphasized the importance of its connectedness to Indian communities and its role in fostering cultural continuity and student self-awareness. She began teaching at the University of California, Berkeley, in 1970, and later became coordinator of Native American Studies there. In 1972 Mann became director of Native American Studies at the University of Montana, where she continues to teach as a full professor. During leaves of absence from Montana, she has taught at the Graduate School of Education at Harvard, and has served as deputy director of the Bureau of Indian Affairs' Office of Indian Education (before resigning to protest Reagan administration policies in 1987) and as interim dean of instruction at Haskell Indian Nations University. Mann has taught in unconventional ways: as a consultant on Indian materials for forthcoming elementary social studies texts from Macmillan/McGraw-Hill; in an interview included in the 1996 PBS documentary *The West;* and as a language coach and Cheyenne consultant for the 1995 feature film *Last of the Dogmen.* In 1991 *Rolling Stone* magazine listed Mann on its Honor Roll of Ten Top Professors Nationwide, and she was one of five twentieth-century women educators featured by the National Women's History Project in 1995.

In addition to her academic work, Mann has been active in service to her people. She has been a member of the Business Committee for the Cheyenne-Arapaho Tribal Council and has assisted in developing educational programs for the Northern Cheyenne of Montana. She has served on city and states. Indian education committees, as a trustee of Bacone College and the National Museum of the American Indian at the Smithsonian, and national coordinator of the American Indian Religious Freedom Coalition. She has been honored as National American Indian Woman of the Year by the American Indian Heritage Foundation (1988), as Outstanding Woman in the greater Missoula area by the local YWCA (1987), and as Cheyenne Indian of the Year at the American Indian Exposition (1982). She is the mother of four children.

An eloquent and sought-after speaker, Mann is truly bicultural; her knowledge of her Cheyenne heritage is as extensive as her academic expertise. She synthesizes both traditions in her life and in her work, consistently demonstrating the contemporary viability of traditional Native American culture and values. She is deeply respected as a person of insight, integrity, loyalty, and wisdom.

References

"Class Distinction." *Rolling Stone* (March 1991): 59–61.

Mann, Henrietta. *Cheyenne–Arapaho Education, 1871–1982.* Niwot, Co. University Press of Colorado, 1997.

Whiteman, Henrietta. "Cheyenne–Arapaho Education, 1871–1982." PhD diss., University of New Mexico, 1982.

———. "Insignificance of Humanity, 'Man Is Tampering with the Moon and the Stars': The Employment Status of Native American Women." In *Conference on the Educational and Occupational Needs of American Indian Women.* Pp. 37–61. Arlington, VA: National Institute of Education, 1980.

———. "Native American Studies, the University and the Indian Student." In *The Schooling of Native America.* Edited by Thomas Thompson. Pp. 104–116. Washington, DC: American Association of Colleges for Teacher Education, 1978.

———. "White Buffalo Woman." In *The American Indian and the Problem of History.* Edited by Calvin Martin. Pp. 162–170. New York: Oxford University Press, 1987.

—Helen M. Bannan

MARACLE, LEE [Bobbi Lee] (b. 1950), and her siblings were raised by her Métis working mother in a poor North Vancouver neighborhood. In her adolescence she rejected the racism imposed upon her by dominant society, rebelled, dropped out of school, drifted into the hippie subculture, worked side by side with Chicanos in the western states, abused drugs and alcohol on skid rows in Canadian cities, and finally became politically active in the Red Power Movement and the Liberation Support Movement in and around Vancouver. Her as-told-to autobiography, *Bobbi Lee: Indian Rebel*, based on eighty hours of tape, was published by the Liberation Support Movement Press in 1975. As the record of the life of one of Canada's oppressed but fighting and resisting peoples, the autobiography is a celebration of Native survival and ranks with the autobiographical and political writings by fellow Métis authors/activists Maria Campbell and Howard Adams. Maracle's book had only limited circulation, went out of print for fifteen years, and was reissued in an expanded version in 1990. It was also published in German translation by Trikont, a small publishing cooperative in Munich in the 1970s.

From the time of her first publication until today, Maracle has been an untiring cultural worker, writer, speaker, and political activist for those oppressed by sexism, racism, and capitalist exploitation. An extended stay in China showed her the strength and dignity a people can win through united struggle built on solidarity against imperialist oppression and internal exploitation. In later years, Maracle focused more and more on her development as a writer, drawing strength from a conscious return to her Native roots and connecting with other Native authors throughout North America. In the early 1990s, she was a full-time student at Simon Fraser University, Vancouver. She taught workshops at En'Owkin Center, the first fully Native-operated school of international writing, in Penticton, British Columbia.

Maracle's second book, *I Am Woman*, is the literary reflection of her struggle for liberation. It draws on the West Coast tradition of Big House oratory as well as on feminism and theories of decolonization, bringing them together in one powerful individual voice that moves easily across the mental boundaries defined as "genre" by Western literary criticism. In 1990 Maracle contributed substantially to and coedited *Telling It: Women and Language Across Cultures*. She has edited other Native authors (Rita Joe) and contributed to anthologies, journals, and magazines. Her 1990 book of short stories, titled *Sojourner's Truth* after the African American liberation activist, contains texts that come out of her own experiences and are dedicated to the womanist struggle for human rights and dignity. Maracle's first novel, *Sundogs* (1992), relates the story of a young urban Native woman who seems to have "forgotten" her aboriginal heritage but is politically and culturally awakened by the events around the Mohawk Reserve at Oka, Queb, in the summer of 1990. The narrative flow follows Marianne's growing involvement in the Native struggle. Against the events of a transcontinental run for solidarity, this historical novel conveys a sense of cyclical time, and it demonstrates that the personal is political.

Maracle's second novel, *Ravensong* (1993), is set in the 1950s on the Pacific Coast near Vancouver. It centers on a young woman's graduation from high school and her last summer in the Native community before venturing to university, against barriers of racism, sexism, and class. Unobtrusively, it blends oral tradition, "dream time," and holistic oneness with living, active nature, using realist depictions of small-town life.

Maracle lives in Toronto and is a full-time writer and critic. She has traveled, lectured, and read widely in the United States, Canada, China, the Caribbean, and Europe.

References

Bohlinger, Janine. "Zeitgenössische Autobiographien Kanadischer Ureinwohner-innen." Inaug. diss., University of Mainz, 1995.

Godard, Barbara. "The Politics of Representation: Some Native Canadian Women Writers." *Canadian Literature* 124–125 (Spring/Summer 1990): 183–225.

Grant, Agnes. "Contemporary Native Women's Voices in Literature." *Canadian Literature* 124–125 (Spring/Summer 1990): 124–136.

Huntley, Audrey. "Native Women Writing for Decolonization: '. . . Reclaiming Our House, Our Lineage, Ourselves. . . .'" In *Ahornblätter 9: Marburger Beiträge zur Kanada-Forschung*. Pp. 157–162. Marburg, Germany: Universitätsbibliothek Marburg, 1996.

"Lee Maracle." In *Contemporary Challenges: Conversations with Canadian Native Authors*. Edited by Hartmut Lutz. Pp. 169–179. Saskatoon, SK: Fifth House, 1991.

Lee, S., L. Maracle, D. Marlatt, and B. Warland, eds. *Telling It: Women and Language Across Cultures*. Vancouver, BC: Press Gang, 1990.

Lundgren, Jodi. "'Being a Half-Breed': Discourses of Race and Cultural Syncreticity in the Works of Three Métis Women Writers." *Canadian Literature* 144 (Spring 1995): 62–77.

Lutz, Hartmut. "First Nations Literature in Canada: Writing Back and Writing Home." In *Ahornblätter 9: Marburger Beiträge zur Kanada-Forschung*. Pp. 129–144. Marburg, Germany: Universitätsbibliothek Marburg, 1996.

Maracle, Lee. *Bobbi Lee: Indian Rebel*. 2nd ed., rev. and enl. Toronto: Women's Press, 1990.

———. *Bent Box*. Penticton, BC: Theytus Books, 2000.

———. *I Am Woman*. Vancouver, BC: Write-on Press, 1988.

———. *I Am Woman: A Native Perspective on Sociology and Feminism*. Vancouver, BC: Press Gang Publishers, 1996.

———. "Just Get in Front of a Typewriter and Bleed." In *Telling It: Women and Language Across Cultures*. Edited by S. Lee, L. Maracle, D. Marlatt, and B. Warland. Vancouver, BC: Press Gang, 1990.

———. *My Home as I Remember*. Toronto: Natural Heritage, 1999.

———. "Oratory: Coming to Theory." In *By, for & About: Feminist Cultural Politics*. Edited by Wendy Waring. Pp. 235–240. Toronto: Women's Press, 1994.

———. *Ravensong: A Novel*. Vancouver, BC: Press Gang, 1993.

———. *Sojourner's Truth*. Vancouver, BC: Press Gang, 1990.

———. *Sundogs*. Penticton, BC: Theytus Books, 1992.

O'Brien, Sue. "'Please, Eunice, Don't Be Ignorant': The White Reader as Trickster in Lee Maracle's Fiction." *Canadian Literature* 144 (Spring 1995): 82–96.

Petrone, Penny. *Native Literature in Canada: From the Oral Tradition to the Present*. Toronto: Oxford University Press, 1990.

Witalec, Jane, ed. *Native North American Literature*. New York: Gale Research, 1994.

—Hartmut Lutz

MARTINEZ, MARIA MONTOYA [Poveka, Yellow Pond Lily] (1886–1980), was born in the Tewa Pueblo of San Ildefonso, New Mexico, the second of five daughters of Tomas and Reyecita Pena Montoya. Baptized a Catholic, as a child, she made a pilgrimage to the Santuario at Chimayo after recovering from smallpox. She attended St. Catherine's Indian School in Santa Fe for two years and learned to make pottery as a child from her maternal aunt, Nicolasa. In 1904 she married Julian Martinez, and they spent their honeymoon at the St. Louis World's Fair—the first of countless times they would demonstrate Pueblo art and culture for Anglo observers. In 1907 Julian began working at the Pajarito Plateau excavations under the direction of Dr. Edgar Hewett. He copied pottery and wall designs from the ruins, and Martinez was asked to reproduce ancient pottery. They were encouraged in their experimentation by the Museum of New Mexico, where they lived and worked from 1909 to 1912. Martinez shaped pots, and when he had finished his janitorial duties, Julian painted them, making famous the *avanyu* (water serpent) design. By 1919 they had developed the black-on-black, matte-and-polish pottery that initiated a major revival of Pueblo ceramics and made them and their Pueblo world famous. Martinez is generally regarded as the greatest of modern Pueblo potters. She is unquestionably the most photographed and written about, and, beginning in the mid-1920s, was the first to sign her pots.

Maria and Julian had four children who survived infancy: Adam, Juan, Tony, and Philip. After her husband's death in 1943, Martinez collaborated with her daughter-in-law Santana (wife of Adam) and, beginning in 1956, with her son Tony, who used his Indian name, Popovi Da. There are now five generations of the Martinez family "making their way with the clay," two of the most famous being her grandson Tony Da and great-granddaughter Barbara Gonzales. They have set new standards and styles for contemporary Pueblo pottery. Beginning with the first Santa Fe Indian Market in 1922, the pottery that Martinez made with various members of her family consistently won prizes and commanded the highest prices. In 1934 she was the first Native American woman to receive a bronze medal for Indian achievement from the Indian Fire Council. This was the first of many national and international awards and honors, including several honorary degrees and four visits to the White House.

Called the "Mother of the Pueblo," Martinez has been credited not only with keeping her family together and improving the economic conditions of her Pueblo, but also with reversing the process of deculturation by engendering a revolution in Pueblo ceramics that transformed a "craft" into an "art." Martinez and her pottery have become important links not only between the traditional and the modern but also between Pueblo and Anglo cultures. Because of her, the role and position of Native American artists and the valuation of indigenous art have changed substantially.

References

Gridley, Marion E. "Maria Martinez: Master Artisan." In *American Indian Women*. Pp. 105–118. New York: Hawthorn Books, 1974.

Marriott, Alice. *Maria, the Potter of San Ildefonso*. Norman: University of Oklahoma Press, 1945.

McGreevy, Susan Brown. *Maria: The Legend, the Legacy*. Santa Fe, NM: Sunstone Press, 1982.

Nelson, Mary Carroll. *Maria Martinez*. Minneapolis, MN: Dillon Press, 1974.

Peterson, Susan. *The Living Tradition of Maria Martinez*. Tokyo: Kodansha International, 1977.

———. *Maria Martinez: Five Generations of Potters*. Washington, DC: Renwick Galleries, 1978.

Spivey, Richard. *Maria*. Flagstaff, AZ: Northland, 1979.

—Barbara A. Babcock

MAYO, SARAH JIM (c. 1860–1945), was a Washoe basket maker who introduced representational designs during the period when Washoe basketry flourished. Her father, Captain Jim, was the most influential spokesman dealing with the whites in the Carson valley during the late nineteenth century. After the death of her husband in 1918, Mayo took back the name of her father. Her proud claims to a prestigious status may have led to some resistance from other women in the tribe.

Mayo's life followed the traditional pattern within the cultural context of the Washoe. In late spring and early summer, they camped on the south shore of Lake Tahoe; in the winter, they returned to the Carson valley of Nevada. Mayo, like other women, worked in ranch houses as a domestic and bartered and sold her baskets to tourists. Her relationship with Margaretta (Maggie) Dressler, whose husband owned a large ranch in the Carson valley, led to Dressler's large collection of Washoe baskets (many attributed to Mayo) and her photography of Mayo. Dressler also photographed a special basket that Mayo made to present to Woodrow Wilson in 1914 when Captain Pete Mayo led a delegation to Washington, D.C., to argue land claims before the federal government. The present location of this basket is unknown.

Mayo introduced representational, or pictorial, designs around 1905, and continued to use them until around 1925, when her eyesight began to fail. Her designs (in contrast to Louisa Keyser's) are characterized by large-scale motifs that usually alternate in an *abab* pattern. The results are powerful and dramatic, with the pictorial images the full size of the design field; she also combined representational images in illusionistic settings and with narrative action and figure groupings. In addition, Mayo experimented with color. She added the brown of undyed bracken root and experimented with yellow, green, gray, and pink-dyed willow. The most documented period of Mayo's artistry is from 1913 to 1918. However, she influenced a significant amount of the Washoe fancy basketry by most major weavers between 1912 and 1925.

References

Cahodas, Marvin. "Sarah Mayo and Her Contemporaries: Representational Designs in Washoe Basketry." *American Indian Art* 6 (Autumn 1981): 52–59, 80.

———. "Washoe Innovators and Their Patrons." In *The Arts of the North American Indian: Native Traditions in Evolution*. Edited by Edwin L. Wade. Pp. 203–220. New York: Hudson Hills Press, 1986.

—Laurie Lisa

McCLOUD, JANET (b. 1934), is a Tulalip woman whose name is synonymous with Indian activism. Born on the Tulalip Reservation, which was created in 1934 for the Duwamish, Suquamish, and other smaller tribes, she has lived in Yelm, Washington, since her marriage to Don McCloud (Puyallup/Nisqually). A mother of eight, she first came to national prominence as a result of her unceasing work on behalf of Indian fishing rights.

Beginning in January 1961, Washington state officials arrested several Nisqually fishermen, in direct violation of long-standing treaties. Two of those arrested were McCloud's brothers-in-law. To maintain a constant presence in the boats, McCloud and other Native women took up fishing as soon as the men were arrested. After their release, the men returned to their boats and McCloud returned to her work with the Survival of American Indians Association (which she had organized in 1964).

By 1968 national Native rights groups were becoming active in the "fish-ins." Many local people, McCloud included, watched as "outside Indians" slowly took over the protests. Eventually, the presence of celebrities turned this very serious issue into a media circus.

However, bigger headlines loomed elsewhere, and McCloud and her sisters persevered until they were again at the helm of their own movement. Now widely known, McCloud was drawn into the national arena to strive for better Indian education; preservation of cultures, languages, and religions; and the rights of Native prisoners. Soon after working on the Native American Rights Fund book *Our Brother's Keeper* (1975), she helped organize the Brotherhood of Indian Prisoners. Concerned at the loss of traditions and startled by the increase in the number of Native women being sterilized, McCloud founded and is still a coordinator for the Northwest Indian Women's Circle. Her lifetime efforts have been rewarded with her appointment to the Elders Circle, an intertribal elders' council that strives to keep traditions alive. Her most recent project has been to expose "plastic medicine men" those who commercialize Native religions.

References

Bomberry, Dan, ed. "Sage Advice from a Longtime Activist." *Native Self-Sufficiency* 6 (1981): 4–5, 20.

Churchill, Ward. "Spiritual Hucksterism." *Z Magazine* 3 (December 1990): 94, 96–98.

Josephy, Alvin M., Jr. *Now That the Buffalo's Gone*. New York: Alfred A. Knopf, 1982.

Payne, Diane. "Each of My Generations Is Getting Stronger: An Interview with Janet McCloud." *Indian Truth* 239 (May/June 1981): 5–7.

Vogel, Virgil J. *This Country Was Ours*. New York: Harper & Row, 1972.

—Cynthia Kasee

McCOY, MELODY L. (b. 1960) is an enrolled member of the Cherokee nation and is a lawyer who has worked in tribal and federal courts. McCoy received her Bachelor of Arts from Harvard University and graduated from the University of

Michigan Law School in 1986. She joined the Native American Rights Fund as a staff attorney later that year. McCoy has argued cases in the areas of tribal jurisdiction and education. She is one of few Native American women to have argued a case before the U. S. Supreme Court in *Strate v. A-I Contractor*. McCoy was also a key part of NARF's Indian Education Legal Support Project. She worked on the Rosebud code, which provides a model for tribes and public schools to work together to set education standards.

References

"NARF Attorney: Melody L. McCoy," *NARF Legal Review* 21:2 (summer/fall 1996): 12.

"Courts rule in two landmark cases affecting tribal court jurisdiction," *NARF Legal Review* 22:1 (winter/spring 1997): 10.

McDANIEL, WILMA ELIZABETH (b. 1918), a poet of Anglo–Cherokee descent, is a native of Stroud, Oklahoma. The daughter of sharecroppers, she grew up in the Creek Nation during the Great Depression. She migrated to California's San Joaquin valley during the Dustbowl exodus of the 1930s, and since settling there she has composed a short novel, several collections of stories, and more than a dozen volumes of poetry. She has also written a regular column for *The Valley Voice*, a central California newspaper. Her work, which James D. Houston has termed "absolutely unique and magical," not only reflects her Creek heritage but also chronicles a childhood lived on the verge of poverty in rural Oklahoma and years of toil as a migrant worker in central California. It speaks to us through richly colloquial language ("Ain't this something, Papa," says Melvin in "Progress," "five years in California / and we have went / from fresh fruit on our / table / to wax apples in a bowl") conveying not merely verisimilitude of place and person but also a universal vision of a world where suffering is mitigated by hope.

References

Cox, Carol. Review of *Toll Bridge*, by Wilma Elizabeth McDaniel. *American Book Review* 3 (May/June 1981): 8.

Haslam, Gerald W., and James D. Houston, eds. *California Heartland: Writing from the Great Central Valley*. Santa Barbara, CA: Capra Press, 1978.

Kates, J. Review of *Sister Vayda's Song*, by Wilma Elizabeth McDaniel. *Village Voice*, January 25, 1983, 42.

McDaniel, Wilma Elizabeth. *Day Tonight/Night Today Presents Wilma Elizabeth McDaniel: A Special Issue of Selected Short Stories*. Hull, MA: Day Tonight/Night Today, 1982.

———. *The Fish Hook: Okie and Valley Prose and Poems*. Big Timber, MT: Seven Buffaloes Press, 1978.

———. *A Girl from Buttonwillow*. Stockton, CA: Wormwood Books, 1990.

———. *Going Steady with R. C. Boley*. Portlandville, NY: MAF Press, 1984.

———. *House with a Gold Door*. Springville, CA: Back 40 Publishing, 1998.

———. *I Killed a Bee for You*. Marvin, SD: Blue Cloud Quarterly, 1987.

————. *The Ketchup Bottle*. St. John, KS: Chiron Review Press, 1996.

————. *The Last Dust Storm*. Brooklyn, NY: Hanging Loose Press, 1995.

————. *Man with a Star Quilt: Poetry*. St. John, KS: Chiron Review Press, 1995.

————. *The Peddlers Loved Almira*. Tulare, CA: Stone Woman Press, 1977.

————. *A Primer for Buford*. Brooklyn, NY: Hanging Loose Press, 1990.

————. *A Prince Albert Wind: Poems*. Albuquerque, NM: Mother Road Publications, 1994.

————. *The Red Coffee Can: Poems and Stories of the Unique Spirit of a San Joaquin Valley People*. Fresno, CA: Valley Publishers, 1974.

————. *Sand in My Bed*. Tulare, CA: Stone Woman Press, 1980.

————. *This Is Leonard's Alley*. Tulare, CA: Stone Woman Press, 1979.

————. *Toll Bridge*. New York: Contact II, 1980.

————. *Vito and Zona*. Parkdale, OR: Trout Creek Press, 1993.

————. *The Wash Tub: Stories of a People Who Knew the Wash Tub as an Integral Part of Life in America*. Fresno, CA: Pioneer, 1976.

————. *Who Is San Andreas: Poems to Survive Earthquakes*. Marvin, SD: Blue Cloud Quarterly, 1984.

Shafarzek, Susan. "Small Press Roundup: Best Titles of 1982." *Library Journal* 107 (1982): 2306.

—Eric Severson

MᴄKAY, MABEL (1907–1993), was born on a ranch in Nice, Lake County, California, where her father, Yanta Boone, a Potter Valley Pomo, worked as a ranch hand. Shortly after McKay's birth her mother, Daisy Hansen, a Long Valley Cache Creek

Mabel McKay

Pomo (often referred to by ethnographers as Patwin) moved with her daughter to Rumsey. There McKay was raised by her maternal grandmother, Sarah Taylor, whose brother Richard Taylor in 1871 initiated the revivalistic Bole Maru and Bole Hesi movements among the Pomo and Southwestern Wintun. Richard Taylor was the first Bole Maru (Dream Dance) doctor and prophet; Mabel McKay would be the last.

McKay began dreaming at the age of five and began her work as a medicine woman at age eighteen. Among the Pomo, she was the last sucking doctor, a doctor who combines song, hand power, and sucking to cast out disease. She began weaving baskets at age seven and today is regarded as the foremost Pomo basket weaver. Her basketry is associated with power and prophecy; she dreamed the designs and patterns, and followed strict rules with her art. She is especially known for her miniatures and feather baskets, which are in permanent collections in museums in the United States and in Europe.

McKay was the last living representative of the Long Valley Cache Creek Pomo, and therefore the last to speak the language and know the history and culture of her people. She was hounded by countless linguists, art historians, folklorists, anthropologists, and others interested in her life and work. McKay taught basketry for nearly fifty years and lectured in numerous colleges and universities. California Governor Jerry Brown appointed McKay to the first board of the California Native American Heritage Commission, on which she served for many years. McKay was known for her witty remarks, through which she reminded people that she was not a relic from a lost past but a contemporary woman living in a world shared by others.

McKay married Charles McKay, a Wintun, and they adopted a son, Marshall. Charles McKay died when Marshall was quite young, so McKay worked for many years in the local apple canneries to support herself and Marshall. She did not stop doctoring and weaving, however, and she worked closely with the Kashaya Pomo dreamer Essie Parrish. Another Pomo once said, "McKay is the old way. She is our history, our hope, our power."

References

Sarris, Greg. *Mabel McKay: Weaving the Dream*. Berkeley: University of California Press, 1994.

————. "On the Road to Lolsel." *News from Native California* 2 (September/October 1988): 3–6.

————. Personal communications with Mabel McKay, 1957–1993.

————. "Strawberry Festival." *National Women's Studies Association Journal* 2 (Summer 1990): 408–424.

————. "The Verbal Art of Mabel McKay." *MELUS* 16 (Spring 1991): 95–112.

—Greg Sarris

MEDICINE, BEATRICE A. [Hin Cha Agli Win] (b. 1924), a Sihasapa Lakota (Sioux), was born on the Standing Rock Reservation, Wakpala, South Dakota. A cultural anthropologist and educator, Medicine has worked to dispel anthropological myths that have tended to oversimplify and homogenize Native American cultures.

Through her writings and teaching, she has sought to depict the diversity of historical and present-day Native American life. She has been especially interested in the changing American Indian family and in Native American women's roles, real and perceived.

Medicine received a BS from South Dakota State University, was awarded MA by Michigan State University, and her Phd from the University of Wisconsin. She has worked with a number of tribes in the United States and Canada. In addition to having taught at levels from kindergarten to university, Medicine has directed American Indian Studies programs at San Francisco State University and the University of Calgary. She has been awarded numerous fellowships and other honors—including an honorary doctor of humanities degree from Michigan State University in 1998—and has been a member of many U.S. and Canadian organizations in her areas of interest. Besides her work as an educator and a scholar, Medicine has dedicated herself to helping to develop Indian leadership and to establishing urban Indian centers.

Even though Medicine has spent much of her life in academe, she has always maintained strong ties to her reservation home. Married and later divorced, she brought up her son, Clarence, in traditional Lakota culture. Having been active in political matters as well as in traditional religious and ceremonial events, Medicine was chosen Sacred Pipe Woman in the revival of the Lakota Sun Dance in 1977.

References

Albers, Patricia, and Beatrice Medicine, eds. *The Hidden Half: Studies of Plains Indian Women*. Washington, DC: University Press of America, 1983.

Gridley, Marion E., ed. and comp. *Indians of Today*. 4th ed. Chicago: ICFP, 1971.

Medicine, Beatrice. "American Indian Family: Cultural Change and Adaptive Strategies." *Journal of Ethnic Studies* 8 (Winter 1981): 13–23.

———. "American Indian Women: Mental Health Issues Which Relate to Drug Abuse. *Wicazo Sa Review* 9 (Fall 1993): 85–90.

———. "The Changing Dakota Family and the Stresses Therein." *Pine Ridge Research Bulletin* 9 (1969): 1–20.

———. "Child Socialization Among Native Americans: The Lakota (Sioux) in Cultural Context." *Wicazo Sa Review* 1 (Fall 1985): 23–28.

———. "An Ethnography of Drinking and Sobriety Among the Lakota Sioux." PhD diss., University of Wisconsin at Madison, 1983.

———. "Higher Education: A New Arena for Native Americans." *Thresholds in Education* 4 (1978): 22–25.

———. "Indian Women and the Renaissance of Traditional Religion." In *Sioux Indian Religion: Tradition and Innovation*. Edited by Raymond I. DeMallie and Douglas R. Parks. Pp. 159–171. Norman: University of Oklahoma Press, 1987.

———. "Indian Women: Tribal Identity as Status Quo." In *Women and Nature*. Edited by R. Hubbard and M. Lowe. Pp. 63–73. New York: Pergamon Press, 1983.

———. "My Elders Tell Me." In *Indian Education in Canada*. Vol. 2, *The Challenge*. Edited by Jean Barman et al. Pp. 142–152. Vancouver: University of British Columbia, 1987.

———. "Native American (Indian) Women: A Call for Research." *Anthropology and Education Quarterly* 19 (1988): 86–92.

————. *The Native American Woman: A Perspective*. Austin, TX: National Educational Laboratory, 1978.

————. "Professionalization of Native American (Indian) Women: Towards a Research Agenda." *Wicazo Sa Review* 4 (Spring 1988): 31–42.

————. "Prologue to a Vision of Aboriginal Education." *Canadian Journal of Native Education* 21 (1995): 42–45.

————. "The Role of Women in Native American Societies: A Bibliography." *Indian Historian* 8 (Summer 1975): 50–53.

————. *Words of Today's American Indian Women: Ohoyo Makachi*. Wichita Falls, TX: Ohoyo Resource Center, 1982.

Trimble, Joseph E., and Beatrice Medicine. "Diversification of American Indians: Forming an Indigenous Perspective." In *Indigenous Psychologies: Research and Experience in Cultural Context*. Edited by Uichol Kim and John W. Berry. Pp. 133–151. Cross-Cultural Research and Methodology Series, no. 17. Newbury Park, CA: Sage, 1993.

—*Elizabeth A. McNeil*

MEDICINE FLOWER, GRACE [Wopovi Poviwah, Tafoya] (b. 1938), was born Grace Tafoya on December 13 at Santa Clara Pueblo, New Mexico, into a distinguished family of potters that includes Camilio Tafoya (her father), Agapita Silva (her mother), Joseph Lonewolf (her brother), and Margaret Tafoya (her father's sister). Fluent in Tewa, she learned English at Santa Clara Day School and graduated from nearby Espanola High School in 1957, after which she took a secretarial course at Brownings Commercial School.

In 1962 Medicine Flower returned to Santa Clara to take up pottery full-time, studying with her father. Her first pieces included miniature bowls and turtles in a plain style with a highly polished red or black glaze.

In the late 1960s, she began carving her ceramic pieces, and in the mid-1970s, she began to etch the surfaces of her pottery with a technique called sgraffito, for which she and her brother have become famous. Sgraffito consists of incising the surface of a pot so that the design is literally scraped away from the polished slip before it is fired. By refining this technique with consummate skill, Medicine Flower transformed pottery making into fine art, assuring herself a permanent place in Pueblo pottery history.

Her designs are integrated to the shape of the pot and may include such delicate and intricate figures as butterflies, hummingbirds, flowers, and deer, or the more "traditional" designs of kiva steps, bear paws, water serpents, and feathers. In the style of her ancestors, she gathers the materials for clay, temper, and slips from the surrounding land of her reservation; hand-builds her pots, and fires them outside. In addition to the classic Santa Clara red, tan, and black, she uses a range of pastels for her pots, including subtle purples and greens that bring out the details of her floral motifs.

In an interview with Jane Katz in 1978, Medicine Flower described how she makes a pot:

> We go to the hills near Santa Clara to get enough clay for a whole season. . . . We put the clay in the sun to dry, soak it in water for about three days, then put it through a fine screen to

get all the impurities out. . . . When the clay has just the right consistency, I begin my pot, using the old coil method. I mold the coils by hand, then use gourds to smooth them. After the pot is formed and completely dry—that takes days—I sandpaper it and wet it down to remove the sandpaper lines. I cover the bowl with a red earth clay. . . . I hand-polish the bowl with stones. . . .

Then it's time to incise designs onto the pot, freehand. . . . I use knives and special tools. . . . fashioned from nails.

The firing is done in the open on the ground. It has to be a really calm day, with no wind. . . . We put wood chips on the ground. Tin cans hold a steel grate, and a wire basket containing the pots is placed on the grate. . . . You have to watch the fire carefully. If the wind blows and soot gets on the pot, it is ruined.

The recipient of dozens of awards over the years, Medicine Flower was especially honored in February 1974, when she was one of twenty-eight Hopi and Pueblo artists invited to the White House. Also in 1974 she was included in the important "Seven Families in Pueblo Pottery" show at the Maxwell Museum of Anthropology at the University of New Mexico. And in 1976, she was one of seven artists chosen for the American Indian Artists film series produced by PBS.

References

Arnold, David. "Pueblo Pottery: 2000 Years of Artistry." *National Geographic* (November 1982): 593–605.

DeLauer, Marjel. "Joseph Lonewolf and Grace Medicine Flower." *Arizona Highways* (August 1976): 42–43.

Houlihan, Patrick T. "Southwestern Pottery Today." *Arizona Highways* (May 1974): 2–6.

Jacka, Jerry, and Lois Essary Jacka. *Beyond Tradition: Contemporary Indian Art and Its Evolution*. Flagstaff, AZ: Northland Press, 1988.

Katz, Jane. *This Song Remembers: Self-Portraits of Native Americans in the Arts*. Boston: Houghton Mifflin, 1980.

LeFree, Betty. *Santa Clara Pottery Today*. Albuquerque: University of New Mexico Press, 1975.

McCoy, Ron. "Homage to the Clay Lady." *Southwest Profile* (March 1990): 21–23.

Monthan, Guy, and Doris Monthan. *Art and Indian Individualists*. Flagstaff, AZ: Northland Press, 1975.

Seven Families in Pueblo Pottery. Albuquerque: University of New Mexico Press, 1974.

Trimble, Stephen. *Talking with the Clay: The Art of Pueblo Pottery*. Santa Fe, NM: School of American Research Press, 1987.

—*Dexter Fisher Cirillo*

MEDICINE SNAKE WOMAN [Natawista-Iksana, Natawistacha-Iksana] (1825–1893), a Blood Blackfeet woman, daughter of Menetokas (Father of All Children), played an important role in maintaining peaceful relations between factions around Fort Union in Upper Missouri (Montana) between 1840 and 1858. She married Alexander Culbertson sometime in 1840, at the age of fifteen. They had five children: Jack, Julia, Nancy, Francisca, and Joseph. Francisca drowned sometime after 1851 in the Missouri River; as a result, the other children were sent to convents and military schools for their education.

Her brother, Seen-from-Afar, rose to the position of head chief of the Blood tribe, and her cousin, Little Dog, was the Piegan chief. Medicine Snake Woman assisted Lewis Henry Morgan, an early anthropologist, when he traveled up the Missouri in 1862 by furnishing him with information on Blackfeet and Gros Ventre kinship systems. In the 1850s Governor Isaac Stevens of Washington Territory chose her husband to accompany and assist his Pacific Railway survey party, in part because of Culbertson's relationship with Medicine Snake Woman. She is represented by white men in journals as having allayed white fear of "those 'most bloodthirsty Indians of the Upper Missouri,'" one who "mixed with the Indians, kept them in good spirits . . . listened to their conversations, and reported their reactions to Governor Stevens through her husband."

Medicine Snake Woman was described by white men as beautiful and intelligent. She is reported, by these same men, to have loved wearing "white women's gowns" and of being fond of colorful jewelry. Her skills as hostess, horsewoman, swimmer, worker in porcupine quills, and diplomat helped bridge the worlds of Anglo–American men and her tribe.

Medicine Snake Woman and Culbertson retired to Peoria, Illinois, in 1858, after he had amassed a fortune in the Indian trade. However, the fortune was soon dissipated, and they returned to the upper Missouri in 1868. Some accounts report such improbable "facts" as that she spoke no English and that her daughters Francisca and Nancy spoke no Blackfeet. It apparently did not occur to these writers of such accounts that mother and children must have had a common language. Eventually, she left Culbertson and lived in the log house of her nephew, Chief Old Moon; in later years, she drew a regular Indian ration from the Canadian government. She died on the Blood Reserve in 1893 and was buried in the Indian cemetery near Standoff, Alberta.

References

Blair, Elizabeth. "Tracking Medicine Snake Woman: Reconstructing Women's Lives from Men's Words." Unpublished manuscript.

Ewers, John E. *Indian Life on the Upper Missouri.* Norman: University of Oklahoma Press, 1968.

———. "Mothers of the Mixed-Bloods." *El Palacio* 69 (1964): 20–29.

McDonnell, Anne. "Mrs. Alexander Culbertson." *Contributions to the Montana State Historical Society* 10 (1941): 243–246.

Morgan, Lewis Henry. *Lewis Henry Morgan, The Indian Journals, 1859–62.* Edited by Leslie A. White. Ann Arbor: University of Michigan Press, 1959.

—*Renae Moore Bredin*

MODESTO, RUBY (1913–1980), was born at Martinez Reservation in the Coachella valley of southern California. Her father was one of the Desert Cahuilla people from this area; her mother was a Serrano woman from the Morongo Reservation. Their family was known as the Dog clan. Modesto's mother took her to the

Moravian church on the reservation and Modesto considered herself a Christian until she later became a Cahuilla *pul* (medicine woman). She then decided that she had to choose between Christianity and the ancient belief of her people that "the power of a *pul*, the Dream Helper, comes from *Umna'ah*," because it became clear to her that the Christians considered her shamanistic power to be witchcraft rather than the blessing she felt it to be.

Modesto's father, grandfather, and great-grandfather had all served as clan *nets*, or ceremonial leaders, and many of her uncles and granduncles were medicine men. Her grandfather Francisco was the last to maintain a kiva before the clan adopted "the white man's law." Although she lived with her husband, David, and their family, Modesto described him as her companion and asserted that as a shaman she was dependent only on Umna'ah.

Besides her shamanistic services to her clan, Modesto taught Cahuilla-language classes. She often provided information to anthropologists, even coauthoring one article, and she was a guest lecturer at local colleges even before 1976, the year she met Guy Mount, with whom she collaborated to create *Not for Innocent Ears*, a book designed for educational purposes in which she hoped to preserve accurate information about her people and her own spiritual beliefs. Her Uncle Charlie, also a *pul*, provides many of the examples of shamanistic ceremonies in the book, but her own autobiographical information and the Cahuilla folktales she recounts offer the most comprehensive picture of her people. The book was published in 1980; shortly after Modesto's death on April 7 of that year.

References

Lando, Richard, and Ruby E. Modesto. "Temal Wakish: A Desert Cahuilla Village." *Journal of California Anthropology* 4 (1977): 95–112.
Mount, Guy, and Ruby Modesto. *Not for Innocent Ears*. Angelus Oaks, CA: Sweetlight Books, 1980.
Wilke, Phillip J. *Late Prehistoric Human Ecology at Lake Cahuilla, Coachella Valley, California*. Contributions of the University of California Archaeological Research Facility, no. 38. Berkeley: *University of California* Department of Anthropology, 1978.

—Thelma Shinn Richard

MOMADAY, NATACHEE SCOTT (b. 1913), is a retired teacher, poet, and painter. Born in Fairview, Kentucky, of Cherokee, French, and English descent, she was educated at Haskell Junior College, Crescent College, and the University of New Mexico. She became a teacher and aspired to be a newspaper reporter. A woman of incredible beauty, she married in 1933, had her only child in 1934, and taught at remote schools in the Southwest. In 1936 she began teaching at the Jemez Day School on the Jemez Springs Reservation in New Mexico, and remained there for twenty-five years. For this service, she was awarded the Bureau of Indian Affairs Service Medal for outstanding achievement. In 1954 she received a BA from the University of California, Los Angeles. In 1975 the University of New Mexico awarded her a doctorate of humane letters.

Since retirement, Momaday has divided her energy among writing, painting, and lecturing. Her children's books include *Woodland Princess*, *Velvet Ribbons*, and *Owl in the Cedar Tree*, about a Navajo boy who paints the stories of his grandfather. In 1972 Momaday edited a critically acclaimed reader for the classroom, *American Indian Authors*, which is thought to be the first such collection of traditional and contemporary stories by Native authors. She has lectured at New York University, City University of Toulouse, and Oxford University. Her paintings in oil and pastel have won prizes in art shows across North America, and she also works in pen and ink and charcoal.

Momaday is the widow of Al Momaday (illustrator of their son's *The Way to Rainy Mountain*) and mother of the Pulitzer Prize-winning novelist, poet, and painter N. Scott Momaday. (Due to the similarity of their names, Natachee Scott Momaday's work is sometimes erroneously identified as her son's.) In 1978 the American Association of University Women named Momaday as one of thirteen women in New Mexico who had made outstanding cultural contributions to that state and the Southwest. She lives in seclusion in the Jemez Mountains with her Belgian shepherd dogs and a very protective black cat.

References

Momaday, Natachee Scott. *At School*. Gallup, NM: Gallup–McKinley County Public Schools, 1975.

———. *Betty, a Navajo Girl*. Gallup, NM: Gallup–McKinley County Public Schools, 1975.

———. *Kee and Jack*. Gallup, NM: Gallup–McKinley County Public Schools, 1975.

———. *Lucky Lobo*. Gallup, NM: Gallup–McKinley County Public Schools, 1975.

———. *My Grandmother*. Gallup, NM: Gallup–McKinley County Public Schools, 1975.

———. *Owl in the Cedar Tree*. Illustrated by Don Perceval. San Francisco: Northland Press, 1975.

———. *A Visit to Grandmother*. Gallup, NM: Gallup–McKinley County Public Schools, 1975.

———. *Woodland Princess*. McHughes, 1931.

———, ed. *American Indian Authors*. Boston: Houghton Mifflin, 1972.

Momaday, N[avarro] Scott. *The Names: A Memoir*. New York: Harper & Row, 1976.

—Jay Ann Cox

MOREZ, MARY (b. 1943), is a Navajo painter whose work reflects the way she has integrated the disparate events of her life into a cohesive whole. She was born near Tuba City, Arizona, on the Navajo Reservation, where she lived with her parents and, following their deaths, with her grandparents. As a young child she moved to Phoenix, Arizona, to live with her adoptive family. As a child Morez spent some time in a Chicago hospital, where she underwent polio-related surgery. Following her return to Phoenix, she graduated from the Phoenix Indian School in 1960, entered the University of Arizona, and attended the Ray Vogue School of Art in Chicago, where she majored in fashion illustration. After she graduated in 1963, she worked as a fashion illustrator and draftsman until turning to painting full-time in 1969.

Morez's paintings reflect her bicultural education and experiences. Unlike a number of Navajo artists, her subjects are not confined to reservation scenes or the problems of the culturally disenfranchised. Instead, Morez explores the abstractions of what it means to her to be Navajo. Although her treatment of this complex topic clearly reflects the influences of Picasso and Wassily Kandinsky, the elements are distinctly Navajo. Her work transcends cultural and tribal boundaries, and successfully explores the universality of human experiences. In this sense, her work reflects her Navajo beliefs and her Navajo sense of herself.

Another theme in Morez's life centers on the Phoenix Indian Hospital, where she is a volunteer. After suffering through her traumatic hospital stay as a child, Morez cared for her second husband, Bill, as he suffered and succumbed to cancer. She has been honored by the hospital as Outstanding Volunteer, is a member of the Phoenix Indian School's Hall of Fame, and has been recognized for her contributions to Indian education at Camelback High School in Phoenix. She is also the former curator of fine art at the Heard Museum in Phoenix.

Since 1970, when Morez held her first one-woman show at the Heard Museum, her work has been shown at the Wheelwright Museum in Santa Fe; the Navajo Tribal Museum in Window Rock, Arizona; and the Native American Art Gallery in New York, among many others. Of her life, Morez said, "When I grow old, I want to know I've left something behind. Not as an artist, but as a human being who loves and cares and tends and helps other human beings. To do that is to walk in beauty."

References

Chase, Katherine. "Navajo Painting." *Plateau* 54 (1982): 24.
Katz, Jane B. *This Song Remembers: Self-Portraits of Native Americans in the Arts*. Boston: Houghton Mifflin, 1980.
"Navajo Artist Will Be Honored at Museum." *Navajo Times*, September 28, 1983.
Niemi, K. Untitled manuscript. Santa Fe: Wheelwright Museum of Indian Art, 1978.
Warner, John Anson. "Continuity Amidst Change: The Navajo Artist Mary Morez." Manuscript collection, Wheelwright Museum, Santa Fe, NM.

—*Laura Graves*

MOUNTAIN WOLF WOMAN [Little Fifth Daughter, Xehaciwinga, Haksigaxunuminka] (1884–1960), a Winnebago, tells her life story—which demonstrates a remarkable ability to value her traditional culture, yet readily adapt to the changes presented to her by the twentieth century—in *Mountain Wolf Woman, Sister of Crashing Thunder*. Born into the Thunder clan at East Fork River, Wisconsin, in her childhood she was cured of a life-threatening illness by a healer named Wolf Woman, and was thereafter given her name. Mountain Wolf Woman's family moved to Black River Falls, and she subsequently attended school for two years in Tomah, Wisconsin. Later her family moved to Wittenberg, Wisconsin, where she remained in her new school only a short time before she married. Her first marriage, arranged by her brother against her wishes, ended after the birth of her second child; she remained in Black River Falls until her marriage to Bad Soldier. After her second marriage, Mountain Wolf Woman moved several times to find better employment or housing, and took several shorter trips to trap muskrats, to dig yellow water-lily roots, to hunt deer, or to pick blueberries and cranberries. She had eleven children, three of whom died, and several grandchildren and great-grandchildren. She was one of the first Winnebago women to own a car, and once took a train to Oregon to visit her daughter. At seventy-four, she flew to Michigan to collaborate on her life story with anthropologist Nancy Lurie.

Mountain Wolf Woman was raised as a traditional Winnebago and participated faithfully in Winnebago ceremonies, including the Scalp Dance and the Medicine Dance. She was also a practicing Christian but counted as her most significant experience her conversion to the Native American Church and her participation in peyote meetings. She died quietly in her sleep on November 9, 1960, at Black River Falls and was given a funeral that epitomized her allegiance to all three religions.

References

Bataille, Gretchen, and Kathleen Mullen Sands. "Culture Change and Continuity: A Winnebago Life." In *American Indian Women Telling Their Lives*. Pp. 69–82. Lincoln: University of Nebraska Press, 1984.

Mountain Wolf Woman. *Mountain Wolf Woman, Sister of Crashing Thunder: The Autobiography of a Winnebago Indian*. Edited by Nancy Ostreich Lurie. Ann Arbor: University of Michigan Press, 1966.

Radin, Paul. *The Autobiography of a Winnebago Indian*. New York: Dover, 1963.

Tsosie, Rebecca. "Changing Women: The Cross-Currents of American Indian Feminine Identity." *American Culture and Research Journal* 12 (1988): 1–37.

—*Joni Adamson Clarke*

MOURNING DOVE [Christal, Christine Quintasket, Humishuma] (1888–1936), was born near Bonners Ferry, Idaho, to Joseph Quintasket (Okanogan) and Lucy Stukin (Colville). In 1912 Christal Quintasket took Morning Dove as a pen name to symbolize the launching of her literary ambitions: she changed the spelling to Mourning Dove in 1921 after she had seen that bird in a Spokane museum. The phonetic spelling of the Okanogan word for Mourning Dove is *Humishuma*.

Her first marriage to Hector McLeod, a Flathead Indian, ended in divorce; in 1919, she married Fred Galler, a Wenatchee. She had no children by either marriage. Her education consisted of short periods at government Indian schools, approximately three years at the Sacred Heart Convent in Ward, Washington, and a course at a business school when she was twenty-four.

In 1914 Mourning Dove met Lucullus V. McWhorter at a Frontier Days celebration in Walla Walla, Washington—a meeting that initiated both a friendship and a literary collaboration for the rest of her life. Founder of the *American Archaeologist* and a scholar of encyclopedic interests, McWhorter encouraged Mourning Dove's literary aspirations. He was instrumental in inspiring her to collect the Okanogan "folklores" that formed the basis for *Coyote Stories* (1933). He also became her mentor and the collaborator on her novel, *Co-Ge-We-A, the Half-Blood: A Depiction of the Great Montana Cattle Range* (1927), published thirteen years after she had completed the first draft. The title page acknowledges that the novel is "given through Sho-pow-tan," a pen name for McWhorter. Indeed, much of the formal and stilted language in the novel and the elaborate notes to the text clearly reflect McWhorter's influence.

However, the novel is Mourning Dove's, from the story—a romance about a mixed-breed female, told from the Indian point of view—to the inclusion of unrecorded stories and beliefs of the Okanogan. Intent upon preserving her tribal heritage but reluctant to divulge restricted material, Mourning Dove found her voice in the medium of fiction.

Her commitment to literature was profound, and she wrote under difficult circumstances. Often working as a migrant agricultural laborer with her husband, she had only temporary shelter at night, but she always took her typewriter with her, so she could work through the night on her stories. Her correspondence with McWhorter is a revealing self-portrait of a woman dedicated to preserving her tribal history and to finding her own voice in the language of fiction.

References

Bernardin, Susan. "Mixed Messages: Authority and Authorship in Mourning Dove's *Cogewea, the Half-Blood: A Depiction of the Great Montana Cattle Range.*" *American Literature* 67 (September 1995): 487–509.

Biedler, Peter. "Literary Criticism in *Cogewea*: Mourning Dove's Protagonist Reads *The Brand.*" *American Indian Culture and Research Journal* 19 (1995): 45–65.

Brown, Alanna Kathleen. "The Choice to Write: Mourning Dove's Search for Survival." In *Old West–New West: Centennial Essays.* Edited by Barbara H. Meldrum. Pp. 261–271. Moscow: University of Idaho Press, 1993.

———. "The Evolution of Mourning Dove's Coyote Stories." *SAIL* 4 (Summer/Fall 1992): 161–180.

———. "Looking Through the Glass Darkly: The Editorialized Mourning Dove." In *New Voices in Native American Literary Criticism.* Edited by Arnold Krupat. Pp. 274–290. Washington, DC: Smithsonian Institution Press, 1993.

———. "Mourning Dove, an Indian Novelist." *Plainswoman* 11 (1988): 3–4.

———. "Mourning Dove, Trickster Energy, and Assimilation Period Native American Texts." In *Tricksterism in Turn-of-the-Century American Literature: A Multicultural Perspective.* Edited by Elizabeth Ammons and Annette White-Parks. Pp. 126–136. Hanover, NH: University Press of New England, 1994.

———. "Mourning Dove's Canadian Recovery Years, 1917–1919." *Canadian Literature* 124–25 (Spring/Summer 1990): 113–123.

———. "Mourning Dove's 'The House of Little Men.'" *Canadian Literature* 144 (Spring 1995): 49–60.

———. "Mourning Dove's Voice in *Co-Ge-We-A.*" *Wicazo Sa Review* 4 (1988): 2–15.

———. "Profile: Mourning Dove (Humishuma) 1888–1936." *Legacy: A Journal of Nineteenth Century American Women Writers* 6 (Spring 1989): 51–58.

Fisher, Alice Poindexter. "The Transformation of Tradition: A Study of Zitkala Sa and Mourning Dove, Two Transitional American Writers." In *Critical Essays on Native American Literature*. Edited by Andrew Wiget. Pp. 202–211. Boston: G. K. Hall, 1985.

Karell, Linda. "'The Story I Am Telling You Is True': Collaboration and Literary Authority in Mourning Dove's *Cogewea*." *American Indian Quarterly* 19 (Fall 1995): 451–465.

Miller, Carol. "Mediation and Authority: The Native American Voices of Mourning Dove and Ella Deloria." In *Multicultural Education, Transformative Knowledge, and Action*. Edited by James A. Banks. New York: Teachers College Press, 1996.

Miller, Jay. "Mourning Dove: The Author as Cultural Mediator." In *Being and Becoming Indian: Biographical Studies of North American Frontiers*. Edited by James A. Clifton. Pp. 160–182. Chicago: Dorsey, 1989.

———. "Mourning Dove: Editing in All Directions to 'Get Real.'" *Studies in American Indian Literatures* 27 (Summer 1995): 65–72.

Mourning Dove. *Co-Ge-We-A, the Half-Blood: A Depiction of the Great Montana Cattle Range*. Boston: Four Seas, 1927. Reprint, edited by Dexter Fisher, Lincoln: University of Nebraska Press, 1991.

———. *Coyote Stories*. Edited and illustrated by Heister Dean Guie with notes by Lucullus V. McWhorter and a foreword by Chief Standing Bear. Caldwell, ID: Caxton Printers, 1933. Reprint, edited by Jay Miller, Lincoln: University of Nebraska Press, 1981.

———. *Mourning Dove—A Salishan Autobiography*. Edited by Jay Miller. Lincoln: University of Nebraska Press, 1990.

———. *Tales of the Okanogans*. Edited by Donald M. Hines. Fairfield, WA: Ye Galleon Press, 1976.

Owens, Louis. "Origin Mists: John Rollin Ridge's Masquerade and Mourning Dove's Mixed-Bloods." In *Other Destinies: Understanding the American Indian Novel*. Pp. 32–48. Norman: University of Oklahoma Press, 1992.

Trafzer, Clifford E., and Richard D. Scheuerman, eds. *Mourning Dove's Stories*. San Diego: San Diego State University Press, 1991.

—*Dexter Fisher Cirillo*

MUSGROVE, MARY [Mary Matthews, Mary Bosomworth] (c. 1700–1763), was a major intermediary between the Creek Indians and the English colonists who settled Georgia in 1733. She was the niece of Brimms, a Creek leader. Her father was a white trader, but in the matrilineal system of Creek society, the fact that her Creek mother was sister to Brimms gave her high status. She was sent to a Christian mission school in Ponpon, South Carolina, at the age of ten. In 1715 she returned to the Creek territory, where she met and married John Musgrove, a member of an English delegation sent to make peace with the Creeks. By 1732 the couple had established an extensive trading post at Yamacraw Bluff, near Savannah.

When James Oglethorpe arrived in 1733, he met Mary Musgrove, and upon discovering that she could speak English, prevailed upon her to negotiate with the leaders of the Yamacraw community to allow him to settle near them and establish the colony he named Georgia. She continued to be an important adviser to Oglethorpe and established a new trading post on the Altamaha River where she could observe the Spanish colonies, which threatened war with the Georgia colony, and rally the Indians in the area to Oglethorpe's side against the Spanish. About 1740 her husband died, and Musgrove promptly married Jacob Matthews, a former indentured servant who had risen to become commander of a group of white soldiers. After the marriage he proved to be a braggart and a drunkard, and his bad reputation in the Georgia colony tarnished Musgrove as well. He died in 1742, at about the same time that hostile Yamasee Indians destroyed her trading post on the Altamaha. Her establishment near Savannah was ruined during the war between Georgia and the Spanish.

When Oglethorpe returned to England in 1743, he gave Musgrove his own diamond ring and £200 with the promise of £2,000 more. He never followed through on the promise, and Musgrove's influence with the government of the Georgia colony declined.

She still had extensive landholdings, however, and she retained her influence with the Creeks. About 1746 she married Thomas Bosomworth, an English ex-minister, and with him set up a new trading station at the confluence of the Ocmulgee and Oconee rivers. They made claims for even more land from both the Creeks and the trustees of Georgia, relying on Musgrove's influential reputation with the Indians and, indeed, ultimately asserting that Musgrove was "Queen of the Creeks." When the Georgia Council failed to honor her claims, despite her veiled threats of an Indian uprising, she took her case to the Board of Trade in England, which in 1759 also disallowed them but gave her £2,100 from the sale of some of the land for her past service to the colony.

Mary Musgrove Matthews Bosomworth died around 1763, partly compensated but mainly thwarted in her attempts to convince the English that she was "Queen of the Creeks" and rightful owner of large tracts of Creek land. Her reputation depended on her family connections and her influence with Oglethorpe, but her motivation in negotiating between whites and Indians seems largely to have been self-interest. Her marriages to three white men, two of whom were of dubious reputation, diminished her standing with whites and ultimately undercut her status with the Creeks.

References

Coulter, E. Merton. "Mary Musgrove, 'Queen of the Creeks': A Chapter of Early Georgia Troubles." *Georgia Historical Quarterly* 11 (March 1927): 1–30.
Todd, Helen. *Mary Musgrove: Georgia Indian Princess*. Savannah, GA: Seven Oaks, 1981.

—*Clara Sue Kidwell*

N

NAHA, PAQUA [Frog Woman] (died c. 1955), was a Hopi–Tewa potter from First Mesa, Arizona. She began making pottery during the Sikyatki revival of Hopi pottery that resulted from J. W. Fewkes's excavations of the historic Hopi villages of Sikyatki and Awatovi on the desert floor below the mesas. Led by Nampeyo, several women from First Mesa studied the excavated pots and shards, and began re-creating historic designs and firing techniques. This effort, encouraged by both Fewkes and a trader named Thomas Keam, served to revitalize Hopi pottery at a time when pottery techniques were dying out. Naha worked in traditional yellow ware and signed her work with a trademark frog in reference to the meaning of her name. Late in life she began experimenting with the white slip that is characteristic of the pottery made by her extended family of descendants, the Navasie and Naha families. These families have maintained and developed the distinctive white ware tradition in Hopi pottery to such an extent that their reputation rivals that of the extended Nampeyo family. Paqua's daughter Joy Navasie and her daughter-in-law Helen Naha (d. 1993) adopted the Paqua white slip for their pottery. Joy Navasie inherited her mother's frog trademark and historic designs, whereas Helen Naha used prehistoric patterns from Anasazi designs and a feather trademark to distinguish her family's work from that of the direct descendants of Paqua, who use variations on the frog.

References

Dillingham, Rick. *Fourteen Families in Pueblo Pottery*. Foreword by J. J. Brody. Albuquerque: University of New Mexico Press, 1994.

Hayes, Allan, and John Blum. *Southwestern Pottery: Anasazi to Zuni*. Flagstaff, AZ: Northland Press, 1996.

Trimble, Stephen. *Talking with the Clay: The Art of Pueblo Pottery*. Santa Fe, NM: School of American Research, 1993.

—Jennifer L. Jenkins

NAMPEYO [Nampayo, Nampayu, Snake Girl] (1859–1942) was a Hopi potter who reintroduced ancient forms and designs, later known as the Sikyatki revival style, to revolutionize her tribe's ceramic art. She was born in Hano on First Mesa, Arizona, the daughter of Qotsvema, a member of the Snake clan, and Qotcakao, a Corn clan woman. Nampeyo married Kwivoya in 1879, but he left her because he feared that her beauty would attract other men. In 1881 she married Lesso (sometimes spelled Lesou).

Nampeyo was first introduced to ceramic art when she watched her grandmother making ollas and other vessels used in everyday activities. She made variations on designs then in use in the tribe, and her work brought good prices from the white traders. Sometime in the early 1890s, Nampeyo became interested in the ancient work of her people and searched for older pieces that she might study. In 1895 her husband was hired to help with the excavation of Sikyatki, an early Pueblo ruin. Nampeyo and Lesso traveled there, as well as to the ruins at Awatovi, Tsukuvi, and Payupki, to find shards to inspire her work. She also began to adapt her pieces to some of the older shapes, such as the low, wide-shouldered jars of Sikyatki. Still, her ceramics were unique, and eventually the bold, fluid designs were characterized by the use of the background space as an essential element that became part of the whole creation.

Nampeyo became a symbol of Hopi culture used in promotional photographs and literature by the Santa Fe Railway and the Fred Harvey Company. According to documented evidence, she left the reservation three times: in 1905 and 1907, to go to the Hopi House at the Grand Canyon, and in 1910, to visit the United States Land and Irrigation Exposition in Chicago. By the end of the first decade of the twentieth century, Nampeyo had been acknowledged in anthropological reports and had been photographed by well-known photographers, and her pots had been collected for the National Museum in Washington, D.C.

Although the height of Nampeyo's career was from 1901 to 1910, she continued to work into her old age. When her eyesight began to fail, she still formed the pottery, and Lesso helped to duplicate her artistry. Nampeyo's daughter, Fannie, carried on the tradition after his death in 1932. Nampeyo died on July 20, 1942. Her four daughters—Annie, Cecilia, Fannie, and Nellie—have carried on the art of ceramics to some degree.

References

Ashton, Robert, Jr. "Nampeyo and Lesou." *American Indian Art* 1 (Summer 1976): 24–33.

Collins, John. *Nampeyo, Hopi Potter: Her Artistry and Her Legacy*. Fullerton, CA: Muckenthaler Cultural Center, 1974.

Colton, Mary Russell F., and Harold S. Colton. "An Appreciation of the Art of Nampeyo and Her Influence on Hopi Pottery." *Plateau* 15 (January 1944): 43–45.

Hirschfelder, Arlene B. *Artists and Craftspeople*. New York: Facts on File, 1994.

Judd, Neil M. "Nampeyo, an Additional Note." *Plateau* 24 (1951): 92–96.

Kramer, Barbara. *Nampeyo and Her Pottery*. Albuquerque: University of New Mexico Press, 1996.

———. "Nampeyo, Hopi House and the Chicago Land Show." *American Indian Art* 14 (Winter 1988): 46–53.

McCoy, Ronald. "Nampeyo: Giving the Indian Artist a Name." In *Indian Lives: Essays on Nineteenth- and Twentieth-Century Leaders*. Edited by L. G. Moses and Raymond Wilson. Pp. 43–59. Albuquerque: University of New Mexico Press, 1985.

Monthan, Guy, and Doris Monthan. "Dextra Quotskuyva Nampeyo." *American Indian Art* 2 (Autumn 1977): 58–63.

Nequatewa, Edmund. "Nampeyo, Famous Hopi Potter." *Plateau* 15 (January 1943): 40–42.

Peterson, Susan. "Matriarchs of Pueblo Pottery." *Portfolio* 2 (November/December 1980): 50–55.

—Laurie Lisa

NAMPEYO, DAISY HOOEE (b. 1910), is Hopi–Tewa and grew up in the Hopi village of Hano on First Mesa, Arizona. She is the daughter of Annie and Willie Healing and the granddaughter of the famous Hopi potter Nampeyo, from whom she learned the art of pottery. At the age of ten, while attending Phoenix Indian School, she was threatened with blindness from cataracts. Anita Baldwin, a patron of the arts, took her to California for surgery and more formal education, and then to study art in Paris.

In 1935, married to Ray Naha and living in Arizona, Nampeyo worked with archaeologists from the Peabody Museum of Harvard University in conjunction with the excavation of Awatovi. The style and designs of her pottery were greatly influenced by the pots that were discovered in this ancient city. In 1938, after divorcing her first husband, Nampeyo moved to Zuni and married Leo Poblano, a prominent local silversmith. She took up sculpting and, together with Poblano, helped to introduce relief settings to the Zuni silversmiths. As the people of Zuni sought to recapture some of their traditions, Nampeyo gave up sculpting and returned to the making of traditional pottery. Her second husband was killed while fighting a forest fire in California, and she subsequently married Sidney Hooee, also a Zuni silversmith.

Nampeyo maintains a workshop at Zuni where the traditional methods and designs of Zuni and Hopi pottery are practiced. She still signs her pottery with the last name of Nampeyo in deference to the talented craftswoman from whom she is descended.

References

Fowler, Carol. *Daisy Hooee Nampeyo, the Story of an American Indian*. Minneapolis, MN: Dillon Press, 1977.

Kramer, Barbara. *Nampeyo and Her Pottery*. Albuquerque: University of New Mexico Press, 1996.

———. "Nampeyo, Hopi House, and the Chicago Land Show." *American Indian Art* 14 (Winter 1988): 46–53.

Peterson, Susan. "Matriarchs of Pueblo Pottery." *Portfolio* 2 (November/December 1980): 50–55.

—Arlon Benson

NARANJO-MORSE, NORA (b. 1953), is a Tewa Pueblo poet and potter. The youngest daughter and last child of Michael and Rose Naranjo of Santa Clara Pueblo, New Mexico, she has six sisters and three brothers, many of whom also are artists. She spent much of her youth in Taos Pueblo, where her father was a Baptist missionary, and graduated from Taos High School in 1971. After sorting mail in Washington, D.C., and selling firecrackers in South Dakota, Naranjo-Morse "came home" to Santa Clara and to "working on clay" in 1976. Her mother and three sisters are potters, and it was her sister Jody Folwell who reintroduced Naranjo-Morse to clay. In 1980 she graduated from the College of Santa Fe with a major in social welfare. By the time she graduated, she had become recognized as a potter and had married Greg Morse, with whom she had twins, Zakary and Eliza. They built an adobe house, and she says that the combination of marriage, children, and building a house has "made [her] flourish" and let herself "follow [her] heart." In the process, her ceramic sculptures have become much larger, but because clay limits the size of what one can do, she is now working in metal as well.

As the youngest in a family of recognized potters, Naranjo-Morse wanted to be different, so she began making small animals and people rather than bowls, combining Taos micaceous clay with Santa Clara clay. She won prizes at the Santa Fe Indian Market in 1979, and in 1980 had the first of many gallery shows at Gallery 10 in Scottsdale, Arizona. She has received fellowships for her art from the Southwest Association on Indian Affairs and from the School of American Research. Her clay people have appeared in two important museum exhibits, "A Separate Vision" at the Museum of Northern Arizona in Flagstaff and "Earth, Hands, and Life: Southwestern Ceramic Figures" at the Heard Museum in Phoenix. Her poems have been published in *Sun Tracks*, in several anthologies of Native American writers, and in her own book, *Mud Woman: Poems from the Clay*. She has read poetry and demonstrated pottery making from Flagstaff, Arizona, to Denmark and Germany, and has been featured in videotapes produced by the Museum of Northern Arizona and the Museum of New Mexico.

Naranjo-Morse describes her art as that of "an American Indian woman trying to make sense of these two cultures" in the late twentieth century, where one day she is reading poetry in New York City and the next gathering clay as Santa Clara women have done for generations. Both the conflict and the humor of this double life are embodied in her clay friend and alter ego, "Pearlene," and in poems such as "Mud Woman Encounters the World of Money and Business." In her "menagerie of characters inspired by culture and personal experience," Naranjo-Morse has taken an important Santa Clara figurative ceramic tradition in a new direction. Her "joyful play" has produced figures and scenes that combine humor with an abstract and refined sophistication. Like the mocking pastiche of Pueblo clown performances, Naranjo-Morse's mixtures of ideas and materials often make a wry, satirical cultural critique of her multiple postcolonial worlds in which "nothing was in place anymore." As both a poet and a potter, Naranjo-Morse subverts traditional and widely accepted conceptions of Pueblo culture, Pueblo women, and Pueblo pottery.

References

Coe, Kathryn, and Diana F. Pardue. "Earth Symbols." *Native Peoples* 2 (Winter 1989): 42–47.

Eaton, Linda B. "A Separate Vision." *Plateau* 60 (Winter 1989): 10–17.

Lichtenstein, Grace. "The Evolution of a Craft Tradition: Three Generations of Naranjo Women." *Ms.* 11 (April 1983): 59–60, 92.

Naranjo-Morse, Nora. *Mud Woman: Poems from the Clay*. Tucson: University of Arizona Press, 1992.

Peterson, Ashley. "Nora Naranjo-Morse: Working with Enchantment." *Santa Fe Reporter*, August 20, 1981, 81–82.

Trimble, Stephen. "Brown Earth and Laughter: The Clay People of Nora Naranjo-Morse." *American Indian Art* 12 (Autumn 1987): 58–65.

—*Barbara A. Babcock*

NAVASIE, JOY [Frog Woman, Yellow Flower] (b. 1919), is a second-generation Hopi–Tewa potter from First Mesa, Arizona. She inherited the nickname "Frog Woman" from her mother, Paqua Naha (died c. 1955), whose name means "Frog Woman." Joy Navasie learned the coil-and-scrape method of forming pots from her mother, and originally signed her work with a flower to represent her Hopi name, Yellow Flower. Around the age of twenty she adopted her mother's frog trademark, thereby establishing the family tradition of the frog signature. She maintains tradition in all aspects of pottery making, from gathering the clay to coiling, scraping and slipping, polishing, and painting with yucca brushes. Her pots are still fired in sheep dung fires rather than in modern kilns. The clarity of design and the striking oppositions of positive and negative pattern on the white slip have led to recognition of Navasie's work in the art world both in and beyond the Southwest. One of her best-known pieces, currently owned by the Heard Museum in Phoenix, is a large Pueblo-style wedding vase in polished white slip with a brown and black design. The white ware has achieved its own museum designation, "Walpi Polychrome," and a secure place in the history of Hopi–Tewa pottery. Navasie's children and grandchildren have learned from her and are producing pottery with the frog trademark.

References

Dedera, Don. *Artistry in Clay: Contemporary Pottery of the Southwest*. Foreword by Jerry Jacka. Flagstaff, AZ: Northland Press, 1985.

Dillingham, Rick. *Fourteen Families in Pueblo Pottery*. Foreword by J. J. Brody. Albuquerque: University of New Mexico Press, 1994.

Hayes, Allan, and John Blum. *Southwestern Pottery: Anasazi to Zuni*. Flagstaff, AZ: Northland Press, 1996.

Trimble, Stephen. *Talking with the Clay: The Art of Pueblo Pottery*. Santa Fe, NM: School of American Research, 1993.

—*Jennifer L. Jenkins*

NEAKOK, SADIE BROWER (b. 1916), educator, community activist, and magistrate, was born and raised in the Alaskan North Slope community of Barrow. One of thirteen siblings, she is the daughter of the American pioneer, whaler, and entrepreneur Charles Brower and his second wife, Assianggataq, an Inupiat Indian. In 1940 she married Nate Neakok, a mechanic and full-blooded Inupiat. In addition to their twelve children, the Neakoks from time to time provided temporary care of foster children.

Though most of Neakok's life has been spent in Barrow, she did venture "outside" in 1930 when her father sent her to San Francisco to finish her education. After receiving a high school degree there in 1934, she returned to Barrow. Her American clothes and "outside" education earned her the epithet "white lady."

Since her return, Neakok has devoted her life to community service as teacher, welfare worker, and state magistrate. Her call to public service came shortly after her return from California. In 1934 she was the first radio announcer to broadcast the news in the Inupiat language. That same year she became involved in the Bureau of Indian Affairs' (BIA) attempts to recruit young Native peoples for a vocational school outside of Anchorage. In 1938, during her sophomore year at the University of Alaska, she was hired by the BIA to teach full-time. Her most important public role came in 1960 when she was appointed by the state of Alaska to be a magistrate. In that capacity, Neakok was instrumental not only in introducing and implementing the American legal system among the Inupiat but also in helping the community learn how to benefit from the system. She served as Alaska's northernmost magistrate for seventeen years, retiring in 1977.

Neakok's unique background and personal experiences helped her to become an important public figure in the Barrow community. She used this position to assist her community in adapting to the changes that were first imposed upon it from the "outside" in the late nineteenth century, and culminated in 1959 with Alaska's entry into the Union.

Reference

Blackman, Margaret B. *Sadie Brower Neakok: An Inupiaq Woman*. Seattle: University of Washington Press, 1989.

—*Faren R. Siminoff*

NELSON, MARGARET F. (b. 1922), an enrolled member of the Cherokee Nation, was born in Claremore, Oklahoma. She attended Oklahoma State University from 1940 to 1942, then married and raised four children. In 1968 she enrolled in Northwestern University, where she completed a BA in English; in 1971 she received an MA in English at Oklahoma State University; and in 1979 she completed a PhD in American folklore at the same institution. She served on the faculty of Oklahoma State University from 1970 until retirement as associate professor in 1990.

Nelson's publications and organizational work have contributed significantly to furthering American Indian education. She was appointed by President Ronald Reagan to the National Advisory Council on Indian Education, and held several offices in the North American Indian Women's Association. Her publications include *Ohoyo Okhana: A Bibliography of American Indian–Alaska Native Curriculum Material*, a guidebook published by the Cherokee National Historical Society, and articles and book reviews for *American Indian Quarterly* and *Studies in American Indian Literatures*. Her many lectures and interviews have addressed Indian education, American Indian literature, and American Indian women's issues.

References

Directory of American Scholars. New York: R. R. Bowker, 1982.

Nelson, Margaret F. *Ohoyo Okhana: A Bibliography of American Indian–Alaska Native Curriculum Material*. Wichita Falls, TX: Ohoyo Resource Center, 1982.

———. *Rural Village Guidebook*. Tahlequah, OK: Cherokee National Historical Society, n.d.

—Helen Jaskoski

NETNOKWA (c.1740/1750–c.1815/1820) was born in the central Great Lakes area and was a member of the Ottawa tribe. She was a respected fur trade "captain," or leader, in the late eighteenth-century Great Lakes fur trade. She traded at Mackinac and led a band of trappers who were her sons and sons-in-law, among them the white captive John Tanner.

As was typical of mature women in Algonquian societies, Netnokwa possessed great wisdom, skills, personal charisma, and strong spiritual power. These enabled her to wield considerable authority within her family. All family property belonged to her; she made all major decisions for the family; and in crises she was able to call on spirit powers in order to affect weather and find game. Besides expertly performing in the skilled tasks for which women were responsible (making rush mats, tanning hides, making clothing, and harvesting, preparing, and storing foods), her duties included the giving of feasts for the first animals of each species killed by her sons and finding suitable wives for her sons.

In the late 1790s Netnokwa decided to go to Red River (present-day Manitoba) to visit relatives of her husband, Tawgaweninne. She persuaded other Ottawa to accompany her, and they were part of a wave of Ottawa and Ojibwa who entered the West about this time. She was widowed during the journey and never remarried, spending the rest of her life leading bands of relatives in the Red and Assiniboine River areas.

Netnokwa's life illustrates Indian involvement in the western fur trade. A plentiful supply of beaver gave her ready access to desired trade goods, but the use of alcohol, one of those goods, in the fur trade was damaging to Native societies. As a trading chief, Netnokwa drank and got others drunk in semiannual drinking parties at trading posts. Her redistribution of alcohol was an adaptation of traditional means of gaining status among Native people, but the drinking parties resulted in accidents and fights that caused many deaths—among them those of her husband and a son-in-law.

Netnokwa died in the Red River valley sometime after 1815. Her forceful character and life history demonstrate that women could and did play vital roles in leadership and decision-making among Algonquian societies.

Reference

Tanner, John. *A Narrative of the Captivity and Adventures of John Tanner During Thirty Years' Residence Among the Indians in the Interior of North America*. Edited by Edwin James. Minneapolis, MN: Ross and Haines, 1956.

—Laura L. Peers

northSun, nila (b. 1951), is a Chippewa–Shoshone poet born in Schurz, Nevada. She graduated from the University of Montana and taught tribal cultural tradition courses in a Missoula, Montana, high school. In addition to writing poetry, her literary career has included coediting *Scree* magazine and writing (with Kirk Robertson) *After the Drying Up of the Water*, a tribal history for the Paiute–Shoshone tribe. She has published two poetry collections, *Diet Pepsi & Nacho Cheese* (1977) and *Small Bones, Little Eyes*, with Jim Sagel (1981). Her poems have been published in numerous magazines, including *Wormwood Review, Pembroke, Sun Tracks, Dacotah Territory, Callaloo*, and *Nitty Gritty*. northSun's work has been included in such anthologies and studies as *Dancing on the Rim of the World, The Remembered Earth, The Sacred Hoop, New Worlds of Literature, Reinventing the Enemy's Language, A Gathering of Spirit, Returning the Gift*, and a number of European collections.

Like other contemporary Native poets, northSun explores themes of disenfranchisement, anger, loss, brutalization, and alienation both from mainstream white culture and from tribal traditions and knowledge. Nevertheless, her poems evoke feelings of ambivalence toward acculturation. northSun's poetry is informed by the conventions of contemporary Native writing in its use of community anecdote and gossip, and her use of colloquial "Reservation English" has been described as rich in idiomatic vocabulary and speech rhythms. Her style is understated and minimalist, and her ironic tone has been characterized as an almost brutal flippancy. northSun often uses humor in an effort to find compromise and reconciliation between the conflicting forces of racism and acculturation and to affirm and celebrate a Native self. Commenting on her own writing and that of others, northSun suggests, "[I]f one were to attempt to find, among the diversity of contemporary Indian writing, a major 'thrust' or 'concern,' perhaps it is to reestablish, within a larger society that all but precludes it, a society linked in harmony with the earth."

northSun began working as the social services director for her tribe in 1989, and she currently directs a teen crisis center on the Stillwater Indian Reservation in Fallon, Nevada, where she lives. Her commitment to work and family had meant placing her writing career temporarily on hold, but in 1992 northSun participated in the Returning the Gift Native Writers' Festival, where she was inspired to revisit her craft. She has since "poked the smoldering writing coals and started writing and submitting again." Her collection of new and old poetry, *A Snake in Her Mouth: Poems 1974–1996*, is the result of that renewed literary productivity.

References

Allen, Paula Gunn, ed. *The Sacred Hoop*. Boston: Beacon Press, 1992.

Brant, Beth, ed. *A Gathering of Spirit*. Ithaca, NY: Firebrand Books, 1988.

Bruchac, Joseph, ed. *Returning the Gift: Poetry and Prose from the First North American Native Writers' Festival*. Tucson: University of Arizona Press, 1994.

Hobson, Geary, ed. *The Remembered Earth: An Anthology of Contemporary Native American Literature*. Albuquerque: University of New Mexico Press, 1981.

Lerner, Andrea, ed. *Dancing on the Rim of the World: An Anthology of Contemporary Northwest Native American Writing*. Tucson: University of Arizona Press, 1990.

northSun, nila. *Diet Pepsi & Nacho Cheese*. Fallon, NV: Duck Down Press, 1977.

———. *A Snake in Her Mouth*. Fallon, NV: Duck Down Press, 1997.

northSun, nila, and Jim Sagel. *Small Bones, Little Eyes*. Fallon, NV: Duck Down Press, 1981.

Speer, Laurel. "Anatomies of Survival." Review of *Small Bones, Little Eyes*. *Small Press Review* 15 (January 1983): 1.

Western Literature Association. *A Literary History of the American West*. Fort Worth: Texas Christian University Press, 1987.

—Vanessa Holford Diana

NUNEZ, BONITA WA WA CALACHAW [Wa Wa Chaw] (1888–1972), was probably a member of the Rincon band of the Luiseño tribe of mission Indians in southern California. A white woman, Mary Duggan of New York City, who was delayed by a winter storm in 1888 while traveling in the area, carried away the newborn baby from the poverty-stricken mother. Nunez was raised by Mary Duggan and her brother, Cornelius Duggan, a prominent New York physician. These two affluent humanitarians and "Indian lovers" raised her as their own daughter, taking care always to dress her as they thought an Indian child should dress. They encouraged both a mystical bent of her mind that they recognized as something extraordinary and her strong artistic abilities.

About the only information available about Nunez and her life is in her diaries, edited in Stan Steiner's *Spirit Woman*. She married and the marriage failed, and she had a child who died at age three. Nunez once danced with Isadora Duncan, performed on the vaudeville stage, visited the White House, and became (and was arrested as) an Indian rights activist. She ultimately journeyed alone to California in search of her real mother and tribe. She lived with her tribe for a time and also with the urban Indians of Chicago, New York, Philadelphia, and other major cities.

One of the earliest and most significant uses to which Nunez's striking artistic ability was put was to draw illustrations of the medical specimens Cornelius Duggan brought home to her. She also was adept at drawing bones, tissues, organs, tumors, and various bacteria. Her method was to meditate upon the subject until she "saw" it with mystical dimensions. She was in demand as a medical illustrator for the best medical journals of the day. As a fine artist Nunez had expressionistic tendencies comparable to those of the Norwegian painter Edvard Munch, but as an early twentieth-century urban Indian activist and spokesperson for ethnically mixed ghetto neighborhoods, she also qualifies as a folk artist who intended her art to be used by the masses rather than preserved in galleries. In her later paintings she used the earthy colors of red, yellow, and brown, as well as black and white, creating a feeling of harmony with the earth and organic unity. Her heavy strokes, thick, dark lines, and bold designs convey strength and energy. Her subjects are often family or group scenes where the members are embracing or holding each other. Ultimately, her paintings speak her personality and experience.

References

Steiner, Stan. *The New Indians*. New York: Harper & Row, 1968.

———. *Spirit Woman: The Diaries and Paintings of Bonita Wa Wa Calachaw Nunez, an American Indian*. San Francisco: Harper & Row, 1980.

—Gretchen Ronnow

O

OSCEOLA, LAURA MAE (b. 1932), a member of the Panther clan, has lived most of her life at the Seminole Reservation in Hollywood, Florida. Because Seminole children were not permitted to attend public school in Florida when she was young, she was sent to the government boarding school for Indians at Cherokee, North Carolina. After completing school she returned to the reservation, and at age seventeen married Max Osceola. She gained distinction as the first Florida Indian girl to apply for a marriage license and to have a marriage ceremony performed in a church. She is the mother of three boys and a girl, and has several grandchildren. Her adopted son, James Billie, is the chairman of the Seminole tribe.

Osceola followed the tradition of service of her uncles Sam Tommie and Tony Tommie (the latter had attended the Carlisle Indian School in Pennsylvania), who were respected Seminole leaders earlier in the twentieth century. She made her own lasting contribution at a time of extreme difficulty, when the Seminoles of Florida faced federal termination proceedings. With her education and ability to speak English, as well as fluency in both Seminole languages, Osceola was selected as the major interpreter for older Seminole leaders during the termination hearings. The Seminoles had no funds for a trip to the nation's capital to defend their lands, so Osceola spoke before numerous church and civic groups to secure donations. She was the only woman member of the tribal delegation that went to Washington, D.C., in 1954 to testify at the congressional hearings on the Seminole Termination Bill. This was a major breakthrough for a woman in a traditionally male-dominated tribal political system. Osceola spoke forcefully for the elders, effectively answering the pointed questions of a joint Senate–House subcommittee and eloquently presenting the Seminole position that they needed twenty-five more years for education and training before they would be ready to manage their own affairs. This convinced the Florida congressional delegation that the Seminoles were not ready for termination of federal services, and the bill was ultimately defeated.

The Florida Seminoles then set out to organize their own government with a federal constitution and corporate charter. Osceola visited all of the reservations, helping to explain what the new tribal government would mean for the people, and it was overwhelmingly adopted. When the Seminole Tribe of Florida was formed in 1957, she was named secretary and treasurer, an extremely influential position that involved setting up the office management and bookkeeping systems, and supervising elections for the new government. She served in that capacity until 1967. Despite the respect and popularity that she gained through her contributions during the early years of tribal organization, Osceola never held an elective office; however, she was generally consulted when important decisions were made by the Tribal Council. She later served for many years as an employment assistance counselor for the Seminole tribe. Her son, Max Osceola, Jr., a tribal councilman from the Hollywood Reservation, continues the family tradition of service to the Seminole people.

References

Gallagher, Peter B. "Hog Farm Signed into Federal Trust." *The Seminole Tribune* [Hollywood, FL], January 13, 1991, 1, 6.

Kersey, Harry A., Jr. *An Assumption of Sovereignty: Social and Political Transformation Among the Florida Seminoles, 1953–1979.* Lincoln: University of Nebraska Press, 1996.

———. "'Give Us Twenty-five More Years': Florida Seminoles from Near-Termination to Self-Determination, 1953–1957." *Florida Historical Quarterly* 68 (1989): 290–309.

Kersey, Harry A., Jr., and Helen Bannan. "Patchwork and Politics: The Evolving Roles of Florida Seminole Women in the Twentieth Century." In *Negotiators of Change: Historical Perspectives on Native American Women.* Edited by Nancy Shoemaker. Pp. 193–212. New York: Routledge, 1995.

Seminole Tribe of Florida. *On The Path to Self-Reliance.* 26 min. 1989. Videotape. Subcommittees of the Committees on Interior and Insular Affairs. *Termination of Federal Supervision over Certain Tribes of Indians.* 83rd Cong., 2nd sess., 1954. S. Doc. 2747. H.R. 7321, pt. 8.

Seminole Tribe of Florida and Seminole Tribe of Florida, Inc. "20th Anniversary of Tribal Organization 1957–1977, Saturday, 20 August 1977." Hollywood, FL: Seminole Tribe, 1977, Mimeo.

—*Harry A. Kersey, Jr.*

OWEN, ANGIE REANO (b. 1946), was born Angelita Reano at Santo Domingo Pueblo, New Mexico, into a family that made jewelry. During the early 1950s, she and her sisters drilled white gypsum for her mother to use in her mosaic jewelry. When she was in the sixth grade, Owen sold the family's jewelry on the porch of the Palace of the Governors in Santa Fe. Educated at Santo Domingo Day School and Bernalillo High School, she graduated from Albuquerque High School in 1965. She worked briefly at a lumber mill before embarking on a jewelry career of her own.

In 1969 she married Don Owen, an Anglo trader and more recently coordinator of the annual Indian Market sponsored by the Southwestern Association on Indian Affairs. Encouraged by her husband and friends, Owen began researching the prehistoric styles of mosaic jewelry created by the Hohokam and Anasazi cultures of the Southwest. She traveled extensively throughout the region, studying early pieces in museum and private collections to learn the techniques of her ancestors.

The mosaic style of jewelry—a pattern of small pieces of turquoise, coral, and other stones cut from the rough stone and set onto shell with epoxy, then ground and polished to a glossy and smooth finish—had been done in the 1940s and 1950s by Owen's mother and a few others at Santo Domingo. It was called "depression" jewelry because the only surfaces available to the jewelers were 78 rpm records and old batteries. Few artists explored the format, however, because "heishi" necklaces of rolled beads were much more popular.

Among the many examples of prehistoric shell jewelry that particularly inspired Owen were the Glycymeris bracelets, which, when cut, became bangle bracelets in any number of shapes that could be etched or overlaid with mosaic. Overlaying a total circumference presented a technical and aesthetic challenge to Owen, as it had to her predecessors. In 1974 she made her first mosaic bangle bracelet on green snail, producing at least one a year following that. It was not until 1978 that she found, in a shell shop in Malibu, California, the same Glycymeris shell used by the Hohokam. And in 1982, she made her first mosaic cuff bracelet out of a tiger cowrie shell.

Recognized early on by museums, traders, and other Indian artists for her single-handed revival of an ancient tradition of mosaic overlay, Owen did not achieve commercial success with her work until the late 1970s. Her work has been widely collected both privately and by museums in the United States and in Europe, including the Albuquerque Museum, the Heard Museum, and the Millicent Rogers Museum. In 1990 the Smithsonian invited her to participate in a special Native American artists series. Owen has received every major award for her work at the various competitions held throughout the Southwest, including Best of Division in Mosaic at the Heard Museum and the annual Indian Market in Santa Fe.

The shells and stones she most frequently uses are black lip and gold lip shell (mother-of-pearl), green snail, spiny oyster, pink mussel, Glycymeris, tiger cowrie, Olivella, Pecten, conch, Conus, clam, turquoise, jet, coral, lapis lazuli, pipestone, serpentine, and ivory.

Owen's talent lies in the fact that her designs are organically determined by the shape of the shells. Though the forms are classic, the aesthetic is modern, and the jewelry she creates is truly timeless. Perhaps even more important, she has launched a jewelry-making revival at Santo Domingo that is providing numerous craftspeople with new opportunities for both artistic expression and economic success.

References

Cirillo, Dexter. "Back to the Past: Tradition and Change in Contemporary Pueblo Jewelry." *American Indian Art* 13 (Spring 1988): 46–63.

———. *Southwestern Indian Jewelry.* New York: Abbeville Press, 1992.

Cortright, Barbara. "Angie Reano Owen." *American West* 1 (February 1987): 68–69.

Jacka, Jerry, and Lois Essary Jacka. *Beyond Tradition: Contemporary Indian Art and Its Evolution.* Flagstaff, AZ: Northland Press, 1988.

Jernigan, E. Wesley. *Jewelry of the Prehistoric Southwest.* Albuquerque: University of New Mexico Press, 1978.

"One Space: Three Visions." Catalog for show curated by Dextra Frankel. Albuquerque Museum, August 5–November 4, 1979.

—*Dexter Fisher Cirillo*

OWL WOMAN (1822–1849) was the daughter of Grey Thunder, keeper of the medicine arrows for the Cheyenne band of Yellow Wolf in the early 1800s. She was "given" in marriage to Colonel William Bent, who had traveled with his brother Charles to establish a fort and/or trading post on the upper Arkansas River in Colorado sometime between 1823 and 1833. The tribal community thought that it would be "a good stroke of diplomacy" to give Bent one of its girls. Bent himself, as well as the family trading company, Bent, St. Vrain & Company, benefited both economically and professionally from this alliance. The Cheyenne also clearly benefited from the close ties with Bent because of his willingness to act as their advocate in dealing with white interests, both while Owl Woman was alive and after her death; Bent eventually acted as agent for the Southern Cheyenne.

Owl Woman and William Bent were instrumental in keeping the peace between area whites as well as among the then battling Kiowas, Comanches, and Cheyennes. Bent's brother Charles, governor of New Mexico Territory at the time of the Mexican and Taos Pueblo uprising, was killed in that conflict. The Cheyenne were apparently eager to assist in "taking revenge" on Taos Pueblo, but Bent managed to dissuade them.

In 1838 Owl Woman gave birth to her first child, Mary. Two other children came shortly thereafter, Robert and George. A fourth child, Julia, was born in 1849. Owl Woman may have died in childbirth, or possibly during the cholera outbreak on the Cimarron. She had apparently willed her children to her mother and her sister. William Bent married the sister, Yellow Woman, which assured his "claim" on his children.

Owl Woman's son George continued as a trader in the area after having been educated, along with his brother, Robert, in St. Louis. George wrote *40 Years with the Cheyenne*, and Julia wrote and published a brief autobiographical piece for the *School News* at Carlisle Indian School in 1881. There is some dispute as to the birth mother of Robert and George. Some have said they were Yellow Woman's children, but it seems more likely that they were born to Owl Woman, then raised as her own by Yellow Woman.

References

Ellis, Richard N. "Bent, Carlson, and the Indians, 1865." *Colorado Magazine* 46 (1969): 55–68.

Grinnell, George Bird. *The Cheyenne Indians: Their History and Ways of Life.* Vol. 1. Lincoln: University of Nebraska Press, 1972.

———. *The Fighting Cheyennes.* Norman: University of Oklahoma Press, 1956.

Seymour, Flora Warren. *Women of Trail and Wigwam.* New York: Woman's Press, 1930.

—Renae Moore Bredin

P

PARKER, CYNTHIA ANN [Preloch] (1827–1870), was born in Clark County, Illinois, the eldest child of Silas and Lucy Parker. In 1832 her family moved to Texas as part of a branch of the Primitive Baptist Church headed by her uncle, John Parker. By the spring of 1834, the congregation had decided to settle at the headwaters of the Navasota River in what is today Groesbeck, Texas. In order to protect themselves from marauding Indians, they built substantial walls around their settlement, which they called Fort Parker, and created a company of Texas Rangers.

On May 19, 1836, Fort Parker was attacked by several hundred Caddo, Comanche, and Kiowa Indians. At least five settlers were killed and five were abducted; among the latter was nine-year-old Cynthia Ann Parker. Within six years all of the captives had been located and returned to white society, except for Parker. She was given to Chatua and Tabbi-nocca, a Tenowish Comanche couple who raised her as their daughter. She assimilated completely to Comanche life, and when attempts were made to ransom her in the 1840s, the band council refused to accept any offer, stating that she stayed with them by her own choice.

In 1845 Parker married Peta Nocoma, a young Quahadi Comanche chief who had led the Fort Parker attack and many other victorious raids. The marriage was apparently successful; although prominent warriors sometimes married two or three women, Parker was Nocoma's only wife. They had two sons, Quanah and Pecos, and a daughter, Topsannah.

Peta Nocoma led many raids into Young, Jack, Parker, and Palo Pinto counties, looting farms and ranches and killing settlers. On December 18, 1860, Captain Lawrence Sullivan Ross attacked Nocoma's camp on the Pease River. Nocoma was wounded, Quanah and Pecos escaped, and Parker and Topsannah were captured and taken to Camp Cooper. She was identified by her uncle Isaac Parker in January 1861 and was taken to his farm in Birdville, Texas.

Although Parker never related her experiences as a Comanche captive, she became a legend in her own day. Many settlers took advantage of her name to publish memoirs, letters, or articles designed to incite anti–Indian sentiment. Others wrote historical fiction that over the years became accepted as fact. Parker returned to white society as unwillingly as she had left it twenty-five years earlier. After her capture by white society she lived with various members of the Parker family but was unable to re-assimilate to a life she had known for only nine years and had forgotten. She never stopped grieving for Peta Nocoma and her sons.

In the fall of 1863, Parker received news that Pecos had died of smallpox; a few months later Topsannah succumbed to influenza. Their deaths devastated her, and she died in 1870, heartbroken and weakened by self-inflicted starvation. Her other son, Quanah, survived his mother and became a notable Comanche war chief who distinguished himself by serving as a member of the Indian police and as a delegate for his people in Washington, D.C. In 1875 he led the Quahada Comanche to a reservation in Oklahoma Territory, and in 1888 he was appointed one of three judges on the Court of Indian Offenses.

Quanah Parker searched for his mother for many years. When he discovered she was dead, he had her remains and Topsannah's remains moved to Cache, Oklahoma, for reburial. On February 21, 1911, Quanah died and was laid to rest at his mother's side.

References

Hacker, Margaret Schmidt. *Cynthia Ann Parker: The Life and the Legend*. El Paso: Texas Western Press, 1990.

Parker family documents. Eugene C. Barker History Center, University of Texas, Austin.

Quanah Parker files. Fort Sill Archives, Lawton, OK.

Waldraven-Johnson, Margaret. *White Comanche: The Story of Cynthia Ann Parker and Her Son, Quanah*. New York: Comet Press, 1956.

Waltrip, Lela, and Rufus Waltrip. *Indian Women*. New York: David McKay, 1964.

—*Joyce Ann Kievit*

PARKER, JULIA F. (b. 1929), tribal scholar, cultural consultant, historian, educator, and basket weaver, was born at Graton, California, and spent her early years moving from tent camp to tent camp with her parents as they followed the crops. When she was six, her father died, followed soon after by her mother, Lily Pete (Kashia Pomo). Parker, two younger sisters and two younger brothers were raised by a foster mother. In the eighth grade boarding school she and her siblings were taken out of public schools and sent to the Bureau of Indian Affairs' boarding school at Stewart, Nevada. Parker was among a group of children who hid out on campus during weekend afternoons to do forbidden "Indian things." At Stewart, she met her future husband, Ralph Parker (Yosemite Miwok/Paiute).

In 1948 Parker moved to Yosemite National Park, where she worked in the laundry and was instructed in Miwok/Paiute tradition by Ralph's grandmother, Lucy Tom Parker Telles, who sometimes demonstrated basketry in the park. One of Telles's baskets, which took four years to complete, was exhibited at the 1939 World's Fair.

In Yosemite, Parker raised four children and assisted with the education and upbringing of two granddaughters and seven grandsons. After Telles died in 1956, the National Park Service asked Parker to replace her as a cultural demonstrator. To prepare for the task, Parker studied basketry with Carrie Bethel and Minnie Mike (both Mono Lake Paiute/Southern Sierra Miwok) and Ida Bishop (Mono Lake

Julia F. Parker

Paiute). She later studied Pomo basketry with Elsie Allen (Cloverdale Pomo), Molly Jackson (Yokayo Pomo), and Mabel McKay (Cache Creek Pomo).

As cultural demonstrator, and more recently as supervisor, for Yosemite's Indian Cultural Program, Parker has been instrumental in preserving Yosemite Miwok/Paiute traditions, including traditional acorn preparation and soaproot brushmaking, basketry, games, and tools. Her baskets are found as far away as Oslo, Norway, and in 1983 she presented Great Britain's Queen Elizabeth II with one of her baskets. Parker has been featured in numerous books and articles, and she is collaborating on a book about traditional Yosemite Miwok/Paiute acorn preparation. She is also assisting in an effort to achieve federal acknowledgment of the Miwok/Paiute.

Parker has taught others how to carry on the "old ways" through classes and demonstrations at Yosemite, other parks, museums, elementary schools, and colleges in such disparate places as Palm Springs, California; Colter Bay, Wyoming; and the Smithsonian Institution in Washington, D.C.

Her legacy is the inspiration she has given others to carry on the traditional ways. In her own words, "We should keep the old way here because of our children and our children's children and generations to come after us."

References

Ortiz, Bev. "It Will Live Forever: Yosemite Indian Acorn Preparation." *News from Native California* 2 (November/December 1988): 24–28.
———. *It Will Live Forever*. Berkeley, CA: Heyday Books, 1991.
———. Oral and taped interviews with Julia Parker, 1983–90.

—*Bev Ortiz*

PARRISH, ESSIE (1902–1979), was born on the Haupt Ranch in Sonoma County, California, where many of the Kashaya Pomo resided before settling on their present reservation. Early on, the Kashaya recognized that Parrish, daughter of Emily Colder and John Pinola, would be the last of four prophets to lead the Kashaya Pomo in political and religious matters. She was raised by her maternal grandmother, Rosie Jarvis, the great tribal historian, and in her early years consulted with her predecessor as tribal leader, Annie Jarvis. Parrish began dreaming in early childhood and treated her first patient at age nine. In 1943, after the death of Annie Jarvis, Parrish became the official religious leader, or dreamer, of the Kashaya people. She doctored the sick and directed all religious activity, including the making of costumes for the numerous religious events and the teaching of rules and traditions associated with those events. This was no small feat; at a time when other tribes of Pomo had stopped most traditional activity and the influences of dominant American culture dissipated tribal cohesion among many Pomo groups, Parrish used her religion and knowledge to keep the Kashaya together. Consequently, the Kashaya Pomo are viewed by most Indian and non–Indian authorities as the most knowledgeable among the Pomo groups regarding religious and historical issues. With well-known anthropologists, Parrish made more than two dozen films on various aspects of the Kashaya Pomo culture, including her dream dances, doctoring, and the use and preparation of acorns as food. Her film on acorn preparation, *Chishkle, or Beautiful Tree*, won the Western Heritage Award in 1965. With the linguist Robert Oswalt, she compiled a Kashaya dictionary and the well-known *Kashaya Texts*, in which many of the Kashaya legends and Parrish's personal experiences are recorded.

Parrish was also a basket weaver of national repute. Her baskets have been collected and displayed in museums throughout the country. She consulted with scholars at the Lowie Museum, University of California at Berkeley, not only on basketry but also on the use of native California plants by the Kashaya Pomo. In 1967 she met Robert Kennedy when he came to the Kashaya Reservation during

Essie Parrish

his campaign for the Democratic presidential nomination. As head of state, Parrish, dressed in ceremonial attire, led Kennedy into the Roundhouse, the Kashaya religious center, and gave him a sacred basket she had woven. Later, after Kennedy left, she told her people that the basket was to help him, because he would not have much time left on this earth.

Parrish was not only a religious and political leader and a scholar who worked regularly with many colleges and universities; she was also a devoted mother of fifteen children. As her daughter Violet Chappell notes, "Mom was one of a kind. She could do anything. Play the piano, the accordion, the harmonica. She could cook. People used to come from the cities just to get her pies. She didn't believe in the word *can't*. And, above all else, she taught us to be proud, how great it was to be Indian and know who we are." As one anthropologist once remarked, summing up the cultural and historical contributions of Essie Parrish, "She was the most important California Indian of the twentieth century."

References

Oswalt, Robert. *Kashaya Texts*. Publications in Linguistics, Vol. 36. Berkeley: University of California, 1964.

Parrish, Otis, and Paula Hammett. "Parrish: A Pomo Shaman." *Native Self-Sufficiency* 6 (1981): 8–9.

Sarris, Greg. Personal communication with Violet Chappell, May 1990.

———. Personal communications with Essie Parrish, 1957–1979.

—*Greg Sarris*

PAUL, ALICE S. (b ?), a Tohono O'odham, is a well-known educator in Arizona. She received her BA in 1958 in elementary education, her MEd in 1968 in elementary education, and her EdD in 1978 in elementary education and educational psychology, all from the University of Arizona.

She is the director of the Tucson Early Education Model Follow-through Program at the University of Arizona College of Education and has been the coordinator of educational development for that model. She has taught in the Tucson public schools and has been an associate professor of teacher education at the University of Arizona.

Paul sees her primary focus as centering on young children and their families. She is especially interested in holding workshops for tribal peoples and parents on how to become involved in their children's educations. She has worked in this capacity with the San Carlos Apache, the Tohono O'odham, and the Choctaw tribal schools, as well as with the Native American Head Start programs in Arizona, Nevada, North Dakota, Utah, and New Mexico. She has been a consultant with the National Head Start Bureau in Washington, D.C., and a reader of American Indian fellowship applications for the U.S. Department of Education. She gives numerous conference presentations on Native American child language development, on facts and myths of the Native American perspective, and on strategies for teaching "at-risk" children and for parenting. She also has published on early childhood intervention and bilingualism.

One of Paul's greatest concerns is to foster an awareness in teachers, students, and parents of the resources Native Americans have in their traditions and in their families. She wants to raise awareness about the many networking opportunities for Native American educators, as well as for educators teaching Native Americans.

References

Paul, Alice. "Development of a Classroom Based Procedure for Assessing Aspects of Intellectual Functioning of First Grade Children." EdD diss., University of Arizona, 1978.

———. "The Transitional Model: Bilingualism Examined." In *Educational Models for Young Children*. Edited by Jaipul Roopnarine and James Johnson. Columbus, OH: Charles E. Merrill, 1987.

———. "Two Decades of Early Childhood Intervention." In *Intergenerational Transfer of Cognitive Skills*. Edited by Thomas G. Sticht, Michael J. Beeler, and Barbara A. McDonald. Norwood, NJ: Ablex, 1992.

Ronnow, Gretchen. Personal communication with Alice Paul. University of Arizona, Tucson, Arizona, October 12, 1990.

—Gretchen Ronnow

PAVATEA, GARNET (1915–1981), like many young Tewa and Hopi girls of her generation, learned to make pottery from her mother. As a young girl she accompanied her mother to Winslow, Arizona, where they sold their pottery to the Anglo tourists at the train station. For some women pottery-making was nothing more than a way to earn money; for Pavatea, however, it became a continuation of a timeless cultural aesthetic, a vehicle for self-expression, and a means of defining herself vis-à-vis her people and the non–Tewa world.

In 1953 Pavatea entered her pottery in a judged exhibition and began what was to become a lifetime association with the staff of the Museum of Northern Arizona in Flagstaff, and its annual celebration of Hopi art, the Hopi Craftsmen Exhibition. Pavatea's polychrome bowls and jars won awards, and her engaging personality gained her the pottery demonstrator's job at the Hopi show for the next two decades. Her pottery blended her sense of cultural aesthetic with forms and decorative motifs popular with American consumers. In addition to the traditional bowl and jar forms, Pavatea made the popular wedding vase, as well as a number of special requests like fruit bowls and bean pots. She favored two decorative styles: One was the popular nineteenth-century Sikyatki revival style, which featured a yellowish-white background with red and black painted geometric and stylized bird motifs. The other was a design Pavatea reintroduced and perfected. Sometime in the early 1960s, she began producing plain, highly polished redware pieces that were often decorated with a punctate band made by pressing the triangular tip of a bottle opener into the damp clay. During the winter of 1981, having narrowly failed to win the Pottery Division award at the 1980 Hopi Show, Pavatea began trying to re-create the "really big" pots her mother had made. She was motivated by the desire to reclaim the prize that had been "hers" and to recapture a talent she felt Hopi potters had lost—the ability to make and fire large vessels. This was her goal despite the fact that she had lost both legs to diabetes and gathering clay had become something of a chore. The disease claimed her life two weeks after she reclaimed "her" prize with the largest jar she had made in years.

Pavatea's artistic talent and her popularity as a demonstrator at the Museum of Northern Arizona ensured that her house at Tewa Village was often visited by Anglo neophytes, as well as connoisseurs who prized her pottery and her friendship. Her humor and graciousness made her house a popular spot for Hopi and Tewa women to stop and visit, their laughter ringing out across the mesa.

References

Allen, Laura Graves. *Contemporary Hopi Pottery*. Flagstaff: Museum of Northern Arizona Press, 1984.

"Garnet Pavatea Exhibit Set at Museum Through October." *The Sun* [Flagstaff, AZ], September 21, 1981.

"Garnet Pavatea 1915–1981." *Museum Notes (MNA)* 28 (Fall 1981).

—*Laura Graves*

PEARSON, MARIA DARLENE (b. 1932), is a political activist, an adviser for programs involving Native American education, and a consultant on cultural preservation and repatriation issues. She was born Darlene Elvira Drappeaux on July 12, 1932, in Springfield, South Dakota, the third of eight children of Joseph Luther Oscar Drappeaux and Winifred May Keeler Drappeaux. A member of the Turtle clan of the Yankton Sioux tribe, she was given the name Running Moccasins by her mother. At her confirmation in the Catholic Church, she was named Margaret Mary. A follower of traditional Native American social and religious practices, she has been adopted into the Hochunk (Winnebago) and Arapaho tribes, and given the respective names Woman Stepping into Water and Whirlwind Woman. The widow of John Pearson, she has six children, seventeen grandchildren, and four great-grandchildren.

Pearson completed her primary and secondary education in South Dakota and Colorado, then took classes at Iowa Western Community College and Iowa Technical College, and continuing education courses at Iowa State University. She worked as a surgical nurse at Iowa Methodist Hospital in Des Moines (1966–1967), and was a health and nutrition specialist at the American Indian Center in Omaha (1970–1974). Pearson also has worked as a keypunch operator, and was the owner/operator of a motel in Georgia and of a restaurant and filling station in Missouri. She lived in Germany for seven years while her husband was there in the military service.

Since 1961 Pearson has advised the Iowa State legislature, the Lutheran Church, the Methodist Church, and various schools and universities on issues of American Indian education, health, and civil rights. From 1980 to 1986 she served on the Juvenile Justice Advisory Council. She is a member of the National Congress of American Indians and the National Indian Board on Alcohol and Drugs. Pearson serves as a consultant to the Yankton Sioux Tribal Council concerning repatriation and other interests in Iowa. She was elected national president of the Governors' Interstate Indian Council (1992–1994).

In 1971 Pearson began the project for which she is perhaps best known: the reburial of Native American skeletal remains from public and private collections. Personally and spiritually outraged by discriminatory handling of Indian versus non–Indian skeletal remains at an archaeological excavation near Glenwood, Iowa, Pearson determinedly set out to transform long-established laws and professional procedures. Her efforts led to significant changes in the Iowa Burial Code requiring reburial of Native American skeletal remains and establishment of an Indian Advisory Committee for the Office of the State Archaeologist. She has chaired that committee since 1974 while concurrently functioning as the Iowa governor's liaison for Indian affairs. Pearson's work in Iowa significantly anticipated the federal Native American Graves Protection and Repatriation Act *(NAGPRA)* of 1990. She helped organize the World Archaeological Congress's First Inter-Congress on the Disposition of the Dead in Vermillion, South Dakota (1989), and was invited to participate in the World Archaeological Congress held in Venezuela (1990).

References

Anderson, Duane C. "Reburial: Is It Reasonable?" *Archaeology* 38 (1985): 48–51.

British Broadcasting Corporation. *Bones of Contention*. Horizons program series. London: BBC, 1995. Television documentary.

Carmack, Patrick J., ed. *The Study of Ancient Human Skeletal Remains in Iowa: A Symposium*. Iowa City: Office of the State Archaeologist of Iowa, 1983.

Frese, Millie. "Maria Running Moccasins Pearson, Indian Rights Activist." *The Goldfinch* 15 (1993): 21–23.

Fruhling, Larry. "Iowan Recalls Fight for Indian Reburial Laws." *Des Moines Register*, April 16, 1989, AI 7.

Gradwohl, David. Interview with Maria Darlene Pearson, Ames, Iowa, December 9, 1996.

O'Shea, James. "Controversy over Bones of Indian." *Des Moines Register*, July 11, 1971, 1, 3.

David Mayer Gradwohl

PEÑA, TONITA [Maria Antonia Peña, Little Bead, Pink Shell, Quah Ah, Quah H. Ah, Tonita Peña A., Tonita P. Arquero] (1893–1949), was born at San Ildefonso Pueblo, New Mexico. She lived there with her parents and attended day school from 1899 to 1905. During an influenza epidemic she moved to Cochiti Pueblo to live with her aunt, Martina Montoya, who is credited with introducing the Cochiti slip to San Ildefonso potters. Under her aunt's tutelage, Peña learned to paint on pottery; at this time she also attended St. Catherine's Indian School in Santa Fe, where she studied art. Peña married Juan Rosario Chavez in 1908 and had two children with him; after his death in 1912, she returned to St. Catherine's to pursue her art studies. From 1913 to 1920 she was married to Felipe Herrera; their son, Joe H. Herrera, became a noted Pueblo artist. After Felipe Herrera's death, Peña taught art, pottery-making, and pottery painting at the Indian schools in Santa Fe and Albuquerque. She married Epitacio Arquero in 1922; with him she raised another family and pursued her career as an artist.

Peña is believed to be the first modern woman watercolorist of the Rio Grande Pueblo peoples. As early as 1909 she was identified as the only female member of the San Ildefonso Group, a group of Pueblo artists that included her cousin Romando Vigil, Alfredo Montoya, and Fred Kabotie, a Hopi. In the 1920s Peña displayed her paintings and pots in the arcade of the Palace of the Governors in Santa Fe, and the nearby La Fonda Hotel bought her work to decorate rooms and suites. Peña painted a series of murals for the Santa Fe Indian School in the 1930s, under the auspices of the Works Progress Administration. These panels were soon moved to the Albuquerque Indian School and then to the Southwest Museum in Los Angeles in 1934. She also painted a commemorative panel for the Coronado Quatercentenary in 1940.

Peña's paintings depict Pueblo dances and pottery designs, and her murals blend Pueblo iconography with images from Anglo and Hispanic colonial history. Her watercolor renditions of seasonal dances place the dancers on a field of white rather than in the panoramic scene of the Pueblo plaza. This isolation of the figures makes them seem timeless and emphasizes the dancer's persona and religious significance. Her paintings on pottery, also on a field of white, have been used as illustrations of Cochiti and San Ildefonso styles. Peña's numerous watercolors serve as valuable documentation of the dances and pottery forms she observed during the thirty years of her career as an artist.

References

Brody, J. J. *Indian Painters, White Patrons*. Albuquerque: University of New Mexico Press, 1971.

Cassidy, Ina Sizer. "Art and Artists of New Mexico." *New Mexico Magazine* 16 (November 1938): 22, 32–33.

———. "Indian Murals." *New Mexico Magazine* 12 (1934); 23–24, 39.

———. "Tonita Peña (Quah Ah)—Julian Martinez." *New Mexico Magazine* 11 (November 1933); 28, 45–46.

Dorman, Margaret. "A Study of the Water Color Paintings of Modern Pueblo Indians." Master's thesis, University of New Mexico, 1932.

Gray, Samuel L. *Tonita Peña: Quah Ah*. Albuquerque: Avanyu Publishing, 1990.

"Indian Drawings." *School Arts* 30 (March 1931): 461–463.

Jantzer-White, Marilee. "Tonita Peña (Quah Ah), Pueblo Painter: Asserting Identity Through Continuity and Change." *American Indian Quarterly* 18 (Summer 1994): 369–382.

"Two Paintings of Tonita Peña and an Article on Her Work." *Christian Science Monitor*, April 22, 1936.

—*Jennifer L. Jenkins*

PETERSON, ANNIE MINER (1860–1939), a member of the Coos Bay (Oregon) Miluk and Hanis tribes, made significant contributions to anthropology and linguistics. Born just after English ships had begun seriously and repeatedly to explore the region, Peterson lived through a time of rapid, sometimes fascinating, and often oppressive cultural change. She was the last living person to speak

Miluk, and for many years before her death, she worked with anthropologists recording the language.

Probably the most famous anthropological work Peterson completed was conducted by Melville Jacobs, an anthropologist at the University of Washington and a former student of Franz Boas. Her facility with both the Miluk and Hanis languages was invaluable to Jacobs and constitutes an important part of his research. Peterson chose not to record her memoirs in English, though she knew it well, but in Miluk, which was translated by Jacobs.

Largely gleaned from these memoirs, interviews with her descendants, and the field notes of Jacobs, a comprehensive account of Peterson's life and culture is now available in a book by Lionel Youst. In the book, *She's Tricky like Coyote*, Youst chronicles Miluk conflicts with white settlers, intermarriage with whites (often accompanied by pronounced gender and racial inequities), healing ceremonies, and social mores. Also included are several Miluk myths and folkloric tales that Peterson told to Melville Jacobs.

A prominent member of the Coos Bay community, at her death in 1939 she was survived by her daughter and sixth husband.

References

Jacobs, Melville. "Coos Ethnologic Notes." Notebooks 93–104, 1933–1934. Melville Jacobs Collection, University of Washington Archives, Seattle.
Youst, Lionel. *She's Tricky like Coyote: Annie Miner Perterson, an Oregon Coast Woman*. Norman: University of Oklahoma Press, 1997.

—Patricia Verstrat

PETERSON, HELEN (b. 1915), was born on the Pine Ridge Reservation in South Dakota. An enrolled member of the Oglala Sioux tribe, she attended a public high school and Nebraska State Teachers College, and graduated with a degree in education from Colorado State College. First employed as a secretary to the head of the Education Department at Colorado State College, Peterson went on to serve as the director of the Rocky Mountain Council on Inter–American Affairs, located in Denver. In this capacity she attended the Inter–American Indian Conference in Peru as an adviser for the United States delegate.

From 1948 until 1950, Peterson directed the Mayor's Committee on Human Relations in Denver, and after becoming an active member of the all–Indian National Congress of American Indians (NCAI) in 1948, she rose to executive director in 1953. Later Peterson returned to Denver as the director of Denver's Commission on Community Relations.

Reference

Philp, Kenneth R., ed. *Indian Self-Rule: First-Hand Accounts of Indian–White Relations from Roosevelt to Reagan*. Salt Lake City, UT: Howe Brothers, 1986.

—Gretchen G. Harvey

PICOTTE, AGNES [Goes In Center] (b. 1935), editor of the papers of Ella Cara Deloria, began collecting letters, stories, and documents by Deloria and other

Agnes Picotte

Dakota writers in 1975. She and Paul Pavich edited Deloria's *Dakota Texts*, reissued in 1978; Picotte's biographical sketch of Deloria is published with the latter's novel *Waterlily;* and she wrote the foreword to Zitkala-Sa's *Old Indian Legends*, reissued in 1985. Picotte's book, *An Introduction to Basic Dakota, Lakota and Nakota*, was published in 1987.

Born at Hisle, South Dakota, Picotte grew up in the Wanblee district on the Pine Ridge Reservation. Her father, Oliver Goes in Center, was of the Oglala tribe; her mother, Mabel Romero Goes in Center, was the daughter of Manuel Romero, originally from Mexico but adopted into the Oglala tribe. Picotte grew up in the traditional way, speaking Lakota and living near her grandmothers, Katie Lip Goes in Center and Florence Hawk Romero. There were a number of white ranchers in the Wanblee area, and the Goes in Center family, who raised cattle, had friendly relations with them during the 1930s.

The youngest of four girls, Picotte, like her sisters, was sent to the Holy Rosary Mission School because the family lived seventeen miles from the nearest public grade school. Her father found occasional construction work in Rapid City and at nearby Ellsworth Air Force Base. She and her family sometimes moved with him. She graduated from high school at St. Paul's Indian School, Marty, South Dakota.

Encouraged by her father to pursue her education, she attended Mount Marty College in Yankton, South Dakota, where she completed a BA in education. She then taught at Red Cloud School on the Pine Ridge Reservation, where she was Indian Studies director.

After receiving a scholarship, Picotte enrolled in graduate school at the University of Oregon, where she assisted in the development of the Ethnic Studies Department. She completed both the MA and the PhD in education there, the first Oglala to earn a PhD.

From 1975 through 1986, Picotte was adjunct professor of history and director of the Ella C. Deloria Project in Indian Culture and Language at the University of

South Dakota. She and her husband, Norbert, live in Chamberlain, South Dakota. They have one daughter, Mabel Grace.

References

Hoover, Herbert, and Susan Peterson. Interviews with Agnes Picotte. Audiotapes 1046–1048. Vermillion, SD: American Indian Research Project, University of South Dakota, 1979.

Picotte, Agnes. "Biographical Sketch of the Author." In *Waterlily*, by Ella Cara Deloria. Lincoln: University of Nebraska, 1988.

———. Foreword to *Old Indian Legends*, by Zitkala-Sa. Lincoln: University of Nebraska, 1985.

———. *An Introduction to Basic Dakota, Lakota and Nakota*. Chamberlain, SD: Dakota Indian Foundation, 1987.

Picotte, Agnes, and Paul N. Pavich. Introductory notes to *Dakota Texts*, by Ella C. Deloria. Vermillion, SD: Dakota Press, 1978.

Who's Who Among the Sioux. Vermillion. Institute of Indian Studies, University of South Dakota, 1988.

—*Norma C. Wilson*

PINKERMAN-URI, CONNIE REDBIRD (b. 1930), is Choctaw/Cherokee who was born near of Wheatland, California. She was raised in a traditional rural Native American community, attended the local public school, and graduated from high school in 1947. After taking classes at Uba Junior College, she attended the University of Arkansas, where she received the MD degree in 1955. She practiced medicine in the Los Angeles area for two decades before returning to college, earning a JD degree from Whittier College in 1979. She was the first Native American woman to hold degrees in both law and medicine.

Pinkerman-Uri has been active Native American civil rights and cultural preservation. In the mid-1960s she organized the first Indian free clinic in the Los Angeles area, in the back of a church. During the same period she participated in an attempt to acquire and convert an abandoned army hospital, Fort McArthur, into an Indian hospital, and worked to alleviate health care problems at Chino State Prison in California. In the 1970s her investigative work concerning the forced sterilization of Indian women helped to bring about new federal regulations on sterilization in 1979. During the reoccupation of Wounded Knee in 1973, she organized a caravan of medical supplies and helped arrange bail for participants who were jailed. Pinkerman-Uri helped the Northern Cheyenne use the Clean Air Act of 1970 to protect their environment from air pollution generated by factories outside the reservation. Throughout her career she has provided medical and legal services to the Los Angeles Indian community, often without charge.

In her professional capacity, Pinkerman-Uri has worked to aid the process of organization within the Native American community. As a committee member of the Association of American Indian Physicians, she advocated the establishment of an Indian medical school. She has been a council member of Indian Women United for Social Justice since 1968. She also has been outspoken on the subjects of racism and sexism in the professional community.

References

Anderson, Owanah, ed. *Ohoyo One Thousand: A Resource Guide of American Indian/Alaskan Native Women, 1982*. Wichita Falls, TX: Ohoyo Resource Center, 1982.

Benson, Arlon. Personal communication with Connie Pinkerman-Uri, March 22, 1992.

Jarvis, Gayle Mark. "The Theft of Life." *Akwesasne Notes* 9 (Autumn 1977): 30–33.

—Arlon Benson

POCAHONTAS (c. 1595–1617), born in eastern Virginia, was the daughter of Powhatan, the most powerful Indian leader of that area. Pocahontas and her people, the Powhatan, began to encounter the English, who had settled at Jamestown in 1607. Because she was the favored daughter of an influential political leader, she traveled freely from her father's village to other Indian towns and to the English settlements; at times she may have visited Jamestown on missions for her father, or she may have gone out of curiosity. There is no clear evidence that she brought food or was enamored of John Smith. When she reached age thirteen, she was placed in an arranged marriage with one of her father's supporters named Kocoum.

Her life changed dramatically in 1613 when she was kidnapped by the English and held in Jamestown for more than a year. During that period she fell in love with an English settler named John Rolfe, who obtained permission from both English authorities and Powhatan to marry Pocahontas. Early in 1614 she was baptized into the Church of England as Rebecca and then married to Rolfe. This significant union, one of three legal Powhatan–English marriages in the seventeenth century, ushered in a brief period of relative peace on England's Virginia frontier. English officials anxious to capitalize on this harmony invited Pocahontas and Powhatan's chief adviser, Uttamatomakkin, to visit England. Included in the traveling party were several other Indians, as well as John Rolfe and the Rolfes' infant son, Thomas. Under the financial sponsorship of the Virginia Company of London, Pocahontas was introduced to English society in 1616; she and Uttatnatomakkin were honored at the king's Twelfth Night masque on January 6, 1617. During her stay in London, Pocahontas became ill, probably from some form of pulmonary disease. She boarded ship for Virginia in March 1617 but sailed no farther than Gravesend, where she was taken ashore. She died there and was buried on March 21, 1617.

Within three years, Pocahontas's story became larger than life through the writings of John Smith, one of Virginia's early leaders. In his 1624 *General Historie of Virginia*, Smith alleged that Pocahontas had rescued him from execution in December 1607. The story is questioned because Smith's two earlier works about Virginia did not mention the rescue. Although the account has been accepted by some historians and rejected by others, modern anthropologists have found no confirmation for it. The basic problem is Smith's capacity for self-glorification— he transforms an Indian girl into a princess intervening on his behalf against the imperial Powhatan. John Smith's reporting also clouds the information about the visit to England because only Smith described his interview in England with Pocahontas. Since romance seems more attractive than actuality, the Pocahontas of reality has become the Princess Pocahontas of novels and plays, as well as a symbol in modern poems by Sandburg, Lindsay, Crane, and Benét. Fortunately, twentieth-century anthropological research has stripped away the legends and returned Pocahontas to her rightful, if less epic, place in history.

References

Barbour, Philip L. *Pocahontas and Her World: A Chronicle of America's First Settlement.* . . . Boston: Houghton Mifflin, 1970.

Feast, Christian. "Pride and Prejudice: The Pocahontas Myth and the Pamunkey." *European Review of American Studies* 1 (1987): 5–12.

Mossiker, Frances. *Pocahontas: The Life and the Legend.* New York: Alfred A. Knopf, 1976.

Rountree, Helen C. *Pocahontas's People: The Powhatan Indians of Virginia Through Four Centuries.* Norman: University of Oklahoma Press, 1990.

———. *The Powhatan Indians of Virginia: Their Traditional Culture.* Norman: University of Oklahoma Press, 1989.

Tilton, Robert S. *Pocahontas: The Evolution of an American Narrative.* New York: Cambridge University Press, 1994.

Woodward, Grace Steele. *Pocahontas.* Norman: University of Oklahoma Press, 1969.

—*James H. O'Donnell III*

POTTS, MARIE [Chankutpan] (1895–1978), was born at Big Meadows, California, now the site of Lake Almanor in Plumas County. She belonged to the Northern Maidu tribe. She was the first California Indian to graduate from the Carlisle Indian School in Pennsylvania. She then returned to northern California, where she married and raised five children.

Throughout her life, Potts worked to improve the lives of all Native Americans. She traveled throughout the country, lecturing on her heritage, urging cultural preservation, and speaking out for the welfare of Indians. She participated in the Indian occupation of Alcatraz Island, and confronted former Governor Ronald Reagan in her quest to use the governor's mansion for a prayer meeting.

Potts played a key role in establishing the American Indian Press Association and was cofounder of the Federated Indians of California Inter-Tribal Council. She was also a member of an ad hoc committee that later became the California Education Association. Potts taught at California State University, Sacramento, where she was considered an expert on American and California Indian history. She also founded *Smoke Signals*, which focuses on the struggle for Indian rights.

In 1975 the state of California honored Potts for her efforts to help Indians. She has also been honored by the establishment of the Marie Potts Journalism Achievement Award, the highest honor in Indian jounalism, given by the American Indian Press Association (AIPA). In 1977 the California State Parks and Recreation Department gave her a commendation at Sutter's Fort. The second floor of the California Health, Education, and Welfare Department building is named for her and includes a permanent lobby display recounting her achievements.

Reference

Potts, Marie. *The Northern Maidu*. Happy Camp, CA: Naturegraph, 1977.

—*Julie A. Russ*

POWER, SUSAN (b. 1961), writer, teacher, and enrolled member of the Standing Rock Sioux tribe, was born in Chicago. Her mother, Susan Kelley Power, a descendent of the Sioux chief Mato Nupa (Two Bears), founded the American Indian Center in Chicago. Her father, Carleton Gilmore Power, worked as a salesman for a publishing house. She was named Miss Indian Chicago at the age of seventeen. Power received BA from Harvard/Radcliffe, a J.D. from Harvard Law School, and an M.F.A. from the Iowa Writers' Workshop.

While recovering from an appendectomy, Power had a vision of a Dakota Sioux woman wearing a sky blue beaded dress. This vision led her away from a lucrative law career and toward creative writing. Her first novel, *The Grass Dancer*, garnered critical praise and earned Power the prestigious PEN/Hemingway Award for Best First Fiction in 1995. Other novels by Power include *Strong Heart Society* and *War Bundles*. Her short fiction has appeared in *The Atlantic Monthly, The Paris Review, The Voice Literary Supplement, Ploughshares, Story*, and *The Best American Short Stories, 1993*. Her works, while focusing on Native American issues and perspectives, also treat politics on a larger scale. Power views herself as "an American writer who happens to be Indian" and notes that "focusing on exotica can distract us from what we all have in common." She cites Louise Erdrich, Toni Morrison, and William Shakespeare (whose *Romeo and Juliet* she had memorized by the age of twelve) as literary influences. Power continues to write fiction and poetry and teach writing. She lives in Cambridge, Massachusetts.

References

Putnam, Anne. "From heart of Chicago, fiction of Native America arrives with great spirit." *Bucknellian Online*, February 20, 1997. <http://coral.bucknell. edu/publications/bucknellian/sp97/2-20-97/lifest/1660.html>

Moseley, Caroline. "*Grass Dancer* evokes past, present." *Princeton Weekly*, March 10, 1997. <http://www.princeton.edu/pr/pwb/97/0310/0310-power.html>

"Q and A: Susan Power." Interview for September 1996 *george, jr.* <http://www. georgejr.com/september/qapower.html>.

—*Matthew Halt Jennings*

PRETTY ON TOP, JEANINE (b. 1949), is known as "One Who Likes Places of Prayer" in her native Crow language. She was one of four children born to teachers working on die Colville Reservation in Washington. Her father was a Crow;

her mother was German–English. In 1970 she received two BAs, one in sociology and one in anthropology, from Central Washington University. She served as a counselor at Navajo Community College in Tsaile, Arizona, in 1971, before serving for three years as director of the Upward Bound Program at Big Bend Community College (Washington). In 1975 Pretty on Top, now married, moved to Havre, Montana. There she became director of the Adult and Continuing Education Commission of the Crow tribe, a post she held for four years.

By 1979 a divorced mother of two, Pretty on Top took two years off work to devote to her children. Her former husband's unemployment forced her to accept public assistance, an experience that made her sensitive to the struggles of the many single, low-income mothers who scrape together resources to further their educations.

In 1981 Pretty on Top moved to Billings, Montana, where she worked in Eastern Montana College's Indian Career Services Department. The following year she launched the institution with which she has become synonymous.

With a tribal mandate, an abandoned house, two trailers, and fifty thousand dollars, Pretty on Top founded Little Big Horn College (LBHC). LBHC has grown into a fully accredited two-year college, serving about three hundred of the Crow Reservation's seven thousand residents every year. Fifteen full-time and several part-time faculty members teach there, and many classes are conducted entirely in Crow. Pretty on Top is president; teaches math, psychology, and English composition; carpools students to the college in bad weather; and mops floors. She donates three thousand dollars of her twenty-six thousand-dollar salary back to the college every year. The college has entered into a partnership with Montana State University to train Crow scientists and to locate a biomedical research lab at LBHC.

Pretty on Top received her MEd and PhD in education from Montana State University. She has honorary doctorates from Hood College (Maryland) and Gonzaga University (Washington). She won the 1987 Outstanding Graduate Achievement Award from Montana State University and the 1988 Outstanding Alumni Achievement Award from Central Washington University. In 1990 the National Indian Education Association named her Educator of the Year. Pretty on Top has served on the boards of the American Indian Higher Education Consortium (she was its president from 1983 to 1985), the Minority Concerns Advisory Commission, and the Phelps-Stokes Fund, and is a trustee of the Smithsonian's National Museum of the American Indian.

Also an activist, Pretty on Top has not avoided controversy. From 1983 to 1986 a Montana court heard the redistricting case *Windy Boy* v. *Bighorn County*. She successfully sued for a review of a redistricting plan to decrease Crow voting strength in nontribal elections and to exclude Crow children from public schools. In 1990 several noted Soviet authors were invited to visit Montana, and the state requested that Pretty on Top host a tour of the Crow Reservation for them. When she found out the authors' anti–Semitic views, she refused the request, citing the need for all minorities to act as advocates for each other. For this, she won an award from the Torah Academy of Suffolk County (New York).

An active member of the First Crow Baptist Church and the Bighorn County Democratic Central Committee, Pretty on Top lives in the reservation community of Lodge Grass with her daughter, Roses, and her son, Vernon.

References

Ebin, Barbara Burkhard. "On Indians and Jews: Cross-Cultural Support." *Jewish Week*, March 1, 1991, 28.

Kleinhuizen, Jeff. "A Boost for American Indians: Tribal Colleges Combine Academics and Heritage." *USA Today*, May 7, 1991, D4.

Mooney, Carolyn J. "Head of Blossoming Tribal College: 'A Product of My Community.'" *Chronicle of Higher Education*, November 29, 1989, A3.

Newell, Kathie. "Youthful Strivers Given Name, 'dream-Maker.'" *Havre [MT] Daily News*, March 21, 1989, 3.

"NIEA Educator of the Year Award." *NIEA Newsletter* 23 (1990): 1.

—*Cynthia Kasee*

PRETTY-SHIELD (c. 1858–late 1930s?), was born near the Missouri River in what is now southeastern Montana. A member of the Sore-lip clan of the Crow Nation and the fourth of eleven children, Pretty-shield was given her name by her paternal grandfather, Little-boy-strikes-with-a-lance, who named her in honor of his handsome war shield when she was four days old.

In 1932, when she was seventy-four years old, Pretty-shield agreed to tell her life story to the Euro–American trapper and hunter Frank B. Linderman. Since so many male warriors had narrated their personal histories, Linderman particularly wanted to hear "a woman's story." Responding to the questions of her amanuensis and with the help of her interpreter Goes-together, Pretty-shield told stories about growing up in prereservation days when her "people's hearts were . . . as light as breath-feathers." As a child, she played with kickballs and dolls, and, with other children, organized a play Sun Dance; she also traveled with her people, fearing and fighting the Lakota, Cheyenne, and Arapahoe, their long time enemies. Pretty-shield described childbirth and child-rearing practices, and the first time she saw white men, whom the Crow at first called Beta-awk-a-wah-cha (Sits-on-the-water—they were first seen in canoes) and then called *Masta-cheeda* (Yellow-eyes). She narrated humorous stories about being chased by an angry buffalo cow and adventurous stories about how her father rescued her from a buffalo stampede. Pretty-shield also shared her vision, explaining the origin of her personal medicine.

The wife of Goes-ahead, a Crow scout for General George A. Custer, Pretty-shield recounted her husband's stories of the Battle of the Little Bighorn. But in order to balance the men's accounts of battle, she told about the little-known Crow women warriors. She described how a battle between the Crows and the Lakota was won by a sixty-year-old Crow woman named Strikes-two and how two Crow women warriors fought with Three-stars (General George Crook) at Rosebud. Pretty-shield is one of the few Native American women who lived during prereservation days to share her life story with an amanuensis.

Dominated by the contrast between then and now, Pretty-shield's life story testifies to the overwhelmingly traumatic transformation suffered by many indigenous people in the late nineteenth century when they were forced onto reservations. The "times have changed so fast," Pretty-shield told Linderman, "that they have left me behind. I do not understand these times. I am walking in the dark. Ours was a different world before the buffalo went away, and I belong to that other world." Even so, Pretty-shield's narrative offers a corrective to the stereotypes of indigenous women by depicting a lively, intelligent woman with a playful sense of humor and a survivor's spirit.

References

O'Brien, Lynne W. *Plains Indians Autobiographies*. Boise, ID: Boise State College, 1973.

Pretty-shield. *Pretty-shield: Medicine Woman of the Crows*. Edited by Frank B. Linderman. New York: John Day, 1932. Reprint of *Red Mother*. Lincoln: University of Nebraska Press, 1972.

—Hertha D. Wong

PUZZ, ANNA (b. 1947), is a Native American community leader in southern California who has focused primarily on Indian health and education. An Assiniboine, she moved to San Diego, California, in 1979 after attending the College of the Redwoods, where she earned her associate in arts degree. She has studied at Humboldt State University and San Diego State University, and is completing her bachelor's degree in literature at Calilfornia State University, San Marcos. In 1980 Puzz went to work at the San Diego American Indian Health Center, serving as executive secretary. In 1985, when HIV infection became epidemic, she helped plan and execute the first American Indian AIDS project in southern California. She soon became the project's director, writing several successful grant proposal that brought funds for the program. In addition to serving as the key administrative officer, Puzz led the HIV Community Education Program, offering informative lectures to adults and children, and scheduling other Native speakers to talk to groups about the cause and prevention of HIV infection.

As the HIV program coordinator, Puzz developed the Women's Enrichment and Empowerment Project, helped set up the HIV Testing Project, and counseled Native Americans about HIV and AIDS. As program director, she wrote numerous reports and monitored cases in addition to her administrative duties. Because of this work, she was appointed to the California HIV Comprehensive Care Working Group, which administers millions of dollars for HIV prevention. For years, Puzz has participated in Indian education programs in southern California. She is a poet and writer of short stories, a storyteller, and a lecturer. Puzz has three children and one grandson. She lives in Santee, California, with her son Skye.

Reference

Trafzer, Clifford E. Personal communication with Anna Puzz, 1996.

—Clifford E. Trafzer

Q

QUEEN ANNE OF PAMUNKEY (c. 1650–1725) is known from legal documents as the leader of the Pamunkey Indians of Virginia during the period from 1706 to 1718. She was the third female ruler of the Pamunkeys during the years between 1656 and 1718. Her primary role was to protect her people against being completely overwhelmed by the surrounding English colonists. Over the years, tribal lands had been reduced to a relatively small area. Faced with a declining population that could not support itself, both because of numbers and because of an insufficient land base, the Pamunkeys often had resorted to selling off land for income. Queen Anne complained that surveyors from Virginia sought to cheat the tribe either by arriving without notice or by surveying more land than actually had been purchased. She also complained that too much liquor had been sold to the people of the tribe.

Consequently, Queen Anne sought to stop the sales both of liquor and of land. If she had had her way, only leases would have been permitted; no more land would have been sold by the tribe. Another source of difficulty for the Pamunkeys was the annual tribute they had to pay to the British government. In light of her tribe's poverty, Queen Anne repeatedly asked that they be forgiven this annual debt. In 1711 the governor of Virginia agreed to forgive the tribute if the Queen of Pamunkey would send her son to be educated at the College of William and Mary. She sent her son and another young Pamunkey to the college.

During her brief term as Pamunkey leader, Queen Anne sought every possible means to guarantee the survival of her people, whether that necessitated land sales or leases, protests to the Virginia governor, or permitting her son to study at the College of William and Mary. If politics may be described as the art of compromise, Queen Anne understood politics and effectively employed that art in protecting her people.

References

Mathes, Valerie Shirer. "A New Look at the Role of Women in Indian Society." *American Indian Quarterly* 2 (1975): 131–139.

McCartney, Martha W. "Cockacoeske, Queen of Pamunkey, Diplomat and Suzeraine." In *Powhatan's Mantle: Indians in the Colonial Southeast*. Edited by Peter Wood et al. Pp. 173–195. Lincoln: University of Nebraska Press, 1989.

Minor, Nono. "The American Indian: Famous Indian Women in Early America."
    Real West 14 (January 1971): 35, 78.
Rountree, Helen C. *Pocahontas's People: The Powhatan Indians of Virginia
    Through Four Centuries*. Norman: University of Oklahoma Press, 1990.

—James H. O'Donnell III

R

RAND, JACKI (b. 1956), Choctaw historian born in Great Falls, Montana, to a Choctaw mother and Anglo-American father. Rand's mother attended Wheelock and Chilocco Boarding Schools. Rand left high school at age fifteen and worked as a waitress and in garment factories. When she was nineteen, she gained admission to the University of Maine. After graduation, she went to work for the Smithsonian Institution National Museum of the American Indian. In 1990 she returned to Oklahoma to pursue a Ph.D. in history, which she received from the University of Oklahoma in 1998, when she completed her dissertation, "The Economic and Cultural Politics of Trade and Found in the Kiowa, Comanche, and Apache Reservation and Allotment Periods, 1867–1910."

In 1995 and 1996, Rand was the recipient of an American Fellowship from the American Association of University Women. She also received the Arrell Gibson Award for Outstanding Student in Western History in 1996 and a grant from the Iowa Arts Council in 2000. Rand also coordinated the first CIC-AIS conference, which was held in Iowa City in April of 2000.

Rand teaches Native American history at the University of Iowa in Iowa City. She has taught courses on federal Indian policy, museum literacy, and American Indian history from pre-contact to the present. Rand lives in Iowa City with her two children, Thomas and Amelia. She is working on her first book, which will be based on her dissertation.

References

Personal correspondence with Jacki Rand, February 27 to March 4, 2001.

Matthew Holt Jennings

RED SHIRT SHAW, DELPHINE (b. 1957), born in Gordon, Nebraska, has written about her Lakota childhood and the paths she has taken in a bicultural world in her autobiography, *Bead on an Anthill: A Lakota Childhood*. She is an enrolled member of the Oglala Sioux and lived on the Pine Ridge Reservation from 1966 to 1975. In the latter year she graduated from Red Cloud Indian School.

Red Shirt Shaw served in the U.S. Marine Corps from January 1977 to January 1978 and was the second woman to enter combat training for field radio operator. She earned a BS in accounting and history from Regis College (Denver) in 1980 and an MA in creative studies from Wesleyan University in Middletown, Connecticut, in 1995. During graduate school, she worked at Yale University as an adviser to Native American undergraduate students and served briefly as a guest columnist for the *Hartford Courant*.

After graduate school, Red Shirt Shaw served as chair of the United Nations nongovernment organization Committee on the International Decade of the World's Indigenous People (1995–1996), and currently she is United Nations representative for the Four Directions Council, an international indigenous organization. Red Shirt lives in Guilford, Connecticut and is married to Richard Shaw: they have a son and two daughters.

Reference

Red Shirt, Delphine. *Bead on an Anthill: A Lakota Childhood*. Lincoln: University of Nebraska Press, 1997.

—Angela Noelle Williams

ROBINSON, WUNGNEMA ROSE (1932–1995), was born on the Hopi Reservation in Arizona, in her tribal village Kykotsmovi; she is a member of the Butterfly clan. She graduated from Carson City High School in Carson City, Nevada, where her family had moved when she was small. She next graduated from Haskell Institute, where she took a scretarial course; subsequently, she was employed by the Bureau of Indian Affairs (BIA) in Aberdeen, S.D. A year later she transferred to the Washington, D.C., main office, where she met and married Richard H. Robinson of the British military. Robinson is survived by three children—Robin R. Shield, Roanne R. Shaddox, and Michael Robinson—and one grandson, Harlan W. Shield.

Robinson left her position as secretary to the BIA deputy commissioner to work for the Indian Arts and Crafts Board, beginning her journalism career by volunteering to type the board's newsletter, *Smoke Signals*. In 1967 she became editor of the publication, which led to her promotion to public information officer for the BIA and editor of the bureau's *Indian Record*. In 1972, when the American Indian Movement took over the BIA building, Robinson stayed inside during the confrontations between the protesters and officials. She joined other Native American journalists to form the American Indian Press Association, and in 1973 was named its executive director.

Robinson's career in philanthropy began in 1976 when she was employed as the director (and later as the vice president) of the Phelps-Stokes Fund. The mandate of the organization included promoting educational opportunities for American Indians. Seeing herself as a "broker" between the Indian world and private philanthropy, she created a foundation news service to help tribal communities and Indian education groups locate private funding. As an editor of *The Exchange* (a magazine that promoted fund-raising), she continued to assist with the identification of financial resources for Indian communities. Robinson was named the National Indian Media Woman of the Year in 1981.

In the mid-1980s she left the Phelps-Stokes Fund to begin a private consulting service. During this era of her career, she published a Native American guide to Washington, D.C., *Robinson's Red Book*, which identified government and private sector offices that worked with/for Native Americans. After serving as a volunteer for the National Congress of American Indians for nearly twenty years, she went to work for it in 1992. During her lifetime she was on a number of boards: American Indian Graduate Program, recording secretary; National Congress of American Indians; American Indian Lutheran Board; and the National Indian Education Association. In 1992 Robinson was a major developer and promoter of the Columbus Quincentenary, an event she felt was her crowning achievement.

Reference

Running Wolf, Paulette. Telephone interview with Mark Trehant, April 1998.

—Paulette Running Wolf and Susan Rae Banks

ROE CLOUD, ELIZABETH BENDER (c. 1887–c. 1964), was born on the White Earth Indian Reservation in Minnesota. The daughter of an Ojibwa mother and a German father, she attended Pipestone Boarding School and later Hampton Institute, from which she graduated in 1907. Following additional course work in education in Hampton, Virginia, and nurse's training in Philadelphia, she found employment as a teacher in the Indian Service at Indian schools in Browning, Montana, Fort Belknap, Montana, and Carlisle, Pennsylvania.

After her marriage to the Winnebago leader Henry Roe Cloud, she worked with him to establish the American Indian Institute in Wichita, Kansas. In 1939 they moved to the Umatilla Reservation in Oregon, where her husband became the agency superintendent. Once there, Roe Cloud founded the Oregon Trails Club of Pendleton, an Indian women's club affiliated with the General Federation of Women's Clubs. She later became the Federation's national chairperson for Indian Affairs.

In 1950, shortly after her husband died, Roe Cloud was honored as Oregon Mother of the Year and American Mother of the Year. As the National Congress of American Indian's (NCAI) field secretary during this period, she directed a workshop in Indian community organization at Brigham, Utah, in 1951. She continued to take part in subsequent Indian community development programs initiated by the NCAI. She died in Oregon at seventy-seven years of age.

References

Bender, Elizabeth. Student file. Hampton University Archives, Hampton, Virginia.
Gridley, Marion E., ed. *Indians of Today*. 3rd ed. Chicago: Towertown Press, 1960.
Hultgren, Mary Lou, and Paulette Fairbanks Molin. *To Lead and to Serve*. Virginia
   Beach: Virginia Foundation for the Humanities, 1989.

—Gretchen G. Harvey

ROESSEL, RUTH W. (b. 1934), was born in Rough Rock, Arizona, on the Navajo Reservation, the daughter of the medicine man Ashishie and Hasbah. While growing up, she learned the traditional values, practices, and crafts of the Navajo; in fact, at the age of five she began weaving, a craft that continues to earn her numerous awards.

Roessel has devoted her life to educating Navajo children and adults in both the academic manner, preparing them for careers, and the traditional Navajo manner, preparing them for family life. This bicultural approach arose from the difficulties she faced as a young woman pursuing her education. Although she had a diploma from the only institution available to Navajo girls, Roessel was refused admission to colleges because her education was considered inadequate. After many letters, phone calls, and favors from understanding individuals, she began her studies in education and received her MA from Arizona State University in 1975.

Roessel has served as a teacher at Navajo Community College, Tolani Lake School, Rough Rock School, Rough Rock Demonstration School, and Pinon School; a director at Rough Rock Demonstration School; and a principal at Round Rock Elementary School. She is a resource teacher at Jeddito Puppy School, where she also served as president of the chapter of American Federation of Teachers.

In addition to teaching, Roessel has written and edited books dealing with Navajo topics, and she started a medicine person training program for the Navajo. She is involved in a number of activities in women's advocacy, including the Navajo Women's Association (president, 1978–1980), the North American Indian Women's Association (charter member and state president, 1976–1977), and Arizona Women in Higher Education. In 1980 Roessel was Navajo Woman of the Year Award.

Roessel, along with her husband, Dr. Robert Roessel, Jr., who works in the Division of Education, remains committed to helping Navajo people maintain elements of their traditional culture. Since 1988, the Roessels have conducted summer workshops centering on Navajo issues such as alcoholism, jealousy, and the Navajo medicine person.

References

Roessel, Ruth. *Women in Navajo Society*. Rough Rock, AZ: Navajo Resource Center, 1981.

———, comp. *Navajo Livestock Reduction: A National Disgrace*. Chinle, AZ: Navajo Community College Press, 1974.

———, comp. *Navajo Stories of the Long Walk Period*. Tsaile, AZ: Navajo Community College Press, 1973.

———, comp. *Papers on Navajo Culture and Life*. Rev. ed. Many Farms, AZ: Navajo Community College Press, 1970.

———, comp. *Stories of Traditional Navajo Life and Culture*. Tsaile, AZ: Navajo Community College Press, 1976.

———, ed. *Navajo Studies at Navajo Community College*. Many Farms, AZ: Navajo Community College Press, 1971.

—*Michelle Savoy*

ROSE, WENDY [Bronwen Elizabeth Edwards] (b. 1948), poet, artist, teacher, and anthropologist, was born in Oakland, California, the daughter of a mixed-blood Miwok mother and a Hopi father. She was raised in an urban environment just out-

Wendy Rose

side San Francisco, and her poetry reflects the experience of a mixed-blood Indian living off the reservation and away from the influence of a tribal culture. After dropping out of high school in El Cerrito, California, she became involved in the American Indian Movement, participated in the occupation of Alcatraz, and began a writing career under the pen name Chiron Khanshendel.

Influenced by a "surrogate father," Rose became interested in anthropology and has attended Cabrillo College, Contra Costa College, and the University of California, Berkeley, where she earned her BA (1976), MA (1978), and PhD from the Department of Anthropology. Her dissertation is an annotated bibliography and analysis of books written by Native Americans.

Rose has served as manager of the Lowie Museum of Anthropology of the University of California at Berkeley, editor of *American Indian Quarterly*, and lecturer in Native American Studies for both the University of California at Berkeley (1979–1983) and California State University at Fresno (1983–1984). Currently, she is the head of the American Indian Studies Program at Fresno City College, where she lives with her husband, Arthur Murata.

Throughout her writing career, Rose has published widely in journals, anthologies, and collections. Her book of poems, *Lost Copper* (1980), was nominated for a Pulitzer Prize. In addition to writing and teaching, Rose is a successful visual artist, having illustrated numerous books and journals, exhibited works around the country, and designed posters, postcards, and sport shirts.

Rose is an active member of Indian organizations and has given many poetry readings in connection with powwows and tribal functions. Her accomplishments in poetry and scholarship have helped to establish Native American writing as a legitimate part of the American literary canon, as well as to reclassify Native American writers as literary artists rather than "literate fossils" or anthropological voices.

References

Allen, Paula Gunn. "This Wilderness in My Blood: Spirituality in the Works of Five American Indian Women Poets." In *Coyote Was Here: Essays on Contemporary Native American Literary and Political Mobilization*. Edited by Bo Scholer. Pp. 95–114. Aarhus, Denmark: University of Aarhus, 1984.

Bruchac, Joseph. "An Interview with Wendy Rose." *Greenfield Review* 12 (Summer/ Fall 1984): 43–75, Reprint, in *Survival This Way*. Edited by Joseph Bruchac. Pp. 87–104. Tucson: University of Arizona Press, 1987.

Gray, Lynn. "The Power of Words: An Interview with Poet/Artist/Teacher Wendy Rose." *Akwesasne Notes* 17 (Winter 1985).

Hunter, Carol. "A MELUS Interview: Wendy Rose." *MELUS* 10 (Fall 1983): 67–87.

Rose, Wendy. *Academic Squaw: Reports to the World from the Ivory Tower*. Marvin, SD: Blue Cloud Press, 1977.

———. *Bone Dance: New and Selected Poems, 1965–1993*. Tucson: University of Arizona Press, 1994.

———. *Builder Kachina: A Home-Going Cycle*. Marvin, SD: Blue Cloud Press, 1979.

———. "For Some It's a Time of Mourning." In *Without Discovery*. Edited by Ray Gonzalez. Pp. 3–7. Seattle: Broken Moon Press, 1992.

———. *Going to War with All My Relations*. Flagstaff, AZ: Northland Publishers, 1993.

———. "The Great Pretenders: Further Reflections on White Shamanism." In *The State of Native America: Genocide, Colonization and Resistance*. Edited by M. Annette Jaimes. Pp. 403–424. Boston: South End Press, 1992.

———. *The Halfbreed Chronicles & Other Poems*. Los Angeles: West End Press, 1985.

———. *Hopi Roadrunner Dancing*. Greenfield Center, NY: Greenfield Review Press, 1973.

———. "Just What's All This Fuss About White Shamanism Anyway?" In *Coyote Was Here: Essays on Contemporary Native American Literary and Political Mobilization*. Edited by Bo Scholer. Pp. 13–24. Aarhus, Denmark: University of Aarhus, 1984.

———. *Long Division: A Tribal History*. New York: Strawberry Press, 1976. Enl. ed., 1981.

———. *Lost Copper*. Banning, CA: Malki Museum Press, 1980.

———. "Neon Scars." In *I Tell You Now: Autobiographical Essays by Native American Writers*. Edited by Brian Swann and Arnold Krupat. Pp. 251–261. Lincoln: University of Nebraska Press, 1987.

———. *Now Poof She Is Gone*. Ithaca, NY: Firebrand Books, 1994.

———. *What Happened When the Hopi Hit New York*. New York: Contact II, 1982.

"SAIL Bibliography No. 2: 'Wendy Rose.'" *Studies in American Literatures* 6 (Spring 1982): 19–23.

Saucerman, James R. "Wendy Rose: Searching Through Shards, Creating Life." *Wicazo Sa Review* 5 (Fall 1989): 26–29.

Wiget, Andrew. "Blue Stones, Bones and Troubled Silver: The Poetic Craft of Wendy Rose." *Studies in American Indian Literatures*, ser. 2, 5 (Summer 1993): 29–33.

—*Michelle Savoy*

ROSS, AGNES ALLEN (b. 1910), was born on the homestead of her parents, John Allen and Ida Wakeman, (granddaughter of Chief Little Crow). The homestead, located west of Flandreau, South Dakota, was sold following John Allen's death to provide money for his nine children.

Ross attended Flandreau Public School, the sole Indian in a class of forty-eight. As a speaker of only the Dakota language, she had to learn English quickly. After graduating in 1929, she enrolled at Haskell Institute, where she earned a teacher's certificate in 1931. For most of the rest of her adult life until retirement, she taught in government Indian schools.

From 1931 to 1933 Ross taught at the Hayward Indian School in northern Wisconsin. When it closed, she was transferred to the Rosebud Reservation and taught in the boarding school there for two years. Resigning from this position, she went to Northern Arizona University in Flagstaff and earned a bachelor's degree in education in 1938. That year she returned to teaching and was placed in a two-year internship in Pine Ridge. When her supervising teacher recommended that the second year be waived, the government agreed, and she was transferred to Horse Creek Day School in White River in 1939. That summer she was selected by the national YMCA to represent American Indian youth at the World's Conference of Christian Youth in Amsterdam, the Netherlands.

She taught at Horse Creek Day School until 1943. Her husband, Harvey Ross, whom she had married in 1939, entered the army in 1943, and she stayed home to take care of their three small sons until 1952.

In 1952 Ross returned to teaching in the Pine Ridge Oglala Community School, where she remained until her retirement in 1972. In 1958 she received an MS in education from Chadron State College in Nebraska. In that year she was selected as Teacher of the Year for South Dakota. She was a teacher, then teacher supervisor, and finally education specialist for the Pine Ridge Reservation.

After her retirement, the Rosses moved back to Flandreau. From 1972 to 1975 she worked for Dakota State University as coordinator of title programs conducted for the Flandreau Indian School. During one of these summers she taught the Dakota language at the University of South Dakota. In 1980 Ross was awarded an honorary by doctorate Oglala Lakota College of Kyle, South Dakota, in recognition of her help in establishing that college.

From 1972 to 1974 she was tribal chair of the Flandreau Indians. In that capacity she was instrumental in having a motel built on the reservation, and initiated tribal housing and health programs.

In recent years Ross is prouder of her four sons' achievements than of her own. Two sons have doctorates and work in education. A third, who has finished course work for the doctorate in mathematics, is budget analyst for the Bureau of Indian Affairs in Aberdeen, South Dakota. The fourth has a master's degree in elementary education. In 1986 the Rosses were honored by Black Hills State University for having four sons who received degrees there.

In October 1996 Ross received an award for her contributions to Indian education from the National Indian Education Association at its regional conference in Rapid City, South Dakota.

References

"Allen-Ross." In *Moody County History Book*. P. 194. Sioux Falls, SD: Jack Kilgore and Associates, 1984.

Marken, Jack. Personal communication with Agnes Allen Ross, August 5, 1996.

Paulson, T. Emogene, and Lloyd R. Moses. *Who's Who Among the Sioux*. Vermillion, SD: Institute of Indian Studies, University of South Dakota, 1988.

Ross, Agnes. *Dakota Language*. Aberdeen, SD: N.p., 1980.

———. *Dakota Language Santee*. Bushnell, SD: Featherstone, 1983. Audio cassette.

—Jack Marken

ROUSSEAU, LORRAINE MAE (b. 1936), has been a leader of the Sisseton–Wahpeton Sioux tribe in the fields of law and politics. She served for many years as a tribal judge and as a family therapist before her election as the first chairwoman of her tribe. Rousseau was juvenile judge and associate judge from 1973 to 1975, and chief judge for the Sisseton–Wahpeton Sioux tribe from 1981 to 1991. As tribal chairwoman in 1992 to 1993, she attacked corruption and promoted economic development. In 1995 she served as special judge for the Turtle Mountain Chippewa tribe in North Dakota. In 1996 she became program manager for the Sisseton–Wahpeton Sioux tribe Child Protection Program.

Rousseau was the fourth of five children born to one of the first racially mixed couples on the Sisseton–Wahpeton Sioux Reservation. Her father, John Greybuffalo, was a full-blooded Sioux, the son of Tatankahota (Greybuffalo) and Sarah. Her mother, Goldie Ella Varnes, was the daughter of Pennsylvania Dutch pioneers who settled next to Greybuffalo's family in the first reservation land run, April 15, 1892. She married Darryl Rousseau in 1966, and is the mother of one daughter and five sons.

Rousseau dropped out of school in the tenth grade, but she completed a high school GED and began college at age thirty-eight, graduating from the University of South Dakota with a bachelor's degree in social work and criminal justice in 1979.

Besides her service as judge, tribal chairwoman, and social worker, Rousseau has been active in national Native politics. In 1986 she served on a Bureau of Indian Affairs task force for improvement of tribal courts, and in 1988 she testified about reservation conditions before the Civil Rights Commission. In 1993 she made a nominating speech for fellow Native woman Ada Deer, President Clinton's choice to head the Bureau of Indian Affairs (BIA). In 1996 she was a BIA federal women employee honoree.

References

Kelley, Matt. "Ex-Tribal Leader Tips Feds on Equipment Deals." *Sioux Falls [SD] Argus Leader*, March 17, 1994, B2.

Lockhart, Gemma. "Woman Gives Reservation a New Look." *Sioux Falls [SD] Argus Leader*, December 6, 1992, A9.

—Jerry Wilson

RUNNING EAGLE [Brown Weasel Woman, Pitamakan] (d. c.1878), known for her skills as a warrior, probably was born during the Hudson's Bay trading era. She was a member of the Piegan tribe of the Blackfeet nation.

Brown Weasel Woman assumed the household duties when her mother became ill, although she disliked domestic routine. At a young age she was taught by her father, a warrior, to shoot a bow and arrow, and accompanied him on buffalo hunts, learning to shoot well enough to kill buffalo. On one of these hunts they encountered an enemy party. Her father's horse was shot as they were retreating to camp; she returned and picked him up, unloading the fresh meat on her horse. They returned to the camp, where she was praised for her bravery. Her father died soon after.

Her mother died after learning of the father's death, and Brown Weasel Woman took over the care of her brothers and sisters. Having no interest in marriage, she brought a widow into her lodge to help with the household and to care for the children. From then on, she carried a rifle inherited from her father and acted as the head of the family.

Brown Weasel Woman's first war experience came soon after her parents' deaths. Crow warriors had stolen some horses, and Blackfeet warriors went in pursuit of them. Told by the warriors to return to camp, she nevertheless trailed behind them. Several days later, the party reached the enemy camp. During the raid, Brown Weasel Woman and a male cousin captured eleven horses. On the return to their camp, while the rest of the party rested under cover, she kept watch on the trail from a nearby butte. When she saw two enemy riders approach the horses, she ran down the butte with her rifle, caught hold of the rope of the herd's lead horse to keep the rest from running away, shot one of the enemy, and forced the other to turn back. Instead of reloading her rifle, she grabbed the fallen enemy's firearm and shot at, but missed, the man as he fled.

Still not accepted as a full warrior, she followed the advice of the wise elders and went out to fast and seek a vision. After four days and nights alone, she received a vision giving her the power necessary for leading a successful warrior's life. From then on, the people considered her a person with special powers guided by the Spirits, and she was named Running Eagle by the chief, Lone Walker. She went on many raids and was allowed to tell of her exploits in the Medicine Lodge Ceremony. She became a member of the Braves Society of young warriors, and led many war parties.

Running Eagle died during one of these raids sometime after 1878. Near the Sun River, in a battle with a large party of Flathead warriors, she was clubbed from behind and killed. Trick Falls in Glacier National Park bore the name Pitamakan in her honor until it was renamed by white settlers.

Her name appears as Running Eagle Pe Tu on the Blackfoot Agency census of 1877 to 1878, but it is absent after that time.

References

Ewers, John. "Deadlier Than the Male." *American Heritage* 16 (June 1965): 10–13.

Hungry Wolf, Beverly. *The Ways of My Grandmothers*. New York: William Morrow, 1980.

Pratt, Grace Roffey. "Female War Chief of the Blackfeet." *Frontier Times* 45 (1971): 22–23, 46.

Schilz, Thomas, and Jodye Lynn Dickson Schilz. "Amazons, Witches and Country Wives: Plains Indian Women in Historical Perspective." *Annals of Wyoming* 59 (Spring 1987): 48–56.

U.S. Department of the Interior, Bureau of Indian Affairs. Blackfoot Agency Census. 1877–1878.

—Audrey M. Godfrey

S

SACAGAWEA [Sacajawea, Bird Woman] (c. 1788–1812/1884), one of the most elusive women in American history, remains obscured by controversial scholarship surrounding every mention of her in historical records, from the spelling and meaning of her name to the assessment of her contributions to the Lewis and Clark expedition. The controversy extends into her postexpedition fate, because verifiable information about her exists only in the journals of the explorers and in a few of Clark's letters after the journey ended. Finally, in some revisionist views, Sacagawea, like Pocahontas and La Malinche, is the embodiment of collusion with the Euro–American invaders.

Sacajawea (Shoshone for "Boat Launcher") or Sacagawea (Hidatsa/Minnetaree for "Bird Woman"), as her name is alternately spelled, was born probably in 1788 or 1789 to Shoshone parents in eastern Idaho, near the present-day town of Salmon. Following Shoshone custom, shortly after birth she was promised in a marriage that was to commence when she reached puberty. When she was about ten or eleven, the Shoshone camp near Three Forks in Montana was attacked by Minnetaree (Hidatsa), and Sacagawea and another girl were taken prisoner. Eventually the two young women were purchased by Toussaint Charbonneau, a French–Canadian fur trader. While they were camped for the winter of 1804 to 1805, at Fort Mandan in present-day North Dakota, Lewis and Clark hired Charbonneau as an interpreter to accompany the expedition. On February 11, 1805, Sacagawea gave birth to a son, Jean Baptiste, and when the Corps of Discovery resumed its westward trek in April of that year, Charbonneau, Sacagawea, and her baby were members of the party.

In their journals, Lewis and Clark appeared to have differing assessments of Sacagawea and her usefulness. Lewis seldom mentions her. Two of his more noteworthy observations illustrate his ambivalence toward her. In the first, he states that she required only sufficient food and a few "trinkets" to make her happy; in the second, he worries that she is dangerously ill, anxious not only for her sake but also because her services would be needed when the Corps reached the Shoshone. Clark, on the other hand, frequently expresses his fondness for her baby, the value of her services to the party, and his concern for her welfare in the face of illness, danger, and physical abuse by Charbonneau. Clark portrays her as self-effacing in most instances, but she argues forcefully and successfully that she should be allowed to travel the final few miles to view the Pacific Ocean and a beached whale after coming so far and enduring so many hardships.

Her specific contributions to the expedition are recounted in Clark's journal. Sacagawea was needed as a translator and negotiator for horses with her own people, the Shoshone, and as a guide through her home territory. The fact that her brother, Cameahwait, was the Shoshone leader enabled the explorers to procure the animals they needed for the mountain portage. Her services as a translator also were utilized among other Indian tribes who had Shoshone prisoners living among them. Maintaining a cool head when Charbonneau panicked, she saved valuable scientific equipment from being swept away when one of the pirogues capsized. On the return trip, she guided Clark through the Bozeman Pass, saving him many miles. When food supplies were scarce, she found edible roots and berries. Perhaps most significantly, the presence of a woman and child on the expedition gave proof of the corps's peaceful intentions. Clark noted, "The Wife of Shabono our interpreter. We find reconsiles all the Indians, as to our friendly intentions. A woman with a party of men is a token of peace." For her efforts, Lewis and Clark named a river for her, and Charbonneau received the sum of $500.33 at the conclusion of the expedition. Clark recognized the inequity in a later letter to Charbonneau: "Your woman who accompanied you that long dangerous and fatiguing rout to the Pacific Ocian and back diserved a greater reward for her attention and serves on that rout than we had in our power to give her at the Mandans."

If Sacagawea were perceived by the Indians whose country the corps traversed as a "token of peace," there is little peace associated with other elements of her life. Stolen from her family and people at a young age, she was sold to a man who abused her. When she was reunited with her brother, Cameahwait, she learned that her family was dead, save for him and her sister's son, whom she adopted. Clark wished to adopt her son, Jean Baptiste, and raise him in civilization. Because the child was not yet weaned, Charbonneau and Sacagawea agreed that one year later they would take the child to Clark in St. Louis. Charbonneau tried farming on land purchased from Clark, but eventually returned to hunting and trapping. Sacagawea appears to have remained in St. Louis for some period of time, but information on the remainder of her life is contradictory.

One theory contends that Sacagawea died of "putrid fever" on December 20, 1812, at Fort Manuel in present-day South Dakota, at the age of about twenty-five, leaving behind an infant daughter. Evidence supporting this theory comes from a notation by trader John C. Luttig and an annotation from 1825 to 1826 in Clark's handwriting on his cashbook as to the fate of members of the expedition. After Sacagawea's name he had written "Dead."

The second theory, promoted by Eva Emery Dye in a popular 1902 novel, and by Grace Hebard, a professor at the University of Wyoming, in a 1933 scholarly work based on oral histories of Indians and whites on the Wind River Reservation in Wyoming, holds that Sacagawea lived a long and fulfilling life after leaving Charbonneau because he took a third wife who displeased her. After traveling to the Comanches, who were linguistically close to the Shoshone, Sacagawea married a Comanche man, Jerk Meat, and bore five more children, two of whom survived. After Jerk Meat's death, her whereabouts are unknown for several years, but she eventually returned to Wind River, where her son Jean Baptiste and her adopted son, Bazil, were living. According to the accounts of Indians, Indian agents, and missionaries on the reservation, the woman they knew as Porivo (Chief Woman) knew many details of the Lewis and Clark expeditions and wore a Jefferson Medal around her neck. She became a highly respected member of the Shoshone tribe and was a close associate of Chief Washakie, attending and speaking at the meeting that led to the Fort Bridger Treaty. The woman's grandson, Andrew Bazil, credits his grandmother with introducing the Sun Dance to the Shoshone. By several accounts, she related her version of the expedition to Grace Irwin, wife of the Indian agent. Sometimes speaking in French, her few mentions of Charbonneau were bitter, but she spoke highly of Captain Clark. Unfortunately, Irwin's document was lost in a fire at the agency office at Fort Washakie in 1884 or 1885. Porivo died April 9, 1884, and was buried in the white cemetery at Fort Washakie because whites perceived her as a friend because of her role in the expedition and because of her advocacy of agriculture as a way of life for the Shoshone in the last half of the nineteenth century. In 1924 the Bureau of Indian Affairs asked Dr. Charles Eastman to determine the location of Sacagawea's grave so that a monument could be erected on it. Taking into account the strong oral tradition among the Shoshone, he concluded that Porivo was indeed Sacagawea.

Because of the passage of time and the scarcity of documentation, the events of Sacagawea's life after the expedition may never be known with certainty. However, the conflict between the theories rests in the tension between scanty, but "authoritative," written evidence of Sacagawea's early demise versus substantial, but "unauthoritative," oral accounts of the Shoshone Indians. In addition, the two women who were early proponents of the longer-lived Sacagawea theory, Dye and Hebard, were frequently referred to as leaders of the women's suffrage movement by opposing scholars, suggesting that the women's scholarship was rendered suspect not simply by Dye's choice of genre or Hebard's methodology but also by their political activism.

References

Anderson, Irving. "A Charbonneau Family Portrait." *American West* 17 (1980): 4–13, 63–64.

———. "Probing the Riddle of the Bird Woman." *Montana: The Magazine of Western History* 23 (1973): 2–17.

Chuinard, E. G. "The Bird Woman: Purposeful Member of the Corps or Casual 'Tag-along.'" *Montana: The Magazine of Western History* 26 (1976): 18–29.

Clark, Ella, and Margot Edmonds. *Sacagawea of the Lewis and Clark Expedition.* Berkeley: University of California Press, 1979.

Coues, Elliot, ed. *History of the Expedition Under the Command of Lewis and Clark.* 4 vols. 1893. Reprint, New York: Dover, 1964.

Dye, Eva Emery. *The Conquest: The True Story of Lewis and Clark.* Chicago: A. C. McClurg, 1902.

Hebard, Grace Raymond. *Sacajawea: A Guide and Interpreter of the Lewis and Clark Expedition, with an Account of the Travels of Toussaint Charbonneau, and of Jean Baptiste, the Expedition Papoose.* Glendale, CA: Arthur H. Clark, 1933.

Howard, Harold P. *Sacajawea.* Norman: University of Oklahoma Press, 1971.

Kessler, Donna J. *The Making of Sacagawea: A Euro–American Legend.* Tuscaloosa: University of Alabama Press, 1996.

Kingston, C. S. "Sacajawea as a Guide: The Evaluation of a Legend." *Pacific Northwest Quarterly* 35 (1944): 2–18.

Ronda, James P. *Lewis and Clark Among the Indians*. Lincoln: University of
    Nebraska Press, 1984.
Schroer, Blanche. "Boat-Pusher or Bird Woman?: Sacagawea or Sacajawea?" *An-
    nals of Wyoming* 52 (1980): 46–54.

—*Kathleen McNerney Donovan*

SACRED WHITE BUFFALO, MOTHER MARY CATHERINE [Josephine Crowfeather,
Ptesanwanyakapi, Ptesan-Wanyagapiwin] (1867–1893), daughter of Joseph Crowfeather, a Hunkpapa Lakota chief, was born near Standing Rock Agency, Dakota
Territory (now North Dakota). From infancy, she was regarded as a sacred virgin
because, just after her birth, her father had carried her into battle for protection, and
they both returned unharmed. Hence her Indian name, Ptesanwanyakapi (They See
a White Buffalo Woman), compared her to the sacred virgin in a Lakota story. As a
youth, she expressed a desire to become a Catholic nun, and for four years she
entered the Benedictine Sisters' School at Fort Yates, North Dakota.

From 1888 to 1890 Crowfeather trained to become a sister under the guidance
of Father Francis M. Craft, a priest of Iroquois ancestry. She shared his vision of
fulfilling the dream of the seventeenth-century Mohawk convert Kateri Tekakwitha, who had wanted to establish an Indian Christian sisterhood. With five other
Lakota women, she attended a Benedictine academy in Avoca, Minnesota, and
then entered the Benedictine novitiate in Zell, Minnesota, where she professed her
vows in 1890. She then served as assistant cook at a Stephan, South Dakota, mission school until internal strife at the novitiate prompted the premature transfer of
the fledgling community to its new convent at Elbowoods, North Dakota, on the
Fort Berthold Reservation.

Sacred White Buffalo,
Mother Mary Catherine

The next year, Crowfeather was elected the founding prioress-general of the new Congregation of American Sisters, and she assumed the title "Mother." Although independent, her community followed Benedictine discipline through convent devotions and missionary work among the Arikara, Gros Ventre, and Mandan. The congregation taught English, cared for the sick, and directed Christian sodalities.

In 1893 Mother Catherine succumbed to tuberculosis. Her young community survived for seven years more and reached a membership of twelve. Despite chronic poverty, illness, and racism during its brief history, the order served to inspire future Native religious workers.

References

Duratschek, Mary C. *Crusading Along Sioux Trails: A History of the Catholic Indian Missions of South Dakota*. St. Meinrad, IN: The Grail Press, 1947.

Ewans, Mary. "The Native Order: A Brief and Strange History." In *Scattered Steeples, the Fargo Diocese: A Written History of Its Centennial*. Edited by Jerome D. Lamb, Jerry Ruff, and William C. Sherman. Pp. 10–23. Fargo, ND: Burch, Londergan, and Lynch, 1988.

Mathes, Valerie S. "American Indian Women and the Catholic Church." *North Dakota History* 47 (1980): 20–25.

—*Mark G. Thiel*

SAILA, PITALOOSIE [Pitalouisa, Pitaloosee] (b. 1942), was born in Arctic Canada on August 11. A well-known Inuit printmaker, she lives at Cape Dorset. Pitaloosie is married to the noted sculptor Pauta Saila and is the niece of Oshoochiak Pudiat and the famed Cape Dorset sculptor and printmaker Pudlo.

In the late 1950s the Canadian artist and author James A. Houston, working as a civil administrator for the Department of Northern Affairs and National Resources, introduced drawing and printmaking to the Inuit people of Cape Dorset. Since then the production of art has been a creative outlet and a means of earning a livelihood for many Inuit people. Pitaloosie belongs to the second generation of Cape Dorset artists. She began drawing in the late 1960s, and her first piece was published in the 1968 Cape Dorset collection. Since that time her prints have appeared regularly in the illustrated catalogs of the annual collections of Inuit art, and her work has been exhibited internationally.

Pitaloosie often draws scenes of seasonal activities, such as hunting and fishing. *Fisherman's Dream*, a 1971 print, was reproduced on a twelve-cent stamp issued in November 1977 by the Canadian government. Pitaloosie is best known, though, for her depictions of mothers and children. In 1983 her print *Arctic Madonna* was selected to be reproduced on a UNICEF Christmas card. Much of her work conveys the Inuit sense of transformation and possibility.

References

Barz, Sandra B., comp. *Inuit Artists Print Workbook*. New York: Arts and Cultures of the North, 1981.

Dorset 79: The Twentieth Annual Cape Dorset Graphics Collection. Toronto: M. F. Feheley, 1979.

Furneaux, Patrick. "Evolution and Development of the Eskimo Print." In *Arts of the Eskimo: Prints*. Edited by Ernst Roch. Pp. 9–16. Barre, MA: Barre, 1975.

Leroux, Odette, Marion E. Jackson, and Minnie Aodla Freeman, eds. *Inuit Women Artists: Voices from Cape Dorset*. Vancouver, BC: Douglas, & McIntyre, 1994.

Rosshandler, Leo. "The Eskimo Print, an Appreciation." In *Arts of the Eskimo: Prints*. Edited by Ernst Roch. Pp. 17–19. Barre, MA: Barre, 1975.

Schuldberg, Jane. "Pitaloosie Saila." Seattle: Snow Goose Associates. (Photocopy.)

—Hertha D. Wong

SAINTE-MARIE, BUFFY (b. 1941), a Cree orphaned as an infant, was adopted and raised by a couple in Massachusetts who lived in a virtually all-white community. Her adoptive mother, part Micmac, spent many hours telling Sainte-Marie her Native American history.

Sainte-Marie's musical interests began early in life. At the age of four she was making up poems and taught herself to play the piano. She began to play the guitar and to write her own songs after her father gave her a guitar for her sixteenth birthday. As a university honors student, Sainte-Marie studied Oriental philosophy while continuing to play the guitar, compose songs, and research her heritage. After graduation Sainte-Marie went to New York to perform in Greenwich Village coffeehouses, and was soon offered nightclub dates and a recording contract.

During the 1960s Sainte-Marie became internationally known as a folk singer and songwriter who had a number of gold records. Besides her popular love songs, she wrote antiwar ballads and many songs that celebrate Native American identity and protest injustices against Native peoples. During the height of the antiwar era, some of her music was banned from radio and television, and her outspokenness brought her an FBI record.

Despite her perceived controversial nature, Sainte-Marie appeared on major television shows during the 1960s and early 1970s, including frequent guest performances on Johnny Carson's *The Tonight Show*. She was also a *Sesame Street* cast member from 1976 to 1981, playing herself. Whenever she appeared in a film, Sainte-Marie insisted that all Indian roles be filled by Indian people, thus opening the door for other Native American performers.

A social and political activist, Sainte-Marie founded the Native North American Women's Association, a group that has sponsored theater, arts, and education projects. She also instituted the Nihewan Foundation, a law school scholarship fund for Native Americans funded by money from her concerts. By 1975 Nihewan Foundation scholarships had sent more than twenty people through law school.

Although less visible during the 1980s, as were the other folk and protest musicians of the Vietnam/civil rights era, Sainte-Marie continued to be active in Native rights movements. For instance, she read the English translations of elders' words in *Broken Rainbow*, Maria Florio and Victoria Mudd's 1985 film about the forced relocation of Navajo and Hopi from their ancestral homeland. Her activisim and her music have earned Saint-Marie "Elvis" status among Native Americans.

Living on Kauai, Hawaii, since the 1960s, Sainte-Marie raised Dakota Starblanket Wolfchild, her son with actor Sheldon Wolfchild. Since the 1980s, besides continuing to record and to perform, mostly overseas, Sainte-Marie has become a digital artist, producing multimedia art that she sells in Europe and Canada.

References

Braudy, Susan. "Buffy Sainte-Marie: 'Native North American Me.'" *Ms.* (March 1975): 14–18.
"Buffy Sainte-Marie." *People Weekly* (June 17, 1996): 132.
Florio, Maria, and Victoria Mudd. *Broken Rainbow*. Earthworks Films. 1985.
Gridley, Marion E., ed. and comp. *Indians of Today*. 4th ed. Chicago: ICFP, 1971.
Sainte-Marie, Buffy. "Buffy." *Talking Leaf* 41 (August 1976): 8–9.
———. *The Buffy Sainte-Marie Songbook*. New York: Grosset and Dunlap, 1971.
———. "The Music of the American Indians." *Sing Out* 17 (June/July 1967): 29–31.
———. "Refuse to Be a Victim." In *The Ethnic American Woman: Problems, Protests, Life-Style*. Edited by Edith Blicksilver. Pp. 339–40. 2nd ed. Dubuque, IA: Kendall/Hunt, 1978.

—*Elizabeth A. McNeil*

SAKIESTEWA, RAMONA (b. 1949), makes weavings that are a metaphor for her life; her family included a Hopi father, a German–Irish mother, and an Anglo–American stepfather. She was raised in Albuquerque, New Mexico, a city that successfully melds past and present and Native American, Hispanic, and Anglo cultures. Her textiles incorporate these environmental influences, as well as the region's rich textile heritage. Her weavings reflect her multicultural environment. The influences are clear in her interpretations of historic Navajo weavings, her abstractions of kachina textile motifs, and her treatments of the southwestern landscape and unique architecture. Each textile bears Sakiestewa's imprint; each is well designed and executed in clean, clear colors.

Sakiestewa grew up surrounded by the Native arts of the Southwest in her home and in her job in an Albuquerque trading post. After teaching herself to weave by reading books written by the anthropologists Ruth Underhill and Kate Peck Kent, she moved to New York to study design. In 1975 Sakiestewa began a project at Bandelier National Monument to replicate the ancient techniques used in the manufacture of a spun turkey feather blanket, and in 1983 she replicated a cotton manta. Before turning to weaving as a full-time profession, she worked as an arts administrator for the Museum of New Mexico, New Mexico Arts Division, and was instrumental in establishing ATLATL, a national Native American arts and cultural services organization. In 1981 she traveled to Peru to consult with weavers on the creation of a weavers' guild. The next year she founded Ramona Sakiestewa Ltd. to produce and market functional textiles. Her studio has transformed Frank Lloyd Wright sketches into fiber realities.

Sakiestewa studies contemporary Pueblo textiles and experiments with historic dyes. She is a member of the New Mexico Arts Commission, the Southwest Association on Indian Affairs, and the board of the Wheelwright Museum of Indian Art in Santa Fe, and is president of the Santa Fe Indian Market; she also has served as a panel member for the National Endowment for the Arts. Her work has won awards at the Santa Fe Indian Market, the Heard Museum, in Phoenix, and the Museum of Northern Arizona at Flagstaff, and is held in many public and private collections. She lives in Santa Fe with her husband Arthur Sze, a poet, and their son, Micah.

References

Baizerman, Suzanne. *Ramona Sakiestewa Patterned Dreams: Textiles of the Southwest*. Santa Fe, NM: Wheelwright Museum of Indian Art, 1989.

Bender, Roberta. "Ramona Sakiestewa: Beyond Limits." *Native Peoples* 2 (Summer 1989): 30–34.

Hammond, Harmony, and Juane Quick-to-See Smith. *Women of Sweetgrass, Cedar and Sage*. New York: Gallery of the American Indian Community House, 1985.

Jacka, Lois Essary, and Jerry Jacka. *Beyond Tradition: Contemporary Indian Art and Its Evolution*. Flagstaff, AZ: Northland Press, 1988.

Traugott, Joseph. "Indian Weaver's Creations Art More Than Artifacts." *Albuquerque Journal*, May 28, 1989.

—*Laura Graves*

SALABIYE, VELMA S. (1948–1996), a Navajo born at Bellemont, Arizona, was educated at Bellemont Hogan School and at St. Michael's. After graduating from high school in 1966, she entered the University of Arizona, from which she graduated with a BA in education in 1971. In 1974 she earned her MLS from the university's Indian Graduate Library Institute, a federally funded program. As part of this program, she interned at the Window Rock Public Library on the Navajo Reservation.

In 1975, Salabiye began planning a library on the reservation that was later known as the Navajo Research and Statistics Center. She was the coordinator for a Special Libraries Association meeting on the Navajo Reservation in 1977. In 1979 she served as evaluator of major American Indian collections in California, and in that year she was awarded a D'Arcy McNickle fellowship at the Newberry Library Center for the History of the American Indian, in order to study the roles and contributions of Navajo women to American Indian society.

Beginning in 1980, Salabiye (Vee, as she was known to family and friends) was the librarian of the American Indian Studies Center, UCLA. In 1988 she became an associate editor of *American Indian Culture and Research Journal*. She wrote, alone or with others, works on American Indian library collections, believing that her major roles were to promote American Indian librarianship and to build a strong American Indian library collection. On October 7, 1987, she was presented a certificate of appreciation by the Office of Educational Research and Improvement, U.S. Department of Education, "in recognition of the outstanding service provided to the Library Services for Indian Tribes and Hawaiian Natives Program."

Salabiye published poetry in *American Indian Culture and Research Journal*, but her promise as an author was cut short by her death in the summer of 1996.

References

"Humor and Joking of the American Indian: A Bibliography." *American Indian Libraries Newsletter* 10 (Fall 1986): 2–4.

Marken, Jack. Personal communications with Velma S. Salabiye, August 7 and December 27, 1990.

Salabiye, Velma. *American Indian Library Resources at UCLA*. Los Angeles: Institute of American Cultures, 1980.

———. "Literature" (seven poems). *American Indian Culture and Research Journal* 19 (1995): 215–222.

———. "Library and Information Resources." In *Community-Based Research: A Handbook for Native Americans*. Edited by Susan Buyette. Pp. 197–232. Los Angeles: American Indian Studies Center, UCLA, 1983.

Salabiye, Velma, and James R. Young. "American Indian Leaders and Leadership of the Twentieth Century: A Bibliographic Essay." *Journal of the West* 23 (July 1984): 70–76.

—Jack Marken

SANAPIA [Mary Poafpybitty, Sticky Mother] (1895–1984), Yapai Comanche medicine woman, was born in a tepee encampment near Fort Sill, Oklahoma, the sixth in a family of eleven children. Her father was a "progressive" Christian Comanche proselytizer, and her mother was a staunch Comanche–Arapaho traditionalist and medicine woman. The maternal influences proved stronger.

As a young child, Sanapia was raised by her maternal grandmother, who stressed the importance of learning and recording tribal traditions, and urged the girl to follow her mother's career as an eagle doctor. Sanapia's uncle, who cured her of influenza in the early 1900s, extracted a promise that she would become a doctor when she regained her health. Seven years of boarding school education at Cache Creek Mission School ended when Sanapia was fourteen. Her training as a medicine woman began the summer before her last year of school and continued for three years after she returned home. By age seventeen, Sanapia had learned all the skills and knowledge she would need as an eagle doctor from her mother, who then transferred her healing power to Sanapia in a formal ceremony. Sanapia could not begin to practice, however, until she had reached menopause.

Once her training was complete, Sanapia's mother and brother arranged a marriage for her that ended shortly after her first son was born. Sanapia remarried within a year and had a son and a daughter before her second husband died in the 1930s. She mourned his death for several years by "roughing it out" in wild, self-destructive behavior that stopped when she began to use her healing powers in the 1940s. She married for a third time as she began her healing career, and was again widowed in old age.

By the late 1960s, Sanapia was the last surviving eagle doctor and had acquired the maximum power and prestige attainable by a woman in traditional Comanche society. She specialized in the treatment of "ghost sickness," an illness increasingly common as Comanches acculturated, that involved facial paralysis believed to be caused by fearful contact with a ghost. Her very effective healing ritual combined elements of psychiatry, herbal medicine, and peyote with songs and prayers to invoke the intercession of spirits and her medicine eagle, a process that reintegrated patients into the traditionalist community and thus restored their health.

As she approached old age, Sanapia began thinking about transferring her power, but no obvious successor appeared ready. She consented to work with anthropologist David E. Jones, whom she adopted as a son, to record her life and preserve her medical knowledge and practices in case she died before she could completely train her successor. This was a wise decision; she probably did not have a chance to formally transfer her power before her death in Oklahoma in 1984.

References

Jones, David E. "Face the Ghost." *New Directions in the Study of Man* 4 (1980): 53–57.

———. *Sanapia, Comanche Medicine Woman*. New York: Holt, Rinehart, and Winston, 1972.

—Helen M. Bannan

SANCHEZ, CAROL LEE (b. 1934), is a Laguna Pueblo/Sioux born in Albuquerque, New Mexico, and raised in the village of Paguate. She later lived in a nearby small Chicano town until she was eighteen. Her mother is a Laguna/Sioux and her father is a Lebanese–American who speaks Spanish and Arabic. A sister of Paula Gunn Allen, Sanchez is a poet, painter, and educator. Her poetry and art are heavily influenced by her multicultural and multilinguistic background. Her writing is also influenced by her experiences in San Francisco since her arrival there in 1964.

Sanchez received her BA in arts administration from San Francisco State University in 1978. In 1975 her book of poems *Conversations from the Nightmare* was nominated for the American Academy of Poets' Edgar Allan Poe Award. In 1981 she was a speaker for meetings of the American Indian Women Painters and Third World Women in Arts. Also in 1981, she was conference coordinator for the National Women's Studies Association at San Francisco State University. She is Affirmative Action Committee chair for the California Association of English. She also has a growing reputation as an arts administrator for her work as coordinator of the First Western States Biennial Exhibition.

Sanchez taught at San Francisco State University from 1976 to 1985. After 1989 she relocated to central Missouri and has taught at the University of Missouri-Columbia; State Fair Community College in Sedalia, Missouri; and Whiteman Air Force Base in Knob Noster, Missouri. She is primarily a teacher of American Indian Studies but has also been active and vocal in the feminist arena, teaching women's and Third World women's literature in addition to lecturing.

References

Allen, Paula Gunn. "This Wilderness in My Blood: Spiritual Foundations of the Poetry of Five American Indian Women." In *The Sacred Hoop: Recovering the Feminine in American Indian Traditions*. Boston: Beacon Press, 1986.

Anderson, Owanah, ed. *Ohoyo One Thousand: A Resource Guide of American Indian/Alaska Native Women, 1982*. Wichita Falls, TX: Ohoyo Resource Center, 1982.

Green, Rayna, ed. *That's What She Said: Contemporary Poetry and Fiction by Native American Women*. Bloomington: Indiana University Press, 1984.

Sanchez, Carol Lee. *Conversations from the Nightmare*. Berkeley, CA: Casa Editorial, 1975.

———. *Coyote's Journal*. Berkeley, CA: Wingbow Press, 1981.

———. *Excerpts from a Mountain Climber's Handbook*. San Francisco: Taurean Horn and Out West, 1985.

———. *From Spirit to Matter: New and Selected Poems, 1969–1996*. San Francisco: Taurean Horn Press, 1997.

———. *Message Bringer Woman*. San Francisco: Taurean Horn Press, 1977.

———. *Morning Prayer*. Brooklyn, NY: Strawberry Press, 1977.

———. *Sex, Class and Race Intersections: Visions of Women of Color*. New York: Women's International Resource Exchange, 1991.

———. *She Poems*. Goshen, CT: Chicory Blues Press, 1995.

———. *Time Warps*. San Francisco: Taurean Horn Press, 1976.

—Lucy Leriche

SAUBEL, KATHERINE SIVA (b. 1920), is a Cahuilla Indian elder born on the Los Coyotes Reservation and raised in Palm Springs, California. She grew up speaking the Cahuilla language and learning tribal traditions from her mother, Melan Seivatily, and her father, Juan C. Siva. After her marriage, she and her husband, Mariano Saubel, helped establish the Malki Museum, the first nonprofit tribal museum on an Indian reservation in California. For many years Saubel served on the Riverside County Historical Commission, which selected her County Historian of the Year in 1986. The next year she was recognized as Elder of the Year by the California State Indian Museum. Governor George Deukmejian appointed her to the California Native American Heritage Commission in 1986, and she has served with distinction, preserving sacred sites and protecting Indian remains. Saubel has testified as an expert on Indian culture and history before the California legislature, the United States Congress, and several boards, commisions, and agencies.

A respected scholar of Cahuilla Indian history, literature, and culture, Saubel was University of California Lecturer at the University of California, Riverside; she has taught at the University of California at Los Angeles, California State University at Hayward, and the University of Cologne in Germany. She has worked closely with the linguist Hansjakob Seiler to preserve the Cahuilla language. Saubel's publications are a result of her interest in "saving remnants of my culture in these books," which are designed "to tell everyone how it was." With Professor Lowell Bean she has published *Temalpakh: Cahuilla Indian Knowledge and Use of Plants, Cahuilla Ethnobotanical Notes: Mesquite and Screwbean, Cahuilla Ethonobotanical Notes: The Aboriginal Uses of Oak*. Her other books include *Kunvachmal: A Cahuilla Tale* and *I'sniyatam Designs*. Saubel is known internationally as a Native American scholar, and is considered one of the foremost Indian leaders in California. In 1993, she was elected to the national Women's Hall of Fame.

References

Bean, Lowell John, and Katherine Siva Saubel. *Cahuilla Ethnobotanical Notes: Aboriginal Uses of Mesquite and Screwbean*. Archaelogy Survey Annual Report. Los Angeles: University of California, Los Angeles, 1963.

————. *Cahuilla Ethnobotanical Notes: The Aboriginal Uses of Oak.* Archaeology Survey Annual Report. Los Angeles: University of California, Los Angeles, 1961.

————. *Temalpakh: Cahuilla Indian Knowledge and Uses of Plants.* Banning, CA: Malki Museum Press, 1972.

Jeffrey, Cheryl. "Katherine Saubel." *Local Daughters of the Desert* 2 (December 1989): n.p.

Saubel, Katherine Siva. *I'sniyatam Designs: A Cahuilla Word Book.* Banning, CA: Malki Museum Press, 1977.

Trafzer, Clifford E. Personal communication with Katherine Saubel, March 1, 1990.

—*Clifford E. Trafzer*

SCHOOLCRAFT, JANE JOHNSTON [Bame-Wa-Wa-Ge-Zhik-A-Quay, Woman of the Stars Rushing Through the Skies] (1800–1841), was born at Sault Ste. Marie, on the border of Michigan and Ontario, to John Johnston, an Irish fur trader, and Ozha-guscoday-way-quay, the daughter of the Anishinaabe (Chippewa) leader Waub Ojeeb. Her education was rich and varied, consisting of her father's tutelage in literature, history, and the classics, and her mother's teaching of their tribe's beliefs, legends, and lore. In 1809 she was sent to Ireland, where she completed her education.

Henry Rowe Schoolcraft arrived at the Sault in 1822 and developed a close relationship with the Johnston family. Jane and her family became interested in Schoolcraft's work in Native American languages and culture, helping him compile his Chippewa vocabulary. Schoolcraft developed a fascination with the tribe's legends and tales, and set out, with Jane's help, to collect them. After their marriage in 1823, the pair continued their literary pursuits. During the winter of 1826–1827, they began publishing the *Literary Voyager* or *Muzzenyegun* manuscript magazine. Developed initially as a diversion for the snowbound people at the Sault, it was also distributed in New York, Detroit, and other cities. The *Literary Voyager* contained both prose and poetry, mostly on Native American subjects. Schoolcraft was a prominent contributor, furnishing essays and poetry under the pen name Rosa Leelinau. The essays trace the traditions of her tribe with authority and accuracy, and remain important sources of information on the Chippewas. For the most part, her poetry can be said to be in the romantic vein; the poems on the death of her two-year-old son William Henry are eloquent expressions of grief.

In spite of her relative isolation, Schoolcraft gained the attention of contemporary writers, including the British authors Anna B. Jameson and Harriet Martineau. Martineau made the difficult journey into the North Woods to meet her. After a lingering illness, Schoolcraft died in 1841.

References

Mason, Philip P. *The Literary Voyager or Muzzenyegun.* Lansing: Michigan State University Press, 1962.

Littlefield, Daniel F., Jr., and James W. Parins. *American Indian and Alaska Native Newspapers and Periodicals, 1826–1924*. Westport, CT: Greenwood Press, 1984.

—James W. Parins

SEARS, VICKIE (b. 1941), Tsalagi (Cherokee)/Spanish/English poet, essayist, short story writer, former therapist and social worker, and children's advocate, was born August 2, 1941, in San Diego, California. In "Toward the Light," an essay in *Names We Call Home: Autobiography on Racial Identity*, she reflects on her trilingual childhood and the racism in her early school days, her family of origin, and her extended family (which, including foster families, encompasses thirty-four distinct racial and ethnic identities). Part of her upbringing was Catholic. "I can't pass a church today without making the sign of the cross," she says, "but I still practice Native spirituality."

Married early (and the mother of two children, now deceased), Sears raised many foster children, dedicating herself to their safety and well-being. With grants from the National Institute of Mental Health, she create and directed Kwawachee, a counseling center for the Puyallup tribe that blends the work of medicine people with current psychotherapeutic practices, conducts outreach in prisons, and offers counseling programs. Sears has testified on children's issues and Native American health issues before the Washington state Senate and has served as a consultant on social services for children's mental and physical health for tribes in Washington, Oregon, and Montana. She has taught courses and workshops on racism, feminism, child abuse, domestic violence, women's literature, and history.

Sears's first book, a collection of short stories titled *Simple Songs* (1990), focuses on children's responses to violent disruptions in family life, particularly sexual abuse. In "Grace," she inhabits the child-narrator Jodi, whose first question to a new foster parent is "Do you use a stick or a strap for spanking?" Sears's work has received attention from feminist, Native American, and mainstream critics and scholars. She is working on a new book, *People We Grow With*, stories about children who benefit from contact with adults and later come to understand the significance of these conjunctions. Sears has poems, stories, and/or essays in *Names We Call Home: Autobiography on Racial Identity; Spider Woman's Granddaughters: Traditions, Tales and Contemporary Writing by Native American Women; Dancing on the Rim of the World; An Anthology of Contemporary Northwest Native American Writing; Talking Leaves: Contemporary Native American Short Stories; Breathing Ground: New Writing and Art by Northwest Women of Color; A Gathering of Spirit: Writing and Art by North American Indian Women; The Things That Divide Us: Stories by Women; and Gay and Lesbian Poets of Our Time.*

Battling diabetes and two recent minor strokes has claimed much of Sears's attention, but she sees her illness in a broader social context. "Diabetes is epidemic among Native people," she says, "and my difficulties are not unusual." Sears lives with her partner, Linda Luster, in Seattle.

References

Brant, Beth. "Giveaway: Native Lesbian Writers." *Signs* 18 (Summer 1993): 944–948.

Carroll, Rhoda. Review of *Simple Songs*, by Vicki Sears. *Studies in American Indian Literatures* 3 (Fall 1991): 76–80.

Gould, Janice. "Disobedience (in Language) in Texts by Lesbian Native Americans." *Ariel* 25 (January 1994): 32–45.

Herzog, Kristin. Review of *Simple Songs*, by Vicki Sears. *MELUS* 19 (Winter 1994): 147.

Sears, Vickie. *Simple Songs*. Ithaca, NY: Firebrand Books, 1990.

Thompson, Becky, and Sangecta Tyagi, eds. *Names We Call Home: Autobiography on Racial Identity*. New York: Routledge, 1996.

—Rhoda Carroll

SEKAQUAPTEWA, HELEN [Dowawisnima] (1898–1990), was born during a turbulent time in Hopi history, a period of rapidly accelerating Anglo influence on the remote mesas of her tribal land. She was the second daughter in a family residing in the most traditional and conservative of the Hopi villages of northern Arizona; her family was forced to move to Hotevilla when a split at Oraibi village ended in eviction of nearly half the families. Hopis resisted sending their children to school, and Sekaquaptewa was hidden from truant officers. She was finally discovered, however, and sent to boarding school at Keams Canyon; her father was jailed for one year for his resistance to government interference in tribal organization and traditional education.

Though, like other children at the time, Sekaquaptewa suffered from illness and the family rupture caused by removal to school, she became a good pupil, and when the opportunity to attend the Phoenix Indian School was offered, she chose to complete secondary school there. She became adept at domestic skills as well as academic subjects, and aspired to open a laundry business on the Hopi Reservation. However, when she returned, her family and other villagers were suspicious of her nontraditional ways, and she felt alienated. She soon married Emory Sekaquaptewa, whom she had met at school, and together they moved to a ranch on the perimeter of the reservation. There they raised a large family, several of whom were to become prominent in tribal politics and cultural studies.

Despite her conversion to Christianity, Sekaquaptewa retained an intense interest in Hopi ceremonialism, and as the matriarch of the Eagle clan she was particularly involved in women's ceremonial life. In her later years she lived in the village of Kikutsmovi on Third Mesa, and her home became a center for clan and family activities. She credited the publication of her autobiography, *Me and Mine*, as the critical factor in her gaining a central place in Hopi society.

References

Bataille, Gretchen M., and Kathleen M. Sands. "Two Women in Transition." In *Native American Women Telling Their Lives*. Pp. 83–112. Lincoln: University of Nebraska Press, 1984.

Hopi: Songs of the Fourth World. Produced and directed by Pat Ferrero. 58 min. New Day Films, 1983. Videotape.

"Iisaw: Hopi Coyote Stories," with Helen Sekaquaptewa. *Words and Place: Native Literature from the American Southwest*. Larry Evers, project director. 18 min. Clearwater Publishing, 1981. Videotape.

Sands, Kathleen M., and Emory Sekaquaptewa. "Four Hopi Lullabies: Method and Meaning." *American Indian Quarterly* 4 (May 1978): 97–106.

Sekaquaptewa, Helen. *Me and Mine*. Edited by Louise Udall. Tucson: University of Arizona Press, 1969.

—Kathleen Mullen Sands

SHANLEY, KATHRYN [Vangen] (b. 1957), born at Wolf Point, Montana, is a professor of English at the University of Montana. She is a member of the Assiniboine tribe and grew up on the Fort Peck Reservation. She received a nursing degree from Metropolitan State University in Minneapolis in 1973. After pursuing nursing as a career, Shanley returned to school to complete a BA degree in English (summa cum laude) at Moorhead State University in Minnesota. She then went on to graduate school at the University of Michigan, receiving her MA in English in 1982 and her PhD in 1987. Shanley was awarded a Frances Allen fellowship at the Newberry Library in Chicago to do research on Lakota written and oral traditions, and in 1985 she joined the faculty of the University of Washington.

Shanley has been a prolific literary critic. Her writings include analyses of contemporary American Indian authors such as James Welch, N. Scott Momaday, Leslie Marmon Silko, and Linda Hogan, as well as traditional Lakota thinkers Black Elk and Lame Deer. She has written a book on politics in the poetry and prose of James Welch, and has published her own poetry and short fiction. In 1988 to 1989 Shanley held a Ford Foundation minority postdoctoral fellowship.

She has worked extensively on curricular transformation, including as a faculty member for three summers at the Cultural Pluralism Institute, funded by the Ford Foundation, at Evergreen State College in Washington. In addition, Shanley has taught tribal college workshops on special topics in American Indian literature as well as at Atlanta University in Georgia. She has developed a project using American Indian autobiographies as primary source material in the teaching of American history and literature, and has led a workshop on this topic for the D'Arcy McNickle Center for the History of the American Indian at the Newberry Library in Chicago. Her work on American Indian literature is innovative, and she is strongly committed to the development of a unique American Indian pedagogy at the university level. During the 1996 to 1997 academic year, Shanley was a Rockefeller Foundation fellow at the Northwest Center for Race Ethnicity, Department of Comparative American Cultures, at Washington State University, Pullman. She is now chair of the Native American Studies Department at the University of Montana.

References

Shanley, Kathryn. "The Lived Experience: American Indian Literature After Alcatraz." *Akwe:kon Journal* 11 (1994): 119–127.

———. *"Only an Indian" Reading James Welch*. Norman: University of Oklahoma Press, 1996.

—Clara Sue Kidwell

SHAW, ANNA MOORE [Chehia] (1898–1975), was born on the Gila River Pima Reservation in Arizona. Her Christianized family was headed by Red Arrow, later known as Josiah Moore, a leader in his tribe. After eagerly following her older brother to a missionary boarding school in Tucson, she attended the Phoenix Indian High School, where she was a student leader. There she met her future husband, Ross Shaw, who subsequently became a freight wagon driver for the Santa Fe Railroad. In 1918 they set up a household in a multiethnic neighborhood in Phoenix where they raised two children. She was not interested in returning to the Gila River Reservation, feeling that she and her husband had an obligation to use their educations in an urban setting and to assimilate into Anglo culture without losing Indian identity. Active in her local community and in church affairs, Shaw was determined to overcome bigotry; her advocacy for intercultural understanding was given strong impetus by a visit from Carlos Montezuma, a well-known Indian spokesman, just before his death in 1922.

As her children became older, Shaw began to regret the loss of traditional Pima stories and to compile her own version of tales she remembered from her youth. Her collection, *Pima Legends*, was published in 1968. Though she was satisfied with life in Phoenix and her fifty-year role as a mediator of two cultures, when her husband retired, she agreed to move to the Salt River Pima Reservation. There she devoted her considerable energies to reviving traditional Pima skills, teaching basket weaving to younger women in the tribe at a time when the techniques had nearly died. She also edited the reservation newspaper, was instrumental in setting up a museum of Pima culture, and continued her activities in the Presbyterian congregation.

During her later years Shaw began to write down a series of episodic recollections about her life. The autobiography, supplemented by interview material and edited in a chronological narrative, was published in 1974. Titled *A Pima Past*, it is characterized by her positive attitude toward life and her dedication to multicultural understanding.

In 1981 Shaw was posthumously inducted into the Arizona Hall of Fame for her work in advocating interracial harmony.

References

Bataille, Gretchen M., and Kathleen M. Sands. "Two Women in Transition." In *Native American Women Telling Their Lives*. Pp. 83–112. Lincoln: University of Nebraska Press, 1984.

Shaw, Anna Moore. *Pima Legends*. Tucson: University of Arizona Press, 1968.

———. *A Pima Past*. Tucson: University of Arizona Press, 1974.

Tsosie, Rebecca. "Changing Women: The Cross-Currents of American Indian Feminine Identity." *American Culture and Research Journal* 12 (1988): 1–37.

—Kathleen Mullen Sands

SILKO, LESLIE MARMON (b. 1948), was born in Albuquerque to Lee H. Marmon (Laguna) and Virginia Marmon (from a Plains tribe). Of Indian–white–Mexican ancestry, she grew up on the Laguna Pueblo Reservation, where she learned the rich cultural lore of the Lagunas through the stories told by her grandmother Lillie and her "Aunt Susie," whose influence was fundamental in shaping Silko's personality.

She attended a Catholic high school in Albuquerque, and in 1969 she received a BA in English from the University of New Mexico. The same year Silko published her first short story, "The Man to Send Rain Clouds," based on a real incident that happened at Laguna, and was awarded a National Endowment for the Humanities discovery grant. She attended three semesters of law school at the University of New Mexico, then decided to devote herself to writing.

Later, Silko taught at Navajo Community College at Tsaile, Arizona, and in the mid-1970s she went to Ketchikan, Alaska, where she wrote her novel *Ceremony*.

She has received numerous grants and awards, including a National Endowment for the Arts fellowship and a MacArthur Foundation award in 1981 to complete her second novel, *Almanac of the Dead*.

Her first book-length publication, the collection of poems *Laguna Woman*, appeared in 1974, and seven short stories were published the same year in one of the first anthologies of contemporary Native American writing, *The Man to Send Rain Clouds*.

Ceremony, Silko's first novel, received enthusiastic praise. It tells the story of a half-breed Laguna World War II alienated veteran who is gradually able to heal himself by reenacting a traditional, yet modified, ceremony with the help of a powerful mixed-blood medicine man who significantly changes the rituals to serve a different reality after the coming of white people. Only these innovations make the ceremony grow and keep it strong. The cycle of restoration leads to a sense of unity between the individual and the land; oral storytelling is seen as a link between past and present in a mythological concept of time. Myths and legends are interwoven with the main narrative, and they are in fact the mythological parallel of what is happening to the protagonist. The ceremonial nature of existence is reflected in the ritualistic use of the storytelling—both ancient and modern—and its healing power. At the beginning of the novel, in a kind a traditional formula, Silko creates a persona of herself—the storyteller who tells a story called *Ceremony* that

Leslie Marmon Silko

the Pueblo creator Thought Woman is thinking. A miscellany of family stories and photographs, *Storyteller* (which includes some of the poems and short stories that had appeared in *Laguna Woman* and *The Man to Send Rain Clouds*), can be considered as an autobiography: a new version, in written form, of traditional oral storytelling.

Almanac of the Dead, whose composition covers a period of ten years, is an ambitious and complex novel, both for its time structure and for its special locations, a radical and revisionary view of the history of the West, of the conquest and the exploitation of the Americas over two continents and through four centuries of Indian life and culture, violence and oppression. "A brilliant, haunting and tragic novel of ruin and resistance in the Americas," as Larry McMurtry defined it, *Almanac of the Dead* offers a grim and utterly bleak view of the contemporary world, in which Silko seems to find no hope to relieve the evil and corruption surrounding our age.

Yellow Woman and the Beauty of the Spirit gathers lucid and articulate essays on Indian communities, the grief of separation—both racial and cultural—Pueblo Indian language and literature, a recurrent discussion of why the people and the land are inseparable, and the injustices inflicted upon Native Americans by the Anglo–American legal system.

References

Allen, Paula Gunn. "The Ceremonial Motion of Indian Time: Long Ago, So Far." In *The Sacred Hoop*. Pp. 147–154. Boston: Beacon Press, 1986.

———, ed. "The Feminine Landscape of Leslie Marmon Silko's *Ceremony*." In *Studies in American Indian Literature*. Pp. 127–133. New York: MLA, 1983.

Barnes, Kim. "A Leslie Marmon Silko Interview." *Journal of Ethnic Studies* 13 (Winter 1986): 83–105.

Blicksilver, Edith. "Traditionalism vs. Modernity: Leslie Silko on American Indian Women." *Southwest Review* 64 (1979): 149–160.

Coltelli, Laura. "*Almanac of the Dead:* An Interview with Leslie Marmon Silko." In *Native American Literatures*. Pp. 65–80. Pisa: Servizio Editoriale Universitario, 1994.

———. "Leslie Marmon Silko." In *Winged Words: American Indian Writers Speak*. Pp. 135–153. Lincoln: University of Nebraska Press, 1990.

———. "Leslie Marmon Silko's *Sacred Water*." *Studies in American Indian Literatures* 8 (1996): 21–29.

———. "Re-enacting Myths and Stories: Tradition and Renewal in Ceremony." In *Native American Literatures*. Pp. 173–184. Pisa: Seu, 1989.

Evers, Lawrence J., and Dennis W. Carr. "A Conversation with Leslie Marmon Silko." *Sun Tracks: An American Indian Literary Magazine* 3 (Fall 1976): 28–33.

Graulich, Melody, ed. *Leslie Marmon Silko: "Yellow Woman."* New Brunswick, NJ: Rutgers University Press, 1993.

Hailey, David E., Jr. "The Visual Elegance of Ts'its'tsi'nako and the Other Invisible Characters in *Ceremony*." *Wicazo Sa Review* 4 (Fall 1990): 1–6.

Herzog, Kristin. "Thinking Woman and Feeling Man: Gender in Leslie Marmon Silko's *Ceremony*." *MELUS* 12 (Summer 1985): 25–36.

Hirsch, Bernard A. "The Telling Which Continues: Oral Tradition and the Written Word in Leslie Marmon Silko's *Storyteller.*" *American Indian Quarterly* 4 (Winter 1988): 1–26.

Jahner, Elaine. "The Novel and Oral Tradition: An Interview with Leslie Marmon Silko." *Book Forum* 5 (1981): 383–388.

Jaskoski, Helen. *Leslie Marmon Silko: A Study of the Short Fiction.* New York: Twayne, 1998.

Lincoln, Kenneth. "Grandmother Storyteller: Leslie Silko." In *Native American Renaissance.* Pp. 222–250. Berkeley: University of California Press, 1983.

Ruoff, LaVonne A. "Ritual and Research: Keres Traditions in the Short Fiction of Leslie Silko." *MELUS* 5 (1978): 3–17.

Sands, Kathleen Mullen. "Indian Women's Personal Narrative: Voices Past and Present." In *American Women's Autobiography: Fea(s)ts of Memory.* Edited by Margo Culley. Pp. 268–294. Madison: University of Wisconsin Press, 1992.

———, ed. "A Special Symposium Issue on Leslie Marmon Silko's *Ceremony.*" *American Indian Quarterly* 5 (February 1979): 1–75.

Seyersted, Per. *Leslie Marmon Silko.* Boise, ID: Boise State University, 1980.

Silko, Leslie Marmon. *Almanac of the Dead.* New York: Simon and Schuster, 1991.

———. *Ceremony.* New York: Viking Press, 1977.

———. *The Delicacy and the Strength of Lace: Letters Between Leslie Marmon Silko and James Wright.* Saint Paul, MN: Greywolf Press, 1986.

———. *Gardens in the Dunes.* New York: Simon and Schuster, 1999.

———. *Laguna Woman.* Greenfield Center, NY: Greenfield Review Press, 1974.

———. *Sacred Water.* Tucson, AZ: Flood Plain Press, 1993.

———. *Storyteller.* New York: Seaver, 1981.

———. *Yellow Woman and a Beauty of the Spirit: Essays on Native American Life Today.* New York: Simon and Schuster, 1996.

Swann, Edith. "Healing via the Sunrise Cycle in Silko's *Ceremony.*" *American Indian Quarterly* 12 (Fall 1988): 313–328.

———. "Laguna Symbolic Geography and Silko's *Ceremony.*" *American Indian Quarterly* 12 (Summer 1988): 229–249.

—Laura Coltelli

SIOUI, ELEONORE MARIE (b. 1925), known as "the spiritual Mother of the Huron–Wyandots," was the first Canadian Indian women to receive a PhD. She is director of the Tecumseh Spiritual Medicine Center at her home on the Village-des-Huron near Quebec City. She grew up among traditionalists at the Forty Arpents Reserve. Her father, Emery Sioui, was a chief and noted hunter, rancher, and guide who taught himself to write and speak English. Her mother, Caroline Dumont, was a healer who taught her daughter traditional values and the power of those things considered sacred by her people.

On June 10, 1946, she married Georges Albert Sioui; they raised seven children in the rich Huron culture. She instilled in her children a love of learning and personal development, as well as the concept of wisdom. They have become recognized leaders among Canada's First Nation peoples in education, art, philosophy, religion, and Native Studies. When her children were grown, Sioui continued her own formal education, studying languages and education at Laval University of Quebec, and international development at the University of Ottawa, where she received a degree in international cooperation. She studied international communications and human resource development at the University of Miami. In 1984 she entered the PhD program at the Union of Graduate Schools, where she completed her degree in 1988 with dissertation on Native American philosophy and spirituality, titled "Life of a Huron–Wyandot Woman: The Realization of an Impossible Dream."

Sioui is known for her books of poetry, including *Andatha, Femme du nord, Femme de l'ile*, and *Corps a couer perdu*, and for her expertise in Native American spiritual beliefs. She is currently completing a major study of traditional Native spiritual medicine and an autobiography. She has lectured throughout the world on Native American spiritual beliefs and is internationally known for her courageous struggle "to win back for her people the dignity that is its own." Sioui is a teacher–scholar who has spent her life studying the ideology behind the historical repression of Native Americans, always returning to her Huron roots for understanding. Her Wyandot name is Andata Tshikonsaseh. She is the grandmother of twenty-one children and has numerous other "relatives" who walk in her spirit.

References

Hammond, Heather. "An Inspiring Guest Visits SIFC: Dr. Eleanor Sioui." *Powwow Times* (1994): 53.

"Sioui, Eleonore Marie." Unpublished manuscript. Office of the Academic Dean, Saskatchewan Indian Federated College, University of Regina, Canada.

Trafzer, Clifford E. Personal communication with Georges Sioui, February 6, 1997.

—Clifford E. Trafzer

SISK-FRANCO, CALEEN A. (b. 1952), a member of the Wintu tribe, was born in Redding, a small town near Mount Shasta in northern California. The seventh of eleven children, she graduated from Shasta Union High School in 1970 and earned her AA degree from Shasta College two years later. After earning her BA degree in physical education from California State University (CSU) at Chico in 1975, she went on to obtain a teaching certificate the next year. Currently, while working full-time, she is completing an MA degree in physical education at CSU, Chico.

From 1976 to 1977, Sisk-Franco was the director of Title V Indian education in Santa Rosa and Richmond, California. In 1977 to 1979 she taught adults at the Indian Education Center in her hometown. In 1979 she returned to teaching kindergarten through twelfth grade, this time in Fort Hall, Idaho. In 1981 Sisk-Franco move back to northern California and taught grades K–4 in Marysville for five years. Since 1986 she has been the American Indian recruiter and adviser at CSU, Chico.

Throughout her years of teaching, recruiting, and advising, Sisk-Franco has worked on behalf of all Native American people and for federal recognition of the Wintu. From 1985 to 1990 she was the chair of the Toyon Wintu Center, Inc., the main tribal organization for the Wintu people. She is a board member of Four

Winds of Education, an Indian-organized community education program in Chico, and a member of the CSU, Chico, Provost's Repatriation Committee. In addition, she belongs to the National Indian Education Association, the Northern California Indian Recruiters Consortium, and the California State Department Indian Education Advisory Board.

As part of her commitment to serving her people, Sisk-Franco has published editorials calling attention to the Wintu struggle for federal re-recognition and land rights. In 1971 the Toyon Wintu Center was built on sixty-one acres northwest of Redding, California, but in 1983 the Bureau of Indian Affairs (BIA) revoked the Wintus' "indefinite use permit." Years of political and legal struggles ensued. In 1985 the BIA declared the Wintus "unrecognized Indians," making them ineligible for BIA health and educational services. In 1989 the Native people still living at Toyon were evicted, and their buildings were bulldozed. On June 18, 1990, Sisk-Franco began a much publicized water-only fast to hasten the state and federal governments' responses to the Wintu appeal for federal recognition and for transfer of the Toyon Wintu Center land base to tribal control. She ended her fast twenty-one days later (July 8, 1990) when she received a letter from U.S. Senator Daniel Inouye, chair of the Senate Select Committee on Indian Affairs, in which he promised to support the California Tribal Status Act of 1990.

In addition to educational and political activism, Sisk-Franco is committed to traditional Wintu spirituality and is raising her son, Michael, to follow Winnemem Wintu traditions. Her leadership provides an important model for other Indian people of how to combine traditional teachings and a university education.

References

Aylworth, Roger. "Two Women Fast for Wintu Recognition." *Enterprise-Record* [Chico, CA] June 29, 1990, A2.

Budman, Matthew. "Going to the Top of the Mountain: A Chico State Administrator's Fast for Indian Life." *News and Review*, June 28, 1990, 15–16.

"SCUC Indian Adviser Ends Successful Fast." *News and Review*, July 12, 1990, 26.

Sisk-Franco, Caleen A. "Toyon Belongs to the Wintu." *News from Native California* 4 (Fall 1989): 10–12.

Wong, Hertha. Interview with Caleen Sisk-Franco, March 20, 1991.

———. Written personal communication with Caleen Sisk-Franco, March 1, 1991.

—*Hertha D. Wong*

SKYE, FERIAL DEER (b. 1940), was born in Keshena, Wisconsin, on the Menominee Indian Reservation. She is the daughter of Joseph Deer, an enrolled Menominee, and Constance Wood Deer, of English–Scots–Irish descent. After elementary education in Milwaukee and Shawano, Wisconsin, she graduated from high school in Shawano in 1958, third in a class of 185 students. She then attended the University of Wisconsin in Madison, graduating in 1962 with a BS (with honors) in secondary education, having majored in dance and minored in English.

Skye continued her education by studying in the Dance Department of the Juilliard School of Music in 1962 to 1963. She attended graduate school in dance at the University of Wisconsin in 1968 to 1969 and 1978 to 1979. She earned an MA in educational psychology and guidance from the University of South Dakota at Vermillion in 1975 and received her EdD from the University of South Dakota in educational psychology and counseling in 1988. Her dissertation is titled "A Study of the Effects of Dance Education on Stress in College-Age American Indian Women."

She is married to Clarence Skye, a Hunkpapa Sioux, and they are the parents of Clifton, born February 5, 1965; Martin, born March 25, 1966; and Wenonah, born September 8, 1967. Besides being a mother, Skye has had a busy life as a school counselor, dance instructor, and professional dancer. From 1977 to 1978 she served as a counselor at the Pierre Indian Learning Center in South Dakota. From August 1982 until January 1988, she was a special education counselor for South Dakota's Crow, Creek, and Lower Brule Sioux tribes.

Skye's dance career began in her undergraduate days. As a college senior in 1962, she was chosen as dance soloist in *Earth-Trapped*, a dance-opera based on a Sioux ghost legend that was choreographed by Forrest Coggan of the University of Wisconsin-Madison. This was presented again in 1971 at Kalamazoo, Michigan, and in 1972 at South Dakota State University in Brookings. Skye presented a dance-lecture demonstration at the South Dakota State Teachers' Convention in Rapid City in 1970 and was a dance participant in the Brookings, South Dakota, Fine Arts Festival in the summers of 1972 and 1973. In 1973 and 1974 she conducted an Indian student dance project, "Dakota Wicohan," sponsored by the South Dakota Arts Council. In 1976 she was a dance soloist in the South Dakota Bi-Centennial Program under Marjorie Weeks at the Kennedy Center in Washington, D.C., performing a ritualistic modern dance that she choreographed to an interpretation of the Sioux national anthem by Curt Jurrens.

In 1987 Skye was appointed to the South Dakota Arts Council, and was re-appointed to a three-year term in 1988. She is a member of educational committees in South Dakota and Wisconsin. From 1989 to 1991 she served as director of multicultural affairs at St. Norbert College in DePere, Wisconsin. In the summer of 1991 she moved back to South Dakota.

References

"Keshena Native to Head SNC Minority Program." *Green Bay Press-Gazette*, December 22, 1989, B2.

"Q & A: Skye Sees Aiding Self-esteem as Important in New SNC Post." *Green Bay Press-Gazette*, January 14, 1990: A16.

Skye, Ferial Deer, Orla J. Christensen, and Joan T. England. "A Study of the Effects of a Culturally Based Dance Education Model on Identified Stress Factors in American Indian College Women." *Journal of American Indian Education* 29 (October 1989): 26–31.

—Jack Marken

SLIPPERJACK, RUBY (b. 1952), was born to Ojibwa parents in northern Ontario (Whitewater Lake). Growing up on her father's trapline, she developed a keen interest in storytelling through the stories told to her by elders. She remembers her mother making napkin dolls as props for stories the children invented. Later, while attending school in an isolated community, Slipperjack wrote little stories on any paper she could get her hands on, using pencils borrowed from school. She was a very clandestine author because writing and reading were not considered useful skills in a traditional hunting and trapping community. In her high school years, she attended Shingwauk Residential School in Sault Ste. Marie and high school in Thunder Bay. She later enrolled at Lakehead University, graduating with BA and BEd degrees in 1989 and receiving her MA degree in education in 1993.

Besides being an accomplished painter, Slipperjack won recognition as an outstandingly gifted and skilled writer for her first novel, *Honor the Sun*, despite the book's limited circulation as a small press product. The central character is Owl, whose experiences from the age of ten until about sixteen are related with great atmospheric density and realism based on careful observation of human nature and details concerning all beings that surround the girl. Social criticism is never presented as such, but the realistic depictions of living conditions in the nameless northern "bush" village by the railroad tracks carry a convincing humanist message, speaking out strongly against the abuse of women and children by males, be they drunken bullies or "nice" blue-eyed teachers. Owl's toughness and optimism carry her through the tragedy of a one-parent family gradually slipping apart like the community that surrounds its members. There is no lament and no attack; the book itself is a celebration of an indomitable will to survive and a creativity that is deeply rooted in a very traditional upbringing in the northern "bush," shared by many Native authors in Canada (Maria Campbell, Tomson Highway, Lenore Keeshig-Tobias). Often humorous and sometimes sad, *Honor the Sun* records an adolescent's curiosity about life's puzzles in a way that achieves a high degree of psychological universality. Owl's exact tribe or band identity is never disclosed, nor would such an ethnic label seem important in the community depicted.

In her second novel, *Silent Words* (1992), a boy named Danny runs away from an abusive stepmother and goes on a picaresque journey in search of his mother. Eventually he returns home to his father as a more mature and seasoned person. Again, Slipperjack manages unobtrusively to give readers a glimpses of various facets of aboriginal reality in contemporary Canada, dealing with Native traditional religion and the influence of pan-tribalism, Christianity, and other ideologies, as well as with traditional trapping and fishing, canoeing, and walking in the northern "wilderness." As in *Honor the Sun*, the psychological profundity and social realism of *Silent Words* are simply "there"—there is no open didacticism or preaching, and readers of any ethnic background will discover more and more layers in a complex parable of First Nations existence today that seems meant for "juvenile" readers only at first glance.

Ruby Slipperjack is married and has three daughters. She lives in Thunder Bay, Ontario.

References

Petrone, Penny. *Native Literature in Canada*. Toronto: Oxford University Press, 1990.

Slipperjack, Ruby. "Coal Oil, Crayons and Schoolbooks." In *All My Relations: An Anthology of Contemporary Canadian Native Fiction*. Edited by Thomas King. Pp. 27–37. Toronto: McClelland and Stewart, 1990.

————. *Honor the Sun*. Winnipeg, MN: Pemmican Press, 1987.

————. "Ruby Slipperjack." In *Contemporary Challenges: Conversations with Canadian Native Authors*. Edited by Hartmut Lutz. Pp. 203–216. Saskatoon, SK: Fifth House, 1991.

————. *Silent Words*. Saskatoon, SK: Fifth House, 1992.

—Hartmut Lutz

SMITH, BARBARA ELENE [Gua Gua La] (b. 1947), is the author of *Renewal: The Prophecy of Manu* and *Renewal Teoni's Giveaway: Book II*. Smith also goes by her Cherokee name, Gua Gua La. An artist, writer, researcher, and instructor, Smith holds a BA in anthropology from the University of Toledo and an MA in health education from the University of Michigan. She has lived in areas ranging from isolated Indian reserves in Canada's Northwest Territories to large cities to the desert of Arizona, experiencing the richness of society that she feels has broadened her perspective on life, peoples, and cultures.

Smith, a widow with four sons, is legally blind and must use special glasses to be able to read. She now lives and works with the Dene Nation in Canada.

References

Smith, Barbara. *Renewal: The Prophecy of Manu*. Pendicton, BC: Theytus Books, 1985.

————. *Renewal: Teoni's Giveaway: Book II*. Pendicton, BC: Theytus Books, 1986.

—Carlos Adams

SMITH, JAUNE QUICK-TO-SEE (b. 1940), of French–Cree/Shoshone descent, was born at St. Ignatius on the Flathead Indian Reservation in Montana. She received a BA degree in art education from Framingham State College (Massachusetts) in 1976 and an MA in painting from the University of New Mexico in 1980. She currently lives in New Mexico.

Smith is a painter whose abstract, nontraditional paintings reflect influences of de Kooning, Miro, Klee, and Picasso, but find their power in traditional images of landscapes, animals, cave paintings, and rock art. She says that she "makes parallels from the old world to contemporary art . . . like being able to speak two languages and find the word that is common to both." She is so successful at merging these disparate worlds that her work is known for its excellence in both New York and Native American art circles. It has been shown and installed in permanent collections throughout the United States and Europe. Smith has had shows at the Corcoran Art Gallery, Washington, D.C.; the Museum of Modern Art, San Francisco; and the Heard Museum, Phoenix. She has had over twenty-five solo exhibits and has been included in more than fifty group exhibits.

Her father, a horseman, horse trader, amateur artist, and collector of Charles Russell prints, was very influential in Smith's becoming an artist. The earthy colors of her paintings are inspired by the hues in the horse tack and bunkhouses of her father's world. The horse images so frequently found in her paintings can also be traced to her father's background as well as to artistic depictions of her own horse, Cheyenne.

Smith is an active lecturer and spokeswoman for traditional and contemporary Native American artist. She founded two artists cooperatives: Coup Marks, on the Flathead Reservation, and Grey Canyon Artists in Albuquerque, which has since become a national organization. She is a supporter of art and education for the Flat-head Reservation, providing scholarships and speaking on behalf of Salish–Kootenai College on the reservation. She has served as a panel member on the - Washington State and Idaho State Arts Commissions and a board member for ATLATL, an Indian organization for the arts. She was cocurator of an Indian wo-men's exhibit for AIR Gallery in New York and of "Sweetgrass, Cedar, and Sage" (with Harmony Hammond) at the Gallery of the American Indian Community House, New York. She also has been involved in founding and curating or jurying many other exhibits. Her awards include honorary professor (Beaumont chair), Washington University, St. Louis (1989); a fellowship from Western States Art Foundation (1988); and the Purchase Award of Arts and Letters, New York (1987).

References

American Indian Artists: Jaune Quick-to-See-Smith, Shoshone French Cree Painter. Produced by PBS Television. 30 min. Native American Public Broadcasting Consortium, 1982. Videocassette.

Bass, Ruth. "Jaune Quick-to-See Smith." *Art News* 83 (March 1984): 224.

Cohen, Ronny. "Jaune Quick-to-See Smith at Kornblee." *Art in America* 68 (March 1980): 116–117.

Galligan, Gregory. "Jaune Quick-to-See Smith: Crossing the Great Divide." *Arts* 60 (January 1986): 54–55.

———. "Jaune Quick-to-See Smith: Racing with the Moon." *Arts* 61 (January 1987): 82ff.

Hammond, Harmony, and Jaune Quick-to-See Smith. *Women of Sweetgrass, Cedar and Sage*. New York: Gallery of the American Indian Community House, 1985.

Hurst, Tricia. "Crossing Bridges." *Southwest Art* 10 (April 1981): 82–89.

Smith, Jaune Quick-to-See. *Jaune Quick-to-See Smith*. Long Beach, CA: University Art Museum, 1989.

Smith, Katherine. "Outside the Pueblo." *Portfolio* 4 (July/August 1982): 52–57.

Zwinger, Susan. "Viewpoint: An Interview with Artist Jaune Quick-to-See Smith." *El Palacio* 92 (Summer/Fall 1986): 51–54.

—Julie A. Russ

SMITH, KATHLEEN R. (b. 1939), tribal scholar, cultural consultant, artist, and writer, is the daughter of Steven Smith, Jr., an Olemitcha (Bodega) Miwok, and Lucyanna Lozinto Smith, a Hihilakawna (Dry Creek) Pomo, she was the sixth of eight children and the first to be born in a hospital (Sonoma County Hospital in Santa Rosa, California).

Smith earned a BFA from the San Francisco Art Institute in 1977 and has worked as a field hand, packing clerk, computer operator, and stockroom clerk.

Advised by her Uncle Manuel Cordova (Dry Creek Pomo) to "work for your people," and taught pride in her Indian heritage by her family, she has also been a Native American observer and archaeology technician, cultural consultant and interpreter, administrative assistant to the Model Urban Indian Centers Project in Washington, D.C., Sonoma County YMCA Native American outreach worker, and organizer of a Dry Creek Pomo language class.

Faced with an Army Corps of Engineers project that would flood the Warm Springs Valley, home to her ancestors for generations (Lake Sonoma was filled in 1985), Smith served as archaeology technician and coordinator for the Native American Advisory Council of the Warm Springs Cultural Resources Study, which sought to preserve and record the traditions and tribal history of her Dry Creek people. Smith's maternal great-grandmother, Juana Cook, was the last family member to live on that land, having been driven from it by U.S. Army troops in an 1850s "death march."

Smith has contributed to her community as a board member and vice chair of the Sonoma County Indian Health Project (1978–1984); a board member of California Indian Rural Health (1979–1981); a commissioner on the Sonoma County Status of Women Commission (1980–1982); a board member of the California State Rural Services Advisory Committee (1981–1983); and a charter member of the Sonoma County Women's Support Network (1981–1987).

Smith designed the logo for the National Women's History Project, was co-author of a biography of Indian health activist Annie Wauneka for the second grade social studies curriculum, and has been a columnist for *News from Native California*, a quarterly publication that provides an inside view of California Indian history and culture.

Smith received the Sonoma County YWCA's Women of Achievement Award in the art category in 1980 and a 1988 to 1989 California Arts Council traditional

Kathleen R. Smith

folk arts master apprentice grant for Pomo basket making. She has been featured in several publications, and her art work has been commissioned and shown throughout central California.

Smith is devoting herself to her painting, which has roots in her cultural traditions; writing a book about her people's foods and history; and coordinating an effort to obtain federal acknowledgment for her Bodega Miwok people. In 1991 she was appointed to the Board of the Olompali People of Olompali State Park.

References

Eisenberg, Bonnie, and Marylynne Slayen. "An Interview with Kathleen Smith." *Women's Voices* 6 (March 1981): 16–17.

Fellman, Debbie. "Indian Tribes Seek Unity, Identity." *The Contra Costa Times* [Walnut Creek, CA] August 22, 1990, A4.

Ingle, Schuyler. "Secrets of the Earth." *New West* 6 (July 1981): 88–93, 126–129.

Johnson, Holly. "Artists Remain Loyal to Heritage." *Sacramento Union*, August 25, 1990, D1.

Ortiz, Bev. "The Art of Life: An Interview with Five Smith Artists." *News from Native California* 3 (May/June 1989): 8–11.

———. Oral and taped interviews with Kathleen Smith, 1987–1990.

Wyss, Dennis. "Miwok Bands Mount Drive for Rights, Respect, Dignity." *Marin Independent Journal* [Novato, CA], July 30, 1990, A1, A7.

—*Bev Ortiz*

SNEVE, VIRGINIA DRIVING HAWK (b. 1933), has written several novels with Native American characters, including *Jimmy Yellow Hawk* and *High Elk's Treasure;*

Virginia Driving Hawk Sneve

received the Distinguished Alumnus Award from South Dakota State University; and was named 1975 Woman of Achievement by the National Federation of Press Women. Born and raised on the Rosebud Reservation, she is an enrolled member of the Rosebud Sioux tribe, attended Bureau of Indian Affairs day schools on the reservation, and graduated from St. Mary's High School for Indian Girls in Springfield, South Dakota, in 1950. She received a BS (1954) and MEd (1969) from South Dakota State University at Brookings.

Sneve taught music and English at a public high school and in a Pierre junior high, as well as English, speech, and drama at the Flandreau Indian School, where she later served as a guidance counselor. She has worked as a consultant producer–writer for South Dakota Public Broadcasting, creating television scripts stressing the ethnic pride and cultural traditions of Native Americans. She is the secondary Title V counselor for the Rapid City School District and a part-time instructor in English for Ogalala Lakota College, Rapid City Extension Services.

Sneve (rhymes with "navy") is married to Vance M. Sneve, a retired Bureau of Indian Affairs employee, who now owns an antiques business; they have three children and four grandchildren.

Sneve has stated that "In my writing, both fiction and nonfiction, I try to present an accurate portrayal of American Indian life as I have known it. I also attempt to interpret history from the viewpoint of the American Indian. In doing so, I hope to correct the many misconceptions and untruths which have been too long perpetrated by non–Indian authors who have written about us."

References

Blicksilver, Edith, ed. *The Ethnic American Woman: Problems, Protests, Lifestyle.* Dubuque, IA: Kendall/Hunt, 1978.

Sioux Falls Argus-Leader, August 5, 1973, C8.

Sneve, Virginia Driving Hawk. *Betrayed.* New York: Holiday House, 1974.

———. *The Chichi HooHoo Bogeyman.* New York: Holiday House, 1975. Reprint, Lincoln: University of Nebraska Press/Bison Books, 1993.

———. *Completing the Circle.* Lincoln: University of Nebraska Press, 1995.

———. *Dancing Teepees.* New York: Holiday House, 1989.

———. The First American series: *The Sioux* (1993); *The Navajos* (1993); *The Seminoles* (1994); *The Nez Perce* (1994); *The Hopis* (1995); *The Iroquois* (1995); *The Cherokees* (1996); *The Cheyennes* (1996). New York: Holiday House.

———. *High Elk's Treasure.* New York: Holiday House, 1972. Reprint, New York: Holiday House, 1996.

———. *Jimmy Yellow Hawk.* New York: Holiday House, 1972.

———. Letter to Edith Blicksilver, July 30, 1990.

———. *The Trickster and the Troll.* Lincoln: University of Nebraska Press, 1977.

———. *When Thunders Spoke.* New York: Holiday House, 1974. Reprint, with illustrations by Oren Lyons, Lincoln: University of Nebraska Press/Bison Books, 1993.

—Edith Blicksilver

SOMERSAL, LAURA (1892–1990), tribal scholar, cultural consultant, Indian hand-game player, and renowned basket weaver, teacher, and lecturer, was born to Mary John Fish Eli (Alexander Valley Wappo) and Bill Fish (Dry Creek Pomo) on the Stone Ranch outside Geyserville, California, where her father was working. Baptized Dolores Ellen Fish in Healdsburg at age five, Somersal was the sixth of seven children. She had two older brothers, Tony Jack and George, and a younger sister Josephine. Three other siblings died before she was born; she also had a half brother, Will Fish. Her first home was a brush house; her last was a trailer at the Dry Creek Rancheria.

Wappo was Somersal's first language. Fluent in several Indian dialects as different as English and Russian, she also understood Spanish and spoke English, learning her "alphabets" from a disabled boy she cared for as a teenager.

Somersal picked hops and fruit throughout her youth; in her teens she worked as a housekeeper at several ranches. Married for the first time at age sixteen and several times thereafter, Somersal had no children of her own but raised several relatives and a foster son.

At about age eight or nine, she began learning to weave baskets from her uncle, Jack Woho (Wappo), later studying its intricacies under the tutelage of her sister-in-law Rosie, "Fernando's daughter." Lacking formal education (Indians weren't then allowed to attend public schools, and her blind mother kept her from being sent to Indian school), Somersal was able to devote herself to her culture. A respected tribal scholar, she taught and lectured about Pomo/Wappo basketry throughout California, including institutions of higher learning, and once traveled to Washington, D.C., to identify baskets for the Smithsonian Institution.

Somersal was instrumental in preserving the Wappo language, overcoming the objections of some of her people to sharing that language with non–Indians; she collaborated with the linguist Jesse O. Sawyer to publish a Wappo/English dictionary in 1965 and other smaller works. She was featured in numerous articles as well as a film, and she was instrumental in a project to transplant basketry and other native plants from an area that the Army Corps of Engineers planned to flood

Laura Somersal

(now Lake Sonoma). Her mother and her brother George were principal consultants for Harold E. Driver's 1936 *Wappo Ethnography*.

In 1978 Somersal was honored with the first Woman of Achievement Award by the Sonoma County Commission on the Status of Women, and received recognition from Women of Color as a woman who had done the most for her community. Her contributions to preservation of Wappo culture were unparalleled. The anthropologist David Peri said of her in 1980: "She's a Picasso of Indian basketweaving, and an Einstein in terms of Indian culture."

References

Beard, Yolande S. *The Wappo: A Report*. Banning, CA: Malki Museum Press, 1979.

Ortiz, Bev. Personal communication with Bette Holmes, 1990.

———. Oral and taped interviews with Laura Somersal, 1985–1990.

———. "With Respect: Laura Fish Somersal." *News from Native California* 3 (November 1990/January 1991): 4–5.

Sawyer, Jesse O. *English-Wappo Vocabulary*. Berkeley: University of California Press, 1965.

Smith, Ray. "Weaving a Future from the Past." *The Press Democrat* [Santa Rosa, CA], October 23, 1980, B1, 7.

—*Bev Ortiz*

STANLEY, DOROTHY AMORA (1924–1990), tribal scholar, cultural consultant, educator, tribal chair, and political activist, was born in Los Angeles, to Alice Carsoner Pruitt and Raymond Dudley. Her maternal grandparents and great-grandmother were descended from families of hereditary Northern Miwok leaders.

Stanley's youth was spent at Bald Rock (near Twain Harte) and the Tuolumne Mewuk Rancheria, where she was raised by her mother; her stepfather, Raymond Fuller; her aunt and uncle Etta and Richard Fuller; and Raymond's mother, Annie Jack Fuller, the wife of Chief William Fuller and Stanley's primary teacher of Northern Miwok culture.

Brought up speaking Northern and Central Miwok, Stanley learned English in public school and attended the Bureau of Indian Affairs boarding school at Stewart, Nevada, as a teenager. Upon graduation, she worked at jobs that included cashier, strawberry picker, and candymaker, eventually becoming employed for twenty-five years as an operator/supervisor for Pacific Telephone.

In the early 1970s Stanley and her fourth husband, Elmer Stanley (Southern Miwok), her teenage sweetheart, returned to the Sierra Nevada. There she chaired the Acorn Festival of the Tuolumne Mewuk Rancheria (1973); was appointed to the Tuolumne County Commission on Aging (1974–1975); served on the Business Committee of the Tuolumne Mewuk Tribal Council (1975–1976); was Native American liaison for the Department of Interior Heritage Conservation and Recreation Services for the New Melones Dam Project (1975–1976); was appointed to the Advisory Council for Area Technical Agency for Aging (1975–1976); served as project director for the Tuolumne Indian Rural Health

Project (1976–1977); and was elected Tuolumne Mewuk Tribal Council chair (1980). Stanley also served on the boards of various employment, mental health, alcoholism, Indian housing, and Indian education agencies and commissions, and was once vice chair of the Advisory Board of the Bureau of Indian Affairs Central Agency. She also fought for years to preserve her people's archaeological sites.

Stanley was a consultant for linguists, ethnographers, archaeologists, and anthropologists, and demonstrated and lectured about her culture throughout the state and as far away as Washington, D.C. In 1980 and 1981 she supervised the Miwok Indian Village at a West Side lumber company, and from 1982 to 1985 she supervised the Indian Cultural Program at Yosemite National Park.

Stanley raised seven children, made substantial contributions to the preservation and continuance of Miwok culture, and worked extensively on behalf of her community. As the ethnographer Craig Bates put it, "She was a link with a people and a past."

References

Bates, Craig. "With Respect: Dorothy Stanley." *News from Native California* 5 (November 1990/January 1991): 6–8.

Ortiz, Bev. Personal communication with Craig Bates, 1990.

———. Oral and taped interviews with Dorothy Stanley, 1988.

———. "Skills Remembered, Cherished, and Continued: Northern Sierra Miwok Food Preparation and Soaproot Brush Making." *News from Native California* 4 (Spring 1990): 16–19.

—*Bev Ortiz*

STEELE, LOIS FISTER (b. 1939), enrolled member of the Fort Peck Assiniboine tribe, began her career as an educator teaching at public schools in various Indian communities in Montana between 1963 and 1969. Although her teaching experience ranges widely—from being an instructor and dean of women at Dawson Community College in Glendive, Montana (1970–1973), to being assistant professor of family at the University of North Dakota Medical School (1984–1985) and clinical lecturer at the University of Arizona, Department of Family and Community Medicine (1986–present)—Steele is best known for her role as director (and consultant) of the Indians into Medicine Program (INMED) at the University of North Dakota (1973–1985). INMED is a unique program that enables young American Indians to pursue undergraduate science degrees and to be placed in schools where they can successfully complete their training for careers in medicine and other health professions. During Steele's years at INMED, she expanded the budget and instituted an outreach program to Indian youth on reservations through INMED's Traveling Medicine Show, featuring puppets and a coloring book based on the traditional mythical figures Coyote and Turtle. At the time INMED began, there were only sixteen Indian physicians in the nation; through INMED efforts, more than sixty Indians have received degrees in medicine and others have received degrees in allied health professions.

Born in Washington, D.C., in 1939, the first daughter of Russell Fister, a Bureau of Indian Affairs official, and Winona Simons (Assiniboine), Steele grew up on the Fort Peck Reservation at Poplar, Montana. She earned a BA from Colorado College in 1961, an MS in science teaching from the University of Montana in 1969, and a medical doctorate from the University of Minnesota in 1978.

After thirteen years of teaching in various capacities and her first term as director of INMED, Steele decided to become a medical doctor. She entered the University of Minnesota Medical School at Duluth, a two-year program at the end of which she earned the Lampson Award as most valuable woman medical student. She finished her studies on the Minneapolis campus in 1978 and fulfilled her residency requirements at Methodist Hospital in Minneapolis and at the University of North Dakota, Grand Forks, in 1984, the latter four years of which she was again director of INMED. She is a board-certified family medicine physician.

Steele served as clinical director for the Pascua Yaqui tribe of Tucson, Arizona, from 1986 to 1991, working to promote the development of a tribally controlled health delivery system while also conducting research on American Indian health concerns. She has coauthored many articles on health research. She developed the Yaqui clinic's substance abuse program, which included methadone maintenance and traditional healing ceremonies, and helped to develop outreach programs for immunizations, Pap smears, and mammograms as well as animal control and sanitation. Currently Steele serves as clinical specialty consultant in areas of colposcopy and women's health, tobacco abuse prevention, clinical research, and medical information for the Tucson Area Indian Health Service (IHS), and as division director of medical media and of information systems development, both for the Tucson IHS.

Steele has received many awards: a commendation medal from the United States Public Health Service for development of AIDS prevention and methadone demonstration programs for the Pascua Yaqui tribe (1993), the American Medical Association's Physician Recognition Award (1991–1994), the Indian Health Service Award for Health Promotion and Disease Prevention Work (1989), the American Indian Science and Engineering Society's Ely Parker Award (1989), the Indian Health Service Award, Aberdeen area (1983), the Distinguished Achievement Award of the Rocky Mountain College Alumni Association (1981), and the Outstanding Educator of America Award (1970).

References

Katz, Jane, ed. *Messengers of the Wind: Native American Women Tell Their Life Stories*. New York: Ballantine, 1995.

Steele, Lois F. "Cross-Cultural Perspectives in Patient Education: Native Americans." In *Patient Education in the Primary Care Setting*. Edited by Mary Nell Currie and Barbara Widmar. Pp. 95–99. Kansas City, MO: St. Mary's Hospital, 1985.

———, ed. *Medicine Women*. Grand Forks: INMED, University of North Dakota, 1985.

—Kathryn W. Shanley

STEWART, IRENE [Glinezbah, Goes to War with] (b. 1907), politician and activist, was born near Canyon de Chelly, on the Navajo Reservation in northern Arizona, to Elenor Bancroft, a weaver, and Jake Watchman, a medicine man. After the death of her mother in 1911, Stewart went to live with her grandmother, who taught her the responsibilities of Navajo a woman.

At the insistence of government officials and the request of her father, Stewart was removed from her grandmother's home and was taken to the Fort Defiance Indian School, from which she graduated in 1922. She continued her education at the Haskell Institute in Lawrence, Kansas, and the Albuquerque Indian School, receiving her diploma in home economics from the latter in 1929. Later that year, Stewart enrolled in a nine-month Bible course in California designed to train assistant missionaries for the Presbyterian Church, an education she continues to draw upon in her work with the Presbyterian Mission in Chinle, Arizona.

While in California, Stewart met and married a member of the Oneida tribe. They had four sons, but the marriage was later dissolved due to differences. In 1942 Stewart married Greyeyes, a Navajo medicine man who was much older than she and followed traditional Navajo customs; this union provided Stewart with the strength and confidence to run for the Tribal Council in 1955. Although she lost this election by a narrow margin, she went on to serve as council secretary for fifteen years.

Stewart has served the Navajo tribe as a warehouse supervisor, a member of the Children's Welfare Foundation, a district loan representative for the Navajo Tribal Council, and as a Chinle representative to the Navajo Nation's Council on Aging.

Reference

Stewart, Irene. *A Voice in Her Tribe: A Navajo Woman's Own Story*. Edited by Doris Ostrander Dawdy and Mary Shepardson. Socorro, NM: Ballena Press, 1980.

—*Michelle Savoy*

STROUD, VIRGINIA (b. 1949), was born in Madera, California, where she lived with a Kiowa family after the deaths of her parents. She later moved to Oklahoma, where she attended Bacone Junior College (1969–1979) and the University of Oklahoma (1971–1976), where she majored in art education. During her college years she was named Cherokee Tribal Princess (1969–1970), Miss National Congress of American Indians (1970–1971), and Miss Indian America (1971).

In spite of urging by an art professor to quit painting Indian subjects, Stroud has created a style of painting that depicts images of everyday life in Indian America. Referring to herself as a "visual orator," she produces work that knows no cultural or tribal boundaries. She paints scenes with Navajo dancers and weavers, Apache sunflower seed gatherers, and Cherokees in wagons. Regardless of the subject, Stroud's work is warm and carries a touch of whimsy, humor, and joy. Her painting *Where from Here*, described as a self-portrait, illustrates the problem of identity faced by many Native Americans and Native American artists today. According to Stroud, as she is quoted in Wade and Strickland: "Indians live in a world where they always have to explain themselves. . . . You work, you accomplish, and you improve your standard of living, and then non–Indians say you aren't Indian any more." For Stroud, art is the medium through which she deals with herself and the world she must live in: "[W]ithout anything to paint and record, we would be drifting, searching for where we fit in."

Stroud's work has drawn a loyal and enthusiastic following. In 1970 she won first prize at the American Indian Artists Exhibition at the Philbrook Art Center in Tulsa, Oklahoma, the youngest artist to receive that prize. Since then she has regularly won honors at the Heard Museum in Phoenix and the Philbrook; in 1982 she was named Artist of the Year by the Indian Arts and Crafts Association. Her work is in the permanent collections at the Heard Museum, the Philbrook Art Center, and the Minneapolis Institute of Art. Her work is collected by many individuals, either as originals or reproductions. She has served as artist-in-residence for the Oklahoma Arts and Humanities Council and has consulted with the Oklahoma Indian Education Association.

References

Jacka, Lois Essary, and Jerry Jacka. *Beyond Tradition: Contemporary Indian Art and Its Evolution.* Flagstaff, AZ: Northland Press, 1988.

Stroud, Virginia. Biographical file. McFarlin Library, University of Tulsa.

————. Biographical file. Philbrook Art Center and Special Collections Library, Tulsa, OK.

————. *Doesn't Fall off His Horse.* New York: Dial Books for Young Readers, 1994.

————. *The Path of the Quiet Elk: A Native American Alphabet Book.* New York: Dial Books for Young Readers, 1996.

————. *A Walk to the Great Mystery.* New York: Dial Books for Young Readers, 1995.

"Virginia Alice Stroud." In *Native American Art Sampler: A Patchwork of Contemporary Art.* Edited by Paul Speckled Rock and Rosemary Speckled Rock. Santa Fe, NM: Wheelwright Museum of Indian Art, 1982.

"Virginia Stroud: Artist Profile." *Four Winds* (Winter 1980): 58–61.

Wade, Edwin L., and Rennard Strickland. *Magic Images: Contemporary Native American Art.* Norman: Philbrook Art Center/University of Oklahoma, 1981.

—*Laura Graves*

SUTTON, CATHERINE [Nahnebahwequay, Upright Woman] (1824–1865), was the daughter of Mary Crane and Bunch Sonego of the Mississaugas, as the settlers called the Ojibwas living on the north shore of Lake Ontario. The family was converted to Christianity, and in the spring of 1826 moved to the Credit River Indian mission just east of Toronto. In the spring of 1837, Sutton accompanied her uncle, the Reverend Peter Jones, a celebrated Ojibwa Methodist missionary, and his English-born wife, Elizabeth, to England. She returned to Canada the next year, and in January 1839, she married an English shoemaker, William Sutton. For six years the couple lived at the Credit River Indian village, where they started their family, and Catherine acted as a Methodist Sunday school class leader. Her fluency in the English language also made her a useful interpreter.

In the summer of 1845, Sutton was adopted by the Newash band at Owen Sound and given title to two hundred acres of land, forty to fifty of which the Suttons brought into a good state of cultivation. In 1852 the family moved to the Garden River Reserve near Sault Ste. Marie, where William superintended the working of a model farm for the benefit of the Indians. Two years later they went to Michigan, where he was in charge of making improvements to a Methodist mission.

In 1857, when the family returned to Owen Sound, they found their property sold, surveyed, and laid out in lots for sale. Catherine was refused a share of the Newash band's annuities because she had married a non–Native and had been absent from the country. Later the same year she was not allowed to buy back her land at public sale because she was Indian.

At a General Council of the Chiefs in Rama, Ontario, in July 1859, Sutton was chosen as their special envoy to petition the British Crown in person for a change in the laws governing landownership. Her election to such a high rank was a great honor for Sutton.

To raise money for the overseas journey and to enlist support for her cause, Sutton gave a series of talks in Canada and the United States. This was no easy feat in a strange city like New York, where she knew no one. But her religious fervor, regal bearing, and intense dedication to her cause soon won her the support of a group of New York Quakers, who financed her trip to England. The *New York Tribune* reported her lecture to Brooklyn's Society of Friends.

In London, too, Sutton captured the imagination of the press as well as the sponsorship of the colonial secretary, the Duke of Newcastle, and several Quaker members of Parliament. On June 19, 1860, Sutton met Queen Victoria. Awestruck and nervous, she forgot to kiss the queen's extended hand. Of the visit, the queen wrote in her private journal, "She speaks English quite well, and is come on behalf of her tribe to petition against some grievance as regards their land." Two months later, while still in England, Sutton gave birth to a son.

As a result of the direct intervention of the British government, the Suttons were granted a deed for three lots in the newly formed Sarawak Township. Sutton continued her activism, writing letters of protest to the editors of newspapers and to her Quaker friends in England, who had them included in Quaker publications, until her death in 1865.

Throughout her life Sutton was an indefatigable worker for the rights of her people, one of the few Indian women of her time to do so publicly. In the long and bitter history of aboriginal land claims in Canada, Catherine Sutton's contribution ranks as one of the earliest.

References

Christian Guardian, January 12, 1848; April 2 and May 28, 1862; November 8, 1865.

Daily Sun Times [Owen Sound, ON], August 30, 1960.

Journal of William Sutton. PAC, R.G. 10, vol. 2877, file 177181. Greg County and Owen Sound Museum, Owen Sound, ON.

Sarawak Township and Keppel Township 1861 Census. R.G. 31, Greg County and Owen Sound Museum, Owen Sound, ON.

Smith, Donald B. *Dictionary of Canadian Biography*. Vol. 9. Toronto: University of Toronto Press, 1976.

"Wesleyan Methodist Church in Canada." Missionary Society *Annual Report*. Toronto: The Society, 1845–1846.

—S. Penny Petrone

SWAN, MADONNA [Madonna Mary Swan Abdalla] (b. 1928), was born on the Cheyenne River Reservation of the Lakota Sioux, and has spent most of her life in Cherry Creek, South Dakota. She went to mission school at Immaculate Conception School in Stephan, South Dakota. In 1944 she was diagnosed with tuberculosis and spent the next six years at the Sioux Sanitorium in Rapid City. She was admitted to the Sanitor at Custer, the "white" TB sanitorium, in September 1950. There, Swan received more advanced treatment. Though the tuberculosis was cured, she has remained susceptible to colds and pneumonia throughout her life. Her autobiography is a testament to the courage and determination with which she faced both the disease and the stigma attached to it.

Despite her health problems, Swan completed her GED, obtained a certificate in horology (clock and watch repair), and completed numerous hours toward a bachelor's degree in education. After leaving the sanitorium, she held several clerical and jewelry repair positions. She accepted a teaching position in 1966 in the Head Start program on the reservation; however, poor health forced her to resign in 1971. She again attempted to complete her bachelor's degree in 1974, taking classes at the University of South Dakota, but again her health failed. Swan remained active, however, serving on the board of the Tri-Community Development Cooperative and tribal employee relations committees. In 1983 Swan received the North American Indian Woman of the Year award.

Swan's autobiography is an important historical document that chronicles Lakota worldviews and values, humanizes tuberculosis statistics, and documents Lakota reservation life in the twentieth century.

Reference

St. Pierre, Mark, ed. *Madonna Swan: A Lakota Woman's Story*. Norman: University of Oklahoma Press, 1991.

—Pattiann Frinzi

SWENTZELL, RINA [Rina Naranjo] (b. 1939), architecture historian and independent scholar, was born in Santa Clara Pueblo, New Mexico, the third of eight children of Rose and Michael Naranjo, a Santa Clara (Tewa) family noted for its artistic and scholarly creativity. After earning her BA in education from New Mexico Highlands University, she taught for several years in public schools and Pueblo day schools. Entering graduate school at the University of New Mexico, she earned her MA in architecture in 1976 and, as a Ford Foundation fellow, her PhD in American Studies in 1982.

The consistent intention of Swentzell's many and diverse books and articles is explication of a Pueblo worldview, emphasizing how basic cultural values are expressed in architecture, art, language, mythology, and social structures, including the family. She has collaborated with several other scholars, most recently her siblings Tessie Naranjo and Tito Naranjo, with whom, as Katrin Lamon Scholars at the School of American Research in Santa Fe in 1995 to 1996, she wrote an analysis of gender as a basic organizing principle of reciprocity in traditional Santa Clara, and how contact with Western culture has affected this. Swentzell and Lekson's *Ancient Land, Ancestral Places* won the 1995 Southwest Book Award of the Border Regional Library Association.

Swentzell is a doer as well as a thinker and a writer. After analyzing the culturally disruptive effects of the institutional design of federal Indian schools, she became involved in the renovation of several Southwestern schools, encouraging student and community participation to make their buildings reflect Native traditions more closely. Her work in this area led to a New Mexico Historic Preservation Award in 1993. Combining expertise as architect and educator, Swentzell has designed schools and curricula that communicate cultural values. She is internationally sought after as a speaker and has consulted on many projects, including museum exhibitions and television documentaries. Swentzell has served on planning committees and governing boards for the Pueblos, the state of New Mexico, and her profession of architecture. She has been honored as Alumna of the Year by the University of New Mexico Indian Alumni chapter, and as 1989 International Woman by UNM's Women Studies Program. She also won a Scholar Award from the New Mexico Endowment for the Humanities in 1994.

Married, with three daughters and a son, and ten grandchildren, Swentzell lives outside Santa Fe, New Mexico, in a house she and her family designed and built. In her life, as well as in her work, she consistently strives to embody traditional Pueblo values of connection, nurturing, and harmony. These qualities, together with her warmth, wisdom, and clarity of expression, have earned her widespread and sincere respect.

References

Gillette, Jane Brown. "On Her Own Terms." *Historic Preservation* 6 (November/December 1992): 26–33, 84–86.

Lichtenstein, Grace. "The Evolution of a Craft Tradition: Three Generations of Naranjo Women." *Ms.* (April 1983): 59–60, 92.

Peterson, Susan. *Pottery by American Indian Women: The Legacy of Generations.* New York: Abbeville Press, 1997.

Swentzell, Rina. *Children of Clay.* Minneapolis, MN: Lerner Publications, 1992.

———. "A Comparison of Basic Incompatibilities Between European/American and Traditional Pueblo World-View and Value System." PhD diss., University of New Mexico, 1982.

Swentzell, Rina, with J. J. Brody. *To Touch the Past: The Painted Pottery of the Mimbres People.* New York: Hudson Hills Press, 1995.

Swentzell, Rina, and Stephen Lekson. *Ancient Land, Ancestral Places: Paul Logsdon in the Pueblo Southwest.* Santa Fe: Museum of New Mexico Press, 1993.

Swentzell, Rina, with Tessie Naranjo and Tito Naranjo. *Sacred to Secular: The Transformation of a Gendered Pueblo World.*

Swentzell, Rina, and Tito Naranjo. "Nurturing: The Gia at Santa Clara Pueblo." *El Palacio* 92 (Summer/Fall 1986): 35–39.

—Helen M. Bannan

T

TALLCHIEF, MARIA (b. 1925), famed Indian ballerina, teacher, and ballet company director, was awarded a prestigious Kennedy Center Honor in 1996. She is best known for her interpretation of the title role of *Firebird* (1949), a role George Balanchine created especially to suit her strength, speed, and athleticism.

Born to an Osage father and Scotch–Irish mother in Fairfax, Oklahoma, Tallchief was raised in Beverly Hills, California, where she received instruction in piano and ballet and trained with Bronislava Nijinska. In 1942 she joined Ballet Russe de Monte Carlo, later becoming a soloist and performing in *Serenade, Gaîté Parisienne*, and *Schéhérazade*.

George Balanchine first noticed Tallchief while choreographing for Ballet Russe, and in 1947 he offered her a position in his new company, Ballet Society, which evolved into the New York City Ballet. She married Balanchine at age twenty, and although the marriage was annulled in 1951, she continued dancing with the New York City Ballet through 1965. While with the company Tallchief performed in numerous pieces, including *Orpheus, The Guests, and Divertimento;* she was a principal dancer in *Miss Julie, The Guests, Theme and Variations*, and *Allegro Brillante*, and danced the role of the Sugarplum Fairy in *The Nutcracker*. Her partners included Igor Youskevitch, André Eglevsky, Francisco Moncion, Nicholas Magallanes, Erik Bruhn, Jerome Robbins, and Rudolf Nureyev.

After her marriage to Balanchine was annulled in 1951, Tallchief married Emourza Natirboff. That marriage ended in 1954, the year Ballet Russe de Monte Carlo offered her a substantial salary to be a guest artist with them for two years. In 1956 she married Henry Paschen, a Chicago businessman with whom she had a daughter, Elise Maria. In 1960 to 1961, she danced and toured as a guest artist with American Ballet Theatre.

In October 1965 Tallchief retired from the New York City Ballet because she felt Balanchine was excluding her from principal roles. In celebration of the sixtieth anniversary of Oklahoma statehood in 1967, Tallchief, along with other Oklahoma ballerinas including her younger sister Marjorie, were honored with a performance entitled *Four Moons*. In 1953, the Osage tribe named had her honorary princess.

Tallchief returned to Chicago after retiring from performance. In 1974 the Chicago Lyric Opera asked her to establish a ballet school and company, and to be the artistic director of the Chicago Lyric Opera Ballet. When the Lyric Opera disbanded the ballet company because of financial difficulties, Tallchief started her own school and company, the Chicago City Ballet. The school used Balanchine's teaching methods and included many of his ballets in the company's repertoire; despite praise from critics, however, it folded in 1987. In 1990 Tallchief was featured in a film titled *Dancing for Mr. B: Six Balanchine Ballerinas.*

References

Croce, Arlene. "All American." *The New Yorker* (December 9, 1996): 80.

Finney, Frank. "Maria Tallchief in History: Oklahoma's Own Ballerina." *Chronicles of Oklahoma* 38 (1960): 8–11.

Gruen, John. "Tallchief and the Chicago City Ballet." *Dance* 58 (December 1984): HC25–HC26.

Kufrin, Joan. *Uncommon Women.* Piscataway, NJ: New Century Publishers, 1981.

Livingston, Lilli Cockerville. *American Indian Ballerinas.* Norman: University of Oklahoma Press, 1997.

Maynard, Olga. *Bird of Fire: The Story of Maria Tallchief.* New York: Dodd, Mead, 1961.

McMillan, Florri. "The Lady in the Black Pajamas." *Chicago* 29 (November 1980).

Tallchief, Maria. *Tallchief: America's Prima Ballerina.* New York: Viking, 1999.

—*Dorie S. Goldman*

TALLCHIEF, MARJORIE (b. 1927), was the third child of Ruth and Alex Tallchief of the Osage tribe. She debuted as a ballerina in 1944 with Lucia Chase and Richard Pleasent's Ballet Theatre in Montreal, Canada. Her skill as a dancer gained her a contract that same year with the Ballet Theatre in New York City. Through her devotion to dance rather than to success, her status as a ballerina rose until in the 1946 to 1947 season she attained the rank of leading soloist for the Original Ballet Russe. In 1947 Tallchief joined the Marquis de Cuevas's Nouveau Ballet de Monte Carlo, where she met her future husband, George Skibine.

After several years with the Ballet de Monte Carlo, interrupted briefly for the birth of twin sons, Tallchief became the first American to attain the rank of *première danseuse étoile* for the Paris Opera Ballet (1957–1962). She continued her career through appearances with several ballet companies until her retirement in 1966.

References

Livingston, Lili Cockerille. *American Indian Ballerinas.* Norman: University of Oklahoma Press, 1997.

"Moon Maidens." *Newsweek* (November 6, 1967): 101–102.

—*Carlos Adams*

TALLMOUNTAIN, MARY (1918–1994), of Athabaskan/Russian/Irish lineage, was born in the last year of World War I, one hundred miles south of the Arctic Circle and two hundred miles west of Fairbanks, Alaska. On a clear day in Nulato, she could see Siberia. TallMountain remembers "pure, wonderful snow" and the Yukon River going by "incessantly." Her mother contracted tuberculosis, and Tall-

Mountain was adopted "outside" at the age of six, psychically ripped from her Native family. It would be fifty years before she could return.

In the early 1970s Paula Gunn Allen found TallMountain working as a secretary in San Francisco, and a curious writerly adoption clicked into place. For a year and a half, TallMountain wrote sixteen hours a day on a typewriter; each Tuesday she brought her work to Allen for tutoring. It was a rebirth of gifted childhood, an elder writer's awakening. Paula Allen introduces *The Light on the Tent Wall: A Bridging* (1990): "Who is this woman, this survivor, this half-breed, this poet, this friend? If you know the land of her origins and the cadences of the People, if you recall the rhythm of Roman liturgy, the solemnity of the Mass, if you read this collection with care, hearing the eerie, powerful silences that surround the words, you will know who she is, what extinction is, and what survival engenders." With pointillist country diction and rattling tree-branch rhythms, TallMountain's voice could sweeten the pit of winter. She counterpoints loss with come-on lyrical lilts. This self-taught writer knows where her cadences lie, when the currents run deep, where the accents trip off the consonants.

The controlling motif of TallMountain's work is a long homecoming poem, "Koyukons Heading Home." Never spending more than two years in any job or dwelling, for over three-quarters of a century TallMountain carried a native trust that would not quit or submit, a Franciscan grit, a Catholic aboriginal faith. She enjoyed her newfound focus and status as a Native elder with words for the younger. She suffered through terrible losses—her childhood untimely torn from the Yukon, her mother's death from tuberculosis, her brother's death from the same disease (she never saw a second brother sent to live in another village), her father's disappearance for sixty years until TallMountain found him in Phoenix, her sense of estrangement on the "outside" of the West Coast, the financial ruin and death of her adoptive physician father when she was a teenager during the Depression, her adoptive mother's suicide not long after, joblessness and hard times and finally legal secretarial work to try to stabilize her life, battles with depression and broken hearts and alcoholism, two bouts with cancer, a quadruple heart bypass . . . from which she awoke laughing, the doctors told her. "In her way TallMountain is Coyote," Allen wrote, "and like that quintessential old survivor, she knows that if you're going to face death, and if you're to engage the sacred, you'd better have your sense of humor intact."

TallMountain died September 2, 1994, in Petaluma, California. She survived much grief and passion, many insights and illnesses, gaining little money or recognition in her own time. The TallMountain Circle, sponsored by the Tenderloin Reflection and Education Center in San Francisco, keeps this singular woman's spirit alive through her writings and the works of those following her. In addition to a complete bibliography of her writings, it has reissued *A Quick Brush of Wings, Listen to the Night: Poems for the Animal Spirits of Mother Earth,* haiku and other poetic forms, *Goddesses We Ain't!: Tenderloin Women Writers* (1992), and *Celebrating Mary TallMountain: A Memorial Tribute* (1995).

References

Allen, Paula Gunn. Introduction to *The Light on the Tent Wall: A Bridging*, by Mary TallMountain. Native American Series, no. 8. Los Angeles: UCLA American Indian Studies Center, 1990.

————, ed. *Spider Woman's Granddaughters: Traditional Tales and Contemporary Writing by Native American Women*. Boston: Beacon Press, 1989.

Bledsoe, Lucy, ed. *Goddesses We Ain't*. San Francisco: Freedom Voices, 1992.

Brant, Beth, ed. *A Gathering of Spirit: Writing and Art by North American Indian Women*. Ithacan, NY: Firebrand Books, 1988.

Green, Rayna, ed. *That's What She Said: Contemporary Poetry and Fiction by Native American Women*. Bloomington: Indiana University Press, 1984.

Lincoln, Kenneth. *Indi'n Humor: Bicultural Play in Native America*. New York: Oxford University Press, 1991.

Nelson, Richard K. *Make Prayers to the Raven: A Koyukon View of the Northern Forest*. Chicago: University of Chicago Press, 1983.

TallMountain, Mary. *Continuum*. Marvin, SD: Blue Cloud Press, 1988.

————. *haiku and other poetic forms*. Edited by Kitty Costello. San Francisco: Grow Like Weeds Press, 1996.

————. *The Light on the Tent Wall: A Bridging*. Introduction by Paula Gunn Allen. UCLA Native American Series, no. 8. Los Angeles: UCLA American Indian Studies Center, 1990.

————. *Listen to the Night*. San Francisco: The TallMountain Circle, 1995.

————. *Matrilineal Cycle*. Oakland, CA: Red Star Black Rose Printing, 1990.

————. *There Is No Word for Goodbye*. Marvin SD: Blue Cloud Press, 1982.

————. *A Quick Brush of Wings*. San Francisco: Freedom Voices Publications, 1991.

————. "You Can Go Home Again: A Sequence." In *I Tell You Now: Autobiographical Essays by Native American Writers*. Edited by Brian Swan and Arnold Krupat. Pp. 1–13. Lincoln: University of Nebraska Press, 1987.

—Kenneth Lincoln

TANTAQUIDGEON, GLADYS (b. 1899), Mohegan scholar of Algonquian Indian cultures and descendant of the seventeenth-century sachem Uncas and the eighteenth-century preacher Samson Occom, was selected by her great-aunt Fidelia Fielding (1827–1908), the last speaker of the Mohegan–Pequot language, and two other elders of the Connecticut Mohegan community to be the bearer of tribal medicinal and other lore. Educated as an anthropologist by Frank Speck at the University of Pennsylvania, she conducted field research on other Algonquian peoples, including the Montagnais-Naskapi of Quebec, the Wampanoag of Gay Head and Mashpee, Massachusetts, the Nanticoke of Delaware, and the Delaware of Oklahoma and Ontario, resulting in published articles on their crafts, medicines, and folklore. Her Mohegan identity aided her in recording the rapidly disappearing traditional knowledge of Eastern Algonquians.

In 1934 Tantaquidgeon became a community worker for the Bureau of Indian Affairs, and later became a specialist in Indian arts for the Indian Arts and Crafts Board on reservations in the Dakotas, Montana, and Wyoming. She returned to her home community in 1947 to assist in the operations of the family-run Tantaquidgeon Indian Museum, which serves as a cultural and educational resource center for and about New England's Native peoples. In 1986 the Women's Studies Program of the University of Connecticut established the Gladys Tantaquidgeon Award in her honor.

References

Fawcett, Melissa. "The Role of Gladys Tantaquidgeon." In *Papers of the Fifteenth Algonquian Conference*. Edited by William Cowan. Pp. 135–145. Ottawa: Carleton University, 1984.

Simmons, William S. *Spirit of the New England Tribes: Indian History and Folklore, 1620–1984*. Hanover, NH: University Press of New England, 1986.

Tantaquidgeon, Gladys. *Folk Medicine of the Delaware and Related Algonkian Indians*. Rev. ed. Pennsylvania Historical and Museum Commission Anthropological Series 3. Harrisburg: The Commission, 1972.

———. "Newly Discovered Straw Basketry of the Wampanoag Indians." *Indian Notes* 7 (1930): 475–483.

———. "Notes on the Gay Head Indians of Massachusetts." *Indian Notes* 7 (1930): 1–26.

———. "Notes on the Origin and Uses of Plants of the Lake St. John Montagnais." *Journal of American Folklore* 54 (1932): 265–267.

—John D. Nichols

TAPAHONSO, LUCI (b. 1951), was born at Shiprock, New Mexico. She has published four volumes of poetry: *One More Shiprock Night, Seasonal Woman* (illustrated by the Navajo painter R. C. Gorman and introduced by John Nichols), *A Breeze Swept Through* (with Klee-like drawings by the Cree/Shoshone artist Jaune Quick-to-See Smith), and *Sáanii Dahataal: The Women Are Singing* (cover by Emmi Whitehorse). During the 1980s, Tapahonso was an assistant professor of literature at the University of New Mexico, Albuquerque. Now teaching at the University of Kansas, she lives in Lawrence with her Cherokee husband and two daughters, Misty Dawn and Lori Tazbah Ortiz.

Tapahonso's poetry meshes naturally shifting voices with transcultural perspectives, a bifocal kind of code-switching poetics. Her verse does not employ formal poetics but cultural aesthetics: why and how to live in *hozhó*, the Navajo term for the good life. Between the old and new Navajo, code-switching to English and back, people know the *feeling of words*, sometimes, but not exactly what they mean. Tapahonso's daughters step in and out of the poems; her subjects consistently retain a sense of family, home, and extended kin—that is, who, and among whom, and where they belong. Tapahonso writes of earthen births, children, siblings, uncles and aunts, parents and grandparents, lovers and husband, girlfriends, rivals, cowboys, coyotes, sheep, and horses. Hers is a gynocratic or woman-empowered tribal strength. Tapahonso's grandmother broke wild broncos, according to one poem, and her mother baked incomparable bread. The poet speaks often of tribal food—husked corn, frybread, mutton and chili, Spam, Diet Pepsi, Hills Brothers coffee.

Tapahonso's English has a lightly broken, pointillist quality, syllable by syllable, as a second language is learned, where the breath "talks." With the title poem, commemorating her two daughters' births, we see in *A Breeze Swept Through* that dawn breeze, first breath, Grandpa's song, the mother's opening poem, and all winds around incorporate what the Navajo call the soul, the "in-standing wind," that breathes life through all creation.

The Southwest animates Tapahonso's verse landscape—arroyos, buttes, mesas, mesquite, chamiza, (brushwood), sagebrush, greasewood, piñons, desert chaparral, and the alluring Chuksa and Lukachukai Mountains. Powwows, rodeos, dance competitions, sudden deaths, desert highways into the sky, Chinle and Albuquerque and Dulce and Gallup locate her poems among real events in Indian places today. The voice is quick, and quick to shift with a woman's sharp wit in nurturings, teasings, gossipings, prayings, hurtings, carings, disciplinings, midnight writings, and dawn pollen blessings. Hers is the humor of a people who delight in going on adventures and are assured of a traditional home—a Navajo people who love and forgive and care for their own over vast journeys, wrenching acculturations, and odd accommodations that prove positive in the long view.

This poet is happy to be alive, to be Navajo, and to be a woman. She will not be embarrassed by elemental delights in a good laugh, unquestioned love for children, her husband's workday return, or her grandfather's quiet song at a dawn birth. She is disarmingly up-front about the goodnesses all around her, above the historical losses: "I drink a lot of coffee/and it sure does it for me." It is this sophisticated innocence, this lyric naturalism, that makes the poems singularly enjoyable, especially Navajo, and specially womanist.

Tapahanso ends her fourth book with "that going home business." She talks her way home: "For many people in my situation, residing away from my homeland, writing is the means for returning, rejuvenation, and for restoring our spirits to the state of *hozhó*, or beauty, which is the basis of Navajo philosophy. It is a small part of the 'real thing,' and it is utilitarian, but as Navajo culture changes, we adapt accordingly."

References

Alexander, Floyce. "A New Voice Among the Navajo." *Greenfield Review* 11 (1983): 191–93.

Allen, Paula Gunn, ed. *The Sacred Hoop: Recovering the Feminine in American Indian Traditions*. Boston: Beacon Press, 1986.

Balassi, William, John F. Crawford, and Annie O. Eysturoy, eds. *This Is About Vision: Interviews with Southwestern Writers*. Albuquerque: University of New Mexico Press, 1990.

Baldinger, Jo Ann. "Navajo Poet: Tapahonso Holds Home in Her Heart." *New Mexico Magazine* 70 (August 1992): 31–35.

Brant, Beth, ed. *A Gathering of Spirit: Writing and Art by North American Indian Women*. Ithaca, NY: Firebrand Books, 1988.

Breinig, Heimbrecht, and Klaus Losch. "Interview." In *Facing America*. Edited by Heimbrecht Breinig and Wolfgang Binder. Pp. 114–130, 333–346. Middletown, CT: Wesleyan University Press 1994.

Bruchac, Joseph. "For What It Is: An Interview with Luci Tapahonso." In *Survival This Way: Interviews with American Indian Poets*. Pp. 271–285. Tucson: University of Arizona Press, 1987.

———. "A MELUS Interview: Luci Tapahonso." *MELUS* 11 (Spring 1984): 88–91.

Lincoln, Kenneth. *Indi'n Humor: Bicultural Play in Native America*. New York: Oxford, University Press, 1991.

Moulin, Sylvie. "Nobody Is an Orphan: Interview with Luci Tapahonso." *Studies in American Indian Literature* 3 (1991): 14–18.

Penner, Andrea M. "The Moon's So Far Away: An Interview with Luci Tapahonso." *SAIL* 8 (Fall 1996): 1–12.

Tapahonso, Luci. *Bah's Baby Brother Is Born*. Washington, DC: National Organization on Fetal Alcohol Syndrome, 1994.

———. *Blue Horses Rush In: Poems and Stories*. Tucson: University of Arizona Press, 1997.

———. *A Breeze Swept Through*. Albuquerque, NM: West End Press, 1987.

———. "Come into the Shade." In *Open Spaces, City Places: Contemporary Writers on the Changing Southwest*. Edited by Judy Nolte. Pp. 73–85. Tucson: University of Arizona Press, 1993.

———. *Navajo ABC: A Diné Alphabet Book*. New York: Simon and Schuster, 1995.

———. *One More Shiprock Night*. San Antonio, TX: Tejas Art, 1981.

———. *Sáanii Dahataal: The Women Are Singing*. Tucson: University of Arizona Press, 1993.

———. *Seasonal Woman*. Santa Fe, NM: Tooth of Time, 1982.

———. *Songs of Shiprock Fair*. Walnut, CA: Kiva Publishing, 1999.

—Kenneth Lincoln

TEKAKWITHA, KATERI [Tekakouitha, Tagaskouita Katherine, Lily of the Mohawks] (1656–1680), was the first North American Indian to be beatified by the Roman Catholic Church. Her mother is believed to have been a Christian Algonquin who was captured by Mohawks about 1653. Married to a non–Christian Mohawk, she gave birth to Tekakwitha in 1656. In 1660 both parents died in a smallpox epidemic; the disease left Tekakwitha's face scarred and her eyesight damaged. The uncle who raised her after this time was strongly anti–Christian; nevertheless, Tekakwitha greatly admired several Jesuits who passed through her village in 1667, and desired to become a Christian.

One of the hallmarks of Tekakwitha's character is the importance she placed on virginity. When she came of age, Tekakwitha refused her family's suggestions that she marry. This conviction probably stemmed from a fascination with the Ursuline nuns' behavior at Montreal, of which she had been told by Christian members of her village. Her refusal to marry and her desire to refrain from working on the Sabbath greatly angered her family; they accused her of not helping to support them and withheld food from her. This persecution increased after her baptism, which occurred at Easter 1676, following an unusually short but intense period of instruction with a Jesuit who was impressed by her preparedness. Following the Jesuit practice of isolating converts, when possible, from their non–Christian relatives, and after a threat on her life by her family, the resident priest persuaded Tekakwitha to escape to the mission village of St. Francis Xavier on the St. Lawrence River in the fall of 1677.

At the mission, Tekakwitha received intense instruction in Christianity. She was seen as an extraordinarily gifted pupil and was admitted to Communion within a few months. Anastasia Tegonhatsiongo, a former friend of her mother's, treated Tekakwitha like a daughter and assisted in her spiritual development, and in this environment Tekakwitha's spirituality thrived. She manifested a spirit of great humility and charity, and practiced continual mortifications of the body—burning herself, standing in the snow, whipping herself with branches—to show her love for Christ. This self-torture may have had additional meanings for Tekakwitha, who lived in an age when Indian prisoners were tortured. The prisoner was expected to remain brave and impassive during torture, enduring pain for personal and family honor; Tekakwitha gave Christian meanings to this traditional behavior. Some of these self-imposed penances were considered extreme, and she was ordered by the Jesuits to modify them. Tekakwitha wished to found a community of Native religious women, but this was considered premature by the priests, and she was dissuaded from it. She was allowed to pronounce a vow of virginity on the feast of the Annunciation, March 25, 1679.

Tekakwitha's mortifications of her body weakened her always frail health, and she died on April 17, 1680, at only twenty-four years of age. At her death, her smallpox-scarred face suddenly became beautiful, and shortly afterward a series of apparitions, healings, and other intercessions attributed to her began. In 1744 Pierre de Charlevoix described her as being "universally regarded as the Protectress of Canada"; devotion to her has increased steadily since then, and hundreds of thousands of people have made pilgrimages to her shrine at the mission of St. Francis Xavier at Caughnawaga, where her relics are kept, and to her natal village at Auriesville, New York. After intensive lobbying, she was declared Venerable by the Church in 1943 and was Beatified in 1980, the first two steps on the path to sainthood. She has also become the focus of the international Kateri Tekakwitha Conference, which fosters the development of a distinctively Native American Catholicism.

Kateri Tekakwitha's life has been closely documented by Catholic clergy, who saw in her intense devotion a symbol of the potential success of their missionary endeavors. She has likewise become a symbol for Native Catholics to whom she represents acceptance of Native American peoples by the Catholic Church and the possibility of a Native American Catholicism. Despite the growth of this Native Catholic movement and the recent change in attitudes by the Church toward Native peoples, biographies of Tekakwitha have not yet dealt adequately with her Native identity and the manner in which she reconciled her new faith with her Native worldview. That she might have been able to truly join aspects of both traditions makes her an even more meaningful figure for contemporary Native peoples.

References

Allen, Christine. "Women in Colonial French America." In *Women and Religion in America*. Vol. 2. Edited by Rosemary Radford Ruether and Rosemary Skinner Keller. Pp. 79–131. San Francisco: Harper & Row, 1983.

Bechard, Henri, S.J. "Tekakwitha." In *Dictionary of Canadian Biography*. Vol. 1. Toronto: University of Toronto Press, 1966.

Blanchard, David. "To the Other Side of the Sky: Catholicism at Kahnawake, 1667–1700." *Anthropologica* 24 (1982): 77–102.

Mathes, Valerie Sherer. "American Indian Women and the Catholic Church." *North Dakota History* 47 (Fall 1980): 20–25.

Peterson, Jacqueline, and Mary Druke. "American Indian Women and Religion." In *Women and Religion in America*. Vol. 2. Edited by Rosemary Radford Ruether and Rosemary Skinner Keller. Pp. 1–41. San Francisco: Harper & Row, 1983.

Shoemaker, Nancy. "Kateri Tekakwitha's Tortuous Path to Sainthood." In *Negotiators of Change: Historical Perspectives on Native American Women*. Edited by Nancy Shoemaker. Pp. 49–71. New York: Routledge, 1995.

The Position of the Historical Section of the Sacred Congregation of Rites on the Introduction of the Cause for Beatification and Canonization and on the Virtues of the Servant of God Katherine Tekakwitha, the Lily of the Mohawks. New York: Fordham University Press, 1940.

—*Laura Peers*

TELLES, LUCY PARKER (c. 1870–1956), was the daughter of Louisa Sam, of Yosemite Valley Miwok descent, and Mack "Bridgeport" Tom, a Mono Lake Paiute. She married Jack Parker, a Paiute from the Mono Lake area, who died shortly after their son, Lloyd, was born in 1902. She married John Telles, a Mexican–American from Texas, in 1914; they had a son, John Telles, Jr., in 1922. When John Telles became ill, Lucy turned to basket making to support her family.

As a small girl, she had learned the art of basketry, an essential part of traditional life among the Miwok and Paiute people. Due to the demand for Native basketry by white tourists to the Yosemite Valley region, Telles (and others) began developing baskets that were not utilitarian but art. She was the first weaver to employ many new and different techniques, including using red and black together in the same design unit; realistic floral, butterfly, and hummingbird motifs; lids for baskets that snap into place; and flattened-top, high-shouldered baskets. By 1912 she had gained a reputation as the best weaver in the region, and by the 1920s other weavers were copying her innovations in design and weaving techniques. In 1929 Telles began a basket that would take her four years to complete. Thirty-six inches in diameter and twenty inches in height, it won first prize at the Panama–Pacific Exposition at San Francisco in 1939. From 1947 on, Telles demonstrated weaving for the National Park Service at Yosemite Valley, and at the time of her death, she was working on a basket that, judging from the size of the base, would have been larger than any basket ever produced in the Yosemite region. In her lifetime Telles produced hundreds of baskets that reflected the perfection of the three-rod basketry technique, innovation in two- and three-color designs, and designs never used before by the Miwok–Paiute people.

References

Bates, Craig D. "Lucy Telles, a Supreme Weaver of the Yosemite Miwok Paiute." *American Indian Basketry* 2 (1982): 23–29.

———. "Lucy Telles, Outstanding Weaver of the Yosemite Miwok–Paiute." *Pacific Historian* 24 (1980): 396–403.

Ross, George. "Lucy Telles, Basket Maker." *Yosemite Nature Notes* 26 (1948): 67–68.

—Julie A. Russ

THE-OTHER-MAGPIE [Mary Buoyer, Magpie Outside] (c. 1849–post 1900), was known for her warrior-like skill and bravery while riding with Crow wolves (army scouts) during the Battle of the Rosebud in 1876. Although both Magpie Outside and The-Other-Magpie can be placed in the same vicinity during the Battle of the Rosebud, it is doubtful they are the same woman. Pretty-shield says that The-Other-Magpie "had no man of her own," and yet Magpie Outside was married to Mitch Buoyer. Magpie Outside is also described by Thomas H. Leforge, her second husband, as a calm woman, whereas The-Other-Magpie is called "a wild one . . . both bad and brave" by Pretty-shield.

Pretty-shield saw the battle in which The-Other-Magpie exhibited her bravery: "I saw the two women, Finds-Them-and-Kills-Them, and The-Other-Magpie, riding and singing with them [the wolves]. . . . The-Other-Magpie [had] a long coup stick, with one breath-feather on its small end." She circled the Lakota while singing her war song and waving her coup stick. When the Lakota closed in on a grounded wolf, The-Other-Magpie rode straight at them, waving her coup stick. "See," she called out, "my spit is my arrows." Then she struck the Lakota with her coup stick and saved her companion. That day she took a scalp and cut it into many pieces, so that the men might have more scalps to dance with when they returned from battle. Her appearance as a warrior was formidable. She wore a stuffed woodpecker on her head, and her forehead was painted yellow.

Magpie Outside, also known as Mary Buoyer, was born in May 1849 into the Burnt Mouth clan of Mountain Crows. She married four times: Mitch Buoyer, or Two-Bodies, a half-breed Sioux who interpreted for Custer and died with him; Thomas H. Leforge, or Horse-Rider, a white who lived with the Crows; Jack, a white who was employed by the Crow Indian Agency on the reservation; and Cold Wind, a full-blooded Crow, born in 1865. Her children were Jim and Mary Buoyer; and Tom (Born-in-Another-Place), Phoebe, and Rosa Leforge.

Unlike The-Other-Magpie, Magpie Outside is described by Leforge as "a true and good wife," "calm," "benignant," with "goodness of heart," one who loved "all human beings," "a special friend of every orphan and decrepit old person in the tribe," and one who exhibited "benevolence, generosity, magnanimity."

She saw that each of her children was educated, and later she became a medicine woman. She died on the Crow Reservation sometime after 1900.

References

Ewers, John C. "Deadlier Than the Male." *American Heritage* 16 (June 1965): 10–13.

Leforge, Thomas H. *Memoirs of a White Crow Indian*. As told to Thomas B. Marquis. Lincoln: University of Nebraska Press, 1974.

Liberty, Margot. "Hell Came with Horses: Plains Indian Women in the Equestrian Era." *Montana: The Magazine of Western History* 32 (Summer 1982): 10–19.

Linderman, Frank B. *Pretty-Shield, Medicine Woman of the Crows*. Lincoln: University of Nebraska Press, 1972.

Mathes, Valerie Sherer. "Native American Women in Medicine and the Military." *Journal of the West* 21 (April 1982): 41–48.

U.S. Bureau of the Census. *Crow Agency, Custer County, Montana. Indian Population*. Washington, D.C., 1900.

—Audrey M. Godfrey

THORPE, GRACE (b. 1921), was born in Yale, Oklahoma, and grew up in the same community (Keokuk Falls) and attended the same Indian boarding schools (Haskell Institute, Carlisle Indian Industrial School) as her father, Jim Thorpe. She is a member of the Sauk and Fox tribe and a descendant of the chieftain Blackhawk. Her degrees include a paralegal certificate from Antioch School of Law in 1974 and a BA from the University of Tennessee, Knoxville, in 1980.

Thorpe joined the Women's Army Corps during World War II and was stationed in New Guinea for more than two years before being selected as a member of the staff for General Douglas McArthur's headquarters command in Japan. During her tour in Japan she married Fred Seeley; they had a son, Thorpe, and daughter, Dagmar. The couple were later divorced. In 1950 she returned to the United States, took up residence in Pearl River, New York, and sold Yellow Page ads to businesses in the New York area.

In the mid-1960s, Thorpe decided to redirect her talents toward helping the Native American community, and she became quite active in the areas of land reacquisition, government and public relations, and community organization. In 1966 she helped to secure the property for Deganawidah-Quetzalcoatl University, an institution designed to meet the specific needs of Native American and Chicano students. Thorpe spent a year with the National Congress of American Indians, working to interest private companies in locating plants on reservations where Indians would be both trained and employed. During the first two months of 1970 she participated in the successful takeover of Alcatraz and the Fort Lawton Museum in Washington state, handling much of the public relations work on both occasions. While working with various women's clubs in 1971, Thorpe helped start the National Indian Women's Action Corps. She served as a legislative assistant to the United States Senate Subcommittee on Indian Affairs and then spent two years with the American Indian Policy Review Board, sponsored by the United States House of Representatives. In 1980 she returned to Oklahoma, where she now serves as a part-time district court judge for the Five Tribes in Stroud, Oklahoma.

Grace Thorpe is vice-president of the Jim Thorpe Foundation and, with her sister Charlotte, worked for the return of their father's Olympic medals. (They were returned in 1983.) She wrote "Jim Thorpe Family History: 1750 to 1904," published in *Chronicles of Oklahoma*.

References

Anderson, Owanah, ed. *Ohoyo One Thousand: A Resource Guide of American Indian/Alaska Native Women, 1982*. Wichita Falls, TX: Ohoyo Resource Center, 1982.

Benson, Arlon. Personal communication with Grace Thorpe, March 17, 1992.

Berman, Susan. "Working for My People: Thorpe's Daughter Indian Activist." *Akwesasne Notes* 3 (March 1971): 27.

Thorpe, Grace. "Jim Thorpe Family History: From Wisconsin to Indian Territory." *Chronicles of Oklahoma* 59 (Spring 1981): 91–105; (Summer 1981): 179–201.

—*Arlon Benson*

TIGER, WINIFRED (b. 1924), an enrolled member of the Eastern Band of Cherokees, grew up in the Paint Town community of rural North Carolina. She was sent to the Cherokee Indian School to complete her secondary education and graduated in 1943. At Cherokee she met a handsome young Seminole from Florida, Howard Tiger, an outstanding athlete and leader. After World War II began, Howard left school and volunteered for the Marine Corps, seeing combat action in the Pacific on Guam and Iwo Jima. In 1946 Howard returned to North Carolina, and he and Winifred were married; the couple had three sons and a daughter.

In 1957 the family moved to Florida, where Howard became a leading political figure in the newly organized Seminole Tribe of Florida, which had just received a federal constitution and corporate charter. He served as a member of the Tribal Council and as president of the board of directors, which supervised tribal business affairs. He was also an avid promoter of sports and recreation activities on the reservations. When Howard died in a heavy equipment accident in 1967, he was so highly respected that the Tribal Council named an annual sports tournament and the first reservation athletic facility in his honor.

Winifred Tiger was not a member of the Seminole tribe, and thus was ineligible to vote or hold office. Nevertheless, she was one of the best educated and most respected women in the Seminole community, and played an important role in improving tribal relations with the local education authorities. From 1966 to 1972 she was employed by the Broward County School Board as liaison with the Seminole tribe, checking Seminole school attendance, solving health and social needs, and finding children who were hiding in the woods or their homes to avoid attending school. When the Seminole tribe contracted its education programs from the Bureau of Indian Affairs, Tiger was selected as the education counselor. In 1985 she was named director of education for the Seminole Tribe of Florida, charged with supervising an expanding staff and new reservation school programs. Among her accomplishments have been achieving full academic accreditation for the Afachkee Day School—an elementary school operated by the tribe on the Big Cypress Reservation—improving the dropout rate for Seminole youngsters attending public schools, and initiating plans for a residential secondary school on the Seminole Reservation. She has also served as an adviser to the Broward County School Board and was a member of the school board for the Intertribal School at Intermountain, Utah. Among the honors she has received are a certificate of recognition from the Broward County School Board, the Human Relations Award of the Broward County Teachers Association, and the Broward County Pioneers Award.

References

Harrington, V. N., to T. M. Reed. BIA Central Office Files, File 13671–1957–Seminole 055, September 15, 1959. Washington, DC: National Archives.
Kersey, Harry. Personal communication with Winifred Tiger, December 3, 1990.
Seminole Tribe of Florida and Seminole Tribe of Florida, Inc. "20th Anniversary of Seminole Tribal Organization 1957–1977, Saturday, August 20, 1977." Hollywood, FL: Seminole Tribe, 1977. (Mimeo).

—Harry A. Kersey, Jr.

TOHE, LAURA (b. 1952), was born at Fort Defiance, Arizona, of the Sleepy Rock people for the Bitter Water clan, and grew up in Crystal, New Mexico, near the Chuska Mountains on the eastern edge of the Navajo Reservation. She was forced to attend boarding schools in the 1950s and 1960s, and the shame she was made to feel for her language and culture suffuses *No Parole Today*, her creative 1993 PhD dissertation at the University of Nebraska. Tohe's poetry moves between the worldviews of two cultures whose languages offer no natural cognates. This is not to say that merging the irreconcilable is a goal. "I'm not from here," insists the child in "No Parole Today," recalling cement floors, roll calls, forced labor, and separation in the prison of her boarding school. In "At Mexican Springs," Gallup, New Mexico, the notorious edge-of-the-reservation strip of bars and motels, becomes another symbol of soul robbery, but a larger view includes the land that stretches "across these eternal sandstones" and ensures that she will live to tell her children the ancient stories. The Dinétah is the severe, radiant landscape that sustains life and restores spirit. In the poem "Blue Horses Running," Tohe says, "Here it's possible to know that you belong to the earth / in a language that names us, / that this place formed you, / and carved the high bones in your face."

Tohe teaches in the Department of English and is affiliated with the Women's Studies Department at Arizona State University in Tempe. Her honors and awards include the Distinguished Service Award from the Goodrich Program at the University of Nebraska, a certificate of recognition from the Wordcraft Circle of Native American Mentor and Apprentice Writers, and the poetry prize from *Blue Mesa Review*. She has given poetry readings throughout the country and scholarly presentations for the Modern Language Association, the Conference on College Composition and Communication, the Popular Culture Association, and numerous local and regional arts and humanities councils. She lives with her two sons in Mesa, Arizona. Today she says, "I believe that we as Indian people have to reclaim what was beaten out of us and what was nearly stolen from us: our voices, our stories, our songs, and most important, our language." Of her own poems and stories she says, "I hesitate to say that I make the invisible visible, because DinÈ women were always visible to ourselves and to other Native people. Our invisibility came as a result of colonization. I reclaim power through the stories and poems that I write."

Tohe has poems, stories, and essays in literary magazines and anthologies in the United States, France, Germany, Canada, and Luxembourg, including *Callaloo;*

Contemporary Arizona Poets; Reinventing the Enemy's Language; The Color of Resistance: A Contemporary Collection of Writing by Aboriginal Women; Braided Lives: An Anthology of Multi-cultural American Writing; Blue Dawn, Red Earth; and many others.

References

Tohe, Laura. *Making Friends with Water*. Omaha, NE: Nosila Press, 1986.
————. *No Parole Today*. Albuquerque: University of New Mexico Press, 1998.

—*Rhoda Carroll*

TOMASSA [Tomasse] (c. 1840–1900), was born into a respectable, wealthy family in the Republic of Mexico. While a small child, she and her cousin, a boy a year or so older, were taken captive by a band of Carissa Comanche. After living with the Comanches for ten years, they were ransomed by the United States government and sent back to Mexico. For some unknown reason, neither she nor her cousin was claimed, so they were left with a wealthy Mexican family who treated them as servants.

After staying in Mexico for about a year, Tomassa and her cousin decided to return to the Comanches. They gathered food they thought would be sufficient for the journey hundreds of miles north, and took one horse. The North Star was their only guide. When their food gave out, they killed the horse, dried the meat, and took the hide along to use in making moccasins. Miraculously, when the last of the dried meat was gone, they stumbled into a camp of the very band of Comanches with whom they had lived.

When she was around fourteen, Tomassa's Comanche mother told her she was to marry Blue Leggings. Tomassa broke Comanche custom and refused to go with Blue Leggings. She stated she wished to marry Joseph Chandler (1823–1873), a half-Cherokee, half-white farmer who owned a farm near what would become Fort Sill, Oklahoma. Chandler bought her from Blue Leggings for three dollars and a crowing rooster. During the Civil War renegades sacked and burned the area, and the Chandlers were forced to flee to Texas. They returned to their land in Oklahoma in 1868.

In 1871 Tomassa was employed as an interpreter for the first school at Fort Sill. She spoke Spanish, English, Comanche, and Caddo, and was of great service to the officials at Fort Sill. Due to their close friendship with the Comanches, Tomassa and her husband were able to warn the Indian Agency of impending Indian raids.

Tomassa was respected by the Indian agents and the Comanches because of her humanity. Once, when two Comanche captives escaped, they went to Tomassa's home for protection. She treated them kindly and later was able to secure their freedom.

Chandler died in 1873, leaving Tomassa a widow with three sons and one daughter. Some years later she married George Conover, a retired army man. She had several more children by him. In 1887 Tomassa was converted to Christianity and joined the Methodist Church. She died in 1900 and was buried on her ranch at the extreme western edge of Grady County, Oklahoma.

References

Butler, Josiah. "Pioneer School Teaching at the Comanche–Kiowa Agency School, 1870–1873." *Chronicles of Oklahoma* 6 (December 1928): 483–528.

Corwin, Hugh D. *Comanche and Kiowa Captives in Oklahoma and Texas*. Lawton, OK: By the author, 1959.

———. *The Kiowa Indians*. Lawton, OK: By the author, 1958.

Methvin, J. J. *In the Limelight*. Anadarko, OK: By the author, c. 1925.

Waltrip, Lela, and Rufus Waltrip. *Indian Women*. New York: David McKay, 1964.

—Joyce Ann Kievit

TREMBLAY, GAIL (b. 1945), of Onondaga, Micmac, and French Canadian descent, was born in Buffalo, New York. A well-known poet and visual artist, she holds a BA in drama from the University of New Hampshire and an MFA in creative writing from the University of Oregon.

The author of numerous collections of poetry, Tremblay has earned a reputation as one of the most striking voices in contemporary American poetry. Her work has appeared in well-known journals including *Denver Quarterly, Northwest Review, Calyx*, and *Maize*, and has been anthologized in a volumes including *New Voices from the Longhouse, Harper's Anthology of 20th Century Native American Poetry*, and *Dancing on the Rim of the World: An Anthology of Contemporary Northwest Native American Writing*. Tremblay has received numerous awards for her writing and has given poetry readings across the country.

Tremblay has also earned a substantial national reputation as a visual artist, particularly in fiber works and weaving. She is best known for her wall hangings, masks, tapestries, and weavings of wood, fiber, and metal. The recipient of numerous awards, Tremblay has exhibited her work in both group and individual shows nationally and in Japan and Switzerland. Her work was a highly acclaimed addition to "Women of Sweetgrass, Cedar, and Sage," an exhibition that toured North America.

Both her poetry and her visual art draw upon the traditional culture of her ancestry. Traditional Native American motifs find a home in her work, juxtaposed to and complementing the most contemporary techniques and modes of expression.

Tremblay is also a vital force in the Northwest educational network. Since 1981 she has been on the faculty of Evergreen State College in Olympia, Washington, where she has been a leader in programs in Native American Studies, multicultural studies, and fine arts. Tremblay frequently gives presentations across the country on the development of multicultural programs. A dynamic educator and nationally acclaimed artist and poet, Tremblay has found a number of media in which to articulate her profoundly spiritual and highly artistic vision.

References

Lerner, Andrea, ed. *Dancing on the Rim of the World: An Anthology of Contemporary Northwest Native American Writing*. Tucson: University of Arizona Press, 1990.

Tremblay, Gail. "Artist's Statement." In *Contemporary Native American Art*. Stillwater: Oklahoma State University, 1983. Exhibit catalog.

————. "Artist's Statement." In *Women of Sweetgrass, Cedar, and Sage*. Phoenix: ATLATL, 1984. Exhibit catalog.

————. "Carrier of Culture" and "Artist's Statement." In *New Directions Northwest: Contemporary Native American Art*. 1987. Exhibit catalog.

————. *Fiber, Metal, and Wood*. Browning, MT: U.S. Department of the Interior, 1988.

————. *Indian Singing in North America*. Corvallis, OR: Calyx Books, 1990.

————. *Indian Singing: Poems*. Covallis, OR: Calyx Books, 1998.

————. *Night Gives Women the Word*. Omaha, NE: Omaha Printing, 1979.

————. *Talking to the Grandfathers*. American Poetry Series, annex 21, no. 3. Omaha: University of Nebraska, 1981.

Zydeck, Frederick, ed. *Close to Home*. Omaha: University of Nebraska Press, 1981.

—*Andrea Lerner*

TSUPU (c. 1815–1890), was born near Petaluma, California. Little is known about either her mother, Tcupi Yomi, a Coast Miwok from the Olum (Bodega) band, or her father, Tsutcuk, a Coast Miwok from the Petaluma band. Nor is much known about the seven brothers and sisters she is reputed to have had. Tsupu survived both the Spanish and the Mexican invasions of Coast Miwok territory, and single-handedly passed her knowledge of Coast Miwok language and culture to her children, particularly to her sons, Tom and Bill Smith, and their families.

Tsupu spoke both Olum and Kashaya Pomo. Undoubtedly, she knew other Coast Miwok languages as well. She first married Tintic (Tomas Comtechal, or Kom-sha-tal), a Kashaya Pomo from Fort Ross. They had four children. Their son Thomas Comtechal (later called Tom Smith) was the last prominent Coast Miwok doctor and spiritual leader. Later, Tsupu moved to Bodega Bay, where she became maid/mistress of Captain Steven Smith, a Quaker settler from Massachusetts who had a Peruvian wife. Smith claimed a large tract of Bodega Miwok land as his own. With Smith, Tsupu had a son, Bill, who established an important and prosperous fishing business with his sons at Bodega Bay.

Tsupu's survival and tenacious memory assured the survival of both a people and their culture. Her granddaughter, Sarah Smith Ballard, who died in the early 1970s at nearly one hundred years of age, was the last fluent speaker of Olum. Sara, in turn, passed much of her knowledge to her grandson, David Peri, a Coast Miwok tribal scholar and professor of anthropology at Sonoma State University. Today over one thousand Indians can trace their ancestry to Tsupu. And because of Tsupu, these Indians can know something about their Coast Miwok history and culture.

Among Tsupu's descendants are many Indian scholars, including David Peri, professor of anthropology at Sonoma State University; Bill Smith, former professor and director of American Indian Studies at Sonoma State University; Kathleen Smith, artist, writer, and tribal scholar; and Greg Sarris, professor of English at University of California, Los Angeles.

References

Kelly, Isabel. *Ethnographic Notes on the Coast Miwok Indians.* Miwok Archeo-
  logical Preserve of Marin, San Rafael, CA, 1991.
Sarris, Greg. Personal communication with David Peri, June 1990.
————. Personal communication with Kathleen Smith, June 1990.

—Greg Sarris

V

VANDERBURG, AGNES (1901–1989), was born in Valley Creek near Arlee, Montana. From an early age, she had an interest in traditional Salish (Flathead) culture. Consequently, she devoted her life to passing on those ways and the Salish language to her five children, to the Salish community, and to anyone who showed an interest. She and her husband, Jerome Stanislaus Vanderburg (1890–1974), were married in 1920 and operated a farm south of Arlee. They were respected and active members of the Salish community. After Jerome's death, Agnes Vanderburg continued to work as a resoource person for the Flathead Culture Committee and to operate what came to be known as "Agnes's camp," at which she taught Salish ways to young and old, Native American and non–Native alike.

Besides maintaining the camp for over twenty years, Vanderburg was featured in several educational video productions and was recognized by the Smithsonian Institution at the Folk Life Festival; she also earned many state and national awards for her work. One such work is *Tales from the Bitterroot Valley*, in which she performs dual roles as storyteller and as interpreter (other storytellers include Ignace Pierre, Jerome Lumpry, and Adele Adams). The collection is composed of a number of traditional Salish folk tales featuring Coyote, Mole, Fox, Raven, and others. Another important work is the posthumously released production, *Coming Back Slow*, in which she discusses the importance of preserving Salish culture and language. Barbara Springer Beck's MA thesis, "Agnes Vanderburg: A Woman's Life in the Flathead Culture," further details the importance of Vanderburg's contribution to the Salish culture and community.

References

Beck, Barbara Springer. "Agnes Vanderburg: A Woman's Life in the Flathead Culture." Master's thesis, University of Montana, 1982.
Coming Back Slow. Pablo, MT: Salish Kootenai College Press, 1995. Video. Originally published as an interview in *Parabola* 5 (1980): 20–23.
Tales from the Bitterroot Valley. Billings: Montana Indian Publications, 1971. Video.

—*Greg Grewell*

VELARDE, PABLITA [Tse Tsan, Golden Dawn] (b. 1918), a famous Tewa Indian painter from Santa Clara Pueblo, New Mexico, is the third daughter of Herman and Marianita Velarde. Her mother died of tuberculosis in 1921. In 1924 Velarde and her two older sisters were enrolled in St. Catherine's Indian School in Santa Fe. During their summers in the pueblo, they frequently stayed with their grandmother, the medicine woman Qualupita, from whom Velarde learned traditional customs and arts. From her father, a respected storyteller, she learned traditional myths and legends, and from the petroglyphs at Puye Ruins, ancestral designs. In 1932 Velarde was enrolled at the Santa Fe Indian School run by the Bureau of Indian Affairs, where she was one of many students encouraged by art teacher Dorothy Dunn to paint from their tribal experience. In 1933 she was selected to work with artist Olive Rush on murals for the Chicago "Century of Progress" World's Fair, and in 1934 she again worked with Rush on Works Progress Administration art projects. After graduating from the Santa Fe Indian School in 1936, Velarde taught arts and crafts at the Santa Clara Day School, and worked again with Rush in 1938 on a mural for the Maisel Trading Post in Albuquerque. In 1939 she was employed by the United States Park Service to paint archaeological and ethnological murals that reconstructed the life of her ancestors in Frijoles Canyon at the Bandelier National Monument Visitors' Center. Velarde married an Anglo man, Herbert Hardin, in 1942, and in 1943 gave birth to a daughter, Helen, who became an artist in her own right, and in 1944 to a son, Herby. The conflict between her Indian heritage and life in the Anglo world, and the conflict between their respective careers, proved too great. They divorced in 1959.

Whether in her "memory paintings" done in tempera or oil or in her "earth paintings," and whether realistic or abstract, Velarde's art re-presents designs, images, and ceremonial and mythic scenes from Pueblo life. What she has remembered and created from her own experience has been supplemented by both historical scholarship and ethnographic research, which has at times been criticized or opposed by tribal members. In 1948 Velarde won her first important prize at the Philbrook Art Center's annual Indian Art Show, and in 1954 she was awarded the Palme Académique by the French government. She won all the top prizes at the Inter-Tribal Indian Ceremonial in Gallup in 1955, including Grand Prize for her painting *Old Father, the Storyteller*. In 1956 she completed *The Green Corn Dance*, a twenty-one-foot mural for the Foote Cafeteria in Houston. During this time, Velarde frequently returned to Santa Clara Pueblo and spent time with her father, listening to and recording his stories. The result of their collaboration was *Old Father, the Storyteller*, an illustrated book of Tewa legends that was selected as one of the best Western books in 1960. Since then, Velarde has received countless honors and awards, including the New Mexico Governor's Award and an Honor Award from the National Women's Caucus for Art. Her paintings and murals are on permanent display at the Indian Pueblo Cultural Center in Albuquerque, and countless Indian artists, especially women, have been inspired and enabled by her example.

References

Dunn, Dorothy. "Pablita Velarde, Painter of Pueblo Life." *El Palacio* 59 (1952): 335–341.

Gridley, Marion E. "Pablita Velarde, Artist of the Pueblos." In *American Indian Women*. Pp. 94–104. New York: Hawthorn Books, 1974.

Nelson, Mary Carroll. *Pablita Velarde*. Minneapolis: Dillon Press, 1971.

———. "Pablita Velarde." *American Indian Art* 3 (1978): 50–57, 90.
Velarde, Pablita. *Old Father, the Storyteller*. Globe, AZ: D. S. King, 1960.
—*Barbara A. Babcock*

VENEGAS, HILDRETH MARIE TWOSTARS (b. 1919), she has spent her life in community service. The daughter of Jemima and David Twostars, she was born in Sisseton, South Dakota, and has spent most of her life there.

After early schooling in Sisseton, she attended Flandreau Indian School for her final three years of high school, graduating in 1938. She then attended Haskell Institute in Lawrence, Kansas, and earned her diploma for a two-year course in business. During World War II she was a civilian employee in the Pentagon.

Over her lifetime Venegas has continued her education. In 1949 she attended the Phoenix Academy of Beauty Culture in Arizona. After graduating, she passed the state board exam and received her beautician's license. She owned and operated her own beauty shops in Arizona and South Dakota. In 1985 Venegas received an associate degree in general studies from the Sisseton–Wahpeton Community College. She continued her education at the University of Minnesota at Morris, where she earned a Bachelor of Arts in Indian Studies with emphasis on anthropology/sociology in August 1994. In 1996 she was accepted into the master's degree program at Northern State University in Aberdeen, South Dakota.

For almost forty years Venegas has worked in government service, primarily in the Indian Health Service. She spent twenty-eight years at the Indian Hospital in Sisseton, most of these as administrative officer, service unit director, hospital director, or health systems administrator. She is one of the few Indian women to have held management positions in the Indian Health Service.

Venegas's life has been filled with honors and awards. In 1970 she was the first Indian woman to be selected South Dakota Merit Mother, an honor repeated in 1981. Also in 1970 she received the title Mrs. Indian Seminar at the first national meeting of American Indian women at Fort Collins, Colorado. She was elected president of the North American Indian Women's Association at their meeting in Chilocco, Oklahoma, in June 1977, the same year she was selected by Haskell for its Outstanding Alumni Award.

In 1978 Venegas was given special recognition and a letter from President Jimmy Carter, who invited her to participate in the White House Conference on Balanced National Growth and Economic Development. On March 31, 1980, she received the Jefferson Award in recognition of outstanding public service, active involvement in community affairs, and continual effort to improve the image of the Indian. In October 1983, Venegas was given a certificate and plaque at the first Indian Women's Recognition Ceremony during the annual convention of the National Congress of American Indians held in Green Bay, Wisconsin. It is fitting that her efforts to establish Indian–white harmony should be honored by both races.

In retirement Venegas has served on the American Lung Association of South Dakota board of directors since 1983, and was its president for two terms (1991–1993). She was selected to receive the Agnes M. Holdridge Award in October

1996, at the annual meeting of the American Lung Association of South Dakota, in recognition of her outstanding work to prevent lung disease and promote lung health. She is a lifetime honorary member of the Human Services Board of the Sisseton–Wahpeton Sioux tribe, and she continues to serve as vice president of the Roberts County (her home county in South Dakota) Heritage Museum board.

At the beginning of the twenty-first century, Venegas says she is continuing her "lifelong endeavors to facilitate more harmonious relationships between the Indian and non–Indian segments of the community to promote the positive image of Indian women and to improve living conditions for the entire community."

References

"Hildreth Venegas." *The University of South Dakota Bulletin*. 1988.

Marken, Jack. Personal communication with Hildreth Marie Venegas.

North American Indian Women's Association. "Message from the President." *Highlights* 1 (June 1977/March 1978): 1.

"SWST Tribal Member Attests to Value of Education." *Sota Iya Ye Yapi* [Old Agency] (February 15, 1995).

"Venegas Accepts Invitation to Participate in 41st Annual National Security Seminar." *The Sisseton Courier*, April 26, 1995.

"Venegas Outstanding Alumna." *The Indian Leader* [Haskell Junior College, Lawrence, KS], May 13, 1977, 1.

—Jack Marken

VOLBORTH, JUDITH MOUNTAIN LEAF [Ivaloo], (b. 1955) is an Apache–Comanche poet born in New York City. She studied at the University of California at Los Angeles, where she honed her skills in prose, poetry, and, particularly, haiku, a Japanese form of impressionistic free verse. Tribal themes dominate her work, and the trickster figure of Coyote is a frequent subject. Though traditional motifs are common in her work, so are images of strong, modern Native women and their unique struggles.

Volborth's synthesis of ancient forms with more contemporary works, *Thunder Root: Traditional and Contemporary Native American Verse*, was published by the American Indian Studies Center at her alma mater, UCLA. In addition to her creative writing, Volborth is an adept writer on the mechanics and styles employed in contemporary Indian literature. Her analysis of the power of sound and language in Native literature appeared in *Native American Literature: Forum 7*, a special publication of Serrizo Editoriale Universitario of Pisa, Italy.

A resident of Santa Monica, California, Volborth is very interested in the performance of her own works and in the meaning of dramatic readings for the preservation of Native culture.

References

Coltelli, Laura, ed. *Native American Literature: Forum 7, 1989*. Pisa, Italy: Serrizo Editoriale Universitario, 1989.

Green, Rayna, ed. *That's What She Said*. Bloomington: Indiana University Press, 1984.

Swan, Brian, ed. Special issue of *Shantih* on Native American literature (1979).
Volborth, Judith Mountain Leaf. *Thunder Root: Traditional and Contemporary Native American Verse*. Los Angeles: UCLA American Indian Studies Center, 1978.

—Cynthia Kasee

W

WALLIS, VELMA (b. 1960), an Athabaskan, was born in Fort Yukon, Alaska. After her father died, leaving her mother with thirteen children to raise and provide for in the remote Alaskan interior, Wallis left school at age thirteen. She later earned her high school equivalency degree and began a promising career as a writer with the novel *Two Old Women*, a version of an Athabaskan legend told to Wallis by her mother. Her second novel, also containing versions of traditional legends, is *Bird Girl and the Man Who Followed the Sun*. Both novels have been translated into several languages, and *Two Old Women* received both a Pacific Northwest Booksellers Award and a Western States Book Award. Each novel deals with the related themes of isolation, survival, cultural rebellion, and cultural reconciliation. Wallis, who is married and has two children, makes her home near Venetie, Alaska.

References

Wallis, Velma. *Bird Girl and the Man Who Followed the Sun*. Anchorage, AK: Epicenter, 1996.
———. *Two Old Women*. Anchorage, AK: Epicenter, 1993.

—Patricia Verstrat

WALSH, MARNIE [M. M. B. Walsh], (b. ?) is a Sioux writer and Dakota native who prefers that her work speak for itself. She avoids releasing personal information, which she once called "biographical garbage." Walsh earned BA degrees in history and English from Pennsylvania State University and an MA in creative writing from the University of New Mexico. During her graduate studies, she was awarded a fellowship by the National Endowment for the Arts.

In 1975 Walsh published her first novel, *Dolly Purdo*. The following year she produced another novel, *The Four Colored Hoop*, and a collection of poetry, *A Taste of the Knife*. Her poetry has appeared in numerous publications, including *From the Belly of the Shark, Voices from Wah'Kon-Tah, Dacotah Territory, Scree, South Dakota Review, Best of the Small Presses, The Third Woman: Minority Writers of the United States*, and *Women Poets of the World*. Her poetry is noted for its starkly realistic depictions of life on Sioux reservations in North and South Dakota.

References

Ahsahta Cassette Sampler: 14 Western Poets Read from Their Ahsahta Volumes.
    Boise ID: Ahsahta Press, 1983. Audiocassette.
Hobson, Geary, ed. *The Remembered Earth*. Albuquerque: University of New
    Mexico Press, 1979.
Walsh, Marnie. *Dolly Purdo*. New York: Putnam's, 1975.
————. *The Four Colored Hoop*. New York: Putnam's, 1976.
————. *A Taste of the Knife*. Boise, ID: Ahsahta Press, 1976.

—*Lois Griffitts*

WALTERS, ANNA LEE (b. 1946), a Pawnee/Otoe/Missouri, is a writer of poems, short stories, novels, and essays. She was born on September 9, 1946, in Pawnee, Oklahoma, the daughter of Luther and Juanita M. (Taylor) McGlaslin. Walters attended the College of Santa Fe from 1972 to 1974. She has worked as a library technician for the Institute of American Indian Arts in Santa Fe, New Mexico (1968–1974); a technical writer for Dineh Cooperatives in Chinle, Arizona (1975); and a technical writer of curriculum development for the Navajo Community College in Tsaile, Arizona (1976–1984). She was employed for a short time in the National Anthropological Archives at the Smithsonian Institution in Washington, D.C.

A prolific writer, Walters is coauthor of a textbook, *The Sacred: Ways of Knowledge, Sources of Life*, and has contributed to many anthologies, including *The Man to Send Rainclouds* (1974), *Warriors of the Rainbow* (1975), and *The Third Woman* (1978). In an interview published in *Wildfire*, she says that one of her primary reasons for writing is to demonstrate the Native American tribal perspective on histories and philosophies to contemporary audiences. She stresses that the tribal view of the world is unique, and that Native Americans adhere to and live according to that nonmainstream view needs to be understood. This serves as one of the major premises of her novel, *Ghost Singer*. In her essay "Odyssey of Indian Time," Walters emphasizes the spiritual, continual, and intangible sense of time in tribal cultures. Her award-winning collection of short stories, *The Sun Is Not Merciful*, chronicles a people—triumphant, not defeated—who come to terms with time, life, and place. Walters, in short, writes in many genres about the people and culture she knows, with a full understanding of what it is to be Native American in contemporary society.

Walters is married to Harry Walters, a Navajo museum curator. They live on the Navajo Reservation in Arizona, where she is director of the Navajo Community College Press. She is the mother of two sons.

References

Algner-Alvarez, Erika. "Artifact and Written History: Freeing the Terminal Indian in Anna Lee Walters's *Ghost Singer*." *SAIL* 8 (Spring 1996): 45–59.
Beck, Peggy V., Anna Lee Walters, and Nia Francisco. *The Sacred: Ways of Knowledge, Sources of Life*. Tsaile, AZ: Navajo Community College Press, 1977.
Carroll, Rhoda. "The Values and Vision of a Collective Past: An Interview with Anna Lee Walters." *American Indian Quarterly* 16 (1992): 63–73.

Farley, Ronnie. *Women of the Native Struggle: Portraits and Testimony of Native American Women*. Introduction by Anna Lee Walters. New York: Orion Books, 1993.

Fiesta, Melissa J. "Solving Mysteries of Culture and Self: Anita and Naspah in Anna Lee Walters's *Ghost Singer*." *American Indian Quarterly* 17 (1993): 370–384.

Hogan, Linda, ed. *Frontiers,* Special issue on Native American women 6 (1981).

Ortiz, Simon H., ed. *Earth Power Coming: Short Fiction in Native American Literature*. Tsaile, AZ: Navajo Community College Press, 1983.

Ryan, Matthew. "Interview with Anna Lee Walters." *Wildfire* 4 (Summer 1989): 16–21.

Steinberg, Marc. "Myth, Folk Tale and Ritual in Anna Lee Walters's 'The Warriors.'" *Studies in Short Fiction* 34 (Winter 1997): 55–60.

Walters, Anna Lee. "American Indian Thought and Identity in American Fiction." In *Coyote Was Here: Essays on Contemporary Native American Literary and Political Mobilization*. Edited by Bo Scholer. Pp. 35–39. Aarhus, Denmark: University of Aarhus, 1984.

———. "Fractured Vessels of a Holy Life." *Christianity and Crises* 49 (1990): 407–408.

———. *Ghost Singer*. Menominee, WI: Northland, 1988.

———. "Odyssey of Indian Time." *Book Forum* 5 (1981): 396–399.

———. *The Spirit of Native America: Beauty and Mysticism in American Indian Art*. San Francisco: Chronicle Books, 1989.

———. *The Sun Is Not Merciful*. Ithaca, NY: Firebrand Books, 1985.

———. *Talking Indian: Reflections on Survival and Writing*. Ithaca, NY: Firebrand Books, 1992.

———. *The Two-legged Creature: An Otoe Story*. Flagstaff, AZ: Northland Publishers, 1993.

———, ed. *Neon Pow-Wow: New Native American Voices of the Southwest*. Flagstaff, AZ: Northland Publishers, 1993.

—Laurie Lisa

WANATEE, ADELINE (1910–1996), is known for her prodigious accomplishments in education, political leadership, and art. She was born Jean Adeline Morgan, a member of the Wolf clan, on December 9, 1910, on the Settlement of the Meskwaki or Red Earth People (also known as the Mesquakie or the Fox) near Tama, Iowa. Her parents were Earl Morgan and Annie Waseskuk Morgan. In 1932 she married Frank David Wanatee; they had four sons and five daughters. In 1993 Wanatee was inducted into the Iowa Women's Hall of Fame, the first Native American woman to be honored by that organization. During the summer of 1996, although in failing health, she summoned the strength to represent her people at Iowa's Sesquicentennial Celebration in Washington, D.C., and Des Moines. She died on October 15, 1996.

Wanatee attended the Sac and Fox Day School, Flandreau Indian School, and Tama public schools, finally graduating from Haskell Institute in Lawrence, Kansas. She returned to Iowa and taught sewing, cooking, Meskwaki language, and art at the Sac and Fox Day School. Wanatee served as chair of the Meskwaki

School Board and was a founding member of the national Coalition of Indian Controlled School Boards. For many years she was a resource person for scholars interested in traditional Meskwaki culture and its twentieth-century continuities: for example, Ives Goddard (Smithsonian Institution) and Amy Dahlstrom (University of Chicago) on Meskwaki language and Algonquin linguistics, Gretchen Bataille (Washington State University) and Kathleen Sands (Arizona State University) on Meskwaki women's roles and the oral tradition, Gaylord Torrence (Drake University) on Meskwaki art, and David Gradwohl (Iowa State University) on Meskwaki material culture and food preparation.

In the political arena, Wanatee is perhaps best known for being the first woman elected to the Meskwaki Tribal Council, serving two four-year terms. She was also the first woman to belong to the Meskwaki Pow Wow Association. Wanatee was appointed to three terms on the Iowa Governor's Advisory Committee. She was a member of the National American Indian Women's Association and a delegate to the National Indian Council on Aging.

Wanatee's artistic endeavors included appliqué, ribbonwork, and weaving of "yarn belts" or sashes by the traditional finger-weaving (warp face braiding) technique. She wove sashes for individuals at the Settlement and also accepted commissions for private collectors and museums. Photographs of her sashes are included in several books on Meskwaki art. Wanatee taught weaving to young people across the state as a member of the Iowa Arts Council's "artist in the schools" program.

Wanatee followed traditional Meskwaki religion, particularly the practices of the Wolf clan Medicine Bundle. She was a staunch guardian of traditional Meskwaki culture and the role of the Meskwaki in contemporary American society. Informed that she had been inducted into the Iowa Women's Hall of Fame, Wanatee commented, "I never realized I did so much. I just did things that were right for my people."

References

Bataille, Gretchen M., and Kathleen Mullen Sands. *Native American Women Telling Their Lives*. Lincoln: University of Nebraska Press, 1984.

Dahlstrom, Amy. *Narrative Structure of a Fox Text. Nikotwasik Iskwahtem Paskihtepayih!: Studies in Honor of H. C. Wolfart*. Algonquin and Iroquoian Linguistics, Memoir 13. Winnipeg: University of Manitoba, 1996.

———. "The Snytax of Discourse Functions in Fox." *Berkeley Linguistics Society, Special Session in Syntactic Issues in Native American Languages*. Pp. 11–21. Berkeley: *University of California*, 1993.

Goddard, Ives, ed. *Leonard Bloomfield's Fox Lexicon: Critical Edition*. Algonquian and Iroquoian Linguistics, Memoir 12. Winnipeg: University of Manitoba, 1994.

Gradwohl, David M. Interview with Donald W. Wanatee, Sr., December 11, 1996.

———. "Shelling Corn in the Prairie-Plains: Archaeological Evidence and Ethnographic Parallels Beyond the Pun." In *Plains Indian Studies: A Collection of Essays in Honor of John C. Ewers and Waldo R. Wedel*. Edited by Douglas H. Ubelaker and Herman J. Viola. Pp. 135–156. Washington, DC: Smithsonian Institution Press, 1982.

Howard, Phoebe Wall. "Hall of Fame: Women Win Recognition for Their Life's Work." *Des Moines Register*, August 5, 1993, M5.

Hykes, Jenny. "Wanatee, Hall of Fame Honoree, Dies." *Des Moines Register*, October 16, 1996, M7.

Torrence, Gaylord, and Robert Hobbs. *Art of the Red Earth People: The Mesquakie of Iowa*. Seattle: University of Washington Press, 1989.

Wanatee, Adeline. "Education, the Family, and the Schools." In *The Worlds Between Two Rivers: Perspectives on American Indians in Iowa*. Edited by Gretchen M. Bataille, David M. Gradwohl, and Charles L. P. Silet. Pp. 100–103. Ames: Iowa State University Press, 1978.

—David Gradwohl

WARD, NANCY [Nanye-Hi, One Who Goes About] (c. 1738–1824), the last Beloved Woman of the Cherokees, was born at Chota, the sacred Mother Town of the Cherokees. She was born into the Wolf clan and was the niece of Attakullakulla, a prudent chief who allowed Moravian missionaries into the Cherokee country only after exacting a promise that they would build schools to teach his people about the ways of the whites. Ward, sometimes called "Wild Rose," is first noted at the Battle of Taliwa in 1755. She was married to Kingfisher, a warrior who was killed in this skirmish with the Creeks. Fighting alongside him, Ward became enraged at the Creeks for his death, and she rallied the Cherokee forces to a decisive victory. For her heroism, she was named "Beloved Woman," a title reserved for wise women who distinguished themselves in battle or who were the wives or mothers of great warriors.

In her role as Beloved Woman, Ward performed such duties as sitting in the General Council (where she had full voice and vote), heading the Women's Council, preparing the black drink for the Green Corn (busk) Ceremony, and acting as a negotiator in treaty parlays. When she met with John Sevier to strike peace terms with the Americans (Little Pigeon River, Tennessee, 1781), she was appalled that he had no women negotiators. He was as appalled that she was trusted with such an important task. Reportedly she admonished him to return to his people and explain the terms to the women, saying, "Let your women hear our words."

As a Beloved Woman, Ward had the right to save a captive condemned to death. In 1780 she saved the life of a Mrs. Bean, a white woman captive about to be immolated. Ward nursed her back to health and then set her free, but not before Mrs. Bean had introduced Ward to the art of weaving in the manner of the whites and to raising cattle as dairy animals. Though these innovations are attached to the name of Nancy Ward with great honor, there is at least one other that calls forth great shame: she was the first Cherokee to have black slaves.

Many years of broken promises on the part of the Americans eventually took their toll on Ward's credulity, and by the Cherokee Council of 1817, she was no longer advising peace. She told the younger people not to cede any more land because already the talk of Indian removal west of the Mississippi was being heard and believed. Fearing removal in her lifetime, Ward took to the trade of innkeeping and married a white man, Bryan (Briant) Ward. They kept a small inn at the Ocowee River's Womankiller Ford. She bore three children and became prosperous before her death in 1824. Her son, Fivekiller, who was with his mother at her death, reported that a white light ascended from her body and flew into the sacred mound at Chota. The same mound was destroyed by the Tennessee Valley Authority's Tellico Dam Project of the 1970s and 1980s. Nancy Ward is buried somewhere near present-day Vonore, Tennessee. Many honors have been bestowed in her name since her death. Among these, the Nashville, Tennessee, chapter of the Daughters of the American Revolution is named for her.

References

Dockstader, Frederick J., ed. *Great North American Indians: Profiles in Life and Leadership*. New York: Van Nostrand Reinhold, 1977.

Felton, Harold W. *Nancy Ward: Cherokee*. New York: Dodd, Mead, 1975.

McClary, Ben Harris. "The Last Beloved Woman of the Cherokees." *Tennessee Historical Society Quarterly* 21 (1962): 352–364.

Tucker, Norma. "Nancy Ward, Ghighau of the Cherokees." *Georgia Historical Quarterly* 53 (June 1969): 192–200.

Woodward, Grace Steele. *The Cherokees*. Norman: University of Oklahoma Press, 1963.

—*Cynthia Kasee*

WAUNEKA, ANNIE DODGE (1910–1997), a public health activist and politician, was born in the Navajo Nation near Sawmill, Arizona. She was the privileged daughter of Henry Chee Dodge, the first elected chairman of the Navajo Tribal Council after the tribe adopted a constitutional form of government in 1923. Although Henry Dodge was a wealthy rancher and an influential politician, he believed that his children should learn Navajo traditions and values. From an early age, Wauneka had chores such as sheepherding, but also received a formal education at the Albuquerque Indian School.

Wauneka grew up fully bilingual. She was equally comfortable in Navajo and English, and was able to act as a cultural translator between the conservative and liberal elements of the tribe. Soon she realized that the way her unique talents could best serve the Navajo was through improving the health of the more traditional segment. Wary of the ways of Indian Health Service physicians, which they thought were witchcraft, many conservatives refused to receive injections or to have their children or grandchildren inoculated. Diseases such as tuberculosis ran rampant, both because of this cultural misunderstanding and because of poor sanitation. For many years, while also holding tribal office, Wauneka dedicated her life to finding common ground for Navajo patients and non–Navajo health professionals. She made visits to isolated hogans to discuss the importance of inoculating children, wrote a lexicon of terms in Navajo to be used by doctors and nurses to explain procedures, and acted in films promoting improved sanitation that were shown throughout the reservation.

Her selfless work on behalf of the Navajo erased any doubts about this daughter of a wealthy liberal politician. Her brother, Thomas Dodge, had been elected tribal chairman 1933, continuing the family tradition of political service. In 1951 Wauneka was elected tribal council representative from the Klagetoh District.

After her marriage to George Wauneka, she became the first woman elected to the Tribal Council. Her work in public health made her the obvious choice to head the council's Health Committee. Her successes garnered her two more terms on the council (1955, 1959). She felt so certain that her talents were needed by the Navajo people that she risked her marriage to continue her work. In 1953 her husband was running for the position Wauneka had been holding, but she felt he was not a good candidate, so she ran against him and easily defeated him.

As she continued her grassroots work with the Navajo Tribal Council Health Committee, Wauneka went to college, eventually earning the credentials to back up her work. She graduated with a BS in public health from the University of Arizona in the mid-1950s. In 1959 she received the Arizona State Public Health Association's Outstanding Worker in Public Health Award, as well as the Indian Achievement Award from the Indian Council Fire of Chicago. In 1960 Wauneka began hosting a biweekly radio show on KGAK in Gallup, New Mexico. The program, completely in Navajo, covered topics of interest to the Navajo Nation, as well as health information. A tireless worker, Wauneka was eventually appointed to the Surgeon General's Advisory Board and served as a board member of the National Tuberculosis Association.

In 1963 Wauneka received the Presidential Medal of Freedom, given to her at the White House by President John Kennedy. She also received an honorary doctorate in public health from the University of Arizona.

References

Anderson, Owanah, ed. *Ohoyo One Thousand: Resource Guide of American Indian/Alaska Native Women, 1982*. Wichita Falls, TX: Ohoyo Resource Center, 1982.

Gridley, Marion, ed. and comp. *Indians of Today*. 4th ed. Chicago: ICFP, 1971.

Nelson, Mary Caroll. *Annie Wauneka*. Minneapolis, MN: Dillon, 1972.

Steiner, Stan. *The New Indians*. New York: Harper & Row, 1968.

Wauneka, Annie D. "The Dilemma for Indian Women." *Wassaja* 4 (September 1976): 8.

Witt, Shirley Hill. "An Interview with Dr. Annie Dodge Wauneka." *Frontiers* 6 (Fall 1981): 64–67.

—Cynthia Kasee

WETAMOO [Namumpam, Tatatanum, Tatapanum, Squaw Sachem of the Pocasset, Wetemoo, Wetamou, Wetamoe, Weetamoo, Weetamou, Weetamoe, Weetammo, Weetamore, Queen Wetamoo] (c. 1635/1650–1676) was born near the Fall River in present-day Rhode Island. Her father (Corbitant?) was a sachem (chief of a confederation of the Algonquian tribes of the North Atlantic coast) of the Pocasset (Pokanoket) village of the Wampanoag Confederacy. When he died, Wetamoo succeeded her father as sachem. She married Wamsutta (Alexander), grand sachem of the Wampanoag Confederacy and brother of Metacom (Metacomet, King Philip). When Wamsutta died, she married Quequequamanchet (Petonowowett, Peter Nunnuit, "Ben"), but she left him because he sided with the colonists in King Philip's War. With her next husband, Quinnapin (Quinapin, Quequequamanchet), a Narragansett, Wetamoo allied with King Philip and led the Pocasset (Pokanoket) and the Narragansett in battle. Quinnapin captured a white woman, Mary Rowlandson, who in her memoirs described Wetamoo's leadership role and regal stature. In 1676, as she was escaping from the Plymouth colonists, Wetamoo drowned in the Fall River. The colonists cut off her head and displayed it on a rod in Taunton.

References

Biographical Dictionary of Indians of the Americas. Vol. 2. Newport Beach, CA: American Indian Publishers, 1983.

Bourne, Russell. *The Red King's Rebellion: Racial Politics in New England, 1675–1678.* New York: Atheneum, 1990.

Church, Colonel Benjamin. *Diary of King Philip's War, 1675–1676.* Edited by Alan and Mary Simpson. Riverton, RI: Lockwood Publications, 1975.

Horowitz, David. *The First Frontier: The Indian Wars and America's Origins, 1607–1776.* New York: Random House, 1978.

Mathes, Valerie Shirer. "Native American Women in Medicine and the Military." *Journal of the West* 21 (April 1982): 41–48.

———. "A New Look at the Role of Women in Indian Society." *American Indian Quarterly* 2 (1975): 131–139.

Rowlandson, Mary. *The Sovereignty and Goodness of God, Together with the Faithfulness of His Promises Displayed; Being a Narrative of the Captivity and Restoration of Mrs. Mary Rowlandson, a Minister's Wife in New England.* London: Joseph Poole, 1682.

—Pattiann Frinzi

WHITE, ELIZABETH Q. [Polingaysi Qoyawayma] (c. 1892–1990), was a Hopi born at Old Oraibi, Arizona, to Sevenka and Qoyawayma (called Fred by the Mennonite missionaries in the area). She was a member of her mother's Coyote clan and a child of her father's Kachina clan. As a child she was raised in the traditional Hopi way, but in her teens feelings of restlessness prompted her parents to allow her to leave home to attend school in the white world. White attended Sherman Institute in Riverside, California, and graduated from Bethel College, a Mennonite school in Newton, Kansas. Most of her white education conflicted with the lifeways of her home, causing her much unhappiness. She worked in the homes of German families to pay her way through school and was surprised at the hard work, equating the Hopi women slaving at their grindstones to the German women slaving at their washboards. She made friends with Elizabeth Schmidt who, upon finding out that Polingaysi did not know her exact birthday, only that it was in the spring, offered to share her birthdate, April 9, with her. At Bethel, White trained to be a Mennonite missionary; when she returned to Oraibi, she built a house from which to do missionary work, but she soon began to feel troubled about her calling among the Hopi.

In 1924 White took a job as a housekeeper at the government day school at Hotevilla; then she began to teach first grade and soon became officially certified to teach in the Indian Service system. In 1941 she was chosen from among all the Indian Service teachers to conduct a workshop at Chemawa, Oregon, for teachers and supervisors from the United States and Alaska. She continued to teach until 1954, and received the United States Department of the Interior's Distinguished Service Award for her long career in Indian education.

She married Lloyd White, part Cherokee, in 1931 at Bloomfield Trading Post near Toadlena, New Mexico, but they soon separated. When she retired from teaching, White turned to music, writing, and pottery making. Her pottery has been displayed in private collections and in major museums, such as the Museum of Northern Arizona and the Heard Museum in Phoenix. She has written several books describing traditional Hopi life and the difficult transitions between cultures. White lived in Flagstaff and founded the Hopi Student Scholarship Fund at Northern Arizona University. She died at the Phoenix Indian Hospital and was buried at Kykotsmovi Cemetery. Chief Tawaquaptewa once called her "the little one who wanted to be a white man."

References

Qoyawayma, Polingaysi. *No Turning Back: A Hopi Indian Woman's Struggle to Live in Two Worlds*. Albuquerque: University of New Mexico Press, 1964.
———. *The Sun Girl: A True Story About Dawamana*. Flagstaff: Museum of Northern Arizona Press, 1978.
Qoyawayma, Polingaysi, and Vada Carlson. *Broken Pattern: Sunlight and Shadows of Hopi History*. Happy Camp, CA: Naturegraph, 1985.
Sweitzer, Paul. "Hopi Authoress, White Is Dead." *The Sun* [Flagstaff, AZ], December 8, 1990, 7.

—*Gretchen Ronnow*

WHITE, MADELINE MELBA (b. 1944), is a prolific artist who has over fifty paintings in the collection of the Tekakwitha Fine Arts Center in Sisseton, South Dakota, and produced over seven hundred paintings between 1968 and 1982. Born in a log cabin at Long Hollow, near Sisseton, she is the daughter of Indian ranchers who raised horses, cows, and chickens, and grew vegetables for sale in town. Her father died when she was five years old, and because her mother was unable to support the family, White was sent to the Tekakwitha Orphanage.

She attended Wahpeton Indian School for her elementary education, and then went to Flandreau Indian School for her high school education. White received no formal art training and began painting in 1968 as a result of an argument with her brother, Cliff, who said he was a better artist than she was. She was befriended by Tino Walkingbull and Paul WarCloud, two noted Sisseton artists, who taught her technique and gave her confidence. She was influenced by the paintings of George Catlin and Frederic Remington.

White says she paints to keep the culture of her people alive. She hopes people will look at her paintings and like them. She does not mind adverse criticism from Indian people, but she dislikes criticism from non–Indians who do not try to understand Indian culture. To her, historical accuracy is important. Her paintings are created not just to be looked at but to be studied. They are expressions of her cultural heritage. The range of her work is very wide. In addition to Indian culture, she paints scenes from biblical literature and portraits of contemporaries. She is an excellent portrait painter, with an outstanding ability to perceive and include details that bring her subjects to life. Her paintings have a striking boldness of line and color.

White lives with members of her family in Indian housing north of Sisseton. After a three-year break from work as a result of illness, she began painting again, working often in the artists' studio at the Tekakwitha Fine Arts Center. Her paintings are in private and public collections in the Upper Plains states.

References

Marken, Jack. Personal communications with Madeline Melba White, May 16 and 28, 1990.

—Jack Marken

WHITEMAN, ROBERTA HILL (b. 1947), a Wisconsin Oneida, has been married since 1980 to the Arapaho artist Ernest Whiteman; they have three children: Jacob, Heather, and Melissa. She received a BA at the University of Wisconsin and an MFA at the University of Montana in 1973. Whiteman taught in the Poets in the Schools programs in Minnesota, Arizona, Wyoming, South Dakota (Rosebud Sioux Reservation), Oklahoma, Montana, and Wisconsin. She taught American literature at the University of Wisconsin, Eau Claire, and completed a doctorate in American Studies at the University of Minnesota, where she now teaches. Her first book of poems, *Star Quilt*, was illustrated by her husband. "I work as hard (consciously, unconsciously) as I can to hear the music of the voice that speaks through me," Whiteman says in *The Third Woman*. She also states, "I sense that I am trying to regain an image of wholeness. Before that can occur, I feel one must be aware of what is left."

The Iroquois word *Oneida* comes from *oneyote a ka* ("people of the erected stone," in upstate New York). Transplanted from Native lands, this poet and mother has learned Coyote's peacemaking patience, ironically composite. In *Star Quilt* she writes iambic verse with a vision courageously decentered, yet stable in personal commitments to her children, husband, and lifework. Her logic skitters, her lines search, her images dissociate. There is lightning in her star quiltings, thunder in Oneida stone origins.

Whiteman's tutor at the University of Montana, Richard Hugo, taught her to trust the strange tongues, the startled insights, Coyote's yellow eyes, and yips toward the losses that bond. "More than land's between us," she said in tribute, in "Blue Mountain," to the middle-aged Anglo poet who asked that their common losses be chanted as collaborative gain. "Chant to me in your poems/of our loss and let the poem itself be our gain," Hugo counseled in *31 Poems and 13 Dreams*, "You're gaining/the hurt world worth having. Friend, let me be Indian." Like her Montana contemporary, James Welch, through Hugo's example and tutoring Whiteman learned the patterned natural rhythms of the blank verse line, the essentially iambic foot of Euro–American traditional verse. She plays off this Western form in much of her poetry.

The Dakota painter Oscar Howe, no stranger to surreal and cubist visions, also served as Whiteman's teacher. For half a century, he taught and painted a wildly beautiful visionary world where inner structures and modern tonal surfaces shared an interplay of planes and forms on the canvas. Whiteman wrote "Woman Seed Player," the penultimate poem in *Star Quilt*, about Howe's painting by the same name: "you said no one had ever gone full circle,/from passion through pattern and back again/toward pebbles moist with moonlight." From all these mentors—lost mother and alcoholic father, children and husbands, Anglo poet and Dakota painter, sea's fire and gray stone's blood—Whiteman asks the contrary's humor to heal her wounds: "Teach me/your crisscross answer/to the crackling of gulls."

If *Star Quilt* makes for slow going, the thick unraveling of a mare's nest of images, of impacted rhythms, and of tangled feelings—from rage to inebriation to ecstasy and grace—the way leads toward rebirth, a renaissance still in the making. "One finds in this work," Carolyn Forché writes in the foreword, "a map of the journey each of us must complete, wittingly or not, as children and exiles of the Americas." Native mothers, their lovers, husbands, and children *re*form new families and "dream of rebirth" from "this slow hunger, / this midnight swollen four hundred years."

References

Bruchac, Joseph. "Massaging the Earth: An Interview with Roberta Hill Whiteman." In *Survival This Way: Interviews with Native American Poets*. Edited by Joseph Bruchac. Pp. 323–335. Tucson: University of Arizona Press, 1987.

Campis, Jack. "Oneida." *In Handbook of North American Indians*. Vol. 15. Edited by Bruce G. Trigger. Washington, DC: Smithsonian Institution Press, 1978.

Fisher, Dexter, ed. *The Third Woman: Minority Women Writers of the United States*. Boston: Houghton Mifflin, 1980.

Lincoln, Kenneth. *Indi'n Humor: Bicultural Play in Native America*. New York: Oxford University Press, 1991.

McCullough, Ken. "*Star Quilt* as Mandala: An Assessment of the Poetry of Roberta Hill Whiteman." *North Dakota Quarterly* 53 (Spring 1985): 194–203.

Niatum, Duane, ed. *Carriers of the Dream Wheel: Contemporary Native American Poetry*. New York: Harper & Row, 1975.

———. *Harper's Anthology of 20th Century Native American Poetry*. San Francisco: Harper & Row, 1988.

Whiteman, Roberta Hill. *Philadelphia Flowers*. Duluth, MN: Holy Cow! Press, 1996.

———. *Star Quilt*. Minneapolis, MN: Holy Cow! Press, 1984.

—*Kenneth Lincoln*

WILLIAMS, ALICE CLING (b. 1953), began a renaissance in Navajo pottery about 1976. Previously, Navajo pottery was strictly utilitarian. Pots had bullet-shaped bottoms, which made them functional as cooking vessels but unmarketable to non–Navajos. The vessel's surface was scraped with a corncob, which produced a rough surface, and the only decoration was a filet around the rim. This was the style of pottery Williams learned to make from her mother, Rose Williams. She took her traditional pots to Bill Beaver, a trader at Sacred Mountain Trading Post, the only trader at the time who bought Navajo pottery. Even though he offered the pots at a very low price, Williams's pots were not very popular. Williams says her pots did not sell because they were ugly.

Because of this, Williams began polishing her unfired vessels with a smooth stone rather than the traditional corncob, and paying closer attention to the manner in which the piñon pitch was applied after the pot was fired. She also gave more thought to vessel shape and overall design. Today Williams's pots are very popular and command among the highest prices paid for Navajo pots. Her vessels are highly polished and have only the thinnest veneer of piñon pitch, a combination that makes the vessels seem as if they are carved from highly polished wood. Her work has won numerous awards at the Museum of Northern Arizona in Flagstaff and the Heard Museum in Phoenix. Because of her success, and because Bill Beaver continued to encourage her and a few Navajo potters as they experimented with their craft, Navajo pottery did not vanish. Indeed, it is a vital craft. Today the largest collection of Alice Williams's work is held at the Arizona State Museum. Williams and her husband live at Shonto, Arizona, on the Navajo Reservation, where she works as a teacher's aide.

References

Bernstein, Bruce D., and Susan Brown McGreevy. *Anii Anaadaalyaa'igii: Continuity and Innovation in Recent Navajo Art*. Santa Fe, NM: Wheelwright Museum of Indian Art, 1988.

Graves, Laura. Field notes. 1980–1990.

Hartman, Russell P. *Navajo Pottery*. Flagstaff, AZ: Northland Press, 1989.

Wright, H. Diane. "Navajo Pottery." *American Indian Art* 12 (1987): 26–35.

Wright, H. Diana, and Jan Bell. "Potters and Their Work." *Plateau* 58 (1987): 24–31.

—*Laura Graves*

WINNIE, LUCILLE JERRY [Sah-Gan-De-Oh] (b. 1905), provides an account of her life story in *Sah-Gan-De-Oh, the Chief's Daughter*. Winnie, a Seneca/Cayuga, was born in Oklahoma and raised on reservations in Oklahoma and Montana. Her father, a teacher whom she lovingly calls "Chief," worked to improve the Indians' education and living conditions on these reservations, and although he died when Winnie was only twelve, his belief in the need to acculturate the Indian people into modern society became the most influential factor in her life. Her autobiography is of her acculturation.

Shortly before her father's death, Winnie left her family to attend her father's alma mater, Haskell Institute, a government school for Indians in Lawrence, Kansas. After seven years there, she left to follow her father's profession and became a teacher for the Indian Service. However, she soon abandoned teaching for a series of jobs in government agencies and private businesses. The greater part of Winnie's autobiography is devoted to her life as a single career woman in a society that was increasingly accepting women into its workforce.

Winnie ends her autobiography with her return to a reservation, thus framing her life story with accounts of reservation life. In 1963 she became the director of arts and crafts on the Northern Cheyenne Reservation in Montana.

Here she worked to help the Cheyenne people become more economically independent by teaching them how to produce and market authentic Indian products. Through this work, Winnie helped accomplish "The Chief's" mission: the integration of the Indian into the American way of life without the loss of individual heritage.

References

Bataille, Gretchen M., and Kathleen M. Sands, eds. *American Indian Women: A Guide to Research*. New York: Garland, 1991.

Brumble, David H., ed. *An Annotated Bibliography of American Indian and Eskimo Autobiographies*. Lincoln: University of Nebraska Press, 1981.

Green, Rayna, ed. *Native American Women: A Contextual Bibliography*. Bloomington: Indiana University Press, 1983.

Winnie, Lucille. *Sah-Gan-De-Oh, the Chief's Daughter*. New York: Vantage, 1969.

—Jeanne Olson

WITT, SHIRLEY HILL (b. 1941), Mohawk academic and public servant, was born and raised on the St. Regis Reservation in New York. She became involved in Indian affairs while an undergraduate student at the University of New Mexico (UNM). In 1961 Witt and nine other Indian students began meeting at the Gallup Indian Center and discussing what role young Indians should play in the emergent Indian rights movement. From those meetings, the National Indian Youth Council was born, and Witt was its first vice president. She and another founder, Herbert Blatchford, continued to work together on Indian rights concerns throughout Witt's years at UNM. Together they became protesters at the fledgling fish-ins starting at the Quillayute River near Puget Sound. They went on to salvage the Gallup Indian Center during its low point in the late 1960s with such programs as the Workshops for Leaders, a youth training program.

Though she is a religious traditionalist, Witt also relates to the common experience of peoples of Catholic culture. For many years, she has worked to forge ties between Indians and Chicanos in the Southwest, calling on them to see the similarities of their ethnic experiences. She served as a conduit between the two groups when Chicano politician Reies Tijerina sought the Indian vote in statewide elections in New Mexico in the late 1960s.

Keeping up with her schoolwork while staying active in community organizing and raising two children as a single parent, Witt received her BA, MA, and PhD in anthropology from UNM. She moved into the national arena of Indian issues when she served as an assistant researcher for the Indian Claims Commission in the 1970s. In recent years, Witt has been the director of natural resources for the State of New Mexico. In addition to her more famous exploits as an organizer and speaker, she is also an active feminist (noting in a Women of All Red Nations publication that the sexism of the United States government in not prosecuting women activists after Wounded Knee II allowed the Indian rights movement to remain intact with national leaders in litigation and in jail), has been a member of the United States Civil Rights Commission, and is a published author.

References

Green, Rayna, ed. *That's What She Said*. Bloomington: Indiana University Press, 1984. "Past Positives and Present Problems." In *American Public Discourse: A Multicultural Perspective*, Edited by Ronald K. Burke. Lanham, MD: University Press of America, 1992.

Witt, Shirley Hill. "The Brave-Hearted Women: The Struggle at Wounded Knee." *Civil Rights Digest* 8 (1976): 38–45.

———. "Native Women Today: Sexism and the Indian Woman." *Civil Rights Digest* 6 (Spring 1974): 29–35.

———. *The Tuscaroras*. New York: Crowell-Collier, 1972.

———. *The Way: An Anthology of American Indian Literature*. New York: Vintage Books, 1972.

—*Cynthia Kasee*

WITTSTOCK, LAURA WATERMAN (b?), was born on the Cattaraugus Indian Reservation and is a member of the Heron clan of the Seneca Nation of New York. She is a political activist for Native American peoples, a journalist, a writer, and an education and programs consultant. She was the founder, developer, and president of MIGIZI Communications, a radio news service providing weekly radio shows on seventeen stations for Native peoples in the Midwest Great Lakes area.

Wittstock has been active in women's advocacy, including work for the Women's Educational Equity Act advisory board and the Harriet Tubman Battered Women's Center. In 1975 she served as a panelist for the United Nations International Women's Year World Conference for Women in Development, held in Mexico City. She has also been active in Native alcoholism programs including the Juel Fairbanks Aftercare in St. Paul (an alcohol treatment program) and the National Commission on Alcoholism and Alcohol Related Problems.

Wittstock is the manager for the Native American Research Institute in the Center V satellite office. Her responsibilities include training and providing technical assistance to recipients of Title IV Indian Education Grants in several of the north midwestern states.

Wittstock has been the director of the American Indian Press Association and editor of *Legislative Review*. She has published in *Media Bulletin, Civil Rights Digest, Indian Voice*, and *Akwesasne Notes*.

References

Anderson, Owanah, ed. *Ohoyo One Thousand: A Resource Guide to American Indian/Alaska Native Women, 1982*. Wichita Falls, TX: Ohoyo Resource Center, 1982.

Wittstock, Laura Waterman. "Native American Women in the Feminist Milieu." In *Contemporary Native American Addresses*. Edited by John Maestas. Pp. 373–376. Provo, UT: Brigham Young University, Press, 1976.

———. "Native American Women: Twilight of a Long Maidenhood." In *Comparative Perspectives of Third World Women: The Import of Race, Sex and Class*. Edited by Beverly Lindsey. Pp. 207–227. New York: Praeger, 1980.

—*Lucy Leriche*

WOLF, HELEN PEASE (b. 1906), half Absaroka (Crow) and half Anglo, was born near Rotten Grass, Montana. Always interested in the adventures of her parents, relatives, and friends, she asked about them and committed some stories to memory and others to paper. In 1989 Wolf published *Reaching Both Ways*, which tells of her and her family's history, primarily in the region that was to become known as Lodge Grass, Montana, and includes a few traditional Crow tales as well as histories of local Natives, settlers, and schools.

Wolf's goals in writing *Reaching Both Ways* were primarily two: to preserve and pass on aspects of early Crow history that might otherwise be forgotten, and, as the title suggests, to show the intricate interrelations of people of several nationalities, people often engaged in common rather than in divisive acts. Wolf's Crow ancestors, in her telling of that history, traveled from what was to become known as the Canadian side of the Great Lakes in the 1500s to the Dakotas and later into the Yellowstone region of Montana and Wyoming. Part of Wolf's European lineage reaches back to the arrival of the *Mayflower*, and from the time of her European ancestors' arrival on the North American continent, there were Indian–Anglo intermarriages. Several of her Anglo ancestors were active in Native affairs, serving as Crow delegates in Washington, D.C. Wolf's mother, Sarah Walker Pease, named her daughter Helen after Helen Phelps Stokes, who was friend and benefactor to Sarah when, as a child, she was sent from her home in Montana to attend Hampton Institute in Virginia (Booker T. Washington was one of the institution's supervisors). Wolf also tells of her mother, at age ten, meeting General George Custer in 1876, two months before the Battle of the Little Bighorn.

At age fifteen, Wolf left Montana to attend Bacone, a Christian school in Muskogee, Oklahoma, at which she completed four years of high school and two years of junior college, graduating in 1931. Although she returned to Montana intending to teach, Wolf instead married Charles Wolf (1900–1977); they had four children, and began ranching in Soap Creek, Montana. Having maintained the ranch for nearly fifty years, the Wolfs retired to Lodge Grass while some of their children took charge of the ranch.

Reference

Wolf, Helen Pease. *Reaching Both Ways*. Cheyenne, WY: Pioneer Printing & Stationery, 1989.

—*Greg Grewell*

WOMAN CHIEF [The Absaroka Amazon] (c. 1806–1858), was born into the Gros Ventre of the Prairie and captured by the Crow around the age of ten. In contrast to the Crow males, who practiced female behaviors and cross-dressing, Woman Chief dressed as a woman but pursued male activities. As a young woman, she was known for her marksmanship and her ability to kill and butcher buffalo in the field. Her foster father seems to have encouraged this behavior because his own sons had died or had been captured in the ongoing hostilities with the Blackfoot. When he died in battle, she became the head of his lodge and family.

Woman Chief (her Gros Ventre and childhood Crow names are unknown) achieved the status of warrior during a Blackfoot raid in which she is reported to have single-handedly turned an ambush and protected a fort that sheltered both Crow and white families. Her reputation made, Woman Chief gathered a group of young men and led guerrilla-style raids on the Blackfoot with great success (measured in horses and human scalps). Soon she was elevated to the Council of Chiefs and given the title by which we know her. Her rank was third in a band of 160 lodges. After the Treaty of Fort Laramie (1851), she was involved in peacemaking efforts with the tribes of the upper Missouri and visited the tribe of her birth, the Gros Ventre of the Prairie. Although a peace lasted for three or four years, Woman Chief died in ambush at the hands of her parents' tribe.

Woman Chief fascinated the white men who encountered her. Because of her rejection of the doctrine of separate spheres of activity for men and women, which whites perceived in the Crow camps along the fur routes, she seemed an exotic and revolutionary figure. These informants compare her to European images of the Amazon, crediting her lack of a husband to her ferocity and tribal status, and making much of the fact that Woman Chief took up to four "wives" to manage the domestic work of her lodge. Many of these assessments must be seen as biased by white doctrines of gender, labor, and domesticity, yet they suggest possibilities for a reexamination of this nearly mythic figure.

References

Capps, Benjamin. *Woman Chief.* Garden City, NY: Doubleday, 1979.

Denig, Edwin Thompson. In *Indian Tribes of the Upper Missouri.* Edited by J. N. B. Hewitt. Bureau of American Ethnology, Forty-sixth Annual Report (1928–1929). Washington, DC: Bureau of American Ethnology, 1930.

———. "Biography of Woman Chief." In *Five Indian Tribes of the Upper Missouri.* Edited by John C. Ewers. Pp. 195–200. Norman: University of Oklahoma Press, 1961.

Kurz, Rudolph J. *Journal of Rudolph Friedrich Kurz: An Account of His Experiences Among Fur Traders and American Indians on the Mississippi and Missouri Rivers During the Years 1846–1852.* Edited by J. N. B. Hewitt. Bureau of American Ethnology Bulletin 115. Washington, DC: Bureau of American Ethnology, 1937.

—Jennifer L. Jenkins

WOODY, ELIZABETH (b. 1959), was born in Ganado, Arizona, of Warm Springs, Wasco, and Navajo heritage. She studied creative writing at the Institute of American Indian Arts in Santa Fe, New Mexico. There her talent was fostered by teachers including Joy Harjo and Phil Foss, as well as fellow students including Phillip Minthorn and Joe Dale Tate Nevaquaya. Later, Woody studied at Portland State University in Oregon with Primus St. John, as well as Henry Carlile, and at Evergreen State College in Washington. Although she credits much of her growth as a writer to her teachers, she also points to the influence of her family, as well as to a long oral legacy that predominates not only her work but also her vision.

Though readers of Northwest literature have long recognized Portland-based Woody as a prominent presence in the literary community, it was the publication of her first book, *Hand into Stone,* that gained Woody's writing national recognition. Awarded the American Book Award and lauded by Simon Ortiz, Barry Lopez, and

Joy Harjo, the book offers its readers a stunning range of emotion and concern. Clearly political in its embrace of the fishing rights issue that concerns so many of the Northwest's Native people, the book also details the destruction of the environment and the hazards of nuclear energy, and offers a compelling renunciation of the ways in which Native people continue to be victimized. Yet Woody's poetry is also profoundly spiritual and ultimately hopeful. With her visions of the ways in which people come together, the power of the earth and its creatures to heal, her words finally become a kind of healing, a kind of song.

Woody's poems have appeared in a number of journals, including *Wooster Review, Mr. Cognito, Contact II*, and *Akwekon;* her work is also featured in a number of anthologies, including *Dancing on the Rim of the World, Sur le dos de la torte: Revue bilingue de littérature amerindienne, Bearing Witness/Sobreviviendo, The Clouds Threw This Light*, and *Songs from This Earth on Turtle's Back.*

Woody has also earned a substantial reputation as a visual artist and a photographer. Her art has been featured in a number of Northwest shows, as well as exhibits in San Francisco, Minneapolis, New York, and Washington, D.C. She has worked closely with Lillian Pitt, one of the most renowned artists in the Northwest. Woody's photographs are featured in a number of books, including *Faces of a Reservation, Songs from This Earth on Turtle's Back*, and *Dancing on the Rim of the World.*

Woody is active in a number of arts, political, and community organizations. An enrolled member of the Confederated Tribes of Warm Springs (Oregon), she is also active in the Native American Arts Council, the Metropolitan Arts Commission, and ATLATL, a national Native American arts organization. In 1988 Woody was a founding member of the Northwest Native American Writers' Association, which has sought to bring together the region's writers and to foster increased opportunities for publication, readings, and collaboration.

References

Bruchac, Joseph, ed. *Songs from This Earth on Turtle's Back: Contemporary American Indian Poetry.* Greenfield Center, NY: Greenfield Review Press, 1983.

Cochran, Jo, J. T. Stewart, and Mayumi Tsutakawa, eds. *Bearing Witness/Sobreviviendo: An Anthology of Native American/Latina Art and Literature. Special issue of Calyx: A Journal of Art and Literature by Women* 8 (Spring 1984).

Lerner, Andrea, ed. *Dancing on the Rim of the World: Contemporary Northwest Native American Writing.* Tucson: University of Arizona Press, 1990.

Van Thienen, trans. *Sur le dos de la torte: Revue bilingue de littérature amerindienne.* Rillieux, France: N.p., 1989.

Woody, Elizabeth. *Hand into Stone.* New York: Contact II Press, 1988.

———. *Luminaries of the Humble.* Tucson: University of Arizona Press, 1994.

———. *Seven Hands, Seven Hearts.* Portland, OR: Eighth Mountain Press, 1994.

—*Andrea Lerner*

WRIGHT, MURIEL HAZEL (1889–1975), well known as a historian and an editor, began her career as a teacher and administrator in elementary and secondary schools in southern Oklahoma. Born at Lehigh, Choctaw Nation, into an affluent Choctaw family, she was educated in the schools of the Choctaw Nation, at

Wheaton College in Massachusetts, and at East Central State Normal School in Oklahoma. From 1912 to 1924 she held teaching and administrative posts, except for one year spent in graduate study at Barnard College of Columbia University.

In the 1920s Wright began a writing career that extended to the end of her life. Her first major effort was *Oklahoma: A History of the State and Its People*, a four-volume work that she wrote with Joseph B. Thoburn. That same year (1929) she published *The Story of Oklahoma*, a public school textbook. From 1929 to 1931 she was employed by the Oklahoma Historical Society to conduct research for the history of the Five Civilized Tribes, and during the next decade she devoted herself to writing. From the 1920s to the early 1970s, Wright produced seven books, including the standard *A Guide to the Indian Tribes of Oklahoma* and dozens of articles, nearly one hundred of which appeared in *Chronicles of Oklahoma*, the journal of the Oklahoma Historical Society.

Throughout her writing career, Wright held significant positions. First, she was active in the affairs of the Choctaw Nation. From 1922 to 1928 she was secretary of the Choctaw Committee, which conducted Choctaw business affairs. She worked to restore and preserve the Choctaw Council House at Tuskahoma. In 1934 she helped to organize the Choctaw Advisory Council and served as its secretary until 1944. Second, Wright assumed editorial responsibilities for *Chronicles of Oklahoma* in 1943. Though officially associate editor until 1955, when she was named editor, she performed all editorial duties from her appointment until her retirement in 1973. A persistent and exacting editor, she exerted a strong influence on the historiography of the Indian tribes of Oklahoma. In recognition of her writings on the American Indian, Oklahoma City University awarded her an honorary Doctor of Humanities degree in 1964, and in 1971 the North American Indian Women's Association recognized her as the outstanding Indian woman of the twentieth century.

References

Arrington, Ruth. "Muriel Hazel Wright." In *Notable American Women, the Modern Period: A Biographical Dictionary*. Edited by Barbara Sicheman and Carol Hurd Green. Pp. 751–752.

Cambridge, MA: Belknap Press of Harvard University, 1980.

Fischer, LeRoy H. "Muriel H. Wright, Historian of Oklahoma." *Chronicles of Oklahoma* 52 (Spring 1974): 3–29.

Wright, Muriel. *Civil War Sites in Oklahoma*. Oklahoma City: Oklahoma Historical Society, 1967.

———. *A Guide to the Indian Tribes of Oklahoma*. Norman: University of Oklahoma Press, 1951.

Wright, Muriel, and Joseph B. Thoburn. *Oklahoma: A History of the State and Its People*. 4 vols. New York: Lewis Historical Publishing, 1929.

—Daniel F. Littlefield, Jr.

WYNNE, MARY T. [Turgeon] (b. 1952) is a Rosebud Sioux judge who has worked in tribal courts. She received her Bachelor of Arts degree from Augustana College in Sioux Falls, South Dakota, and graduated from the University of Minnesota Law School in 1978. Since that time, Wynne has held many prominent judicial positions. She has served as the chief judge of the Colville tribal court, a member of the board of directors of the Native American Rights Fund, and president of the Northwest Tribal Court Judge's Association. She is currently the president of the National American Indian Court Judges Association and a justice for tribal courts in the Northwest.

With her work in tribal courts, Wynne has attempted to "define and apply tribal custom and tradition within the mixed structure of today's tribal courts." Her work asserts the importance of tribal law in a wider context. She is a member of the advisory board of the Tribal Law and Policy Institute and one of the primary authors of the Tribal Legal Code Project.

References

"New NARF Board Member: Mary T. Wynne," NARF *Legal Review* 22:2 (summer/fall 1997): 17.

"Non-Indian Launches Suit Over Authority of Tribe," *The Ojibwe News* 3/27/1998 v.10; N.24 p.2

—*Kerry Kennedy Wynn*

Z

ZEPEDA, OFELIA (b. 1952), a Tohono O'odham and professor of linguistics and former director of the American Indian Studies Program at the University of Arizona, is also a poet and one of the foremost scholars of Tohono O'odham language and literature. Raised in Stanfield, near Casa Grande, Arizona, close to both the Tohono O'odham and Pima reservations, Zepeda took three degrees in linguistics (BA, MA, and PhD) at the University of Arizona after graduation from public schools. She was the first Tohono O'odham to receive a doctorate in linguistics and has regularly taught Tohono O'odham at the university since 1979, and since 1978 in the Papago Reservation Teacher Training Program. She has been instrumental in establishing centers for undergraduate and graduate Native American students and in developing a cross-disciplinary, cross-cultural degree program.

In addition to her university service, Zepeda has worked with her tribe to improve literacy in both English and Tohono O'odham. In 1983 she developed *A Papago Grammar* from tapes of Native speakers because no textbook existed for the classes she taught. Her work with the reservation committee for Tohono O'odham language policy yielded an official policy that encourages the speaking of the Native language at all grade levels. She also regularly participates in the summer American Indian Language Development Institute, which encourages Native Americans to complete their teaching certification.

Zepeda also writes poetry that blends English with Tohono O'odham oral tradition. She is a frequent recipient of grants and fellowships for linguistics, education, and humanities projects on her tribe's language and literature, which will promote literacy in both English and Tohono O'odham into the twenty-first century. In 1999, Zepeda was awarded a fellowship by the prestigious MacArthur Foundation.

References

Alvarez, Manuel, Ofelia Zepeda, et al. *The Tohono O'odham Language Policy*. Tohono O'odham Nation Sells, Arizona, 1988.

Evers, Larry, ed., with Ofelia Zepeda, et al. *The South Corner of Time*. Tucson: University of Arizona Press, 1983.

Zepeda, Ofelia. "The Continuum of Literacy in American Indian Communities." *Bilingual Research Journal* 19 (Winter 1995): 5–15.

———. *Ocean Power: Poems from the Desert*. Tucson: University of Arizona Press, 1995.

———. *A Papago Grammar*. Tucson: University of Arizona Press, 1983.

———, ed. *Mat Hekid o ju: When It Rains. Papago and Pima Poetry*. Sun Tracks, vol. 7. Tucson: University of Arizona Press, 1982.

———, comp. and trans. *Sand Papago Oral History Project*. Tucson, AZ: Western Archeological and Conservation Center, 1985.

—Jay Ann Cox

ZUNI, FLORA (1897–1983), was born into the Badger clan of the Zuni on July 1, 1897, the third child of her parents. Her father was a member of the Bear clan and an accomplished artist, and her mother, Lina, was an accomplished potter. She received her education at the boarding school at Black Rock and became one of the few Zuni of her time who could speak English. Later, this skill allowed her to become an interpreter for several different groups, including anthropologists, Bureau of Indian Affairs employees, Public Health Service employees, missionaries, and teachers. In 1915 she married a man from the Sun clan, and in 1918 she went to work as a teacher at the Zuni Day School. Her first husband died in 1939, and two years later she married a man from the Deer clan. Zuni had six children, two of whom predeceased her.

Noted as an interpreter and storyteller of great skill, Zuni worked with the anthropologists Alfred L. Kroeber, Ruth Benedict, Ruth Bunzel, and Elsie Clews Parsons in collecting Zuni folk tales, prayers, and linguistic material. Bunzel said of Zuni, "Flora had excellent command of English and translated her own texts and interpreted for her father, mother, and sisters and helped with the revision and analysis of all texts." Zuni also became an entrepreneur and saleswoman who took in boarders and sold turquoise on commission to help support her family.

Zuni remained a traditional Zuni throughout her lifetime, sponsoring several initiations into the kachina society and her medicine society, and attending summer and winter dances. She strongly believed in the importance of passing traditions from one generation to the next.

References

Bunzel, Ruth. "Anthropologists at Zuni." *Proceedings of the American Philosophical Society* 116 (August 1972): 323.

———. *Zuni Texts*. Publications of the American Ethnological Society, vol. 15. Edited by Franz Boas. New York: G. E. Stechert, 1933.

Pandey, Triloki Nath. "Flora Zuni—A Portrait." In *American Indian Intellectuals: 1976 Proceedings of the American Ethnological Society*. Edited by Margot Liberty. Pp. 217–225. St. Paul, MN: West Publishing, 1976.

—Joni Adamson Clarke

Selected Bibliography

Ahenakew, Freda, and H. C. Wolfart, eds. *Kôhkominawak Otácimowiniwâwa/ Our Grandmothers' Lives: As Told in Their Own Words*. Saskatoon, SK: Fifth House, 1992. Includes narratives by Glecia Bear, Irene Calliou, Janet Feitz, Minnie Fraser, Alpha Lafond, Rosa Longneck, and Mary Wells, all Cree women of western Canada. The texts are presented in both Cree and English.

Albers, Patricia, and Beatrice Medicine, eds. *The Hidden Half: Studies of Plains Indian Women*. Washington, DC: University Press of America, 1983. Essays on Plains tribal women covering such topics as slaves, male/female roles, work division, women's production of ceremonial objects, women's political roles, and the changing status of Plains women.

Allen, Paula Gunn, ed. *Grandmothers of the Light: A Medicine Woman's Sourcebook*. Boston: Beacon Press, 1991. This is a collection of Native American women's stories and the myths that have guided women's religious views through history. Allen connects myth, medicine, and the sacred to describe the roles of Native women through time.

————. *The Sacred Hoop: Recovering the Feminine in American Indian Traditions*. Boston: Beacon Press, 1986. Analysis of the gynocentric character of precontact Pueblo culture and the erosion of women's power through imposition of European patriarchal systems. Discussion of the role of American Indian women writers within the context of contemporary Indian women's cultures.

————. *Spider Woman's Granddaughters: Traditional Tales and Contemporary Writing by Native American Women*. Boston: Beacon, 1989. Allen has collected traditional tales, biography, and contemporary short stories that demonstrate the relationships of women writers with their communities.

Amberly, Julia V. *Thresholds of Difference: Feminist Critique, Native Women's Writings, Postcolonial Theory*. Toronto: University of Toronto Press, 1993. Critical examination of Native women's writing in Canada, and feminist and postcolonial theory. Interprets Native, Métis, and Inuit writing. Includes material on Jeannette Armstrong, Maria Campbell, and Beatrice Culleton.

Anderson, Owanah, ed. *Ohoyo One Thousand: A Resource Guide of American Indian/Alaska Native Women, 1982*. Wichita Falls, TX: Ohoyo Resource Center, 1982. Biographical sketches of over 1,000 American Indian/Alaskan Native women indexed according to area of expertise.

Axford, Roger, W. *Native Americans: 23 Indian Biographies*. Indiana, PA: A. G. Halldin, 1980. Includes interviews with and statements by Ida Carmen, Betsy Kellas, Clara Sue Kidwell, Veronica L. Murdock, Joanne Linder, Vivian Ayoungman, Yvonne Talachy, Gay Lawrence, Carol Allen Weston, and Roxie Woods.

Axtell, James, ed. *The Indian Peoples of Eastern America: A Documentary History of the Sexes*. Oxford, UK: Oxford University Press, 1981. This collection of essays documents various gendered tribal beliefs from 1632 to 1918 under the headings birth, coming of age, love and marriage, working, peace and war, heaven and earth, and death.

Bataille, Gretchen M., and Kathleen M. Sands. *American Indian Women: A Guide to Research*. New York: Garland, 1991. A comprehensive bibliography of over 1,500 annotated entries including bibliographies, reference works, ethnography, cultural history, social roles, politics, law, health, education, employment, visual and performing arts, literature and criticism, autobiography, biography, interviews, film, and video.

———. *American Indian Women: Telling Their Lives*. Lincoln: University of Nebraska Press, 1984. Examination of American Indian women's personal narratives and the centrality of women in tribal cultures. Focuses on eight autobiographical texts and speculates on emerging forms of autobiography by American Indian women.

———. *Native American Women: A Biographical Dictionary*. New York: Garland, 1993. This dictionary presents a wide selection of Native American (including Canadian) women who have influenced and currently influence lives inside and outside their culture. The dictionary includes a selected, annotated bibliography and four indices that list the women by their area of specialization, decade of birth, birth place, and tribal affiliation.

Bowker, Ardy. *Sisters in the Blood: The Education of Women in Native America*. Newton, MA: WEEA Publishing Center, Education Development Center, 1993. Report on study of nearly 1,000 women and their experience in the education system in an attempt to understand the high dropout rate of Indian women.

Boyer, Ruth McDonald, and Narcissus Duffy Gayton. *Apache Mothers and Daughters: Four Generations of a Family*. Norman: University of Oklahoma Press, 1992. Focuses on the life stories of four women, each of a different generation in the same Chiricahua Apache family, within the context of the roles each played within the ceremonial and everyday life of the tribe.

Bradford, C. J., and Laine Thom. *Dancing Colors: Paths of Native American Women*. San Francisco: Chronicle Books, 1992. Personal statements about their lives by Native American women and stories about women illustrated by historical photographs and traditional clothing and art, much of which is housed in museums.

Brant, Beth [Degonwadonti], ed. *A Gathering of Spirit: Writing and Art by North American Indian Women*. Ithaca, NY: Firebrand Books, 1988. Brant has gathered narratives, poetry, and art from over fifty Native American women. The collection includes well-known writers and artists as well as emerging writers.

Buchanan, Kimberly Moore. *Apache Women Warriors*. El Paso: Texas Western Press, 1986. This publication in the Southwestern Studies series focuses on Apache women such as Lozen, as well as lesser known wives and mothers within the tribe.

Castillo, Susan, and Victor M. P. Da Rose, eds. *Native American Women in Literature and Culture*. Porto, Portugal: Fernando Pessoa University Press, 1997. Twenty-five contributions are divided into three sections—Native American Women in Literature, Native American Women: Historical Perspectives, and Current Research. This is the Proceedings of an international conference held in Oporto.

Dearborn, Mary V. *Pocahontas's Daughters: Gender and Ethnicity in American Culture*. New York: Oxford University Press, 1986. A study of gender and ethnicity in American culture with specific references to Native American women writers and their relationships with other ethnic women writers.

Devons, Carol. *Countering Colonization: Native American Women and Great Lakes Missions, 1630 to 1900*. Berkeley: University of California Press, 1992. Study of the missions in the Great Lakes area and their role in colonization, and how gender relations within the tribes were influenced by the missionaries.

Dockstader, Frederick J. *Great North American Indians: Profiles in Life and Leadership*. New York: Van Nostrand Reinhold, 1977. An extensive compilation of 300 biographies; includes photographs and biographies of many Indian women.

Donovan, Kathleen M. *Feminist Readings of Native American Literature: Coming to Voice*. Tucson: University of Arizona Press, 1998. Includes analysis of works of Joy Harjo, Paula Gunn Allen, and other Native American writers, providing a study of the intersection between women's voices and Native American literature.

Emberly, Julia V. *Thresholds of Difference: Feminist Critique, Native Women's Writings, Postcolonial Theory*. Toronto: University of Toronto Press, 1993. Emberly focuses on Native, Métis, and Inuit women of Canada in this study of the relationships between Native women and non–Native researchers. Includes commentary on Jeannette Armstrong, Maria Campbell, and Beatrice Culleton.

Farley, Ronnie, ed. *Women of the Native Struggle: Portraits and Testimony of Native American Women*. New York: Orion Books, 1993. Anna Lee Walters wrote the introduction to this collection of photographs and words from Native American women who represent a broad cross section of views, tribes, and experiences.

Fife, Connie, ed. *The Colour of Resistance: A Contemporary Collection of Writing by Aboriginal Women*. Toronto: Sister Vision Press, 1993. Nearly fifty Native women represented by poetry, fiction, and nonfiction.

Fisher, Dexter [Alice Poindexter], ed. *The Third Woman: Minority Women Writers of the United States*. Boston: Houghton Mifflin, 1980. One of the first collections to include contemporary Native American writers such as Leslie Marmon Silko, Elizabeth Cook-Lynn, Janet Campbell, Wendy Rose, Joy Harjo, and Paula Gunn Allen.

Foreman, Carolyn. *Indian Women Chiefs*. 1954, Reprint. Washington, DC: Zenger, 1976. Foreman summarizes the roles of women in several tribes and discusses well-known Indian women such as Nancy Ward and Sarah Winnemucca as well as lesser-known figures.

Godard, Barbara Thompson. *Talking About Ourselves: The Literary Productions of Native Women of Canada*. Ottawa: Canadian Research Institute for the Advancement of Women, 1985. Godard uses oral narratives from over twenty Native women to redefine the canon to be more inclusive of Native and women's cultural forms.

Green, Rayna. *Native American Women: A Contextual Bibliography*. Bloomington: Indiana University Press, 1983. A briefly annotated bibliography of over 600 entries covering political, social, cultural, and biological issues.

————. *Women in American Indian Society*. New York: Chelsea House, 1992.

————, ed. *That's What She Said: Contemporary Poetry and Fiction by Native American Women*. Bloomington: Indiana University Press, 1984. Includes the work of fifteen Native American writers.

Gridley, Marion E. *American Indian Women*. New York: Hawthorn Books, 1974. General introduction and chapters summarizing the lives of nineteen American Indian women.

Hanson, Elizabeth I. *Forever There: Race and Gender in Contemporary Native American Fiction*. New York: Peter Lang, 1989. Hanson includes chapters on Leslie Marmon Silko, Paula Gunn Allen, and Louise Erdrich in this study on colonialism and its effects on Native cultures as portrayed in contemporary literature.

Harjo, Joy, Gloria Bird Patricia Blanco, et al. *Reinventing the Enemy's Language: Contemporary Native Women's Writing of North America*. New York: W. W. Norton, 1997. This collection of more than eighty voices originated from conversations among Native American women about their tribal, professional, and personal experiences. It includes well-known and new writers as well as political activists.

Hogan, Linda, ed. "Native American Women." Special issue of *Frontiers* 6 (1981). This special issue of *Frontiers* is devoted to Native American writers of fiction, poetry, and criticism.

Hungry Wolf, Beverly. *The Ways of My Grandmothers*. New York: Morrow, 1980. Hungry Wolf records the lives of the women of the Blood people of the Blackfoot Nation, including personal accounts, tribal history, and photographs documenting the lives of these women.

Jacobs, Sue-Ellen, Wesley Thomas, and Sabine Lang, eds. *Two-Spirit People: Native American Gender Identity, Sexuality, and Spirituality*. Urbana: University of Illinois Press, 1997. Native Americans, non–Indians, anthropologists, and others explore gender issues within Native societies, particularly as they relate to lesbian, gay, transgendered, or otherwise "marked" Native people. The study links sexuality, gender, and spirituality, and relates all to both traditional and contemporary experiences and perspectives.

James, Caroline. *Nez Perce Women in Transition, 1877 to 1990*. Moscow: University of Idaho Press, 1996. James combines archival records with interviews of Nez Perce women aged twenty to ninety in order to document changes in the lives of these women in the Pacific Northwest.

Jamieson, Kathleen. *Indian Women and the Law in Canada: Citizens Minus*. Ottawa: Ministry of Supply and Services Canada, 1978. A documented history of the Indian Act in Canada and the efforts to change it to accord Native women their rights and identity. Jamieson asserts that to be poor, Indian, and female in Canada is to be the most disadvantaged minority in Canada—"a citizen minus."

————. *Native Women in Canada: A Selected Bibliography*. Ottawa: Social Sciences and Humanities Research Council of Canada, 1983. Over 400 entries covering books, articles, and films on Inuit, Indian, and Métis women of Canada. Prepared in conjunction with the Workshop on Research on Women at Simon Fraser University in 1982.

Katz, Jane, ed. *Messengers of the Wind: Native American Women Tell Their Life Stories*. New York: Ballantine, 1995. Twenty-five Native women recount their histories, both personal and communal.

Keeling, Richard, ed. *Women in North American Indian Music: Six Essays*. Bloomington, IN: Society of Ethnomusicology, 1989. Six experts in Native music provide analyses of the roles of women in Shoshone, Ojibwa, Navajo, Gros Ventre, Algonquian, and Yurok music, contradicting the stereotypes of male dominance in music performance.

Klein, Laura F., and Lillian A. Ackerman, eds. *Women and Power in Native North America*. Norman: University of Oklahoma Press, 1995. Collections of essays on gender issues among Inuit, Tlingit, Chippewa, Seneca, Navajo, Pueblo, and other tribes. All of the authors address issues of gender equality within Native American cultures.

Leroux, Odette, Marion E. Jackson, and Minnie Aodla Freeman, eds. *Inuit Women Artists: Voices from Cape Dorset*. Vancouver, BC: Douglas & McIntyre, 1994. Biographical sketches of Pitseolak Ashoona, Lucy Qinnuayuak, Kenojuak Ashevak, Qaunak Mikkigak, Napachie Pootoogook, Pitaloosie Saila, Oopik Pitsiulak, Mayoreak Ashoona, and Ovilu Tunnillie. Includes essays on the history and voices of Inuit women as well as accounts of contemporary roles.

Medicine, Beatrice. *The Native American Woman: A Perspective*. Austin, TX: National Educational Laboratory, 1978. A contemporary perspective by a Lakota anthropologist who has been a spokeswoman for Indian women's rights.

Mihesuah, Devon A. *Cultivating the Rosebuds: The Education of Women at the Cherokee Female Seminary, 1851 to 1909*. Urbana: University of Illinois Press, 1997. The Cherokee Female Seminary in eastern Oklahoma, with its focus on acculturation, trained Native women during the transition period from removal to reservation life.

Moss, Maria. *We've Been Here Before: Women in Creation Myths and Contemporary Literature of the Native American Southwest*. Hamburg: North American Studies, 1993. Traces both Navajo and Pueblo creation myths and the depiction of women by Leslie Marmon Silko, Paula Gunn Allen, and Natachee Scott Momaday.

Niethammer, Carolyn. *Daughters of the Earth: The Lives and Legends of American Indian Women*. New York: Collier Books, 1977. Women's cycle of life in traditional Indian cultures is described and analyzed. Childbirth, childhood, courtship, marriage, homemaking, power roles, arts, religious practices, aging, and death are described for several North American cultures.

Ohoyo Resource Center. *Words of Today's American Indian Women: Ohoyo Makachi*. Wichita Falls, TX: Ohoyo Resource Center, 1982. Collection of conference proceedings and speeches by American Indian and Alaska Native women who attended a major conference in Tahlequah, Oklahoma, in 1981.

Perreault, Jeanne, and Sylvia Vance, eds. *Writing the Circle: Native Women of Western Canada*. Norman: University of Oklahoma Press, 1990. Collection of the works of over fifty Native women of Canada with an introduction by Gloria Bird and preface by Emma LaRocque.

Perrone, Bobette, H. Henrietta Stockel, and Victoria Krueger. *Medicine Women, Curanderas, and Women Doctors*. Norman: University of Oklahoma Press,

1989. The stories of ten Native American and Hispanic women healers who demonstrate through their own practices and beliefs how traditional means of healing can complement modern medicine.

Peters, Virginia Bergman. *Women of the Earth Lodges: Tribal Life on the Plains.* North Haven, CT: Archon Books, 1995. Study of the women of the upper Missouri River villages during the first half of the nineteenth century. Much of the information comes from Buffalo Bird Woman and her family, but Peters has brought in historical information about a number of other Native American women of the region and period.

Poelzer, Dolores T., and Irene A. Poelzer, eds. *In Our Own Words: Northern Saskatchewan Métis Women Speak Out.* Saskatoon, SK: Lindenblatt and Hamonie, 1986. The editors taped and edited conversations with Métis women in northern Saskatchewan who spoke freely about their communities and the changes in resource development, employment, religion, social life, and education.

Powers, Maria N. *Oglala Women: Myth, Ritual, and Reality.* Chicago: University of Chicago Press, 1986. An anthropological study of Oglala Sioux women that contradicts the stereotypes of subservient women and discusses religion, economics, medicine, political life, and the role of women in the culture.

Pulford, Florence. *Morning Star Quilts: A Presentation of the Work and Lives of Northern Plains Indian Women.* Los Altos, CA: Leone Publications, 1989. This glossy, full-color book contains women's quilting work from tribes including Gros Ventre, Assiniboine, Cree, Mandan, and many more. Pulford states her personal reactions upon meeting each of the artists.

Roessel, Ruth. *Women in Navajo Society.* Rough Rock, AZ: Navajo Resource Center, 1981. Written by a Navajo woman, this book describes the contemporary roles of Navajo women and the historical and traditional influences on these roles. Based on many of the author's experiences in Navajo culture.

St. Pierre, Mark, and Tilda Long Soldier. *Walking in the Sacred Manner: Healers, Dreamers, and Pipe Carriers—Medicine Women of the Plains Indians.* New York: Simon and Schuster, 1995. Study of the role of Plains women in the religious life of Northern Plains tribes—Lakota, Cheyenne, Crow, and Assiniboine. The conclusions of the authors are based on interviews with women who participate in Plains religious ceremonies.

Sarris, Greg. *Keeping Slug Woman Alive: A Holistic Approach to American Indian Texts.* Berkeley: University of California Press, 1993. In a collection of essays, Sarris recounts his personal history and those of women in his family, as well as the historical studies of Pomo women, basketmaking, and traditional life in the area of Santa Rosa, California.

Secretary of State of Canada. *Speaking Together: Canada's Native Women.* Ottawa: Hunter Rose, 1975. Published in conjunction with the celebration of International Women's Year, this book includes brief biographical sketches, personal statements, and photographs of twenty-nine Canadian Indian women.

Shoemaker, Nancy, ed. *Negotiators of Change: Historical Perspectives on Native American Women.* New York: Routledge, 1995. This collection of essays includes work by scholars such as Clifford Trafzer, Harry Kersey, and Clara Sue Kidwell. Each essay discusses women in particular tribes such as Cherokee, Choctaw, and Navajo.

Silman, Janet, ed. *Enough Is Enough: Aboriginal Women Speak Out*. Toronto: The Women's Press, 1987. Thirteen women speak out about their lives as Native women from the Tobique Reserve in New Brunswick who campaigned to change the Indian Act, which denied them status and rights.

Sonneborn, Liz. *A to Z of Native American Women*. New York: Facts on File, 1998. This reference book includes entries about popularly recognized Native American women. In addition to several black-and-white photographs, Sonneborn includes a map of North American labeled with tribal locations for easy reference.

Spittal, William Guy, ed. *Iroquois Women: An Anthology*. Ontario: Irocrafts, 1990. This book contains a collection of reprinted essays on histocial and present-day attributes, problems, etc. of the Iroquois woman. It also includes several black-and-white photos.

Stockel, H. Henrietta. *Women of the Apache Nation: Voices of Truth*. Reno: University of Nevada Press, 1991. Study of the women of the Chiricahua Apache with focus on the puberty ceremony, history of Apache women, and contemporary views of these women about their personal and collective futures.

Swann, Brian, and Arnold Krupat, eds. *I Tell You Now: Autobiographical Essays by Native American Writers*. Lincoln: University of Nebraska Press, 1987. Includes personal statements by Mary TallMountain, Elizabeth Cook-Lynn, Paula Gunn Allen, Diane Glancy, Linda Hogan, Wendy Rose, and Joy Harjo.

Telling It Book Collective, ed. *Telling It: Women and Language Across Cultures*. Vancouver, BC: Vancouver Press Gang, 1990. This collection from a conference includes Jeannette Armstrong, Lee Maracle, and Louise Profeit-LeBlanc in addition to other Canadian women writers.

Terrell, John Upton, and Donna M. Terrell. *Indian Women of the Western Morning: Their Life in Early America*. New York: Dial Press, 1974. Descriptions of the various roles of American Indian women with examples from different culture areas. Includes many Pan-Indian generalizations.

Wall, Steve. *Wisdom's Daughters: Conversations with Women Elders of Native America*. New York: HarperCollins, 1993. Native American women spiritual leaders convey their philosophies about life and their roles as women within their cultures. Includes representatives of ten from the Southwest to the Northeast.

Waltrip, Lela, and Rufus Waltrip. *Indian Women: Thirteen Who Played a Part in the History of America from the Earliest Days to Now*. New York: David McKay, 1964. Biographical sketches of thirteen Indian women from 1535 to the 1960s.

Watchful Eyes: Native American Women Artists. Phoenix, AZ: Heard Museum, 1994. This book includes an essay by curator Theresa Harlan about the preservation of Native art and an additional essay by painter Jolene Rickard about her work, as well as a lengthy section on individual artists with full-color, glossy photographs, a biographical section on the artists featured, and an extensive bibliography.

The Woman's Way. Alexandria, VA: Time-Life Books, 1995. This book includes several large color photographs and illustrations of American Indian women. The contents are divided into three chapters—"Sustainers of the People," "A Bridge Between Two Worlds," "Keepers of the Faith"—and several shorter essays. There are a substantial bibliography and several appendices.

Contributors and Editors

JULIE LAMAY ABNER has a PhD in English composition and American Indian literatures, and is an instructor at Chaffey College. Her text *The Four Directions of American Indian Education* will be published by Four Directions Press. She frequently publishes and presents on the topics of composition and pedagogy.

CARLOS ADAMS is a doctoral candidate in American Studies at Washington State University.

LAURA ADAMS is working on her PhD in English at the University of California, Santa Barbara. She received her BA and MA from California State University, Stanislaus. She has twice been awarded a University of California president's predoctoral scholars fellowship.

BARBARA A. BABCOCK is the director and associate professor of Women's Studies at the University of Wisconsin at Oshkosh. She received her PhD from the University of Chicago. Her major publications include *Pueblo Mothers and Children: Essays by Elsie Clews Parsons, 1915 to 1924; Daughters of the Desert: Women Anthropologists and the Native American Southwest, 1880 to 1980* (with Nancy Parezo); and *The Pueblo Storyteller: Development of a Figurative Ceramic Tradition* (with Guy and Doris Monthan).

SUSAN RAE BANKS is an assistant professor of special education within the Department of Teaching and Learning at Washington State University (WSU). She also serves as the faculty liaison for the Northwest Indian College and WSU Partnership in Native Teacher Preparation. Her research interests are in early childhood special education, teacher preparation, and parent/caregiver involvement in education, with emphasis on quality service delivery for American Indian and Alaskan Native children and families.

HELEN M. BANNAN is director of the Center for Women's Studies and associate professor of history at West Virginia University. She received her PhD in American Studies from Syracuse University. She edited *Women in the West: A Guide to Manuscript Sources*. Her published articles include "Patchwork and Politics: The Evolving Roles of Florida Seminole Women in the Twentieth Century" (with Harry Kersey), in Nancy Shoemaker, ed., *Negotiators of Change*; "Newcomers to Navajoland: Transculturation in the Memoirs of Anglo Women, 1900 to 1945," in *New Mexico Historical Review*; and "Spider Woman's Web: Mothers and Daughters in Southwestern Native American Literature," in *The Lost Tradition: Mothers and Daughters in Literature*.

GRETCHEN M. BATAILLE is senior vice president for academic affairs for the University of North Carolina system. Her publications include *American Indian Women Telling Their Lives* and *American Indian Women: A Guide to Research*, both with Kathleen M. Sands.

DAWN BATES, an associate professor at Arizona State University, received her PhD from the University of Washington. She edited (with Thom Hess and Vi Hilbert) *Lushootseed Dictionary* and the proceedings of the Tenth West Coast Conference on Formal Linguistics.

ARLON BENSON earned his BA and MA in English from Arizona State University. He served as a research assistant on Gretchen M. Bataille and Kathleen M. Sands, *American Indian Women: A Guide to Research*, published in 1991 by Garland.

BETHANY BLANKENSHIP is a PhD candidate at Washington State University, where she teaches advanced rhetoric and composition. She has published in the *Washington English Journal* and *Encyclopedia of Popular Culture*.

EDITH BLICKSILVER retired as an associate professor of English at Georgia Institute of Technology. She is a member of the book review staff of the Atlanta *Journal-Constitution*, an organizer and first secretary of MELUS, and president of the Georgia/South Carolina College English Association. Her book *The Ethnic American Woman: Problems, Protests, Lifestyle* was cited as the Best Non-Fiction Book of the Year in 1979; in 1989 it came out in a fifth edition that includes two new chapters and twenty additional works.

RENAE MOORE BREDIN received her BA from the University of Utah, her MA from Rutgers University, and her PhD from the University of Arizona.

RHODA CARROLL is a professor of English and supervises independent study projects in writing and literature in the Adult Degree Program at Vermont College of Norwich University in Montpelier, a low-residency, interdisciplinary, project-based BA program for adult learners. Her undergraduate degree is from the State University of New York at Albany, and her graduate degrees are from the University of Arizona. She has published poems, short stories, and essays in a wide variety of literary magazines, journals, and anthologies.

DEXTER FISHER CIRILLO received her PhD in English from the City University of New York. She has served as director of Gallery 10 of Arizona in New York City and as coordinator of art exhibitions and special events at museums and sites throughout the country. In addition to numerous articles and book reviews on art, education, and literature, her publications include (under the name Dexter Fisher) critical introductions to *American Indian Stories* by Zitkala Sa/Gertrude Bonnin and *Co-Ge-We-A* by Mourning Dove. She edited *The Third Woman: Minority Women Writers of the United States, Minority Language and Literature — Retrospective and Perspective*, and (with Robert B. Stepto) *Afro–American Literature: The Reconstruction of Instruction*. Her books are *Southwestern Indian Jewelry* (1992) and *Across Frontiers: Hispanic Crafts of New Mexico* (1998).

JONI ADAMSON CLARKE is a professor of English at the University of Arizona, where she received her PhD. She received her MA degree from Brigham Young University. Her book *The Middle Place: American Indian Literature, Environmental Justice, and Ecocriticism* is forthcoming from the University of Arizona Press.

LAURA COLTELLI is an associate professor of American literature at the University of Pisa. Her publications on Native American literature include two studies on Leslie Marmon Silko's fiction; *Winged Words: Native American Writers Speak*; the Italian edition of N. Scott Momaday's *The Names*; and *The Spiral of Memory: Interviews*. She is a general editor of a series devoted to contemporary Native American writers. A former Fulbright visiting professor at the University of Boston and at UCLA, she has held a postdoctoral fellowship from the Institute of American Cultures and American Indian Studies Center of the University of California at Los Angeles. She received the Faculty Enrichment Award (1988/1989) from the International Council for Canadian Studies.

JAY ANN COX is a senior lecturer in the English Department at the University of Arizona. Her publications include "Dangerous Definitions: Female Tricksters in Contemporary Native American Fiction," in *Wicazo Sa Review*, and "The Native American Trickster" (with Barbara Babcock), in *Dictionary of Native American Literature*.

VANESSA HOLFORD DIANA is a PhD candidate at Arizona State University, studying nineteenth- and twentieth-century American women's literature. Her publications include book reviews and two articles—on Paula Gunn Allen and Leslie Marmon Silko—in *Studies in American Indian Literatures*. She earned an MA in English from Lehigh University (1992) and a BS in English and secondary education from East Stroudsburg University (1990). She is a teaching associate in the English Department at Arizona State University.

KATHLEEN MCNERNEY DONOVAN is a doctoral candidate at the University of Arizona. She is studying American literature, with an emphasis on Native American literature. She received her MA from the University of Nebraska.

PATTIANN FRINZI is a freelance researcher and evaluator. She collaborates with her husband, Michael Sikes, in the evaluation of programs where education and culture intersect. They work with nonprofits, including museums and arts and humanities organizations. Previously, she worked in the Division of Public Programs at the National Endowment for the Humanities. She received an MA in interdisciplinary humanities and a certificate in scholarly publishing from Arizona State University, and a BA in music from Florida State University.

JANET PETERSON GERSTNER received her BA in English from the University of Colorado at Denver (1990) and her MA in English from Arizona State University (1994), and is a PhD candidate in nineteenth-century American literature at Arizona State University. She is a teaching associate in the English Department at Arizona State University.

AUDREY M. GODFREY earned a BS and MS from Utah State University. Her publications include *Women's Voices: An Untold History of the Latter-day Saints, 1830 to 1900* (with Kenneth W. Godfrey and Jill Mulvay Den); "Uncle Sam's Most Foolish Expedition," in *This People*; and "Housewives, Hussies, and Heroines, or the Women of Johnston's Army," in *Utah Historical Quarterly*.

DORIE S. GOLDMAN is a PhD candidate in English at Arizona State University, specializing in Southwestern regional literatures, folklore, and art. She is also a graduate teaching associate. She received her MA in English from Southwest Texas State University in 1992 and her BA in anthropology from the University of Arizona in 1989.

DAVID MAYER GRADWOHL is professor emeritus of anthropology at Iowa State University in Ames. He graduated from the University of Nebraska with majors in anthropology and geography, studied at the University of Edinburgh, and completed his PhD at Harvard. He is the author of *Prehistoric Villages in Eastern Nebraska* and "Shelling Corn in the Prairie-Plains: Archaeological Evidence and Ethnographic Parallels Beyond the Pun," and editor of *The Worlds Between Two Rivers: Perspectives on American Indians in Iowa* (with Gretchen Bataille and Charles L. P. Silet) and *Exploring Buried Buxton: Archaeology of an Abandoned Iowa Coal Mining Town with a Large Black Population* (with Nancy M. Osborn).

AGNES GRANT holds BA, BEd, MEd, and PhD degrees. She is editor of *Our Bit of Truth: Anthology of Canadian Native Literature* and author of *James McKay: Métis Builder of Canada, No End of Grief: Canadian Indian Residential Schools*, and *Using Literature by American Indians and Alaska Natives in Secondary Schools*. She is author (with La Vina Gillespie) of *Joining the Circle: A Practitioner's Guide to Responsive Education for Native Students*. She is a professor of education and Native Studies at Brandon University, Brandon, Manitoba.

LAURA GRAVES is an instructor in the History Department at South Plains College, Texas. Her publications include *Contemporary Hopi Pottery* and "Navajo Rugs: A Marketing Success." She received her PhD from Northern Arizona University.

GREG GREWELL earned an MA in English literature from San Jose State University in 1992 and then, for five years, taught composition, critical thinking, and introductory literature courses at San Jose State and California State University, Hayward. He is a candidate for the PhD in English at Washington State University, with emphases on early American and nineteenth-century American literature. In addition, he has edited (with Irina L. Raïca) a reader/rhetoric, *Transitions: Lives in America* (1997).

LOIS GRIFFITTS received her BA in English literature from the University of Idaho and her MA in literature from Arizona State University, focusing on critical theory and ethnic writers, primarily Maxine Hong Kingston. She is a quality engineer in the automotive industry.

GRETCHEN G. HARVEY received her PhD in history at Arizona State University and is instructor of history at North Dakota State University, Fargo. Her dissertation is a biography of Ruth Muskrat Bronson.

HELEN JASKOSKI received her PhD from Stanford University. She is a professor of English and comparative literature at California State University, Fullerton. Jaskoski edited *Early Native American Writing: New Critical Essays* and is the editor of the quarterly *Studies in American Indian Literatures*. She is the author of "From the Time Immemorial: Native American Traditions in Contemporary Short Fiction."

JENNIFER L. JENKINS is a member of the faculty of the Interdisciplinary Humanities Program at the University of Arizona. She studied at the University of Chicago and University of Arizona, where she received the PhD in 1992. She has published in *Intertextuality and Contemporary American Fiction* and *ESQ*.

MATTHEW HOLT JENNINGS is a Ph.D. candidate at the University of Illinois at Urban-Champaign. His research interests include race and ethnicity in Colonial North America and Native Americans in the colonial era.

CYNTHIA KASEE has contributed to *Encyclopedia of the American Wars* and *Anthology of Contemporary Cherokee Prose*. Her poetry has appeared in *The Eagle*. Kasee received her PhD in American Indian Studies from The Union Institute in Cincinnati, Ohio.

HARRY A. KERSEY, JR., is a professor of history at Florida Atlantic University. He received BA and MA degrees from the University of Florida and a PhD from the University of Illinois. His publications include *Pelts, Plumes and Hides: White Traders Among the Seminole Indians, 1870 to 1930; The Florida Seminoles and the New Deal, 1933 to 1942*; and *The Seminole and Miccosukee Tribes: A Critical Bibliography*. Kersey served as a member of the Florida Governor's Council on Indian Affairs for ten years.

CLARA SUE KIDWELL is a professor and director of the American Studies Department at the University of Oklahoma. She received her MA and PhD degrees from the University of Oklahoma. Kidwell has held numerous pre- and postdoctoral fellowships, including the Smithsonian Institution fellowship, the Newberry Library summer fellowship, and the University of California humanities fellowship. She is on the board of trustees for the National Museum of the American Indian and a member of the American Historical Association and American Society for Ethnohistory.

JOYCE ANN KIEVIT received her BA from Hope College in Holland, Michigan. She is working on her graduate degree and is a research assistant at the University of Houston, Clear Lake.

LUCY LERICHE graduated with an MA from the Interdisciplinary Humanities Program at Arizona State University in 1992. She has been an instructor at Arizona State University; Johnson State College in Johnson, Vermont; and Trinity College in Burlington, Vermont. Leriche is executive director of the Lamoille Housing Partnership, a nonprofit, affordable housing development organization in Morrisville, Vermont. She resides in Hardwick, Vermont.

ANDREA LERNER received her PhD in English at the University of Arizona and an MA in creative writing from Stanford University. She is the editor of *Dancing on the Rim of the World: Contemporary Northwest Native American Writing*.

KENNETH LINCOLN received a BA from Stanford University in 1965 and an MA and PhD from Indiana University in 1967 and 1969. He is a professor of English and American Indian Studies at UCLA, where he has taught since 1969. Professor Lincoln has directed the UCLA American Indian Studies Graduate Program, edited *The American Indian Culture and Research Journal*, and chaired the Faculty Advisory Committee to the UCLA American Indian Studies Center. He has gathered, edited, and written prefaces for eight volumes of poetry in UCLA's Native American Series. The Modern Language Association published his monograph *Native American Literatures: "old like hills, like stars,"* in Houston Baker's *Three American Literatures*. He has published *Native American Renaissance, The Good Red Road: Passages into Native America* (with Al Logan), *Indi'n Humor: Bicultural Play in Native America*, and the autobiographical memoir *Men Down West*.

LAURIE LISA received her BS degree from the University of Illinois at Champaign and her MA and PhD degrees from Arizona State University. She is editor (with Gretchen M. Bataille and Miguel A. Carranza) of *Ethnic Studies in the United States: A Guide to Research*.

DANIEL F. LITTLEFIELD, JR., is a professor of English and director of the American Native Press Archives at the University of Arkansas at Little Rock. His publications include *Alex Posey: Creek Poet, Journalist, and Humorist; Ke-ma-ha: The Omaha Stories of Francis La Flesche*; and *Seminole Burning: A Story of Racial Vengeance*. With James W. Parins, Littlefield has published *American Indian and Alaska Native Newspapers and Periodicals, 1826 to 1924* (and two more volumes covering the years 1925 to 1970 and 1971 to 1985), *A Biobibliography of Native American Writers, 1772 to 1924* (with a supplement published in 1985), and *Native American Writing in the Southeast: An Anthology, 1875 to 1935*. He received his PhD from Oklahoma State University.

K. TSIANINA LOMAWAIMA received her undergraduate degree from the University of Arizona (1976) and her graduate degrees from Stanford University (MA 1979, PhD 1987), all in anthropology. She is the author of *They Called It Prairie Light: The Story of Chilocco Indian School* and several articles, including the chapter "Educating Native Americans" in J. Banks's *Handbook of Research on Multicultural Education*. She was guest editor of a special issue on boarding school education for *Journal of American Indian Education*. She is an associate professor in the American Indian Studies Program at the University of Arizona.

HARTMUT LUTZ holds an English teacher's degree (SUNY Fredonia and Teachers College, Kiel, 1969), a PhD in English literature (University of Manchester, England, and University of Tubingen, 1974), and habilitation (a German postdoctoral degree) from UC Davis and the University of Osnabrück (1989). He has published articles in anthologies and periodicals in Britain, Canada, Denmark, Germany, Switzerland, Sweden, and the United States. His publications include *William Goldings Prosawerk; D-Q University: Self-Determination in Native American Higher Education; "Indianer und Native Americans"; Minority Literatures in North American* (with W. Karrer); and *Contemporary Challenges: Conversations with Canadian Native Authors*. He also has been editor of OBEMA (bilingual series). He holds a chair in American and Canadian studies, Anglophone literatures and cultures of North America at Ernst-Moritz-Arndt University, Greifswald, Germany.

JACK MARKEN is professor emeritus of English at South Dakota State University. He received his BA from the University of Akron and his MA and PhD from Indiana University. Among his publications are *The American Indian: Language and Literature* and *Bibliography of the Sioux* (with Herbert T. Hoover). His essay "Literature and Legends of South Dakota" is in *Centennial Planning Project of the South Dakota Committee on the Humanities*, and "The Lore of South Dakota" is in *South Dakota: Changing, Changeless 1889 to 1989*. He is general editor for the Native American Bibliography Series and the Native American Bibliography Series published by Scarecrow Press.

ELIZABETH A. McNEIL received her MFA degree in the Creative Writing Program at Arizona State University and is in the PhD program in English, where she serves as the undergraduate academic adviser. McNeil has published "The New and Golden Harvest: Margaret Fuller's Call for an 'American Literature' Fulfilled" in *Critically Speaking*, as well as reviews of *Annie John* by Jamaica Kincaid and *Skokie: Rights or Wrong* (a documentary film) by Sheila Chamovitz, both in *Explorations in Sights and Sounds*.

DEVON A. MIHESUAH is a professor of Native American history at Northern Arizona University. She received her PhD from Texas Christian University with a dissertation titled "History of the Cherokee Female Seminary: 1851 to 1910," and is a former Ford Foundation dissertation fellow. Her journal articles and chapters in books include "Too Dark to Be Angels: The Class System Among the Cherokees at Female Seminary," in *American Indian Culture and Research Journal*; "'Commendable Progress': Acculturation at the Cherokee Female Seminary," in *American Indian Quarterly*; "Indians in Arizona," in *Politics and Public Policy in Arizona*; and "Despoiling and Desecration of American Indian Property and Possessions," in *National Forum*. In addition to writing book reviews and serving as an editorial consultant for journals, Mihesuah published *Cultivating the Rose Buds: History of the Cherokee Female Seminary, 1851 to 1909*.

JOHN D. NICHOLS, professor of Native Studies and linguistics at the University of Manitoba, received his PhD from Harvard University. He is the editor of the quarterly *Algonquian and Iroquoian Linguistics*. He also has edited *An Ojibwe Text Anthology; Statement Made by the Indians: A Bilingual Petition of the Chippewas of Lake Superior, 1864*; Leonard Bloomfield's edition of *The Dog's Children: Anishinaabe Texts Told by Angeline Williams*; and Maude Kegg's *Nookomis Ga-ainaajimotawid/What My Grandmother Told Me* and *Portage Lake*.

JAMES H. O'DONNELL III is a professor of history at Marietta College and author of numerous books, articles, and monographs, including *The Southern Indians in the American Revolution; The Georgia Frontier, 1773 to 1783; The Cherokees and the American Revolution in North Carolina*; and *Southeastern Frontiers, 1540 to 1840*. In addition, he has received many grants and fellowships, such as the American Philosophical Society research grant and the Huntington Library fellowship. His latest work is *The Noise and Miseries of War: The Northern Indians, 1774 to 1783*. O'Donnell received his PhD from Duke University.

JEANNE OLSON received her BA from Eastern Montana College and her MA at Arizona State University. She is a teaching associate in the Department of English at Arizona State University.

BEV ORTIZ is an ethnographic consultant under the auspices of Cabrillo College, California State Polytechnic University, Dominican College, and San Jose State University, and a naturalist for the East Bay Regional Park District. In addition, she is a skills and technology columnist for *News from Native California*. She has published *It Will Live Forever: Yosemite Indian Acorn Preparation* and "Mount Diablo as Myth and Reality: An Indian History Convoluted," in *American Indian Quarterly*. She has also served as a board member of Oyate (Indian education), a member of the executive committee and president of the Miwok Archaeological Preserve of Marin, and chair and commissioner for the Walnut Creek Park and Recreation Commission.

JAMES W. PARINS is a professor of English at the University of Arkansas, Little Rock, and director of the American Native Press Archives there. His publications include *John Rollin Ridge: His Life and Works*, *American Indian and Alaska Native Newspapers and Periodicals, 1826 to 1984* (in three volumes), and *A Bio-bibliography of Native American Writers, 1772 to 1924* (the latter two with Daniel F. Littlefield, Jr.). He has edited the works of B. N. O. Walker (Wyandot) and Francis La Flesche (Omaha), and has written on other Native American figures. Parins received his PhD from the University of Wisconsin.

JAMES ROBERT PAYNE is a professor of English at New Mexico State University. He received his PhD from the University of California at Davis. He is the editor of and contributor to *Multicultural Autobiography: American Lives*, and is the editor of *Joseph Seamon Cotter, Jr.: Complete Poems*. Payne has also published "Hamlin Garland," in *Heath Anthology of American Literature*; "Perceptions of Multicultural America in Personal Narratives of Hamlin Garland," in *A/B: Auto/Biography Studies*; and "Griggs and Corrothers: Historical Reality and Black Fiction," in *Explorations in Ethnic Studies*.

LAURA L. PEERS received her MS in Canadian history, studying at the universities of Winnipeg and Manitoba. Her publications include "Secondary Sources, Subsistence, and Gender Bias: The Saulteaux," in *Proceedings of the National Symposium on Aboriginal Women*; "The Western Ojibwa, 1821 to 1870," in *Proceedings of Conference on Aboriginal Resource Use in Canada*; *The Ojibwa of Western Canada, 1780 to 1870*; *Sacred Encounters: Father De Smet and the Indians of the Rocky Mountain West* (with Jacqueline Peterson).

S. PENNY PETRONE is professor emerita of English at Lakehead University, Thunder Bay, Ontario. She received her PhD in English literature from the University of Alberta. Her publications include *Breaking the Mold*; *Native Literature in Canada*; *Northern Voices: Inuit Writing in English*; and *First People, First Voices*.

BERND PEYER received his PhD in American Studies from Johann Wolfgang Goethe University, Frankfurt. He is currently a lecturer in the Institute for English and American Studies at the same university. Peyer has published several articles and monographs on Indian literature and art, and he edited *The Singing Spirit*, published by the University of Arizona Press.

STEVEN R. PRICE is a student in the English MA program at Arizona State University. He received his undergraduate degree from the University of Wisconsin, Oshkosh.

DEAN RADER earned a BA in English from Baylor University and an MA and PhD in comparative literature from the State University of New York at Binghamton. He has published articles on Wallace, Stevens, Octavio Paz, Emily Dickinson, Leslie Marmon Silko, Luci Tapahonso, and Simon Ortiz. He is an assistant professor of English at Texas Lutheran University.

THELMA SHINN RICHARD is a professor of English and Women's Studies at Arizona State University. She received her MA and PhD degrees from Purdue University. In addition to many articles and chapters in books, Shinn has published *Worlds Within Women* and *Radiant Daughters: Fictional American Women*.

SUSAN L. ROCKWELL is director of the National Office of the National Association for Ethnic Studies (NAES) and is a faculty associate at Arizona State University. She received her BA and MA in English literature from the University of Alabama at Birmingham, and is a PhD candidate in American literature at Arizona State University. In addition to serving as editor of the NAES newsletter, *The Ethnic Reporter*, and as managing editor of the NAES journal, *Explorations in Ethnic Studies*, she has published "The Delivery of Power: Reading American Indian Childbirth Narratives," in *American Indian Culture and Research Journal*, and "Writing the Oral Tradition: Leslie Marmon Silko's *Storyteller*," in *Explorations in Ethnic Studies*.

KENNETH M. ROEMER, a professor of English at the University of Texas at Arlington, received his BA in English from Harvard and his MA and PhD in American civilization from the University of Pennsylvania. His books include *Approaches to Teaching Momaday's "The Way to Rainy Mountain"* and *Native American Writers of the United States*, as well as three books on utopian literature. His articles and essay reviews on Native American literature have appeared in journals such as *American Literature, American Literary History, American Quarterly, SAIL*, and *American Indian Culture and Research Journal*.

GRETCHEN RONNOW has published "John Milton Oskison," in *The Dictionary of Native American Literature*; "Tayo, Death, and Desire: A Lacanian Reading of Leslie Silko's *Ceremony*," in *Narrative Chance: Postmodern Discourse on Native American Indian Literatures*; and "John Milton Oskison, Cherokee Journalist: A Singer of the Semiotics of Power," in *Native Press Research Journal*. Ronnow received her PhD at the University of Arizona.

PAULETTE RUNNING WOLF is an assistant professor in the Department of Educational Leadership and Counseling Psychology at Washington State University, Pullman.

JULIE A. RUSS received her undergraduate degree from Ohio State University. She is enrolled in the MA program in English at Arizona State University.

KATHLEEN MULLEN SANDS is a professor in the Department of English and affiliated faculty in the Department of Anthropology at Arizona State University, where she teaches folklore, American Indian literatures, and interdisciplinary courses. She is the author (with Gretchen Bataille) of *American Indian Women Telling Their Lives* and *American Indian Women: A Guide to Research*. She is the editor of *Circle of Motion: Arizona Anthology of Contemporary Indian Literature*; senior editor of *People of Pascua*, by Edward H. Spicer; and editor-interpreter of *Autobiography of a Yaqui Poet*, by Refugio Savala. She also has published numerous articles on American Indian literatures and folklore.

GREG SARRIS received his PhD in modern thought and literature from Stanford University. His essays and articles have appeared in *College English, MELUS, American Indian Quarterly, Studies in American Indian Literatures, National Women's Studies Association Journal, De/Colonizing the Subject: Race, Gender, and Class in Women's Autobiography, The Ethnography of Reading, In Writing*, and *News from Native California*. He also has published *Keeping Slug Woman Alive: A Holistic Approach to American Indian Texts; Grand Avenue*; and *The Sound of Rattles and Clappers: A Collection of New California Indian Writing*. He is a professor of English at the University of California, Los Angeles.

MICHELLE SAVOY received her BA in English from the University of Wisconsin, Milwaukee. She is currently enrolled in the graduate program in English at Arizona State University.

CHRISTOPHER SCHEDLER received his BA from Wesleyan University in Connecticut, and his MA from the University of California, Santa Barbara; he is completing his PhD in English at UCSB. His dissertation, "Modernist Borders of Our America," examines the intersections between American modernism and Native American and Mexican American literature.

ERIC SEVERSON received his BA from Pennsylvania State University and his MA in American literature from Arizona State University.

KATHRYN W. SHANLEY is an enrolled member of the Assiniboine. Her graduate degrees were earned at the University of Michigan, and she teaches American and American Indian literature in the English Department at Cornell University. She has published "The Lived Experience: American Indian Literature After Alcatraz" and *"Only an Indian," Reading James Welch*.

PATRICK B. SHARP is a Marion L. Brittain postdoctoral fellow at the Georgia Institute of Technology in the School of Literature, Communication and Culture, where he teaches American minority literature and science and technology studies. He holds a PhD from the University of California at Santa Barbara.

MICHAEL SHERFY is a Ph.D. candidate at the University of Illinois at Urbana-Champaign.

RODNEY SIMARD received his PhD from the University of Alabama. Author of *Postmodern Drama: Contemporary Playwrights in America and Britain* and *The Whole Writer's Catalog: An Introduction to Advanced Composition*, he has published widely on a variety of topics.

FAREN R. SIMINOFF has a JD degree from Syracuse University College of Law. She is a candidate for an MA degree in history at New York University.

RYAN SIMMONS is a PhD candidate at Washington State University, where he is completing a dissertation on the twentieth-century political novel in the United States. He teaches composition and literature.

WINONA STEVENSON received her MA from the University of British Columbia and is completing her doctoral studies at the University of California, Berkeley. She has published "Rebirth of Women Warriors" and "Dreamers Who Inspire," in *Saskatchewan Indian*. Her other articles include "SUNTEP Students and Universal Education: The Global Experience of Mixed Blood Peoples," in *New Breed*.

MARK G. THIEL is an assistant archivist for the Native American Catholic Collections at Marquette University in Milwaukee, Wisconsin. He received his BS degree in sociology/anthropology and his MAT in history from the University of Wisconsin, Stevens Point. A certified archivist, he is coauthor of *Guide to Catholic Indian Mission and School Records in Midwest Repositories*, and author of "The Marquette Initiative: Saving Catholic Archives of the Indian Americas," in *Mission Studies*.

CLIFFORD E. TRAFZER has served as professor and chair of ethnic studies, and director of American Indian Studies at the University of California, Riverside. He holds a PhD in history from Oklahoma State University. Trafzer received the Washington Governor's Book Award for *Renegade Tribe*, as well as numerous teaching and research awards. His published work includes *The Chinook, California's Indians and the Gold Rush*, and *A Trip to a Pow Wow* (under the pen name of Richard Red Hawk).

KAY TRONSEN is a PhD candidate at Washington State University. She received her MA in composition and rhetoric in 1998.

CATHERINE UDALL has served as managing editor of the National Association for Ethnic Studies publications and assistant editor for *Native Peoples* magazine in Phoenix, Arizona. She received her BA in English and history from Brigham Young University and her MA in history from Arizona State University.

PATRICIA VERSTRAT is a PhD candidate in literature at Washington State University. She graduated from Northern Michigan University with a BA in 1992 and an

MA in 1994. Her dissertation explores intersections of masculinity and disability in twentieth-century American literature.

ANGELA NOELLE WILLIAMS received her BA in history and rhetoric from the University of California at Berkeley and an MA and PhD in English from the University of California at Santa Barbara. She is an assistant professor at San Jose State University. Her work has appeared in *MELUS* and in the *ADE Bulletin*. Her dissertation focuses on the use of parody by minority communities.

JERRY WILSON is a professor of English and communications at Mount Marty College in Yankton, South Dakota. He holds a PhD in English from the University of Oklahoma and has published numerous short fiction pieces, as well as essays on literature, politics, and the environment. He is completing a book about life along the Pan American Highway from Winnipeg, Manitoba, to Canita, Panama.

NORMA C. WILSON, a professor of English at the University of South Dakota, received her PhD from the University of Oklahoma. She has published a collection of poems, *Wild Iris*, as well as essays on the work of N. Scott Momaday, Leslie Marmon Silko, Linda Hogan, Lance Henson, and other writers in publications such as *Denver Quarterly, Mickle Street Review*, and *A: A Journal of Contemporary Literature*. In addition, she was a contributing editor to the *Heath Anthology of American Literature* and has published essays in *The Dictionary of Native American Literature* and *Approaches to Teaching Momaday's "The Way to Rainy Mountain."*

HERTHA D. WONG is an associate professor in the Department of English at the University of California, Berkeley. She received her MA and PhD degrees from the University of Iowa. Her articles include "Pictographs as Autobiography: Plains Indian Sketchbooks of the Late Nineteenth and Early Twentieth Centuries," in *American Literary History*; and "N. Scott Momaday's *The Way to Rainy Mountain*: Contemporary Native American Autobiography," in *American Indian Culture and Research Journal*. Two articles appear in anthologies: "Adoptive Mothers and Thrown Away Children in the Novels of Louise Erdrich," in *Narrating Mothers: Theorizing Maternal Subjectivities*, and "Plains Indian Names and the 'Autobiographical Act,'" in *Autobiography and Postmodernism*. Her book *Sending My Heart Back Across the Years: Tradition and Innovation in Native American Autobiography* was published by Oxford University Press.

KERRY KENNEDY WYNN is a Ph.D. candidate at the University of Illinois at Urbana-Champaign.

BELLA ZWEIG, senior lecturer in humanities at the University of Arizona, received her PhD in classics from Stanford University. Active in various phases of Native American educational and cultural support work, she has combined her academic and experiential areas of interest in her teaching—designing multiethnic humanities courses that examine cross-cultural issues—and in her research, "The Primal Mind: Using Native American Models to Study Women in Ancient Greece," in *Feminist Theory and the Classics*, edited by N. S. Rabinowitz and A. Richlin.

Appendix 1
Entries by Primary Areas of Specialization

ACTIVISM

Abeyta, Pablita

Allen, Paula Gunn

Aquash, Anna Mae Pictou

Aquino, Ella Pierre

Armstrong, Jeannette

Baker, Marie Annharte

Bennett, Ramona

Black Bear, Matilda

Blackgoat, Roberta

Bonnin, Gertrude Simmons

Brant, Beth

Brass, Eleanor

Brave Bird, Mary

Chrystos

Covington, Lucy Freidlander

Deer, Ada

Dixon, Patricia A.

Gould, Janice May

Hailstone, Vivien

Harjo, Suzan Shown

Harris, LaDonna

Hatch, Viola

Hogan, Linda

Horn, Kahn-Tineta

Jemison, Alice Lee

Keeshig-Tobias, Lenore

LaDuke, Winona

Lavell, Jeannette

Maracle, Lee

McCloud, Janet

Neakok, Sadie Brower

Nunez, Bonita Wa Wa Calachaw

Pearson, Maria Darlene

Pretty on Top, Jeanine

Puzz, Anna

Red Shirt Shaw, Delphine

Stanley, Dorothy Amora

Sutton, Catherine

Thorpe, Grace

Wauneka, Annie Dodge

Witt, Shirley Hill

Wittstock, Laura Waterman

ANTHROPOLOGY

Archambault, JoAllyn

Deloria, Ella Cara

Medicine, Beatrice A.

Peterson, Annie Miner

Rose, Wendy

Smith, Barbara Elene

Tantaquidgeon, Gladys

Witt, Shirley Hill

ARCHITECTURE

Swentzell, Rina

ARTS

Abeyta, Pablita

Ackerman, Maria Joseph

Allen, Elsie

Archambault, JoAllyn

Arrington, Ruth

Ashevak, Kenojuak

Ashoona, Pitseolak

Bahe, Liz Sohappy

Bennett, Kay Curley

Bighorse, Tiana

Bird, Gail

Bird, JoAnne

Blue Legs
Burns, Diane M.
Burton, Jimalee Chitwood
Carius, Helen Slwooko
Chouteau, Yvonne
Chrystos
Cordero, Helen Quintana
Dat-So-La-Lee
Dick, Lena Frank
Dietz, Angel DeCora
Endrezze, Anita
Erdrich, Angie
Folwell, Jody
Gonzales, Rose
Hailstone, Vivien
Hardin, Helen Bagshaw
Hill, Joan
Howe, LeAnne
Isom, Joan Shaddox
Jennings, Vanessa
Kegg, Maude Mitchell
Kimball, Yeffe
Lewis, Lucy
Littleman, Alice
Loloma, Otellie
Martinez, Maria Montoya
Mayo, Sarah Jim
McKay, Mabel
Medicine Flower, Grace
Medicine Snake Woman
Morez, Mary
Naha, Paqua
Nampeyo
Nampeyo, Daisy Hooee
Naranjo-Morse, Nora
Navasie, Joy
Nunez, Bonita Wa Wa Calachaw
Owen, Angie Reano
Parker, Julia F.
Parrish, Essie
Pavatea, Garnet
Peña, Tonita

Roessel, Ruth W.
Rose, Wendy
Saila, Pitaloosie
Sakiestewa, Ramona
Sanchez, Carol Lee
Slipperjack, Ruby
Smith, Jaune Quick-to-See
Smith, Kathleen
Somersal, Laura
Stroud, Virginia
Telles, Lucy Parker
Tremblay, Gail
Velarde, Pablita
Wanatee, Adeline
White, Elizabeth Q.
White, Madeline Melba
Williams, Alice Cling
Woody, Elizabeth

BUSINESS

Bordeaux, Shirley
Robinson, Wungnema Rose

CAPTIVE

Malinche
Parker, Cynthia Ann
Tomassa

CHRISTIAN LEADERSHIP

Sacred White Buffalo, Mother Mary
    Catherine
Tekakwitha, Kateri

COSMETOLOGY

Venegas, Hildreth Marie Twostars

CULTURAL INTERPRETATION

Allen, Elsie
Brant, Molly
Buffalo Bird Woman
Cuero, Delfina

Davidson, Florence Edenshaw
Dorion Woman
Freeman, Minnie Aodla
Green, Rayna Diane
Greene, Alma
Highwalking, Belle
Juneau, Josette
Kavena, Juanita Tiger
Kegg, Maude Mitchell
Kellogg, Laura Cornelius
Lowry, Annie
Medicine Snake Woman
Mountain Wolf Woman
Owl Woman
Parker, Julia F.
Pocahontas
Pretty-shield
Sacagawea
Schoolcraft, Jane Johnston
Sekaquaptewa, Helen
Smith, Kathleen
Somersal, Laura
Stanley, Dorothy Amora
Tomassa
Tsupu
Vanderburg, Agnes
Wolf, Helen Pease
Zuni, Flora

EDUCATION

Ahenakew, Freda
Akers, Donna L.
Alberty, Eliza Missouri Bushyhead
Allen, Minerva
Anderson, Mabel Washbourne
Archambault, JoAllyn
Armstrong, Jeannette
Arrington, Ruth
Ayoungman, Vivian
Bell, Betty Louise
Broker, Ignatia

Bronson, Ruth Muskrat
Brown, Catharine
Brown, Emily Ivanoff
Callahan, Sophia Alice
Cleghorn, Mildred Imoch
Cobb, Isabelle
Cochran, Jo Whitehorse
Cook-Lynn, Elizabeth
Cuny, Sister Genevieve
Dauenhauer, Nora Marks
Deer, Ada
Dietz, Angel DeCora
Erdrich, Heid E.
Erdrich, Louise
Francisco, Nia
Hailstone, Vivien
Hale, Janet Campbell
Hampton, Carol Cussen
Harjo, Joy
Harnar, Nellie Shaw
Heth, Charlotte Anne Wilson
Hilbert, Vi
Hilden, Patricia Penn
Hogan, Linda
Hungry Wolf, Beverly
Hunter, Mary Jo Brooks
Isom, Joan Shaddox
John, Mary
Kidwell, Clara S.
Kilpatrick, Anna Gritts
Kirkness, Verna J.
Krepps, Ethel C.
LaFlesche Picotte Diddock, Marguerite
LaFlesche Tibbles, Susette
LaRoque, Emma
Loloma, Otellie
Mann, Henri
Medicine, Beatrice A.
Momaday, Natachee Scott
Neakok, Sadie Brower
Nelson, Margaret F.
Parker, Julia F.

Paul, Alice S.
Peterson, Helen
Picotte, Agnes
Potts, Marie
Power, Susan
Pretty on Top, Jeanine
Roe Cloud, Elizabeth Bender
Roessel, Ruth W.
Rose, Wendy
Ross, Agnes Allen
Sanchez, Carol Lee
Saubel, Katherine Siva
Shanley, Kathryn
Silko, Leslie Marmon
Sioui, Elenore Marie
Sisk-Franco, Caleen A.
Sneve, Virginia Driving Hawk
Somersal, Laura
Stanley, Dorothy Amora
Steele, Lois Fister
Swan, Madonna
Swentzell, Rina
Tiger, Winifred
Velarde, Pablita
Wanatee, Adeline
White, Elizabeth Q.
Witt, Shirley Hill
Wright, Muriel Hazel
Zepeda, Ofelia

FUR TRADE

Ainse, Sally
Anahereo
Netnokwa

HERDER

French, Alice

HISTORIAN

Child, Brenda, J.
Eaton, Rachel Caroline

Parker, Julia F.
Rand, Jacki
Wright, Muriel Hazel

LAW

Arthur, Claudeen Bates
Hunter, Mary Jo Brooks
Krepps, Ethel C.
McCoy, Melody L.
Neakok, Sadie Brower
Pinkerman-Uri, Connie Redbird
Rousseau, Lorraine Mae
Thorpe, Grace
Wynne, Mary T.

LIBRARY

Salabiye, Velma S.

LINGUISTICS

Ahenakew, Freda
Brink, Jeanne
Deloria, Ella Cara
Hilbert, Vi
Zepeda, Ofelia

LITERATURE/CRITICISM

Abeita, Louise
Allen, Minerva
Allen, Paula Gunn
Anauta
Anderson, Mabel Washbourne
Anderson, Owanah
Armstrong, Jeannette
Awiakta, Marilou
Bahe, Liz Sohappy
Bell, Betty Louise
Bennett, Kay Curley
Bighorse, Tiana
Bird, Gloria
Blaeser, Kimberly M.
Bonnin, Gertrude Simmons

Brant, Beth

Brass, Eleanor

Brigham, Besmilr Moore

Brown, Emily Ivanoff

Burns, Diane M.

Burton, Jimalee Chitwood

Callahan, Sophia Alice

Campbell, Maria

Cardiff, Gladys

Carlo, Poldine Demoski

Chrystos

Clements, Susan Deer Cloud

Cochran, Jo Whitehorse

Cook-Lynn, Elizabeth

Crying Wind

Culleton, Beatrice

Dauenhauer, Nora Marks

De Clue, Charlotte

Dietz, Angel DeCora

Endrezze, Anita

Erdrich, Louise

Evans, Mary Augusta Tappage

Fife, Connie

Francisco, Nia

Fry, Maggie Ann Culver

Glancy, Diane

Goose, Mary

Gould, Janice May

Green, Rayna Diane

Hail, Raven

Hale, Janet Campbell

Harjo, Joy

Henry, Jeannette

Hogan, Linda

Howe, LeAnne

Hungry Wolf, Beverly

Isom, Joan Shaddox

Joe, Rita

Johnson, Emily Pauline

Johnston, Verna Patronella

Keams, Geraldine

Keeshig-Tobias, Lenore

LaDuke, Winona

LaFlesche Tibbles, Susette

LaRoque, Emma

Lone Dog, Louise

Mann, Henri

Maracle, Lee

McDaniel, Wilma Elizabeth

Medicine, Beatrice A.

Mourning Dove

Naranjo-Morse, Nora

northSun, nila

Rose, Wendy

Sanchez, Carol Lee

Schoolcraft, Jane Johnston

Sears, Vickie

Shanley, Kathryn

Shaw, Anna Moore

Silko, Leslie Marmon

Slipperjack, Ruby

Smith, Kathleen

Sneve, Virginia Driving Hawk

Stewart, Irene

TallMountain, Mary

Tapahonso, Luci

Tohe, Laura

Tremblay, Gail

Volborth, Judith Mountain Leaf

Wallis, Velma

Walsh, Marnie

Walters, Anna Lee

White, Elizabeth Q.

Whiteman, Roberta Hill

Winnie, Lucille Jerry

Wittstock, Laura Waterman

Woody, Elizabeth

Wright, Muriel Hazel

Zepeda, Ofelia

MEDICINE (WESTERN)

Bronson, Ruth Muskrat

Cobb, Isabelle

Erdrich, Angie
Ignacio, Carmella
Jumper, Betty Mae
Krepps, Ethel C.
LaFlesche Picotte, Susan
Pinkerman-Uri, Connie Redbird
Shanley, Kathryn
Steele, Lois Fister
Wauneka, Annie Dodge

MEDICINE (TRADITIONAL)

Billie, Susie
Chona, Maria
Coocoochee
Jarvis, Rosie
Lozen
McKay, Mabel
Modesto, Ruby
Parrish, Essie
Sanapia
The-Other-Magpie

MISSIONARY WORK

Brown, Catharine
Cuny, Sister Genevieve
LaFlesche Picotte, Susan
Stewart, Irene
White, Elizabeth Q.

MUSIC

Gould, Janice May
Hail, Raven
Heth, Charlotte Anne Wilson
Kilpatrick, Anna Gritts
Lawson, Roberta Campbell
Little Coyote, Bertha
White, Elizabeth Q.

PERFORMANCE

Blackstone, Tsianina Redfeather
Horn, Kahn-Tineta
Jones, Rosalie Mae

Keams, Geraldine
Sainte-Marie, Buffy
Skye, Ferial Deer
Tallchief, Maria
Tallchief, Marjorie

PHOTOGRAPHY

Woody, Elizabeth

SOCIAL WORK

Deer, Ada

STORYTELLING

Hilbert, Vi
Keeshig-Tobias, Lenore
Slipperjack, Ruby
Tohe, Laura
Zuni, Flora

TRIBAL LEADERSHIP

Awashonks
Dixon, Lorena Lucille Majel
Hopkins, Sarah Winnemucca
Jimulla, Viola Pelhame
Jumper, Betty Mae
LaFlesche Farley, Rosalie
Mankiller, Wilma
Musgrove, Mary
Osceola, Laura Mae
Queen Anne of Pamunkey
Tiger, Winifred
Ward, Nancy
Wauneka, Annie Dodge
Wetamoo

WARRIOR

Dahteste
Lozen
Running Eagle
The-Other-Magpie
Woman Chief

Appendix 2
Entries by Decades of Birth

BEFORE 1840

Ainse, Sally

Alberty, Eliza Missouri Bushyhead

Awashonks

Big Eyes

Brant, Molly

Brown, Catharine

Buffalo Bird Woman

Coocoochee

Dat-So-La-Lee

Dorion Woman

Juana Maria

Juneau, Josette

Lozen

Malinche

Medicine Snake Woman

Musgrove, Mary

Netnokwa

Owl Woman

Parker, Cynthia Ann

Pocahontas

Running Eagle

Sacagawea

Schoolcraft, Jane Johnston

Sutton, Catherine

Tekakwitha, Kateri

Tomassa

Tsupu

Ward, Nancy

Wetamoo

Woman Chief

1841–1860

Chona, Maria

Cobb, Isabelle

Hopkins, Sarah Winnemucca

Indian Emily

Jarvis, Rosie

LaFlesche Tibbles, Susette

Mayo, Sarah Jim

Nampeyo

Peterson, Annie Miner

Pretty-shield

The-Other-Magpie

1861–1880

Anderson, Mabel Washbourne

Bonnin, Gertrude Simmons

Callahan, Sophia Alice

Dahteste

Dietz, Angel DeCora

Eaton, Rachel Caroline

Jimulla, Viola Pelhame

Johnson, Emily Pauline

Kellogg, Laura Cornelius

LaFlesche Farley, Rosalie

LaFlesche Picotte, Susan

LaFlesche Picotte Diddock, Marguerite

Lawson, Roberta Campbell

Lowry, Annie

Sacred White Buffalo, Mother Mary Catherine

Telles, Lucy Parker

1881–1900

Allen, Elsie

Billie, Susie

Blackstone, Tsianina Redfeather

Bronson, Ruth Muskrat

Cuero, Delfina

Davidson, Florence Edenshaw
Deloria, Ella Cara
Dick, Lena Frank
Evans, Mary Augusta Tappage
Fry, Maggie Ann Culver
Greene, Alma
Highwalking, Belle
Lewis, Lucy
Martinez, Maria Montoya
Mountain Wolf Woman
Mourning Dove
Nunez, Bonita Wa Wa Calachaw
Peña, Tonita
Potts, Marie
Roe Cloud, Elizabeth Bender
Sanapia
Sekaquaptewa, Helen
Shaw, Anna Moore
Somersal, Laura
Tantaquidgeon, Gladys
White, Elizabeth Q.
Wright, Muriel Hazel
Zuni, Flora

1901–1920

Anahereo
Aquino, Ella Pierre
Ashoona, Pitseolak
Bighorse, Tiana
Blackgoat, Roberta
Brass, Eleanor
Brigham, Besmilr Moore
Broker, Ignatia
Brown, Emily Ivanoff
Burton, Jimalee Chitwood
Carlo, Poldine Demoski
Cleghorn, Mildred Imoch
Cordero, Helen Quintana
Covington, Lucy Freidlander
Hailstone, Vivien
Harnar, Nellie Shaw
Henry, Jeannette

Hilbert, Vi
Jemison, Alice Lee
John, Mary
Johnston, Verna Patronella
Kegg, Maude Mitchell
Kilpatrick, Anna Gritts
Kimball, Yeffe
Little Coyote, Bertha
Littleman, Alice
McDaniel, Wilma Elizabeth
McKay, Mabel
Modesto, Ruby
Momaday, Natachee Scott
Nampeyo, Daisy Hooee
Navasie, Joy
Neakok, Sadie Brower
Parrish, Essie
Pavatea, Garnet
Peterson, Helen
Ross, Agnes Allen
Saubel, Katherine Siva
Stewart, Irene
TallMountain, Mary
Vanderburg, Agnes
Velarde, Pablita
Venegas, Hildreth Marie Twostars
Wanatee, Adeline
Wauneka, Annie Dodge
Winnie, Lucille Jerry
Wolf, Helen Pease

1921–1940

Abeita, Louise
Ackerman, Maria Joseph
Ahenakew, Freda
Allen, Minerva
Allen, Paula Gunn
Anderson, Owanah
Arrington, Ruth
Ashevak, Kenojuak
Awiakta, Marilou
Bennett, Kay Curley

Bennett, Ramona

Blue Legs

Campbell, Maria

Carius, Helen Slwooko

Chouteau, Yvonne

Cook-Lynn, Elizabeth

Cuny, Sister Genevieve

Dauenhauer, Nora Marks

Deer, Ada

Dixon, Lorena Lucille Majel

Freeman, Minnie Aodla

French, Alice

Hail, Raven

Hampton, Carol Cussen McDonald

Hardin, Helen Bagshaw

Harris, LaDonna

Hatch, Viola

Heth, Charlotte Anne Wilson

Horn, Kahn-Tineta

Isom, Joan Shaddox

Joe, Rita

Jumper, Betty Mae

Kavena, Juanita Tiger

Kirkness, Verna J.

Loloma, Otellie

Mann, Henri

McCloud, Janet

Medicine, Beatrice A.

Medicine Flower, Grace

Nelson, Margaret F.

Osceola, Laura Mae

Parker, Julia F.

Pearson, Maria Darlene

Picotte, Agnes

Pinkerman-Uri, Connie Redbird

Robinson, Wungnema Rose

Roessel, Ruth W.

Rousseau, Lorraine Mae

Sanchez, Carol Lee

Sioui, Elenore Marie

Skye, Ferial Deer

Smith, Jaune Quick-to-See

Smith, Kathleen

Sneve, Virginia Driving Hawk

Stanley, Dorothy Amora

Steele, Lois Fister

Swan, Madonna

Swentzell, Rina

Tallchief, Maria

Tallchief, Majorie

Thorpe, Grace

Tiger, Winifred

1941–1965

Abeyta, Pablita

Akers, Donna L.

Aquash, Anna Mae Pictou

Archambault, JoAllyn

Armstrong, Jeannette

Arthur, Claudeen Bates

Ayoungman, Vivian

Bahe, Liz Sohappy

Baker, Marie Annharte

Bell, Betty Louise

Bird, Gail

Bird, Gloria

Bird, JoAnne

Black Bear, Matilda

Blaeser, Kimberly M.

Bordeaux, Shirley

Brant, Beth

Brave Bird, Mary

Brink, Jeanne

Burns, Diane M.

Cardiff, Gladys

Child, Brenda J.

Chrystos

Clements, Susan Deer Cloud

Cochran, Jo Whitehorse

Crying Wind

Culleton, Beatrice

De Clue, Charlotte

Dixon, Patricia A.

Endrezze, Anita

Erdrich, Angie
Erdrich, Heid E.
Erdrich, Louise
Fife, Connie
Folwell, Jody
Francisco, Nia
Glancy, Diane
Goose, Mary
Gould, Janice May
Green, Rayna Diane
Hale, Janet Campbell
Harjo, Joy
Harjo, Suzan Shown
Hilden, Patricia Penn
Hogan, Linda
Howe, LeAnne
Hungry Wolf, Beverly
Ignacio, Carmella
Jennings, Vanessa
Jones, Rosalie Mae
Keams, Geraldine
Keeshig-Tobias, Lenore
Kidwell, Clara S.
LaDuke, Winona
LaRoque, Emma
Mankiller, Wilma
Maracle, Lee
Morez, Mary
McCoy, Melody L.
Naranjo-Morse, Nora
northSun, nila

Owen, Angie Reano
Power, Susan
Pretty on Top, Jeanine
Puzz, Anna
Rand, Jacki
Red Shirt Shaw, Delphine
Rose, Wendy
Saila, Pitaloosie
Sainte-Marie, Buffy
Sakiestewa, Ramona
Salabiye, Velma S.
Sears, Vickie
Shanley, Kathryn
Silko, Leslie Marmon
Sisk-Franco, Caleen A.
Slipperjack, Ruby
Smith, Barbara Elene
Stroud, Virginia
Tapahonso, Luci
Tohe, Laura
Tremblay, Gail
Volborth, Judith Mountain Leaf
Wallis, Velma
Walters, Anna Lee
White, Madeline Melba
Whiteman, Roberta Hill
Williams, Alice Cling
Witt, Shirley Hill
Woody, Elizabeth
Wynne, Mary T.
Zepeda, Ofelia

Appendix 3
Entries by State/Province of Birth

ALASKA

Ackerman, Maria Joseph
Brown, Emily Ivanoff
Carius, Helen Slwooko
Carlo, Poldine Demoski
Dauenhauer, Nora Marks
Neakok, Sadie Brower
TallMountain, Mary
Wallis, Velma

ALBERTA

Ayoungman, Vivian
LaRoque, Emma

APACHERIA

Dahteste
Lozen

ARCTIC

Ashoona, Pitseolak
French, Alice
Saila, Pitaloosie

ARIZONA

Arthur, Claudeen Bates
Bighorse, Tiana
Blackgoat, Roberta
Chona, Maria
Francisco, Nia
Ignacio, Carmella
Jimulla, Viola Pelhame
Keams, Geraldine
Loloma, Otellie

Morez, Mary
Naha, Paqua
Nampeyo
Nampeyo, Daisy Hooee
Navasie, Joy
Paul, Alice S.
Pavatea, Garnet
Robinson, Wungnema Rose
Roessel, Ruth W.
Salabiye, Velma S.
Sekaquaptewa, Helen
Shaw, Anna Moore
Stewart, Irene
Tohe, Laura
Wauneka, Annie Dodge
White, Elizabeth Q.
Williams, Alice Cling
Woody, Elizabeth
Zepeda, Ofelia

ARKANSAS

Alberty, Eliza Missouri Bushyhead
Anderson, Mabel Washbourne

BAFFIN ISLAND

Anauta
Ashevak, Kenojuak

BRITISH COLUMBIA

Armstrong, Jeannette
Davidson, Florence Edenshaw
Evans, Mary Augusta Tappage
John, Mary
Maracle, Lee

CALIFORNIA

Allen, Elsie

Bird, Gail

Bird, JoAnne

Burns, Diane M.

Chrystos

Cuero, Delfina

Dat-So-La-Lee

Dick, Lena Frank

Dixon, Lorena Lucille Majel

Dixon, Patricia A.

Endrezze, Anita

Gould, Janice May

Hailstone, Vivien

Hale, Janet Campbell

Hilden, Patricia Penn

Jarvis, Rosie

Juana Maria

McKay, Mabel

Modesto, Ruby

Nunez, Bonita Wa Wa Calachaw

Parker, Julia F.

Parrish, Essie

Pinkerman-Uri, Connie Redbird

Potts, Marie

Puzz, Anna

Rose, Wendy

Saubel, Katherine Siva

Sears, Vickie

Sisk-Franco, Caleen A.

Smith, Kathleen

Somersal, Laura

Stanley, Dorothy Amora

Stroud, Virginia

Telles, Lucy Parker

Tsupu

CAPE HOPE ISLANDS

Freeman, Minnie Aodla

CHEROKEE NATION

Brown, Catharine

Lawson, Roberta Campbell

Ward, Nancy

COLORADO

Hogan, Linda

CONNECTICUT

Tantaquidgeon, Gladys

FLORIDA

Billie, Susie

Jumper, Betty Mae

Osceola, Laura Mae

GEORGIA

Musgrove, Mary

IDAHO

Mourning Dove

Sacagawea

ILLINOIS

Parker, Cynthia Ann

Power, Susan

IOWA

Goose, Mary

Wanatee, Adeline

KENTUCKY

Momaday, Natachee Scott

MANITOBA

Baker, Marie Annharte

Culleton, Beatrice

Kirkness, Verna J.

MEXICO

Malinche

Tomassa

MICHIGAN

Brant, Beth

MINNESOTA

Broker, Ignatia
Child, Brenda J.
Erdrich, Angie
Erdrich, Heid E.
Erdrich, Louise
Kegg, Maude Mitchell
LaDuke, Winona
Roe Cloud, Elizabeth Bender

MISSISSIPPI

Brigham, Besmilr Moore

MISSOURI

Glancy, Diane

MONTANA

Allen, Minerva
Blaeser, Kimberly M.
Cardiff, Gladys
Highwalking, Belle
Jones, Rosalie Mae
Medicine Snake Woman
Pretty-shield
Rand, Jacki
Shanley, Kathryn
Smith, Jaune Quick-to-See
Steele, Lois Fister
Vanderburg, Agnes
Wolf, Helen Pease

NEBRASKA

Bordeaux, Shirley
Dietz, Angel DeCora
LaFlesche Farley, Rosalie
LaFlesche Picotte, Susan
LaFlesche Picotte Diddock, Marguerite

LaFlesche Tibbles, Susette
Red Shirt Shaw, Delphine

NEVADA

Harnar, Nellie Shaw
Hopkins, Sarah Winnemucca
Lowry, Annie
Mayo, Sarah Jim
northSun, nila

NEW MEXICO

Abeita, Louise
Abeyta, Pablita
Allen, Paula Gunn
Bennett, Kay Curley
Cordero, Helen Quintana
Folwell, Jody
Gonzales, Rose
Hardin, Helen Bagshaw
Lewis, Lucy
Martinez, Maria Montoya
Medicine Flower, Grace
Naranjo-Morse, Nora
Owen, Angie Reano
Peña, Tonita
Sakiestewa, Ramona
Sanchez, Carol Lee
Silko, Leslie Marmon
Swentzell, Rina
Tapahonso, Luci
Velarde, Pablita
Zuni, Flora

NEW YORK

Ainse, Sally
Brant, Molly
Clements, Susan Deer Cloud
Horn, Kahn-Tineta
Jemison, Alice Lee
Tekakwitha, Kateri
Tremblay, Gail

Volborth, Judith Mountain Leaf
Witt, Shirley Hill
Wittstock, Laura Waterman

NORTH CAROLINA

Henry, Jeannette
Tiger, Winifred

NORTH DAKOTA

Buffalo Bird Woman
Sacred White Buffalo, Mother Mary
    Catherine

NOVA SCOTIA

Aquash, Anna Mae Pictou
Joe, Rita

OKLAHOMA

Akers, Donna L.
Anderson, Owanah
Archambault, JoAllyn
Arrington, Ruth
Blackstone, Tsianina Redfeather
Bronson, Ruth Muskrat
Burton, Jimalee Chitwood
Callahan, Sophia Alice
Cleghorn, Mildred Imoch
De Clue, Charlotte
Eaton, Rachel Caroline
Fry, Maggie Ann Culver
Hail, Raven
Hampton, Carol Cussen McDonald
Harjo, Joy
Harjo, Suzan Shown
Harris, LaDonna
Hatch, Viola
Heth, Charlotte Anne Wilson
Hill, Joan
Howe, LeAnne
Isom, Joan Shaddox
Jennings, Vanessa

Kavena, Juanita Tiger
Kidwell, Clara S.
Kilpatrick, Anna Gritts
Kimball, Yeffe
Krepps, Ethel C.
Little Coyote, Bertha
Littleman, Alice
Mankiller, Wilma
Mann, Henri
McDaniel, Wilma Elizabeth
Nelson, Margaret F.
Sanapia
Tallchief, Maria
Tallchief, Marjorie
Thorpe, Grace
Walters, Anna Lee
Winnie, Lucille Jerry
Wright, Muriel Hazel

ONTARIO

Anahereo
Greene, Alma
Johnson, Emily Pauline
Johnston, Verna Patronella
Keeshig-Tobias, Lenore
Lavell, Jeannette
Schoolcraft, Jane Johnston
Slipperjack, Ruby
Sutton, Catherine

OREGON

Peterson, Annie Miner

QUEBEC

Coocoochee
Sioui, Elenore Marie

RHODE ISLAND

Awashonks
Wetamoo

SASKATCHEWAN

Ahenakew, Freda
Brass, Eleanor
Campbell, Maria
Fife, Connie

SOUTH DAKOTA

Black Bear, Matilda
Blue Legs
Bonnin, Gertrude Simmons
Brave Bird, Mary
Cook-Lynn, Elizabeth
Cuny, Sister Genevieve
Deloria, Ella Carak
Medicine, Beatrice A.
Pearson, Maria Darlene
Peterson, Helen
Picotte, Agnes
Ross, Agnes Allen
Rousseau, Lorraine Mae
Sneve, Virginia Driving Hawk
Swan, Madonna
Venegas, Hildreth Marie Twostars
White, Madeline Melba

TENNESSEE

Awiakta, Marilou
Cobb, Isabelle

TEXAS

Big Eyes
Chouteau, Yvonne

Green, Rayna Diane
Indian Emily

VERMONT

Brink, Jeanne

VIRGINIA

Pocahontas
Queen Anne of Pamunkey

WASHINGTON

Aquino, Ella Pierre
Bahe, Liz Sohappy
Bennett, Ramona
Bird, Gloria
Cochran, Jo Whitehorse
Covington, Lucy Freidlander
Hilbert, Vi
McCloud, Janet
Pretty on Top, Jeanine

WASHINGTON, D.C.

Steele, Lois Fister

WISCONSIN

Deer, Ada
Juneau, Josette
Kellogg, Laura Cornelius
Mountain Wolf Woman
Skye, Ferial Deer
Whiteman, Roberta Hill

Appendix 4
Entries by Tribal Affiliation

ABENAKI

Brink, Jeanne

ACOMA

Lewis, Lucy

APACHE

Cleghorn, Mildred Imoch
Dahteste
Indian Emily
Lozen

APACHE/COMANCHE

Volborth, Judith Mountain Leaf

ARAPAHO

Hatch, Viola

ASSINIBOINE

Allen, Minerva
Puzz, Anna
Shanley, Kathryn
Steele, Lois Fister

ATHABASKAN

Carlo, Poldine Demoski
TallMountain, Mary
Wallis, Velma

BLACKFEET

Ayoungman, Vivian
Hungry Wolf, Beverly
Jones, Rosalie Mae

Medicine Snake Woman
Running Eagle

BLACKFEET/MOHAWK/SENECA

Clements, Susan Deer Cloud

CADDO

Hampton, Carol Cussen McDonald

CAHUILLA

Saubel, Katherine Siva

CAHUILLA/SERRANO

Modesto, Ruby

CARRIER

John, Mary

CHEMEHUEVI/CHIPPEWA

Burns, Diane M.

CHEROKEE

Alberty, Eliza Missouri Bushyhead
Anderson, Mabel Washbourne
Awiakta, Marilou
Bell, Betty Louise
Bronson, Ruth Muskrat
Brown, Catharine
Burton, Jimalee Chitwood
Cardiff, Gladys
Chouteau, Yvonne
Cobb, Isabelle
Eaton, Rachel Caroline

Fry, Maggie Ann Culver
Glancy, Diane
Green, Rayna Diane
Hail, Raven
Henry, Jeannette
Heth, Charlotte Anne Wilson
Isom, Joan Shaddox
Kilpatrick, Anna Gritts
Mankiller, Wilma
McCoy, Melody L.
McDaniel, Wilma Elizabeth
Momaday, Natachee Scott
Nelson, Margaret F.
Sears, Vickie
Smith, Barbara Elene
Stroud, Virginia
Tiger, Winifred
Ward, Nancy

CHEROKEE/CREEK

Hill, Joan

CHEROKEE/MUSKOGEE

Harjo, Suzan Shown

CHEYENNE

Highwalking, Belle
Little Coyote, Bertha
Mann, Henri
Owl Woman

CHICKSAW

Hogan, Linda

CHIPPEWA

Blaeser, Kimberly M.
Child, Brend J.
Erdrich, Louise
Johnston, Verna Patronella
Kegg, Maude Mitchell
Schoolcraft, Jane Johnston

CHIPPEWA/SHOSHONE

northSun, nila

CHOCTAW

Akers, Donna L.
Anderson, Owanah
Brigham, Besmilr Moore
Howe, LeAnne
Rand, Jacki
Wright, Muriel Hazel

CHOCTAW/CHEROKEE

Pinkerman-Uri, Connie Redbird

CHOCTAW/CHIPPEWA

Kidwell, Clara S.

CHOCTAW/SIOUX

Bordeaux, Shirley

COCHITI

Cordero, Helen Quintana

COEUR d'ALENE

Hale, Janet Campbell

COLVILLE CONFEDERATED TRIBES

Covington, Lucy Freidlander

COMANCHE

Harris, LaDonna
Parker, Cynthia Ann
Sanapia
Tomassa

CREE

Ahenakew, Freda
Kirkness, Verna J.
Sainte-Marie, Buffy

CREE/MÉTIS

LaRoque, Emma

CREE/OJIBWA

Brass, Eleanor

CREE/SHOSHONE

Smith, Jaune Quick-to-See

CREEK

Arrington, Ruth
Callahan, Sophia Alice
Harjo, Joy
Musgrove, Mary

CREEK/CHEROKEE

Blackstone, Tsianina Redfeather

CROW

Pretty on Top, Jeanine
Pretty-shield
The-Other-Magpie
Wolf, Helen Pease

CROW/CREEK/SIOUX

Cook-Lynn, Elizabeth

DELAWARE

Lawson, Roberta Campbell

DIEGUEÑO

Cuero, Delfina

GROS VENTRE/CROW

Woman Chief

HAIDA

Davidson, Florence Edenshaw

HIDATSA

Buffalo Bird Woman

HO-CHUNK

Hunter, Mary Jo Brooks

HOPI

Loloma, Otellie
Nampeyo
Robinson, Wungnema Rose
Sakiestewa, Ramona
Sekaquaptewa, Helen
White, Elizabeth Q.

HOPI/TEWA

Naha, Paqua
Nampeyo, Daisy Hooee
Navasic, Joy
Pavatea, Garnet

HURON/WYANDOT

Sioui, Elenore Marie

INUIT (INUKTITUT)

Anauta
Ashevak, Kenojuak
Ashoona, Pitseolak
Carius, Helen Slwooko
Freeman, Minnie Aodla
Saila, Pitaloosie

INUK

French, Alice

INUPIAT

Neakok, Sadie Brower

IOWA

Dorion Woman

IROQUOIS

Brant, Molly

ISLETA

Abeita, Louise

KICKAPOO

Crying Wind

KIOWA

Jennings, Vanessa
Krepps, Ethel C.
Littleman, Alice

LAGUNA

Silko, Leslie Marmon

LAGUNA/SANTO DOMINGO

Bird, Gail

LAGUNA/SIOUX

Allen, Paula Gunn
Sanchez, Carol Lee

LUISEÑO

Dixon, Lorena Lucille Majel
Dixon, Patricia A.
Nunez, Bonita Wa Wa Calachaw

LUMMI/YAKIMA

Aquino, Ella Pierre

MAIDU

Gould, Janice May
Potts, Marie

MENOMINEE

Chrystos
Deer, Ada

Juneau, Josette
Skye, Ferial Deer

MESKWAKI

Wanatee, Adeline

MESKWAKI/CHIPPEWA

Goose, Mary

MÉTIS

Campbell, Maria
Culleton, Beatrice
Maracle, Lee

MICMAC

Aquash, Anna Mae Pictou
Joe, Rita

MILUK/HANIS

Peterson, Annie Miner

MIWOK

Stanley, Dorothy Amora
Tsupu

MIWOK/HOPI

Rose, Wendy

MIWOK/PAIUTE

Telles, Lucy Parker

MIWOK/POMO

Smith, Kathleen

MOHAWK

Anahereo
Brant, Beth
Coocoochee
Greene, Alma
Horn, Kahn-Tineta

Johnson, Emily Pauline
Witt, Shirley Hill

MOHAWK/ALGONQUIN

Tekakwitha, Kateri

MOHAWK/DELAWARE

Lone Dog, Louise

MOHEGAN

Tantaquidgeon, Gladys

MUSKOGEE/CREEK

Kavena, Juanita Tiger

NAVAJO (DINÉ)

Abeyta, Pablita
Arthur, Claudeen Bates
Bennett, Kay Curley
Bighorse, Tiana
Blackgoat, Roberta
Francisco, Nia
Keams, Geraldine
Morez, Mary
Roessel, Ruth W.
Salabiye, Velma S.
Stewart, Irene
Tapahonso, Luci
Tohe, Laura
Wauneka, Annie Dodge
Williams, Alice Cling

NEZ PERCE

Hilden, Patricia Penn

NICOLEÑO

Juana Maria

OJIBWA

Baker, Marie Annharte
Broker, Ignatia

Erdrich, Angie
Erdrich, Heid E.
LaDuke, Winona
Lavell, Jeannette
Roe Cloud, Elizabeth Bender
Slipperjack, Ruby
Sutton, Catherine

OJIBWA/POTAWATOMI

Keeshig-Tobias, Lenore

OKANAGAN

Armstrong, Jeannette

OKANOGAN/COLVILLE

Mourning Dove

ONEIDA

Ainse, Sally
Kellogg, Laura Cornelius
Whiteman, Roberta Hill

ONONDAGA/MICMAC

Tremblay, Gail

OSAGE

De Clue, Charlotte
Kimball, Yeffe
Tallchief, Maria
Tallchief, Marjorie

OTTAWA

Netnokwa

PAIUTE

Harnar, Nellie Shaw
Hopkins, Sarah Winnemucca
Lowrey, Annie

PAMUNKEY

Queen Anne

PAPAGO

Chono, Maria

PAWNEE/OTOEMISSOURI

Walters, Anna Lee

PIMA

Shaw, Anna Moore

POMO

Allen, Elsie
Jarvis, Rosie
McKay, Mabel
Parker, Julia F.
Parrish, Essie

PONCA/OMAHA

LaFlesche Farley, Rosalie
LaFlesche Picotte, Susan
LaFlesche Picotte Diddock, Marguerite
LaFlesche Tibbles, Susette

POWHATAN

Pocahontas

PUYALLUP

Bennett, Ramona

SALISH

Vanderburg, Agnes

SAN ILDEFONSO

Peña, Tonita

SAN JUAN

Gonzales, Rose

SANTA CLARA

Folwell, Jody
Hardin, Helen Bagshaw

Medicine Flower, Grace
Naranjo-Morse, Nora
Swentzell, Rina

SANTO DOMINGO

Owen, Angie Reano

SAUK AND FOX

Thorpe, Grace

SEMINOLE

Billie, Susie
Jumper, Betty Mae
Osceola, Laura Mae

SENECA

Wittstock, Laura Waterman

SENECA/CAYUGA

Winnie, Lucille Jerry

SENECA/CHEROKEE

Jemison, Alice Lee

SHOSHONE

Sacagawea

SIOUX

Archambault, JoAllyn
Bird, JoAnne
Black Bear, Matilda
Blue Legs
Bonnin, Gertrude Simmons
Brave Bird, Mary
Cochran, Jo Whitehorse
Cuny, Sister Genevieve
Deloria, Ella Cara
Medicine, Beatrice A.
Pearson, Maria Darlene
Peterson, Helen
Picotte, Agnes

Power, Susan

Red Shirt Shaw, Delphine

Ross, Agnes Allen

Rousseau, Lorraine Mae

Sacred White Buffalo, Mother Mary
    Catherine

Sneve, Virginia Driving Hawk

Swan, Madonna

Venegas, Hildreth Marie Twostars

Walsh, Marnie

White, Madeline Melba

Wynne, Mary T.

SKAGIT

Hilbert, Vi

SODA CREEK

Evans, Mary Augusta Tappage

SPOKANE

Bird, Gloria

TEWA

Martinez, Maria Montoya

Velarde, Pablita

TLINGIT

Ackerman, Maria Joseph

Dauenhauer, Nora Marks

TOHONO O'ODHAM

Ignacio, Carmella

Paul, Alice S.

Zepeda, Ofelia

TULALIP

McCloud, Janet

WAMPANOAG

Awashonks

Wetamoo

WAPPO/POMO

Somersal, Laura

WARM SPRINGS/ WASCO/NAVAJO

Woody, Elizabeth

WASHO (WASHOE)

Dat-So-La-Lee

Dick, Lena Frank

Mayo, Sarah Jim

WICHITA

Big Eyes

WINNEBAGO

Dietz, Angel DeCora

Mountain Wolf Woman

WINTU

Sisk-Franco, Caleen A.

YAKIMA

Bahe, Liz Sohappy

YAQUI

Endrezze, Anita

YAVAPAI

Jimulla, Viola Pelhame

YUPIK

Brown, Emily Ivanoff

YUROK/KAROK

Hailstone, Vivien

ZUNI

Zuni, Flora

Index